HISTORIC WORCESTER STREETS

HISTORIC WORCESTER STREETS

Their history and the people
who lived and worked in them

Listings of Worcester streets recorded
from the earliest times up to 1940

By Terry Wardle

Published by
TWP

Historic Worcester Streets
First published in the UK in 2014 by
Terry Wardle Publications,
MTC, PO Box 665, Worcester WR1 3WN

(c) Terry Wardle

ISBN : 978 0 9553809 4 5

Cover Illustration:
All Hallows about 1820 by Powell
Courtesy of Worcester City Museums and Art Gallery
And with thanks to Stephen Beacham

Contents

Preface

There has never before been a book dedicated to Worcester's historic streets, so readers may wonder why there is felt to be a need for one now. There are several answers that could be given, not least that as time moves on, as it always does, it is easy for the past to be forgotten in the daily rush to cope with the present. Streets are named in the here and now, for those activities, events and people that are significant at the time, but as times and fashions change and memories fade, it is easy for so much that was important to be lost, and for the motivation behind our street names to be forgotten.

The Victorians began a fashion for aspirational street names, which was often continued in the twentieth century, by naming streets after poets, areas of natural beauty or rustic reminders of our largely vanished rural past. The Victorians however, had a very different idea of what was aspirational. They named their streets after heroes of empire, military commanders and civic leaders; the people they felt that everyone would aspire to be like, in a century when they could have no conception of the modern cult of instant celebrity.

Prior to the nineteenth century, street names were usually purely descriptive. Streets on the outskirts of the city often described where a thoroughfare was or led from or to, or what inn or landmark was there or nearby, while city centre street names described what trade or activity people carried on there, Today some of the past activities after which streets were named are as mysterious to us as an IT technician would be to a medieval man or woman, and many of the names of former heroes have faded in memory. So it seems that the time is right to remind ourselves of what we and our city have lost and forgotten.

This is especially important, because our streets and their history are a record of the history of the city, and of its people throughout the centuries. Some streets have disappeared over the years, whilst others have stayed, but changed their course or their name or both. They record the stories of the people who lived in them; they sometimes show who built the houses, shops and factories; they explain what trades and pursuits they followed, who were their local and national heroes, what their life was like back then, living in streets we are familiar with today, but at a time when they were very different.

All this and more can often be gleaned from our street names and their histories. And until science produces a time machine, this is the closest we can come to travelling back into the past.

Terry Wardle
Worcester
September 2014

Acknowledgements

Though there has been no previous volume on this subject, this book does owe a considerable debt to past local historians, whose names and works are recorded in Further Reading. A number of them have touched on the subject, and some have examined it in detail: most notably Valentine Green, who recorded many of the medieval street names in his eighteenth century history of the city; former Worcester mayors John Noake and Hubert Leicester, both authors of books on Worcester's history; city headmaster, alderman and former mayor Bertram Brotherton, whose series of articles, mainly concerned with council members for whom streets were named, appeared in the *Worcester News* in 1962; the authors of detailed studies of Friar Street and Blackfriars in the 1980s; Joan Knowles who told the story of Lansdowne Crescent in the 1990s; Bill Gwilliam, who distilled a lifetime of knowledge of Worcester's history into his book *Old Worcester : People and Places* in 1993; and Dr Pat Hughes, whose valuable work includes a comprehensive conjectural map of the city as it was likely to have been in 1575, which was based on extensive research. Other map makers also deserve our thanks for the knowledge they have vouchsafed to us, especially John Speede, John Doharty, Valentine Green and the unnamed surveyors and cartographers of the Ordnance Survey.

Grateful thanks for help and facilities which were essential to the research for this book are due to the staff of the Worcestershire Local History Centre on Trinity Street, which has now sadly been swallowed up by The Hive. Thanks are also due to James Dinn and Sheena Payne-Lunn of Worcester City Council Conservation Dept; Mike Grundy of the *Worcester News*; David Beacham, the historian of All Saints Church; Simon Shearburn for use of his research on St George's Square, and Ian Pattison of St George's Church; the city council staff at the Guildhall; Worcester Cathedral Archaeologist Chris Guy; Marcus Roberts of the Oxford-based JTrails project; Roz Sherris of the Museum of London; Bob and Joyce Lampitt of Redditch, for valuable help with sourcing twentieth century Worcester street plans; John Sermon, chairman of the Surman Family History Society; Christine Sylvester; Claire and Dale England; and the authors, mapmakers, directory publishers and others whose hard work in past centuries has enabled me to complete this volume.

We live in a visual age and illustrations are vitally important in a book such as this. For the provision of pictures used in this volume, grateful thanks are especially due to the late antiquary and collector *extraordinaire* Ron Shuard, whose sad loss robbed the city, and writers such as myself, of someone with a deep knowledge of Worcester's past and great generosity in sharing that knowledge. Thanks are also due to Mike Grundy and the *Worcester News*; Philippa Tinsley and Worcester City Museums and Art Gallery; Worcester City Council and especially the Guildhall staff; the late Bill Gwilliam; Brian Standish, a collector of Worcestershire images; HarperCollins Publishers for use of mid-twentieth century maps; Martin Smith; Linda from Lee Design; Worcestershire County Cricket Club; Ian Narraway; Paul Griffith; the late Hubert Leicester; Carol Bundy; and the late Mrs Gladys Green of York Place. Picture Credit abbreviations are listed at the back of the book. Every effort has been made to acknowledge ownership of images and assistance with information during the long research process, but where acknowledgements have not been possible or have inadvertently been overlooked, it is hoped that such errors will be excused in the cause of illuminating the history of a great city. All rights remain with owners of the images used.

Finally I have to thank Marianne Wardle for the considerable time she gave to help me create the listing of street dating and information which formed the basis of this book, and for much further help with research along the way, without which this book could not have been written.

A Note on Sources

Researchers who wish to take some aspect of this work further may wish to have some guidance on the sources used to compile the information in this book, especially since footnotes and references were regarded as unduly cumbersome and impractical given the working method. Some readers may also wish to know how the information was gathered.

The research work was completed in several main phases. In phase one a list was compiled of all the streets from the earliest times to around 1940, which could be found in maps, street directories, voters lists, building control applications and similar documentary sources. The aim in this phase was to compile as complete a list as could be made of street names which exist or have existed in the city, together with such dating and development evidence as could be obtained from these sources. All the information included on that list is in the book, in direct or summary form.

Phase two involved collecting all the information relating to city streets which could be found in so-called 'secondary' sources, which included published and unpublished books and pamphlets on the history of the city from the earliest times to the present day, research papers and summaries, archaeological evidence, collections of old photographs – which are vital source material - old newspapers and periodicals, building listings, some family history material, and a limited amount of oral history, together with site visits. All the written sources used in this phase are listed in Further Reading. Phase three involved adding further information about people and trades/professions to be found in streets in past times, which mostly came from street directories, carrying out site visits and conducting a substantial amount of picture research.

Where the correct spelling or punctuation of street names has been in doubt the onus has been put on the planners, and the version given on the street sign has been taken as correct, except where the street signs just add to the confusion, for example in Wyld's Lane or St Swithin's Street, where there are signs both with and without an apostrophe, in which case a judgement has had to be made about which is more appropriate now. There is also often confusion about which person actually inspired a road name. In 1962 Alderman Brotherton was convinced that Wood Terrace was named for best-selling, Worcester-born, Victorian novelist Mrs Henry Wood, but it is much more likely that the name refers to builder, mayor and long-serving city councillor Joseph Wood. However, it is not possible to say with absolute certainty which of them inspired the name, and in many cases we can only make an educated guess.

Ideally a book such as this would also have been based on a complete survey of all the city property deeds which are available in county archives, but such a task would be beyond the ability of any one person to complete within a realistic timescale. Where information from deeds has been available from work that the author has done elsewhere, or that others have completed, then it has been included in the book, but there is much more material yet to be found. If in the future someone sets about organizing a 'research your street' project on a large scale, then much more valuable information can be brought to light. We are also now seeing digitisation of Worcester's valuable newspaper archive, which will unlock a treasure trove of material for local and national historians. This book is therefore simply a first step along a road that others will hopefully follow and map more accurately in the future.

Historic Worcester Streets

Introduction

Worcester sits at the head of the tideway of the longest river in Britain, and its location on the Severn's gravel terraces, as the only major town in the middle Severn district, has been a major factor in its existence and development as a settlement. It may have been a town as early as 100AD, though a very different one, bounded roughly by Copenhagen Street, Friar Street and Severn Street, and little or nothing remains of what the Romans called our streets, nor of what the Britons knew them as, though the names Severn and Teme have Celtic origins. By the seventh century the Britons had been displaced by the Anglo-Saxons, who had established themselves in Worcester by the 660s or before, and it is from them that we derive many of our names for outlying areas of the city, though their city centre names have mostly either been lost, or corrupted over time into modern equivalents that they would find unrecognisable, because of changes in pronunciation, usage or fashion.

By 680 this was an important regional administrative centre and a cathedral city, a new episcopal see covering Worcestershire and parts of Gloucestershire and Warwickshire, with a market that would have drawn people from many miles around, and thus it was a place of importance and influence. Worcester's other great claim to importance was its situation as an inland port, though the point at which this began is more difficult to determine. Certainly the Romans would have used water transport to bring in fuel and iron ore to their iron industry along Pitchcroft, and take out smelted iron, and no doubt they shipped Droitwich salt from here, as the Anglo-Saxons and Normans did for centuries afterwards. The real heyday of river transport was probably to come however, and was due to Worcester's position closer to the manufacturing West Midlands than either of the other great Severn towns, Shrewsbury and Gloucester.

Goods from Birmingham and the Black Country came across country to the Severn at Worcester for transshipment to the port of Bristol, while imported goods from around the world could be shipped up the river, for distribution across the West Midlands. When roads were poor, inland shipping had no rival. It was a lucrative trade on which Worcester often prospered, until the coming of the railways, though oddly it has left very little evidence in our street names, apart from Quay Street and the quays. Birdport did derive its name from the port, but that name disappeared back in the 1960s. Some commercial river traffic continued into the twentieth century, but nothing like the amount which had once existed. Worcester was also important for its bridge, which may have first been built by the Romans somewhere near the cathedral, and was no doubt built in timber on a site between Tybridge Street and Newport Street in the eleventh century or before. In the early fourteenth century, when it was re-built in stone, there was no other bridge across the Severn between Gloucester and Bridgnorth, placing the city at the centre of an important road network.

In the year 904, when a charter conferred on the Mercian earl the site of a fort in north Worcester, to protect the settlement from river-borne Norse raiders, we get a picture, though unfortunately a word picture rather than a visual one, of the city as it then was. The charter confirmed Worcester's status as a burh or burgh, a defended settlement, protected by a wall and surrounded by a deep ditch. The structure of fortification around the settlement, which was put in place by the Anglo-Saxons, was the basis of the later medieval town, though how closely the boundaries of the two were related is yet to be agreed by academics. A conjectural map of the city about the year 900, published in 1958, appeared to show that Worcester then had boundaries similar to those which existed in the medieval period, but another conjectural map from 2004 drew a rather different picture, and it remains to be seen which is the most accurate. At present there is no certain knowledge of the extent of the Anglo-Saxon city. At that time land ownership in the city must have been split between the bishop and the king, and they may have had rival markets, since the High Street must have been a market area, but it was claimed by Jones in the 1950s that the Anglo-Saxons' main market was beside St Alban's, near the boundary of the cathedral's extensive Sanctuary. Later specialist markets for different types of goods spread out around the city centre, and streets were named accordingly, though most of these old names have been lost. Only Mealcheapen Street, the meal, flour and oats market, the later Cornmarket, and Fish Street, the street of the fishmongers, still have their old names. The old Dish Market, once full of crockery stalls, is now Church Street; Garden Market for vegetables is St Nicholas Street; Cornchepyn, the old corn market, is Queen Street; and Goose Lane, the former poultry market, is now St Swithin's Street.

The street pattern of Worcester, as it existed within the medieval city walls, is more certain than that of the Anglo-Saxon city. No map of the city existed prior to 1610, and detailed street plans did not appear until the eighteenth century, but the surviving sections of wall, and the archaeological work carried out before the building of the City Walls Road in the 1970s, have given us a clear picture of where the medieval wall was. It ran from the Severn just north of Dolday, and followed the line of gates to reach the Severn once more near Severn Street. It has been conjectured that the city wall in Anglo-Saxon times had only three main gates, aside from fortification at the river crossing. They were Foregate to the north, St Martin's Gate to the east and Sidbury Gate to the south.

Historic Worcester Streets

By the medieval period there appear to have been seven city gates. In addition to the three main gates, there was also a small postern gate by St Clement's Church on the riverside at the bottom of Dolday, near to what was then the site of the bridge; Trinity Gate, which was apparently a postern gate at what is now St Nicholas Street, leading onto Lowesmoor; Friar's Gate, off Friar Street, which was also a postern, giving access to the friars' graveyard outside the walls; and Frog Gate, probably also a postern, just east of the castle, plus powerful defences on the bridge. A number of these gates have left their mark on the city with street names: The Foregate and Foregate Street, Sidbury, and St Martin's Gate, which will hopefully not be lost with the 'rebranding' of the area as St Martin's Quarter. We also have Trinity Street and The Trinity, but they are likely to have been named for their connection with the Trinity Guild and chapel rather than the gate, which probably took its name from the Guild. There are representations of some of these gates on seventeenth and eighteenth century maps, though how accurate they are is unknown, but sadly no contemporary illustrations exist of any of the old city gates. This is a sad contrast with the city of Hereford, where there are good illustrations of two former gates.

Worcester castle, built soon after the Conquest, was never one of the great Norman citadels, though it saw action in a number of domestic disputes in the twelfth and thirteenth centuries. It consisted of a motte on a former Roman and Anglo-Saxon tump, near the present Severn Street, within an irregularly shaped, vaguely rectangular bailey. By the mid-fifteenth century stone from the site was being robbed out to repair the city walls, though the site eked out a living as the county prison until the opening of a purpose-built replacement in Castle Street in the early nineteenth century. The castle was subsequently demolished and left no mark on our street plans, except for Castle Place, which is just the entry to the King's School car park. Oddly the monastery, an important monastic establishment for hundreds of years, has also left no mark on city street plans, though the monks' great rivals, the Greyfriars, are remembered by Friar Street, and the Blackfriars were remembered until the 1990s, when the Crowngate Centre replaced the awful concrete shopping mall which bore the last reminder of their name.

The medieval boundaries of Worcester were partly determined by an important geographical feature which disappeared from view in the early nineteenth century, though most of us will have passed it by many times without realising. Frog Brook, which ran across the east side of Worcester and joined the Severn south of the castle, became the water supply for a section of the Worcester and Birmingham Canal when it opened in 1815, but it had previously dominated the landscape to the east of the city, and there was a Frog Lane, though that has long since become Severn Street. The valley of the brook was inclined to be marshy, and tradition has it that, in the event of a threat to the city, damming the brook to flood the valley would quickly turn the area into a muddy swamp. It has been said that the city walls were lower to the east because there was thought little likelihood of an attack from that direction, and even in September 1651 there was no attempt to take the city from that side, despite what later maps suggest. The future Charles II was only able to make his famous escape from Worcester because the Royalists still held St Martin's Gate, even when the city had effectively fallen. When the brook was merged into the canal, it opened the way for the great industrial expansion of the city to the east, and the canal provided the cheap transportation for raw materials and finished goods which made the area between Lowesmoor and St Martin's Gate the wealth-producing heart of Worcester through much of the nineteenth century.

It was Godfrey Giffard, Bishop of Worcester between 1268 and 1302, who is credited with first setting about the improvement of Worcester's streets. At that time all the city's thoroughfares had a natural earth surface, which was flattened and hardened by centuries of foot traffic in alleys and lanes, but became rough and uneven from the passage of vehicles on main thoroughfares. To overcome this problem the bishop ordered that main routes should be covered with cobblestones, firmly set in the surface, and Green said he laid the first stone himself on 27 April 1281. These then became known as streets, from the Latin *strata* meaning a paved way, while those routes which retained their earth surface continued to be known as lanes. A section of the city's original old cobblestones could still be found in The Avenue in the city centre in 1935, and historian and former mayor Hubert Leicester urged in that year that it should be preserved for posterity. Needless to say, it hasn't been.

There were no street signs or published street plans in Bishop Giffard's day, and some of the medieval street names – in fact most street names up to the past century or so - could be regarded more as nicknames than street names as we know them. This means that streets might often be known by several names. It also means that in some cases those people who frequented a street may have known it by a particular name, though other residents who did not frequent it may not have referred to it by that name, or in some cases may not have wished to refer to it at all. This would doubtless have applied to Worcester's vanished dockside 'red light' district, behind All Saints Church, referred to in the eighteenth century as Grope Lane, and likely to have been known in the medieval period as something even more colourful. Those who frequented this lane,

Historic Worcester Streets

or lived there in the humble timber-framed cottages which lined it, presumably had no objection to the frank terms in which it was described, and those too polite to use such terms would probably not have wished to go there, or even acknowledge its existence.

Most other street names had a similar descriptive purpose, though usually a more socially acceptable one. Medieval tradesmen tended to group together, or were required to do so by the city authorities, at least until the seventeenth century, and most medieval streets had Old English names which described the activities that went on there, such as Cucking or Cooking Street, for cooked food shops, now Copenhagen Street, or Baxter or baker's Street, later to become the Shambles when the butchers moved in. By the end of the fifteenth century the city boundaries were much as they were to remain until 1837. Beyond the city walls, many outlying areas retained manorial names still in use today, such as Timberdine, Battenhall and Barneshall, which all have their roots in the names of the first Anglo-Saxon settlers.

Some ancient names were corrupted over the centuries into quite different forms. One way in which this seems to have happened is through the substitution of a more modern word for an older one which may no longer have been relevant, and was certainly no longer understood. When this happened the new name often had no relevance to the location, but the new word was substituted because it made sense to contemporary English speakers, when the old one didn't. Birdport is an example of this, having been corrupted from burhport, the port of the defended settlement of Anglo-Saxon Worcester. Another example is Rainbow Hill, a charming name with no relevance to its location, which must have derived from Old English *rainow*, or raven hill, which lost its relevance when ravens were no longer so widely distributed, and lost its meaning when Old English was no longer spoken. In this way, names that made sense but had no meaning were introduced to the city's street maps. An even stranger substitution was Harbour Hill, shown on a map of 1838 between Tolladine Road and Newtown Road, which was nowhere near any stretch of water. Doubtless this was another meaningless substitution, this time for Old English Herdeberge meaning herdsman's hill, and Hagley has a similar corruption to Harborough Hill.

By 1575, when Elizabeth I visited Worcester, the city had not changed greatly in structure from the medieval period, but it had increased the density of its population, and this would be the continuing pattern of development over the following centuries, with more and more people packed into increasingly insanitary and disease-ridden courts and tenements, and spilling out onto the approaches to the city. There are believed to have been only around 2,000 people in Worcester at the time of the Norman Conquest, but this had more than doubled by the mid-sixteenth century, and was estimated to have doubled again to around 8,000 within a century. These figures were dwarfed by the many thousands who packed into the city in the nineteenth century. The city's courts, in which many of these people would have been condemned to live, could make a complete history in themselves; probably no-one has ever counted them all as yet. As late as 1937 Kelly's Directory was still listing 92 courts in the city, and others may have gone by that date. A court could consist of up to 12 or 14 modest rooms around a small courtyard, in each of which as many as 12 people might eat and sleep, sharing whatever rudimentary sanitary facilities there were with the rest of the court. Pat Hughes quotes a description of conditions in St Andrew's parish as 'the tenements being of the vilest description, and their occupants the most deprived class'. It was a way of life almost inconceivable to us now, and not surprisingly, none of the courts are remembered in street names.

By 1772 Worcester had water access to Birmingham on the Staffs & Worcs and Birmingham Canal, via the Severn, but the canal age really came to the city with the belated opening of the Worcester and Birmingham Canal in 1815. This was planned as a much easier way of bringing goods from Birmingham to Worcester, for transhipping down the Severn to Bristol, but the cost per mile of construction had been vastly higher than that of any other English canal, and within 20 years Worcester faced serious threats to its traditional position as Birmingham's port. Being at the farthest extremity of the Severn's tidal flow, the city suffered most at low water, and when the tide was out horses could drink in the centre of the river, the water barely covering their hooves. This was nothing new, though the recent proliferation of weirs on the Severn had not helped, but the Industrial Revolution had quickened the pace of commerce, and no-one had time to wait for the tide to come in anymore. In 1840 a body was formed which became the Severn Commissioners in 1843, and in another three years it had established locks at Diglis to regulate the flow of the river at Worcester. In the meantime however, the coming of the railways gave Birmingham manufacturers other shipping options, and in 1836 plans were set out for a line from Birmingham bypassing Worcester, and going direct to Gloucester. The early nineteenth century investment in deep water docks there had enabled more economical shipping by larger vessels, which could avoid heavy trans-shipping charges at Bristol, but these vessels were too big to come up to Worcester. There was outrage in the city, but the line went ahead as planned, and Worcester had to await the arrival of the Oxford, Worcester and Wolverhampton Railway in 1850.

Historic Worcester Streets

As the centre of a large rural hinterland, Worcester inevitably had early industries which used the raw materials and by-products of agriculture. In the time of Henry VIII the city was the greatest cloth-making centre in England, producing the finest cloth from Herefordshire Ryeland sheep, and in the sixteenth century clothiers like the Wyldes, Nashs and Berkeleys were the wealthiest families in the city, and all are remembered in street names. When the topographer Leland visited the city in 1539 he wrote: 'The wealthe of the towne of Worcester standeth most by draperinge, and no town in England at this present tyme maketh so many cloths yearly as this towne doth.' The city suffered badly in the Civil War, both through damage to its fabric and heavy losses to its citizens, but it later acquired various street names which recalled that period, including Cromwell Street at Shrub Hill, and a string of them around London Road where the fighting of 1651 was fiercest, from Fort Royal Hill, Prince Rupert Road and Hamilton Road, to Camp Hill and the Cromwells at Oliver's Mount.

The traditional clothing industry went into decline in the seventeenth century, as Ryeland sheep fell out of fashion with landowners, and by the mid eighteenth century it was dead. A directory of 1790 said the trade 'at one time employed 1500 Broad-cloth Weavers, and now not one in the City!' Gloving and leather processing were to continue as important industries for the next two centuries, but the end of the cloth trade left a major gap in the city's economy, and there was much unemployment. Dr Wall's china manufactory at Warmestry Slip, established in 1751, was a giant job creation scheme funded by the well-off, who feared rising poor rates and, above all, social unrest. The scheme worked. By 1780 the factory employed 200 people, and in 1800 Worcester Porcelain was said to be one of the three biggest employers in the city, the others being Fownes Gloves and Three Springs Tannery.

Industrial development then moved fast. By 1815 when the Worcester and Birmingham Canal opened, Grainger's porcelain and the Worcester Foundry were growing employers, and from that date there was a surge of enterprise as more porcelain works, boot and shoe makers, vinegar makers, organ builders, carriage makers, engineers and retail clothiers all opened their doors. Some of the city's most famous businesses began in this period; Hill, Evans vinegar works and Lea & Perrins' Worcestershire Sauce production both began in the 1830s. Gloving had been hit hard in 1826 by the ending of barriers to imports, and only the biggest, such as Fownes, would survive by creating a factory system from what had been a traditional outworking trade, but engineering continued to grow, and both entrepreneurs and industries gave rise to new street names, as also did the momentous Battle of Waterloo in 1815, though most of those names were in the Blockhouse, and have since disappeared. As they had done down the centuries, the city's watermen had continued to contribute to Worcester's prosperity, shipping coal and iron ore from as far afield as Staffordshire and the Forest of Dean down the Severn to Bristol, and bringing back the construction materials which helped build Georgian and Victorian Worcester.

Until the eighteenth century the city's buildings, aside from the cathedral and churches, would mainly have been timber-framed, since this was the only cost-effective means of building, though the occasional 'great house' might be of timber and stone. Brick was too expensive for ordinary folk, except perhaps to build fireplaces and chimney stacks, and even then people commonly used lime-plastered oak for fireplaces where they could, and the city had to pass a series of ordinances in the fifteenth and sixteenth centuries, trying to outlaw the dangerous practice. Those who built in brick, such as Cardinal Wolsey at Hampton Court, west of London, were demonstrating their enormous wealth. This was not so much because all bricks then were hand-made, since those who made them would have been paid a pittance, but because of the cost of transport. The only practical means of inland transport was by pack horse, and it has been estimated that bricks doubled in cost after 17 miles, due to the cost of transportation. This changed in the eighteenth century, when some automated brick manufacture began, and canals began to make possible cheap transportation of bulk goods. Suddenly the preserve of the rich was available to all, and the timber-framed or 'half-timbered' buildings we now prize were regarded as hopelessly old-fashioned until they were given a nice fashionable brick front. A prime example of the 'brick mania' can be seen in the seventeenth century cottages on the corner of Little London, which received brick frontages in the eighteenth century. Bricks became so popular that an opportunist government taxed them in 1784, and the tax was increased in 1794, 1797 and 1805, but there was no stopping brick, and since the tax was repealed in 1850 it has been the standard building material. The city still had many timber-framed buildings from past centuries, but sadly most of them have since disappeared.

As the city underwent massive expansion in the nineteenth century, street names became more diverse; some were named after national heroes, some after factories or the local wealthy and powerful, many after owners of the land on which housing was developed, and sometimes builders or developers, responsible for most or all of the houses in a particular street, took their chance to snatch immortality by naming it after themselves. The story of the builders of Victorian Worcester has never yet been told, but it would be a mistake to think it was all a matter of big property developers and massive developments. There were some larger, though still mostly amateur developers, but many of the entrepreneurs were builders who sponsored small scale schemes of a few homes, or small businessmen who put their savings behind building two houses to live in one and sell or let off the other to make back their investment, and many streets were built a house or two at a time over many years.

One practice which has sadly long since disappeared is that of small investors proudly naming the small terraces of cottages they built, often after the places they came from or had perhaps visited, or after wives, mothers or daughters, or even after politicians they admired! Many of these names can still be seen on houses, and some of these small terraces, or even single villas, gave their names to fast-developing streets, such as Melbourne Street, which must have taken its name from two Melbourne Cottages on the corner of Crown Street, probably named for a former prime minister, which were recently demolished to make way for a medical centre. No doubt some property investors prospered, but certainly not all, and the risks they ran were considerable. Despite the undoubted boom in Victorian property development, there were a number of streets begun in the 1860s, 70s or 80s where building stalled, and there was no further development until the 1960s, 70s or 80s. Unlike us, the Victorians were not land poor, and there was little or no incentive for developers to complete stalled developments while new ones were starting, especially since the incidence of unoccupied houses even in boom times suggests that the supply of houses often outstripped demand for them, or at least outstripped the ability or willingness of poorer citizens to pay the higher rents which were inevitably demanded for new properties.

However, with no local transport system, workers had to go where the work was. As business had moved east following the coming of the canal, so workers had to follow, and development of the now-vanished Blockhouse suburb before the 1820s. The massive Victorian expansion of Worcester began with a vengeance in the early 1860s. In 1864 *Worcester Herald* sub-editor and local historian John Noake told *The Builder* magazine that 'immense blocks of buildings, like little towns' had suddenly sprung up in Sansome Walk, Chesnut Walk, the Blockhouse, Happy Land, the Moors, London Road and Barbourne, which 'have so transformed the place that you would scarcely recognise it now'. One reason for this was that the city's population of less than 30,000 had rapidly grown to 35,000, and even faster growth, in building and population, was to come in the 1880s and 1890s. But another reason for urgency in commencing building schemes in the early 1860s was the imminence of development controls, which arrived in December 1865.

The records of these regulations are referred to as planning applications in the index at the archives, but they were apparently building control applications, required by city by-laws made under the Local Government Act 1858, and only concerned with matters such as road access and sewage. Unfortunately it is not possible to check the detail of the regulations made in Worcester, because they seem to have been lost, but there seems little doubt that they were very unwelcome in some quarters when they were first introduced. Developers were given more than seven years after the Act was passed before the city put its precepts into practice, and Worcester could have introduced measures even earlier, under a similar Act of 1848, which certainly seems to suggest a distinct reluctance to act on the part of the city authorities. This may well have been because those who stood to gain most from delaying introduction of regulation were sitting in the council chamber, but it was also inevitable that the housing improvements brought about by greater regulation increased rents beyond the means of many poor people. There were probably also those who prophesied that greater regulation would disastrously stem the flow of new homes, but in the late Victorian boom building applications for more than 3,000 homes were submitted between 1878 and 1901.

Though much more information on city streets became available during the nineteenth century from maps and published sources, writing the history of the main expansion of the city in that period proved far from straightforward. Often streets and roads, especially those in the suburbs, began as lanes and 'cut-throughs', but their names were not recorded until urban development began in the area, and they then formed the basis of our road network. For that reason main roads out of the city, which clearly existed for centuries past, did not appear in listings until substantial development began there. Sometimes it is possible to date the naming, or renaming, of a street to a particular event, as when the ancient Cucking, Cooken or Cooking Street was renamed Copenhagen Street in honour of that battle's victor, Lord Nelson, who visited the city in 1802. But in other cases old names could persist for long periods, as happened with the ancient Salt Lane, which was renamed Castle Street in the early nineteenth century, but was frequently referred to by the old name throughout the rest of the century. Consequently exact dating of street names can be difficult.

There was also often confusion in the naming of streets in the nineteenth century. Early street directories, which were the telephone directories or online databases of their day, often named as streets what were in fact terraces of houses, which were subsequently incorporated into developing streets and were heard of no more in later directories, though others continued to be listed separately for many years. It has been difficult to know how best to deal with some of these early names; whether to remove them from the book or include them and explain what happened to them. In the end it was felt best in most cases to include them under the streets of which they form or formed part. However, obsolescent names which clearly applied to streets have usually been listed separately. Building applications show that streets were often referred to by a variant of the 'official' name; Sansome Walk for example, was often referred to as Sansome Fields or its previous name, Sansome Fields Walk, and confusingly after Sansome Fields Walk became Sansome Walk the original name was given to another street which still exists. Often the same or similar names were used in different parts of the city; Spring Gardens for example, which in the nineteenth century existed both in the Moors and St Martin's Gate, and Mill Street, which existed both in Barbourne and Diglis. Street, Road, Terrace and Place were often treated as interchangeable, and frequently a modern Street started as a Lane or Terrace, and changed its name after a few years – sometimes more than once.

Fast-developing streets often sprouted extensions or offshoots. Barbourne Terrace, the Butts, Park Street, the Quay, Severn Terrace and the Tything all acquired 'Upper' extensions, of which only Upper Park Street and Upper Tything remain. Meanwhile Bath Road sprouted a 'Lower' extension, not now to be found on the street map, because it has become Diglis Road, while other streets acquired 'Little' variants, some of which have survived, though the eighteenth century Little Angel Street was widened into Angel Place in the early twentieth century. Sometimes the confusion was inexplicable. Late nineteenth century street directories listed Lion Row, but not Lion Walk, of which it was said to be an offshoot. In the late twentieth century this situation had reversed, and Lion Walk was to be found on the street map, while Lion Row had disappeared, though this is somewhat academic now, because the whole area has recently been redeveloped. There does also tend to be a distinct shortage of records in relation to some streets, which could be because some areas only became part of the city after extensions of the boundaries in the 1830s, 1880s and at various later dates, though in other cases it appears that records of building applications must either have been lost or were never submitted in the first place. All of this does tend to cause some confusion for the researcher.

Another area of confusion is over who actually named streets. In many entries it has not been possible to do more than speculate about the reasons for a street name. The point has already been made that in earlier times street names appear to have been arrived at by some sort of consensus between users and residents over a period of time. But since public records became more detailed in the nineteenth century, readers are bound to ask who had the right to name new streets, and where are their decisions recorded. Anyone who knows anything about choosing street names now, will know that by law the local authority has the final say, and certainly that right extends back into history. For much of the Victorian period it was accorded by the Towns Improvement Clauses Act of 1847, which consolidated powers that city authorities had under earlier acts, but that is far from the whole story. The clause on naming of streets seems vague, to say the least, and it is questionable how far the city authorities could or did rely on it, especially since there is little in the way of recorded examples of them exercising these powers.

This is not to say that this process was never recorded, or that the council never had any say. Where the streets concerned were within the old city centre, then the council had a traditional right to control what happened there, and was likely to assume that included a right to rename the streets if it saw fit. It rarely did, but in 1877 John Noake blamed 'the meddling of a very incompetent party then in the Town Council' for a spate of apparently recent name changes that he thoroughly disapproved of. He doesn't list too many examples however. The only changes he lists which seem attributable to this 'same remorseless dauber' are one of the city's several Back Walks becoming part of The Butts (subsequently to become Upper Butts, then Farrier Street); Butts Walk becoming Cherry Tree Walk; Grope Lane becoming Group Lane; Salt Lane becoming Castle Street; and Turkey, the Causeway and Cripplegate becoming Tybridge Street. Nor is it clear over what period these changes took place, since 'a few years ago' seems to be a phrase Noake uses whenever he doesn't have the exact date.

However the situation with new roads and streets was quite different. These were always on private land outside the traditional city centre. Consequently it seems to have been assumed that the land owner had the legal right to call parts of their land whatever they cared to. So as odd as it may seem, the naming of most new Victorian streets seems to have been regarded as a private matter. Streets Committee minutes contain records of developers applying for previously named and developed streets to be adopted as public roads, and the committee grew increasingly tough in its demands for proper pavements, drainage and so on, but no instances have been seen of Victorian councillors overturning the developer's choice of street name. This again may be the result of councillors and developers being the same people, and no doubt there was some collusion, since the 1890s saw a spate of streets being named after mayors.

Given that there is no public record of how the names of many of our street were determined, readers might well ask how they were arrived at for this book. In some cases the task was not too difficult. With Ashcroft Road for example, the building applications for creation of the street and building of the houses were submitted by builder Bert Ashcroft, so it is clear that Mr Ashcroft gave his family name to the road. Here, as elsewhere, the guiding principle was, if it seems just too obvious to be a coincidence, then it is pretty likely that it isn't. In that case there was also confirmation from an elderly resident who had grown up in the street and knew Mr Ashcroft's son.

In other cases, it has not been so obvious, and the search has had to be widened. Some streets – George Street and Pheasant Street for example – were clearly named for pubs in the area at the time they were created. A number of other options were also looked at. Was the street name taken from a field name, the name of a large house in the area, or a natural feature such as a brook or spring? All these have given rise to street names. Where it was obvious that a street had been given a family name, the search began with property professionals – builders, surveyors, solicitors, land agents – and sometimes one or other of these produced a result. Most often however, it is not surprising that the name was traced to a wealthy local individual or family who probably supplied the finance for the development, or owned, leased, or bought the land on which it was built. In one or two cases – Shaw Street, and possibly Surman Street for example – it is possible that naming of the street may have been part of the deal under which the owner of leases surrendered them in order that a building project could go ahead. Much that has had to be surmised can hopefully be confirmed in the future, if the opportunity arises for a much more extensive examination of city property deeds and leases than would have been possible during the preparation of this book.

Another area where more work could be carried out in the future is in the listing of residents. The listings used here to describe the occupations of residents are, with a very few exceptions, taken from street directories. These are valuable, but they can be misleading because only the head of the household is shown, suggesting that there was only one occupant or breadwinner to a house. In fact most small houses could be packed with up to 10 or 12 family members, relatives and lodgers, most of whom worked. So listings of residents give only a rough idea of the sort of community that existed in a street in the past, and a much more detailed picture can be obtained by looking at census returns and other records, but again the time that would take has not been available in the preparation of this book, nor was the space available in the book for that level of detailed information. Consequently there is plenty of scope for those with the time and inclination to research the history of individual streets, and hopefully the information here will at least provide a starting point.

The task of starting to recreate some of the central areas of the city as we know them today largely fell, in the late nineteenth century, to city industrialist George Henry Williamson. One of two brothers who ran a tin plate manufactory at the Providence Works in the Blockhouse, he was a leading member of the city corporation for 40 years, and mayor in 1893. During his years as Chairman of both the Streets and Electricity Committees he took a major role in transforming Worcester's cramped, medieval central streets into wide, attractive thoroughfares lit by electricity, for which he facilitated the building of the first municipal power station. This all had the effect of creating attractive open spaces within the city centre, but at the cost of sweeping away many old buildings. In the early twentieth century Elgar's boyhood friend and neighbour Hubert Leicester took up the baton, campaigning for the clearance of slum areas, and many of the old courts and tenements of slum housing were demolished in the 1920s and 30s, while much new building went ahead in the suburbs. Both men have had streets named after them.

Redevelopment in the 1960s led to the wholesale demolition of long-established areas, including the destruction of a whole block of largely medieval buildings in Lich Street at the heart of the city, and the much-loved Public Hall in the Cornmarket. In all, during the 1960s the city lost much that it has had cause to regret losing, though not until the history of this period is written will we truly be able to understand why this devastation took place.

Today the city has grown far beyond its Roman, Anglo-Saxon, medieval and even Victorian boundaries, but the city as it existed in past centuries is still the heart of our community. Many of us still work within the line of the medieval city walls, and for all of us it is the focus for commerce, finance, culture, entertainment, shopping and leisure. It is sad that we have lost so much of what once existed in old Worcester, but the better we understand our past, the better we may preserve what remains of it in the future.

Historic Worcester Streets

HISTORIC WORCESTER STREETS PAST AND PRESENT

First recorded from earliest times to 1940

(Bold capitals indicate that a street still exists. Bold italics indicate either that a street
no longer exists or that the name is no longer in use. Streets referred to within an
entry, either in bold or bold italics, have their own entry. Only the first mention is bold.)

ABBEY ROAD

This road was the site of a former timber framed manor house, after which **Great House Road** was also named, which was apparently on this site from the seventeenth century. City council experts have identified

The Great House pictured around 1904, shortly before it was demolished - RS

this house on **Malvern Road** as the building shown on late nineteenth century maps standing exactly where this street is. The house was originally the manor house of Hardwick Manor, which once held a large area of St John's, and was said by Victorian local historian Noake to have been a replacement for an earlier house burnt down during the Civil War. It ceased to be a manor house in the eighteenth century, after this part of the manor was purchased by the Vernon family, who built themselves a home further along Malvern Road.

The old manor house here apparently continued to be known as Great House, but for some reason it was also referred to as The Priory in the late nineteenth century, perhaps because this was originally monastic land. Presumably this monastic connection accounts for the street name, though why it isn't Priory Road is a mystery. In its later days the building housed a tannery and glove making business.

A building application to create this road was submitted in 1902, after the site was purchased by the city for redevelopment. The old manor house was demolished in 1904, and in 1906 an application to build six houses was submitted. These were the six cottages of Abbey Terrace, which were in existence when the road was first listed in a street directory of 1912 under Malvern Road. Residents then included an engine driver, three draymen, a bricklayer, and a brewer. These Edwardian cottages still exist, but the development didn't go well, and nothing further was built here until modern times.

ALBANY ROAD

First mentioned in the 1830s, and listed in a street directory in 1840, this was one of several roads in the city, and many others around the country, named for Frederick, Duke of York and Albany , second son of George III, who died in 1827. As a military field commander he was not a great success, said to be the subject of the satirical rhyme:

> *The grand old Duke of York,*
> *He had ten thousand men.*
> *He marched them up to the top of the hill*
> *And he marched them down again.*
> *And when they were up, they were up.*
> *And when they were down, they were down.*
> *And when they were only halfway up,*
> *They were neither up nor down*

He blamed his lack of success on the state of the military, and became a very popular commander-in-chief of the army, whose thorough reforms, including the establishment of the Royal Military Academy, Sandhurst, were credited with laying the foundation for the defeat of Napoleon.

Frederick, Duke of York and Albany

Like many city streets, this was built piecemeal over a long period. In 1885, when it was listed as Albany Street, there appeared to be 28 houses already built, and the Mission Room and school of the Rev James Davenport. Residents were mostly workmen and small tradesmen, including engineers, railwaymen, coopers and a cabinet maker, plus an alderman, and photographer E.J. Morley. Five building applications for a total of 20 more houses were submitted between 1886 and 1904, but there wasn't room for all of these, and by 1912 or before the road was complete with the 41 homes which still exist.

ALBANY TERRACE

Albany Terrace and York Place in December 1835

Named for Frederick, Duke of York and Albany (see **Albany Road**), the development of this street and the neighbouring York Place was being planned when he died in 1827, and a lease on the land was taken on 21 May, by Worcester businessman John Rowlands and Shropshire landowner Henry Wilding. Around that time the east side of **Britannia Square** was shown on a map as Albany Road. This street was apparently based on the adjoining **Britannia Square** development, with building plots being sold to speculators or aspiring home owners, but it did not prove as popular, perhaps because the houses here were too small to be split into apartments or lodgings, as often happened in the Square. Whereas Britannia Square was largely completed in 20 years, it was more than a century before this street was anything like complete.

Building began slowly in the 1830s and it was listed in a street directory of 1840, but while many streets were numbered in 1841 with the introduction of the penny post, Albany Terrace was not, presumably because it was nothing like complete, though the north side was shown complete on a map of 1840. A building application for four houses was submitted in 1884, but other houses were not built until the twentieth century.

By 1912 all the homes here now were listed. Residents included a commercial traveller, an engineer, an inland revenue officer and a brush manufacturer, but 10 residents were ladies, either Miss or Mrs, with no stated occupation, presumably supported by income inherited from parents or late husbands.

Two house plots then remained. One plot was finally occupied by the United Reformed Church in 1963, and the adjoining plot was until 2014 occupied by a temporary building of WWII vintage, erected as an emergency food store. At the time of writing, the site is being redeveloped for housing.

H.H. Lines - MAG

The most famous resident was Victorian landscape artist Henry Harris Lines, who lived here for some 35 years, from 1855 at the present No. 27, and spent the last decade of his long life with his daughter at the present No. 14.

ALBERT ROAD

Prince Albert

A building application for the new road was submitted in 1897, named for Queen Victoria's late consort, Prince Albert. He had died 36 years earlier, but the Queen's Diamond Jubilee in that year, celebrating her sixtieth year on the throne, resulted in a wave of public affection for the long widowed monarch, and Albert and Victoria streets sprang up all over the country; the adjoining **Victoria Avenue** also went ahead at this time. Development proceeded quickly, with a building application for 12 houses submitted in that same year, and another for 14 houses in 1899, by which time some of the homes were already built. It was first listed in a street directory in 1900, with eight homes and four more 'in course of erection'. Residents listed in 1900 included a works manager, Royal Porcelain Works foreman John Austin, Howard John Hadley of porcelain manufacturer James Hadley & Sons, a china modeller, several clerks, a commercial traveller and a dairyman. The rate of development then slowed. Further building applications were submitted for five houses and a shop in 1901, four houses in 1904 and another three in 1905. In 1905 there were 24 homes, with 28 by 1912. Development then stalled, and nothing further was built until the 1930s, and development at the south end is all modern. The shop on the corner of Victoria Avenue was still open in the 1990s, but has since been converted to a home.

ALEXANDER ROAD

Homes in this small road must have been built in the 1920s, probably around the time that **Bromwich Road** was created as it is now, since the first building applications found were for additions in 1929 and 1935, by which time the houses must have been built, and all the homes here are built with the 'black and white' cladding reminiscent of the twenties, but no records have been found for the original construction of the road or the homes, and no listings for it were found in directories before the Second World War. The homes here may originally have been developed to let, since there would probably have been more variety of construction if plots had been sold and building carried out by various developers or owners. The road must take its name from Alfred Norman Alexander, who lived at the Old Orchard, Lower Wick, and was presumably responsible for this development. The firm of A.N. Alexander Ltd submitted close to 90 building applications involving hundreds of city homes in the first half of the twentieth century, especially in the 1930s and 1940s, but the company was not found listed in city or county trade directories, and whether Mr Alexander was a property developer in his own right, or acted on behalf of others is not known.

All Hallows

Now part of **Deansway**. The name is an old form of All Saints, the church which it adjoined. This ancient name referred to an area between All Saints Church and the end of Broad Street, now mostly beneath the roadway. It probably originated in Anglo-Saxon times as a market, and may have been a cattle market then, as it was later.

The dedication of the church probably resulted from its closeness to the quay and the bridge, meaning many of its worshippers would have come from far and wide, with many different dedications to their parish churches. The present church, called by Pevsner 'A fine introduction to Worcester as one crosses the bridge', is believed to be at least the third on the site. It was built 1739-1742 to replace a building much damaged in the Civil War, but retains from that building the base of the fifteenth century tower, some medieval stained glass, a chained bible of 1538, and an effigy of Edward Hurdman, Worcester's first mayor in 1621. The earliest surviving registers date from 1560. Until the nineteenth century this area consisted of large half-timbered houses (see cover illustration), and the church was built to be imposing and tower above its neighbours.

All Saints Church in the late eighteenth century and a map of the area in 1884

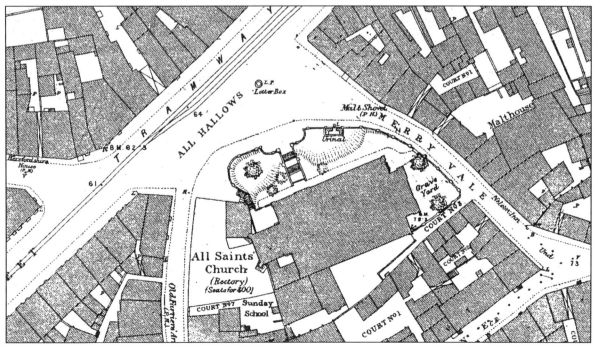

For centuries this had been one of the sites from which citizens could access the city's water supply, and this had a significant effect on the street name. There had long been wells in each ward, and a city ordinance of

1551 required the appointment of 'credible persons' to ensure their maintenance, but in 1612, during a period of severe drought throughout England, the city authorities ordered that pumps be installed, and the one at the end of **The Shambles** gave its name to **Pump Street**. Here however, the original name stuck, and in 1790 the street was still listed as *All-hallows well*. A small, square, domed building on the roadside, which housed the pump from which citizens could collect water in barrels at certain hours, was still in existence at that date. The pump was superseded in the early nineteenth century, and the small pump house was presumably removed, since the cover painting of about 1820 does not show it. Officially then the area became known simply as All Hallows, but far into the twentieth century older people still referred to this area as 'the well'.

The small, square domed building in this late eighteenth century print was 'The Well' where residents could draw water on. Below, an effigy of the first Mayor Edward Hurdman in All Saints Church - TW

All Saints was the largest, most populous parish in the city, with many courts housing poor people, which quickly became slums. In 1779 there were 1944 inhabitants in the parish, living in 352 tightly-packed houses. Many of the houses in this area were pulled down around 1835, including that of Edward Hurdman, who lived at the end of Broad Street

opposite All Saints Church. This street name survived until the early 1960s when redevelopment created **Deansway**. The current All Saints Road is an extension of **Dolday** and doesn't actually pass the church. Much of the street in the late nineteenth century was used as business premises.

There were many pubs here over the years. The Dun Cow was listed here in 1790, and the Hen and Chickens was also said to be an eighteenth century house. In 1885 there were 14 business premises listed here and three pubs, the Brewer's Arms, the Malt Shovel Inn and the Nelson, at the junction with *Merryvale*. There was also a stationers and newsagent, a confectioner, a clothes dealer and a fruiterer. The Malt Shovel, a pub which opened in the 1820s as the Press Inn because it was next door to Potter's Printing Press, was situated across the road almost due east from the church. It closed in 1906 and became the Empire Dining Rooms. By 1958, not long before the Deansway redevelopment, all that was left of this street was Potter's Printing, and the Car Park Cafe serving the massive car park which had been created from the site of the cleared slums of St Andrew's parish.

ALMA STREET

Originally this was just a lane beside the **Droitwich Road** pub, one of many pubs around the country named after the British military victory at the Battle of Alma, the first battle of the Crimean War, which took place at the River Alma on 20 September 1854. The lane may have begun to be developed soon afterwards, about the same time as the pub, but it was not first listed in a street directory until 1873, becoming Alma Street by 1884, though a street directory of that date seemed to be confused as to exactly where it was, and listed many properties in the general area under this street. By 1896 there were 23 homes listed here, surrounded by a good deal of open space. Residents at that time included five labourers, a shunter, building tradesmen, a stoker, two glovers, a tin plate worker, a cellarman, a laundress, a charwoman and a hay trusser. A group of four cottages or villas called Cypress Place in 1884, probably gave their name to **Cypress Street**. Long-time resident Henry Cale at No. 3 was a potter. There has been a good deal of further development here on the remaining house plots in modern times.

The Battle of Alma 20 September 1854, after which the pub and the street were named

ANGEL PLACE

This was originally a much narrower lane called *Little Angel Street*, but the present name gradually replaced it, and the street was largely widened by the early twentieth century. The name Angel Place appears to have come into existence originally in the late eighteenth or early nineteenth century, and was first found in a street

The fruit and veg market in Angel Place, later a small shopping mall and now a restaurant - RS

directory of 1840, but then it referred only to the area from Angel Street to The Butts, which is still partly of the original width. The rest of what is now this street continued as Little Angel Street until 1913, when it was widened.

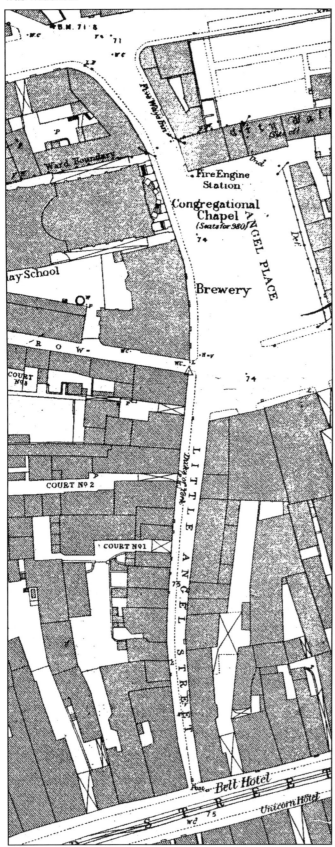

Little Angel Street in 1884 before it was widened into Angel Place during which the Bell Hotel was demolished

Up to the mid fourteenth century the land to the west, leading down to the river, was known as Belassis, old French for beautiful place. In 1347 it was given to the Blackfriars who established a friary here on a substantial site bounded by **Broad Street** and **The Butts**, and running down towards the Severn (see ***Blackfriars Street***).

An area at the north end of the street, where there is now a Chinese restaurant, has had various uses over the centuries. It was once an orchard held by the Black Friars, but was purchased by Worcester Corporation in 1625 for use as a burial ground, though it may not have been consecrated until 1644. It appears to have been the first cemetery established to supplement the cathedral burial ground, which was the only one in the city in the medieval period, and continued in use until 1804.

This area used to be known as the old Sheepmarket, since it served that function after the graveyard closed. In 1920 a building was put up for a fruit and veg market, which operated until 1981, when it became the Angel Mall shopping arcade for some years. Old city folklore identified this as the site of the plague pit from the last great plague outbreak of 1637, in which about one fifth of the city's population lost their lives, but no evidence has been found to support this claim, and it is regarded as unlikely.

The Congregationalists were established here in the late seventeenth or early eighteenth century. The date of 1687 has been given and their earliest registers, for christenings and marriages, date from 1699, though their first purpose-built chapel has been said to date from 1708, which may mean they were originally meeting in a house in this street, perhaps because of difficulty in obtaining the land they needed for the chapel at a time when dissenters were not popular. There is a story told by Bill Gwilliam, that when the dissenters were refused permission to build here, they obtained land for a chapel next door to the home of a leading member of the corporation, after which the land here was quickly released.

The chapel may have provided some of the earliest education for poor children in Worcester. When Rev George Osborn came to Worcester as minister he noticed large numbers of children in the streets, and in 1797 began a Sunday School for boys, soon followed by one for girls, at which youngsters were taught to read, write and spell, and there were rewards of clothing for well-behaved children at the end of each year. This did not go down well with the establishment, who believed education would make the poor dissatisfied and foment revolution, and Osborn was forced to defend himself in the pulpit.

The chapel was rebuilt in a striking, robust, classical style in 1859 at a cost of £6,000, £1,000 of which was contributed by Richard Padmore, after whom **Padmore Street** was named. A striking new building for the Sunday School was built in 1887-88 to the design of Aston Webb, regarded as the greatest architect of the late Victorian period. The plan for the chapel to become a nightclub was unveiled in 1983, to considerable opposition from local publicans.

Immediately north of the bus station entrance is the nineteenth century building which was Lewis Clarke's brewery, founded in 1846, which became Malpas, Lewis, Clarke & Co in 1884. Brewing ceased here when it was taken over by Burton brewers Marstons in 1937. The southern end of the building was altered during the Crowngate redevelopment, but otherwise it is almost unchanged. The pub on the corner of The Butts – now the Angel – was then the Five Ways, with the Norwich Union Fire Station next door, and auctioneers Wooldridge and Joseland and a number of smaller business premises were nearby.

The Scala Picture House cinema opened on the corner in November 1922, partly owned by wealthy businessman George Gascoyne, who lived in **Barbourne Terrace**. It closed in 1973. Until a new bus station opened as part of the Crowngate development, this street was busy with buses picking up and dropping off from stops on the east side. The Midland Red had an enquiry office here from 1928 or before, with a clock on the outer wall supplied by city mail order business Kay's. The office closed some years ago, but the clock is still here.

Angel Place after 1922 when the Scala cinema on the left opened - RS

ANGEL ROW

An old alleyway from **Angel Place** to *Blackfriars Street*, formerly *Smock Alley* or Smoke Alley, the name was changed in the nineteenth century, according to Noake, who in 1877 wrote disparagingly of it having 'of late been dignified' with this name. The new name was first found listed in a street directory of 1840. It still exits Angel Place in much the same spot, but due to redevelopment it now runs beside the Crowngate bus station entrance and serves only as a back route into the shopping centre, though its use has increased since the opening of The Hive on 2 July 2012, to which it is linked by a pedestrian bridge over The Butts.

ANGEL STREET

A very ancient street or lane. In past centuries *Little Angel Street* linked the west end of the street to **Broad Street**, since **Angel Place** was not completed until the early twentieth century, so locations we would think of as in Angel Place were often described in past centuries as being in this street.

The Theatre Royal, Angel Street,
described as The Opera House on
this Edwardian postcard - RS

THE OPERA HOUSE.   WORCESTER   1272.

Historic Worcester Streets

In Anglo-Saxon times it was believed to be Agga Strete, a lane leading to the Earl of Mercia's fort, agga or haga, created by a charter of 904 to protect the settlement from Norse raiders coming up the Severn. In the mid-1950s it was believed that the fort was on the north side of Broad Street, but 60 years later academics moved it to the south side of Broad Street, though there seems to be no certain evidence of exactly where it was. The fort, wherever it was, must have become obsolete after the Norman Conquest, when a castle was built at the other end

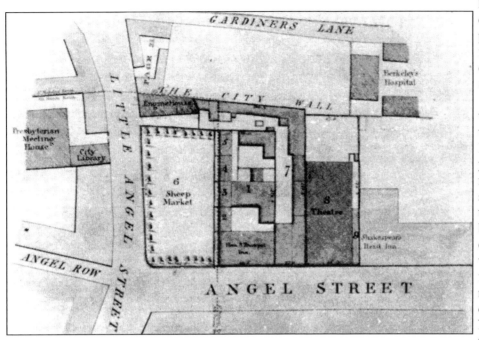

Angel Street after 1789 when the theatre opened

of the city, but it has been suggested in recent times that there may have been urban expansion onto the fort site even before the Norman Conquest.

This street was recorded as Angel Lane in 1625 and on a map of 1764. The city wall was its northern boundary until the walls were slighted by parliamentary forces after the Civil War. By 1790 it had become a Street, presumably having been paved, perhaps as its shops and taverns attracted more people.

This street presumably took its name from the fifteenth century Angel tavern on the south side of the street, which in 1517 was owned by Bordesley Abbey, near Redditch. It was opposite where the HSBC Bank is in Broad Street, since there was an Angel Passage beside the pub, passing between the two streets, which was built over in the 1960s by the present bank building. The entrance to the alley is still here but is not now open to the public.

An area at the bottom of the street, now in Angel Place, was a graveyard in the seventeenth and eighteenth centuries, later a sheep market, and in the twentieth century a fruit and veg market and a shopping mall, before becoming a restaurant (see picture on Angel Place entry).

Immediately to the east of this site in 1646 was built a large house belonging to Robert Stirrop, who was mayor in the following year. He was said to have prospered during the Civil War, and spent £400 on construction of his house, which has been identified by building historian Pat Hughes as The Horn and Trumpet pub, which she described as the earliest brick building in the city. There was originally a large brick-built workshop range to the rear, long since demolished. In 1790 this was the shop of James Clark, described as 'musician, horn and trumpet', which presumably accounts for the name of the pub which had opened here by 1822. This was an important inn in the nineteenth century for country carriers, taking goods and passengers to outlying villages. The building acquired an outer brick skin in the nineteenth century, but the original brickwork can apparently still be seen in the attic.

In 1812 inquests were being held in this street at the Currier's Arms, though there is no further information about this hostelry. In 1864 the Journal mentioned the Crystal Palace Spirit Vaults, not otherwise known, which seems from a crime report to have been a haunt of 'ladies of the night'. In 1885 there were four inns in the street, the Shakespeare Hotel, the Horn and Trumpet, the Fountain Inn and the Ewe and Lamb Vaults. The office of the Surveyor of Taxes was also here, together with a maltster, a seed warehouse, a hop warehouse, plus various small businesses.

The street long offered entertainment aside from inns and taverns. In 1779 Mr Whiteley, manager of the King's Head theatre in the **High Street**, which was in a poor state, built The Theatre Royal here at a cost of £1,000, funded by subscription. It opened in 1780 and had 70 very successful years, attracting large audiences and all the leading actors of the day, until provincial theatres declined in the 1850s. In 1875 a new theatre was built on the same site, but it burnt down two years later. It became 'Royal' in 1884 when it was taken over by an amateur group and rebuilt, after which it was so fashionable that the audience were expected to

Burgess's shop at No. 3 Angel Street in 1906 - RS

wear evening dress. The Theatre Royal closed in 1955 and was demolished in 1960, when provincial theatres once more declined with the advent of television. The theatre site was taken over by Colmore Depot for a car showroom, but building works caused some problems. The excavation of the site to a depth of 15 – 20 feet (4.5 – 6m) badly affected the historic Berkeley's Hospital site on **The Cross**, and the chapel and two almshouses were in imminent danger of collapse, until the trustees got a court order to stop the work. A supermarket has occupied the site since the 1980s. The Congregationalists were established here in the late seventeenth or early eighteenth century, on a site which is now in Angel Place. The city's first public library was started here in 1790 by the Presbyterian Society. It was a subscription library, and claimed 120 subscribers and 600 books. Initially it thrived, becoming known as the City and County Library, and moved to **Pierpoint Street** in 1831. The Corn Exchange was built in 1848 at a cost of £5,000. It was built in competition to another Corn Exchange in the **Cornmarket** which was being built by the corn merchants, while this was built by the farmers, who wanted to

take control of this valuable trade, and it was said to have been put up in just four months. There was a grand opening on 26 August, at which around 500 farmers, gentry and nobility toasted their success. It was this spacious building that subsequently took the business, and the building in the Cornmarket became the Public Hall, but within 50 years this building was struggling for business as the trade fell off, and during 1900-1930 it was used for boxing bouts and as an auction room. It was converted into shops as part of the Crown Passage development.

ARBORETUM ROAD

This road is situated on part of what was formerly the mid nineteenth century Arboretum Pleasure Grounds. In the eighteenth century this was part of the Sansome Fields estate, owned by Sir Charles Trubshaw Withers, who lived on what became **Sansome Walk**.

Later part of the estate was bought by the Worcester Public Pleasure Grounds Company, which despite its name was a private company. The company employed leading landscape gardener William Barrow to lay out the 25 acres in terraces, promenades and flower beds, with medieval-style entrance gates, a cricket ground, bowling green, archery butts, a large central fountain similar to one at Witley Court, and an arboretum of American conifers, which gave the area its name. The entrance, off Sansome Walk had an entrance lodge, still in existence, and imposing iron gates and railings by Hardy and Padmore, now at the Infirmary site in

Castle Street. The entrance drive, now this road, led to a crystal pavilion on the site of the present **East Street**.

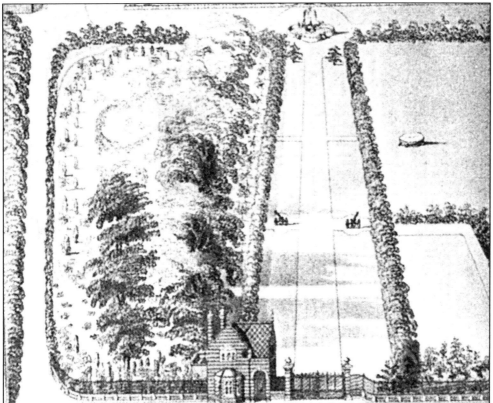

The entrance drive to The Arboretum, now Arboretum Road. The lodge still exists.

When completed, the gardens were regarded as amongst the finest in the provinces. They were opened on 30 July 1859 by the Mayor of Worcester, Thomas Rowley Hill, after whom **Rowley Hill Street** was named, in a lavish ceremony with 200 guests. The council had put £1,000 into the project, which earned citizens free access on one day a week, though that day turned out to be Monday. The rest of the week the public had to pay to attend events including shows, fetes, performances, firework displays and a well-attended horticultural show, but the venture was not profitable and after four years the company went bust. The council then had the opportunity to buy the park, and Lord Dudley put up more than a third of the purchase price, but the council didn't seize the opportunity, and in 1866 the site was sold for redevelopment. Given the history of the site there were many interesting possibilities for street names, but instead the streets were mostly given commonplace compass references, **East Street**, **Southfield Street**, **Northfield Street**.

The land was split into lots for sale, and the first recorded building applications, for three houses, were submitted in the following year, but development proceeded slowly, though building was also going on in the other streets round about, and in 1869 there was a reference to the Arboretum building estate. Between 1868 and 1896 there were 27 building applications for 60 homes here, many for just one or two houses, the largest being two separate applications for eight houses. Vigornia Terrace**, a** terrace of eight houses between **Middle Street** and Sansome Walk, was listed separately for some years from 1880.

In 1884 there were 33 homes in the road, but by 1904 this had increased to about 80. In 1884 the residents included Rev John Anderson, assistant minister at the Countess of Huntingdon's church, and a mixture of commercial clerks, railwaymen, tailors and dressmakers, a revenue officer, a brewer, a tinman, and two ladies, presumably widows, offering apartments to let.

Around the end of the century No. 30 was home to the British Employees Co-operative Society, which claimed to have 'a practical solution for the servant problem'. The organisation operated as a cross between a friendly society and a recruitment agency, charging employers for supplying suitable servants, and providing benefits for members who were sick or out of work through no fault of their own.

ARROWSMITH AVENUE

This street must have been named for city councillor and local solicitor Arthur Arrowsmith Maund, after whom **Maund Street** is likely to have been named in the 1880s. He was city council member for the Claines ward, Under Sheriff of the city in 1896 and Sheriff in 1901, and sat on the Streets Committee. He was a partner in the law firm Maund & Coombs. The street was first found in a street directory in 1937, when there were 43 homes listed.

Historic Worcester Streets

Artichoke Fields

An old name for the area where the Infirmary in **Castle Street** was built. The site was in use as an artichoke field until shortly before construction began.

ASH AVENUE

Part of a 'tree' estate off **Brickfields Road**, though on the opposite side of the road from the rest of the estate. It was first found listed in 1937, when it was already complete.

Ashcroft Road today - TW

ASHCROFT ROAD

Builder Herbert Ashcroft, who lived in **Lansdowne Road**, possibly in a house he built himself, built this street and gave it his family name. He had already been involved in other large-scale projects, such as the building of 16 houses in **Waterworks Road** and **Barbourne Walk**, for which a building application was submitted in June 1888. In 1896 he submitted building applications for a new road here, a shop and 11 cottages which were called Coburg Terrace, and were listed separately in directories for many years from 1900. In 1898 he submitted a further building application for 31 houses.

By 1908 or before, Blundell's general store had opened on the west side of the street, where there is now a hairdressing salon. From the 1920s to the 1950s or later it was run by Vera, the daughter of the original owners, Mrs Emily Blundell and her husband. On the opposite corner was Bacon's grocery and fruit and veg shop, run by James and Louisa Bacon, and from the 1940s by their daughter Molly.

In 1912 residents of the street included a van man, a prison warder, a foreman maltster, a printer, an iron fitter, a glover, a laundryman, a chimney sweep and an artists' colourman's assistant. Homes in the street were built to rent, and an elderly former resident recalled that none were sold until the late 1920s when Mr Ashcroft's son had taken over the business after his father's death.

ASTWOOD ROAD

This road has an ancient name; in Old English Astwood meant Eastern Wood. A reference of 1392 connects it to Wystan or Whitstones, an early name given to **The Tything**, which suggests that the land was held by the White Ladies convent there. In the nineteenth century much land in this area was owned by wealthy city lawyer and philanthropist William Laslett, after whom **Laslett Street** was named. It was he who gave 20 acres of land to the city to create Astwood Cemetery, and burials were taking place from 1858. Alice Ottley, after whom the school she ran in the **Tything** was formerly named, was buried here in 1912.

The road was first found in a street directory in 1873, and there was a steady flow of small-scale building applications into the next century, mostly for 1 or 2 houses. Stately home Astwood House stood in its own ample grounds on what is now **Brickfields Road**, on the north side a little way past the railway bridge.

A street directory of 1912 showed that the list of residents' occupations in this lengthy road read like a roll call of trades, including a good many railwaymen. Alfred Edward Brown was then master of the Rainbow Hill School at the end of Green Lane.

Astwood Road, looking towards Rainbow Hill, probably around 1910, showing the parade of shops on the left. The Co-op had the supermarket (extreme left) and the butcher's shop until the early 1980s - RS

Athelstan, an artist's impression from a nineteenth century engraving

ATHELSTAN ROAD

This road must have been named after the grandson of Alfred the Great, who is widely regarded as the first king of England. He reigned between 924 and 939, though scholars date his reign as King of the English from 927. In that year he conquered the Viking kingdom of York to rule over the whole of England, and in 934 he conquered the Scots, but he is also known for his reforms of government, law and learning, and he is credited with laying the foundations for Benedictine reform of the monasteries later in the century. These days his name is most often spelled with an initial 'Ae'.

He grew up in the Anglo-Saxon kingdom of Mercia, which included Worcester, and he may have indirectly contributed to the naming of **Dolday**. It is possible that this road's closeness to **St Dunstan's Crescent**, named for a former Bishop of Worcester believed to have been a relative of Athelstan via his mother Ecgwynn, may imply an intention to create an Anglo-Saxon themed estate here, even though there was apparently 17 years between the creation of the two streets. In any event, the theme was not continued in surrounding streets.

A building application to create this road was submitted in 1902. It was first listed under **Battenhall Road** in 1912, when there were three villas, St Wulstan's Lodge, Lucerne and Ingledale, occupied by a stock broker, a clerk and the Misses Hughes. A fourth was added in the next 12 years. The remainder of the development here is modern.

AUTUMN TERRACE

First found on a map of 1838, this street was shown in street directories from 1840 as a terrace of five houses, listed under **Spring Hill**. Occupants in 1885 were an engine fitter, a seamstress, a labourer, a compositor and a Mrs Lucy Yapp letting out apartments at No. 3. These have since been cleared, but the main feature of this little cul-de-sac is the imposing Nightingale House, a former nurses home now split into flats.

Nightingale House on Autumn Terrace - TW

AVENUE ROAD

This road was first found listed in a street directory in 1884, shown under **Bransford Road**, when there were four homes, whose residents included a glove manufacturer, a telegraph inspector for the GWR, and a lay clerk of the cathedral. The remainder of the plots were not built on until modern times.

AVENUE, THE

This small, city centre cul-de-sac seems to have been created soon after the middle of the eighteenth century, although it is possible it could have been earlier. It seems never to have been a through route. It appears to be shown first on a 1779 map. In the mid 1880s the directory and railway guide publishers Littleburys were partly based here. There was also a book binder, two solicitors, two land agents and a local office of Burton brewers Ind, Coope. In 1935 local historian and former mayor Hubert Leicester said there was still a section of the old cobbled road surface here, which he claimed was the last to survive in the city, and should be preserved for posterity, but it has unfortunately since disappeared.

Back Lane

Blockhouse. Shown on a map of 1824, running parallel with **Carden Street** and **Charles Street** midway between them, it subsequently became ***Foundry Alley***, and ***Little Charles Street*** beyond ***Portland Place***.

Back Lane

Now **Hebb Street**. This lane ran across the north side of **Britannia Square** and **Albany Terrace**, and must have been created as a rear access to houses in those streets and **York Place**. It was listed in street directories from 1840 until the 1880s, and Hebb Street was first listed in 1898. In 1884 there were seven homes listed here, housing two upholsteresses, a journeyman baker, two grocers and a greengrocer.

BACK LANE NORTH

This lane was first found in the health board streets list of 1872, and listed in a street directory in 1897 as access to the rear of houses in **Britannia Square** and **Albany Terrace**.

BACK LANE SOUTH

First found in the health board streets list of 1872, and in a street directory of 1884, when six homes were listed here, including two Woodland Cottages and Beaufort House. Residents included a tailor, a clerk, a labourer, a carpenter, a foreman at the local board of health and a businessman.

BACK WALK

First listed in a street directory in 1840, it originally included the present **Back Walk** and what is now **Brewery Walk**. Eleven homes were listed here in 1897, three of them empty. Residents were either small tradesmen or manual workers. They included a butcher, a painter, two labourers, two laundresses and a glover.

BALLIOL ROAD

See *Elbury Road*.

BANK STREET

Originally part of ***Powick Lane***, this street must have been named for the Old Bank, which opened in 1765. This street name was first found in a street directory in 1790. It is now cut off by Crowngate, but formerly curved around to the back of the Countess of Huntingdon's chapel. In the seventeenth century the Globe inn stood at the top of the street, much frequented by senior councillors, who feasted the new MP there in 1655. The street seems to have been largely rebuilt in the late 1860s or early 1870s. It is now dominated by the entrance to Crowngate, but a good deal of interest remains on the north side. Beside the entrance to the

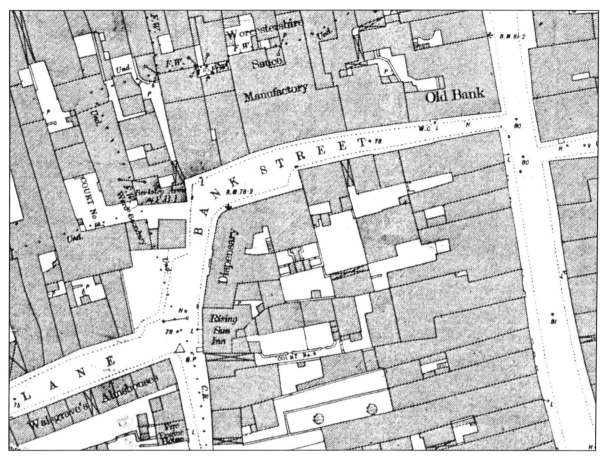

Map of the Bank Street area in 1884, and below, Bank Street, then part of Powick Lane, in 1800 - HL

shopping arcade is all that remains of what was the Berkeley Arms, apparently known locally as the Blood Hole, a pub first listed in 1873, and closed about 1970, named for a family of wealthy clothiers who lived in **Mealcheapen Street** and bought country estates.

Nearby is the former grocery warehouse of Richard West, dated 1872. Next door Lea and Perrins had their first Worcestershire Sauce factory, behind their **Broad Street** shop, though part of the factory has been redeveloped as offices.

The street was widened in the late nineteenth century by demolishing buildings on the south side.

The Worcester Old Bank was the city's oldest known bank, and stood on the **High Street** corner where W.H. Smith is now situated. It was also often known as Berwick's Bank, since it was founded in 1765 by Joseph Berwick, who held the lucrative post of Receiver-General to the County of Worcester, collecting Crown debts, and Samuel Wall, a silk mercer.

They were joined in partnership in 1781 by Elias Isaac, after whose family **Isaac Walk** was named, and various other people became partners over the years.

The bank was amalgamated with the Capital and County Bank in 1906, and in 1918 was absorbed into Lloyd's Bank, but the original premises remained open for almost 200 years, until 1962.

Bank Street and Powick Lane in Edwardian times, home to wholesale confectioners Norton & Whitton. Below, old house on High Street corner, later replaced by Simes' and since by a department store - RS

In 1822 the Worcester Dispensary and Provident Medical Institution opened here, with a doctor and a pharmacist on staff, to provide medical advice and medication for poor people who could not afford doctors' fees. Home visits could be arranged, vaccinations given, and women having difficult births could be attended. Funding was obtained by subscription and by charity events. The Dispensary was extremely popular and had to be rebuilt in 1850. In 1873 a Provident branch was added, which had 9,000 members, while 30,000 prescriptions were dispensed in that year.

The building was demolished around 1968. It stood on a corner site where Debenhams enters the shopping arcade. Next door, to the south of where the Dispensary stood, was the Rising Sun Inn, which was first found listed in a 1790 directory, and closed around 1930.

In 1884 the street also housed a number of small businesses, and a row of three homes, called Herald Cottages, whose residents included a compositor and a plumber.

Bank Street
Barbourne. Now **New Bank Street**.

BARBOURNE CRESCENT
The first record found of this street was a building application of 1901 for a single house, with another for two more in the following year. It was first listed in a street directory in 1908, when there were four villas named Thorncroft, Calshot, Renthorpe and Tintagel, occupied by a cigar merchant, a carpet designer, and two ladies who were presumably widows. However, the substantial Thorneloe Court could be earlier than that. On the 1928 Ordnance Survey map there appears to be six houses on the east side, and

one plot which is still vacant to this day. Two more substantial villas were added on the same side, probably in the 1930s, but the other side has had to wait for development until quite recently.

BARBOURNE LANE

This lane was first found in a street directory in 1840. There were just three building applications for five homes in the ten years from 1867, but in 1880 there were suddenly five applications for 20 houses, after which there was little more activity throughout the rest of the century, and most of the homes applied for weren't built at that time. In 1884 there were just seven homes listed here, whose residents included a hop porter, a tailor, a horse dealer, a bricklayer, a glover and a blacksmith. That number has since more than doubled.

BARBOURNE ROAD

The road took its name from Barbourne Brook, which in ancient times was called Beaverbourn, or beaver stream, since there were beaver here until around the fourteenth century, after which the name was corrupted to its present form, though it was simply known as Barbourne, the Road not being added until 1896.

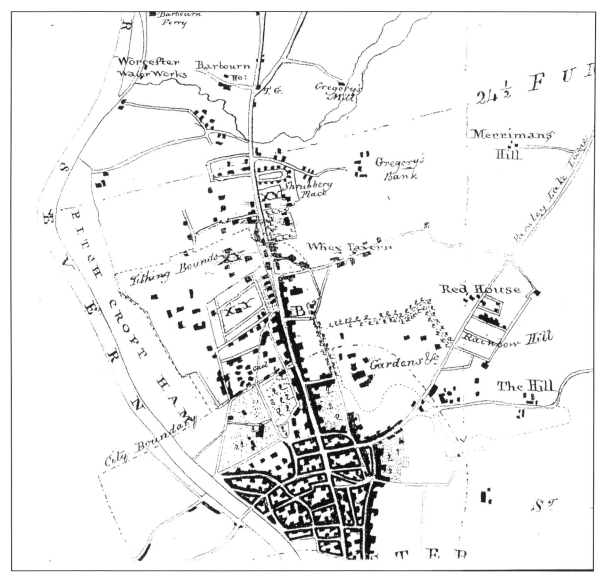

North Worcester about 1830

For many centuries Barbourne was outside the city. The south side of Castle Street was the furthest extent of city governance, until the city boundary was moved to Barbourne Brook in 1837, and to the south side of Bilford Road in the 1880s. The area may have been a manor within the bishop's manor of Northwick in medieval times, but was not a parish in its own right. In early times it may have been a chapelry of St Helens in Fish Street, but in 1218 it became part of Claines, when that chapelry became a parish, and it remained so until it became part of the Tything parish between 1875-1977. There was once said to be a gallows almost opposite the end of **Shrubbery Avenue**, at a site called Gallows Pools, shown on a map of 1751.

From Roman times until the eighteenth century this was part of the 'saltway', by which salt - then a valuable and vitally important commodity for medicine and food preservation - was carried by cart from Droitwich to the River Severn, so this road was kept in a much better state of repair than many others in the county. In Anglo-Saxon times the area was the homestead of the Ludadingas, meaning Ludad's people, a small tribe or extended family group of probably 30 or 40 people, who are estimated to have held all the land from **Vine Street** to Shrubbery Avenue, together with Pitchcroft.

Barbourne Road looking north from Little London about 1903. On the left is the tower of Spreckley's Brewery and on the right beyond The Talbot is Barbourne's 'High Street' Paradise Row - RS

During the medieval period the surrounding area was largely owned by the church, including the White Ladies convent in **The Tything**, and will have been given over to farming, as it no doubt had been since Roman times, with a few cottages and an occasional more substantial house as the only development. Barbourne Lodge on **Barbourne Walk** was probably a farmhouse originally, though by 1712 it was a Bedlam or mental hospital, and was later used by cockfighting teams.

By 1751or before, access to the north was constrained by toll gates on **Droitwich Road** and **Ombersley Road**, and a joint gate at the end of this road was built around 1814, of which the toll house still remains. During the 1750s grand houses were being built in **Barbourne Terrace**, and Thorneloe House nearby must also date from this period. By the late eighteenth century Barbourne had become a fashionable hamlet outside the city. It then needed a fashionable High Street, which it acquired with the building of an elegant Georgian terrace named **Paradise Row**, beside **Little London**, though ironically this was then in The Tything. Barbourne now begins beyond Little London, but in the nineteenth century it extended south only as far as the site of Shrubbery Avenue.

The area around this road was largely rural as late as the early nineteenth century, with ribbon development of grand houses, surrounded by grazing and market gardening, such as onion growing around the brook. **St George's Square** was developed in this period on pasture land for a dairy herd. It was during the course of the nineteenth century that this road and the area around it saw intensive development, with building going ahead rapidly in surrounding streets, and on the Shrubbery estate in the 1890s. There was also considerable additional building on this road, with building applications for more than 70 homes and six shops being submitted between 1866 and 1903. To care for the health needs of the poor in this community, the Barbourne Dispensary, probably an offshoot of a very successful **Bank Street** institution, was opened on the corner of **Sunnyside Road** in 1905, in a property which still exists.

Historic Worcester Streets

West of the junction of Droitwich Road and Ombersley Road lay Barbourne House, a mansion in substantial grounds which subsequently became Gheluvelt Park. A house was built on the site in the early sixteenth century, probably by the Cookes family who owned the land. In the early 1750s much of the park was in industrial use, with a whitening yard for textiles, and a mill on the brook. The house was rebuilt about 1788, and was then occupied by the Rev Thomas Cookes. The house was subsequently leased to a Col

Barbourne House - RS

Newport, who was famous for having a fine cellar of port, but it remained in the ownership of the Cookes family until it was sold to John Pearkes Lavender (see **Lavender Road**) in 1837.

Around 1850 the house was occupied by Admiral Hastings, the hero of the storming of Acre in the 1840s, and later by the Smith family who had nurseries in St John's which were reputedly the largest in the world. In 1881 the estate was sold again, and from 1883 became Barbourne College, a school for boys, which continued until 1908. During the First World War it was a military HQ.

In 1918 the estate was purchased for the city, and the house was demolished. In 1922 the estate was opened as Gheluvelt Park, a memorial to the men who fought in the Great War, with a name recalling a gallant victory of the Worcestershire Regiment. Gheluvelt was a

Covent Garden House, now a laundrette, in the early twentieth century - RS

Belgian village where Second Battalion, Worcestershire Regiment, lost 189 men and three officers in October 1914, preventing the German army reaching the Channel ports and turning the Allied line.

The new park had a row of homes for former soldiers, and the opening, on 24 June 1922, was a very grand affair, attracting thousands of people and being attended by wartime commander Field Marshall Sir John French, the Earl of Ypres. Other buildings with notable history include Baskerville House and Thorneloe House. The former was named for the great Worcestershire-born printer John Baskerville, by High Street bookseller William Smart, who lived there for some years. Alfred Bate Richards, the first editor of the Daily Telegraph in 1855, was born there in 1820. It is now split into flats. Thorneloe House was named for the family who were said to be its first occupants, and probably owned other land in the area. Mr Thorneloe was frequently mentioned in the Journal of the time as a well known city attorney. Between the 1760s and 1792 or later, a Miss Harris ran a school there, and one of her earliest pupils was Sarah Kemble, who became famous as a tragic actress under her married name, Sarah Siddons.

The house was occupied in the 1860s by Edward Evans of the former Hill and Evan vinegar works at **St Martin's Gate**. Between 1940 and 1995 it was the city's eye hospital, and it is now used as offices. The former Bishop Perowne School building is on the site of Thames House, demolished in the 1920s, which had been home for many years to businessman and JP Francis Dingle.

A large site beyond Paradise Row was home in the nineteenth and early twentieth centuries to Spreckley's Worcester Brewery. Claimed to have been the first public brewery in Worcester, it was founded as Britannia Brewery by the Stallard family at a date before 1851, and was taken over by the Spreckley Brothers from London in 1871. The brewery tower, built by the brothers, became a well-known local landmark. By 1897 the company had 57 pubs in and around Worcester. The business was taken over in 1958 and had closed within two years.

Sarah Siddons

Some of the buildings have survived as part of a residential development completed in 1987, but most of the site was cleared, and a vehicle repair shop and an office building are now situated here.

The Talbot is an historic inn, where county justices often sat in an area at the back once known as the Justices Room. It was here that the inquest was held on the Oddingley Murders. There was once a large field behind the inn where entertainments and political meetings were held. Coaches ran from here in the 1820s to Kidderminster, Birmingham, Wolverhampton and Dudley. The Swan is also believed to be long established, though the present building appears to be mostly twentieth century.

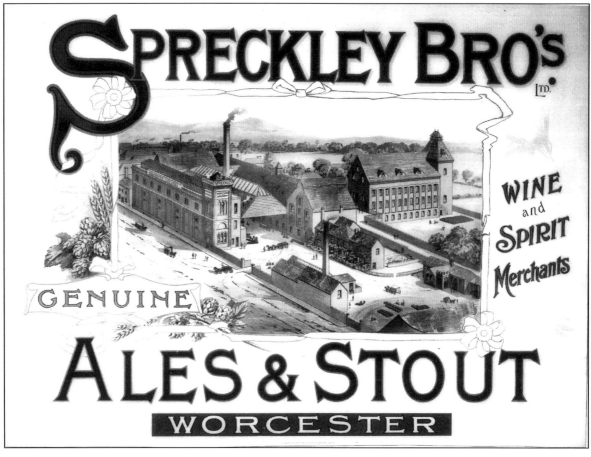

Next to the Talbot, now a sandwich shop

This road can claim a famous royal connection. In 1651, as the future Charles II fled from defeat at the Battle of Worcester, he paused at Barbourne Bridge to determine which road to take.

Had he taken Droitwich Road – along which most of the defeated royalist army was fleeing - he would almost certainly have been captured and executed, as most of his army was.

Instead he took Ombersley Road, and lived to return to England in triumph in 1660. Thus it could be argued that the continued existence of a British monarchy was thanks to a decision taken on this road!

BARBOURNE TERRACE

The building of grand houses here can be dated at least to 1759 from the earliest deed to a property in the county archives. Some of the city's wealthiest families then lived here, or had 'country houses' here as well as a house in the city. In 1840 there were just nine homes listed here in a directory, whose residents included a leather factor, a printer and five ladies, Miss or Mrs, presumably widows or bereaved single ladies.

An *Upper Barbourne Terrace* was fist listed in 1880, but by 1896 it had been partly cleared to create access to adjoining roads, and the remaining properties were incorporated into the Terrace.

One of the grandest houses in its day was Terrace Villa, now called Lindisfarne House, built by local architect Henry Day, who completed several other impressive local houses, but regarded this as his finest work.

It was commissioned in the late 1850s by Thomas Chalk, who was already living elsewhere in the street. He was part-owner of the *Worcester Herald*, then the pre-eminent county newspaper. The house was a fine Italianate mansion with extensive ornamental gardens in the style of a grand country estate, and was considered the finest house in Worcester in its heyday.

Lindisfarne House, Barnourne Terrace, as it was originally, with ornamental gardens - RS

In 1909 it was purchased by George Gascoyne, wealthy founder of a very successful city hop and seed business. He and his family were much involved in the social life of the city, and there are many photographs of large gatherings of local societies in the gardens. The house still exists but the gardens have largely been built over.

BARBOURNE WALK

Barbourne Lodge when the Burneys lived there

This probably began life as a lane leading to Barbourne Lodge, at the junction with **Pitchcroft Lane**, but it became known as the route from **Barbourne Road** to the Waterworks, which moved to the area in the 1790s. Barbourne Lodge was said to have been a farmhouse originally, but by the early eighteenth century it had become a bedlam, or mental institution and a dirt track named Bedlam Lane led to it from Barbourne Road. But by 1712 it had presumably become a private residence, though still called Bedlam, which had a cockpit used by county teams for the brutal 'sport' of cockfighting. In February of that year the Journal reported fights over two days between the gentlemen of Worcestershire and Herefordshire.

In the 1750s it became home to the Burney family. Richard Burney, who had five sons and three daughters, ran a school at the Lodge for dancing and music. The family were very active in local society, had connections to many of the leading scholars and authors of the day, and were related to the novelist Fanny Burney. Several of the children were gifted musically or artistically.

The house later became a fever hospital, known as Barbourne Hospital for Infectious Diseases. This was

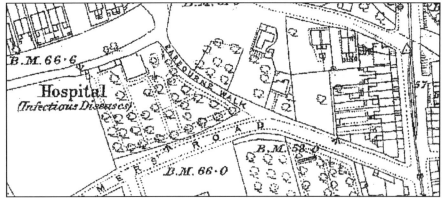

Barbourne Walk in 1884

considered an ideal location for such an institution since isolation was the only known means of limiting the spread of infectious diseases at that time. This street was first listed in a street directory in 1880, but then and throughout the remainder of the century no other properties were built here, since local people feared being anywhere near the hospital.

Despite this, the hospital grounds provided a pleasant environment for those patients well enough to enjoy it, with spacious tree-lined walks. Improvement of the city water supply in 1894 brought many infectious diseases under control, and at the end of the century the hospital was transferred to Newtown Road. The Lodge was offered for sale, but no-one would buy it, and in 1905 it was gutted by fire to destroy any lingering germs, before being demolished.

No nineteenth century building applications were found for this street. In 1897 the only listing here was for Barbourne Hospital for Infectious Diseases, but in 1900 – by which time the hospital had closed – there were seven listings. At Graydon Villas were a commercial clerk and a machinist, and at Alden Villas were an organ builder and a law clerk. Opposite, where shops still stand, were butcher Robert Bailey, general dealer Mrs Elizabeth Alford and shopkeeper Mrs Augusta Furness.

BARKER STREET
The street name must come from the nearby Barker's Brick Works, beside the canal, known in the nineteenth century as the Worcester Patent Brick Works. David Wilson Barker was listed there in a directory of 1879, and was living nearby at Mayfield House, which will have given its name to **Mayfield Road**.
The two villas which constituted this street in 1896, Belmont and The Laurels, must have been built prior to 1880, since they were listed then in **Belmont Street**. The Laurels still exists, though incongruously incorporated into a block of c. 1970s flats. This street was first found in a street directory in 1896. The Goodrest pub must have been built before 1930, when the nearby **Goodrest Walk** was first found listed, and must be on the site of Belmont.

BARN CLOSE
This street is on land which had been part of Smith's nurseries. It was first found in the health board streets list of 1872, and in a street directory in 1896, when five homes were listed, whose occupants included a 'professional waiter', two gardeners and a fitter. These must originally have been nursery cottages, for workers at Smith's nurseries, which must have been demolished later, and all the development seen here now is modern.

BARNES WAY
Named for the ancient manor of Barnes (see **Barneshall Avenue**), this street was first found in a street directory in 1937, when there were 23 homes listed.

BARNESHALL AVENUE
This street takes its name from the manor of Barnes, known to the Normans as Le Baryns, because as the name suggests it was a livestock or dairy farm. The manor was not mentioned separately in Domesday Book, probably because it was included as part of the manor of Whittington (see **Battenhall Road**). It was known as the manor of Barnes, but must have had a manorial hall at an early date, as a result of which it became known as Barneshall. The manor was given to the priory at Worcester in 1327 by Richard de Bickerton and John de Bransford, vassals of Richard the Mercer. At the Dissolution it was granted to Sir John Bourne of Holt, from whom it passed to Lord Chancellor Sir Thomas Bromley, who had presided at the trial of Mary, Queen of Scots.
In 1767 it was purchased by Worcestershire historian Rev Treadway Nash. Barnshall was listed in a directory of 1790, though whether that was the hall or the estate is not clear. In the early nineteenth century the estate came into the possession of the Somers family, descendants of a seventeenth century Lord Chancellor, after whom **Somers Road** was named, and they held it for a century or more.
Barnes Hall was still listed in a street directory in 1908 and the land was farmed by George Smith. At that time there were just seven houses in the area. Mr Smith continued to farm the estate until at least 1928. The Avenue was first found in a street directory in 1932, when there were six houses listed, including Buena Vista, the home of Lt. Col. G.H. Goddard DSO.

BARRY STREET
This street name presumably comes from the Barry family, who seem to be connected with Himbleton and Tibberton in the eighteenth and nineteenth centuries, and later with Dudley. Robert Barry was in the Worcestershire Militia in the nineteenth century, and the Barrys would seem to be a well-off county family, though what their connection is here, whether as landowners or financiers behind this development, is not known.
The land here was part of the mid nineteenth century Arboretum Pleasure Grounds, with their entrance drive on **Arboretum Road**, which were sold for redevelopment in 1866, but the area closer to the canal was not developed until some years later. The first record found of this street was a building application for two houses in 1887, and there was another for five houses and a shop in the following year. In the period 1891-96 there were a further three applications for another 25 houses.
The street was first listed in a street directory in 1896, when there were just 16 homes, but by the following year there were almost 40 – certainly more than the surviving records show applications for – which were built in a number of blocks of about half a dozen cottages or villas. There were some fascinating contrasts; Shakespeare Villas, probably named for a local builder, stood next to Bismark Villas, presumably named for the former German Chancellor. In both years photographer Henry Terry was living at No. 1. There were

also a number of building tradesmen, along with a brushmaker, a manager, a glove cutter, a litho artist and a coach builder.

Edwardian Barry Street, with a corner shop in the distance - RS

BATH ROAD

This was mostly known in past times as the Tewkesbury or Gloucester road, doubtless taking its present name in the eighteenth century when Bath became popular as a spa, and Worcester would have been on the stagecoach route to it from the West Midlands. Documents have identified this area as the site of siegeworks during the wars of Stephen and Matilda in the twelfth century, though their exact location is unknown. Expansion to the south outside the city walls was shown on a map of 1610.

By the reign of George III a fashionable residential suburb had grown up here called *Bath Row*, where building had begun as early as 1740. The suburb was listed 'off Sidbury-st' in 1790, and still exists as the first section of Bath Road.

In the eighteenth century a joint turnpike tollgate with **London Road** was built at the bottom of the hill, but as the city expanded further it moved twice, first around 1800 to near where the Albion pub now stands at the junction with **Diglis Road**, and then about 1860 to just north of what is now **Timberdine Avenue**.

Occupants of the street in 1840 included straw hat maker Harriet Townsend, carrier and coal dealer John Hood, timber and coal merchant John Lee and oil and lead dealer Henry Webb, along with milliners, a wine merchant, a hop dealer, a schoolmaster and a grocer.

Much of this area continued as open fields well into the nineteenth century. As late as 1885 a building application was submitted for new farm buildings within the city boundary of that time, and two years earlier another application had been submitted for a blacksmith shop for George Knight, near the

Samuel Butler

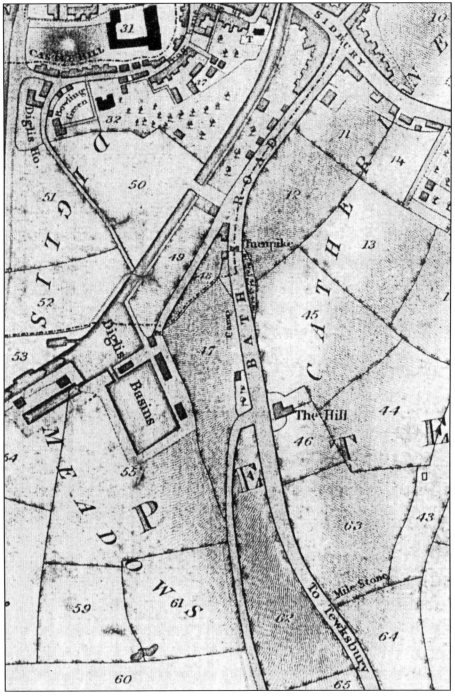

Map of Bath Road in 1822, surrounded by open fields and with a turnpike gate

public weighing machine, which was beside No. 18, on the west side of the street.

The slow pace of change was mirrored in the building applications for this road. Between 1886 and 1905 there were 27 mostly small-scale building applications for just 63 homes, and development did not creep much beyond Timberdine Avenue until the 1930s.

The Ketch public house is said to have been an inn since at least the seventeenth century. Cromwell's troopers are supposed to have drunk here, and seventeenth century Worcestershire-born satirist Samuel Butler is supposed to have written part of his great work, Hudibras, beside a window here looking out over the Severn.

Aside from The Albion, which may have been established before 1834, the other well-known pub on Bath Road was the Berwick Arms, on the corner of **Stanley Street**, the name of which presumably related to ownership of Worcester's first bank in **Bank Street**. It was first found listed in 1873 but closed early in 2011.

South Bank, a large Victorian house in substantial grounds, was owned by John Wheeley Lea of Lea and Perrins in **Midland Road**. Anny Mary Wheeley Lea left the property to be used as a nursing home, and it opened in 1920. Elgar was treated here for cancer in 1934. It became an NHS convalescent home in 1948, but closed in 1983, and the site was then redeveloped as a private hospital which opened in 1986.

Bath Row

The principal terrace of a residential suburb on **Bath Road**, said to have been fashionable in the reign of George III, though building obviously began earlier than that, since the double-fronted Haresfield House is dated 1740, 20 years before George came to the throne. Residents over the years included porcelain manufacturer Robert Chamberlain, whose works at **Severn Street** later became Royal Worcester Porcelain. This row of Georgian houses still exists as the first section of Bath Road.

Historic Worcester Streets

BATTENHALL AVENUE

This street was first found in a directory in 1924, when it was described as a continuation of **Camp Hill Road**. There was just one house, Highfield, on the west side, and seven large villas on the east side, including the rectory of St Martin's Church in London Road. These homes have been described as late-Victorian, though that seems too early, especially since the church was not built until the twentieth century, and Edwardian seems more likely. The nearby Battenhall Grange, a timber-framed seventeenth century building, which was demolished in the 1960s, had once been the parish workhouse, but had subsequently been converted into a private residence, and in 1924 was home to Capt. Saville Richard. Further large-scale development was planned but did not go ahead at that time. In the 1960s a road link was created between this street and **Sebright Avenue**, and an estate of houses and bungalows was built.

BATTENHALL PLACE

A charming cul-de-sac, situated just off **London Road**, above **Greenhill**. It was first found in the health board streets list of 1872, and in a street directory of 1884, listed under London Road. At that time there were three maiden ladies here; Miss Anna Farrell at No. 1, Miss Catharine Mary Breay at No. 2, and Miss Theodosia Egan at No. 3.

BATTENHALL ROAD

This road was developed in the nineteenth century, though the area had a fascinating history for centuries before that. It was named for the manor of Batenhale or Battenhall – an Anglo-Saxon name meaning the hall on the heath of a man nicknamed Bata - which was recorded as early as 969, when it was in the possession of the church at Worcester as a game enclosure, and was leased by Bishop (Saint) Oswald to a clerk named Wulfgar.

The manorial estate began at the south wall of the church of St Peter, beside the city wall off **Sidbury**, and continued for more than a mile south and east. It was closely associated with the manor of Barneshall, both of which may have formed part of the manor of Whittington, and were thus not mentioned separately in Domesday Book. The land then seems to have been held by the Poer family, best known as the holders of Wichenford Court, one of the largest houses in the county in the fifteenth century.

The estate passed, apparently by marriage, to Worcester citizen Richard the Mercer in 1306, and in 1327, probably after his death, the manor passed with Barneshall to the priory of Worcester, which created a deer park, and surrounded the manor house within the park with a moat and well-stocked fish ponds. This road will then have been a lane leading to the manor house from **London Road**.

Eighteenth century historian Valentine Green said: 'Here was an ancient park, now destroyed, which formerly served for the retirement of the priors of Worcester monastery'. Retirement meant relaxation, and one prior spent up to 19 weeks of his year here. After the Dissolution both manors passed in 1545 to Sir John Bourne, a Secretary of State under Queen Mary. Queen Elizabeth came here to hunt in 1575, but it was not so well stocked since the priors departed, and she found the game very sparse. The manor house was rebuilt in the sixteenth century, possibly by Bourne, but by the eighteenth century it had been destroyed.

By 1614 the estate was in the possession of William Sebright of Besford, a wealthy London merchant with Worcestershire roots, and it remained with that family for two and a half centuries. It was the Sebrights, after whom **Sebright Avenue** was named, who began the development of land here as a residential area, which started with a modest development of perhaps five villas, which were built at the north end of this road, near London Road, probably in the 1820s.

The Sebrights must also have played a major role in bringing to Worcester an event which really put the city and this area on the map. In 1863 Battenhall hosted the Royal Show, a national agricultural show held annually for 70 years from 1839. In later years it was always held at Stoneleigh, Warwickshire, but in its early days it moved around between various venues. Bringing it to the outskirts of Worcester was a major coup for the city, drawing around 70,000 people here during the five days of the show.

Siting of the show here may have been encouraged by the fact that one of the Sebrights had been a noted agriculturist and breeder, whose work influenced Darwin. It was only possible though because of the railway, which ran across the estate, and a special siding was constructed for the show.

This road was widened as the approach road to the site, and was lined with trade stands and refreshment booths. The entrance to the showground is believed to have been where No. 60 is now. The main stands stood to the south of **Timberdine Avenue**.

The show popularised this area of the city, and from 1864 more housing was built here, though it was mostly a steady rather than a hurried process; as stately as the homes being built. There seem to have been a number of houses built in 1864-65, but after building control applications began in late 1865 only one application for

The Royal Show at Battenhall in 1863

a single house was submitted in the next two decades. No. 51, built in 1865 as the manse of the Congregational Church in **Angel Street**, was an early work of Aston Webb, one of the finest architects of the late Victorian period. The road acquired its present name in 1869.

In the early 1880s the Sebrights decided to sell off the Battenhall Estate, and it was auctioned at the Star Hotel on Saturday, 13 September 1884. Eleven of the 20 lots were purchased by solicitor Frederick Corbett for £13,000. The pace of building quickened in the second half of the 1880s and throughout the 1890s. Further improvements to the road were sought in 1886, and from then to the end of the century there were ten building applications for 22 homes. Building went on into the twentieth century, but it is the stately Victorian villas that give the area its distinctive character, though many of their generous gardens were reduced in the twentieth century with in-fill housing.

Battenhall Mount as a rehabilitation centre in the 1914-18 war - BG

In 1897 there were 33 homes here, including three empty and two being built. They were mostly occupied by residents who may have been living on inherited wealth, and either didn't have occupations or didn't feel any need to give details of them to directory publishers. Of the few who did, Walter Thomas Lewis at Ravendale was a manufacturer's manager, Richard William Deacon at Boeboetan was an engineer and James Bradnee Bate at St Wulstan's Lodge was a commercial traveller.

There were also a couple of clergymen and at Holmden, Miss Alice Woodward was running a ladies' college. By 1938 there were 59 homes here. The finest of the houses here is undoubtedly the impressive Battenhall Mount, standing in grounds covering 15 acres, which was built around 1865 for wealthy local draper William

Spriggs. In 1889 it was purchased by Percy Allsopp, MP for Taunton, and a member of a wealthy Burton-on-Trent brewing family which had purchased Hindlip Hall. He spent a good deal on extending and improving the house, and much of the excellent interior work was carried out by H.H. Martyn, who was born in *Lich Street*. Mr Allsopp's lavish hospitality was legendary in the locality, but it was to prove his undoing, and he went bankrupt in 1913.

The house was taken over by the Red Cross as a convalescent home for soldiers in the First World War, and in 1933 was purchased by the nuns of a French teaching order as a convent school, which it continued as until 2014.

BATTLE ROAD

The name recalls the Civil War Battle of Worcester of 1651, which saw fierce fighting around Red Hill and Perry Wood. The south side is entirely taken up with the grounds of St Mary's convent school. There was a building application in 1893 for a lodge here, but nothing was built until the modern development of the north side.

Above, Vesta Tilley as Burlington Bertie - PG. Below, a map of Beaver Row in 1884.

Bean's Entry

A long vanished alley leading from **Newport Street** to the eighteenth century waterworks at the riverside, last found on a map of 1764. The alley ran from beside the house of Arnold Bean, a wealthy clothier and river transport owner, who also built adjoining tenements to rent out. Historian Pat Hughes said that the city's worst ever outbreak of plague in June 1637, in which 1,505 people died, began here.

Beaver Row

This vanished street off **Wyld's Lane** fell victim to the redevelopment near **Dent Close** in the 1960s. It was the birthplace of one of Worcester's most famous daughters, Matilda Alice Powles, better known as music hall star Vesta Tilley, who was born here in 1864. There is a commemorative plaque nearby on a building in Wyld's Lane. She is usually said to have been born in the Blockhouse, but that name was used very loosely in the nineteenth century, and was often applied to everything east of the south of the city. She was the second of 13 children of china gilder turned music hall artiste and manager Harry Powles, and his wife Matilda. She began performing before the age of five as a comic male impersonator, and by the age of ten was on stage twice nightly in London.

She performed for more than 50 years until 1920, and died in 1952, aged 88.

This street obviously existed by 1864, but it must have been built after 1838, since a map of that time shows open fields around Wyld's Lane.

In 1884 there were 13 modest homes here, housing several boatmen, no doubt working on the canal, plus labourers, sawyers, a brush maker, an iron moulder, a letter carrier, a French polisher and a gloveress.

BECKETT CLOSE
This and the other Becketts may have been named for Charles Stevenson Beckett, who was living in **Bilford Road** in 1930. He presumably had a connection to the land in this area, though it has not been traced. All three Becketts were first listed in 1937, when there were 15 homes here.

BECKETT DRIVE
First found listed in 1937, when there were 12 homes here.

BECKETT ROAD
First found listed in 1937, when there were 33 homes here.

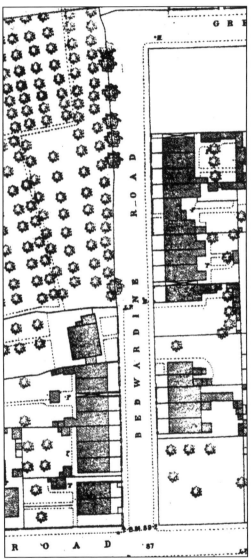

Bedwardine Road in 1884

BEDWARDINE ROAD
Development of this road seems likely to have begun in the early 1860s. The first record found of it was a building application for one house in 1867, but when it began to appear in street directories there were more houses listed than applications have been found for, which suggests that building began before development control records started in 1865. There were nine small-scale building applications for 16 homes between 1867 and 1889, but in 1896 a street directory listed 28 homes. Residents then were mostly small tradesmen and manual workers, including glovers, building workers, gardeners, two millers and a blacksmith, but there was also a nursery foreman, no doubt at Smith's nurseries, and a lay clerk at Worcester cathedral. This still left a substantial area on the west side, which was not developed until the 1930s.

BEECH AVENUE
Tree names were in vogue in the 1930s, which might explain the name of this street, which was first found in a street directory in 1930 when there were just four listings, for The Bungalow, Newhaven, Kuduna and Dean House.

BELMONT STREET
This street must have taken its name from Belmont, one of a pair of villas which pre-dated the street, though their exact date is unknown. By 1896 they began to be listed in **Barker Street**. In 1884 this street was already lined with about 40 homes of all types, from humble cottages to more substantial villas, and the occupants were a wide social mix. At Belmont villas a saw mill proprietor was living next door to a grocer's assistant. At Ashburton villas, a blacksmith was living next door to a railway inspector and a baker. There were a good many railwaymen of all trades, plus a dressmaker, a prison clerk, and various tradesmen and women. The schoolmistress of the Belmont Road School also lived in the street. Belmont must have been on the site now occupied by the Goodrest pub.

BELMONT WALK
This small cul-de-sac off **Droitwich Road** almost opposite **Blanquettes Avenue**, is not shown on most city street maps, which may explain why it passed most directory publishers by. It may also pass delivery drivers by, since residents say it cannot be found using satnav. There are no nineteenth century building records, probably because it was already complete with the present 11 homes by the 1880s when this area first became part of the city, but it was not found in a street directory until 1930, and was not listed under the present name until 1937. The name Belmont is old French for 'lovely hill', and was often used in the nineteenth century for house or street names.

Historic Worcester Streets

BERKELEY STREET

This street must take its name from the Berkeley family of wealthy clothiers, who are thought to have lived in **Mealcheapen Street**, and founded Berkeleys almshouses in **The Foregate**.

The street was shown unnamed with no development on a map of 1884, but the first records found were two building application for a total of three houses in 1886, and there were a further three small-scale applications for a total of six houses up to 1892.

In 1896 when it was first found listed in a street directory, there were 14 residents listed, including clerks, carpenters, glovers, a foreman and Mrs A. Smith, teacher of pianoforte.

BERWICK STREET

Cherry Orchard. No doubt this street takes its name from the nearby Berwick Arms pub, the name of which must in turn be related to the ownership of Worcester's first bank in **Bank Street**.

The pub was first listed in 1873, and this street was first found listed as Berwick Terrace in a street directory in 1880, when Kingston Terrace, a terrace of 17 houses, had already been completed here. Berwick Cottages in Bath Road, near **Stanley Street**, were also listed as Berwick Terrace in the late nineteenth and early twentieth century. The pub closed early in 2011.

Except for some land at the north-west end, this street was shown as largely complete – but unnamed - on a map of 1884. Also completed then were the four Hope Cottages almshouses for women, erected by Thomas Rowley Hill, after whom **Rowley Hill Street** was named. Near the almshouses was a corner shop, kept in 1896 by Mrs Matilda Priest.

This was not found listed as 'Street' until 1896. In 1900 there were 20 homes, whose residents included mostly manual workers, plus a post office clerk, a commercial clerk and a policeman. This originally formed the main access off **Bath Street**, but that has since been blocked.

BILFORD AVENUE

See **Bilford Road**. The first mention found of this street in a directory was in 1932, but there was no listing until 1937, when 36 homes were listed here.

BILFORD ROAD

It must have long existed as Bilford Lane, which is how it was first found listed in a street directory in 1900, since the Bilford family were leading Worcester citizens as long ago as the sixteenth century: Richard Billford was one of the two bailiffs or city administrators in 1524 and 1528.

The area stretching away to the north of the lane was parkland, then well outside the city boundary, and remained so into the twentieth century. It was probably held in the medieval period by the White Ladies convent in **The Tything**.

The Bilford family must have held the estate after the Dissolution, and this lane must have marked its southern boundary. By the late eighteenth century the land had passed to the Wakeman family, who built the neo-classical Perdiswell Hall off **Droitwich Road** about 1787.

The land on the south side of the lane became part of the city in the 1880s, but continued to be farmed. The farmhouse was shown on an 1880s map south of the road, just west of where the canal bridge is now situated. No. 66 is probably seventeenth century, according to listing information, and may have been the farmhouse, or at least part of the farm buildings.

In 1900 there were just three listings here, for cottages housing two gardeners and a boatman. It wasn't listed as Road until the 1920s. In 1922 the area was still rural. Edwin Farmer was farming then at Moat Farm, and his stockman was living nearby. Walter Whitehouse was then serving as lock keeper at Bilford Lock. As late as 1940 the north side of the road was still beyond the city boundary, so that half the road was in the city and half wasn't.

The city side was developed in the later 1920s or 1930s, but such development as exists on the other side did not take place until much later in the century.

During the Second World War the adjoining Perdiswell estate became an RAF training base, and in September 1942 the road was blocked for some days when a Dakota transport plane, said to have been carrying Hollywood movie star Clarke Gable, crash-landed on the airfield, slid through a boundary fence, across the road and in to a rubbish tip. The plane was finally dismantled and carted away on a low loader.

BIRCH AVENUE

Part of a 'tree' estate between **Tolladine Road** and **Tunnel Hill**, this street was first found in a street directory in 1937, when there were 34 homes listed.

Birdport

Now part of **Deansway**. In Anglo-Saxon times the area was named Burhport, a defended settlement around the port, which was situated alongside the site of the present-day College of Technology. At that time the

St Andrew's church, late eighteenth century

most important market in Worcester is believed to have been here, beside St Albans Church. By the medieval period the street was called Burport or Birdport, in which form it continued into the twentieth century, running from the present-day **Copenhagen Street** to roughly where the Deansway entrance to Crowngate is situated. It has been shown sometimes as Bridport, and in the eighteenth century was also known as Cor Street, though the derivation of that name is not clear. It was listed still in 1960, but by 1965 had become part of Deansway.

In the medieval and Tudor period many leading families in the city lived here in large, fine, timber-framed houses with pleasant riverside gardens, but as the city's population increased the rich moved out and the poor moved in. The large houses were split into slum tenements and the pleasant gardens were built over with cramped, insanitary courts. A number of small tradesmen were listed here in 1790, including a baker, a bricklayer, a chimney sweeper, a maltster, a muffin maker, a sedan chair man, a snuff maker and a 'taylor'. There were at least three pubs in the street, the Cock, the Dragoon and the King David, and possibly also one called the Quiet Woman.

This street was at the heart of the populous parish of St Andrew's, the second largest in the city, stretching roughly between the High Street and the Severn, which in 1779 had

The 'Model Dwellings' - WN

The slums of Birdport around 1900 - WN

1845 inhabitants, of whom 1,483 were claiming poor relief in 1812, packed into 327 houses. At an average of roughly six to a house this might not seem too bad, but most of these 'houses' might have been single rooms. The only thing ever likely to have been described as spacious in this area in the nineteenth century was St Andrew's cemetery, where many of the inhabitants ended up before their time.

An attempt was made to overcome this situation, at least for some, in the mid nineteenth century. In 1854 BMA founder Dr Charles Hastings and others founded the City of Worcester Association for the building of

Historic Worcester Streets

Dwellings for the Labouring classes, which built what were known as the Model Dwellings near St Alban's Church, between Copenhagen Street and **Warmestry Slip**. This was essentially a block of flats built around a courtyard, and Bill Gwilliam described it as a 'grim barracks'. Nevertheless it succeeded in its twin aims of providing decent housing for working people and improving their health.

The scheme's main drawback was that it was never financially viable, and it had accommodation for only nine families. However this and other factors caused the death rate in the area to drop by half in ten years. The Model Dwellings continued to be occupied until the late 1930s, and were later taken over as housing for the poorest people in the city. They were finally demolished in 1953 and the College of Technology now stands on the site.

Birdport shortly before it was demolished - WN

In 1873 there was the first listing of the Red Cow, presumably another old pub called the Dun Cow with a new paint job, though it did no good, the pub had closed by 1900. Also listed in 1884 were the Plume of Feathers, which closed within a few years, and the Duke of Wellington, next door to the chapel. At that time there was a wide range of small businesses in the street including several clothes dealers, shopkeepers, a signwriter, a greengrocer, a box maker, Mrs Weeks' coffee house and Mrs Amelia Smith, whose occupation was mangling.

An old house on the corner of Birdport, pulled down in the early twentieth century, had been the home of Christopher Dighton, who was High Bailiff of Worcester when Queen Elizabeth came here in 1575. The slums to the west were cleared in the 1920s and 30s, leaving the eighteenth century St Andrew's Church without its parish, and it was demolished in the 1940s, though its spire, a much-loved landmark nicknamed the 'Glovers Needle', was retained and is the focus of riverside gardens. By the end of the 1950s little remained of the old Birdport, except the Duke of Wellington inn, which closed soon afterwards.

What is now a live music venue was formerly the chapel of The Countess of Huntingdon's Connexion, an evangelical sect with Methodist links. The movement grew out of the evangelical work of Selina, the widowed Countess of Huntingdon, initially within the Church of England. Her followers first came to Worcester in 1767 and she visited the city herself in the following year. Her reforming zeal struck a chord with the poor and many flocked to hear her followers speak, which led to the founding of a chapel here in 1773. When it opened large crowds besieged the chapel and many had to be turned away. In 1781 the Countess left the established church and two years later founded the sect which bears her name. The sect was very popular, and a larger chapel had to be built in 1804 to accommodate 1,000, and even that had to be extended in 1815 to accommodate 1500, some sources say 2,000 people. Though it was faithful to the traditions of the sect, the chapel was independent, and was prevented by the provisions of a founding trust from identifying itself legally with the Connexion. It closed in 1976 and is now a performing arts venue.

The Birdport area being cleared. Top left is the riverside, bottom right is the Hounds Lane School - WN

Blackfriars Street

Previously *Friers Alley*. Known simply as Blackfriars in the eighteenth and nineteenth centuries, but listed as Street in some sources by 1880, it ran to the site of a former Dominican Friary, roughly where the bus station is now. The friars there didn't acquire their popular name by wearing black habits; in fact they wore white habits, but with a black mantle over them. The site was west of what is now **Angel Place**, and the street ran from **Broad Street**, roughly where the entrance to the northern side of Crowngate is located now.

Established here in 1347 on land given by William de Beauchamp of Elmley, the black friars were a teaching and preaching order, which had a surprisingly substantial site between the present day Angel Place and the river, bounded by Broad Street and **The Butts**. The order developed close links with the Clothiers guild, whose members dried treated cloth on racks alongside the riverside and The Butts, giving rise to the name **Rack Alley**. By 1538, when the priory was closed in the Dissolution, it had few brothers and few possessions.

The buildings were purchased by the Bailiffs and Citizens of Worcester in the following year. The stone from the site was probably used to repair the city walls and the old stone bridge, but the city also had a real bonanza selling off materials, and nothing remains of the friars' buildings.

By the eighteenth century the site was covered with the modest houses and workshops of artisans, but these had good gardens. By the nineteenth century the gardens were covered with a patchwork of cramped, insanitary tenements and courts. In 1884 residents included both labourers and small tradesmen in a wide range of occupations from gloving and chimney sweeping to porters and seamstresses.

Pemberton & Son's brush factory was in this area, and the eighteenth century Falcon Vaults was on the Broad Street corner until 1908, but seems to have had an unsavoury reputation.

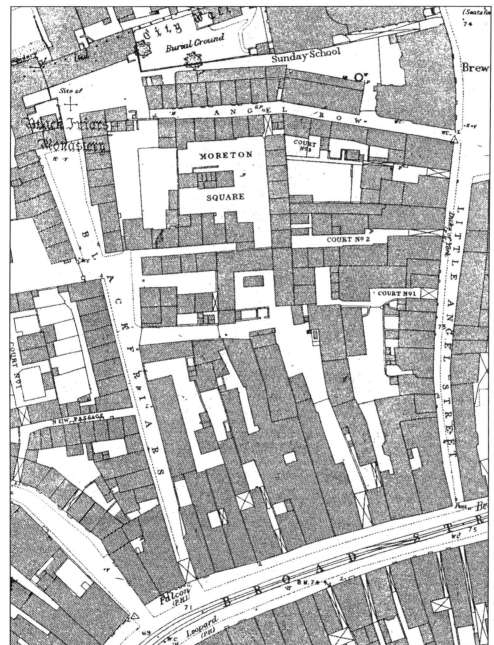

In the nineteenth century it was the haunt of prostitutes, and in January 1861 two of them were given a month's hard labour for robbing a young groom they had got drunk at the Falcon and lured to a brothel. Much of the slum housing here would have been cleared in the early twentieth century. The Blackfriars redevelopment plan was drawn up around 1967, and a stark and entirely unprepossessing concrete shopping mall took over the friary site, but at least it kept the Blackfriars name alive.

In the 1990s that was replaced by the north side of the Crowngate Centre, since when the Blackfriars name has disappeared entirely from the city map.

Blackfriars Street in 1884, then just called Blackfriars

BLACKTHORN ROAD

Part of a 'tree' estate north of **Brickfields Road**, this street was first found in a street directory in 1937, when 16 homes were listed.

BLACKPOLE ROAD

This would have been an Old English name, likely to have meant 'black pool'. In some parts of the country a pool might be described as black because of discolouration by peaty soil, but the pool here would have been in woodland, and either overshadowed by trees or discoloured by fallen foliage and rotting bark.

The first listing found in a street directory was in 1915, when there were 15 homes listed, whose occupants included a moulder, a grocer's manager, a skin sorter, a dental operator, a market gardener, plus seven railwaymen with various roles. Development accelerated in the 1930s, and by 1937 there were close to 40 homes listed here.

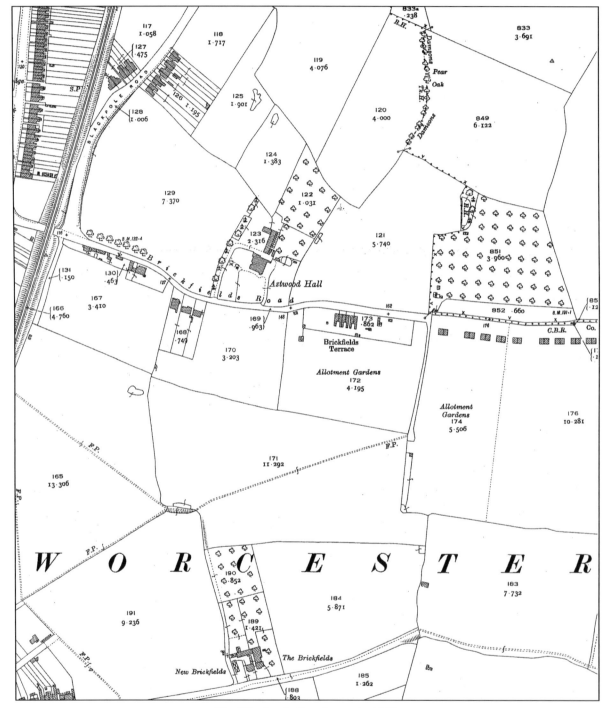

The Blackpole Road area in 1928

BLAKE STREET

The Blakes were a wealthy nineteenth century Worcestershire property-owning family, and may have been involved with development in this area. This street was first found in a street directory in 1897, but served only as a route to rear entries of houses in adjacent streets. It is in the area at the crest of Red Hill known as Oliver's Mount, since Oliver Cromwell is said to have made his camp here during the Battle of Worcester in 1651, so that he could see over the whole city and direct his troops.

BLAKEFIELD GARDENS
See **Blakefield Road**. First found in a street directory in 1937, when there were four homes listed here.

BLAKEFIELD ROAD
This name in Old English meant 'black field', probably because of dark clay soil, and was presumably the field name here before the road was created. The first record found of this road, listed as 'street', was a building application of 1868 for two houses. By 1884 applications for 14 homes had been submitted, but by that date around 35 homes seemed to be listed in a street directory in blocks of from four to ten houses, so either development had started before 1865 when building control began, or some developers were not submitting applications. Residents at that time included a police constable, china workers, seamstresses and clerks.

BLAKEFIELD WALK
This seems to have been created slightly later than **Blakefield Road**, but it was included in the health board streets list of 1872. The first building application found was in 1881 for four houses named Shrawley Cottages, which still stand and have a plaque with that date. The building applications found up to 1884 exactly match the 23 homes listed in a street directory of that year. The street was mostly built in blocks of four cottages,

Blakefield Walk in 1884

with names such as Thrifts Cottages, Thrifts Place, Claremont Cottages and Shrawley Cottages. Residents at that time included two police constables, a fireman, gardeners, bakers, a dressmaker, a glazier and a leather dresser. Building applications for a further 18 homes had been submitted by 1904, but modern redevelopment of the street has reduced it almost to its original size.

BLANQUETTES AVENUE
See also **Blanquettes Street**. First found listed in a street directory in 1912, when there were just five homes, and the Rev Sydney Phillips was living at The Blanquettes. Later the avenue was extended, and curved to the south at its eastern end to avoid The Blanquettes. By 1930 the avenue was largely complete, with 28 homes. The Blanquettes is believed to have been demolished in the 1960s.

BLANQUETTES STREET
See also **Blanquettes Avenue**. On part of an estate once owned by the Blankett family, who held land in the bishop's manor of Northwick, and gave their name to this land. Osbert Blankett is recorded as holding an estate near Barbourne from the late twelfth or early thirteenth century. Robert Blankett was recorded about 1280, and was the holder of the estate in 1299. Agnes Blankett was recorded here in 1327, and John Blankett in 1339. The family continued to hold the estate until around 1484, but then disappeared from the record, perhaps having backed the wrong side in the Wars of the Roses, but their name has stuck to the estate ever since. At that time the estate came into the hands of Humphrey Frere or Friar, and his family held it for five generations, during which it became a manor in its own right around 1548.

Richard Frere and his wife Anne sold the estate in 1589, and it then passed through various hands. The Blankets had built a mansion here, and during the Civil War siege, which ended in July 1646, the Parliamentary commissary, Major John Smith, based himself at the house, and cattle acquired for the Roundhead army were grazed in what were then fields in this area. The manor house was shown on a map of 1751, and was rebuilt later in the eighteenth century as The Blanquettes, the 'Frenchified' version of the name that has been used ever since. The hall stood just west of where the canal runs, and is believed to have been demolished in the 1960s.

Some time after 1831 the estate was bought by the Stallard family of landowners and lawyers, who improved the land, and may have been responsible for dividing up part of the estate for building. The cottages on the south side of this street could have been built around that time, and certainly by the 1850s or 60s. When the street was first found listed in a street directory in 1896, the cottages were occupied by manual workers. In 1904 a building application was submitted for a further eight homes, which had been built by 1910 or before. Nothing more was built here until the east end of the street was developed in modern times.

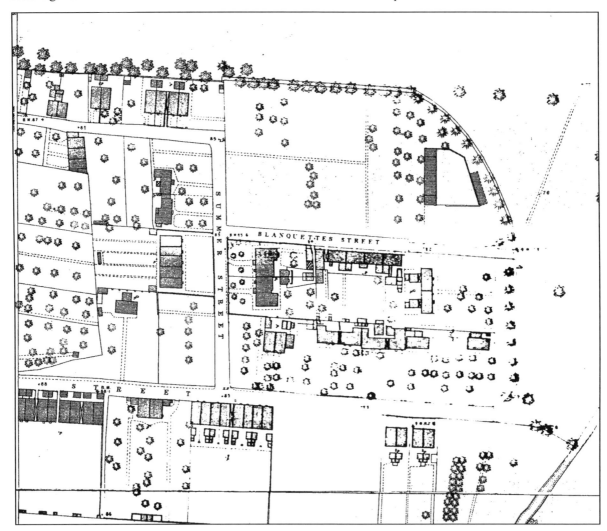

Blanquettes Street area in 1884

Blockhouse

Blockhouse was not a street, but an area of housing for poor working families, built in the first half of the nineteenth century in the area of Blockhouse Fields, beyond the city wall, on land once owned by the Greyfriars, and known in the medieval period as Friar's Meadows. Today it could be described as the area between **New Street** / **Friar Street** and the canal, bounded roughly by **St Martin's Gate** to the north and **Claire Street** to the south, though other surrounding areas, including **Wyld's Lane**, were often regarded as part of it in the nineteenth century.

Before the area began to be developed for housing it was an extra-parochial district – which it was still in 1840 - taking its name from a blockhouse or fort at Friar's Gate which was a feature of the Civil War defences. There has been some confusion about its location amongst later historians, but the remains of the blockhouse apparently still existed in 1764 when local historian Valentine Green drew a map of the city and referred to 'Frier's-gate, or Blockhouse'.

Historic Worcester Streets

The Friars' postern gate, above, on a map of 1610 had become the blockhouse, below, on a map of the city's 1651 defences

This gate was originally a simple postern giving access to the graveyard of the grey friars, which was outside the city wall, and it was shown as such on a map of 1610. But on a later map showing the city's defences as they were said to be at the time of the Battle of Worcester in 1651, the postern has clearly been replaced by the blockhouse, a square fort which strengthened an otherwise weak point in the wall. The later map was apparently not printed until the eighteenth century and may not have been made until then, but the blockhouse was still in existence at that time, so the mapmaker could have based the illustration on the actual building.

It is not clear when exactly the blockhouse was built. The date of 1643 has been suggested, though 1651 might seem more likely. Since Green said it was still in existence in 1764, it must have been one of the last city gates to be demolished.

The land on this side of the city was inclined to be marshy because of the Frog Brook, which ran right around the east side of the city, and the medieval walls were said to be lower here because an attack was not expected from this direction. The land was farmed in part, but had to be intersected with drainage ditches to channel away the waters of the brook. Bill Gwilliam said one of these ditches still existed in the 1850s, and the path alongside it, known as Withy Walk, became **St Paul's Street**. Frog Brook had made large-scale development here impossible throughout most of the city's history, and the only person listed as living here in 1790 was gardener Henry Taylor, but landowners were soon beginning to see the future potential.

Around 1800 much of the land here was divided between Josiah Palmer, who may have been a **New Street** glove manufacturer, and a member of the Carden family, though there is some confusion about which one. However historian David Whitehead, whose research on this area is admirably detailed, said the larger part of the land here was held by New Street surgeon John Carden. But he also refers to Alderman Carden, that is former mayor Thomas Carden, after whom **Carden Street** was named, being regarded by the corporation as the 'real' creator of the Blockhouse. It seems likely that surgeon Carden was the son or grandson of Alderman Carden, and that the two of them may have worked together on the project. By 1811 land here began to be divided into plots for sale to builders and investors. By 1815 or before the brook was diverted into the new Worcester and Birmingham Canal, which gave a major boost to business in the city. In the following year houses in the Blockhouse began to be offered for sale. They were modest 'two up, two down' industrial cottages with little in the way of gardens, and were mostly built to rent, with leases often sold in groups of six or twelve at a time.

Development of the remainder of the area had apparently begun by 1816, and seems to have gone ahead quickly at first, but to have stalled in the 1830s, though it seems likely to have been completed by the 1860s, when pubs were being built on almost every street corner, which could not have survived without customers. Many of the workers of the Worcester Foundry, the Vulcan Works, the vinegar works, the Providence Works

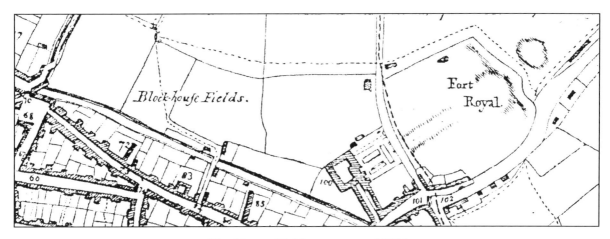

Blockhouse Fields on a map of 1764

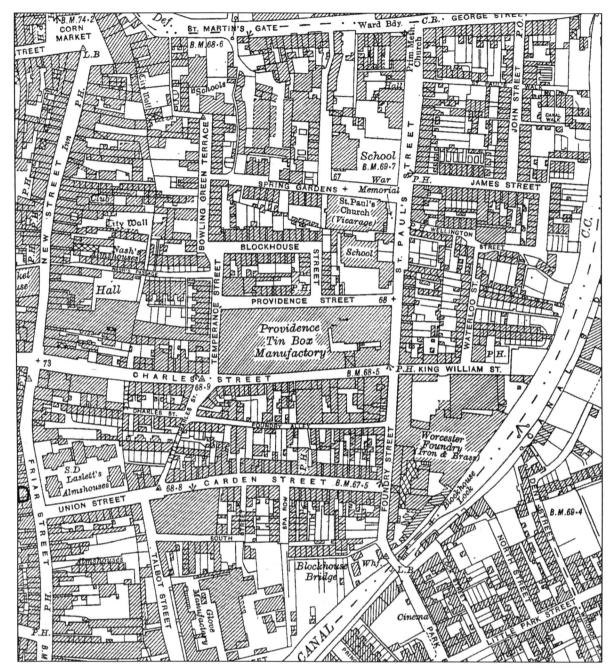

The Blockhouse area in 1928

and the railway will have lived here, with **Lowesmoor** as their high street and entertainment centre, though there were a good many corner shops and pubs in this area.

By 1820 **Union Street** had been created as a route from Friar Street into the Blockhouse, and by 1824 a map showed substantial development around **Charles Street** and Carden Street, including *Back Lane* and *Spa Row*, and probably also *Spa Gardens*, though building was in some cases far from complete, and land to the north and south was still open. In many cases, streets followed the pattern of footpaths which existed in the fields before the builders arrived. By 1829 *St Paul's Street*, *Wellington Street*, *Waterloo Street and King William Street* had appeared on the map.

Building stalled in the 1830s, but by 184*0 Fourfoot Row* and *Waterloo Gardens* were listed. Again these streets may not have been complete and a great deal of building probably continued into the 1860s. It is likely that *Portland Place*, *Little Charles Street*, *James Street*, *John Street* and *Canal Walk* were also complete by late 1865, when building control regulations were introduced, since there was very little further evidence of building throughout the rest of the century, and many of these streets had pubs built in them or nearby in the 1860s, which mostly means streets will largely have been completed already.

The Blockhouse is usually said to be the birthplace of one of Worcester's most famous daughters, Matilda Alice Powles, better known as music hall star Vesta Tilley, but in fact she was born around the corner at ***Beaver Row*** off **Wyld's Lane** which was not strictly part of the Blockhouse, though in the nineteenth century anything east of the south of the city tended to be described in that way.

The area succumbed to re-development in the 1960s, the 'Blockhouse clearance plan' being drawn up in 1964, though the area is recalled by **Blockhouse Street** and Blockhouse Close.

BLOCKHOUSE STREET

This was probably contemporary with the development of the ***Blockhouse***, and may have been completed by 1865. This small street running from ***Bowling Green Terrace*** to **Providence Street**, had almost 40 homes in 1884, and the Nag's Head pub, which closed in 1912. Residents at that time were working families of glovers, blacksmiths, building workers, clothing workers, a hairdresser and cutler George Adams who was also the town crier. The area was cleared in the 1960s, and this is now just an unnamed footpath behind the church.

BOLSTON ROAD

The name is probably based on that of an individual or family who held the land here before it was developed, or was involved in the development of the street, but no trace has been found of this surname in either city or county records. This could mean that Bolston was the surname of the financier of the development who came from outside Worcestershire.

A building application to create the road was submitted in 1893, and over the next two years six building applications were submitted for a total of 28 homes and a shop. In 1896, when it was first found in a street directory, there were 13 homes in existence, three of them empty awaiting occupants. Eight more houses were being built, and builders Hill & Mutlow had a base in the street, while boss George Hill had taken a house next door. His neighbours then were mostly building workers, including a plasterer, a labourer and a carpenter, plus a compositor. Grocer and beer retailer Frederick Noble had the shop. No house names were listed in 1896, but it had acquired some by 1900, and Percy Ward, chef at the Star Hotel, was then living at The Lindens.

BOUGHTON AVENUE

See **Boughton Street**. First found in a street directory in 1922, when just two homes were listed.

BOUGHTON CLOSE

See **Boughton Street**. First found listed in a street directory in 1937, when there were 14 homes here.

Boughton House

BOUGHTON STREET

This street began to be developed in 1811 as a garden suburb, with the sale of leases for plots around 300 square yards in size by landowner William Welles gent. Builders and local businessmen were amongst the purchasers, who could lease a plot for a year for five shillings (25p) and extend their lease once they had built on the land. A small group of rural villas was erected, similar to those built in other parts of the city in that decade, and between 1815 and 1817 the street was laid out. The Berkeley Arms pub around the corner could date from the same period. The Methodists built a small chapel here in 1854, later converted to a house.

It was often referred to as the Boughton Gardens or Boughton Fields development throughout the nineteenth century, though neither seems ever to have been an accepted street name. As also happened with other developments of this time, the project ran out of steam and it seems to have been several decades before any more building took place here, and much of the street was probably completed between the 1860s and 1880s. In 1884 there were around 50 homes and a Wesleyan chapel which had been built in 1841, though unusually for a Victorian street of this period, there seem to have been no corner shops and no pub. Residents were an eclectic mix of white and blue collar workers, including commercial travellers, labourers, gardeners, railwaymen and a police constable, a watchmaker, a bank clerk, a wheelwright, a carriage builder, a seamstress, a cutler, a rate collector and a law clerk.

It takes its name from Boughton Park, the home since 1926 of Worcester Golf and Country Club. Boughton, an Anglo-Saxon name meaning 'farm with enclosure', or a defended farm probably with a moat, was originally part of the bishop's manor of Wick Episcopi, but by 1546 it was described as a manor in its own right, and was owned by Henry Gower, whose family built the first house here and held the estate until 1729. It was sold in that year to city merchant Joseph Weston, who had twice been Mayor of Worcester. In 1810 city banker Elias Isaac, after whose family **Isaac Walk** was named, bought part of the estate and he had mostly bought the remainder by 1814. In 1818 he joined the council and was elected mayor the following year. In 1821 he was elected High Sheriff of Worcestershire. He died at Boughton House, now part of the golf club, in 1841. Various other members of the family joined the bank, and the Isaacs were a very influential family in the city. The family remained here until 1925. During the Second World War part of the golf course was ploughed up to grow crops, and the remainder was used to graze sheep.

BOURNE STREET

City builder John Bourne is likely to have named this back entry after himself, probably after building some of the **Ombersley Road** houses for which this is a service road. He had a yard and office at *Spring Gardens* off **Britannia Road**, and was probably from the family involved in Bourne & Grove, a large timber yard and builders' merchants in **Hylton Road.** This street was first found listed in 1896, when it was shown in a street directory as 'newly formed'.

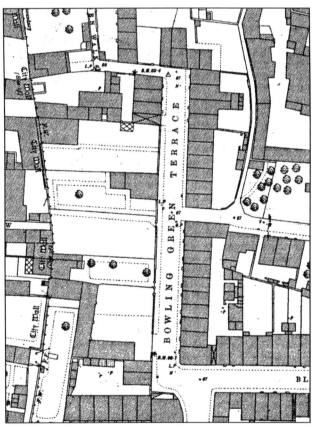

Bowling Green Terrace in 1886

Bowling Green Terrace

The bowling green was behind the Pheasant inn in **New Street**, and was used by members of the corporation, who also had a cockpit here, until it became illegal. The city ditch outside the medieval wall ran here, and was excavated in 1969. The lane may have existed from the eighteenth century, but development here was first recorded in a building application of 1872 for just one house, though housing here was probably largely complete before 1865. It was first found in a street directory of 1880, when there were almost 30 homes here for working families. Residents' including an organ builder, a straw bonnet maker, a sauce maker, a leather brusher, an iron worker, a soda water manufacturer, a tin plate worker and a compositor. Bowling Green Walk was listed in 1884, running from the Terrace to **St Martin's Gate**, with eight homes listed there. Both were demolished to make way for the **City Walls Road** in the 1970s.

BOZWARD STREET

Likely to have been named for a long-serving late nineteenth century councillor named John Lloyd Bozward, who was sheriff of the city in 1884, and subsequently chairman of the council's Streets Committee. He was also clerk to the Upton Snodsbury highway board. He had an office at 13A **Cornmarket**, next door to the Exchange pub, and lived at Cedar House, 32 **Henwick Road**.

This street was first found in a street directory in the year that he was sheriff, when it was a modest community of almost 20 mainly quaintly named cottages, chiefly built in pairs, such as Cedar Villas and Fern Villas, all built in 1879, two Hawthorn Cottages and several Strawberry Cottages. A Mirapore Villa suggested an Indian connection for one investor. These homes will mainly have been built to rent, and most residents seem likely to have found their employment locally. There were several gardeners, a china potter, a leather dresser, a signalman, a carpenter, two shopkeepers and a laundress, as well as several labourers. Four building applications for a further 11 homes were submitted between 1891 and 1902, to complete the street with around 30 homes.

BRANSFORD ROAD

A Victorian view of Bransford Road - RS

This road must have existed for centuries as a rural lane leading out of **St John's** to the west, known in early times as *suth street*. In earlier centuries there would probably have been a modest amount of development near St John's, but urban development did not begin to spread along this road until the late eighteenth or early nineteenth century. Historian David Whitehead said homes began to be built along the south side of the road in the 1780s and 90s. Development at nearby **Boughton Street** began as early as 1811, and Spring Terrace, a row of six cottages beside Ivy House in this road, were probably built around the same time. More development no doubt took place before late 1865, when building applications were first required, since there were only nine building applications throughout the rest of the century, mostly for two houses. This cannot entirely be explained by the failure of city boundaries to reach some areas until later.

By 1884 there were well over 100 homes here, Most of the residents were working families, listed as labourers or small tradesmen, interspersed with named villas housing small business people, or those with administrative or managerial jobs. At Ivy House, near **Avenue Road**, lived horse dealer Thomas Cook, and a few doors

The joint turnpike toll gate for the Malvern and Bransford roads - RS

down was John Haynes, who was collector of the poor rates. At Albion Place, near Boughton Park, lived straw hat maker Mrs Harman, and her lodger, John McCanlis, was a professional cricketer. At No.20 lived fellmonger (dealer in hides) Henry Badgery, whose family later took over Ward's tannery in **Pope Iron Road**. At the far end of the road in those days there was a Whitehall police station, where PC Christopher Williams served.

At the east end of the street, in the area where a garage now stands, there was an old patch of common land called St John's Green. This was where a cattle fair was held, and the St John's Mop Fair took place every year, on Old Michaelmas Day in October. The Mop was a hiring fair, and this Mop was accounted one of

Above, old cottages in Bransford Road-RS, and below, the lower end of the road in 1884

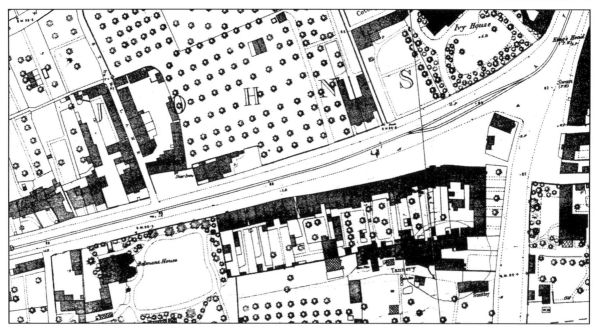

the two most important in the county, St John's being considered the best for hiring domestic servants, and that at Hanbury for hiring farmhands. In past centuries some servants and farmhands were contracted for a year, and then needed to find a new employer. Males and females, dressed in their 'Sunday best', paraded on opposite sides of the road, carrying emblems to show their trade – a tuft of cow hair for a milkmaid, a length of whipcord for a waggoner – while farmers and their wives went amongst them looking for likely candidates.

According to tradition, a servant with no particular skills would carry a mop head, and the emblems worn by others came to be known as 'mops'. A hired servant would remove their mop and wear bright ribbons to show they were no longer available for employment. They would be paid a small amount of money to seal the deal, which no doubt was spent on the many food stalls and amusements at the fair. The Mop is said to have declined soon after the 1860s.

The company which was once the city's biggest employers opened premises in this road in 1957. Kay's purchased land behind the Cinderella works on **Watery Lane** and built a warehouse at No. 202. As part of the deal they also got the Cinderella sports ground, original home of the Worcestershire County Cricket Club, until it moved to **New Road** in 1899. In 1968 another even larger warehouse was opened at No. 250, between here and **Bromyard Road**. All have since closed of course.

The Portobello was a country inn in the nineteenth century, and a favourite of St John's folk taking a country stroll. It then had ornamental gardens where patrons could stroll or sit during good weather. These pleasure gardens were very popular with the young and well-off in the city, and were compared favourably with similar gardens in London, but they were closed in the 1850s. This may have long been a roadside inn, but its present name recalls the taking of the Spanish naval base at Porto Bello, Panama, in late 1739, by Admiral Edward Vernon, who may have been a distant relative of the Worcestershire Vernon family. This was regarded as a major victory against a long-standing enemy and commercial competitor, and there were said to have been more medals struck for Admiral Vernon than for any other eighteenth century figure. When news of the victory reached Britain in 1740 there were wild celebrations, as a result of which Portobello Road in London was created and Rule Britannia was composed. This pub no doubt took its name at that time.

Other pubs in the road in 1884 included the Royal Oak; the nineteenth century Herefordshire House; the Star inn near **Star Lane** which was listed as early as 1822; the Express at No. 58, which became a store and off-licence in 1930; the Crown at St John's Green and the Whitehall inn at Rushwick, in existence from at least 1873.

The road once had its own railway station on the Worcester to Malvern line, which was closed in the 1960s Beeching cuts. It was said by the Journal in 1963 to be used by more than 300 passengers.

BREWERY WALK

This was originally part of *Back Walk*, and ran behind Spreckley's Brewery on **Barbourne Road**. This name was first found in a street directory in 1896. At that time there were three homes here, Albany Lodge, home to china painter Chas. Emery, Paradise Cottage, home to plumber Edward Garrard, and Paradise House, which is still here, though the other two homes have disappeared in modern redevelopment.

BRICKFIELDS ROAD

A largely rural area up to the twentieth century, this must have been where clay was dug for brickmaking at the brickworks at **Gregory's Bank**. In the nineteenth century the Brickfields estate was owned by wealthy

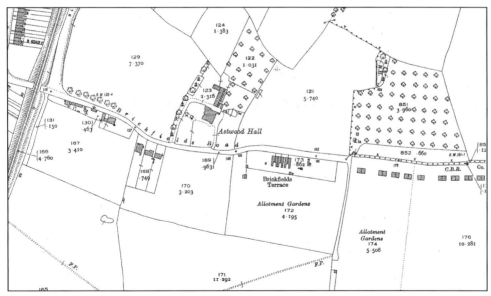

Brickfields Road in 1928

Pierpoint Street solicitor Richard Price Hill, who lived nearby at Ronkswood House, **Newtown Road**. The land on which the Elbury Hill reservoir was created was part of the Brickfields estate. The land for the reservoir was purchased by the city because the Rainbow Hill reservoir, created following the building of a new city waterworks at

Barbourne in 1858, proved inadequate to meet the city's needs.

This road will originally have been a lane or trackway across the estate, and was called Green Lane on a map of 1838. It was first found listed in a street directory in 1884 as 'Brickfields', the Road being added by 1896. There was still open farmland to the north of the road, with Brickfields Farm situated roughly between where Oak Avenue and Walnut Avenue now stand. The farmer then was Thomas Wyatt, and the farm bailiff was

Joseph Robinson. To the north of the road stood Astwood Hall in its own substantial grounds, and some distance to the south was another mansion, The Brickfields.

To the south of the road by 1884, immediately on the east side of the railway bridge was a modest ribbon development of homes, including two small rows of cottages housing an iron turner, a wheelwright, two labourers and two signalmen, plus two villas named Springfields and Glenthorn, the second of which was the home of solicitor George Adam Bird. Urban development in the area only began in the 1930s

BRICKFIELDS WALK
A footpath first listed in 1912.

Bridewell
A city gaol which existed for a time in the mid eighteenth century on *Warmestry Slip*.

Bridge-place
Another name for *The Pinch*, off **Hylton Road**, according to Noake, though the name actually seems to have applied to the area from there to **Tybridge Street**, and the name was also shown on a map of 1838 as the area between Tybridge Street and **New Road**. The Farmers Arms alehouse stood in this area until it was demolished to make way for part of the new power station.

BRIDGE STREET
This street was created as the eastern approach to the new bridge, opened in 1781, by clearing *Rush Alley*, a notorious slum area between *All Hallows* and the river. It was originally called New Bridge Street, because

Gwynn's bridge in 1824

before the opening of this bridge, **Hylton Road** was often referred to as Bridge Street, since it was the approach from Hallow to the old stone bridge, which was built in the early fourteenth century, upstream between **Newport Street** and **Tybridge Street**, where an earlier bridge had also been sited. Raising the money for repairs to the old bridge was always a problem for the city authorities, and there were regular complaints about its condition, in pursuance of pleas for funds from the Crown. On a map of 1768 it was described as 'dangerous by its narrowness and decayed by its antiquity', and the city managed to get responsibility for building a new bridge largely transferred to a group of trustees representing the county gentry. In 1769 John Gwynn R.A. of Shrewsbury, a friend of Dr Johnson, who was also constructing bridges at Shrewsbury and nearby Atcham, and would subsequently build one at Magdalen, Oxford, was chosen as Worcester's bridge architect. The trustees may well have been impressed by Gwynn's 1766 book *London and Westminster Improved*, which proposed more than 100 separate schemes for the improvement of the capital, many of which were subsequently carried out, though Gwynn had no involvement in them. However this spirit of improvement was now to be applied to Worcester's new bridge and riverside.

The foundation stone of the new bridge was laid in 1771. It was to be 270 feet in length with five arches, but would take ten years to build and cost more than four times the original estimate. In February 1779 Gwynn's

John Gwynn, and Bridge Street about 1910 - WN

plans for the approach roads were approved, and work soon began on the foundations, but there were many problems over compensation to owners of buildings to be demolished in Rush Alley. On 17 September 1781 the bridge was opened, after the appointment of a William Nichols as bridge cleaner and lamp lighter at one shilling a day. On the west side were two small, domed toll houses in classical style, designed to defray some of the cost of the bridge by collecting tolls from travellers. The foot tolls were always unpopular and were ended in 1809. All tolls were discontinued in 1827, but the toll houses remained until the 1930s and were by then held in some public affection.

Gwynn also reconstructed the quays, at a total cost with the bridge of £30,000. The city authorities were delighted, and he was given the freedom of Worcester. He died in February 1786, worn out by the work, and is buried at St Oswald's in **The Tything**. Nothing had then been done in this street since foundations of houses went in in 1780, but after a number of advertisements in

newspapers locally, and in Birmingham and Gloucester, plots began to sell in 1788, though the houses that were built on them had to conform entirely to John Gwynn's plans and specifications.

The street was completed in 1792, and had sewers much earlier than most of the rest of the city, thanks to John Gwynn. In accordance with Gwynn's scheme, this was initially a commercial development for city tradesmen, with every house having a room at the ground floor front which served as a shop, with a workshop behind, though from the beginning it seems that some houses served as accommodation. In 1790 Mary and Catharine Stephens were shopkeepers, and Ann and Mary Amphlett were mantua makers (superior dressmakers), but one house was occupied by the rector of Grafton Flyford, and another by someone styling himself 'gentleman'. There was also attorney Robert Mussendine, and 50 years later there were three solicitors, plus a butcher, a milliner, a surgeon, a saddler, a baker, a spirit dealer, a dentist, a schoolmaster and a seminary, amongst others.

A fixture of the street from the start was the Bridge Inn, at No. 3, a short distance along from the bridge on the south side, held by Robert Lewis in 1840, which survived for almost two centuries but closed around 1970. In the 1880s, on the west corner facing the bridge, was Mellor & Co's sauce manufactory. Next door to the inn at that time was the Midland Advance Office of infamous moneylender Isaac Gordon, said to be the most dangerous member of his trade, whose nefarious and extortionate practices helped lead to tighter regulation of moneylending.

John Gwynn's bridge was effectively obliterated by the widening work which took place in the early 1930s, but this street still stands as testament to the quality of his work.

Britannia Place

A row of five houses at the east end of **Back Lane South**, near to the entrance to Britannia Square, first found in a street directory of 1840, when residents included clerk Thomas Clutterbuck, shopman George Palmer and James Southall 'sole licencie for the newly invented waterproof process (county of Worcester)'. These houses were demolished in the 1960s as part of the *Spring Gardens* redevelopment.

BRITANNIA ROAD

This existed before it was first found listed in 1873, as a lane or footway giving rear access to houses in **The Tything**, but it acquired an additional role after the creation of **Britannia Square**, as an access road to it from **Castle Street**, and building probably took place here on the west side of the road before 1865. In 1884 there were a number of shops and small businesses at the Castle Street end of the road, including a poultry dealer, a fly proprietor, a pump maker and a shoemaker, plus two shops, one a greengrocer. Printers Ebeneezer Baylis also had a printing office here, and carriage makers McNaught & Smith from **The Tything** had a carriage repository. Further along were 14 modest homes, including a terrace of five homes called Australian Place, which were home in 1884 to a glover, a compositor, a groom, a fishmonger's assistant and a cooper. All of this fell victim to redevelopment in the 1970s. Probably best remembered will be the former McNaught & Smith premises, which became the Britannia Hall, a dance hall which was home to popular Saturday night 'hops'. It was also used at one time for indoor practice by the Worcestershire County Cricket Club, and the last occupants were storage and removals firm Frederick Winwood, which the Journal said in 1972 was behind the £100,000 redevelopment of the area.

Britannia Row

A row of 10 modest houses running west off **Britannia Road**, opposite the back of the Green Dragon, now on the site of an office development. In 1884 it was home to three labourers, a coachman, a saddler, a yardsman, a bricklayer, a seamstress and a miller, amongst others. Two years later groom Arthur Wyatt was living here when his wife Sarah gave birth to a son, George, who went on to be a First World War Victoria Cross winner. The family moved from Worcester when George Wyatt was about six years old, and he later moved to Yorkshire and joined the police. Despite repeatedly putting his life in danger during the war to protect his comrades, he survived and returned home to complete a long career in the police force.

BRITANNIA SQUARE

Probably the site of a large villa in Roman times, this affluent neighbourhood must have been named after Britannia House in **The Tything**. It was one of Worcester's first planned housing developments, in the sense that the whole scheme for the square was planned, though the land was sold in plots and the form of construction of individual houses was largely left to owners or builders, except that all were required to have a fashionable stucco finish, then called Roman cement.

The site was owned originally by the Bishop of Worcester who held all the land from Love's Grove to Stephenson Terrace, which was to fuel the start of the nineteenth century northern expansion of Worcester. At the beginning of the century the land was still split, as it had been since medieval times, into three large meadows, the Pound Fields. In the eighteenth century the land had been leased out to a number of holders for agricultural uses, and the square was built on a field formerly planted with flax. In the second half of the eighteenth century the Ingram family acquired most of these leases.

Historic Worcester Streets

An auction was held at the Hop Pole Hotel, now Victoria House, **Foregate Street**, on 24 August 1807, at which the auctioneer, a Mr Handy of The Tything, purchased the lease of the Second or Middle Pound Field, perhaps after it failed to reach its reserve price. In 1810 Handy was able to buy out the bishop's interest in the land and become the freeholder for the sum of £1,627 4s 6d. By October 1815 he had borrowed £2,000 to carry out the preparatory works required for such a prestigious project, including provision of roads, and piping from the river the same fairly polluted water that the rest of the city was drinking.

Britannia Square December 1835, and an 1873 advertisement which might indicate that one family finally achieved success here

By 8 September 1817 the house plots had been marked out, and at the Hop Pole Hotel on that date they were auctioned off. The average price per square foot was just under 5s (25p) which suggests that the whole development sold for the substantial sum of about £10,000. Some building work began very soon afterwards. A builder named Benjamin Buckley quickly put up a house on a plot for which he had probably paid £200 or less, and sold it for £1,260 to a Maria Kilvert, who herself sold the house within a year or two for £1,545, making a profit of £285, a sum of money on which you could then live in some style for a year.

Many of the houses in the square were built speculatively by builders and developers, but not all. One man who probably bought the site and had a house built for himself on it was dancing master Louis Harvey d'Egville, and his story gives some idea of the lengths people would go to to obtain such a prestigious address - and also explains why owners often sold out after just a year or two.

The house he had built was probably Albion House, perhaps the finest house in the square, actually built on two house plots. d'Egville soon found himself so stretched by the cost of building his house that he had to start borrowing money.

Within a couple of years he owed £650 and was forced to sell his house to repay the debt, though it has been estimated he made a massive profit of £1,750.

But the family did not give up. By 1873 a Mr W.H.H. d'Eqville, a 'Professor of Dancing, Calisthenics and Deportment',

Mr. W. H. H. d'Egville

(Cousin and only Pupil of Madame Michau, of London, teaching in Malvern, Worcester, and Neighbourhood),

Professor of Dancing, Calisthenics, and Deportment.

Albion House,
Britannia Square, Worcester.

perhaps Louis's son, was advertising his services at Albion House.

All the houses on the south side of the square were built by Claines builders Edward Smith and Nicholas Willoughby. Willoughby's son lived in Westminster and it has been suggested that this London connection may account for the metropolitan style of buildings on this side of the square. By 1822 the south and east sides of the square are believed to have been completed and a map of that time showed that the road on the east side of the square was known as Albany Road. The west side was completed in 1826. A map of 1835 shows a number of vacant house plots on the north side, but building does seem to have been mostly completed by 1840, though a building application for two further houses was submitted thirty years later.

One of the most notable early residents of the square was Worcester's first modern mayor, Christopher Hebb (see **Hebb Street**), who lived for many years at No. 49. Other notable early residents of the square included Harvey Berrow Tymbs, publisher of Berrow's Worcester Journal, at No. 1 and John Rowlands, the original developer of **York Place** at No. 37. There were quite a number of houses which listed single occupants, no doubt with a staff of servants caring for them, but it appears that right from the start there may have been some difficulty in finding enough residents with the budget to match the generous size of these stately villas. Numbers 18 and 19 were lodging houses in 1842 and numbers 8 and 9 housed a ladies' boarding school.

Analysis of the 1851 census data shows that the largest economic grouping was those living on unearned income, comprising 27 householders including 14 widows. At No. 15 in 1842 was a police office where the chief constable R.R. Harris and his deputy John Lane were based. No. 11 was acquired by the Catholic church in 1848 and was occupied for some years as accommodation for teachers at the Catholic school and, for about a decade from some time in the 1850s, was itself the site of a school, described initially as a 'Middle Class School for Girls', though it must also have opened its doors to boys since its pupils included not only Lucy and Pollie Elgar but also their brother Edward who took piano lessons there with Miss Pollie Tyler. The composer's uncle Henry, of Elgar Brothers music shop in the **High Street**, was living in a rented apartment at No. 1 in 1885.

Springfield, the large house at the heart of the square, was not begun until 1829 and a map of about that time shows that there had been a proposal to build a chapel on the site, but perhaps commercial considerations took precedence; at any rate, the plan came to nothing. In 1890 the house was rented by the Worcester High School for Girls, later the Alice Ottley School, as a boarding house for 18 boarders. It was run initially by Mrs Vincent, a former governess in Lord Beauchamp's household. In 1904 it was taken over by Mrs Druitt and in 1910 by Miss Tuke, former head of Derby High School. In 1911 the house was purchased by the school. In 1924 it housed 14 boarders whose families paid fees of 18 guineas (£18.90) a term.

Springfield - TW

BROAD STREET

A very ancient street, though its buildings are now Georgian and Victorian or later, however it has more good Georgian buildings than any of the other central shopping streets. Known as Brade Strete in Old English, when pronunciation was different from ours, but otherwise the name has apparently been unchanged across the centuries.

This must always have been the route by which goods were carried to and from the busy quays to the central area of the city. Much of the city in past times was densely-packed with tenements, so an open route to the **High Street** would have been vital for the flow of goods.

Its importance also grew as a centre for commerce and trade, and by the sixteenth century it was second only to the High Street in importance. The opening of the new bridge in 1781 and the building of **Bridge Street** must also have helped to channel business into this street, and it was also widened somewhat at the lower end, and the gradient was reduced to link with the new street. There must have been many alleyways then linking to surrounding streets, but only the former *Little Angel Street* remains, now widened to **Angel Place**.

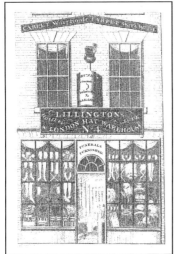

Advertisements for the businesses at No. 4 Broad Street in 1820, above, and 1920, below

It had also been Hooper's grocers in 1896, below, and before that Skarratt's watchmakers, and the founder of Kay's then lived above the shop. It's now a shoe shop.

This was once a street packed with inns and hostelries. The Vintorne was recorded as long ago as 1696, and historian Pat Hughes said the Antelope was here even earlier, in 1577, either at No. 55 or 57, which would make it a forerunner on the south side of the street to the later Unicorn. The Butcher's Arms, at the lower end of the street, was mentioned by the Journal in 1713, but nothing more is known of it. In the nineteenth century the London Vaults and the Dolphine were on the north side, to the west of Angel Place, while the Crown Hotel was on the east side, and the Malt Shovel, the Beauchamp Arms, and the Long Stop were all on the south side of the street. When police applied to close the Falcon Inn here in 1906, it was said that there were then 33 licensed houses within 240 yards.

This street was the centre of transport and communication in the eighteenth and early nineteenth centuries, with three of the city's leading coaching inns, the Unicorn, the Crown, and the Bell, and remnants of the first two still remain. The Unicorn was an old and important coaching inn, but it struggled after the railway arrived in the 1850s. The coach entrance to the Unicorn is now the entrance to the Crowngate shopping centre, with its accommodation used as offices, but the Unicorn sign is still on the exterior, above the top floor windows. The Unicorn was still listed here in 1905, but by 1906 it had become the printing house for the Journal, which moved here from the High Street. The paper moved to its present home in **Hylton Road** in 1965.

Across the road was the stuccoed Crown Inn, another major coaching inn, which had a large coachyard and stables, commercial rooms, a glee room where local musical societies met, and even a 'Men Only' room. The railway originally came no closer to the city than Spetchley, and coach buses ran from here on a jolting, uncomfortable, hour-long journey with 15 passengers to Spetchley Station on the Birmingham to Bristol line. From the 1850s passengers were able to catch the train more conveniently at Shrub Hill, but oddly mail for Worcester continued to be dropped at Spetchley until 1940. The Crown closed in 1973, unable to afford the substantial cost of implementing new fire regulations, and later in the 1970s was converted into a shopping arcade and offices, though there is still a lengthy and attractive street facade, and the charming William IV lamps are still above the entrance. The other main inn here was the Bell, on the west side of the entrance to the present Angel Place, which was demolished when that street was widened before the First World War. It was popular as a market inn, and had a large yard which was full with farmers' carts and gigs on market day. In the early nineteenth century, when

Historic Worcester Streets

The Bell Hotel, demolished in 1913 - WN

they took their politics seriously, this was the main resort of members of the Whig party, and in 1831 it was the scene of a political riot. In that year it was the election HQ of dashing soldier Colonel Lygon, who had fought at Waterloo, and been elected five times unopposed as a county MP. But times were changing, and the crowd which assembled outside was not all that friendly. Irritated by shouts from the street, one of the colonel's friends at an upper window threw a decanter, and the furious crowd stormed the inn, smashing all the windows. The colonel didn't win the election.

The bottom of Broad Street in 1903, when tracks were being laid for the electric tram service. The buildings in the centre of the picture were demolished to make way for the Crowngate Centre, but those on the left still survive. Richard Creese's draper's shop is now an Indian restaurant - RS

The Bell Hotel was purchased by the city in February 1912 and demolished in the following year when Angel Place was widened.

At the east end of the street, No. 70, probably an early nineteenth century building, has a medieval stone cellar given to the priory around 1448. At the other end of the street, Edward Hurdman, one of the city bailiffs in 1619-20 and the first mayor in 1621, lived opposite All Saints Church from 1618 until his death in 1635, but his house was demolished around 1835.

Mayor Jas. Taylor, who held the office in 1648, lived in a four bedroom house, with two 'top-lofts' near the Blackfriars. Another mayor, Alderman Lowbridge, built Nos. 59/60, an attractive four storey Georgian building, in 1736.

The most attractive building in the street, and one of the oldest, is Cupola House, opposite the HSBC bank, which has a domed roof and keystones decorated with striking, brightly-painted, sculpted heads. Bill Gwilliam believed these were similar to the sculpture at the Guidhall and therefore dated the building to around 1720,

Historic Worcester Streets

Cupola House - TW

Crowngate, formerly the Unicorn - TW

though the listing authorities suggest c. 1740. In the nineteenth century this building was nicknamed 'the Synagogue'; perhaps a bit of rustic humour prompted by one of the sculpted heads, which has something of the appearance of a 'stage Jew' of that time.

There has been a bank on the site of the HSBC Bank building since 1864. In that year a branch of the Stourbridge and Kidderminster Bank opened here. It subsequently became the Birmingham Banking Company and later the Midland Bank, and in 1876 it was rebuilt in the French Renaissance style. The present building, which dates from 1969, was expanded from the previous one and built over an ancient passage into Angel Street, which, it has been claimed, gives the owner of that passage the right to walk through the bank.

The oldest business here must be Kitsons Pharmacy, which traces its foundation to the 1740s, and celebrated its 250th anniversary in 1999. It is believed to have been founded by chemist Samuel Chayasse, but it was not until 1869 that the business, then at No. 51, was taken over by Edward John Kitson. In 1884 his son, also Edward John, moved to a prime site at No. 1, and became the city's first cash chemist, declining credit which was normally provided by chemists, and thus reducing his prices to the lowest in the city, to the consternation of other pharmacies. His son, George, practiced as a chemist for some 50 years, and was still there in 1948, but he was the last Kitson involved in the business, which he sold in that year. The shop moved to its present location in 1975.

Undoubtedly the best known business to have been based here was another pharmacy, that of Messrs Lea and Perrins. John Wheeley Lea was a farmer's son who had worked for chemist George Guise at No. 68, and in 1823 he went into partnership there with William Henry Perrins. They were very successful, opening branches in Kidderminster and Cheltenham, but in 1837 they launched their famous Worcestershire Sauce which became a world-wide success, and by 1865 they had given up the pharmacies to concentrate on the sauce, which has

Broad Street about 1903 - RS

THE **CROWN HOTEL**

Broad Street

WORCESTER

Family and
Commercial

::::::

GARAGE

CENTRALLY SITUATED.   Established 200 years.
In close proximity to Cathedral, Royal Porcelain Works, River,
and other places of interest. Good Cooking.

Telephone No. 3938.   Manageress—Miss M. HUDSON.

**A 1939 advertisement for the Crown, and below,
Broad Street in the 1930s - RS**

been manufactured at **Midland Road** since 1897. Their shop still existed in the mid-1960s, when it was occupied by chemists George & Welch, but sadly the site has since been redeveloped, and is now a sports shop.

Next door in the 1960s were Skan's tobacconists, who had been in Foregate Street at the start of the century. The shop they occupied still survives, recently selling Cornish pasties.

Opposite at No. 3, now a shoe shop and No. 4, from 1814 was watchmaker John Skarratt, who moved here from **St Swithin's Street**, and increased the width of the building here, as well as adding a storey.

By 1883, when the firm was in the hands of John Martin Skarratt, the grandson of the founder, William Kilbourne Kay was employed here and lived above the shop. In 1886 he took premises in **Foregate Street**, and started Kay's of Worcester, which grew into the massive mail order empire, and 10 years later he took over the

firm that he had worked for. The premises were then occupied by grocers Hooper & Co.

The city post office was here for some years. It moved from **Shaw Street** to a shop near the top of the street where Thomas Lewis sold stationery. He was the last person in the city to hold the lucrative post of Stamp Distributor, which meant that he received a commission on all stamps used on legal documents and even on receipts. He was the only shopkeeper in the city allowed to sell stamps. The Post Office remained there until the 1920s, before moving down to the other end of the street.

Older residents might remember Beards grocery stores in the late 1950s at No. 4, an address which had seen many different businesses over the years. At that time Curry's was at No. 9, listed as cycle and radio dealers, and at No. 12 was Halfords, which closed in the 1990s, after they established an out-of-town store.

This was an important area for men's fashion. Forshaw's gents outfitters was next door to the Crown, Thomas & Spencer were at No. 24, Creeses outfitters, drapers and tailors were at 33/34, Norton's gents outfitters was at No. 48, Glenns was at No. 70 and tailor G.H. Mogridge was at No. 64. The Worcestershire Farmers Club was at No. 66. Knowles' sports shop at No. 50 was established in 1884 and is still here today, with a second shop across the road.

BROADWAY GROVE

First found in a street directory in 1937, when there were 17 homes listed.

BROMSGROVE STREET

The name of this street is presumably due to it being just off the road to Bromsgrove. It must have been created as a back entry to properties on **Droitwich Road**, and as a result there are homes only on the east side. There are no building applications for most of the homes, because this area did not become part of Worcester until the 1880s, but building could have begun at the same time as **Crown Street**, in the 1860s or 70s. It was first found listed in a street directory in 1880. In 1884 it was listed with 26 homes housing working families. Almost half the residents were labourers, the rest were building workers, iron workers, shoemakers, a tailor, a grocer's assistant and a glover. There was also a staff sergeant and at No. 1, army pensioner Edwin Chetwin. Unusually for this period, it had no shop and no pub, though it did have a back entrance to the Crown Inn on Droitwich Road. The only nineteenth century building application found was for two cottages in 1899. Modern redevelopment has left only 15 of the original homes.

BROMWICH LANE

First found listed in 1912, when there was the Worcester Corporation Sewage Disposal Works, but also five cottages or villas, and a market garden behind Avenue House run by Mrs Hannah Griffith.

In 1912 Bromwich Lane was still largely rural, with market gardening and a few cottages - RS

BROMWICH ROAD

This was not created as the road we know until the twentieth century, but it existed earlier as a lane meandering across riverside meadows held by the Dean and Chapter, and was known in the eighteenth century as *Swan Post Lane*. The post referred to must have been the liberty post, marking the boundary of the city's liberties, since the lane ran immediately to the west of the city boundary of that time.

By 1838 it was known as *Swan Pool Lane*, since the city boundary had advanced further out, though both names had probably been in use for some time. The Swan Pool, near **Swan Pool Walk**, belonged to the manor of Hardwick, which once covered much of **St John's**, and must have supplied fish for the monks' Friday mealtimes in past centuries.

The meadow in which it lay must have been hedged, and there was a mention of the gate leading to the pool in the Journal of December 1861.

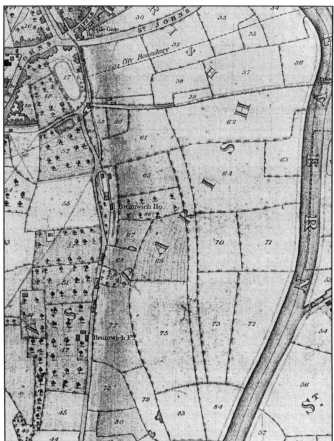

Above, map of Swan Pool Lane later Bromwich Road in 1822, with Bromwich House in the centre and Bromwich Farm lower. Below, view from Bromwich Farm in 1781.

This road must have been named for the de Bromwich family who presumably once held land in the area. A Lady Agnes de Bromwich was Prioress of the White Ladies convent in **The Tything** until her death in 1308. This position usually went to a nun who had given a valuable gift of land to the convent on entry. This was probably a lane leading to or though the family's land. A 1781 engraving of the city from 'Bromwych Farm' showed that this area was then open fields.

The road was not created until about 1928, according to Gwilliam, who remembered it as a new road when a teenager, but there was a modest amount of semi-rural development here earlier. In 1790 William Elt was living at Bromwich Hall. Bromwich House stood in its own grounds on the east side of the road, occupied in the late nineteenth century by Rev Thomas Littleton Wheeler, hon. canon of the cathedral, and there were also a few other villas. The nearest thing to urban development was the Hardwick's Spring Cottages, beside **Slingpool Walk**, which in 1884 housed a scripture reader, a painter, a seamstress, a gunsmith, a labourer and a shoemaker. The cottages were demolished in the 1920s when this road was straightened and widened.

There was nothing between the cottages and Lower Wick in the nineteenth century, but early in the twentieth century what was then the corporation sewage works was set up at **Bromwich Lane** opposite **Coventry Avenue**. To build the sewage works the city had to purchase Bromwich Farm from Henry Portman, and the works opened in 1909. They originally had a small narrow guage railway, which ceased operations in 1968. It wasn't until the early 1960s that Weir Lane appeared, and the development to the south of it is later than that. Bromwich Lane was first found listed in 1912.

The Bromyard Road turnpike toll gate about 1850

BROMYARD ROAD

This will long have been a lane leading west out of **St John's**, mentioned as long ago as 963. It was no doubt a drove road, along which livestock was brought into the city. It was shown on a map of 1741 as the road to Cotheridge. There was some modest development near St John's Church in 1835, and on **Bromyard Terrace** possibly as early as the eighteenth century, but otherwise there was an uninterrupted vista of open fields stretching into the distance on either side of the road.

That began to change with the **Happy Land** development in the 1860s, which included a pub on this road originally called the Sand Pits, but changed to The Bedwardine in the 1960s. The Garabaldi, further along the road and named for the great Italian patriot who was a popular hero in this country, was also built at about the same time. This road's first appearance in a street directory in 1873 thus probably acknowledged the

St John's Post Office at the bottom of Bromyard Road about 1900 - RS

A Sentinel steam lorry - RS

beginnings of urban development here.

A building application was submitted in 1872 for the St John's girls' school near **Bromyard Terrace,** just across the way from the infants; a sign that population was growing in the area. Some land here formed part of the extensive holdings of Frances Williams of Henwick Grange, sold in 1875, and building permission was sought for development of one lot here in 1876. Development along this road appears from the records to be less than dramatic, with 28 mostly small building applications for a total of 55 homes over the next 33 years, but the records clearly do not tell the whole story, mainly because much of the road was outside the city until later boundary revisions.

In fact there was fairly rapid development here, especially around the St John's end of the road, with around 80 homes completed by 1884 and almost 100 by 1910. These were spacious suburban villas with generous gardens and elegant names, such as Malvern Villa and Fir Tree Cottages, which attracted a mainly middle class community of clerks, commercial travellers, managers, business people and even the occasional 'gentleman'. William Birch, clerk of the Hop Market, lived here in 1884, as did Frederick Page, proprietor of the Unicorn Hotel Billiard Room, and Albert Buck, a future mayor of the city, after whom **Buck Street** is likely to have been named, who lived next to the Sand Pits, now the Bedwardine. In 1910 St John's Post Office was at No. 2, and land agent Col. William Stallard was nearby at St John's House.

In the 1880s there was little beyond the Bedwardine, aside from Grove Farm, where the land was then farmed by William Rimell, and the St John's Steam Mills, just beyond the railway bridge, which by 1910 had ceased operation as a flour mill, and was being used by the Worcester & Midlands Ice Co., as a result of which the building has been known since as the Ice House.

Engineering firm Alley & McLellan became established on what was later the Kay's site at the west end of the road, just before the railway bridge, in 1922, making Sentinel steam lorries. These were enormously powerful vehicles, and the city council streets department had at least one, but they were also extremely slow and lumbering, and by the late 1930s the firm was forced to move over to production of diesel lorries. The

An Edwardian view of Bromyard Road - RS

factory, which employed 380 people, closed in 1963 when production was moved to the owners' Scottish plant. The massive Kays warehouse, which came to dominate the west end of the road, was built in the early 1980s on the 11-acre Alley & McLellan site, and only the building used for offices remained from the original engineering plant. After Kay's closed, work to demolish all the buildings on the site began in 2008 and continued for two years.

Alongside the Kay's building is what was once the Cinderella sports ground, but back in the nineteenth century it was the first home of the Worcestershire County Cricket team, where W.G. Grace once played. The team moved to **New Road** in 1899. The pavilion was built in 1866, and was once used by a visiting Australian national team, but it was only narrowly saved from threatened demolition in the last few years because a council official found birds nesting in the rafters as the bulldozers moved in. Developers have now given the council a 25 year lease on the ground, and it is to be hoped that it can be saved for future generations.

The Joy Mining business is on the site of Worcester's only fatal bombing raid of the Second World War. It was then the Mining Engineering Co (Meco), with a wartime role making aircraft parts. On 3 October 1940 a single German plane, diverted from fog-bound Coventry, bombed the factory killing seven people and injuring 60 more. The raid also damaged houses in Happy Land.

BROMYARD TERRACE

The first record found of development here was a building application of 1868, for conversion to houses of an existing building, possibly a warehouse, but it seems certain that this was the site of a tannery, which could have been established here in the eighteenth century or before, though no details of it have been traced. There were only three building applications for four homes in the 1870s, but 18 homes were listed here by 1884, suggesting some may have been built before building control began in late 1865. Newbold House is dated 1887 and the adjoining Newbold Cottages 1888. In total, four applications for eight homes were submitted up to 1890, and they were probably built fairly quickly. The listing for 1910 still showed just 24 homes here, including 11 cottages in Tanyard Terrace. Residents were invariably manual workers, with the largest single group being labourers, but by 1910 James Tegg at No. 10 was working as an electrician. There were also brewers, fitters, glovers, a baker, a vanman, a shoemaker, a stoker and a carriage trimmer. William Clark was also in a 'new' business, doing motor repairs at Newbold House, Edmund Dunn made wrought iron fencing at No. 1, and there was a shop near **Bromyard Road**, on a site now redeveloped. The Grosvenor Arms pub at the north end, on the corner of **Henwick Road**, was built in the early 1870s, when **Grosvenor Walk** was developed, and was first listed in 1873. Modern redevelopment has swept away around half of the original homes in the street.

Broode Street

Medieval name for Broad Street.

BROOK STREET

Named for the nearby Barbourne Brook, this was a new street 'near Swan inn, Barbourne', mentioned in a building application for three houses in 1879. This was the first record found of the street, but it was not listed in a street directory until 1896, when there were half a dozen cottages, two of which may have been new-built, since they were empty awaiting occupation, while two others were occupied by widows letting rooms, and one was occupied by GWR goods inspector George Naish.

On the north corner of the street in the early twentieth century was the hairdressing salon of Fred Homer, a well-known local character who built up a modest property empire. A bald-headed barber with a ginger beard, Mr Homer had opened a tobacconist's shop next door to his salon by 1910, and had a couple of adjoining cottages in the former Swan Terrace, between his salon and the Swan Inn, which were let to other businesses, including a butcher, a boot maker and a general dealer. The area was later cleared and is now mostly occupied by flats.

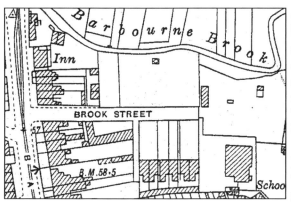

Brook Street in 1928

BROWN STREET

This street was probably named for a city councillor, sculptor Charles Frank Brown, who had a business at 39 **St Nicholas Street**, primarily specialising in memorials, and was representing St Nicholas' Ward on the city council in 1930. It was first found in a street directory in 1932, when seven homes were listed.

Albert Buck - TW

BUCK STREET

Developed on land which was formerly part of Ivy House Farm – see **Comer Road** – this street was presumably named for **Pierpoint Street** land agent and surveyor Albert Buck, who was mayor of Worcester in 1898, and a member of the Streets Committee. He lived nearby in **Bromyard Road** and may have been involved in the development of this street.

A first short section of the planned street running off **McIntyre Road** was shown unnamed on a map of 1884, but the street name was first found recorded in a building application of 1900 for four houses. It was first found listed in a street directory in 1903, when there were five homes. Residents then included a fitter, a tailor, two letter carriers and grocer and beer retailer John Price. Three more homes had been added by 1910, and development moved slowly into the northern end of the street, beyond **Rowley Hill Street**, but as late as 1928 this end of the street was still very much incomplete, though it was developed in the following decade, apparently by the city council.

BULL ENTRY

The Bull and Sun Inn, often just called the Bull, was in the High Street from at least the eighteenth century until around 1850, near where the entrance to Crowngate is now, and this alleyway ran from the pub to *Birdport*, now part of **Deansway**. Following modern redevelopment only a remnant exists as a driveway beside the former police station, which is now part of the College of Technology.

In the nineteenth century this was a densely populated area of extremely poor housing and sanitary conditions.

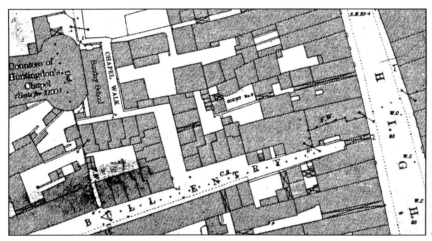

Bull Entry and Chapel Walk in 1884

It was inspected in 1846 by Henry Austin, secretary of the Health of Towns Society, who found that there was just one toilet between 15 families. He described it as 'one of the most terrible examples of loathsomeness and indecency' he had ever witnessed. In 1884 there were nine families here with breadwinners in manual occupations, plus Martin & Co's sauce manufactory, and Weaver and Co's fancy box manufactory. Residents' occupations included chimney sweep, charwoman, gloveress, dressmaker, paperhanger, labourer, brush maker and hay trusser.

Fred Dancox, a hay baler who won the Victoria Cross in the First World War, lived here at No. 5 with his family. Unfortunately he didn't live to collect his medal, being killed in action shortly before he was due to return to England for the presentation. His bravery is recalled by a commemorative plaque at the Deansway entrance to the Crowngate centre.

BULL RING

From at least the medieval period until the nineteenth century almost every town and village in the country had a bull ring, where the barbaric 'sport' of bull baiting was practiced.

The ring here was probably at the base of the hill, at least until **New Road** was created as a raised causeway in the 1780s. Regular 'baits' attracted large crowds of all classes, and there was always frantic betting on the outcome.

The bull was secured to a stake and bulldogs specially bred for the purpose were set upon it, intent on 'pinning' the bull, by grabbing and holding its nose to immobilise it. The enraged bull would respond by trying to throw off the dog and toss it in the air.

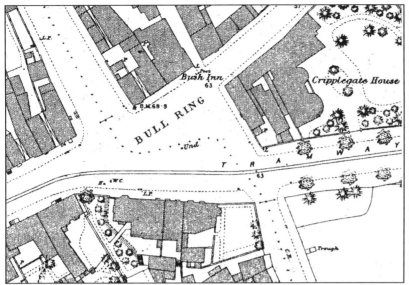

Often dogs were left with terrible injuries, but punters in pursuit of some wager would force them into the attack again and again. Win or lose, the bull would be slaughtered, and baiting was thought to make its meat more tender, so much so that it was said Worcester butchers would be fined for selling meat from an unbaited bull. Historian John Noake said the Mayor of Worcester had a duty to ensure that there were enough bulls available for baiting. Bull rings were also known to host boxing matches, and 'baits' with bears and other animals.

It is not known why the bull ring was located here, but such activities were often based outside city boundaries, and this was also on the drove route, since for many centuries cattle were driven into **St John's** over the drove roads from mid-Wales.

Bull baiting probably ceased here in part because of the creation of New Road, but public opinion was also turning against the 'sport'.

It was not banned until 1835, but a bill to outlaw it was defeated

The Bull ring mapped in 1884, showing Cripplegate House and the tram route, and pictured in the 1890s. Below, part of the Bull Ring and New Road in the 1930s - RS

by only 13 votes following a heated debate in Parliament in 1802.

Despite public sentiment, some local butchers continued to organise 'baits' on Pitchcroft, and one of the last of these in 1816, in which the bull was said to have been 'barbarously

mangled', was roundly condemned in the local press.

In 1840 milliner Eliza Beach was in business here, as were skinner Samuel Thorn and plumber S. Raven. The Bush inn was also here, but has been dealt with under **Bush Walk**.

The city tram depot is invariably referred to as having been at the Bull Ring, as is the Co-op supermarket which replaced it, but this road ends at the junction with **Henwick Road**, so both are dealt with under **St John's**.

BUNNS ROAD

There were several members of the Bunn family in the city at the time this street was created. Samuel Bunn lived in **Grosvenor Walk** in the 1930s, and other members of the family mostly lived in St Johns. Presumably someone in the family was involved in the creation or development of this street. It was first found in a street directory in 1937, when there were 54 homes listed, so it was presumably being built from about 1930 on.

BUSH WALK

This name was first found listed in the census of 1851, but it may have existed since the eighteenth century as a trackway leading to a tannery east of what is now **Henwick Road**, a little way south of St Clements Church, though the tannery was there before the church, and possibly before the road. It was owned in the first half of the nineteenth century and perhaps before by the Allies family. The walk must have been an unnamed path which took its name from the Bush pub, which has closed in recent times. The pub was probably built originally in the early eighteenth century, but may have been earlier. An application was made in 1899 to rebuild and enlarge it. A street directory of 1884 showed the Hancock Brothers, plumbers and painters, at the **Bull Ring** end of the walk, plus a row of nine cottages called St Clement's Place, housing two labourers, a clerk, a gardener, a charwoman, a plumber, a dressmaker and a seamstress.

Butcher's Market

A covered market between the **Shambles** and **High Street** created in 1804.

Butchers' row

Listed in 1790, but not found on maps of the time. Presumably a popular name for the **Shambles**.

Butler's Square

Blockhouse. The only mention was in a directory of 1840, and no directory listings of residents have been found.

BUTTS, THE

This street was originally an unnamed trackway or footpath running outside the city wall from the riverside to the Foregate, the main gate of the medieval city, and sections of the city wall can still be found incongruously set into the rear of workshops on the south side of the street. It is likely to take its name from an area for practice firing by archers, which existed in this area in past centuries.

Respected city historian David Whitehead has come up with another explanation for the meaning of the name, but it doesn't seem to fit with many of the facts. He claims the name derives from Middle English *butte* meaning an irregularly shaped end piece of land. However, the Oxford English Dictionary shows the word as French in origin, and describing a hillock or rising ground. Certainly this street is on rising ground, but it is unclear why this area would acquire a French name. Poulton Smith suggests that *butte* actually refers to mounds of earth around the butts,

In any event, this is typical of a practice firing area, since it is just outside the city wall, where hopefully no-one would get injured by stray arrows, and close to The Foregate for access. A city ordinance of 1549, issued by order of Edward VI, shows that there were also butts outside Sidbury Gate, Frog Mill Gate, Friar's Gate and St Martin's Gate, as well as two pairs of butts across the river. Since there certainly were butts in this area, it is questionable whether there would be any other reason for the name of this street.

Nevertheless, the butts here, where the targets were placed, do not seem to have been on this street as it exists now. Mid eighteenth century maps show this street name given to a short, dead-end section of what is now **Farrier Street**. The existence of a Butts Walk, now under Orchard House, might suggest that archers were firing in the direction of **Infirmary Walk**. This seems a sensible arrangement, since otherwise archers would have had to walk downhill to retrieve their arrows, and back up again to fire them once more. Nineteenth century city historian John Noake said the use of bows and arrows had "very nearly died out" by the end of the sixteenth century, and the butts must have become disused soon afterwards, if indeed they weren't already.

Historic Worcester Streets

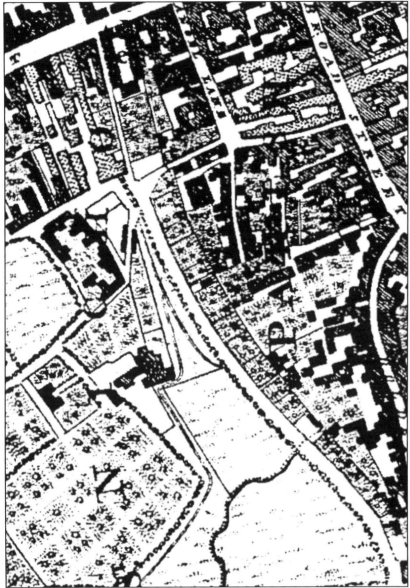

The Butts is not named on this 1799 map but is the lane running up through the centre of the map until it meets the narrow Gardiners Lane, also unnamed. The short dead-end section running off to the left was also once known as The Butts but is now part of Farrier Street.

Aside from houses on the main road, the gardens of which ran down to the line of Farrier Street, this area was still rural in the eighteenth century, with extensive orchards either side of **Castle Street**, and a large arable area to the west, and this street was then an unnamed footpath running down to the riverside.

In the early nineteenth century the footpath was straightened and widened into a street, and urban development began, though Farrier Street also had this street name throughout most of the century.

There was once a bath house on the south side of this street, utilising the waters of what had been known long ago as the Holy Well, no doubt because of a connection with the Blackfriars who had their pigeon house nearby.

In 1719 innkeeper Shadrath Pride obtained a lease of land here and built a house, diverting the spring water into a bath house to create Pride's Cold Baths. The bath water was presumably very cold, but would have been clean and pure, at a time when purity was not a quality that most city water possessed.

The house, known as North Wall House because it utilised the old city wall as the north wall of the cellar, was taken over in 1779 and enlarged for use as a flax-dressing business, and the spring was converted into a public pump in 1790. In the nineteenth century the house was enlarged again for a girls' grammar school, and today is used for offices, though it is much altered from the house that Pride built. Gwilliam said the bath house still existed in the 1970s, but was in ruins.

Cattle and horse trading came here in 1838 with the opening of the Cattle Market, which covered an area of more than four acres. Previously *All Hallows* is believed to have been a cattle market, but the trade was periodically banned from the city because of the mess.

A well-known feature of the market was the sale ring, surmounted with a clock tower, which was demolished in 1963. The Cattle Market closed around 2000, with the opening of a new market on Nunnery Way, well outside the city centre.

Leading city builder Joseph Wood, after whom **Wood Terrace**, was likely to have been named, had a builders yard with a large woodworking department here in the nineteenth century, next door to the cattle market, on the site which later became a council depot until 2009.

One building still survives from Joseph Wood's yard, which was used as accommodation when the council took over the site. The nine Nash's almshouses, erected behind Wood's yard, were demolished in 1975.

Since 2012 this has become the site of The Hive, said to be the first centre of its kind, combining university and public libraries, and artefacts from Wood's yard are on display there.

Historic Worcester Streets

A Samuel Netherton built Netherton House here c. 1775-1780. Historian David Whitehead said that by 1803, when Netherton's widow, Elizabeth, renewed the lease, 'the house had been joined by a miscellaneous collection of buildings, shops and 'Butts House', possibly a pub.

By 1884, there was a mix of modest cottages and substantial villas in the street, along with businesses providing for travellers visiting the city, with carriage building and repair and horse stabling. At the top of the street were Goodman & Ward ironmongers, Tustin's livery stable and blacksmith Abell Thomas. There were several shops around the Paul Pry pub, saddlers and harness makers, carriage builders, wheelwrights and horse breaker Herbert Bartlett. At the bottom of the street were modest homes for working families, in which most of the breadwinners were labourers.

This street didn't boast many pubs – only two have definitely been traced. The Ewe and Lamb was a Victorian pub opposite the Cattle Market, which closed about 1970. The Paul Pry takes its name from a muckraking journalist who was a character in a popular Victorian play, which was probably presented around the corner at the Theatre Royal in **Angel Street**. An application to rebuild the pub was submitted in 1900 and the new building is dated 1901.

CAMBRIDGE TERRACE

This terrace does not seem to have had any houses on it, and does not even have a road sign, though it is shown on street plans. It was first mentioned as a new road off **Severn Terrace**, beside what is now a restaurant, in a building application of October 1887, at a site referred to as 'Jews Patch', which a contemporary plan suggests was beneath the present Pitchcroft car park to the rear of this street.

'Jews Patch' was a term often used for a former Jewish cemetery, though there is no further evidence to confirm that use of the land here. Such a cemetery could have dated from the existence of a small Jewish community in the city between 1158 and 1275, and would then have been outside the city boundary and at the junction of several parishes, which is what the authorities at that time would have been likely to require. The application to create the street was submitted by William Good Pike, an estate agent with offices at **The Avenue**. A further application was made in 1895 for 28 houses at 'Cambridge Crescent' and Severn Terrace, but if these were built they are on Severn Terrace, since they are clearly not here.

CAMP HILL AVENUE

See also **Camp Hill Road**. This street was first mentioned in 1936, but the first listing found for it was in a street directory in 1937, when there were 24 homes here.

CAMP HILL ROAD

This may have been the nearest Parliamentary camp to the south of the city during the siege of 1646, when the Roundheads placed a battery of guns on **Green Hill**, Bath Road. The Royalists learned from this, and in 1651 set up a strongpoint on what is now Fort Royal Park, forcing the enemy to retreat back up the hill and make camp on Oliver's Mount near the crest of Red Hill.

Housing development here went ahead at much the same time as interest revived in building at **Battenhall Road**. This road was first found recorded in a building application of 1886 for just one house, and between then and 1892 there were 10 small building applications for 17 homes. Historian Pat Hughes said the land was previously rented by Peter Foxwell, who was involved in the development here and at **Foxwell Street**.

In 1896 residents included a retired builder, a mechanic, an engineer, a cattle dealer, a jeweller, a draftsman and Thomas Duckworth, librarian of the Free Library in **Foregate Street**.

Living at Ethelbert Lodge then was Joseph Sharman Wood, after whom **Sharman Street** was probably named. He was mayor of the city in 1885 and a JP.

Samuel Southall, who was Town Clerk for 50 years from 1881, and had **Southall Avenue**, and once also a **Merrimans Hill Road** school named after him (now Bishop Perowne School), lived here then at Radcliffe. By 1904 he had moved to a newly-built house called The Elms.

The founder of the Kay's catalogue empire, William Kilbourne Kay, died at this house in 1927, after it had become the home of one of his sons. **Battenhall Avenue** was first found listed in 1924 as an extension of this road. Camp Hill Avenue was first found listed in 1936.

Canal Walk

This small street ran off *John Street* and consisted of fourteen cottages, which in 1884 were housing shoemakers, labourers, tailors, a railway guard, a bricklayer, a wagon maker, a brush maker, a tailor, a milk seller and a drayman. The street will have been cleared at the same time as John Street.

Historic Worcester Streets

CANNON STREET

This street is in the area at the crest of Red Hill known as Oliver's Mount, since Oliver Cromwell is said to have made his camp here during the Battle of Worcester in 1651, so that he could see over the whole city and direct his troops. A battery of cannon was placed nearby.

There is no record of applications to build here before 1897, but clearly development went ahead earlier because the first street directory entry in 1896 appears to show 15 homes here, a mix of modest cottages and more affluent villas. Residents included a sawyer, a laundress, a labourer, a railway fireman, a bricklayer, an engine driver, a gardener, a butcher and a painter. At Lilburn Villas, perhaps named for an officer in the Parliamentary army, was a school attendance officer, and at May Bank was a clerk at the Vulcan Works in **Padmore Street**.

A building application was submitted in 1890 for a Mission Room, a sort of outlying chapel. There was a shop and bakery then on the corner of **Foxwell Street**, and on the other side of the road was the Carpenters Arms pub at No. 21, which closed around 1960. The Baptists built a chapel here in 1891, which has been superseded in modern times by one on the St Peter's estate, and the chapel here has since been converted to residential use.

CARDEN STREET

This street was built between 1820, when **Union Street** was created to link **Friar Street** with *The Blockhouse*, and 1824 when it was first found on a map, and a good deal of building had gone on around it. It was originally an extension of Union Street, but the **City Walls Road** now divides them.

The street must have been named for long-serving councillor and former mayor Thomas Carden, who was regarded by the city corporation as the creator of the *Blockhouse* area. He was born in 1738 and came to Worcester in 1755 or 6 to set up a clothing business, which he ran for many years, listed in the 1790s as Carden & Bishop woollen drapers, at 31 **The Cross**.

He served the city in various public offices for half a century. In addition to councillor, he was city magistrate, mayor in 1790, and for many years governor of the Guardians of the Poor or Hop Market Guardians, who oversaw the running of the city workhouse off **Sansome Street**.

Despite these commitments he obviously prided himself on keeping fit, and won the admiration of contemporaries when he walked from Worcester to

Thomas Carden - TW; below Carden Street in 1886

Birmingham at the age of 70. By 1820 he had amassed sufficient wealth to style himself a gentleman, and he lived in **Mealcheapen Street**. He finally retired from the council in 1828, aged 90, and died aged 98 in 1836.

This street was the basis of much of the development in the *Blockhouse* area, which Carden seems to have overseen in partnership with a surgeon named John Carden of **New Street**, who was presumably his son or grandson.

Part of the street is believed to have been part of the Greyfriars graveyard, and many bones were found when Sigley's sweet factory was built on what is now the south east corner in the nineteenth century. John Sigley, a long-serving councillor in the All Saints

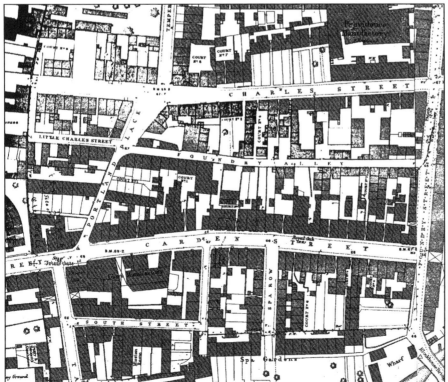

John Sigley - TW

ward, is believed to have founded his factory in the 1870s, using steam-powered machinery and employing around 200 people to produce confectionary products which were said to have a national reputation. The factory was gutted by fire in the last century, but the shell, or part of it, was refurbished and in recent times has been a pine warehouse and a furniture showroom.

In 1884 there were around 65 homes here and about a dozen shops. Many of the residents were shoemakers, possibly working at the Cinderella factory in **College Street**. There were also building and clothing workers, and several file cutters, whose work would be essential to surrounding factories.

There was a Cannon Inn here in 1864, referred to in a Journal report when the landlord, Francis Rudninzski, a former police officer, assaulted a police sergeant. There was obviously some personal grudge between the men, but the landlord was nevertheless fined 20 shillings and costs, with 14 days hard labour if he didn't pay up. Of the other pubs in and around the street, there was the Royal Oak at No. 22, the Freemason's Arms at No. 10. and the Odd Fellows Arms on the corner of **South Street**. The first of these closed after 1930, but the others survived until around 1960, so the area must have been cleared about that time, and aside from what is left of Sigley's factory, there is nothing here now of any antiquity.

Castle Lane
Now **Castle Place.** Lane leading to the old castle site off **Severn Street**.

CASTLE PLACE
Previously *Castle Lane*, leading to the castle, which was on the riverside just to the north of **Severn Street**. It now leads to the King's School car park. The remains of the castle were removed in 1853, and the name changed some time after 1880, when it was last found listed under the original name.

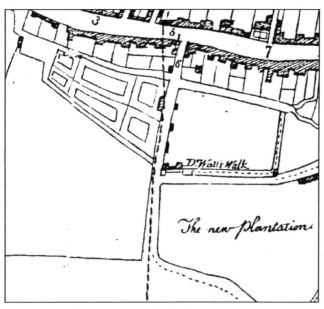

Salt Lane, now Castle Street, in 1764, when there was no development aside from the rear of houses on Foregate Street and The Tything

CASTLE STREET
The land around this ancient lane was entirely rural from earliest times to as late as the eighteenth century. Archaeological excavations in the 1990s produced evidence of a small settlement of late Iron Age round houses here, which remained in use until the first or second century, and evidence of farming by the people who lived here was found in **Love's Grove**. In the Roman period a domestic compound stood on what is now the site of the police station. In the eighteenth century there were orchards at either hand to the east and arable land to the west, and as houses were built in **Foregate Street** in the eighteenth century this rural hinterland became a pleasant area for summer evening walks for the doctors and lawyers living on the main road, with little or no development here until the Infirmary was built in the second half of the century.

From ancient times until the nineteenth century this was Salt Lane, part of the route by which salt - then a vital commodity for medicine and food preservation - was carried by cart from Droitwich to a salt quay on the River Severn at the bottom of the lane, for shipping down the Severn. The lane lay immediately beyond the end of the city liberty, an area outside the walls where city governance was still in force. The route may have been used to avoid the tolls which would have been charged if salt had been taken into Worcester and shipped from its quays, though the shippers still apparently had to pay some dues to the city. A canal route to take water-borne cargoes direct from Droitwich to the Severn was opened in 1771, making the saltway obsolete.

Historic Worcester Streets

The former county prison in Castle Street - RS

The name change resulted from the opening of the new county prison here in 1813, built in the style of a castle, perhaps because the city's castle off **Severn Street** had been the previous home of the prison. John Noake called it 'a very unnecessary and silly alteration of probably the most ancient name in the city'. However, directories, building applications and maps continued to refer to Salt Lane throughout the rest of the century. Possibly the new prison opened behind schedule, because a hanging in April 1812 had to be held in the fields nearby. It was a substantial building with 90 cells, and another 80 were added in 1839. Only one prisoner ever escaped, and he was quickly returned. Executions were held here in public until 1863, the last of which must have been the hanging of 70-year-old tailor William Ockold of Oldbury on 2 January, for the murder of his elderly wife. Afterwards hangings were held out of the public gaze inside the prison, the last execution at Worcester being of Chinaman Djang Djang Sung on 3 December 1919, for murdering a fellow countryman at Warley, to steal his Post Office book.

Popular Quaker prison and social reformer Elizabeth Fry visited the prison in 1824. She was mobbed by a massive crowd outside the prison and was actually allowed to address the prisoners in the chapel. One prisoner

Edwardian Castle Street, with the Three Tuns pub on the left, which closed around 1930, the prison in the centre, which closed in 1922, and the Victorian Christ Church Presbyterian chapel on the right - RS

who was very unpopular with the authorities was the Salvation Army's first city commander, Captain Osborne, who was gaoled for preaching in the street without a licence. The whole army contingent in the city, with their band, began marching round and round the prison on Sunday afternoons, singing and playing, until the authorities were glad to let him out.

Thereafter the Salvation Army played every Sunday afternoon near the prison until it closed in 1922. The building was then used to house homeless people. The facade was demolished in the 1930s, but Bill Gwilliam said several cells remained until 1987.

In 1939 part of the site was used to build Austin House, a substantial car dealership building with a clock tower topped by an attractive open lantern. This building still exists as a furniture showroom.

The prison was arguably the most imposing building in the street, but the most important was the Infirmary, built on a former artichoke field between 1768-1771. It was designed by architect Anthony Keck, builder of

St Martin's Church, at a cost of £6,000, and replaced an earlier building in **Silver Street**, which proved just too small.

In 1832, in the hospital boardroom, Charles Hastings and other local doctors founded the Provincial Medical and Surgical Association, which later became the British Medical Association. The Infirmary served the local community for more than 250 years, until the Worcestershire Royal Hospital opened in 2002. The original buildings

The Infirmary about 1900 - RS

now form part of the University of Worcester. During work on the site a tunnel was rediscovered linking the hospital to the prison. This was said to have been built to allow bodies of executed prisoners to be taken for dissection, but there were never large numbers of hangings taking place in the nineteenth century - between 1868 and 1900 for example, there were just 8 hangings – though there were probably more in the eighteenth century, and there may regularly have been many more deaths due to disease, especially 'gaol fever' or typhus.

Between **Love's Grove** and **Foregate Street** stood Summer Place, a terrace of eight houses, on the site of the present police station, which was listed separately in 1840. In 1884 residents there included an auctioneer, a wine merchant's manager, a horse dealer, a commercial traveller and a clerk.

West of **Britannia Road**, on the site of the present magistrates court, was a large bowling green, probably associated with the Saracen's Head on **The Tything**, and Christ Church, a Presbyterian chapel with a Sunday School behind.

On the east side of **Farrier Street** was the eye hospital, which later moved to **Barbourne Road,** and opposite was the Three Tuns pub which had opened by 1818 on land that had formerly been Lord Sandys garden on the corner of **Infirmary Walk**. It closed around 1930. On the other side at the top of the street was the Foley Arms, a Victorian pub demolished around 1900.

There is a folktale, probably from the early nineteenth century, of the Salt Lane Witches, two old ladies who produced folk remedies and cured ailments.

In front of their cottage was said to be a deep and boggy hole in the road which never dried up, even in the hottest summers, and trapped many passing carts, but in return for sixpence from the carter the old ladies would magically persuade the horses to pull the cart out of the mire.

Causeway, The

Now **Tybridge Street** and **New Road**. The name used in the eighteenth century for both the street leading from St John's to the old bridge, opposite **Newport Street**, which had been raised to avoid flooding, and to the road leading to the new bridge when it was first created, and again raised to try to avoid flooding.

CAVENDISH STREET

The name may be the result of involvement in the development of this street by a family of this name which is mentioned in the county archives, though very little is known about them. The first documentary reference found for this street was a building application for four houses in 1890, but an 1884 map, which did not name the street, showed it largely complete on the west side, but with much open ground on the east side.

Further development continued steadily, with nine applications for a total of 32 homes over the six years to 1896, though when it was fist found listed in a street directory in that year there appear to have been more than 50 homes here, mostly modest cottages with a few villas. Unusually for this period, there was no shop and no pub, but there was the Albion Dairy near **Orchard Street**, and coal dealer George Cullis near **Berwick Street**. Other residents included labourers, building workers, glovers, china workers and metal workers. It was a sign of the times and improved public health that there was also a water inspector at Berwick Villas.

CECIL ROAD

Believed to be named for the son of a city businessman. When James Roberts took over the Three Springs Tannery off **Wylds Lane**, across the canal from the **Blockhouse**, in 1877, he also acquired the land between **Midland Road** and roughly where **Vincent Road** is now, and later developed it for housing. At that time, though there was some development along the canalside, and along Wyld's Lane as far as **Richmond Hill**, the land he had purchased here was completely open, save for Field House, a mansion opposite Richmond Hill. An application for creation of three roads – this road, **Stanley Road** and **Vincent Road** - was submitted in 1890. Tradition has it that these roads were named for his two sons, Cecil and Stanley Vincent.

Only two building applications for five houses were recorded in the next few years, but by 1896 there were 10 homes here. Most of the residents were railwaymen, including a guard, two engine drivers, and a permanent way inspector. By 1910 the road had been completed with 15 homes, but there were only two railwaymen left, with other residents being a carpenter, a machine minder, a blacksmith, a packer, a skin dresser and a fitter. There was also a dairy which by 1922 was held by Mrs Bond, and is now a general store.

CEDAR AVENUE

Part of a 'tree' estate off **Brickfields Road**, this street was first found in a directory in 1937, when there were 35 homes here.

Chapel Walk

An alleyway which snaked between the intensive development at the rear of the High Street from **Bull Entry** to **Bank Street**, and will have taken this name after the Countess of Huntingdon's Chapel opened in *Birdport* in 1773. In 1910 nine homes were listed here. Nearly all the residents were labourers, but for two draymen and Mrs Eliza Wedgbury, a horsehair weaver, who must have worked at Webb's factory in **Copenhagen Street**. The name is no longer on the street map, but is still used for the walkway through the south side of the Crowngate Centre.

CHARLES STREET

This street once ran directly from **New Street** to **Foundry Street**, but was split in two by the **City Walls Road** in the 1970s, and there are now oddly two separate streets of the same name, which are treated as one here.

There is no clear evidence for the naming of this street. No trace has been found in archives of a family of this name, and the most likely explanation is that it was named for Prince – later King – Charles who made his escape from near here after the Battle of Worcester in 1651.

Initial development took place between 1820, when **Union Street** was created to link **Friar Street** and the *Blockhouse*, and 1824 when this street was shown on a map. The land had been divided into plots, but some on the south and most on the north side had not then been built on. At that time all the plots had good gardens, and the land to the north was still a meadow. Building was presumably completed before 1865, when building control was introduced, since there were only two building applications for three houses throughout the rest of the century. In 1884 there were almost eighty homes in the street and more around it in seven courts, occupied by working families including labourers, builders, glovers, shoemakers, factory workers, laundresses, a fish dealer and a hair weaver, presumably making wigs. There were also two pubs, the Horn and Trumpet and

The future Charles II in the 1650s

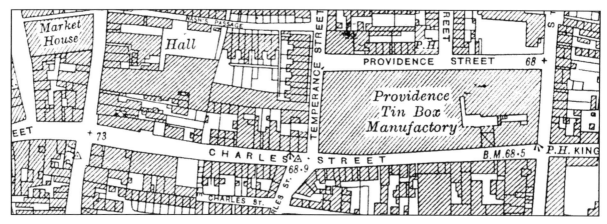

Charles Street in 1928

the Thistle Vaults, with a third, the Fish Inn, at the end of the street, fronting on to **Friar Street**, and in existence from at least 1822.

The street would have been dominated then by the two buildings of the Williamson tin plate manufactory, the Providence Works, between here and **Providence Street**, since demolished, and the firm's offices here, in an 1858 building which thankfully still exists.

The street probably connected originally with **Friar Street** and **New Street** only as an alleyway, but it was extended or widened to connect with them as a street in 1895, causing the demolition of four houses in those streets, as well as the Fish Inn. The homes here must have been demolished in the slum clearances of the early twentieth century – certainly The Horn and Trumpet was gone

Plaque remembering J.J. Cam - TW

by 1912 - and no-one lives here now.

Recent research under the auspices of the Worcester Tourism Association has revealed the significance of John James Cam, an inventive engineer who once worked in the **Shambles**, and established a business here in purpose-built premises at No. 4 on the south side around 1900, which is now commemorated with a blue plaque.

He built motorcycles, and up to the First World War, when his factory was commandeered for war production, he pioneered many improvements to the carburettor, the radiator and handlebar controls. He also built machinery for the clothing industry, and engines for the organs at the Cathedral and the former Public Hall in the **Cornmarket**. In his spare time he was a founder member of Worcestershire Camera Club.

CHECKETTS LANE

The name came from the land on which it stands, which was known as Checketts Field. Presumably it had been held by members of the Checketts family, who had been city tradesmen for centuries. A Thomas Checketts was a smith in the city in 1631, making locks and nails, and another Checketts, a carpenter by trade, lived in Britannia Square in the late nineteenth century.

The lane had probably long existed as a field-side footpath between **Droitwich Road** and **Ombersley Road**. The area was then outside the city, and the only nineteenth century building application found was for a new road and sewers, submitted in 1899 for Barbourne Nurseries owner Sir Offley Wakeman, but house building had clearly begun by 1880 or before, since it had been listed in a directory of 1884. At that time there appear to have been just over 20 homes here, whose residents included building tradesmen, gardeners, labourers, a wheelwright, a blacksmith, an iron fitter, a brewer and a maltster. This little community had two shops, kept by William Bowden and Mrs Mary Woodward, neither of which is open now. It was listed as Street in 1884 but Lane from 1896, by which date it had doubled in size.

When building began here the lane was entirely outside the city, and even as late as 1928 it was still 'partly out of the city', with the south side in Worcester, and the north side in Droitwich. As a result, building of Victorian and Edwardian villas went ahead fairly rapidly on the north side of the lane, but the south side was not developed until the 1930s, probably by the city council. Older residents might remember the chip shop about midway along the lane on the north side, but it closed some years ago.

In its early days the lane was much affected by flooding. In the early 1890s the city had raised the adjacent section of Droitwich Road to avoid this important route being affected by flooding, which caused the water to run off into the lane. It was inundated so often that some wag advertised it as suitable for boating and fishing! Clearly the developer was not going to foot the bill for this, and there was a decade-long wrangle between the county and the two borough councils over who was going to pay for sewers to clear the flood water, which was not settled until 1902.

Cherry Orchard

Not a street but the name of an area off **Bath Road**, which was developed in the 1880s and 90s on former orchard land. In 1327 the orchard belonged to the Sheriff of Worcester, and was therefore known as 'Sheriff's Orchard'. Presumably the name changed when it passed into other ownership, and it clearly remained as an orchard for many centuries, just as the area to the west remained as riverside meadows, which were liable to flood.

The area probably grew from the existence of a lane giving rear access to properties on **Bath Road**, which became **Orchard Street**. Intensive urban development had already begun by 1880, and went on over the next few years. Kingston Terrace, a terrace of 17 houses in **Berwick Street**, was listed by 1880, as was

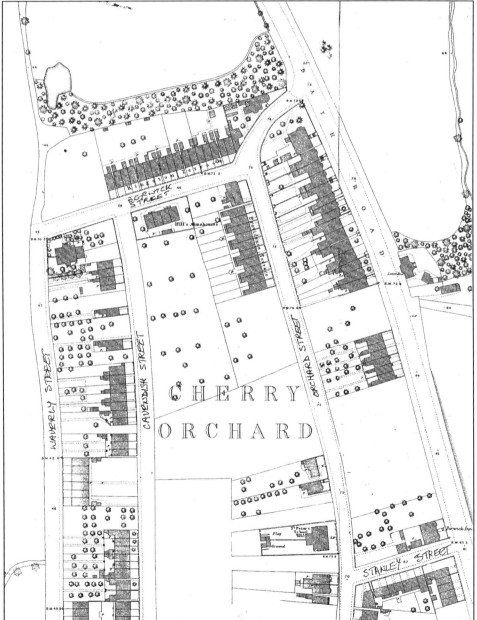

Providence Terrace, a terrace of 10 houses in Orchard Street, both just off Bath Road.. Two of the streets, Berwick Street and **Waverley Street**, were shown as Terraces in an 1880 directory, but none of the other streets were listed then. The school in Orchard Street opened as early as 1883 with 38 pupils. A map of the area from 1884 shows **Stanley Street** apparently complete, and the upper part of **Berwick Street** largely complete, as was **Cavendish Street** on the west side and on the south, though there was still nothing but open riverside meadows to the north between Cherry Orchard and Diglis, and to the east also.

None of the streets were named on the 1884 map, and a directory of the same year showed all development under Cherry Orchard. It

Map of Cherry Orchard in 1884. Despite many homes already built the street names were not published, but were added in by the author during research

wasn't until the 1890s that individual street names came into general use here, and building on still vacant plots continued for some years. Usually memories have survived of how early developments came about and who was behind them, but unfortunately no such memories seem to have survived about the development of Cherry Orchard, nor can definite information be given on the reasons for the names of Cavendish Street or Stanley Street.

CHERRY STREET
This street was first found listed in 1932, when there were 12 homes here.

CHERRY TREE WALK
Formerly known as Back Butts, but renamed about 1870, 'thereby supplanting the proper name,' according to Noake. It was included in the health board streets list of 1872, and first found in a street directory in 1880. In 1884 there was a mix of commercial development and modest homes. Charles Williams ran a commercial day school here then, and William George Dinsdale was a cab proprietor, though probably only of his own cab. Most of the other residents were labourers, plus a blacksmith, a seamstress and a laundress. All the homes here have since been swept away by redevelopment.

CHESHIRE CHEESE ENTRY
The eighteenth century **Foregate Street** pub which gave its name to this alley closed around 1829, but surprisingly the name has survived. There was a large yard at the pub, and John Noake noted a tradition that the first Worcester to London coach departed from there, though no record was found of it having been a coaching inn. It stood on part of the site now occupied by the Odeon cinema, and was demolished before 1834, when the Athaeneum opened in Foregate Street on the site of the pub.

CHESNUT STREET
The rural setting of this area was no doubt once similar to that of **Chesnut Walk**, but development here seems to have been slightly later, since unlike Chesnut Walk, this street was not listed in 1840. The street was first found recorded in three building applications in 1872 and 1873 for a total of 14 homes, and was listed in the health board streets list and in a street directory in those years. Sale of land went ahead around the same time as development of parts of the Arboretum estate, such as **Northfield Street** and **Wood Terrace**.

Land here was split into lots for sale, possibly around 1872, and in 1874-5 there were references in building applications to Lot 1, Lots 33 and 35 North Side, and Lot 36. This almost certainly applied also to land at **Lower Chesnut Street** and **Little Chesnut Street**. Between 1872 and 1879 there were 15 mostly small-scale building applications for 47 homes, but it is difficult to know how many were for this street, and how many for the other Chesnuts. When the first full residents' listing appeared in 1884 it became obvious that building had gone ahead on many of the lots not mentioned in building applications, apparently without any permission being sought, unless applications have been lost, and 58 homes had been built here.

Residents were slightly more 'white collar' than in surrounding streets, though with plenty of working men and women. The Misses Davis at No. 3 were machinists and baby linen makers, Thomas Nicoll at No. 17 was a reporter, John Nott at No. 51 was a commission agent, next door to sewing machine agent Charles Newman, and four doors down from John Austin who was a musician. There was also a police sergeant, shoemakers, tailors, dressmakers, building tradesmen, a sheriff's officer, print workers, glovers, a mason and a watchmaker.

CHESNUT WALK
Named for the chesnut trees growing here until urban development overtook the area, which seems to have happened in the early 1860s. The name was first listed in a street directory of 1840, but it is unlikely there was any development here at the time, and this is confirmed by a writer in the *Worcester Herald* of the late 1920s, who said that it was still a mere footway in the 1850s, and in the spring it was 'a vision of chestnuts, hawthorns and golden chain'.

By 1864 however, John Noake, a journalist from the same newspaper, said there had recently been considerable development here. This seemed to slow after building development regulations came into force in 1865, since over the rest of the century there is only an occasional building application recorded, mostly for two houses. As a result no records have been found of how the development proceeded initially, though it was common to auction off building plots.

In 1884 there were more than 40 homes here, mostly described as villas rather than the more humble 'cottages', with a mix of white-collar and skilled occupations, and even one resident who styled himself 'gentleman'.

There were a number of clerks, a stonemason, an engineer, a cashier, an accountant, a coachsmith and an auctioneer. Some residents had a strange mix of occupations to make ends meet; James Taylor at Sydenham Villa was a coal dealer and boot and shoe maker; John Bishop at Elmley House was a carpenter and lodging house keeper.

The Foresters Arms may have been built at much the same time as the street, and was first found listed in 1873. It closed around 1990, though the building still remains as student accommodation. Edward Elgar lived nearby at Loreto Villa, on the corner of **Chesnut Street**, between 1879 and 1883, with his sister Pollie and her husband, William Grafton. There is a claim that he first composed *Land of Hope and Glory* here, but 1901-2 is generally accepted as the date of that composition, so the story seems unlikely.

CHRISTCHURCH ROAD

The meaning of this name is obvious now – but the reason for choosing it originally is more of a mystery. This is now one of a small estate of streets named for Oxford colleges, including Balliol, Keble. Oriel, Merton and Somerville, but this street was started in the late 1920s, around 40 years before most of the estate, and the only other adjacent street built at that time was then called *Elbury Road* - clearly not an Oxford college - so it is questionable whether this was originally chosen as an Oxford college name. It is more likely that it was chosen originally for a connection to Tolladine's Christ Church, though that wasn't built until around 20 years later at nearby Rowan Avenue. Whatever the reason for this choice of name, the fact that it was coincidentally an Oxford college name probably accounts for the names of the adjacent streets, including the later renaming of Elbury Road as **Balliol Road**.

The road was first found in a street directory in 1922, when there were 18 homes listed, which were shown on an Ordnance Survey map of 1928. Residents at that time included a painter, a cooper, a policeman, a printer, an electrician and a labourer. With Elbury Road, first listed at the same time, it formed the first phase of a planned Garden City, designed to occupy the Portfields between here and **Newtown Road** (see **Tolladine Road**). The remainder of the 'Oxford colleges' estate was first found on a street map of the early 1970s, when Elbury Road was also renamed.

St Barnabas Church and Vicarage, Church Road, about 1900 - RS

CHURCH ROAD

This road was first found recorded in 1884 as an unnamed track leading off **Astwood Road**, but by the following year construction of St Barnabas Church was underway and the road had taken its present name, though it was some time before there was any house building going on here. A building application for the vicarage was submitted in 1888, and the school buildings – which were demolished in the 1980s - were built around the same time. It wasn't until 1903 however that there was a building application for 24 houses, but construction then went ahead quickly and they were all completed and occupied by 1905. Nearly half of the original residents were railwaymen. Charles Dowler at No. 16 was a farm bailiff, and his neighbours included a pattern maker, two foremen, several smiths, a bricklayer and a gardener. At No. 1 was the shop of greengrocer Henry Starr. At that time the vicar of St Barnabas was Rev William Worster.

CHURCH STREET

It was formerly the *Dish Market* where crockery was sold, one of the city's ancient street markets, though this one may have been at **The Cross** in earlier times. The present name was in use by 1790, and may have come into use in the 1730s when St Swithun's Church in **St Swithin's Street** was rebuilt. The west end of the street was widened in the twentieth century by reducing the width of building plots on either side, but

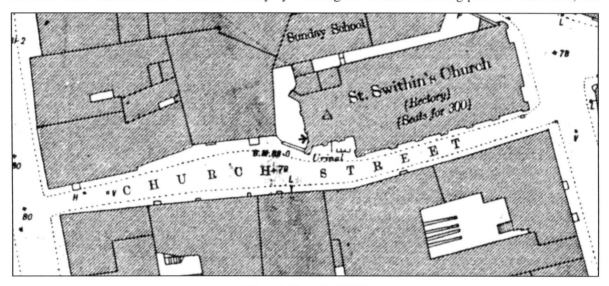

Church Street in 1884

otherwise the width of the street is pretty much as it was, and the east end beside the church gives a very good idea of the width of many city streets in times past.

Unfortunately the architecture has undergone a complete transformation since 1900, and not for the better. All that remains now of any age is the church and the Georgian church house, recently completely refurbished, where the Worcester Royal Grammar School was housed in a single room until it removed to **The Tything** in the late nineteenth century.

On the south side of the street at the junction with **High Street**, from at least 1820 for more than a century, were the offices and print works of the Berrow's Worcester Journal, which had begun life in **Sidbury**, and was moved to **St Swithin's Street** by Harvey Berrow. By 1820 it had moved here, and by 1840 it had been taken over by the Deighton family, who had been wealthy clothiers as long ago as the sixteenth century, when Christopher Dighton was a city bailiff during the visit of Elizabeth 1 in 1575.

The Deightons' print works remained here for the rest of the nineteenth century, but the Journal moved to No 43 in the 1860s, where it remained until it moved to **Broad Street** early in the twentieth century. The site of Deightons print works was redeveloped in the 1960s, and is occupied by Barclays Bank.

Beyond the print works was an old inn called the City Arms, which was held by John Baylis in 1790 and by William Harding in 1840. It closed around 1960 and a clothes shop now stands on the site. Beyond that was the side elevation of a superb timber-framed building fronting onto the **Shambles**, long occupied by ironmongers J. & F. Hall. That was also demolished in the 1960s, despite a public outcry.

The City Arms was the only listing for the street in 1790, which may suggest that the other properties here at that time were homes of wealthy citizens. But by 1840 on the north side of the street were shoemaker James Stockall, cooper Thomas Barnett and silk dyer John Halling.

By 1884 the same properties were occupied by Munt's cabinet makers, Butler & Co outfitters and John Butler's house. The building occupying the northern corner site was rebuilt in 1903, and by 1940 was occupied by Hardy's furniture store. The ground floor is now largely occupied by Superdrug, but part of the frontage onto this street a century ago was the Central Arcade, which ran through from **St Swithin's Street**, and was later the Arcade Cinema. The street became a pedestrian precinct in February 1973.

CHURCH TERRACE

First found on the health board streets list of 1872, and in a street directory of 1884, though there was probably some development here earlier than that. At that time the Terrace was a narrow lane surrounded with orchards, and half of the homes were spread around them, whilst half were grouped into the 12 Coucher's Cottages at the end of the Terrace, from where a footpath ran past Ivy House to **Bransford Road**. Near the cottages was the St John's Working Men's Club, which still exists, and then seems to have been at the home of gardener Benjamin Elvin, with the vicar, Rev Walter Raleigh Carr, as president. Next door lived Charles Mortimer Downes, receiver in bankruptcy. Not surprisingly, given the semi-rural environment, there were a number of gardeners living here, but also building workers, seamstresses, labourers and a millwright. Much is now 1930s or later, but there are still some nineteenth century homes here.

CHURCH WALK

First found on a map of 1838, and shown in a street directory of 1840, it may have been created as a footway through to what is now **Tybridge Street** to make it easier for residents of that populous area to get to the new church on Henwick Road, opened in 1822, though this lane may have been even older than that, providing a route to the new section of **Henwick Road**. The east end now connects with St Clement's Close.

According to John Noake, this lane was known in the nineteenth century as Cold Comfort, though Gwilliam believed the nickname actually applied to a group of cottages here, and was due either to poor soil in the gardens, or to lack of amenities. In 1884 there were 27 homes listed here, including 10 cottages named *St Clement's Gardens*, behind the church, to the north of the Walk, which were set amongst orchards, like a mini garden city, creating what must have been a very pleasant environment. Residents then included building tradesmen, seamstresses, glovers, a fireman, a brushmaker, a wood turner, a tailor, a baker, a charwoman and a china packer. Gwilliam said this was also known later as 'School Walk', though that must have been because of confusion with *School Walk*, which actually ran further west. The Parish Hall midway along the Walk probably dates from the 1820s, but is now disused and deteriorating. Everything else around the Walk now is modern redevelopment.

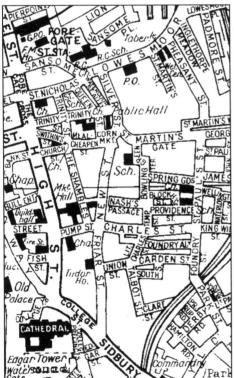

The area through which City Walls Road was to run, shortly before it was created - HC

CITY WALLS ROAD

Not an historic street, but its creation along part of the line of the medieval city walls in 1975 ended the existence of a number of streets that were, though archaeological excavation at this time did discover new information about the medieval city defences. The streets demolished to make way for the road (from north to south) were *Watercourse Alley*, *Bowling Green Terrace*, *Little Charles Street*, *Portland Place* and *Talbot Street*; and **Silver Street**, **South Street** and **Claire Street** were badly affected.

Clapgate

Old name for **St Martin's Gate**, listed in a street directory as late as 1840, and still in general use in the 1870s, to judge from building applications.

CLARE STREET

This small street was on the fringe of the *Blockhouse* area. It survived that clearance in the 1960s, but was badly affected by creation of the **City Walls Road** in 1975, and is now nothing more than an access road to a car park.

The name must have some connection, probably through ownership of the land here, to the Clare family, who were established at Caldwell, Kidderminster, in the sixteenth and seventeenth centuries. Sir Ralph Clare was a zealous Royalist who fought at Worcester in 1642 and 1651, and was accorded royal honours after the Restoration in 1660. Timothy Clare was shown in documents of 1732 in the county archives as a gentleman of Worcester, and also held land at Hallow. All of the building applications found, including three applications for a total of five homes, were all submitted in the period 1883 – 1886, and building probably went ahead soon afterwards. It was first found listed in a street directory in 1896, when the five homes applied for were listed, plus the Worcester New Co-operative and Industrial Society Bakery, for which a building application had been submitted in June 1883. At Spafield Cottage next door to the bakery lived Edwin Moody, manager of the co-operative stores, and there were four Argus Cottages, housing a railway guard, a gloveress, a gardener and a foreman.

COLE HILL

In the medieval period this whole area was known as Cole Hill, after William Cole who gave 30 acres of land here to the hospital at the Commandery in 1310. At that time a windmill stood on the hill. The hilltop was renamed **Fort Royal Hill** in the seventeenth century, for a Royalist strong point situated on the site of the present park during the Civil War.

It was laid out as a housing estate in the 1860s, and the record of development here began in 1867. In that year there were five building application for just nine houses, with another one in the following year and just two more through the rest of the century. This strongly suggests that a good deal of the street had been built hurriedly before building control applications became compulsory in 1865.

In 1884 there were more than 30 homes here, one shop and a pub, plus two ladies, presumably widowed, letting out rooms. The residents were a fascinating social mix. There was a schoolmaster at No. 14, but at No. 4 was an assistant inspector of schools. There was also an architect, a businessman and a John Emperor who styled himself 'gentleman'. But elsewhere in the street there was a builder, a watchman, a clerk and an engine fitter. The pub was the Plumbers Arms, on the corner of *Wyld's Lane*, which opened before 1873 and still survives.

COLIN ROAD

The development here must have been planned and built by **Northwick Road** builder Ronald William Morris, who presumably chose the road name, perhaps for a member of his family, as must also have happened with the adjacent **Leslie Avenue** and **Dorothy Crescent**. The road was first found in a street directory in 1937, when there were already 25 homes here, and Mr Morris had an estate office here for house sales.

COLLEGE GREEN

Now a green behind the cathedral, this was originally the burial ground of the monks from the nearby monastery. When Urse D'Abitot, the first Norman Sheriff of Worcester, built Worcester Castle in 1069, on a site near **Severn Street,** the bailey encroached on the cemetery. Archbishop Ealdred of York, a former bishop of Worcester, was so incensed by this that he cursed the sheriff, who died fighting in Normandy soon afterwards.

COLLEGE PRECINCTS

A superb row of Georgian houses, leading to what were known in past times as St Mary's Steps, because of the dedication of the cathedral. The houses have inevitably attracted clerical occupants over the years, and in 1790 there were a brace of prebendaries, but most striking was the number of female householders. In that year there were seven widows living here and one miss, to just two male householders. In 1884 occupants included the District Registry of the Court of Probate at No. 4, solicitors Hooper & Hooper at No. 7, and the Servants' Home and Registry Office at No. 11 with Mrs Annie Collis as Lady Superintendent. More humble residents included a warehouseman, a glover, a commercial clerk, a foreman, and Mrs Charlotte Salt whose occupation was mangling.

COLLEGE STREET

Much of it was formerly regarded as **Sidbury**, this street having only been created at the end of the eighteenth century. It was named for the college established by a charter of Henry VIII and now called King's School. It is situated in what was originally the cathedral Sanctuary, which ran from the Bishop's Palace up to the castle, near **Severn Street**, much of which consisted of the cathedral's lay cemetery, north of the building, which accommodated most of the population of Worcester until the Reformation, and remained in use until 1804.

The see was established in 680 and the cathedral was rebuilt by both its saintly bishops, Oswald and Wulfstan. Amongst the best known of its many historic features are the Norman crypt, the Chapter House, its fine tower and the tomb of King John. The cathedral library has the second largest collection of medieval manuscripts

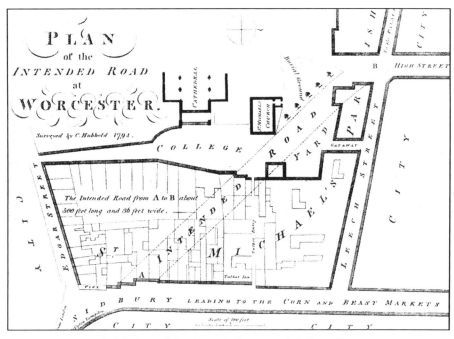

A 1794 plan of the intended route of College Street

in the country, some dating back as far as the seventh century, and also has many early printed books and a fine music collection. King John's will and a book printed by Caxton, the first English printer, are amongst the highlights of this collection.

Prior to the construction of this street all traffic coming through the Sidbury Gate to the city centre had to turn sharply into *Lich Street* and then sharply again into **High Street**. Around 1782 city linen draper Timothy Gillam and the landlord of the Talbot Inn, Thomas

Williams, proposed a new route direct into the High Street, to improve the traffic flow. Perhaps the two men hoped to bring coaching business to the Talbot, though that did not happen.

There was already a footpath leading from the Talbot through the Sanctuary and the graveyard into the High Street, but opening this up to traffic needed the sanction of the Bishop and the Dean and Chapter, and it was not until 1792 that the mayor was authorised to spend 100 guineas on preparatory work. One obstacle in the street's path was College Grates, a gatehouse with tenements over, situated at the south end of High Street and forming the entrance to College Yard, at the front of the cathedral. An Act of Parliament was needed to

Old St Michael's Church beside the cathedral, this engraving must be from shortly before it was demolished about 1840, after which a replacement was built on the other side of College Street

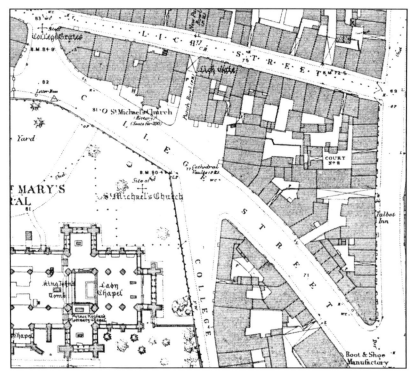

demolish it, which was obtained in 1795. A plan of 1794 showed the course of the intended new street, and the intended line was also shown on Valentine Green's map of 1795. It must have been created shortly afterwards, no doubt before 1800.

The exemption from city rates afforded by church land attracted a number of the city's wealthiest citizens to this street in the eighteenth century, and the south side of the street nearest the cathedral retains some interesting homes from that era.

The opposite side of the street must also have had many buildings dating from the eighteenth century or earlier.

In 1709 the five houses adjoining the inn were occupied by an apothecary, a smith, a hatter, a pin-maker and a widow probably letting rooms. Unfortunately this

Above, College Street from Palace Yard to the Cinderella Works, 1884. Below, College Street about 1905, with the Cinderella Works in the centre of the picture - RS

side of the street suffered much from 1960s redevelopment.

The widening of the street to a dual carriageway had received planning consent by March 1962, to be completed by September 1965. The plan, which was part of the ***Lich Street*** development, involved the demolition of many older buildings. The one property marked for preservation had, and still has, the street's oldest business, the Talbot Hotel, a very ancient inn in part, though much altered over the years. Situated at the edge of the graveyard, it may have been one of the buildings of the monastery, perhaps providing food

The later St Michael's Church and the Cathedral Vaults pub which closed in 1908 - WN. And an 1896 advertisement

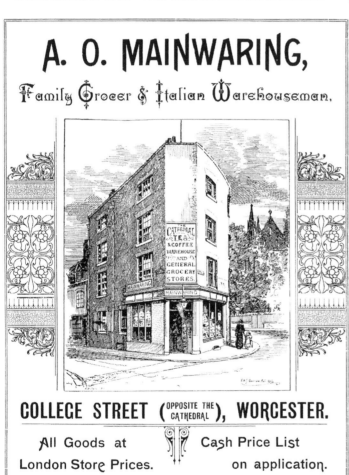

and drink and lodgings to pilgrims, so it was natural that it should become an inn after the Dissolution. In 1555 it was one of only ten licensed inns in the city, though there were 44 licensed ale houses frequented by the poor, and unlicensed ale houses were the haunt of the destitute drinking classes.

In 1649 it had a hall for public events, several bars and parlours, 13 rooms and stabling for 40 horses. Magistrates often sat there in the Justices Room, when there was no space at the castle nearby, or the 'gaol fever' (typhus) was particularly severe there. In 1758 a meeting was held at the inn which led to the formation of the Worcestershire Regiment.

Almost opposite stands the former Cinderella shoe manufactory, built in 1866 on the site of the old Cross Keys inn, beside which was the house, then in **Sidbury**, where the city's oldest newspaper was published. Cinderella was founded by Henry Willis, who was joined by his brother James in 1860. It was one of the largest boot and shoemakers in the city, and is regarded as one of the first firms to establish a brand name for its products, which were sold all over the UK and overseas. At its height the firm employed more than 350 people. It moved to **Watery Lane** in 1914, and the building here is now apartments.

The church of St Michael Bedwardine stood on this street. It was originally at the north-east end of the cathedral, and was traditionally regarded as the parish church of the cathedral sanctuary, but in 1837 a guide book described it as 'a very old structure, but possessing no beauty of architecture'. In 1840 the old church was demolished and a new one built opposite on the east side of the street. It closed during the twentieth century, but served for a time as the Bishop's Registry, before being demolished about 1960 and replaced by a retail development. Just south of the church was the Cathedral Vaults, a late eighteenth or early nineteenth century pub, which closed in 1908.

COLLEGE YARD

The cathedral still owns the street and most of the houses, so this is all that now remains of what was once Worcester Cathedral's extensive medieval Sanctuary, which stretched from **Sidbury** to the Bishop's Palace, now in **Deansway**, and from *Lich Street* to the Severn. Rights of Sanctuary were granted to the cathedral in 712, and though much of this area later lay within the medieval city walls the city authorities had no jurisdiction here. Only the bishops of Worcester had authority over the Sanctuary, and their rights were confirmed by successive monarchs, including Henry IV, who ordered in 1400 that 'No bailiffs, serjeants, ministers or other persons of the City of Worcester shall hereafter carry or bear any mace or maces (here), but only in the presence of the King'. This meant that the city had no authority over the prior and monks at the monastery, which was founded about 960 and dissolved in 1540.

Those in danger were supposed to find safety here, and when a mob beat a man almost to death within the Sanctuary in 1302 they were compelled to do what one writer called 'a most ignominious penance' at the gate of the cathedral. Rights of Sanctuary were abolished in the reign of James I, but the cathedral chapter was still asserting its rights over the area in 1671. The area of the Sanctuary became the parish of St Michael in Bedwardine, since St Michael's, built close to the cathedral in 826, had always been regarded as the parish church for the cathedral precincts. The area did not become part of the city until 1837.

Buildings historian Pat Hughes has identified the late seventeenth and early eighteenth centuries as the period in which most of the present houses here were built. The building of No 10 has been dated to 1687, and most of the adjacent houses had been built by 1700.

Over the centuries the ground level in the area had risen dramatically due to the many burials, with a flight of steps needed to descend to the cathedral's north door. In 1866 the north approach to the cathedral was reduced by more than four feet, to restore it to the original ground level when the cathedral was built, which is why the houses here are at a much higher level than the roadway.

Near the north porch once stood the chapel of the cathedral charnel house, an upper room of which was used from 1636 to 1641 as a schoolroom for King's School, and beneath it was a crypt containing bones. The 'ruinous' charnel house had been taken down by 1696, but when cellars were being investigated for air raid shelters during the Second World War, the cellar beneath No. 10 was found to be still full of bones, and more of the ancient crypt runs beneath the roadway.

Mrs Emily Studdert Kennedy, widow of **St Paul's Street** clergyman and World War One legend 'Woodbine Willie', lived here at 5a for many years until her death in 1964, and despite frail health she was active in the WVS, and the Worcester Cathedral Guild of Embroiderers.

COMER AVENUE
Off **Comer Road**, first shown in a street directory in 1937, though there were no listings before the Second World War, and development does not seem to have taken place here until the 1950s.

COMER GARDENS
See also **Comer Road**. This street was built in the 1850s, as a garden suburb of homes set back behind long gardens, either side of a lane, said to have been built when some folk decided to leave the city after the cholera epidemic of 1848; the second in 16 years.

It was an isolated community - though not entirely devoid of urban amenities - in a beautiful rural location set in meadows and orchards, and it became the dormitory home of a colony of working families, reached by what were originally farm tracks from **Bromyard Road** and **Henwick Road**, now known as **Comer Road** and **Oldbury Road**.

Industrialist William Morris was born in Comer Gardens - WN

The street was built too early for building control records, which began in 1865, and anyway was not in Worcester then. It was not found in a Worcester street directory until 1880, and no building control record was found until 1897.

It was still in Hallow Parish in 1884 when the first full listing of residents was published. There were around 80 homes here at that time, mostly in small terraces of two to five cottages or villas, no doubt built by different developers and named to suit their personal tastes.

There were three cottages in Albert Terrace, five Croydon Villas, two homes in Summer Place, two in Montreal Villas, three in Providence Place. There were also South View Villa, West View Villas, Sherwood Cottages, Temperance Cottages, Spring Hill Cottages, Clarah Villas and Rose Cottages. There were also a number of detached homes, which were probably the first to be built in the area.

Residents were very much a social mix, with many gardeners and labourers, laundresses and building workers, but also a couple of people styling themselves as gentlemen, which usually meant that they didn't need to work.

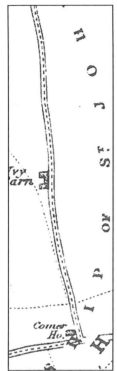

Above, the future site of Comer Road in 1840, then part of Ivy Farm. Comer Road about 1900 - RS

Others included lamplighter John Moon, cabinet maker Thomas Pates and china painter John Hundley. There was a Free Church, erected in 1865, and alongside it was a Day School run by Miss Matilda Brown. At Kent House, on the corner of **Maund Street**, Samuel Whiting was a shopkeeper and beer seller, and three doors down was greengrocer John French.

At South View in 1898 was Thomas Sayce, captain of the Worcester fire brigade – then apparently a part-time job, since he was also partner in a business.

William Morris, the founder of car manufacturers Morris Motors, was born in 1877 at No 47, where there is a blue plaque. When he was three the family moved to Oxford, but he never forgot the city of his birth, and in his lifetime he would always give generously to good causes in Worcester.

COMER ROAD

The name Comer is found in three early forms, as Combire in 1240, as Comer in the Knights Templars' former manor of Temple Lawern in 1316, and as Colmore in 1649. Nothing has been made of the first two names, but the last means 'cool lake' in Early English, and is the most likely origin of the name, probably referring to a small lake or manorial fish pond long since drained, which would have been fed by a spring, remembered by Spring Hill Cottages.

This road marked part of the boundary of the ancient township of St John's, and will have long existed as a country lane – still referred to as Lane up to 1880 - leading from **Bromyard Road** to the isolated farms and mansions around the present **Oldbury Road**. The lane will have acquired greater significance with the building of **Comer Gardens** in the 1850s, but a map of 1884 shows it was still largely surrounded by open fields, with Comer Farm, often also called Ivy House Farm, on the west side beside a track which has since become **Laugherne Road**.

The modest amount of development which then existed on this road was around the southern end. At Comer House, beside the southern end of the road, was a preparatory school run by Miss S.M. Newton. Before and just beyond the railway there were less than 20 homes, with another three being built. They were mostly in small terraces with

suitably rustic and romantic names, such as Rose Cottages, May Cottages, Ivanhoe Cottages, Ivy Terrace and Windsor Terrace. Though there were some gardeners amongst the residents, others may have been commuting into the city daily, either on foot or from Henwick station. They included a glover, a fancy box manufacturer, a railway clerk perhaps at Henwick, an organ builder and building tradesmen. Census records show that at that time this area was part of Hallow.

Over the next 12 years there were 20 mostly small-scale building applications, and around 1890 development of **Laugherne Road** began. By 1896 there were more than 50 homes here, spreading along the west side of the road. The farm still existed, with William Giles as the farmer, but urban expansion was pressing in around it, with three more houses being built nearby, and in that year a building application was submitted for development on the farmland of several streets, subsequently named **Rowley Hill Street**, **Buck Street** and **Hopton Street**, and Ivy House Farm became Ivy Lodge. By 1922 there were 60 homes listed here, though as late as 1928 there were open fields and orchards on the east side of the road, which were not developed until later in the century.

On the corner of **Lambert Road** in 1922 was greengrocer Fred Stockall, and on the corner of **McIntyre Road** was Mrs Mary Greening's grocery shop. It was clearly becoming a select area, as an estate agent might say. Residents included Foregate Street Stationmaster Charles Richards, theatre manager Thomas Bell and John Tyler, chief clerk to the county surveyor. There was also a medical practice at Richmond House, with Drs Williams and Davidson.

Opposite **Nelson Road** is the Brewer's Arms, which may have long existed as a country pub serving St John's folk taking a pleasant stroll on summers' evenings, though there seems to be no information about its history. The present building is of the same age as the surrounding terrace of housing.

COMPTON ROAD

Builder Joseph Compton clearly named the street after himself, having submitted a building application in 1890 for the new road and 16 houses, and an application for another 12 houses in 1892. He was a busy man in the 1880s and 90s, submitting 24 building applications in those decades, including house building in **Carden Street**, **Wyld's Lane**, **Tunnel Hill**, **Stanley Road**, **Nash's Passage**, **Midland Road**, **Hamilton Road**, **Albert Road** and **Albany Road**.

This road was first listed in a street directory in 1896 when there were 12 homes and a corner shop here, whose residents included engineering and railway workers, a commercial clerk, an ironmonger's assistant, a potter, a pattern maker and a 'body maker', who probably made bodices for womens' garments. By 1910 all 28 homes applied for were listed, and a couple more were added shortly afterwards to complete the road. The corner shop was still open in the 1980s, but has since become a house.

COOMBS ROAD

First found in a street directory in 1930, when 27 homes were listed, this road was probably named for Henry Coombs of **Battenhall Road**, an estate agent and auctioneer with an office at 59 **Foregate Street**, who was serving as city councillor for St Peter's Ward in that year.

COPE ROAD

This road was first found in a street directory in 1930, when 22 homes were listed. It was probably named for city councillor Arthur Cope of **Woolhope Road**, who was serving as a member for St Peter's Ward in that year, alongside Henry Coombs after whom **Coombs Road** was probably named, and in 1922 was on the Streets Committee..

COPENHAGEN STREET

This street originally ran right down to the river, but it was cut off by the **Deansway** development in the 1960s. It may once have been known as Huxterstrete, the street of traders or hawkers, which was close to what may have been the city's main market near St Albans Church in Anglo-Saxon times, though Noake identifies Huxterstrete with *Little Fish Street*.

By 1464 it was Cucking, Cooken or Cooking Street, the street of the cooks, and there is documentary evidence of cooks based here. This was most probably the area where cooked food shops could be found. Fast food is nothing new, and every medieval city had an area providing cooked bread and pies. Pudding Lane in London was the most famous of these streets, mainly because the Great Fire of London started there. City authorities in Worcester were sensible to locate a cooked food area on the outskirts of the old city, and as close as possible to the main water supply, the river, should a fire break out. The street's modern name was inspired by one of England's greatest naval heroes.

Historic Worcester Streets

There has been a modern theory that the proximity of this street to the River Severn meant it was named as the route to the cucking- or ducking-stool, which was said to be situated near the Wherry Inn, but medieval streets were named for the trades carried on there. There is in any case some further confusion about this device. Modern researchers suggest that the ducking stool and the cucking stool were not just alternate names for the same thing, but

Copenhagen Street now ends at Deansway but on the map of 1884 it ran on down towards the river, where the Wherry Inn was converted in 1923 into the St Andrew's Institute, on the left of the picture - WN

similar devices with different purposes; the cucking stool being used to wheel its unfortunate occupants around the town for public humiliation, with no ducking involved. A record from 1570, referred to by Hughes, shows that the device used in the city at that time was designed to be moved from place to place, so it may not have been used for 'ducking'.

At the east end of the street was a site called the Earl's Post, now partly the site of Marmion House, beneath which there are remnants of medieval cellars. There was an eighteenth century theory that this was the site of a house to which the Earl of Worcester moved from the castle in the medieval period, but there was no Earl of Worcester during most of the medieval period, and this spot owes its name to another earl. In the mid seventeenth century there was an inn on this corner called the Earles Post, the sign for which was a bear and ragged staff or post, the heraldic device of the Earls of Warwick, the hereditary sheriffs of the city, major landowners in the county, and in the case of the then earl at least, a good friend to the city. This continued as an inn or tavern until the mid eighteenth century. This spot was said to be the legendary site of the last stand of the Royalists at the Battle of Worcester in 1651.

The street assumed its modern name thanks to one of Nelson's most famous victories. On 2 April 1801 the great naval hero defeated a joint Danish and Norwegian fleet at the Battle of Copenhagen, thus helping to end the League of Armed Neutrality which supported trade with Britain's arch enemy, Napoleonic France. During the battle Nelson was ordered to retreat, but famously put his telescope to his blind eye and said 'I do not see the signal'.

When he visited Worcester for a few days in August of the following year Nelson was cheered wherever he went, and the ancient street was subsequently renamed in his honour, probably because it led directly to Worcester's own maritime connection, its inland port. An old inn near the top of the street, just off the **High Street**, was renamed The Mouth of the Nile, recalling perhaps his most important victory, at the Battle of the Nile four years earlier. This hostelry, which closed around 1930, was

Lord Nelson

just one of no less than eight pubs in this street at various times. Along from the 'Nile' was the Old Porter Stores, which closed around 1955, almost opposite the Dolphin, which had closed by 1908. Close neighbours near the Deansway junction were the Ship, an old inn also closed around 1908, and the Glos'ter Arms, which

closed a few years later. Beyond Deansway, on the corner of *Birdport*, was the Plume of Feathers, which closed in the nineteenth century. Another old hostelry beyond that, the Cock Inn, dating back to at least the eighteenth century, was rebuilt around 1900 but closed around 1938.

The riverside Wherry Inn was a popular hostelry, used by watermen in the eighteenth century, and as a better class inn, attracted custom from Bath-bound coach travellers in the nineteenth century. It was also believed to be the haunt of smugglers landing their wares at the nearby slip during the eighteenth century. The riverside could be a dangerous place for other reasons before street lights, and in the early nineteenth

Advertisement for the Worcestershire Chronicle 1847

century hunting parson Rev. Benjamin Dent mistook his way as he left the inn – it was said in the fog – and plunged into the river, dying from the effects of this soaking. In the mid nineteenth century the landlord was gifted stained glass artist George Rogers, whose work is in Worcester and Gloucester cathedrals and many parish churches. In 1923 the inn was converted into the St Andrew's Institute, a club for local men and boys, which had a spacious billiard room on the upper floor. The building was demolished about 1939.

Near the Wherry was said to be a ducking stool. Opposite the Wherry in the eighteenth century was the city Bridewell or prison. It was still in existence in 1778, but by 1784 it had become a stoneyard. In 1841 the St Andrew's Monitorial School for Girls was built on the site, but it closed when the Hounds Lane Board School opened in 1873.

Stallards had a connection with this street for many years. The firm is reputed to have been founded in 1642, but it came here in 1808 to open its wine and spirits premises, with a vast, labyrinth of historic cellars below. The firm also had a distillery at *Warmestry Slip* nearby, and had opened the Britannia Brewery in **Barbourne**

Historic Worcester Streets

Copenhagen Street has historic links to the days when the city had its own police force : above, a plaque remembering it; below, the former entrance to the police station - TW

Road by 1851. In 1969 it merged with Malpas & Co, but the Stallard name was still to be seen over a wine shop here in the 1990s.

The radical Worcestershire Chronicle began publication every Wednesday at No.5, behind the Guildhall yard on 3 January 1838, in the wake of the Reform Act of 1832. Published by Messrs Knight and Arrowsmith, it had a large sale and continued for many years. Isaac Arrowsmith, who was the printer and no doubt also the editor, had been the chief spokesman for the Worcester Political Union during the campaign for reform.

There had been rioting in the city in November 1831, when the Reform Bill was rejected by the Lords. When they turned it down for the second time a massive demonstration was organised on Pitchcroft on 14 May 1832, at which Arrowsmith gave the opening address.

He was involved in agitation for further reform at the Guildhall in 1837 and 38, and was a prominent member of the Chartist movement in 1848. He retired to Bristol in 1864, where he published railway guides and 'shilling shockers', the Victorian equivalent of today's lurid paperback novels, several of which he wrote himself.

After his retirement the paper moved to **Broad Street** and James Knight cultivated a more mainstream liberal stance for it. There are copies up to the end of 1913 in the county archives.

The city's first purpose-built police station for the city police opened here in 1862 behind the Guildhall, and the police sign can still be seen above a doorway, though it was much smaller than the substantial building later built farther along. An application to build a gymnasium in the street was submitted in 1884.

The last of Worcester's carpet mills, Webb's Horsehair Carpet Factory, was located here until 1935. The firm was started exactly a century earlier by twenty-eight year old Edward Webb, later mayor and an enthusiastic supporter of healthcare and the arts, credited with inspiring the 'Worcester School' of landscape painters which included B.W. Leader.

The firm was based initially in an eighteenth century house in the street, but within a decade employed 70 weavers and had begun to expand. The payroll eventually rose to 100, including many children, but it was reputed to be the only factory in the city providing schooling for youngsters, albeit in evening classes after a ten-hour working day.

The firm made carpet for 10 Downing Street, and the wedding of the Duke of York in 1893, and foot rugs for almost every railway company in the land. It moved to **Sheriff Street** in 1935 and the factory site was used to build new police and fire stations.

Slums around the west end of the street towards the river were demolished in the 1930s.

Many of the old buildings have gone, but there is an historic Dutch-gabled house at No. 7. It was built in 1558 for Christopher Dighton, who was bailiff of the city in 1560. He leased the site from the Dean and Chapter of Worcester Cathedral, and built the house to let.

By 1649 the Dean and Chapter were letting out the house themselves. In that year it was let to a Mr Thomason, and on his death in 1697 his widow, Margaret, turned it into an alehouse called the Phoenix, in which role it continued until 1717, when it was partly rebuilt.

It was subsequently let to glovers, a solicitor and shoemakers. From the early twentieth century until around 1940 it was occupied by barber Abraham Harding, and city councillors would often pop out the back of the Guildhall during meetings to get their hair cut. The refurbishment of the property won a city award in 1986.

CORNMARKET

The name can be traced back to the time of Elizabeth I, but it may have existed earlier than that as a trading centre for corn merchants. The corn market may originally have been in **Queen Street**, but moved slightly to the south, no doubt in search of more space. Though once smaller than it is now, this must always have been an open market space.

The Cornmarket about 1840, and St Martin's church in the late eighteenth century

Public punishments were carried out here, usually on Saturdays when the corn merchants were not trading or finished early. The pillory stood here, where miscreants were pinioned while the crowd amused themselves by hurling abuse and rotten vegetables.

It must have had a fair amount of use, for in 1585 a new pillory was ordered, with the lead from the old one being used on yet another new pillory at **The Cross**.

There must have been room for more than one miscreant, since in 1791 John and Mary Venables were set in the pillory together for an hour, after imprisonment for keeping a brothel.

Public whippings with the 'cat-o'-nine-tails', usually for minor thefts, were also held here, and offenders were sometimes whipped around the city at the cart's tail. In 1722 one shilling (5p) was paid by the city for a new whip. In December 1761 the Journal reported that a woman was whipped for stealing tallow, and a young man for stealing 'wearing apparel'.

Historic Worcester Streets

As far as we know, executions were never held here; they were always outside the city walls, at Red Hill and from 1738 at Pitchcroft, but were transferred to the new County Prison at **Castle Street**, when it opened in 1813.

The site of the pageant houses, where the carts and costumes were housed for the annual mystery plays presented around the city by the trade guilds in the medieval period, is believed to have been in the area where a large furniture store now stands. The area was redeveloped around 1584, and the buildings now on the site may date from as early as the 1720s.

The original St Martin's Church was built in the early twelfth century, according to Valentine Green, who said it was 'principally constructed of timber and of a very irregular form'. His remarks suggest it was timber-framed, like most buildings in the city at that time. Local legend has it that Shakespeare married Anne Hathaway at that church in 1582, after obtaining a special licence from the Bishop of Worcester. The records which would prove this claim have not survived, but there is no record of the marriage in the parishes around Stratford either, so St Martins' claim cannot be disproved, though it probably doesn't attract much support outside Worcester.

Shakespeare married Amme Hathaway at St Martin's Church, according to local legend

The present church was built at a cost of £2,215 in 1768-72 by Infirmary architect Anthony Keck in brick, which had become very fashionable. Like many other city churches, its parishioners had moved out to the suburbs by the start of the twentieth century, and a new St Martin's was started in **London Road** which opened in 1911. To avoid the two being confused this was dubbed Old St Martin's, but it ceased to be a parish church, and was classified as a chapel to St Swithin's. However St Swithin's ceased to be a parish in 1978, so this once more became a parish church, now called Worcester St Martin in the Cornmarket.

In the south east corner stands a fine timber-framed house now called King Charles House, since he is said to have escaped from here after the Battle of Worcester in 1651, dashing out of one door as the Rounheads stormed the other in **New Street**.

It was built in 1577 by wealthy brewer Richard Durrant, whose grandson Edward had it at the time of the Civil War, when Charles made it his headquarters. It was once said to be the home of the Berkeleys of Spetchley, but they lived in **Mealcheapen Street**.

The original building was entirely timber-framed and of three storeys, but when the central section was later destroyed in a nineteenth century fire it was rebuilt in brick, and the other parts were reduced to two storeys. It will be remembered by most city folk as J.W. Holtham, a firm founded in 1801 as seedsmen and horticultural suppliers, which continued here until around a dozen years ago.

What became known as the Public Hall was built here in the nineteenth century, on what is now a car park. The entrance faced New Street, and the building filled what is now a car park outside St Martin's Church, extending back as far as **The Trinity**.

It was originally intended as an indoor corn market, on the site where an outdoor market had existed for centuries, and was built in 1848-9 at a cost of £7,000 raised in £10 shares, but the business went instead to the rival farmers' Corn Exchange in **Angel Street**, which opened in 1848. The building here was sold, and by 1851 it was a music hall. Charles Dickens gave two readings here in 1869. In 1870 it was purchased by lawyer William Laslett, after whom **Laslett Street** was named, and sold to the city for a reasonable sum, to be turned into a performance

An 1869 advertisement

venue. It was said to have a fine organ and a resident orchestra, and attracted leading performers. Souza, the 'march king', gave a farewell performance here; both Dvorak and Elgar conducted their own compositions in the hall. Between 1900 and 1902 the Public Hall showed the first movies in the city, newsreels of 'our soldiers in South Africa', which were actually likely to have been mocked-up in this country, but nevertheless

The Public Hall in 1920

drew large crowds. During the Second World War it became a British Restaurant, providing good, solid meals to workers who no longer had time to go home for lunch, and in any case, probably didn't have the ration coupons. The Public Hall had become one of the much-loved treasures of Worcester, which didn't prevent it being knocked down in 1966.

A Green Dragon inn was mentioned here about 1720, but nothing further is heard of it, though there were two other inns of the same name around that time, in **Foregate Street** and **High Street**, so this one may have changed its name subsequently. Of the two pubs which exist here now, the Exchange, formerly the Royal Exchange, is in an imposing nineteenth century building and has a fine Edwardian tiled exterior. The pub next to the church is housed in an older building, probably eighteenth century, and was formerly the King Charles II, before that The Tubs and previously Edwards Vaults.

CORNMEADOW GREEN

First found in a street directory in 1937, off **Cornmeadow Lane**, there were already 23 homes listed here at that time.

CORNMEADOW LANE

This had probably long been a lane linking **Ombersley Road** to Claines Lane, which became a street as the farmland north of **Checketts Lane** began to be rapidly developed for housing in the 1930s. When the street was first found in a street directory in 1937 Mrs A. George was still farming at Cornmeadow House, which gave its name to the street, but there were already 45 homes listed here.

Thomas, 1st Lord Coventry, a prominent seventeenth century lawyer and politician

COVENTRY AVENUE

This street was first mentioned in a street directory in 1932, but there were no listings until 1937, when there were already 60 homes here. The land-owning Coventry family had a long association with the city, and members of the family often served in public offices. In 1930, around the time this street must have been created, the Hon. John Bonynge Coventry of Pirton Court, Wadborough, was Mayor of Worcester, and the street was probably named for him.

Cripplegate

Now part of **Tybridge Street**.

CROFT ROAD

This road was first listed by this name in the health board streets list of 1872, and in a street directory of 1873, though it is undoubtedly much older. It was so named because it leads to Pitchcroft, originally an enclosed area of land or croft probably belonging to the Norman Pyche family. For many centuries citizens had customary rights to use footpaths across Pitchcroft, but the land didn't come into full public use until 1899. Traditionally freemen of the city had the right to graze their cattle on Pitchcroft between July and the beginning of February, and may still have that right, although they don't generally exercise it. A small triangle of land, now serving as a car park with its entrance under the viaduct, was known in past times as Little Pitchcroft. This was traditionally open space and attempts to build on it provoked a riot in 1818. An *Old Croft Road* was formerly to be found off the **Butts**.

CROFT WALK

This had probably long existed as a footway leading from **Croft Road** to the trackway which became **The Butts**, but by the late nineteenth century it found itself sandwiched between the Cattle Market and Wood's timber yard, which explains why it is narrower at the Butts end. The Wheelers Gardens almshouses, listed in **The Butts**, were off the Walk, behind the woodyard.

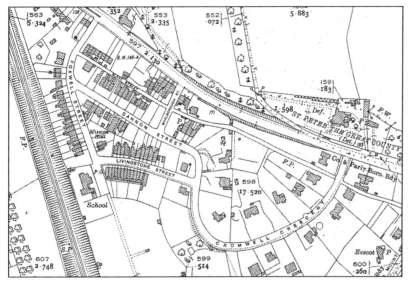

Cromwell Crescent and the surrounding area in 1928

CROMWELL CRESCENT

In the area at the crest of Red Hill known as Oliver's Mount, since Oliver Cromwell is said to have made his camp here during the Battle of Worcester in 1651, so that he could see over the whole city and direct his troops.

This was part of an estate which included **Foxwell Street**, **Cannon Street** and **Marlborough Street**, but while these other streets were developed in the mid 1890s, there is no evidence of building here until 1910. It was first recorded in a building application of 1888 for a new road. It had been created by 1896, but by 1897 had been named Oliver's Mount, and was not listed with its present name until 1910, when five detached homes had been completed, with names such as Winterdyne, Malvern View, St. Nazaire and Redgate. Residents then included a headmaster, a clerk and a cashier sharing, and three people who either didn't need professions, or didn't feel inclined to give details of them. Little further building took place until the 1920s, when in a few years the street was completed.

CROMWELL STREET

One of three thoroughfares in the city named after the man who beheaded Charles I and turned Britain into a republic for a few years. It was probably a path or lane over **Tallow Hill** to **St Martins Gate** even before the Birmingham & Worcester canal was cut in 1815, since a canal bridge was placed here. From 1857 it provided access to the canalside premises of the Vulcan Iron Works, at the end of **Padmore Street**. The firm was started in 1857 by Thomas Clunes as iron and brass founders, but in 1861 he was joined by former railway

Oliver Cromwell

employees McKenzie and Holland, who took over in the 1870s, and they began specialising in railway engineering.

The company expanded to cover the triangular site bounded by **Shrub Hill Road** and the canal. A railway branch on the Vinegar Works line ran from the works through a tunnel under the road, and the company had its own locomotive. The firm merged in 1901 and was closed in 1921.

The site became part of Heenan & Froude in 1936, but after it became Redman Heenan Froude in the 1970s the engineering work ceased and the company went into property development, letting off units on the site, and later taking the name St Modwen after another takeover. The railway branch closed in 1958, and though the tunnel is still there it is blocked. Some years ago the Worcester builders' merchant Underwoods, now Bradfords, occupied a canalside building on the site.

Cromwell Street was first listed in a street directory in 1880, but it was not until the following year that there was a building application for the road. In

The Vulcan Works, which opened in 1857

1884 there were 10 homes here including six cottages in a terrace called Winter Place, one of which was home to photographer George Evans. Other residents included labourers, building tradesmen, a blacksmith, a glover, a letter carrier, a tin plate worker and a porter. The Holy Trinity School and school house of Holy Trinity Church in **Shrub Hill Road**, were built soon afterwards. The Great Western Hotel, built around 1860, stands at the end of this street and the Wine and Spirit Vaults there no doubt attracted some custom from residents here, but there were also pubs in the surrounding streets, and a sub post office nearby.

The homes here, and the nearby sub-post office and The Railway Arms and Prince of Wales pubs, were demolished in the 1960s when the clearance of *Lower Street* and *Regent Street* took place, and there is little here now apart from warehouses, so this street is a shadow of its former self. The area down to **Pheasant Street** was a car park for more than 30 years, until the present retail park was built.

CROOME ROAD
Croome Court, now a National Trust property, was the home from the mid eighteenth century of the Earls of Coventry. This street was first found in a directory in 1937, when there was just one listing, for Alan Walker at Langdale.

CROSS, THE
This was referred to in 1299 as Crocker Street. A *crocca* was an Anglo-Saxon earthenware vessel, which presumably means this street was the original site of the city's crockery market, before it moved in the medieval period to what is now **Church Street**. It must have taken its present name not long afterwards from the Grass or grace Cross, which in the Middle Ages stood opposite where **The Avenue** is now. The odd name of the cross must have resulted from English misinterpretation of the Norman French pronunciation of grace with a short vowel.

This cross seems to have been a very grand affair, standing on a roofed dais and engraved with heraldry, and was one of a number situated around the city streets and environs to remind people of religious devotion as they went about their daily lives, though this was the only one to leave its memory in the history of our street names.

Engravings of The Cross, in the late eighteenth century, above, in 1820 and in 1872

The cross must have been a hindrance to traffic, standing as it did in the middle of the street. Historian Pat Hughes has found a record of a city ordinance to remove it in 1578, though it must still have been there a century later, since Noake recorded that the city made an agreement in 1689 with John Hadley of West Bromwich to erect a new waterworks and lay pipes under the streets, for which he was allowed use of the material from the old waterworks and from the cross. He erected a cistern or reservoir at the Cross with a capacity of 200 hogsheads (approximately 10,800 gallons or 49,000 litres). This must have been in the nature of a water tower since the city had specified that the market there must be able to continue under it.

The city also specified that Hadley must not 'meddle with, hurt or cover the statue of the King thereby standing'. Noake suggests that this must have been a statue of either Charles I or Charles II, and that it was initially preserved in a special niche on the reservoir, and later transferred to the new Guildhall in the **High Street**.

The site was an important gathering point in the city centre. Archers were said to have mustered here before going to **The Butts** to practice. In 1558 a pillory was placed here to supplement that in the **Cornmarket**. According to Gwilliam, it was the place where May Day was celebrated and war and peace declared. There was a street market here for butter and cheese, and the annual Hop and Cheese Fair was held here in September, which attracted many country people to the city for a day of merriment. It was also the place where workmen could stand to be hired.

The east side of the street still has some fine buildings. The oldest of these is the handsome building at No. 2, which was built or substantially rebuilt in the 1750s, which was reputedly designed by Guildhall architect Thomas White. Due to some nineteenth century confusion with numbers, it was also referred to as No. 4. One of the city's earliest banks moved here in 1812 from **Mealcheapen Street**, where it had opened in 1795. It is referred to either as Farley's Bank or Farley, Lavender, Owen and Gutch's bank since George Farley, John Pearkes Lavender (after whom **Lavender Road** was named), John Owen and John Matthew Gutch were involved at various times in its management. It went bust in 1857. The building was later occupied by the Union Club, which opened there in 1878.

The building now occupied by NatWest, at No. 1, dates only from

Edwardian views of The Cross - above RS, below BG

Historic Worcester Streets

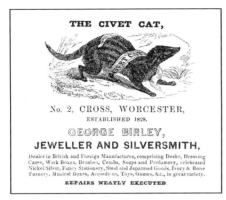

An 1856 ad for the Civet Cat store, and below, the store and St Swithin's Street, pictured prior to 1890 - RS

1890, but earlier buildings on the site have a fascinating history. The building here was owned in the early seventeenth century by wealthy city businessman Richard Inglethorpe (see **Sansome Street**), and since his death in 1618 it has been owned by the charity he set up. It was rebuilt by glover Richard Case in 1714 as the White Hart inn, and was later the subject of a court case which prompted an investigation uncovering many instances of fraud by members of the city corporation.

In 1732 the inn and land at Sansome Street, also belonging to the Inglethorpe charity, were acquired by shady local hop merchant John Garway, who was fraudulently profiting from his position as a leading member of the corporation as well as a trustee of the charity. He sold the inn at a handsome profit, but the charity saw none of the money. In 1827 a commission of enquiry came to Worcester, and found many instances of fraudulent corporation dealings with charity assets, as a

result of which the Lord Chancellor took control of all Worcester municipal charities, and in 1836 handed their administration to the newly created Worcester Municipal Charities body, which has controlled them with admirable probity ever since. However the Inglethorpe Charity had to take legal action to recover No. 1.

From 1828 it was The Civet Cat store, which sold jewellery and fancy goods, and was run by a family called Birley. The last of the family, Alderman G. Birley, died in 1889, and it was then taken over by Alderman Cassidy. It was rebuilt in 1890, and he moved the business to 64 **High Street**. In the twentieth century it was the International Stores, before being occupied by the bank.

The Rectory for St Nicholas Church formerly stood next to the church, but around 1855 the site was sold to raise much-needed funds, and the Rector moved to **Lansdowne Crescent**. A striking new classical building was then erected for the Worcester City and County Bank, one of the earliest joint stock banks, founded in 1840, which moved here from **Foregate Street** in 1863. It has a splendid front and superb carving by William Forsyth of **The Tything**. The City and County name is still above the door, but it was later taken over by Lloyd's Bank.

In 1713 there was an inn here named the Talbot, from which coaches ran to London three times a week, on Mondays, Wednesdays and Fridays. The coaches set out at 4am, and the journey took two days, with an overnight stop in Oxford.

The coffee house at the end of **Trinity Passage** is believed to have been the site of the Trinity Chapel (see **The Trinity**). Historian Pat Hughes believes that after the Trinity Guild was dissolved, the chapel may have been purchased by Robert Steynor, one of the two city bailiffs in 1584 and 1586, and used as a house. Later it became an inn called the Golden Cross, which is thought to have been founded by Steynor's widow. Around 1713 the Golden Cross was kept by John Andrews, in succession to the late landlord Thomas Taylor, and must have had a reasonable amount of land attached, since an advertisement in the Journal said there was room enough for clients to turn their coach or wagon.

Historian John Noake lists this inn as one of those used in the 1734 election, and a later Journal advertisement of around 1764 said it had "good cellars, a large vault and stabling for 100 horses". No further trace of it has

J. J. Williams & Co.

THE CROSS,
WORCESTER.

TEA
and
COFFEE
Specialists.

GROCERS
and
Italian
Warehousemen

WINE
and
BEER
Merchants.

AGENTS FOR W. & A. GILBEY'S WINES AND SPIRITS.

The City Provision Stores,
PRICE LISTS FREE.

J.J. Williams were on the corner of The Cross until 1921 when the store was taken over by grocery chain International Stores. NatWest Bank is here now.

been found, and in the nineteenth century there was an outfitters here, though the inn name was still used for the building, which may suggest that the original building still existed then. Unfortunately the old building was demolished in the late nineteenth or early twentieth century, and The National Provincial Bank of England was built on the site by 1908. The original chapel foundations were said to have been found during construction of the bank.

CROWN STREET
This street was first listed in 1880 as Lane, but existed earlier than that as an unnamed lane beside the former roadside inn on **Droitwich Road**, which had existed from at least the early nineteenth century. Building here had begun in the 1870s and possibly even the 1860s. It was listed as Street by 1884, when more than 30 homes were shown here. Eight of the residents then described themselves as labourers. There were also railwaymen, porters, building tradesmen, a fitter, an iron dresser, potters and a commercial clerk. At the Droitwich Road end of the street was Mrs Myra Leek's corner shop, and milk seller Henry Rudge. Older residents might remember the chip shop on the south side. Victoria Cross winner Fred Dancox was born here, and christened at St Stephen's Church on 23 November 1878. He may also have attended St Stephen's School. He later lived at various places around the city, and his family seem to have been at **Bull Entry** at the time of his death in action in 1917. The Crown was rebuilt as the Deer's Leap in the late 1970s or early 80s, but was closed in 2011 to make way for a medical centre.

CUMBERLAND STREET
This street name may be due to ownership of land here or financing of development by the Duke of Cumberland, a title which had been given in the sixteenth century to the Clifford family, who held land at Severn Stoke. The Worcestershire Militia archive shows that the Duke commanded the Severn district in 1803, but no information was found in city or county archives on his nineteenth century land holdings.
The first record found of the street was a building application for two houses on the south side in 1867, but possibly most of the building had been started before building control commenced in late 1865, since applications here bear no relation to what was actually built.
By 1884 only four homes had been applied for, but 26 had been built, plus a shop and a pub. All the named homes, which are likely to have been the earliest built, were at the west end of the street. There was Endswell Villa, home to an accountant in 1884, the two Radnor villas, and the nine Brighton Villas, all on the north side, and the two Portland Cottages opposite. Residents then included three warders from the prison in **Castle Street** and two police constables, building tradesmen, clerks, a coach builder, a compositor, a brewer, a shoemaker, a tailor, a messenger and a verger at the cathedral.
On the corner of **Lansdowne Street** was the Peep O' Day Inn, which was built around the same time as the street, in the 1860s or early 70s, and closed around 1970. On the corner of Somerset Place was shopkeeper and coal dealer William Henry Smith. In the 1920s and 30s the shop was run by Mrs Mary Ann White, known to locals as Granny White. There was an application to build two further houses in 1889, which had been built by 1896.

Cut-throat lane

A name commonly given to isolated lanes by rustic humorists, jokingly attempting to unnerve travellers. The poet John Masefield recalled in *Grace Before Ploughing* that there was such a lane in Ledbury when he was a lad. The name is used in several parts of Worcester. It was apparently used up to a map of 1829 for **St George's Lane North** or possibly **Lansdowne Road**, or perhaps both. It was also used for **Swinton Lane**.

CYPRESS STREET

This street seems likely to have taken its name from Cypress Place, the home of potter Henry Cale in **Alma Street**, just to the north. This street was not found listed until 1884, when there were six homes and a shop here, with a good deal of open space surrounding them, and the remains of orchards. On the corner of **Crown Street** was Daniel Denley's shop. Residents included a seamstress, a glover, a locksmith, a wood turner and a carpenter.

CYRIL ROAD

This name remains a mystery. The building application for the development of this road was submitted in 1902 by Walter Henry Aston of Eversley Villas, **Stanley Road**, while applications in 1903-4 to build 25 houses here were submitted by William Aston of **George Street**. The Astons were actively involved in Worcester property development during the building boom from the late 1880s on. William Aston had a saw mill in *James Street*, and it seemed likely to be another member of the family who first developed **Himbleton Road**.

The development here went well. By 1905, when the first full listing of residents was published in a street directory, 23 homes had been built, and a corner shop at the junction with **Lansdowne Road**, kept by Joseph Barron. It was an estate entirely of villas, as opposed to more humble cottages, and six were still empty, in fact one was still empty in 1908. 1905 residents had a real mixture of occupations, including a railway guard, an engine driver, a watchmaker, a tile manufacturer, a boiler maker, a carpenter, a gardener, a coach finisher, a couple of tinsmiths, a tailor and a commercial traveller.

The area where Deansway was to be created, shown towards the end of the 1930s, just before Palace Row was renamed as the first section of Deansway - HC

DEANSWAY

The first short section was created at the end of the 1930s, but Deansway as we know it was not created until the 1960s, though had the Second World War not intervened it would probably have been created in the 1940s.

Around 1939 *Palace Row*, between *Palace Yard* and **Fish Street**, was renamed Deansway, and in the 1960s the Deansway redevelopment swept away three more ancient streets, *Birdport*, *Merry Vale* and *All Hallows*. The palace is still known as the Bishop's Palace, but it was sold to the Dean in 1846, and was still in use as the Deanery when the first section of this street was renamed. It ceased to be the Deanery in 1941, but the 1960s planners still extended the name the first section already had.

This area was once so densely populated that there were three separate parish churches west of the roadway; All Saints, St Andrews and St Albans, and just the first two of these parishes had a third of the city's population in the 1750s.

In the seventeenth century and before this area had fine houses occupied by some of the leading families in the city, but they moved out as the area began to fill up, and their houses were split into squalid tenements and pleasant riverside gardens were built over with cramped courts.

Slum clearance in the area between the roadway and the river began in the mid-1920s, and by 1928 the block between *Hounds Lane* and *Birdport* had gone. By the end of the 1930s the clearance had been completed. Both *Hounds Lane* and *Hares Lane* had gone, and little remained aside from St Andrew's Church and graveyard and Hound's Lane School.

Construction of the first phase of Worcester Technical College, as it was then called, went ahead in 1959, covering the site of these old streets and of *Little Fish Street* and *Warmstry Slip*. The design was controversial for such an historic site, but the architects insisted that the facing would weather within 50 years to blend with the stonework of the cathedral and Bishop's Palace.

It has been suggested that the original St Alban's Church dated from Roman times, and that the present building has stonework from the Anglo-Saxon and early Norman periods, but there is no definite evidence for any of this, and the present building appears twelfth century.

The first St Andrew's Church was believed to have been built in the eleventh century, and the tower is from the fifteenth century. The spire, nicknamed the 'Glovers Needle' is the slenderest in the country for the size of its base, which is only 20 feet (6m) in diameter, while the spire soars to 155feet 6in (47.4m) in height.

St Alban's Church, late eighteenth century

DENT CLOSE

Named for a wealthy nineteenth-century glove manufacturer named John Dent. He was born in 1777, the eldest of four sons of a Worcester glover, also called John. The family lived at 26 **Sidbury**, and young John served an apprenticeship with his father, completed in 1798, and by 1807 was a glove manufacturer in his own right. He was later joined in the business by his brother William, to become J. & W. Dent, with premises in **High Street** by 1820.

John was first elected to the corporation in 1814, and in the same year he and his brother purchased a more fashionable residence at No. 34 **Foregate Street,** which they owned for more than 40 years. Now a leading citizen, John held many public offices in the city and beyond. In 1818 he was elected to the Clothiers' Company, and was High Master in 1827. He was Sheriff of Worcester in 1824, and mayor in 1825.

John Dent - TW

He became a city magistrate in 1836, and was also a magistrate of Worcestershire and Gloucestershire. In 1839 he was elected as the first president of the newly-formed Chamber of Commerce, an office he held for the rest of his life.

His brother was also a city magistrate and mayor in 1833, as well as High Sheriff of Gloucestershire in 1851. In 1837 the brothers purchased Sudeley Castle in Gloucestershire, the final resting place of Henry VIII's sixth wife Catherine Parr, and in1846 they sold the major gloving firm they had built up, on condition that it would continue to bear their name. The firm then moved to *Warmstrey Slip* off what is now **Deansway**.

Though the youngest by some seven years, William died first in 1854. At the beginning of October 1855 John Dent 'took cold' while travelling from Worcester back to Sudely, and 'sank and died'. He left £10,000 to local charities.

The first listing was in 1840, but it was then 'Street', and curved to run alongside the canal. In 1896 there were around 40 homes here, including 10 in Willow Place. Fifteen of the residents in 1896 were labourers. There were a number of building tradesmen, two fitters, two gloving workers, a signal fitter, a shoemaker, a platelayer, a skinner, an iron moulder, a needle fitter, an upholsterer, a laundress, a cook, a soldier and a hairdresser. One house was being rebuilt at that time, perhaps after a fire. Mrs Jemima Hazard had a shop at No. 5, and iron worker John Price had another at No. 24. At No. 3 was a pub called the Black Lion, on which Gwilliam has no information.

In the 1960s, when the adjacent **North Street** was demolished, this street was cleared and shortened, becoming a cul-de-sac, which prompted the name change, and the whole area was redeveloped.

DERBY ROAD

This road was part of a development promoted by glove manufacturer Robert Bach of *Great Park Street* and six other investors, which included **Hamilton Road** and **Prince Rupert Road**. A building application for a new road here was not submitted until 1885, but there had been five small building applications for a total of 12 homes in 1881, which together with two shops had been built by 1884 when the first full street directory listing for the street was published.

There were four Derby Cottages, which had probably given their name to the road, and two May Cottages, one of which housed shopkeeper Charlton Newton Jones, plus various other unnamed cottages, and Carleton House at the corner of **Hamilton Road**. The other shop, at the corner of **Park Street**, was kept by George

Fowler. Residents at that time included a labourer, an engine fitter, a china potter, a shoemaker, a fireman, a horse hair dresser, a commercial traveller and a porter.

An engraving of Worcester from 'Digley Fields' in 1781

Diglis

Not a street but an area. In ancient times the Diglis area was Duddan Leah, the meadow of an Anglo-Saxon called Dudda. By the eighteenth century this was corrupted to Digley, which caused some authors to claim that the name had come from 'd'eglise' meaning church land. It was certainly church land, held by the bishops of Worcester to provide grazing and hay for winter feed, but the Anglo-Saxon name is older, and so more likely to be correct than the Norman one.

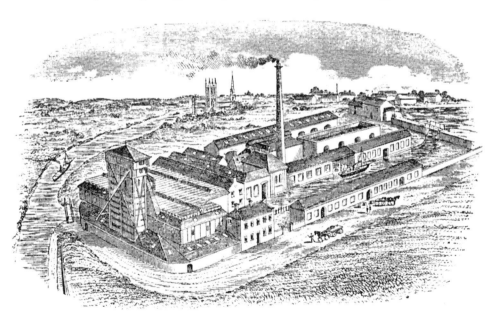

Henry Webb's Chemical Manure Works at Diglis in 1896

The bishop's riverside meadows extended some distance along the river and so did a track known as Green Lane, which was the forerunner of **Diglis Road**. This was a pleasant riverside area which would have been much frequented by city folk in the summertime, and a bowling green and pleasure grounds near **Severn Street** were very popular in their day.

It wasn't until the early nineteenth century, with the arrival of the Worcester & Birmingham Canal in 1815, and the construction of the Diglis Basin, that the name began to be applied specifically to the area around the basin.

The area soon became industrialised, and by 1840 11 water carriers were listed here, and there were about sixty departures a week. Large businesses moved in which could benefit from the use of river transport to

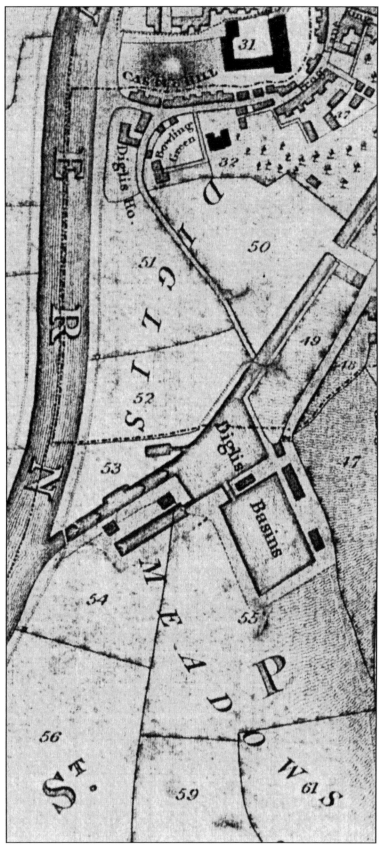

Map of Diglis Road in 1822

bring in raw materials and take out finished goods. Atlas Mills, originally owned by Lewis & Co, and by 1884 Beck & Co, which made pickles and sauces. The massive Worcester Chemical Manure Works was owned by agricultural chemist Henry Webb. The Severn & Canal Carrying Company had an agent here, and the Severn Commission had a collector of tolls, who in 1884 was John Bradley. The area has seen much redevelopment more recently.

DIGLIS AVENUE

This pleasant riverside terrace was first found listed in 1908, with six Florence Villas and six Gordon Villas. Residents then included a rare listing for a fisherman, Fred Jenkins. There was also a packer, a labourer, two glovers, a bookbinder, a gardener and a carpenter. Construction of the other 12 villas, consisting of six Stanley Villas and six May Villas, must have begun very soon afterwards, and they were finished, occupied and listed by 1910.

DIGLIS LANE

This was a name by which **Diglis Road** was commonly known in the past, and is a continuation of that road on the line it formerly took as an old track. In 1896 there were two building applications; one for the eight cottages on Beauchamp Terrace, and a second for Lygon Villa. Within two years they had been built, plus two Malvern View Villas, with two more homes being built. There was one labourer amongst the residents, but they were mostly skilled men, including a cabinet maker, an iron moulder, a china gilder, a fitter, a paperhanger, a painter, a boatman, two potters and an insurance agent.

DIGLIS ROAD

The bishop's riverside meadows extended some distance along the river and so did a track known as Green Lane, which was the forerunner of this road. By 1840 the area had become known as Diglis.

When this road was first listed in a street directory in 1880 it was as *Lower Bath Road*, though it was already being referred to locally either as Diglis Lane or by its present name, which was also shown on a map of 1884. The area was boosted by development of the Diglis Basin after the canal arrived in 1815, but a map of 1838 showed there was still little development here at that time. By 1884 however there were around 40 homes and businesses lining the road. Only four building applications for a total of 13 homes have been found from 1866 up to 1884, so it must be assumed that much of the building went ahead before building control began in late 1865.

The first five premises on the west side of the road were Ewins' corner shop, a shoeing smith, two coal dealers and a fly proprietor, and beyond that was Mrs Bird's lodging house. The importance of coal as the only widely available heating fuel at that time, and the importance of the Severn to bring it in to the city, was emphasised by the fact that there were five coal dealers along this road, including Mrs Sarah Marston, who also kept the Anchor Inn, which may have been established before 1834.

Unusually there was no other inn on this road at the time, but there was the Albion on **Bath Road**. Residents at that time were invariably manual workers, labourers, building tradesmen and factory workers, though Joseph Hail at the end of the road was a master mariner. The Anchor is still here, and a handful of the original homes still remain, but the area has seen massive redevelopment in recent years.

Diglis docks in 1890 - BG

Dines Green cottage probably about 1910 - RS

DINES GREEN
This was a rural area well outside the city for most of its history. Development began here in 1954.

Dish Market, The
The former city crockery market, now **Church Street.**

DOLDAY
An ancient street, just within the medieval city wall. It probably developed originally as a rear service road for premises in **Newport Street**, though over the centuries it took on its own character. Unlike many streets, this has never been

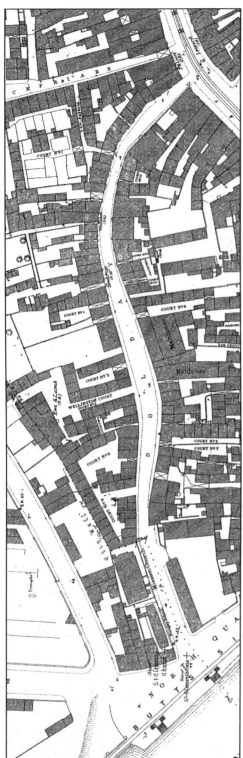

Dolday in 1884

known by any other name since it was first recorded in the thirteenth century, and even the differences in the variants used over the centuries - Doldey, Doldy and Doldy Street – have been slight. So this is certainly an ancient street, possibly first created in the tenth century when the city's defences were reorganised, but scholars have not been able to explain its name, or relate it to any elements found in Celtic, Anglo-Saxon or Old English names.

One local historian suggested that doles or charitable gifts of food or money given to the poor by the black friars, whose priory was just to the south of this street, might have given rise to the name, but since the name was first recorded in 1272 and the friars didn't arrive in the area until 1347, that clearly can't be the explanation.

It seems more likely that the name relates to a saint with some local connections, who would have been popular around the time the street was probably created. St Samson of Dol was born in South Wales about 490, and lived as a hermit beside the Severn, before becoming a bishop and working in Cornwall and France, where he founded the monastery of Dol in Brittany.

In the 930s King Aethelstan, who was brought up in the Mercian kingdom of which Worcester was part, acquired some of St Samson's relics, which could have given the saint new-found popularity in England, and even cult status in Worcester thanks to his links to South Wales and the Severn.

Traditionally the riverside church which stood here is supposed to have been founded in the Anglo-Saxon period, probably after the city's defences were strengthened in the early tenth century, just about the time when Aethelstan was acquiring the saint's relics, so the church might originally have been dedicated to St Samson of Dol.

In the Tudor period there was probably little development on this street, but a good deal was built here in the seventeenth and eighteenth centuries.

Like **Newport Street**, this was an area where cloth dyers settled, and many people working in the cloth industry lived here, but by the eighteenth century the work had dried up, and this became an area of poverty and deprivation. Most parishes had a parish workhouse to provide relief for the poor, and the All Saints workhouse was here near the Severn, in a timber-framed building which still existed around 1930, though it must have been demolished soon afterwards.

The pig market was held here in past centuries, but would have moved to the cattle market when it opened in **The Butts** in 1838. Much of the housing here was very poor, consisting of cramped courts and slum tenements.

Up until 1930, when they were cleared, there were 13 courts around this street, housing some of the poorest people in the city. The houses along the street however were occupied by tradesmen running their own businesses, living and working alongside their servants and apprentices.

Based here in 1790 were Alderman Haydon, brick maker Robert Allen, comb maker Thomas Poole, glover John Pumphrey, sail and tarpaulin maker Samuel Broughton and water bailiff and coal weigher John Broadfield. Along the street in 1884 were a variety of businesses, from Francis Dingle's wine merchants to fish dealer Thomas Mason and Durkin & Gaskin, marine store dealers.

The riverside church was later dedicated to St Clement, a saint with links to water and maritime affairs. It stood at the western end of the street, near the river and the old bridge. The medieval church was so close to the city wall that when that was slighted by the parliamentarians after the Battle of Worcester in 1651, they

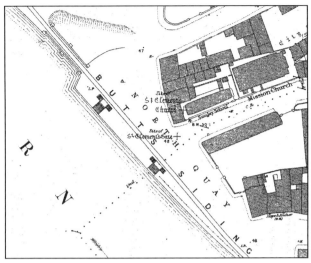

brought down the church tower as well, and Gwilliam said it was replaced by a wooden one, which was painted to make it look like masonry. There was a city gate by the church, probably a postern, which was also slighted, though its ruins remained until the late eighteenth century.

An 1884 map of the site of St Clement's Church, and the church in the late eighteenth century

The old church was much troubled by flooding, and since St Clement's parish lay on both sides of the river, and most of its parishioners had probably moved over the bridge, a new church was built in **Henwick Road** in 1822-3.

Most of the old church was demolished, but it is said that enough of the walls were left to form a cottage, which existed until the site was needed to mount a gun covering the bridge in the event of invasion, during the Second World War. The exact site of the old church cannot now be traced, but it was north of where the Severn View Hotel is now.

There were several pubs in the area. The Catherine Wheel, near St Clement's Church, opened in 1787. The Ewe and Lamb was up an alleyway to Wellington Court, on the north side of the road. Another old inn, the Britannia, stood almost opposite, on the south side of the road. It dated back to at least the eighteenth century, but closed between 1851 and 1873.

Further along, where the road bends, just a few doors apart, were the Sow & Pigs, another eighteenth century inn, which closed around 1912, and the Woolpack Inn, probably of early nineteenth century date but rebuilt around 1898, which closed around 1970. The first of these was formerly the house of brushmaker Abraham Pemberton, who built himself a banqueting house looking over the city wall, which was no doubt enjoyed by

All Saints Parish Workhouse in Dolday about 1930 - WN

pub patrons. Somewhere near these last two, though not marked on the map, was the Ten Bells, a nineteenth century pub which closed around 1925. Also listed in 1790 were the Coach and Mares, the Carpenter's Arms and the Waggon and Horses.

At the west end of the street, partly on the site of the old St Clement's Church, was the nineteenth century Watermen's Church, with the Sunday School beside it. Both of them fell victim to the modern redevelopment of the area and there is nothing left of this street as it was.

This street played host for a few years to the last remnant of great Worcester department store Russell & Dorrell, which once dominated the southern end of the **High Street**. After the store closed the furniture department hung on here for a few years, until it ceased trading in April 2012, in a building towards the west end of the street which may be remembered as Midland Shires Farmers, and at the time of writing is being taken over by the College of Technology.

DOROTHY CRESCENT

This would have been part of a development planned and built by Northwick Road builder Ronald William Morris, which also included the adjacent **Colin Road** and **Leslie Avenue**. No doubt Mr Morris was naming these streets for members of his family. This street was first found in a directory in 1937, when there were nine homes here.

An early photograph of The Drive, when the whole area was referred to as Checketts Field - RS

DRIVE, THE

The name suggests this was the entrance driveway to a nearby house, perhaps the lodge which is now The Perdiswell. The street was not found in a street directory until 1937, when there were 27 homes listed here, but the street is much older than that.

The earliest dated cottages are from 1880 and another is from 1884. The photograph above, probably taken in the early 1890s, when the roadway was still a muddy track, shows about 10 homes here, but that number had more than doubled within a few years, with infilling of vacant plots at the north end of the road. The rest of the street is all modern.

The reason the street was not listed earlier may be that it had not been officially named. When the photograph mentioned above was used on an early picture postcard, it was referred to as 'Checketts Field', which was the name given to the **Checketts Lane** area in its early days. Miss Mabel Bridgman was keeping a corner shop at No. 1 in 1937, which was later the local chip shop, but is now a house.

DROITWICH ROAD

This was part of the ancient Saltway leading into the outskirts of Worcester (see **Barbourne Road**), and the city's vital main route to the north, though urban development did not begin here until the late nineteenth century.

This toll house was built about 1814 with gates on both the Ombersley and Droitwich roads - TW

In the mid-nineteenth century much of the land along this road as far as Perdiswell was still owned and worked by the large fruit growing business Barbourne Nurseries, but urban development was gradually spreading beyond the brook as people fled overcrowding and disease in the city, though the city boundary did not reach Barbourne Brook until the 1830s, and did not advance again to the south side of **Bilford Road** for half a century, so there are few building records relating to the road.

In 1714 the Droitwich Turnpike Trust sited a toll gate close to the junction with **Ombersley Road**, said to be the first in Worcestershire, which was superseded by a joint gate for both roads on the junction around 1814, where the toll house still standa.

The gate was taken down at the end of 1877, though the toll house is still there. In the late nineteenth century the right hand side of this road was known as North Barbourne, and there was much housing development in the area.

St Stephen's church was created to serve this new community, thanks to the generosity of the daughters of businessman and banker John Pearkes Lavender, after whom **Lavender Road** was named. Designed by Worcester architect Mr Preedy, it was consecrated by Bishop Philpott on 20 August 1862. The first vicar was Rev T.G. Curtler of Bevere.

By 1884 there were around 75 homes along the road, ranging from grandly named houses to smart villas to humble terraced cottages.

The well-to-do were ensconced in mansion such as Barbourne Knoll and Clifton House, at the southern end of the road, while homes such as Belmont Place and Park Cottages, near **Perdiswell Street**, housed labourers and other manual workers.

Near **Checketts Lane** lived reporter Henry Augustus Runicles, next door to surveyor and valuer William Birch. Thomas Roberts, divisional superintendent of the Great Western Railway lived near **Gregory's Mill Street** in 1898.

St Stephen's Church in 1920

The Crown inn, near **Crown Street**, is no longer with us, having been demolished and rebuilt as the Deers Leap in the 1970s, and demolished again in 2010 to make way for a surgery, but the Victorian Alma inn further along is still going strong. The Raven inn is in a building which probably dates from around 1900, but an inn on the site dates at least from the eighteenth century, and may have existed earlier than that as a hostelry serving travellers on the main road into the city from the north.

The shop on the corner of **St Stephen's Street**, now a hairdressers, was held by grocer Samuel Joseph Ranford in 1898. Older residents might recall it as Mr Taylor's supermarket in the 1960s and 70s. On the other side, just past Crown Street was a small parade of shops. In 1884 Frederick Marshman had a grocery store here, and Henry Ricketts had the bakery, which survived until the 1970s, but is now a nursery. In 1898 hairdresser Edward Lee was on this parade.

An entrance on the right, just past **Bilford Road**, formerly led to Perdiswell Hall, a neo-classical mansion designed by George Byfield and built in 1788, which was home to the Wakeman family for many years. It was set in parkland stretching along the east side of the road as far as Fernhill Heath, with a large lake created in the eighteenth century.

During the first half of the twentieth century the Perdiswell estate became a centre of aviation. Flying was apparently taking place here as early as 1914. In the 1930s it became a municipal airport, said to be the first

Perdiswell Hall in its later days - WN

in the world, which some sources date to the 1920s, though specialist author Mick Wilkes dates it to 1931. In any event, the grass field was just not suitable for commercial services, though it did provide a base for light aircraft, which is something Worcester doesn't have now. During the Second World War it became RAF Worcester, and served as a flying training school, with Perdiswell Hall as the officers' mess.

The station's most famous incident took place in September 1942, when a plane said to have been carrying Hollywood movie star Clarke Gable crash-landed at Perdiswell. The Dakota transport plane slid on wet grass, ploughed through a boundary fence, across **Bilford Road** and into a rubbish dump. Gable, who was shaken up but unhurt, was in the co-pilot's seat but was apparently in training at that time, and had hitched a ride with General Spaatz, Commander of the US Air Force, who broke his foot in the crash. Bilford Road was blocked for some days until the plane could be dismantled and carted away. After the D-Day landings in 1944 wounded soldiers were flown here direct from Normandy, to be taken to Ronkswood Hospital on **Newtown Road**.

The RAF handed back the estate in 1945, but for many years the air cadets had aircraft outside their base at Perdiswell; first a Spitfire, which was taken away in 1967 to take part in the movie *Battle of Britain*, then a Javelin jet fighter until 1987. The hall was gutted by fire in 1956 and the shell was demolished. The coach house, built in a similar style to the hall, still exists and is used as offices. The lake was drained in the 1960s and the land was used first as a refuse tip, and now as a golf course.

DUTTON STREET

This small street connecting **Rainbow Hill** and **Wilson Street** is likely to have been named for Samuel Telford Dutton, who was city council member for the area in the 1890s, and lived opposite the street at Marl Bank, **Rainbow Hill**, which was later home to composer Sir Edward Elgar. He was from mechanical engineering firm Dutton & Co, which was based in **Shrub Hill Road**, and specialised in railway signalling. He does not seem to have been a large scale property developer. The only two building applications in his name were for creating **Rogers Hill** and widening **Lansdowne Walk**.

In 1884 this was shown on a map as an unnamed track, though there were probably plans at that time to develop it, which didn't then go ahead. The street was first mentioned in a street directory in 1896, but nothing was built here until around 1980.

EARLSDON ROAD

The road was being developed in 1931, when an application was submitted to construct the sewers, though the name of the developer is not known. It was first found in a street directory in 1937, when there were 12 homes listed here. The name may have been chosen by someone who had connections to Earlsdon, a suburb of Coventry.

EAST COMER

Part of the **Comer Gardens** development, which began in the 1850s, though this was not found listed until 1896, said then to be off **Comer Gardens**, but some of the homes, such as South View, Arundel Villa and the three Ventnor Cottages, were listed in 1884 under Comer Gardens and had probably been built some years before that.

Boat builder and market gardener Elijah Everton was at one of the Ventnor Cottages in 1884, and his next door neighbour was warehouseman George Turner. By 1896 14 homes were listed here. At Arundel Villa was printer's machinist George Richardson, and other residents included gardeners, labourers, a porter, a commercial traveller and market gardener Mrs Caroline Hundley. Houses here had substantial gardens, and as late as 1928 a map showed that a good deal of the land to the north of the street was given over to orchards.

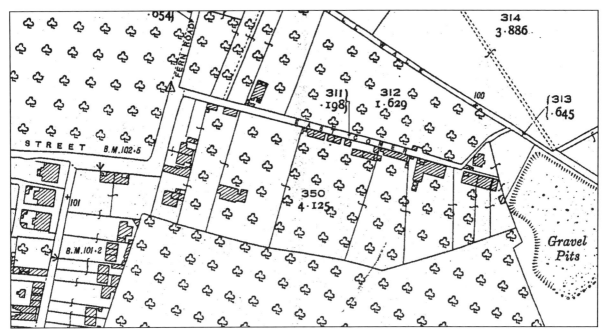

Map of the East Comer area in 1928

EAST STREET

This site was part of the mid nineteenth century Arboretum pleasure grounds. The crystal pavilion of the pleasure grounds stood here, at the end of the entrance drive, now **Arboretum Road**. In 1866 the pleasure grounds' 25 acre site was sold for redevelopment, and the crystal pavilion was taken down and sold.

A skating rink was built in 1870 on the pavilion site, where Waterloo House now stands, constructed of corrugated iron sheeting with cast iron pillars, and described by Bill Gwilliam as one of the ugliest buildings in the county. It also doubled as a tennis court, and circuses and public meetings were held there.

Towards the end of the century some of the great political figures of the day came to speak there, but by 1900 it had been converted to commercial use, housing the City & County Laundry in 1900, next door to wholesale boot and shoe manufacturer Edward James Olds producing 'Arboretum Brand' footwear at the City Boot Works.

In 1913 the Journal reported that the rink had been acquired as 'a depot for motor coaches', or bus garage. This was evidently very much at the start of the development of buses, as the Journal said 'motor coaches will be increased in numbers shortly for extensions of this type of traffic covering a wide radius'. The building was to be 'considerably extended' at that time, said the Journal. It was demolished in 1972, and the site was later redeveloped.

The street was listed in the health board streets list of 1872, but there were no recorded building applications for homes here until 1878, when there were three applications for four houses. The street was first listed in a directory in 1880, and in 1884 there were some 26 homes and small businesses here.

Just down from **Southfield Street** was the forge of smith Robert Warren, with two Verna Cottages and Rink Cottage, and the workshop of carver and gilder William Bennett next door to the rink. On the other side of the rink were the eight Utopian Villas, and the shop of James Rimmer.

On the corner of Arboretum Road were the dying workshops of Davis & Whitlam, the three May Fair Villas and seven cottages on Westwood Terrace. A good many of the residents were skilled or managerial workers, including a china painter, a builder, a grocery manager, a reporter, a foreman, a gas inspector, a coach smith, a stone sawyer, a china painter and an engine driver.

There was still vacant land around the southern end of the street, but development to fill it continued slowly, with five small applications for 15 houses up to 1898. In 1896 a building application was submitted for a mission hall for the railway mission, which was listed in that same year, but has now been split into flats. By that date the area had also acquired a pub, the Arboretum Inn on the corner of **Northfield Street**, now closed, and on the other corner was a shop kept in 1900 by John Grove.

EASY ROW

This street was developed soon after the building of the County prison, which opened in 1813, and probably owes its name to the attractive view it had to the west over Pitchcroft, though to the east was the grim prison wall. It was listed in a street directory of 1840, and was shown with an intensive development of small houses with gardens on a map of 1843.

It was probably intended originally to house prison staff, but subsequently had more general occupation, and by 1884 there was only one warder here, but there were four householders offering lodgings, which may have accommodated other prison staff, and there were four shops and a pub which no doubt counted prison staff amongst their customers. The shopkeepers were potted meat and sausage maker Henry Blundell, baker and brewer Mrs Ann Brindley, grocer Mrs Caroline Foster, and the corner shop of Miss Amelia Hemming.

The pub was the Rose and Crown Inn, probably built around the same time as the street, but closed around 1912. Other residents in 1884 included a brewer, two seamstresses, a cab driver, an ostler, a stay maker, a clerk, a glover, a commission agent, a sawyer and an iron moulder. Local historian Bill Gwilliam was born here in 1912, the son of a former boxer. The houses here were demolished during twentieth century slum clearance in the city, and the street has recently been redeveloped.

This photograph of Edgar Tower was said by Gwilliam to have been taken about 1860, and is said to be by a photographer named Bedford, whose 'developing wagon' is seen on the left - BG

EDGAR STREET

This street was originally known as Knoll's End Lane, since it led from Knoll's or **Knowles-end** in the area where the **City Walls Road** junction is now. It led to the great entrance gate of the medieval castle and monastery, and was shown by its present name as early as 1764, which is odd, since the gate tower, now called the Edgar Tower – hence the street name - was known as St Mary's Gate until the late nineteenth century, because of the dedication of the cathedral. Presumably it was popularly known as Edgar's Tower long before that.

Edgar was an Anglo-Saxon king, known as 'the Peaceful', though he was not averse to using force when necessary to enforce his will. He was crowned by Oswald, Bishop of Worcester in 959, and ruled until 975.

He is often known as the first true English king, since he ruled the three major Anglo-Saxon kingdoms of Northumbria, Wessex and Mercia, in the last of which Worcester was situated.

By tradition the gate tower was built on the orders of King John, who was buried in the cathedral in 1216, following the destruction of the previous gateway in a fire in 1202, but the present building dates from the fourteenth century, and the statues date from the restoration of 1910, though that of Edgar is said to be a faithful reproduction of an earlier figure which was badly decayed.

Another oddity about the tower; the door on the southern side has the address 1 College Green, but the door on the northern side is No. 16. A pub called the Coach & Horses adjoined the east side of the tower in 1751, squeezed between it and the steps leading to **College Street**. It was subsequently demolished and partly converted into a registry office, which was also later pulled down, and the site is now a school maintenance store.

A horse market was held here in past centuries. There were inevitably always a few clergymen here, because of its proximity to the cathedral, and perhaps for the same reason, there only ever seems to have been the one inn here. Residents in 1790 included architect Thomas Johnson, enameller John Strephon, fruiterer Ann Severn, glover William Allen, lamprey potter Elizabeth Pound and musician James Radcliff.

At No. 4 in 1840 was solicitor Morwent Baron, at No. 15 was vocalist Catherine Davis and at No. 17 was calisthenics professor William Lewis. By 1884 education was playing an increasing role in the life of the street.

At Nos. 2 & 3 Samuel Benoni Brewer had the Edgar Street Collegiate School, Mrs Bradley taught dancing at No. 5, the Misses Jackson had a ladies' school at No. 7 and Miss Eliza Parker had another at No. 9.

The King's School has long been based nearby. It was originally a school within the monastery, and was probably mainly for educating novice monks, though some sons of leading families also attended.

After the Dissolution, this was replaced with a king's school, under statutes of Henry VIII. One of its most famous former pupils was John, Lord Somers, a seventeenth century Lord Chancellor of England, after whom **Somers Road** was probably named, who spent much of his childhood at Whiteladies farm in **The Tything**. It was mostly known throughout its history as the College School or Worcester Cathedral Grammar School, but at the end of the nineteenth century it reverted to Worcester Cathedral King's School, to avoid confusion with the Worcester Royal Grammar School in the Tything. In 1971 girls were first admitted to the sixth form, and in 1991 the school became fully coeducational.

ELBURY PARK ROAD

Elbury Hills extend from the north-east section of the Brickfields estate to beyond the Virgin Tavern on the **Tolladine Road**, and in Victorian times were said to be a picturesque waste of gorse, bracken and briar. Elbury Mount, which was near the site of the earliest settlement in the Worcester area around 2,000 BC, was enclosed as parkland, probably in the eighteenth century.

Victorian antiquary Jabez Allies believed the name Elbury was derived from the ancient sun god 'El', and that the summit was a sacred place to druids. A Parliamentary battery was placed in this area at the time of the siege of the city in 1646, during the Civil War, but remains of the camp created here at that time are believed to have been destroyed during the creation of a covered reservoir on the Mount in the late nineteenth century. The area of the mount is now a Local Nature Reserve. This road was first found in a directory in 1937 when 32 homes were listed.

Elbury Road

Now **Balliol Road**. This road was first found in a street directory in 1922, when there were seven homes listed, with 18 by 1930. Residents in 1922 included an accountant, a foreman, a draughtsman, a linotypist, a manager, a fitter and a railway clerk. With **Christchurch Road**, on which development had also begun before 1922, it formed the first phase of a planned Garden City, designed to occupy the Portfields between here and **Newtown Road** (see **Tolladine Road**).

Most of the development here took place in the 1930s. In the 1960s a footpath still ran from here to Newtown Road. The name was changed when a number of adjacent streets were created, including Keble. Oriel, Merton and Somerville, to make an estate named for Oxford colleges, which was first found on a street map of the early 1970s.

ELLIS ROAD

This road must have been named for Bernard Joseph Ellis, who was city councillor for Claines ward in 1930, and lived at Tredennyke in **Barbourne Terrace**. It was first found in a street directory of that year with six listings.

Historic Worcester Streets

ELM ROAD
First found in a street directory in 1930, when there was just one listing, for sausage skin manufacturer David Parnum. Tree names were in vogue at that time, and this is one of a number of such names found in the city.

ELTRIC ROAD
The meaning of this name has been a mystery which has occasioned many hours of fruitless documentary research, and though a local legend about the creation of the road has shed some light on the matter, one mystery still remains.

The road was mostly built in the 1930s, on land formerly covered by orchards, but two houses at the end of the road appear to have been built around 10 years earlier. According to local legend, passed down by elderly ladies who have lived in the street over the years, these two houses were the first in Worcester to be all electric. As a result, the legend says, this was intended to be called 'Electric Road'.

This is an entirely plausible explanation, since these two homes look to date from the 1920s, when gas would doubtless not have been piped this far out of the city. Unfortunately the legend doesn't explain how 'Electric' was corrupted to 'Eltric' as early as May 1931, when it was shown in this form in a building application for a house. Maybe a clerical error somewhere along the line led to the present name. The 1937 directory listing, the first found, showed the road around two-thirds completed, with 22 listings, and it must have been finished soon afterwards since the homes are all of much the same date.

Exchange Street
This short street, which must have taken its name from the corn exchange in the **Corn Market**, ran from **Silver Street** to **Queen Street**, behind the Public Hall, a route which was originally part of **The Trinity**. This may have been created as a separate street after the Corn Exchange was built in 1848, but it was not shown on the 1884 Ordnance Survey map or found listed until 1897.

It housed only businesses, including in 1897 wardrobe dealer Mrs Lucy Leach, Batten's fish stores, and the iron warehouse and workshop of ironmongers J. & F. Hall, who had a shop in **The Shambles**. It probably disappeared when the Public Hall was demolished in 1966, or when the **City Walls Road** was created soon afterwards.

Factory Walk
Back alley leading from **St Martin's Gate** to **Pheasant Street**, first found listed in 1840.

Cllr Fairbairn - TW

FAIRBAIRN AVENUE
This will be named for long-serving councillor and JP Richard Robert Fairbairn. He was a councillor for St John's from around 1900, for more than 30 years. In 1930 he was living in **Park Avenue**. This street was first found in a street directory in that year, when 51 homes were listed.

FARLEY STREET
George Farley was the founder of Farley's bank, which opened in **Mealcheapen Street** in 1795, and went bust in 1857. Presumably his descendants had some money left after the bank crashed, and got involved in the development of this street. It was part of the **Comer Gardens** development, shown unnamed on a map of 1884, with 12 homes on the north side, some substantial with generous gardens, and an orchard on the south. By 1896 the homes here housed a dairyman, labourers, an engineer, a lamp lighter, a laundress, a machinist, an engraver, and a hay trusser. A further seven homes had been built on the orchard by 1910, and one more was added soon afterwards.

FARRIER STREET
This street was originally known as **The Butts**, and the short dead-end section of it that existed off **Shaw Street** in the eighteenth century was shown by that name on maps. What existed of this street in earlier times must have been the practice firing area for archers known to have been in this area, so it actually was 'the butts', though the name was eventually given to the lane leading down to the riverside. The butts must have fallen into disuse some time before the eighteenth century.

In the nineteenth century this became a through route of sorts, originally a narrow, uneven lane, snaking its way through to **Castle Street**. It was shown in a street directory of 1880 as ***Upper Butts***, but was still shown as The Butts on the first large-scale Ordnance Survey map later in the decade. Clearly it was known by various names in that period!

By 1896 however it was listed under its present name. It must have taken this name from the Farriers Arms pub on the corner of Butts Walk, a small alleyway off **Infirmary Walk** which is now under Orchard House, but it is likely that the pub took its name from the trade mainly carried on here. The pub was first listed in 1822, well after firing would have ceased at the butts, and closed around 1965. Directory listings in 1896 show this as a populous street housing both businesses and homes, and with three courts of housing scattered around it.

Many of the businesses were to do with farriery. There were two horse breakers, two or three shoeing smiths, livery stables, rear delivery entrances to the Star hotel and Griffith & Millington's auction house, and a number of cab proprietors and carriage hire businesses – here you could rent anything from a fly or delivery wagon to a hearse. No doubt many of the gentry from country areas found it convenient to stable their horses and park their carriages here while they shopped.

Just off The Butts was Goodman & Sons ironmongers, next door to Grisman & Son, builders and coffin makers. Nearby was John Waring's corner shop. Many of the residents were manual workers, including charwomen, metal workers and a brewer. At the Castle Street end was another pub, the Three Tuns, a late eighteenth or early nineteenth century pub which closed around 1930. The street was widened after the Second World War by demolishing the west side, and all of the homes have gone. By the 1970s car businesses had entirely taken over from horse businesses, and in recent years transport has given way to offices.

FERN ROAD

Presumably either there were ferns growing here before the road was created, or a developer thought this name struck the right sort of semi-rural note for marketing the development. The road was listed in a street directory of 1904, with just four listings, including a market gardener, a cattle dealer and a jobbing gardener, but as late as 1928 the road was largely surrounded by orchards, and little or no further development took place here until after the Second World War.

FERRY BANK

This steep path led to what was known as the Dog and Duck Ferry, though that pub has since been converted into a house. Prior to the ferry, which conveyed travellers across to Pitchcroft, it was known as Ford Bank and travellers could then cross on stepping stones at low tide. The ford here was long established, and was probably that referred to in an Anglo-Saxon charter of 816. After the establishment of the Severn Commission in 1843, dredging was carried out and locks installed at Diglis to deepen the river, making it no longer fordable, and the ferry was the only means of crossing here.

The former Dog and Duck pub, at the bottom of Ferry Bank, is on the left of this 1930s photograph - RS

FIELD TERRACE

Accessed by a footpath off **Bath Road**, this small street was apparently developed in the 1850s. Local historian Jeff Carpenter said 'properties were faced in cement, coloured and jointed like those recently built in Kensington', also somewhat reminiscent of the properties built in **Britannia Square** 30 years earlier, though of a more modest size. In 1896 there were listings for seven villas, occupied by a wine merchant, the collector of market tolls, a foreman, a commercial clerk and two widows.

FIELD WALK

This was first found in a street directory in 1937, when this area would have been fields not long before. There were 10 homes listed here at that date.

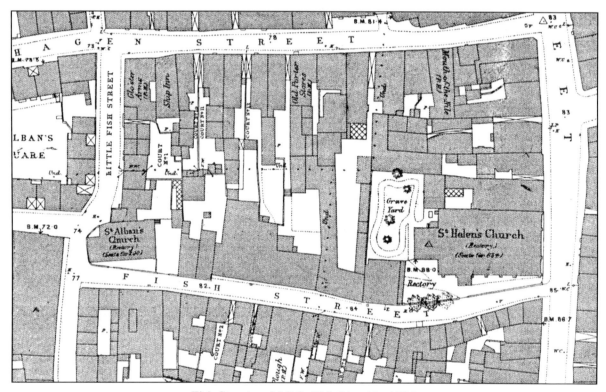

Fish Street and Little Fish Street in 1884

FISH STREET

The ancient street of the fishmongers, though in early times it was Corvisers Lane, the street of the cordwainers or boot and shoe makers. It originally ran from the High Street to just past St Albans church, but it was cut off by the **Deansway** redevelopment in the 1960s. There was also a *Little Fish Street*, which ran behind the church to link with *Birdport*, but that fell victim to the 1960s redevelopment of the area.

Fishmongers must already have been trading here in the medieval period, and in 1544 the city authorities ordered that they must trade only in the parish of St Alban's, on pain of a very substantial fine of 100 shillings. Presumably someone on the corporation really objected to the smell of fish in the city centre! It was a tradition that no fish was sold until it had been sniffed by an alderman to ensure it was fit for consumption. Any that was judged to have 'gone off' was given to prisoners at the gaol, or to the poor.

The most common fish sold was salmon, which was plentiful in the Severn in past times, and in Henry VII's time the fisherman paid one penny for his market pitch, and another halfpenny to the city Swordbearer for every salmon sold. Fishmongers' Hall, the hall of the fishmongers' guild, was a large, timber-framed building, said to be the finest building in the street and to date from the medieval period. In its later days however, it fell into disrepair and was split into nine slum tenements. Gwilliam said it finally collapsed in 1905.

Residents of the street in 1790 included two barbers, two glovers, a brush maker, a hair manufacturer, a maker of 'sheers', a hop merchant and alderman Thomas Giles. Fifty years later there was still one glover in the street, but no barbers, and no listings of purely residential properties. There were however two women running businesses – dressmaker Mary Walters and straw hat maker Jane Williams. There was an Inland Revenue office here in 1896, about half-way down on the south side.

Until Deansway was driven through it in the 1960s, this was a street with a church at either end – St Alban's to the west, and St Helen's to the east. Only the latter is now in the street. St Helen's is believed to be the original mother church of the city, claimed to pre-date all the other parish churches, though there is some controversy about this.

The original church may have been Anglo-Saxon, dating from about 680, when the Worcester diocese was founded, and it has been suggested that there may even have been an earlier Roman church on the site, built at the wish of the mother of emperor Constantine. The present building is mostly fifteenth century, but suffered badly in an 1879 restoration. The building beside the church was once the rectory, but by 1896 had become the Parish Room and Sunday School.

The 8pm curfew was rung at this church every night up until 1939, when it was stopped because ringing church bells was the signal that invasion had begun. Local folklore has it that when the elderly bellringer was indisposed Edward Elgar, then a teenager living in the **High Street**, would deputise for him.

St Helen's Church, late eighteenth century

Old houses in Fish Street in 1899, the Fishmongers Hall on the right

Following the clearance of St Helen's parish it was united with St Alban's in 1882, then with St Andrew's and All Saints just before the Second World War. St Helen's closed as a church in 1950 and later became the County Record Office for some years, before that moved out to the County Hall site, since when the church hosts occasional events, but has not found a role.

At the west end of the street was an old inn called the Stonemason's Arms, where the first Masonic lodge in Worcester was set up in 1757. The inn was still listed in street directories in the early nineteenth century, but it was afterwards either demolished or perhaps renamed, since The Plough inn had appeared in listings by 1840.

Also still in existence is the Farrier's Arms, in what was originally two houses. The main range to the right is of sixteenth century date, with an upper storey added between 1666 and 1678. Later additions and alterations were made around 1700, in the nineteenth century, and in the late twentieth century. Congregationalists in the city originally met at a house at the end of this street, before moving to **Angel Street** in 1687.

FLAG MEADOW WALK

This must have been part of the land brought to the medieval White Ladies convent in **The Tything** by Lady Alice de la Flagge, a member of a wealthy Claines land-owning family, who was prioress of the convent 1308-1328.

On her election to that post she was described as 'a woman of discreet life and morals, of lawful age, professed in the nunnery, born of lawful matrimony, prudent in spiritual and temporal matters'.

She was probably not a young woman seeking a vocation, but an older lady who had been married and entered the convent after she was widowed.

Some accounts claim that the land grant she made to the convent stretched as far as Perdiswell, and this may have been the dowry she originally brought to her marriage. At the Dissolution, in the 1530s, the nunnery became Whiteladies farm.

Being referred to as a meadow, this must have been a pasture, as was the land around **St George's Square**. It was listed in the health board streets list of 1872, and the street could have been substantially complete at that time despite what building records seemed to suggest. The building application for a new road here was not submitted until 1882, and there is no record of any housing applications prior to 1892, but a map of 1884 shows the street already complete opposite the present school sports ground, with around 35 homes, which could have been built as early as the 1860s.

Clearly the homes were originally built alongside what was little more than a track, and the 'new road' application would have been for widening and improving the street. Further north was still open ground, and it must have been for this land that a number of small-scale building applications were submitted in 1892-3. The first listing in a street directory was in 1896. Residents then were mostly skilled workers, including a lithographer, a marble mason, shoemakers, glovers, an organ builder, a baker, a tailoress and a picture frame maker. Mrs Maria Price at No. 14 had lodgings available. The Worcester Royal Grammar School had acquired the meadow as a sports ground by 1915.

FOLEY ROAD

This road in the Vernon Park area must have been named because of a connection between the land-owning Foley family, once owners of Witley Court, and the Vernons, who held the land here. The area was open land up to the start of the twentieth century, probably worked by some of St John's many market gardeners. By 1915, when the road was first found listed in a street directory, there were around 60 homes here, so building must have been going on for a few years previously. There were a good many villas, usually the preserve of the middle classes – and there were some clerks, a bookkeeper and a grocer's manager listed – but this was largely a street of skilled tradesmen and women, with building tradesmen, a cooper, a dressmaker, metal workers, a woodwork instructor, a couple of police constables and three van salesmen.

Thomas Foley 1617 - 77

FOLEY WALK

This footway was first mentioned in a street directory in 1930, but then as now it served only as a rear access to houses in **Malvern Road** and **Foley Road**, without even a street sign, though it is listed on street maps.

FOREGATE, THE

This was the area within the main gate of the city, from which it took its name. It was first recorded as a street name on a map of 1764, though it must have had this name for many centuries before. The Foregate in the medieval wall was the only entrance to the city from the north, and was situated where the Hopmarket development now stands, roughly where the entrance is.

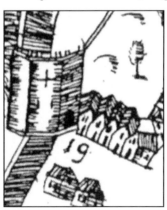

This was one of the original gates in the city wall which must have been rebuilt in stone at some time during the medieval period, though we have no certain information about it. Both the gate and the wall were badly damaged in the Civil War, but clearly the city authorities thought the gate was worth keeping and it was repaired afterwards.

They soon changed their minds however, and it became the first city gate to be demolished in 1702. Sadly no-one thought to describe or sketch this or any other city gate before it was taken down, so we have no evidence of what it was like except a small sketch on a seventeenth or early eighteenth century map.

Twentieth century city historian Hubert Leicester made a sketch of what he imagined it might be like after seeing the massive foundations, which were exposed during construction of the Hopmarket Hotel, as it then was.

The Foregate, from a map of the city's 1651 defences Beyond this the city also controlled the land up to the 'liberty post' which was on the south side of **Castle Street**. The liberty posts were supposedly set a

Historic Worcester Streets

What Hubert Leicester imagined the Foregate might have been like. Below, a Victorian photograph of The Foregate - WN

bowshot from the city walls, though it would have needed a good archer to shoot that far.

This was typical of many narrow city streets, and was far narrower than **Foregate Street**, which created a hindrance to traffic, so the city corporation had the whole east side of the street demolished and erected the range of Edwardian buildings here now, which included the then Hop Market Hotel, now split into apartments, and Barclays Bank, which has since moved down the road. The Hop Market courtyard was opened as a retail development in 1981.

Much of the west side of the street was early nineteenth century, until the building on the corner of **Angel Street** was demolished in recent times. The most striking buildings here are the attractive Berkeley's almshouses. The Berkeley family were wealthy city clothiers who lived in **Mealcheapen Street**, and acquired a country estate at Spetchley. One of the best-known family members was Sir Robert Berkeley, who became a leading judge. His teenage son, Thomas, fought for the Royalists in the Civil War, but after the city was forced to surrender in 1646 he went abroad and married a catholic, causing his staunchly protestant father to disinherit him.

The Berkeley estate was thus settled on the judge's infant grandson, who died as a young man, leaving money to found the almshouses, a project which his widow supervised, and is said to have completed before her death in 1709.

The buildings may be on land which was previously owned by the Gardiner family who gave their name to *Gardiners Lane*, later **Shaw Street**, since there is a record of the Gardiners' land being conveyed to the Berkeleys in 1704. If this land was used for the almshouses, it must mean they could not have been completed earlier than 1705 or 6, not the date of 1703 which the chapel bears.

Above, a 1920 ad for chemists Anderson & Virgo

Left, an 1896 ad featuring the building on the corner of The Foregate, though the address is given as The Cross.

Below, shoe shop Lennards in the same building in 1939.

They cost £2,000 to build and a further £4,000 was given to endow them, which proved to be a good investment since they have stood for more than two centuries, albeit somewhat less than straight these days. The statue on the front of the chapel is of Judge Berkeley.

In 1840 occupants of this street included ironmonger Jas. Lloyd, boot and shoe maker John Rushton, chemist George Anderson, hop and seed merchants Wheeler & Giles, solicitors M & C Elgie and woollen draper William Parry.

Also here at that time, in the building decorated with shields, was the showroom of the Grainger porcelain company of **St Martin's Gate**, and the founder, Thomas Grainger, lived in the rooms above. For many years until the 1990s this building was occupied by W.H. Smith.

FOREGATE STREET

This was regarded as a very fine street in the eighteenth century, when it was lined with the elegant Georgian 'out of town' houses of the city's well-to-do. It became a fashionable, eighteenth-century promenade for city folk, and was nicknamed *The Mall*. It stretched from the Foregate in the city walls, just south of **Sansome**

Foregate Street in the eighteenth century

Street, (see **The Foregate**) to the Liberty Post, near *Salt Lane,* which is now **Castle Street**. This was the area outside the wall over which the city still had authority.

This area and **The Tything** were laid out as a planned suburb by the Bishop of Worcester around the year 1100, and originally it was called Forest Street, since Feckenham Forest, which once covered most of Worcestershire, would still have encroached on land to the east of the road leading out of the city. It was only much later, when the city began to extend north, that the name Foregate Street appeared. In the seventeenth century the open land to the west of the street was referred to as Windmill Field.

Its neighbour, the Tything, had become a foul-smelling slum by the sixteenth century, and during the Civil War all the buildings beyond the city wall, which would definitely have included those here, were cleared to deny cover to the Parliamentary forces. When rebuilding of Worcester's northern suburb began after the restoration of the monarchy in 1660, it was to become a very different suburb, with fine houses for the wealthy. The county justices had tried to rid this area of the poor in 1635 before the Civil War, and in 1662, after the restoration of Charles II, they decreed that all tenants not contributing to poor rates must leave the area, leaving the way clear for the middle classes to move here in their place.

The establishment of a 'poor house' here in 1702 also helped to remove the poor from other sites in the vicinity.

Hearth tax showed that many of the houses boasted five or more hearths and were occupied by gentlemen using the title Esq. Eighteenth century physician Dr John Wall, of Malvern water and Worcester Porcelain

Foregate Street in the early nineteenth century

VICTORIA HOUSE, and West-Midland Mourning Warehouse.

SCOTT & ORAM.—By Appointment.—Importers of French Silks, General Drapers, &c.

An 1869 advertisement for Victoria House

fame, built himself a house in the area in front of the Green Dragon Inn, now marked by a plaque. A pleasant walk from the rear of his house down to **Castle Street** near **Love's Grove** was known as Dr Wall's Walk, and presumably marked the route where he regularly strolled. Directory listings for 1790 show Foregate Street contained an eclectic mix of attorneys, glovers, hairdressers, physicians and surgeons, plus a horse dealer, a corn factor and a couple of tailors, amongst others. The Green Dragon inn was also the excise office in the early eighteenth century.

The first building on the west side of the street, on the corner of **Shaw Street**, is now an office building but has a fascinating history. In 1749 the Hop Pole Inn was built or rebuilt here. It was the city's finest hotel in its day, an elegant and spacious building, attracting a clientele of county families, local Tories, visiting celebrities and even royalty. The Tories made it their HQ, Nelson stayed here during his visit in 1802, and Princess (later Queen) Victoria stayed in 1830 while visiting the music festival. Soon after 1842 the inn closed, and following substantial alterations it opened – with a nod to the building's royal connection - as a very high class shop called Victoria House, a name which has stuck ever since. Older residents might remember Fearis's the grocers on the ground floor.

The Whitehouse Hotel was formerly the Star, and originally the Star and Garter, one of the leading coaching inns of the early nineteenth century city, with a history believed to stretch back four centuries. The city was on most of the main north-south coach routes, and there was a good deal of excitement as coaches arrived and departed, with crowds gathering to see the rapid, skilled changing of teams, and stages competing to produce the best travel times. This was a principal inn for cockfighting, until it was made illegal in the early nineteenth century. Nearly opposite in the late eighteenth century was Tom's coffee-house, which was well provided with an assembly room and bowling green, and kept by a Mr Yardley in 1778.

Around 1685 the Carmelites opened a chapel of St George in this area, making their register one of the earliest catholic registers in the country. The chapel was said by Noake to be where the corner of **Pierpoint Street** is now, though Hughes

Worcester's first public library and museum in Foregate Street - BG

Foregate Street in 1915

prefers 14-16 **The Tything**. It was the first Roman Catholic place of worship in the city since catholic Queen Mary died in 1558, and its registers opened only six years after Father John Wall had been brutally executed on **Red Hill** for saying mass, but catholic James II was now on the throne.

When the king came to Worcester in 1687 he attended the cathedral, but then took mass at this chapel, much to the disgust of the protestant mayor and corporation, who refused to accompany him and spent the time drinking nearby at the Green Dragon. When James was deposed in 1688 a mob destroyed the chapel and the Carmelites had to flee and didn't return until 1690. They remained until around 1720 when Jesuit priests returned after an absence of some years, and thereafter the Jesuits remained in control of the parish until 1990. By 1741 the chapel had moved to a site near the present church in **Sansome Place**.

On the other corner of Pierpoint Street in the eighteenth century was the home of leading city glove maker Timothy Bevington. No 23 was rebuilt in 1793 for city solicitor Moses James.

The site of the Odeon Cinema has had a fascinating history. The Athenaeum, a forum for local participation in science and the arts, was opened in April 1834 on the former site of the eighteenth century Cheshire Cheese pub, now occupied by the cinema, with an address by Christopher Hebb, after whom **Hebb Street** was named. Behind it was a cramped court of working class housing, grandly named Athenaeum Court, which probably helped meet the running costs of the institution. The Athenaeum also hosted art exhibitions, and Constable exhibited here, though he only sold one small painting.

In 1836 the premises of the Worcestershire Natural History Society opened on the same site. The society established the Hastings Museum, named for BMA founder Dr Charles Hastings, who lived nearby and was much involved in the project. The premises were taken over by the council in 1880 as a public library. The City and County Library, the first public library in the city, opened in 1881, having been started in **Angel Street** in 1790 as a subscription library.

It transferred to the present library building when it opened in 1896, and the natural history collections of the Hastings Museum formed the basis of the present city museum, which was on the site formerly occupied by Acacia House, where the Misses Hughes, Mary and Catherine, had been running a boarding house. The museum and library were just a part of the massive Victoria Institute complex, the opening of which in 1896 was a major event for the city, and the culmination of a 40-year dream. It included the School of Art on **Sansome Walk**, now apartments, and a Technical School. The library moved to The Hive at **The Butts** in 2012, leaving the museum and art gallery here.

Historic Worcester Streets

Quarter Sessions in progress at the Shirehall in 1845 - BG

Later in the nineteenth century the Empire Music Hall occupied the Athenaeum site, and by the early twentieth century it had begun showing the exciting new moving pictures, causing it to be claimed by some as the city's earliest cinema, though the Public Hall in the **Corn Market** also showed early movies. By 1915 the former music hall had become the Silver Cinema. It was the city's finest cinema, and had a ballroom above, with of course an orchestra. By 1936 the Gaumont cinema had opened across the road; it closed in the 1970s and has been a bingo hall since, but it is still well remembered for hosting pop concerts in its later days, featuring most of the big stars of the 1950s and 1960s, including Buddy Holly, the Everly Brothers, Roy Orbison, Jimi Hendrix, Engelbert Humperdinck, Little Richard, the Beatles, the Rolling Stones (who were fourth on the bill!) and David Bowie. There were also orchestral concerts and ballet. The Silver closed in 1938, when the site was bought by the Odeon chain. The building was demolished, along with the buildings on either side, to build a new Odeon, but only the shell of the new building had been completed on the outbreak of the Second World War, and it was used for the storage of aircraft parts manufactured in the area. The new cinema didn't finally open until January 1950. Nearby in 1662 was a pub called the Rose & Crown – no doubt owing its 'royal' name to the renewed enthusiasm for the monarchy after the Restoration. It was still here in 1778, but had gone by 1822.

Two famous Foregate Street doctors, John Wall, founder of Worcester Porcelain, and Charles Hastings, founder of the BMA

The imposing classical Shire Hall was built in 1835 to house the city and county assizes, which had long sat in much more cramped conditions at the Guildhall. It was a big improvement for the city's legal fraternity, but its location here caused some political complications.

A shire hall was of course supposed to be within the county it was serving, but this hall was actually in a different county, since until 1974 Worcester was a county in its own right, known as the County of the City of Worcester. To resolve the problem, this patch of the city had to be declared legally part of Worcestershire, and in the days when city and county had separate police forces, which they did until 1967, it had to be the county police who were on duty here, since the city police had no jurisdiction. The Shire Hall was also used for balls and public meetings in the nineteenth century, but has not been used in that way for many years. The statue of Queen Victoria in the forecourt was executed by leading Victorian sculptor Sir Thomas Brock, the son of a Worcester builder who attended the school of design in **Pierpoint Street**, and was said to have executed more statues of Queen Victoria than anyone else.

The street is perhaps best known today as the site of one of the city's two main railway stations. The railway had arrived at Shrub Hill about 1850, but didn't get here until 1860, showing that train delays are nothing new. The station is built on a viaduct, so space is inevitably limited, and oddly the two platforms are for services on different lines, not in different directions. Services from Platform 1 can only go east to Shrub Hill and the national services from there, while services from Platform 2 also go east, but on the Droitwich line which doesn't pass through Shrub Hill.

Historic Worcester Streets

The original home of Kay's - TW

The street's most famous residents were both doctors. John Wall, of Malvern Water and Worcester Porcelain fame, had an 'out of town' house here in front of the Green Dragon, and BMA founder Charles Hastings also lived here in the nineteenth century. There are plaques to both of them on the house.

However another of the street's claims to fame seems to be little remembered. No. 4, now an estate agency, is very little changed since in 1886 it became the first home of Kay's of Worcester, the firm which grew into the giant Kay's mail order business, once the city's leading employer.

William Kilbourne Kay came from Leicestershire, and by 1883 was working for a watchmaker in **Broad Street**, and living over the shop. In 1886 he established his own business here, which progressed by producing a catalogue and adopting innovative sales methods, including the 'club' system which became the standard operating system for many big mail order businesses. It also had a contract to supply clocks and watches to the GWR, and there is still a Kay's clock on Platform 2 at Paddington Station, London.

The business grew rapidly, and in 1894 Kay's moved to larger premises at **Shrub Hill Road,** and in 1908 to **The Tything.** Mr Kay died in 1927, but his firm continued to prosper, with several premises in Worcester, and others in Glasgow, Bristol, Newtown, York, Lancaster, Leeds and Bradford. The firm was taken over by Great Universal Stores in 1937.

Legend has it that the GUS MD, on business in the city, admired Kay's offices, and demanded to see Kay's MD, waving his cheque book and offering to pay whatever he had to to buy the firm. Kay's was the city's leading employer for many years, but its last Worcester premises closed in 2007.

FORT ROYAL HILL

In the medieval period the area was known as Cole Hill, after William Cole who gave 30 acres of land here to the hospital at the Commandery in 1310. At that time a windmill stood on the hill. The hill was renamed in the seventeenth century for a Royalist strong point, on the site of the present park during the Civil War, though the original name is kept alive by **Cole Hill**, slightly to the east.

The southern approaches to the city were vulnerable to artillery attack from the higher ground around Perry Wood, but in 1646 it is saisd the attackers had brought their guns even closer in, to **Green Hill**, Bath Road, so this strong point was needed to keep the Roundheads at a distance. Unfortunately this was also an ideal location for attackers, from which the whole city could be bombarded, so it was vital that the Royalists held this position.

There were said to be defensive works here as early as 1642, but the main defences were hurriedly erected before the Battle of Worcester, 3 September 1651. At various times during the Civil War workers were brought from outlying areas, and in 1651 it was men from Ripple who were urgently brought to the city to dig the earthworks, since Worcester had been ordered to level its defences in the previous year, after the future Charles II landed in Scotland. Fort Royal was rather too grand a name for what was put in place. It was not a building as such, but earthworks dug in a star shaped pattern, with gun emplacements, which may have been shored up with timber inside and fortified with wooden spikes on the outer face. There was also an outer line of defensive earthworks to the east of the fort, and this street follows that line.

One officer called it a 'very fair and large fort' and it was strongly manned by 1,500 men under Sir Alexander Forbes, but it had been created quickly, and was probably still unfinished at the time of the battle. Further earthworks ran to the Severn at Diglis, and to the city wall on the east, close to Greyfriars in **Friar Street**, but they were by no means fully defended when the battle commenced.

After an afternoon Royalist attack, led by Charles himself, was forced back from Perry Wood and Red Hill, the fort here was stormed and overrun by the Essex Militia, the defenders were cut down and the guns turned on the city. Other troops advancing from Diglis stormed the **Sidbury** gate, forced their way into the city and won the day, forcing the young Charles to flee back into exile abroad. Six months later the men from Ripple were summoned back to level the earthworks they had dug before the battle. Two future US presidents, Thomas Jefferson and John Adams visited here in April 1786. The two staunch republicans inevitably saw the battle here as a great victory for liberty, and Adams was appalled that local people he spoke to knew little about it. He gave a speech saying that everyone should visit the site once a year.

A small semi-rural community had grown up in this area by the 1830s, with a view across riverside meadows to the south, and to the north as far as Tallow Hill. This street existed then, but under the name Park Place, and only as far as the crest of the hill, where it met the boundary of the parkland which surrounded it. The present name was first found in a building application for one house in 1868 – the only application found during the nineteenth century, which suggests building had taken place before building control began in 1865. It was first listed in a street directory in 1873. In 1884 the first large-scale Ordnance Survey map showed the east side of the street almost complete, but development on the west side took place at various later dates, some quite recently.

A mansion named Fort Royal was built in the park in the mid nineteenth century, and still exists as the basis of a housing development. Local businessman Henry Corbett was living there in 1884. Other residents of the street at that time were mainly skilled men and women in manual work at the top of the hill, white collar workers at the lower end. George Mason's corner shop, now a hairdressers, was at the bottom of the hill, at the junction with **Wyld's Lane**, but the two pubs were at the top. On the corner of **London Road** was a Victorian pub best known as the Fort Royal, though it was also the London Vaults in 1886, and the Ale & Porter Stores ten years later. It has also had a number of names in modern times, including the Little Sauce Factory. On the corner of **Upper Park Street** was another Victorian pub, the Park Tavern, which closed some years ago. The park, which had continued to belong to the Commandery since it was given by William Cole, was given to the city in 1913.

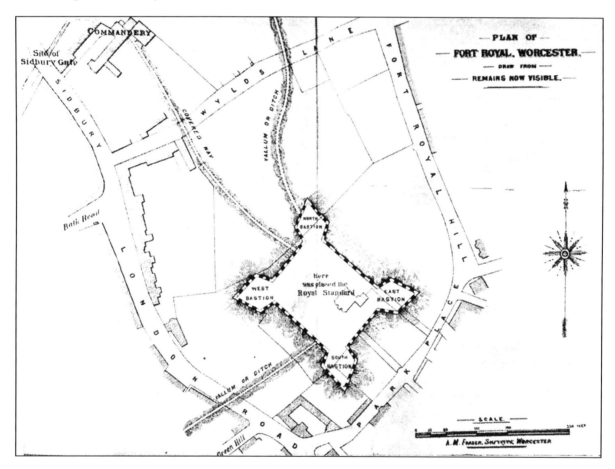

A Victorian plan of streets built around the 1651 Fort Royal defences

FORT ROYAL LANE

Like **Fort Royal Hill**, it was shown on a map of 1838, but at that time this lane was unnamed and served only as an access track to a rural villa. It was first found listed by name in the health board streets list of 1872, and in a street directory of 1880.

In 1884 nine villas and more modest cottages were listed here, housing a foreman glover, a gentleman, an Inland Revenue supervisor, a coachman, a potter, an engine driver, a guard, a clerk and local businessman Ephraim Chetwyn.

Foundry Alley

Blockhouse. An alley which ran from **Foundry Street** to *Little Charles Street*, first found as *Back Lane* on a map of 1824. It was shown under this name in a street directory of 1840. It was demolished in the 1960s.

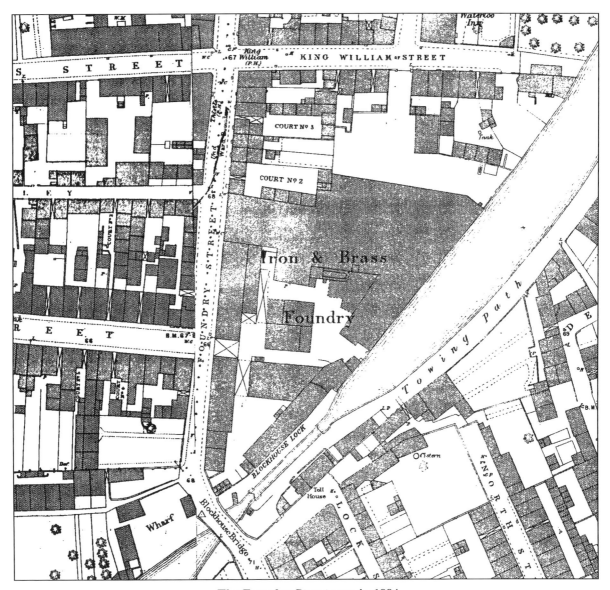

The Foundry Street area in 1884

FOUNDRY STREET

In the *Blockhouse* area. This street must have been part, with **St Paul's Street**, of an old path called Withy Walk, which ran across Blockhouse Fields from **St Martin's Gate** to **Wyld's Lane** in the days when this was open farmland. It may have become a street early in the nineteenth century, once it led to the Worcester Iron Foundry, which was founded here in 1814 by Scots Robert and John Hardy.

The street must have been created when the foundry opened, since a canal bridge, variously called Blockhouse or Foundry Bridge, had been provided to create a route to the area from Wyld's Lane, where foundry workers may then have lived. A map of 1824 showed that **Charles Street** and **Carden Street** had recently been created, and the area to the west had considerable development, though to the east there was nothing then other than the foundry. Development on that side had begun by 1829.

In that year Robert and John Hardy went into partnership with Richard Padmore, after whom **Padmore Street** was named, to form Hardy & Padmore, which traded until 1967, and is best-known for constructing the Blackpool Tower.

The firm's day to day work involved making products such as stoves, kitchen ranges and weighing machines. The street retains what is said to be one of the original foundry buildings, now occupied by Orillo, the plumbers' merchants.

The Worcester Foundry in 1860, and 1920 Foundry Street advertisement

In 1884 there was a corner shop and a bakery here, by the junction with *King William Street*, opposite Charles Street, and two other shops along the street. There was also the Thistle Vaults on the corner of Charles Street, and the Beehive at the corner of Carden Street, which had closed by 1908 and become a butcher's shop. Beside the canal bridge was the yard of hay and coal dealer Noah Dayus, and there were about a dozen residents in the street, who were mostly glovers or labourers. There is little left now of the street as it once was.

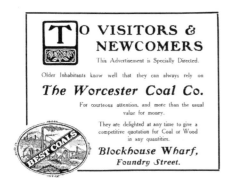

Fourfoot Row

Blockhouse. A narrow alleyway, hence the name, which provided access to a terrace of 19 homes off *Waterloo Street*, first listed in a street directory in 1840. In 1885 it housed mostly labourers, with a bricklayer, two tinmen (tinplate workers, no doubt at the nearby works in **Providence Street**), a shoemaker, a hawker and a glover. The street was demolished in the 1960s.

FOXWELL STREET

This street must have taken its name from Peter Foxwell, who according to historian Pat Hughes formerly rented the land on which it was built. He was living at 48 London Road in 1892, and was possibly a member of a wealthy Malvern family. Very little is known about him, but he was involved in a modest amount of property development around **London Road** in the 1880s and 90s. Building control records show he applied to build two houses at Red Hill in 1886, and to put a new bathroom in St Wulstan's Lodge, Battenhall, in 1891.

Documents in the county archives show the Foxwells as one of the families involved in property development in the London Road/**Sebright Avenue** area in 1893-6, and in this street especially in 1895. They are also believed to have been involved in the development of **Camp Hill Road**.

A map of 1884 shows some development around this area, but no sign of this street. By 1896 however, there were 18 terraced cottages and a villa here. Residents at that time were mostly manual workers, including three labourers, a shunter, a carpenter, a warehouseman, a painter, a gardener, a potter, a stonemason, an engine driver, a maltster, an engine fitter, two police constables and a china moulder.

There was a building application for two more houses in 1905. All this development was at the northern end of the street near London Road. The rest of the street, which is most of it, is all 1930s.

There was a shop and bakery at the end of **Cannon Street** in 1890 and on the other side of the road was the Carpenters Arms pub, which closed around 1960.

In 1897 Harvey Banner had a shop on the corner of **Livingstone Street**. The school opposite Livingstone Street opened around 1896. It is now a social club, and modern homes have been built on the playground. Jazzman Kenny Ball, who had a string of hits in the 1960s, lived here as a youngster before the Second World War, and attended **Stanley Road** school.

FRIAR STREET

This is one of the most interesting and historic streets of the city. It was originally, with **New Street**, called *Glovers Street*, but this street must have changed its name after the Greyfriars came here in 1239. They were given land here by William de Beauchamp of Elmley Castle, the sheriff of Worcestershire and castellan of Worcester. He or a descendant was said to have been buried in the friars' cemetery in 1298, though there is

Above, Friar Street in 1878

Below, Greyfriars about the same date

no certain evidence for this. The friars took their popular name from the grey habits they wore.

No contemporary plan of their buildings exists, but they fronted onto the street and were known to extend to the city wall.

The friars had their graveyard outside the walls, and a church or chapel dedicated to St Lawrence, and they were allowed a postern gate giving access to it, which may have survived into the eighteenth or even the nineteenth century.

The site of the gate was at the end of **Union Street**, but it is now under the **City Walls Road**.

This became an important house in the Francisan order, supervising others in the region. It was dissolved in 1538, and the site was granted to the Bailiffs and Citizens of the city in the following year. Some buildings were leased out and passed through various hands in the following centuries, though others were sold for building materials, and Robert Ewell, subsequently built Nos. 17 to 23, after purchasing friary building materials. In the seventeenth and eighteenth centuries the city prison was sited here. The friary refectory formed part of the prison and was still in existence in 1788, said to be unchanged since the friars were there.

Historic Worcester Streets

Residents in this street in 1790 included two bakers, three maltsters, a carpenter, a glover, a barber, a hop dealer, a printer, a midwife, two 'taylors', a leather colourer, two London carriers, several victuallers, Thomas Evett 'dealer in spirituous liquors', and the mayor's servants, James and John Spike. Two inns were listed at that date – the Fish and the Cross Keys which had been mentioned by the Journal around 1714 – of which more below.

In 1822 the friary buildings were demolished and a new city gaol was built on the site, but by the Worcester Prisons Act of 1867 it was amalgamated with the county prison in Castle Street. A much fuller listing of residents in the street was published in 1840, which showed, amongst other things, some of the odd combinations of occupations which people followed at that time to 'make ends meet'. Henry Clements at No. 2 was a schoolmaster and clothes salesman, while next door John and James Gummery were both builders and pump makers. Other residents included beersellers, shoemakers, tailors, a butcher, clothes dealers and a chemist.

Laslett's Almshouses, beside Greyfriars, were subsequently established on the prison site thanks to a nineteenth century philanthropist. On 19 September 1868 Worcester lawyer William Laslett, after whom **Laslett Street** was named, purchased the old gaol for £2,225, and converted it into almshouses for 33 poor people. In 1912 the old gaol building was taken down, and four blocks of almshouses and a chapel were built, which still exist. The first three houses in the street and No. 1 **New Street** were demolished in 1895, to make way for the extension of **Charles Street**.

In the eighteenth and nineteenth centuries many of the fine old timber-framed houses were divided into tenements and fell into a sad state of disrepair. One of the worst was the now magnificent, timber-framed Greyfriars, which dates from about 1480. Rain came in through holes in the roof, and part of the timber-framing actually fell into the street.

Greyfriars in a sad state in 1946

By the 1960s it was in danger of demolition, having fallen into a dreadful condition, but was restored to its present splendid state by J. Matley Moore and fellow members of the Worcestershire Archaeological Society.

Mr Moore's research into the building suggested it had been built by the friars, perhaps as the friary guest house, and the date of construction would have made this feasible.

However, research in the 1980s suggests that the Friary buildings were on the site of the present Nos. 11-25, and that Greyfriars was never part of the friary, having been built by wealthy brewer Thomas Green.

Another of the street's ancient buildings is the Tudor House Heritage Centre. Dating from around 1575, the timber-framed house, originally three terraced houses, still has wattle and daub infill and a fine Tudor ceiling. It has been home over the centuries to weavers, clothiers, brewers, bakers and a painter. From 1654 the part of the building to the right of the entrance became licensed premises, known from around 1714 or before as the Cross Keys Tavern, which existed until 1908.

From 1909 to 1920 **Rose Hill** resident Richard Cadbury, son of one of the Quaker founders of the chocolate firm, opened a coffee house here, hoping to tempt people away from the many pubs then found in this poor area. Its subsequent closure was due to First World War rationing.

From 1921 to 1971 it was a school clinic, and the school dentist and the nit nurse were based here. It was a warden post and billeting office during the Second World War. In 1971 it was taken over by Worcester City Museums Service, but closed as a museum in 2003. Since 2004 it has been run by the Worcester Heritage Amenity Trust and their splendid volunteers.

Almost opposite Tudor House was Wyatt's Hospital, a row of early eighteenth century cottages for six poor men, built by a charity founded by Edward Wyatt, city mayor in 1696. The almshouses were still here in the nineteenth century but have since been merged with Nash's almshouses in **New Street**.

The first meeting house of the Society of Friends was established here, next to the site of Wyatt's almshouses, possibly in 1655 when Quaker George Fox first visited the city. Persecution of nonconformists was still rife, and in 1681 one of the leaders was imprisoned for holding an unlawful gathering at the meeting house here.

Eighteenth century woman soldier Hannah Snell came from Friar Street

Those who opposed the Quakers claimed that they went naked through the streets and ran into churches during services, to abuse the ministers, but it has to be remembered there was a good deal of prejudice against dissenters at the time. They moved to **Sansome Place** in 1701.

The Cardinal's Hat has claims to be one of the oldest pubs in the city, going back to the medieval period, though the present building dates from 1766. It was first recorded as an inn in 1544, when it was held by James Bannister and his wife Margery. It became the Coventry Arms about 1685, but reverted to its old name about 1960. Folklore suggests it was a brothel at one time, though the line between tavern and brothel was probably more blurred in the medieval period, and this may have applied to many ancient hostelries.

The Eagle Vaults, on the corner of **Pump Street**, is an excellent example of a late Victorian tavern, with a tiled facade and etched windows, though the building is actually much older. It was probably built in the 1740s, on the site of an earlier building. In 1764 it was purchased by John Young and converted into a hostelry, under the name Young's Mug House. During the nineteenth century it was briefly the Volunteer, around the time of Waterloo, then the Plummer's Arms, and the Friar Street Vaults from 1859. The building has been much altered over the years, and the late Victorian pub conversion was carried out in the period 1890 – 1900.

A probable seventeenth century resident of the street was Dud Dudley, illegitimate son of the fifth Baron Dudley and his mistress. He invented a new way of smelting iron, but bad luck and opposition from other ironmasters meant he got little benefit from his patent. He was a Colonel in the Royalist army during the Civil War, and was captured, but escaped to Bristol, posing as a doctor. After the Restoration he probably spent his last years here, and was buried at St Helen's. A timber-framed building, just down from Tudor House, has been suggested as his home, though there is no evidence for this.

Hannah Snell, the woman soldier, whose story caused a sensation and made her a celebrity for a time in the eighteenth century, was born in this street. A site near Wyatt's almshouses has been suggested as her birthplace, but again there is no firm evidence.

Friar Street about 1900 - BS

Historic Worcester Streets

Friers Alley
An alleyway of poor tenements running off Broad Street, around the west side of the medieval house of the Black Friars. It was not found listed later than a map of 1764, and became ***Blackfriars Street*** in the nineteenth century. Today it lies beneath the northern part of Crowngate, probably not far from the Broad Street entrance, and is remembered by the name Friary Walk.

Friers Gate
See **Friar Street** and *Blockhouse*.

Frog Lane
Now **Severn Street**. It was named for the Frog Brook, which formerly ran around the east of the city to the Severn near here, but since 1815 has run into the Worcester & Birmingham Canal. Originally the lane must have run only a short distance to the city wall, where there was probably a postern Frog Gate, and the continuation beyond the wall seems to have been called ***High Timber Street***, though both names seem to have been used at various times. Residents listed in 1790 were a bricklayer, a coal merchant, two fishermen, a sedan chairman, and two pubs; The Fish and the Mason's Arms. In June 1812 the Journal reported that the Worcester Church of England School opened here in a spacious building which was formerly a riding school. The report said there were initially 117 boys and 148 girls, "and the number is daily increasing".

Garden Market
The site of the old city vegetable street market, now **St Nicholas Street**. The name probably changed after the church was rebuilt in the eighteenth century, though the old name was still shown in directories of 1790 and 1840. It was also known as Gayle or Gaol Lane in the sixteenth century, since it led to an old city gaol believed to have been in a gatehouse tower of the Trinity Gate. Residents in 1790 included cheesemonger and seedsman Thomas Andrews, gardener Ann Taylor, glovers Hopkins & Kinnersley, a couple of hop merchants and two pubs; the Holly Bush and The Pack Horse, which is still with us, though renamed.

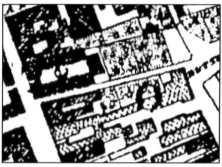
Gardiners Lane on a 1799 map

Gardiners Lane
Now **Shaw Street**. Named for the Gardiner family, whose home may have been on the site where Berkeley's almshouses on **The Foregate** are now. Pat Hughes' 1975 map of the city in Tudor times shows a substantial house with a large garden covering the whole of the almshouses site. A Phillippe Gardiner, apparently a clothier, seems to have been the first member of the family in the city, according to surviving county archive records. He came from Evesham, where the family founded a charity, and in 1616 passed a house in **Mealcheapen Street** to his son Edward. Phillip Gardiner, a clothier and probably Edward's grandson, may have purchased the land here in 1671, which subsequently passed to his son, whose name is not known. He had died by 31 October 1704 when the freehold of the land on which his widow's house stood was conveyed to the estate of Sir Robert Berkeley. If that was the land on which the almshouses stand, then it suggests that they were built later than the 1703 date on the chapel, which is also the view of current charity chairman Paul Griffith. This was still listed as Gardiners Lane in 1840, but shortly afterwards William Shaw gave the lease of land on the north side of the lane to the city so that it could be widened, and the street was then named after him.

Gayle Lane
Now **St Nicholas** Street.

GEORGE STREET
This was once regarded as part of *Clap Gate* or **St Martin's Gate**, and must have existed for many years as a trackway from the city to **Tallow Hill**, which was a favourite picnic spot with city folk, but it is likely to have been widened and improved in the late eighteenth century, to link St Martin's Gate to the new House of Industry at the top of the hill.
It takes its name from an old inn here called The George, which dated back at least to the eighteenth century. This had closed by 1850 but there were still a number of pubs remaining. Gwilliam lists four; the Carpenter's

Arms, which closed around 1908; the Telegraph, which closed around 1925; and the Locomotive and the New Inn, both of which closed around 1970. The New Inn was a canalside pub probably built to attract the boatmen, the Carpenter's Arms and the Telegraph were side by side close to St Martin's Gate, and the Locomotive was near **St Paul's Street**.

On the north side of the street a terrace of housing for working families had been built as early as the 1820s. Development here gained a real boost in the boom of the 1880s, with building applications for 30 homes submitted in 1881-3. This was a populous street by 1884, with 50 homes and small businesses listed, and two courts off it. Registrar of births and deaths Eustace Baylis lived here, as did Salvation Army captain John Ward.

Most of the residents worked on the railway or in the city's iron working, engineering, gloving or clothing industries. Businesses included bill posters and advertising agents, a packing case and crate maker, a watchmaker, and a ginger beer manufacturer. On the corner of St Paul's Street was a Primitive Methodist chapel, which had been built in the previous couple of years. There were several shops, including tobacconist and newsagent Francis Smith, hairdresser Albert Gardner and butcher William Smith, all on a small parade next door to the Locomotive,

The street was cleared in the early 1970s, at the time that the **City Walls Road** was created, and the recent work to create the retail park on Tallow Hill has totally reconfigured the east end of the street and done away with the little 'hump-backed' canal bridge built before 1815.

GEORGINA AVENUE

Named for Lady Georgina Sophia Baillie-Hamilton, daughter of the tenth Earl of Haddington, and wife of Harry Vernon - see **Vernon Park Road**. This street was first found in a street directory in 1937, when 25 homes were listed.

GHELUVELT PARK.

OPENING BY EARL OF YPRES.

City's Freedom for Distingu'shed Soldier.

Worcester gave a cordial welcome to Earl Ypres on Saturday when he attended to open Gheluvelt Park, the new recreation ground which is so designated to mark the signal achievement of the 2nd Worcesters in October, 1914.

The Earl of Ypres came into the City from Madresfield, where he had been staying with Earl Beauchamp. They were met at the City boundary by Col. A. T Anderson, who commands the Royal Artillery of the 48th Division, and is the senior serving officer in the county. So escorted, the Earl of Ypres proceeded to the Guildhall, where already a large company had assembled at the Mayor's invitation to meet their noble guest.

The Assembly.

Those who accepted invitations of the Mayor and Mayoress were:—

Members of the Corporation: The High Sheriff and Mrs. P. J. Roberts, the City Chamberlain (Mr. R. Haughton) Ald. and Mrs. J. S.

The Journal reports the lavish opening of Gheluvelt Park in 1922

GHELUVELT PARK

Formerly the park of Barbourne House, **Barbourne Road**. The house was demolished when the public park was created, but it became a residential address again when homes were built for Great War veterans in the park, which was opened in a grand ceremony on 17 June 1922. The name recalls a First World War battle honour of the Worcestershire Regiment.

GILLAM STREET

Probably named for local solicitor John F. Gillam, who lived nearby in **Lansdowne Crescent**, and may have had a hand in the development of this street. He had an office at 5 **Foregate Street** and clearly acted for clients with an interest in property, since he made an unsuccessful bid to buy the Arboretum Pleasure Grounds in 1865.

This street was first found listed in a street directory in 1885, when there were 16 homes here, mostly referred to as cottages.

Residents then included a number of railwaymen, a timekeeper, a drayman, a charwoman, a carpenter and a coachman.

Two buildings applications for a total of 24 houses were submitted three years later, and another for 14 houses in 1895. The street was largely complete by 1928, but there has been a little modern infill development.

GLENTHORNE AVENUE

This street was no doubt named for a large villa on Brickfields Road, which was home in 1884 to solicitor George Adam Bird, who had an office at 15 **Foregate Street**, on the floor below the office of Elgar's boyhood friend, chartered accountant and five times mayor Hubert Leicester, after whose widows' charity **Leicester Street** was named. This street was first found in a directory in 1937, when almost 110 homes were listed.

Glovers Lane
Now **New Street**. Originally both New Street and **Friar Street** formed this lane. It appears as a past name for the street on a map of 1764. The street was re-developed during the latter part of the sixteenth century, at which time it may have acquired its modern name.

Gaol Lane
Now **St Nicholas Street**.

GOODREST WALK
Named for the Goodrest pub in nearby **Barker Street**, this street was first found in a directory in1930, when 25 homes were listed.

Goose Lane
Now **St Swithin's Street**. The name first appeared in the sixteenth century, when this was the site of the city's poultry street market. Also called Gosse Lane and Goosethrottle Lane, since in the days when there was no simple means of preserving food, the live birds would be driven to market and your chosen goose would be throttled on the spot. The present name was established in the nineteenth century.
Residents in 1790 included a baker, a brush maker, a collar maker, a glover, a linen draper, a pawnbroker, three shoemakers, two tallow chandlers, an upholsterer, a watchmaker, printer James Grundy and Mrs Nelme, who proudly boasted she was 'pastry cook to their Majesties', presumably having supplied her wares to the royal family during their visit two years earlier.

GORSE HILL ROAD
Situated north of Gorse Hill, this road was first found in a street directory in 1930, when 30 homes were listed.

GRAHAM ROAD
This name must have been chosen by the developer, but has not been traced as a surname, though it could be a first name. This road was first found listed in 1937, when there were 34 homes here.

GRANDSTAND ROAD
Racing began here in the early eighteenth century, with 27 June 1718 being given as the official date of the first race, but early viewing platforms left a lot to be desired. This entrance road was first found in the health board streets list of 1872, after the first permanent grandstand was built on the race course.

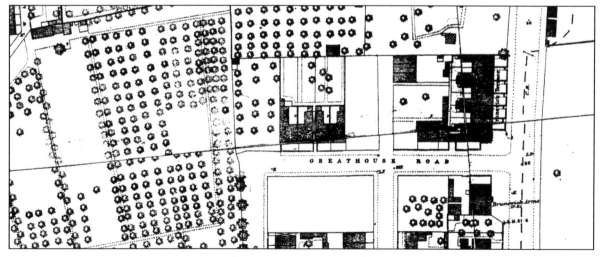

Great House Road in 1884

GREAT HOUSE ROAD
Both this street and **Abbey Road** must have been named for a manor house on **Malvern Road,** which once controlled much of St John's. The Great House was the manor house of the once extensive manor of Hardwick, and was demolished in 1904. This road was first found in the health board streets list of 1872, and in a street directory of 1880, but building records are meagre, and non-existent before 1888. Construction probably

started in the 1870s, though it could have begun in the 1860s at the same time as the adjacent **Bedwardine Road**.

Either way, it proceeded slowly. By 1884 there was still nothing on the south side but the rear of the Brunswick Arms, with just seven homes on the north side, and the street extended west only as far as Bedwardine Road, with the extensive orchards of Smith's Boughton Nurseries stretching out beyond.

Three cottages called Summer Place, just off the main road, were home in 1884 to two gardeners and a smith, and the four villas of Crowther Place, near Bedwardine Road, housed a compositor and two householders styling themselves as gentlemen, with one villa unoccupied.

A small amount of additional building had gone ahead by 1928, and development on **Bransford Road** had left the orchard to the rear of the street as an isolated, enclosed fragment of its former self, which had disappeared by 1940 when the street had been completed.

There was a shop at London House on the Malvern Road corner in 1884, kept by Thomas Monk, who doubled as a carpenter. A building application for a public house was submitted in 1868, and the Brunswick Arms pub was probably built by 1870, and must have taken its name from Brunswick Terrace, a row of six cottages on Malvern Road, which were probably built in the early 1860s. The Brunswick arms were the arms of Queen Victoria, who was a member of the House of Brunswick.

Great Park Street
It became part of **Park Street** between 1885 and 1896. In the late nineteenth century it ran from **Wyld's Lane** to **Derby Road**, intersecting **Little Park Street**.

GREENHILL
A Georgian suburb off **London Road**, begun around 1828-9, which because of the steep gradient was built on two terraces. The lower terrace is accessed from **Bath Road**, and the upper terrace from **London Road**. They were found in 1840 listed as two separate streets, Greenhill Terrace, Bath Road and Greenhill Place, London Road, but both have been named Green Hill since at least 1880, and though they are still separate streets they share a common name, and have therefore been dealt with together here. The name was used for the hill long before the streets were created.

Nineteenth century author Jabez Allies identified Green Hill as the site of siegeworks during the wars of Stephen and Matilda in the twelfth century, which were said to exist still in 1796, though it is more likely that what he saw was from the seventeenth century Civil War. Green Hill, Bath Road was known as Windmill Hill in the seventeenth century, and during the Civil War siege of the city in 1646 the Parliamentary forces set up a battery on this hill to fire on the city. Learning from that experience, the Royalists set up a strong fortification at Fort Royal in 1651, forcing the Roundheads to keep their distance.

Neither terrace was developed quickly, though they had been largely completed by 1884. An 1840 listing of residents showed just nine. Off Bath Road were organ builder J. Nicholson, Mrs E. Jennings, clerk Robert Young, supervisor Thomas Williams and (commercial) traveller John Girvan. Off London Road were wine merchant J. Chamberlain, clerk Benjamin Bulford, upholsterer Thomas Bewley and timber merchant J. Rowley.

In 1884 a Greenhill Terrace was listed off Bath Road, and a separate terrace of the same name off London Road. Off Bath Road were six cottages whose residents included a painter, a builder and a foreman. Off London Road were nine cottages whose occupants included a manager, a kilnman, a cabinet maker, an artist, two clerks and an architect. By that date however there were also three listings as Green Hill, five for Green Hill Place and 12 for Green Hill Gardens. Listings were better organised by 1896, and there were then 11 listings off Bath Road, including a number of substantial villas.

Aside from the 1884 listing, Greenhill Place was not first found listed separately until 1930, though it is clearly much older. Hill House, off London Road, which is said to have given its name to **The Hill Avenue**, was the home of a much-admired colonial bishop.

GREEN LANE
This name was commonly used for lanes in rural areas on the edge of towns and cities, and there were several such lanes around Worcester in past centuries; **Diglis Road**, for example had this name as late as 1838.

This lane was also shown on a map at that date, but not named. It had probably long existed as a track over Merriman's Hill from Blackpole to Barbourne, but must have owed its creation initially to the need for a roadway to provide a northern access to **Mayfield Road** which was largely complete by the early 1880s. Certainly this street does not seem to have been created as a housing development in its own right, since when it was first shown by name in a street directory of 1884, it had just 12 residents listed, and further development was very slow in coming. It must have been a very pleasant semi-rural location, but there was clearly no urgency to build more housing here. Perhaps it was just too remote from the city, in the days before buses and trams, or not fashionable enough as a site for villas to attract the affluent middle classes. Residents in 1884 included labourers, gardeners, a tailor, a glover, a fireman, a seamstress and a nurse.

Much of the south side of the lane at the east end was taken up from the 1880s with the church, listed under **Church Road**, and the adjoining schools. Construction of St Barnabas Church was underway in 1885. A building application for the vicarage next door was submitted in 1888, and the school buildings were begun around the same time. The schools moved up the road to a new building in 1987, and the old buildings here were demolished and replaced with housing, but the fence around the schoolyard still encloses the homes.

A street directory of 1922 showed no more development than had been here 40 years earlier, but slum clearance in the city centre was suddenly creating a need for housing in the suburbs. A map of 1928 showed that development had received a sudden boost, and around 40 homes had sprung up on the north side. These semi-detached houses had generous gardens, but were so newly built that most gardens had not been fenced off yet. By 1930 there was also a small number of homes listed on the south side, but development went only as far as Mayfield Road until the through route was created in the 1950s.

The secondary school was opened in 1937, with separate schools for boys and girls, and was named Samuel Southall in honour of a long-serving town clerk. It became a mixed school in 1965, and Bishop Perowne has since taken over the building.

St Barnabas Schools around 1900 - RS

GREGORY'S BANK

This street, which takes its name from the nearby Gregory's Mill, originally followed the line of the lower end of what is now **Merriman's Hill**, but was diverted to its present position in the 1950s. On its original line it was part of a track or footpath from at least the eighteenth century, which linked to **Green Lane**. It was first shown with this name on a map of 1830, though as late as 1884 it was listed in a street directory under **St George's Lane North**. In the early twentieth century there was a miniature rifle range in this area. The area to the north was dominated by Barker's Barbourne Brickworks, owned by David Wilson Barker, after whom **Barket Street** was named. The brickworks' brick-built chimney, 150 feet (about 46m) tall and built with 100,000 hand-made bricks, was a well-known local landmark until it was demolished in 1961, to make way for an extension to the Redman Tools factory.

In the 1880s just a few cottages clustered near the canal on the south side, which in 1884 housed two foremen and a labourer. By 1896 the little community had grown and homes and residents had gone up in the world. Alongside five cottages, housing a manager, a coach painter, a carriage trimmer, a porter and a labourer, there were now two named villas, Holly Mount and Exbury House, home to Hugh Parkinson, company secretary to the brickworks. After the creation of Merriman's Hill in the 1950s what had been this street became part of it, and this name was given to a new street created across what had been the brickworks site.

Gregory's Mill, early nineteenth century

GREGORY'S MILL STREET

This name did not 'officially' appear until the late nineteenth century, but had no doubt been used locally long before that, since the mill to which it led was known as Gregory's Mill from at least the early nineteenth century, and this lane leading to it from **Droitwich Road** no doubt existed before that.

The lane had probably been in existence since a grist mill was built in 1369 on Barbourne Brook by William Frebara, Master of St Oswald's Hospital in **The Tything**. It was about half a mile upstream from Barbourne Bridge, and was rebuilt in the seventeenth century, after being destroyed in the Civil War. The new mill was a small, timber-framed building, with a similar-sized brick addition, probably of eighteenth century date, which no doubt provided accommodation for the miller and his family. Thomas Gregory probably took over the mill at some time in the eighteenth century, and it became known as Gregory's Mill, being shown by that name on a painting done before 1825, and a map of about 1830.

The lane to the mill continued to be listed as Mill Lane or Street until 1896, when the present name was shown. Listings at that time showed two small rows of cottages, Albert Terrace and Eld Cottages, plus around eight other modest homes. Residents then included two coal agents, no doubt getting supplied by canal, a number of labourers, a cashier, a county court clerk, a shoemaker, a lithographer, a carpenter and two railwaymen. The mill was still grinding corn during the First World War, but closed by 1919, and was completely demolished by 1950.

This was primarily an area of commercial development, which most notably included a company called Windshields, whose works stood between **Raglan Street** and **New Bank Street**. During the Second World War the company made windscreens and turret housings for famous British bombers, here and on sites throughout the city. After the war it reverted to making car windscreens, but perhaps like so many British companies in this period it suffered because of foreign competition, and ceased to trade around the 1980s. A housing development now stands on the site of Windshields works.

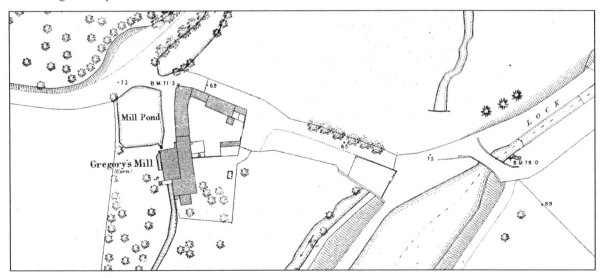

Gregory's Mill in 1885

Grope Lane

A now vanished lane which ran behind All Saints Church from *Merry Vale* to **Quay Street**, in an area which was busy in past centuries with sailors and water-borne trade. For centuries this was Worcester's dockside red-light district, with a name which meant exactly what it said. The medieval version of the name was likely to have been even more colourful, and would be regarded now as far too rude to print in a family publication. It would have been shortened to Grope Lane in the sixteenth century, and was shown as Street in a deed of

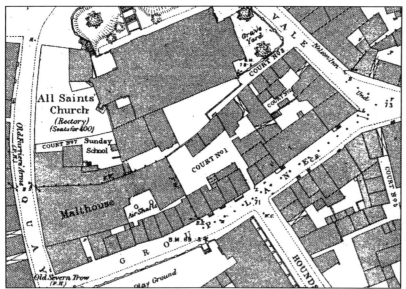

Above, 'Group' Lane in 1884

Below, cottages in Grope Lane, late nineteenth century - RS

1600 but Lane on a map of 1764. By 1840 it had been euphemised into Group Lane, and the prostitutes had moved elsewhere in the city, as the port lost its importance and urban development created new business opportunities. There was a row of timber-framed cottages here, and residents in 1884 included several labourers, a laundress, a plumber, a painter, a letter carrier and Mrs Maria Strickland's lodging house. The area will have been cleared in the 1920s or 30s.

GROSVENOR WALK

The first building applications here date to 1872-3, so construction probably began soon afterwards. It must have been named for the terrace of three Grosvenor Cottages here, which certainly existed in 1884, at the time of the first directory listing, when this was shown as St John's Walk. The cottages may have been named for the Grosvenors, the Dukes of Westminster, who held lands in Worcestershire and many other counties, and may have supplied some finance to the developer. The present name was first found listed in 1896. At that time Grosvenor Cottages housed a charwoman, a potter and a driver, and Broughton Terrace had two glovers and a salesman. Other residents included bricklayers, potters, a glover, a porter and an engine driver. There are still 13 of the original cottages on the north side, but the south side wasn't developed until the twentieth century.

Group Lane

Euphemistic Victorian version of *Grope Lane*.

GROVE, THE

There may have been a woodland copse here before the street was built, but it's more likely that the developers choose this as a suitably rural name for marketing purposes. The street was first found in a directory in 1937, when 17 homes were listed here.

HALLOW ROAD

Hallow was known to the Anglo-Saxons as Halhagan, which scholars have translated somewhat obscurely as 'enclosure on the nook or corner of land'. Land at Hallow was included in a large grant made to the Bishop of Worcester by King Offa in the eighth century.

Then or later Hallow became a manor in its own right, taking in land as far as Henwick, and thus including this road. The road was well outside the city boundary for much of its history, and no building records were found for it prior to 1897.

The first street directory entry found for it was in 1924, when the few listings included George Pery Jn. at Henwick House, Richard Murray at Eldersfield, James Mordan at South vil, Mrs Jacomb at Hallow Bank and Col L.J. Blandford at Bleabeck.

When building applications began to be submitted, they were fairly small and infrequent. The first found was for 4 houses in 1897, and over the next seven years there were five applications for a total of just 10 homes, but by 1924 only eight villas were listed here. However, by 1930 more than 30 were listed, and there were 47 by 1937 as development went ahead quickly. By that date Drs Spalding & Davies had a practice at No. 44. By the mid 1950s there were almost 60 homes listed, mainly on the west side. There has been a good deal of development since on the east side

HAMILTON ROAD

Named for William, the second Duke of Hamilton, a Scottish lord who fell during the Battle of Worcester 1651, and died of his wounds at the Commandery in **Sidbury**. He was born in 1616 and succeeded to the dukedom in 1649. He had a colourful history during the English Civil War and the concurrent Scottish wars. He was appointed Secretary of State for Scotland in 1640, but three years later he was arrested on the orders of Charles I for supporting the Presbyterians.

He subsequently signed a treaty which led to the Second Civil War, which he helped organise, and when the future Charles II lost, Hamilton fled abroad, but returned with Charles in 1650 and raised an army of about 300 men from his estates.

William, Second Duke of Hamilton

Charles appointed him Royalist Commander in Chief, and they entered Worcester on 22 August 1651. Hamilton made his headquarters at the Commandery.

On the afternoon of the Battle of Worcester, 3 September 1651, Charles was on the cathedral tower and saw Cromwell moving troops to the west where his line was weak. Seizing this chance Charles led a charge up Red Hill, while Hamilton led an attack on parliamentary forces in Perry Wood, which had some success until Cromwell hurried back to rally his forces.

Retreating back into the city, Hamilton was badly wounded in the thigh, and was taken to the Commandery, by then a dressing station for wounded men.

Accounts differ of what happened next. An anti-Cromwell version of events told later, said that after the battle Parliamentary physicians told Hamilton amputation of his leg was the only way to save his life, but the Scotsman insisted on a Royalist surgeon, and Cromwell refused this.

In reality there were two Royalists doctors in attendance, including the King's physician, who were ready to carry out the operation, and it was Cromwell's personal physician, not the general, who said it wasn't necessary. He was wrong, and Hamilton died on 12 September of gangrene and blood poisoning, aged just 34.

He was buried under the altar at the cathedral, where a brass plaque was unveiled in 1913 to mark his grave. When the Commandery became a museum in 1977 it was opened by the fifteenth Duke of Hamilton.

The road was developed by Robert Bach of **Great Park Street**, a glove manufacturer who became much involved in property speculation, and with six other investors built 86 houses here and in **Derby Road** and **Prince Rupert Road** over the next five years.

This road was first referred to in a November 1881 building application for two houses at 'a new road off Wyld's Lane'. In the following year the road had to be extended, and development continued quickly, with eight applications for a total of 38 homes by 1884. It was first found listed in a street directory in that year, by which time 28 of the homes had been built.

The east side of the road, which included the 12 cottages of Hamilton Terrace, seems to have been complete, but only seven homes existed on the west side, though three more were under construction. Residents were mostly a mix of clerks, factory workers, glovers, shoemakers, metal workers and railwaymen. John Coombs at Hamilton House gave his occupation as scripture reader. By 1896 all 38 homes applied for had been built, plus one additional one.

HANBURY AVENUE

This street off **Hanbury Park Road** was first found in a street directory in 1937, when 10 homes were listed here.

HANBURY PARK ROAD

The Hanbury estate took its name from the Vernons of Hanbury, who bought the manor of Lower Wick, which included the land here, in 1746. They built themselves a house called Vernon Hall on **Malvern Road**, roughly opposite where this road is now, which was demolished after 1884.

The Vernons retained Lower Wick for more than 150 years, but in the early twentieth century the estate was sold, and the land in this area began to be developed in the 1930s. This road was first found in a street directory in 1937, when seven homes were listed.

HAPPY LAND

The development of these streets was described in an article in the Worcester Herald of 1910, quoted by Bill Gwilliam. In the 1850s land here was bought for building purposes by three Watkins brothers, who were a solicitor, a surveyor and an auctioneer. They first decided to exploit the site for sand and gravel extraction, and it proved so profitable for this that the area was given the ironic nickname California, after the American state where gold had been discovered in 1848. When they began to build on the site it was popularly renamed, according to tradition, from an ironic bit of old Black Country doggerel, which may have been thought appropriate because of the sand and gravel connection:

Gornal is a happy land,
Breaking stones and wheeling sand,
Far, far away.

Victorian local historian and journalist John Noake said there was a great deal of building going on here about 1860, and Happy Land was first found listed in a street directory of 1873. There was also a Sand Pits Inn in **Bromyard Road**, recalling the early history of the area, which changed its name to the Bedwardine in the early 1960s. By 1884 there seem to have been around 60 homes listed under Happy Land in a street directory. They were mostly in small terraces of between two and four homes – 16 of them in all – which must have been built by individual investors, who named their terraces according to their individual taste, with names such as Eastnor Cottages (2), Brunswick Terrace (3), Laughern Terrace (4), Broxash Cottages (4) and Belle Vue Place (3). Many of the residents were clerks, building tradesmen, laundresses, glovers and tailors, but James Penson at Ivy Cottages was a station master, William Meredith at Cromwell Villa was an accountant, and F. Mason at Belle Vue Place was a photographer.

From an early stage the development was split into two adjoining streets, but the separate 'North' and 'West' names were not found listed in a street directory until 1896. In that year Mrs Ann Pritchard had a shop on the corner of Knight Street, now converted to a house. The Second World War bombing raid on Meco in **Bromyard Road** in 1940 also damaged some houses here, and blinded a small child in one eye.

Hardwick Spring

This old name, relating to an area to the east of what is now **Bromwich Road**, where Hardwick's Spring Cottages were once located, has long since disappeared, along with the spring. The name recalls the ancient manor of Hardwick, which once extended from the central area of St John's to where Laugherne Brook crossed **Bransford Road** and **Bromyard Road**. When St John's became a parish church in 1371 it was within the manor of Hardwick. In Anglo-Saxon, Hardwick, or herdwick, was a wick or farm for herds of livestock, probably having both sheep and cattle. The Norman family who held land here took their name from the manor. About the time of Henry III Plulip de Hardwick resided here, and the manor was undoubtedly the most important west of the Severn. It was Edward II who gave the manor to the priory at Worcester. After the Dissolution it continued as a large dairy farm into the nineteenth century. The cottages must have been demolished when Bromwich Road was straightened and widened in the 1920s. The manor is recalled by Hardwicke Close off **Hylton Road**.

Christopher Hebb, aged 65 in 1837 - TW

Hare's Lane

An offshoot of the ancient *Hound's Lane*, now under the college of technology, first found in a street directory of 1840, though it must have been older than that. The slum housing surrounding both lanes in the nineteenth century was cleared in the 1920s and 30s.

HEBB STREET

Formerly called *Back Lane*, this street must have acquired its present name as a result of a charity with two small almshouses here, which was founded on funds given by popular nineteenth century city doctor and mayor Christopher Hebb, who lived around the corner in **Britannia Square**.

These cottages were probably the first properties fronting onto this street, and must have been built more than three decades before it was named.

Above, Back Lane, later Hebb Street, in 1884. The cottages of Hebb's widows' charity are on the bottom left, facing the end of the road. Below, Blundell's store on the corner of Ashcroft Road, now a hairdressers - LL

Dr Hebb was born in London in 1772, and came to practice medicine in the city about 1793. He was an accomplished French speaker and translated into English what was then regarded as the standard work on heart disease, by the French Imperial physician Corvisart.

He was highly regarded in the city and in his profession, becoming secretary of the Provincial Medical and Surgical Association, forerunner of the British Medical Association.

In January 1836 he became the first modern Mayor of Worcester, and was again elected unanimously for a second term in July 1837.

He founded a number of charities, including the one based here which housed widows, and at his death in 1861 he left the substantial sum of £8,000 to local charities.

The charity founded here was Hebb's Municipal Widows' Asylum, which provided two small cottages to serve as almshouses for poor widows. If this charity was established with Hebb's bequest, as seems likely, then these cottages must have been built around 1862 or 3.

They were built in part of the back gardens roughly behind Nos. 58-60 **York Place**, facing east directly down this street.

Dr Hebb was well placed to arrange this, since he was an investor in the York Place scheme, which built houses for rent, and he may have owned those particular houses. There was also a third cottage beside them, which was not one of the almshouses. The charity was last listed in a directory in 1900, and presumably ceased to operate.

In 1905 these homes were listed as Hebb Cottages. At that time they housed a clerk and two ladies, presumably widowed, one of whom was working as a charwoman. As the widows died the cottages came into more general occupation. They were demolished around 1970, and garages now stand on the site.

The street was first found in a street directory in 1898. At that date the residents were mostly clustered around the east end of the street, in modest cottages which have since been demolished. Fern Cottages, housing a shoemaker, a labourer and a dressmaker, were here before 1884 on the site where an electricity sub-station was placed within a few years, for what was then the Worcester Corporation electricity supply system.

On the other side of the road, in cottages that were demolished around the 1960s to widen the access to **Barbourne Road**, lived a labourer and a baker. Beyond the entrance to Britannia Square lived a tailor, in a cottage since demolished. The old cottage still standing in this area, on the south side of the street, was

These cottages at the east end of Hebb Street were demolished in the 1960s to widen the junction - RS

originally an outbuilding of Albany House on **Albany Terrace**, probably accommodation for grooms or gardeners. The pairs of pleasant late Victorian villas on the north side of the street were built, occupied and listed by 1900, then housing two prison warders at the prison in **Castle Street**, a letter carrier, a coal agent, a tailor, an organ builder, two carpenters and a stonemason.

On the west corner of **Ashcroft Road** soon after 1900 was Blundell's general store, run by Mrs Emily Blundell and her husband, and later, until at least the 1950s, by their daughter Vera. The Saturday delivery boy had to collect ice from **Bank Street** which was used to make ice cream that he delivered around the area. On the opposite corner was Bacon's greengrocers.

HENRY STREET

The first record found for this street was a building application of 1878, submitted by Henry Tyler, who presumably decided to name the street after himself. There were several Henry Tylers in the city at that time, all shopkeepers, but the most likely to be behind this application seems to be Joseph Henry Tyler, chosen because other building applications were also submitted by a J.H. Tyler, and he was the only one found. He had premises at **Mealcheapen Street**, where he ran a diverse business, being oil and water colour merchant, grocer, hop dealer and insurance agent.

He was apparently not involved in a great deal of property speculation - only two application for six houses seem likely to have been submitted by him, though he may have owned other houses to rent – but being first in this street, and possibly having bought the land for sale as building plots, apparently won him the right to name it.

A map of 1884 showed eight homes here, which had doubled by 1896, when residents included bricklayers, labourers, a gardener, a boatman, a cooper, a wheelwright, several travelling salesmen, a watchman, a glass cutter, and sauce bottler Mrs Anne Williams. There was a building application for a further two cottages in 1898, which were built soon afterwards, largely completing the street. The building at the north end, on the east side of the street, now part of the Myriad Centre in **St George's Walk** was previously a nursery, and before that a private school, but was originally part of St George's School, and by the 1920s had become the St George's Church Institute. Though it now fronts onto the next street it was listed here through much of its history.

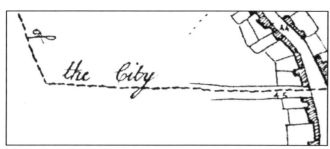

Rosemary Lane in 1764, apparently running only a short distance out of St John's, along the then city boundary

HENWICK ROAD

The Henwick area was church or monastic land from very ancient times, being mentioned in an Anglo-Saxon land grant made by King Offa of Mercia to the Bishop of Worcester between 757 and 775. Henwick, or Higna-wick meant a farm or settlement of monks, and in the twelfth and thirteenth centuries, and probably earlier, it was a dairy farm of the monastery at Worcester.

Henwick fell into two broad areas, Henwick Hill, the high ground above the Severn, and Lower Henwick, where the land fell away to the south and west. Documents are said to have identified Henwick Hill as the site of siegeworks during the wars of Stephen and Matilda in the twelfth century, though their exact location is unknown. The riverside flood plain below the hill, and **Hylton Road** which ran across these meadows, had always been liable to flood, but this sort of thing presented major problems for eighteenth century turnpike trusts, and their clients the stagecoach operators, who relied on the speed of their coaches to attract passengers, and had no time to wait for flood waters to recede.

The southern end of this road existed as a lane for centuries past, known in the eighteenth century as *Rosemary Lane*, but it owes its modern existence to the turnpike trust which created it as a major thoroughfare between

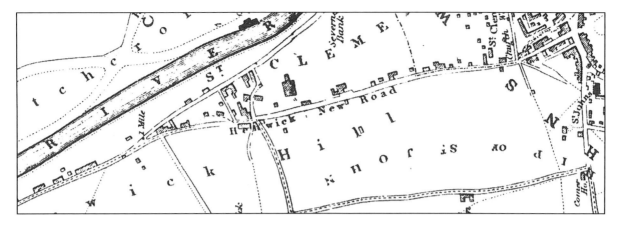

Above, by 1840 development was spreading along what was by then known as Henwick New Road.
Below, the Bull Ring and the lower end of Henwick Road in 1884

1781 and 1790, when it was shown on a map as a new road to Ludlow, which was free from steep gradients (once the **Bull Ring** had been negotiated!) and was well away from flooding. It was referred to throughout most of the nineteenth century as Henwick New Road, to distinguish it from the old Henwick Road beyond Hylton Road. There was a turnpike gate at Henwick Hill, a little way beyond the junction with Hylton Road.

The few homes here in 1790 were occupied by the well-to-do, mostly styling themselves gentlemen. There was also glover Thomas Giles, draper and woollen manufacturer James Southan and surveyor of highways William Giles.

St Clements Church was built in 1822-3 as a replacement for a riverside church standing by the east end of the old bridge between **Tybridge Street** and **Newport Street**. It is said to have been designed by Thomas Ingleman, who is otherwise unknown, and was designed in a neo-Norman style which according to Pevsner was almost unheard of before the 1830s and was not fashionable until the 1840s.

This road was never short of hostelries, to cater for travellers and strollers out of St John's. Near the railway is the Grosvenor Arms, which was built in the early 1870s, around the same time as **Grosvenor Walk**. Beyond the junction with Hylton Road was the Wheatsheaf inn and the Dog & Duck at **Ferry Bank**, and on Henwick Hill the well-known Porto Bello Gardens, which must have dated from the same period as the Portobello in **Bransford Road**, and was famous for its public breakfasts during race meetings, which were held on the bowling green.

Entertainment also included concerts, and dancing in the evenings, when the gardens were illuminated with coloured lamps. During the 'season' there were always boats on hand to take visitors across the Severn to the gardens.

A cholera hospital was set up under canvas at Henwick during the cholera outbreak of 1832, with the involvement of Dr Matthew Pierpoint after whom **Pierpoint Street** was named. Despite this attempt to isolate the disease, 79 people died in the outbreak, and were buried in a mass grave at **Tallow Hill**.

This terrace opposite St Clement's Primary School probably dates from the late eighteenth or early nineteenth century. The house the Edwardian postman is standing outside, and the one on the right, have both gone, as have others further along, but four remain - RS

Above, St Clement's Church 1920. Below, the Royal Albert Orphanage about 1900 - RS

As late as 1838 much of the land around the road was pasture and orchards. Once St John's had been left behind there was the occasional roadside cottage or villa on the east, enjoying a very pleasant view towards the Severn and the city, but virtually nothing on the west except open fields. A listing of 1840 showed that the population was on the increase, but it was still mostly the well-off clustering around Henwick Hill. Two schools for young ladies had made an appearance in this fashionable spot; A.M. Tearne's ladies' seminary near the Porto Bello Gardens, and E. & E. Cottrill's ladies' school, near which was a Vapour and Shower Baths kept by Mary Lewis.

Urban development here really began with the sale of the former estate of Francis Williams at Henwick Grange. It was split into 12 large lots for auction at the Star Hotel in Foregate Street on 24 June 1875. Two

prominent local developers, Lowesmoor stonemason John Rouse and solicitor John Stallard were amongst those behind the scheme. These lots were then split into smaller lots for sale to house builders or prospective owners. By 1884 there were around 80 homes listed here.

There was still an air of affluence in some areas – at Cedar House was John Lloyd Bozward, sheriff of Worcester and the man after whom **Bozward Street** was likely to

146

have been named, next door to Francis Wyatt Dyer, high sheriff of the county courts, at Wren's Nest – but many folk with humbler professions had also moved in, at least some of whom were clearly commuting into the city for work. By 1873 the Grosvenor Arms pub had opened near what was then Henwick Station, and still exists, though the station doesn't.

Henwick was the first station on the Worcester to Hereford Railway. Its opening was complicated however by government inspectors refusing to pass the new bridge across the Severn as safe. Consequently a locomotive and carriages had to be transported through the city by road, so that the first train could run from Henwick to Malvern on 25 July 1859. Henwick had its own ticket office, waiting room, stationmaster and porters, and in later years was used by many Kays employees working at the company's site in **Bromyard Road**. In 1882 the single fare from Worcester was 3d. in third class and 4d. in second. The station closed in the late 1960s.

The imposing Royal Albert Orphanage, now a YMCA hostel, was built in 1869, at a cost of £4,000. It was a time when poor parents might well die young, or abandon their children in despair when times were hard. The orphanage was established at a house nearby in 1862, but larger premises were needed, and Richard Padmore, after whom **Padmore Street** was named, put up the money to build this massive institution for 38 boys and 38 girls, which still had 70 youngsters in the 1940s, but closed in the 1950s as numbers dwindled. To the east of the road in the nineteenth century, just north of the orphanage on the opposite side, was a house which was later called Hardwick Manor. The manor once held much of the land west of the river, but this was not the manor house. That was said to have been burnt down during the Civil War, and its replacement was on **Malvern Road** beside St John's Green, but was demolished in the early twentieth century. The owner of this house then took the name.

Worcester from Portobello Gardens in 1781, with the river at low tide

The Guildhall in 1877

HIGH STREET

This street has long existed as Worcester's most important thoroughfare and centre of business. Anglo-Saxon historian A.E.E. Jones said it was originally known, probably from Roman times and into the Anglo-Saxon period, as Magno Vico, the main or most important area of the town, and the Oxford place names historians of the 1920s said this use continued up to the thirteenth century in city charters.

Built on high ground above flood level, it inevitably became known by its present name to English speakers. The regular pattern of this street and its intersecting streets has led to suggestions that at least the top end was laid out on a grid pattern by one of the later Saxon bishops, possibly Saint Oswald. The stocks once stood outside No. 27, and a public well was dug in that area in 1567. The street was paved or re-paved in 1596.

At the end of the eighteenth century it was opened to traffic direct from **Sidbury** by the creation of **College Street**, which much altered the southern end of the street. It was widened in the late nineteenth century and a building control application was submitted in 1896 for pavements and street lights. In the 1960s it was

Above, the top end of the High Street in 1860. Below, the Elgar Brothers music shop - BG

again altered at the southern end by the *Lich Street* redevelopment. Prior to that, this street extended to the cathedral precincts and connected with **College Yard** and College Street, but has since been curtailed to allow space for a traffic island. The street was once a major traffic route in the city, but has since been pedestrianised.

A town or guild hall was recorded in 1249 on the site of the present fine Guildhall, but an administrative building may have been sited here hundreds of years earlier, originally enforcing the authority of Anglo-Saxon Mercian kings over the burh, or defended settlement.

This role would have come to an end with the Norman Conquest and the building of a Norman castle off the present **Severn Street**, and the building here would then have taken the local administration role that buildings on this site have had throughout the centuries since.

The building here prior to the present one was half-timbered and longer than the present Guildhall. It was once fronted by a piazza, and had a range of shops at either end, facing the High Street, though historian Pat Hughes has shown that it also later had a range of shops built in front of it.

The ground level around it must have risen sharply after that hall was built, since a flight of almost 20 steps descended to the main entrance at the south end. Inside, the building had a medieval hall open to the roof, lit by a large window at the north end. It served both the civil authority – with a council chamber above – and the legal, with two courts on the ground floor.

There were prison cells below the piazza, and opposite was the home of the gaoler, whose residence also doubled as a public house.

Historic Worcester Streets

The Guildhall in the Edwardian period

FANCY DRESS AND SILK WAREHOUSE.
(Established upwards of Half-a-Century.)

C. C. W. GRIFFITHS,
SILK MERCER, DRAPER, UNDERTAKER, &c.,
29, HIGH STREET, WORCESTER.

Griffiths silk warehouse, next door to the market hall

It has been said that the statue of Queen Anne on the front of the present building was formerly in the old hall, but if so it can only have been there a few years, since Anne only reigned from 1702 until 1714.

The present Italianate Guildhall was built between 1721 and 1723 to the designs of important local architect Thomas White, who had been a pupil of Sir Christopher Wren. Though very much of its time, it actually echoes many of the features of the older building it replaced, having a large hall to the front, with court facilities below and a council chamber above. Outside, two fairly plain projecting wings enclose a piazza which sets off the building. As with the older building, there are cells below, with a narrow stairway leading up to the court room.

As shocking as it may seem to us, there was a move in the 1870s to demolish this fine old hall and replace it with a 'nice new' Victorian building. Thanks to the efforts of city journalist John Noake and others, the plan was defeated and the Guildhall was refurbished at a cost of £22,000 in 1880, while Noake was mayor.

The Guildhall has many portraits of past civic leaders, but oddly there isn't one of the journalist who helped to save the building for posterity.

Though this street would always have been a centre of commerce, it would also have been home to many citizens, who either lived above the shops, or in homes on or just off the street. The Newdicks, a family of wealthy clothiers, had a house here by 1530, on the site of what is now the 'Cathedral Plaza' shopping mall. By 1577 however it had become an inn called the Sign of the Lyon, the lion being a device in the Newdick family coat of arms. Before 1678 22 small cottages were built on a plot at the rear of the inn, which became known as Newdix Court, the entry to which was between numbers 3 and 4 in the 1930s. They were demolished when the site was redeveloped in the 1960s.

The street housed a wide cross-section of trades in the past. In 1790 there were apothecaries, bakers, booksellers, cabinet makers, carpet manufacturers, a cutler, a cork cutter, a dentist, druggists, ten glovers, grocers, hair dressers, hosiers, mercers, milliners, musicians, a physician, a plumber, a sausage maker, shoemakers, a stay maker, a stone mason, 'taylors', a toy warehouse, a watchmaker, a wine merchant and

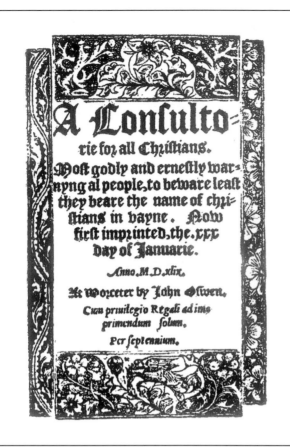

two woollen drapers. Some had an odd mixture of occupations. William Roper was a grocer and shot maker, Samuel Wall was a linen draper and snuff maker, Richard Wainwright was a plumber and glass seller and Edward Connop was a 'taylor' and cheesemonger. By 1840 financial services had made an appearance, with offices of a number of life and fire insurance companies.

This was a centre of printing for centuries. The first printer in Worcestershire was John Oswen, a radical protestant who arrived here from Ipswich in January 1549, making the city one of the earliest in the country to have a printing press. He remained at premises in this street for four years and printed 29 books, but his religious views were not popular when catholic Queen Mary came to the throne, and he swiftly fled. Orders were subsequently given for all his books to be destroyed, and anyone found with them was to be treated as an outlaw, so not surprisingly there are few copies left.

In January 1794, at No. 72, William Holl began publishing the *Worcester Herald*, which became the biggest selling newspaper in the county in the nineteenth century, but was taken over by the *Journal* publishers in the early 1930s. The *Worcester News* was set up here in 1861, but merged in 1869 with its neighbour the *Worcestershire Advertiser* at No. 44, which merged with the *Journal* publishers in 1937 to create the *Worcester Evening News and Times*, now just the *Worcester News* again. At No. 43 in 1884 were Charles Henry Birbeck & Co., publishers of the *Worcester Daily Times*. At No. 53 were Deighton & Co., booksellers and stationers who had been publishers of the *Journal*. There was also W.E. Tucker, colour and general printers at No. 15 in 1884, though the firm later moved to massive premises at **Northwick Avenue**, where it did not thrive.

It is odd that there is not a single pub left here, since hostelries were an important feature of the life of this street in past centuries. There was a Globe inn here in the late seventeenth century, to which a butchers' market moved from **The Shambles** in 1671, and the inn was still here around 1714, when it was mentioned in the Journal as being taken over by Thomas Hassell, who had moved from the White Horse at **St Martin's Gate**, leaving his son James to run that inn. The King's Head, opposite the Guildhall, was a leading inn in its day, and in 1714 the Journal noted it had

Above, the first book printed in Worcestershire, a Consultorie for All Christians, printed by radical Protestant John Oswen in 1549. Below, an ad for the Worcester Herald, 1856.

THE BEST MEDIUM FOR ADVERTISEMENTS IN GENERAL

IN THE

COUNTY AND CITY OF WORCESTER

IS

The Worcester Herald,

Established in 1794.

The WORCESTER HERALD has been for years at the head of the Worcestershire Press, having a circulation *nearly double* that of *any other* paper published *in the County*; and contains a complete digest of the news of the week, with ample details of interesting local events. The HERALD is entirely independent of political party, and circulates among all classes and individuals of every shade of opinion.

AGRICULTURAL AND COMMERCIAL INTELLIGENCE

Forms an important feature in its columns, and besides the principal Markets of the week the

LONDON AND LIVERPOOL CORN MARKETS OF FRIDAY

ARE REPORTED BY ELECTRIC TELEGRAPH.

THE HERALD IS PUBLISHED EVERY FRIDAY EVENING AT

72, HIGH STREET, WORCESTER.

Historic Worcester Streets

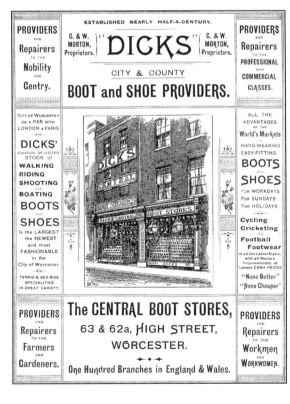

become the new home of the Wool Market, which moved across the road from the Guildhall. In 1761, when the inn was to be sold at auction, the annual rent, including three adjoining tenements in **The Shambles**, was said to be around £56. Gwilliam said it was presided over in the mid nineteenth century by the Widow Price. In the first half of the century newspapers were expensive due to a tax on them, and many could not read, so public readings of newspapers were held at this and other inns around the city.

A small wooden building, adjoining a stable behind one of the street's leading inns, the King's Head, was for many years the site of Worcester's only theatre, and the place where legendary tragedian Sarah Siddons gave her fist performance around 1766, as Ariel in The Tempest. Many other leading thespians of the day also acted there. In 1779 the theatre manager, Mr Whiteley, raised £1,000 by subscription to build the Theatre Royal in **Angel Street**.

This inn then had what may have been Worcester's first off-street general market, which opened in the yard after the theatre moved out. This created a public appetite for a purpose-built market hall, and in 1804 the King's Head was demolished and a market was built running through to The Shambles, with a fine stone frontage and a glass roof, costing more than £5,000 in total.

In 1849 the mayor, Richard Padmore, after whom **Padmore Street** was named, presented the city with a public clock for the frontage. In 1857 the hall was rebuilt in a style inspired by the Crystal Palace, though retaining the same frontage. After the Second World War it was replaced with what Bill Gwilliam called 'a most nondescript building surrounding a passage called an 'arcade'', which has been rebuilt in the past decade and is still fronted by Padmore's clock.

The Golden Lion nearby started life as a house, and is said by buildings historian Pat Hughes to have been one of the earlier domestic buildings existing in the city, owned in the sixteenth century by wealthy clothier John Walsgrove who founded almshouses in *Powick Lane*. It was converted to a pub by the seventeenth century. Built as a timber-framed house, it has since acquired a brick 'skin', probably in the eighteenth century. It was a popular drinking haunt of nineteenth century radicals, and though it closed as a pub in the 1980s and is now a coffee house, the building still retains the inn sign and the figure of a lion, which was re-gilded in 2011.

The Bull and Sun inn, at the head of **Bull Entry**, existed from at least the eighteenth century and possibly before, and was said to be part of the smugglers' cellar complex, by which goods were supposed to have been smuggled to High Street shops from **South Quay** without paying duty on them. The inn closed about 1850, and the building became the Central Coffee Tavern, but was demolished around 1935. Near the southern end of the street was the Stationers Arms, frequented by printers, which had closed by 1925, and nearby was the Swan, which closed around

1960. In 1763 the Journal mentioned another inn called the Rose and Crown, but it is not clear where that was.

The Shakespeare cafe opened in the 1920s, having been given a mock-Tudor front which the building still has, and it was a popular rendezvous for many years, but is now a mobile phone shop.

The street's most famous former shop was the Elgar Brothers music store, near the southern end of the street, where a handsome plaque marks the spot. The shop was founded by Elgar's father, and the young composer lived here from 1863 to 1879, and helped out in the shop as he grew older.

The shop remained in the family until 1928. Sadly it fell victim to the *Lich Street* redevelopment in the 1960s. The statue of Elgar, which has become such a familiar feature of the street, was unveiled by Prince Charles in 1981.

Older residents will no doubt remember Russell & Dorrell's department store at 15-21, near what became the Lychgate shopping precinct, and more recently has been renamed Cathedral Plaza.

MacFisheries was at No. 47 in the mid 1960s, with Littlewoods a couple of doors down, and Greig's the grocers was at No. 53, next door to Lawley's china shop, and near the southern end of the street were a couple of furriers, from the days when fur coats were fashionable. Many people will remember the Cadena Cafe from those days, in the basement below what is now the Alliance & Leicester.

Top, a 1920s ad for the once popular Shakespeare Cafe.

Middle, north end of the High Street after the first phase of widening went ahead, early 1890s. The next phase, including the demolition of Edward Sparks music store (right) went ahead just before the First World War - HL

Bottom, the market hall between High Street and Shambles-BS

152

HIGHLAND ROAD

This name was presumably chosen because it accurately describes the high ground to the east of the city, around Gorse Hill. This road was first found in a street directory in 1930, when there were five villas here.

High Timber Street

Now **Severn Street**. Probably a continuation of *Frog Lane*, beyond the city walls. The name was last found in 1840.

HILL AVENUE, THE

This street was said to take its name from Hill House, on **Bath Road**, which was the home of the Feild family, whose most famous member was a much-admired colonial bishop. Edward Feild was born in 1801 and brought up in that house.

He was consecrated in 1827, and proved himself to be an energetic and hard-working clergyman, so it was hardly surprising that in 1844 he was appointed Bishop of Newfoundland in eastern Canada, where he spent the rest of his life.

There he recruited and trained clergy, built a school, a cathedral and 27 parish churches, and journeyed ceaselessly around his massive diocese, until his health finally broke down, and he died in 1876.

The first record of the avenue is a building application of 1893 for a new road, submitted by developer John Stallard. In the same year there were two other applications for eight houses.

Above, Edward Feild Left, The Hill on Bath Road in 1838

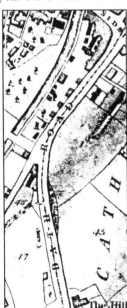

Over the next six years development progressed steadily, with 15 applications for 29 houses, mostly being built two at a time, but in 1901 there was an application for a continuation of the road and plans for the building of 26 more houses were unveiled over the next two years.

Building applications continued to be submitted, and by 1910 there were almost 70 homes here and five more were being built. There was also a site earmarked for a primitive Methodist chapel on the corner of **Bath Road**, though it was never built.

By 1922 there were 74 homes, many of them individually named villas, with occupants in skilled and managerial positions. At Kinghurst was postal superintendent Roger Charles Knight, at St. Denis was Rev Greenhalgh of the Countess of Huntingdon's chapel, at Rosary was Henry Carmichael from the well-known coach building business, at Omega was reporter Frederick Davies, at Leighton was artist Edward John Raby, at Westbury was Albert Edward Holiday, district cashier for the GWR, at Strathmore was excise office Frank Ball and at Chesleigh was gunsmith Frank Clarke. This was not the sort of street to have shops or a pub - tradesmen would be happy to call at these prosperous addresses – but there does seem to have been a shop on the corner of **St Dunstan's Crescent**.

HILL STREET

The name came from the fact that this street crossed **Spring Hill** and **Tallow Hill**. It originally connected to **Cromwell Street**, but the northern part was demolished in the 1960s or early 70s, when *Regent Street* and *Lower Street* were cleared, and the rerouted roadway and a retail park were built over the site in the 1990s. It was first found in the health board streets list of 1872, and in a street directory of 1873. In 1884 the first full street directory listing showed a dozen homes here. The six cottages in a terrace called Providence Place, and the five in Milton Terrace all appeared to be at the north end of the street, between Cromwell Street and Tallow Hill, but a map of around the same date shows a dozen more cottages at the southern end of the street which were not listed, perhaps because they were not built until after the listing was prepared, which meant development here was progressing quickly, though there were still orchards to the west of this end of the street. Residents in 1884 included labourers, seamstresses, a wheelwright, a laundress, a drayman, an iron moulder, two foremen and an engine driver. Mrs Ann Abbott had a bakery on the corner of Cromwell Street, and Mrs Ann Heeks had a greengrocers on the corner of Tallow Hill, opposite the Beehive pub – once described as 'cheap, cheerful and cosy' - which was in existence by 1873 and closed around 1990. Modern redevelopment has changed the face of the northern end of the street, but the southern end is still as it was.

HILL VIEW ROAD
Off **Hanbury Park Road**, looking towards the Malverns, this road was first found in a street directory in 1937, when seven homes were listed.

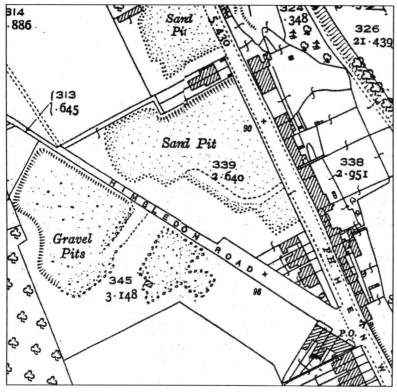

Himbleton Road in 1928, referred to as Himbledon

HIMBLETON ROAD
There may have been a farm track or lane here in past centuries, but this began life as a road through a development scheme which clearly didn't go to plan. A building application was submitted in June 1896 for eight houses in this new road, across land which had previously been exploited for sand and gravel extraction. No doubt many more building applications would have followed for this road, if things had gone well.

The developer was Joseph Aston, who must also have chosen the road name, for reasons best known to himself. He must have come from a family much involved in property development during the late Victorian boom. William Aston, who had a saw mill in *James Street*, which gave him ready access to building materials, submitted a dozen building applications in the 1880s and 90s, while Walter Henry Aston submitted around 20. Between them they applied to build more than 150 houses. James Aston, who had the Lansdowne Hotel in **Lowesmoor** in 1896, submitted only one application, for an addition to a workshop at the saw mill, but may have been involved in many of the others.

Joseph had been involved in the development of 15 houses in **Vincent Road** in the previous couple of years, and also submitted plans for more than 20 houses in **Belmont Street** and **Comer Gardens** in that same year. But perhaps the finance for this plan wasn't forthcoming or fell through, and in February 1897 he resubmitted the housing application, while the application for the new road was submitted on the same date by solicitor John Stallard Snr, either on his own behalf or representing someone who may have been financing purchase of the land.

Things still didn't go to plan however, and only a short section of roadway was constructed, together with four houses at the junction with **Henwick Road**, housing in 1922 Mrs Potter's corner shop and post office, electrical engineer Edmond Bayham, the Misses Walker at Redlands and schoolmaster David Rabjohns next door. This must have been a disaster for Joseph Aston, and may have been the reason that he apparently never submitted another building application.

Perhaps the reasons for the failure of the scheme were to do with the site itself. This was certainly a pleasant spot, with a view over the Severn at the front, and open fields and orchards stretching away to the west at the rear, but it was well out of town, and there were those extensive sand and gravel pits to fill, beginning just beyond the point that the roadway had been constructed to. Which presumably explains why development of the road wasn't completed until the second half of the twentieth century. Oddly, the 1928 Ordnance Survey map gave the name as Himbledon Road.

HOLLY MOUNT

Part of a small 'forest' estate of streets with tree names, presumably based around this street which was probably the first. The street may have been created at around the same time as **Tunnel Hill**, in the 1850s or 60s, though house types suggest that the 1870s or early 1880s may be more likely. A map of 1884 showed that only the west end existed at that time, and much of it was taken up with the gardens of substantial villas fronting onto Tunnel Hill, though there was a terrace of nine Holly Mount Cottages. Residents at that time included four labourers, a porter, a painter, a platelayer, a coach painter and a laundress. By the 1920s the road was extended and additional homes built on the south side. In 1922 there were 60 homes here, but there were still some vacant plots which have only been filled in modern times.

HOLLY MOUNT ROAD

This road was first listed in 1915, when 18 homes were shown here, but the road wasn't shown on a 1928 Ordnance Survey map! All the development here now appears to be from the 1920s or 30s, though the original homes are presumably still here somewhere.

HOLY WELL HILL

The Holy Well at Henwick was a spring which was said to have medicinal properties, and over the centuries people visited it from far afield in search of relief from eye trouble. It was dubbed 'holy' because of its connection to the monastery at Worcester which owned the land in the area. Its water, regarded as the purest in Worcester, was piped to the monastery through lead pipes as drinking water, and in 1461 the prior set up baths for the monks. The lead pipes were said to have been ripped up by Parliamentary soldiers during the Civil War siege of Worcester, and used to make bullets. From about 1750 the water was used by a brewery in **Hylton Road** producing porter, a type of stout very popular in the eighteenth century. In 1790, according to a local directory, its porter was 'esteemed the first outside the Metropolis (London)', but unfortunately the brewery was severely damaged by fire in the following year. The well was bricked up in the 1870s during development here. The site of the well has been identified as being in the garden of Tripleton Cottage.
The street was first found in the health board streets list of 1872, and in a street directory of 1880. By 1884 there were five homes here, which were probably built in the 1870s, plus John Handley's shop on the corner of **Henwick Road**, which has disappeared under modern redevelopment, though some of the original homes remain here.

HOMEFIELD ROAD

This may have been a field name originally, before the builders moved in. The road was first found in a street directory in 1930, when there were eight homes listed.

HOOD STREET

This street probably owes its name to a local business long based here, and there was a reference to a J. Hood & Sons in a building application of 1868, but no further information about them has been found. This small road has long existed as a route from **Quay Street** to the Quay, and from the 1790s served as a rear access to the houses in **Bridge Street**. There was a slipway here in the eighteenth century, but by the 1880s there was just a flight of steps down to the water. No listing was found for the street until 1884, at which date it mostly housed businesses, except for Mrs Emma Dowler's lodging house on the quayside. Above that was wool merchant John Hillman, Gardner & Roan maltsters, sack contractors Brown & Son and hot water engineer Richard Ward.

HOPTON STREET

The Hoptons seem to have been descended from a Herefordshire family of that name who had an estate at Canon Frome near Ledbury, from the sixteenth century. In the eighteenth and nineteenth centuries the Worcestershire Hoptons held land around Rushwick, and in St John's. John Hopton - John was a common name in the family - held land in **Bransford Road** and his name appeared on an 1889 building application for St John's Mill in **Bromyard Road**.
The first housing here was built by Herbert Ashcroft, who built **Ashcroft Road** and named it after himself, but no doubt the development here was financed by John Hopton, who named the street for himself or his family.
It was developed on land which was formerly part of Ivy House Farm – see **Comer Road**. It was one of three new streets for which a building application was submitted in 1896, and once it got started, development proceeded fairly quickly here. The street was first recorded by name in a building application of 1902 for six

houses. They were built by the following year, when the street was first found listed in a directory. Residents then included an engineer, a bricklayer, a labourer, a painter, a county court bailiff and a glover. By 1905 there were a dozen houses, and by 1910 the street had 17 homes, though the south end was not developed until the 1930s, apparently by the city council.

Horne Lane
Shown on a map of 1751 as an old name for **Lansdowne Road**, though it was listed in the 1880s off that road near **Lansdowne Crescent**,

Hounds Lane
Also referred to as Dogs Lane. In Anglo-Saxon times this was said to be Wodesteare Street, translated as the street of the wood lathes. The later version of the name was no doubt Old English in origin but is certainly obscure. In the early sixteenth century, up to 1539, it consisted of gardens for nearby houses, but by 1560 it was built up with housing for renting to the poor. It continued as an area of overcrowding and deprivation into the twentieth century. The slum housing surrounding the lane was cleared in the 1920s and 30s. However the Hounds Lane Board Schools for boys, girls and infants, which had opened by 1884, continued in existence until education was reorganised and elementary schooling became a thing of the past. The late Worcester historian Bill Gwilliam, who was born in 1912, attended Hounds Lane School. This is now part of the college of technology site. By 1955 only one person was still living here; Jeanette Farrant at No. 2.

HUNGERPIT WALK
The name Hungerpit is certainly older than this late nineteenth century alleyway, and must come from a feature in a field here before development began. It seems to suggest a mass grave from some ancient famine, and there were certainly a number of those in the Anglo-Saxon and medieval periods, but no folklore has come down to us about this site, and hunger crops up in old names around the country, most often referring to land with poor soil or poor grazing. Without other evidence we have to assume a meaning of that sort here.

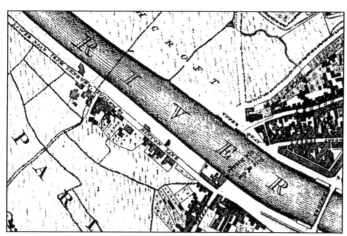

Hylton Road, then called Hinton Lane, in 1799

HYLTON ROAD
In the late tenth century a farm named Hultun, or Hill Farm, stood on the ridge to the east of Laughern Brook, towards the Severn, reached by a lane which became known as Hultun or Hilton Lane, sometimes referred to in the eighteenth century as Hinton Lane. It was listed in street directories as Hylton Street in 1840 and Road by 1873.

It was often also referred to as Bridge Street in the eighteenth century when it gave access to the medieval bridge between **Tybridge Street** and **Newport Street**, but that use ceased after the present bridge crossing opened in 1781, and the present **Bridge Street** was created as an approach to it, though there was still a thriving community here around the former bridgehead on this side of the river.

The area between the old and new bridges was shown on a map of 1838 as ***Bridge Place***. Only later was this road extended to the new bridge. Immediately west of where the old bridge stood was an old pub called the Red Lion, which dated from at least the seventeenth century.

Many of the premises along the road in the eighteenth century were on the east side, serving river traffic. Around 1750 a much praised porter brewery was established near **Holy Well Hill**, but it was badly damaged by fire in 1791. In 1790 two coal merchants were listed here, timber merchant John Bellamy, John Grout's coopery and Edward Broughton, pleasure boat builder and supplier. There was also a riverside hostelry called the Severn Trow which was still listed around 1840, but is said to have closed by 1841, though it may have changed its name to the Mug House, which was in the same area until about 1915.

By 1840 the creation of the 'Bridge Place and Hylton Street Wharfs' had led to a concentration of coal merchants in this area, and seven were listed. But times were hard as river traffic fell off, and J. Lessimore combined coal dealing with keeping the Severn Trow at the southern end of the road, while J. Smith three doors along at the Royal George also doubled as a bricklayer, but his pub did at least survive until 1955, when

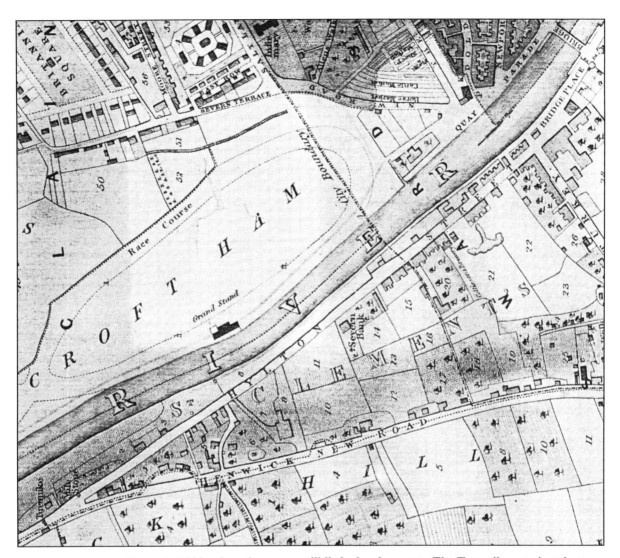

Hylton Road, then Street, in 1822, when there was still little development. The Turnpike gate is at bottom left, just beyond the junction with Henwick Road.

the business moved to **Tunnel Hill**. Between them were the shops of grocer Benjamin Gorle and butcher Josiah Taylor. Further up the road was Collisson, Trimmer & Tolley's Worcester Brewery, probably on the site of the former porter brewery. Other pubs listed by Bill Gwilliam were the Chequers, on the corner of **Tybridge Street**, which was in existence by 1873 but had closed by 1920; the Wheelwright's Arms opposite the Mug House, which closed around 1925; and the Crown & Anchor, towards the northern end of the road, which may have been established originally in the eighteenth century, and is the only one of these pubs to have survived to the present day.

A two-span bridge was built by 1859 to carry the Worcester to Hereford railway line across the Severn. However there were considerable problems with the foundations, and when it was completed the government inspectors found problems with the cast iron spans and refused to pass it as safe. Consequently a locomotive and carriages had to be transported through the city by road, so that the first train could run from Henwick Station in **Henwick Road** to Malvern on 25 July 1859. Considerable further work had to be carried out on the bridge before the Journal could report in late 1861 that repairs should soon be completed. It was replaced by the current bridge in 1905. The viaduct is 935 yards long with 68 brick arches.

The area to the north of the Tybridge Street junction housed, from at least the eighteenth century, a poor housing development called ***The Pinch***, which was cleared in the early twentieth century. It was at *The Pinch* that the cholera outbreak of 1832 started, from which 79 people were to die.

This street was raised in the late nineteenth century to try to prevent flooding, though this was not very successful, and further flood alleviation works have had to be put in place in the past few years. The area on the riverside was named Henwick Parade in 1922. Buildings by the railway arches were demolished in 1959 and the land on the east side of the road was cleared between 1965-1970 to create the riverside gardens.

A reminder of the power station, which was on **Tybridge Street** until 1979, is the small riverside water inlet and pumping station, beside which is the only surviving stairway in the Georgian river wall, created when the new bridge development was carried out in the 1770s and 80s. Today development is mostly modern and commercial, and little is left of the residential community which once thrived here.

Hylton Road flooded, with the power station at the junction with Tybridge Street in the background - RS

INFIRMARY WALK

The Infirmary on **Castle Street** was built on a former artichoke field, and this might well originally have been a path running along the side of fields here. The change in its alignment at the southern end may be the result of the path curving around one of the bastions of the medieval city wall. Until **Farrier Street** became a through route, this walk would have been the only direct route from Castle Street to **The Butts**, and would have become an important access route from the city centre to the hospital when it opened in 1771, at which point it must have acquired its present name. Historian David Whitehead said the path was originally Dr Wall's Walk, a reference to a pathway used by John Wall, who lived in Foregate Street from 1761 to 1774, but only part of this path coincided with his walk, which was clearly there before this time.

As late as 1884 there was open land between the Infirmary and the railway, though additional accommodation for nurses was subsequently built on it, and more recently accommodation for students. Beyond the railway bridge on the west was a school set up by St Nicholas's parish, which was rebuilt in 1894. Though the school closed with the end of elementary education, the building still exists. Next door are Lea's Almshouses, endowed by sauce manufacturer John Wheeley Lea of Lea & Perrins, built around 1874 to house six poor women.

The substantial Grove House, to the east of the walk, on the corner of Castle Street, was home in 1884 to Edward John Kitson, of the **Broad Street** chemists, but by 1896 was occupied as nurses' accommodation, and is now used as offices. An application for the 18 houses between there and the railway was submitted in 1903, but there were homes here earlier. The 1960s nurses' accommodation near the railway bridge was formerly the site of Magdala Terrace, a small square of 13 homes and a shop, probably built in the 1860s or earlier. Residents in 1884 included a watchmaker, two seamstresses, a potter, two shoemakers, a polisher, a police constable, a carpenter, a cab proprietor and greengrocer Henry Aaron.

Also listed under this walk was Netherton Place, though it was some distance to the west, next to Wood's sawmill in The Butts. It consisted of 13 modest homes in three small terraces beside the railway, on a site now redeveloped, which in 1884 housed several labourers, a laundress, several seamstresses, a porter, a shoemaker, an iron worker, a waggoner and a clerk.

Inglethorpe Meadow

A street off Lowesmoor Place, between **Pheasant Street** and **Padmore Street**, named for seventeenth century city businessman Richard Inglethorpe (see **Sansome Street**), presumably because it was built on land owned by the charity he founded. This street existed from 1870 or before, and was first found in the health board streets list of 1872. At the end of the street was Inglethorpe Square, which consisted of two terraces of modest industrial cottages with no gardens, 21 in all, with a narrow alleyway between. In contrast, the street itself had just four cottages in Inglethorpe Terrace, equally devoid of gardens.

In 1897 the street's occupants were a drayman, a fitter, a labourer and a gloveress, and the square housed four labourers, a gardener, a foundryman, two draymen, a riveter, a laundress, a gloveress, a goods foreman, a tinman (tin plate worker), a basket maker and a plasterer. Both Meadow and Square were listed as separate street names in the nineteenth century, but between 1910 and 1922 Inglethorpe Terrace was demolished and replaced with commercial premises. Inglethorpe Square remained, but from then on only Meadow was used as a street name. The street was replaced by commercial premises in the 1970s, occupied by Courts Furnishing for many years, and now a supermarket.

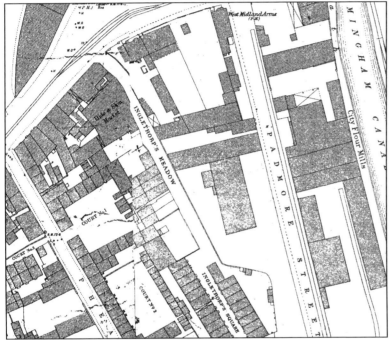

Map of Inglethorpe Meadow and Square in 1884

Inglethorpe Square

See *Inglethorpe Meadow*.

ISAAC WALK

Named for a family founded in Worcester by banker Elias Isaac. He was born in 1755 and came to Worcester in 1781. In that same year he became a partner in Berwick's Bank, more often known as the Worcester Old Bank, established in 1765, and situated on the corner of **Bank Street**. Its other partners were Joseph Berwick, who held the lucrative post of Receiver-General to the County of Worcester, collecting Crown debts, and Samuel Wall, a silk mercer. Isaac lived originally in **Broad Street**, but he moved to 30 **The Tything** in 1790. He married but had no children. Within three years of coming to the city he became a member of the council, and he later became chamberlain, sheriff and finally mayor in 1799 and 1800. He probably retired in the latter year since his nephew, also Elias Isaac, became a partner in the bank in that year. He died in 1803. His nephew purchased Boughton Park soon afterwards and the family remained there until 1925 (see **Boughton Street**).

The street was not found in a street directory until 1922, when just 10 homes were listed, housing journalist Fred Bolwell, engineer William Lewis, confectioner Arthur Palmer, boot operator John Simpson, brewer's clerk Alfred Attwell, labourer Alfred Mills, checker William McManus, compositor Harold Lewis and pattern maker Percival Sanders. Development seems to have gone ahead rapidly, to complete the street soon afterwards.

IVY STREET

The name of this small street was probably chosen as a botanical complement to **Lavender Road**, though that was named for a family rather than the flowering plant. The street was first found in a street directory of 1885, but the first building application was in 1894, for 12 houses here and in Lavender Road. Nothing had been built here by 1900, but four homes on the west side were listed in 1905, whose occupants included a stoker, a mechanic and a gardener. Development on the other side is modern.

James Street

Blockhouse. This street, off **St Paul's Street** almost opposite **Spring Gardens**, was probably built at the same time and completed by late 1865, when building control began, since there is only one small building application for it throughout the rest of the century. It is likely to have been built at the same time as *John*

Street, and their names may also link them, though no explanation for the names has been found. They were of course the names of two of the 12 disciples of Jesus, but could also be the names of builders or developers of the street.

In 1884 there were more than 40 homes here, plus two shops and a bakery. Residents were manual workers and small tradesmen of all sorts, including labourers, builders, railwaymen and iron workers, plus a bill poster, a china painter, an ostler, a signal fitter and a fireman. Timber merchant William Aston's Steam Saw Mill was also based in the street. He was a member of a family heavily involved in property speculation late in the century, and his saw mill gave him ready access to building materials. He submitted a dozen building applications in the 1880s and 90s, including the largest submitted in that period, for 47 homes in **Vincent Road**, while Walter Henry Aston submitted around 20. Between them they applied to build more than 150 houses. The Croft Inn here had its own small brewery, which continued to operate until around 1970, when the street was cleared and the site subsequently redeveloped.

John Street

Blockhouse. This street was probably built at the same time as *James Street* and completed by 1865, since there is only one small building application throughout the rest of the century. Their names may also link them, though no explanation for the names has been found. In 1884 there were around 40 homes here and three shops. Residents included a number of shoemakers, iron workers, fitters, tin plate workers and printers. There were few women listed as heads of households, but there was a gloveress, a seamstress and a charwoman. As with James Street, the area was cleared in the twentieth century.

King George V

JUBILEE ROAD

This road must have been started or at least planned in 1935, the year in which much-loved monarch George V celebrated his Silver Jubilee, after 25 years on the throne. His leadership during and after the First World War, and his concern for ordinary working people during the Depression of the early 1930s, endeared him to the nation. A Silver Jubilee had never before been marked publicly by a monarch, but he saw it as an opportunity for celebration after years of economic gloom, and it added greatly to his popularity. There was great public sadness when he died in 1936. This road was first found listed in a street directory in 1937, when there were 24 homes here.

Kain Street

An early variant of **Quay Street**.

KENDALL STREET

The street must have taken its name from Alfred Kendall, who from at least 1872 lived across the road at a large house called Sunnyside, since demolished, on the corner of **Lansdowne Crescent**, and presumably was involved in the development of this street.

He was a wine merchant with premises at 54 **Broad Street**, and was probably a member of the family listed in county archives which held property in Worcestershire from at least the late seventeenth century. There was also a Kendal House near the end of this street, which he presumably built or renamed, though the listed spelling is slightly different, but that may have been a directory error.

In 1884 there was still open land stretching from **Rainbow Hill Terrace** to the railway bridge, and this was an unnamed footway leading to a track beside the railway. It was not until 1896 that it was found listed in a street directory, when there appear to have been three substantial homes here, housing Benjamin Giles, superintendent of the GWR locomotive department; engine fitter John Wales, and at Kingston House, Rev Jas. Edwin who was minister at the Countess of Huntingdon's chapel in *Birdport*.

In the following year there was an odd building application for nine more houses, which certainly could not have fitted here unless all the existing homes were to be demolished. They have since been demolished anyway, probably in the 1970s, presumably to make way for new homes on **Rainbow Hill**, and there is nothing here now, not even a road sign.

Key, The

Seventeenth century name for **South Quay**.

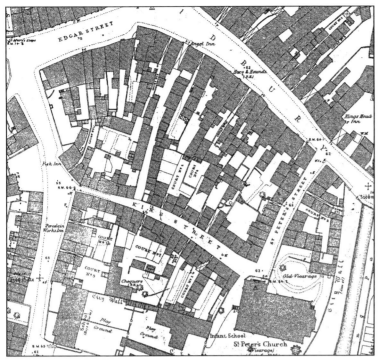

KING STREET

Probably named because of the nearby King's School, founded by Henry VIII, which went by various names but was inevitably known as the king's school. Development of housing here for rent to working families is believed to date from the early seventeenth century. This was a narrow street of old timber-framed houses, until the mid twentieth century when the area was 'cleared'. In 1896 there were around 30 homes here. Many of the residents were labourers, but there were also a couple of fish hawkers, china workers, a laundress, a waterman, a baker, a leather parer or cutter, and a number of shoemakers, probably at Cinderella shoes on **College Street**. There were six courts of tightly-packed housing around the street, and of one of these, on the south side, was near the Chequers pub, which was listed as early

**Above, King Street and the site of Frog Gate (lower left) 1885.
Below, King Street in 1935 - RS**

as 1790, and was last seen on a map of 1885.

King William Street in 1886

King William Street

Blockhouse. This street ran to the canal from **Foundry Street**, opposite **Charles Street**, roughly where the northern end of Blockhouse Close is situated, and was probably created between 1830 and 1837, while King William IV was on the throne. It was a street with a pub at either end. At the east end, on the corner of *Waterloo Street*, was the Waterloo Inn, which pre-dated the street, since it was first listed in 1822, and must have been a bargemen's pub, serving ale to those waiting their turn to go through Blockhouse Lock. It closed around 1950. Nearby was the Waterloo Wharf, where Mrs Amelia Smith was a coal dealer and boat owner. At the west end of the street, on the corner of Foundry Street, was the King William IV pub, built in the 1860s, which was the last thing in the street to go, being demolished in 1975, though it had then been closed for several years. In 1884 there were more than 20 homes and a shop here, including nine cottages in a terrace called Waterloo Gardens. Residents of the street included six other women who were heads of households, two working in the gloving trade, one a laundress, two charwomen and Mrs Jane Perkins who offered lodgings. Other residents included labourers, shoemakers, a painter and a fish hawker. The street was cleared in the 1970s and the site was subsequently redeveloped.

KNIGHT STREET

There is a good deal of material in county archives about a Knight family, and a Sir F.W. Knight was Honorary Colonel of the 1st Volunteer Battalion of the Worcester & Warwick Artillery Volunteers in 1896. The family were presumably involved in financing or development of this street, and gave it their family name, though no firm evidence has been found.

It was first listed in a street directory in 1884, when there were 20 homes here, six of them empty so probably newly built. Residents then were nearly all small tradesmen, including carpenters, a bricklayer, a miller, a glover, a sawyer, a shoemaker, and a tinman, or tinplate worker. There was also someone who gave his occupation as 'billiard marker', which presumably meant he marked up the scores in a billiard hall. On the corner of **Lambert Road** was The Dove, a beer retailer and shop, now a general store. By 1896 there were more than 30 homes listed, and between 1894 and 1901 there were three building applications to build a further seven houses, though only about half of these were built.

Knowles-end

The name given in the seventeenth and eighteenth centuries to an area at the junction of **Sidbury** and **Edgar Street**. The Cock inn was here in the sixteenth century, occupied by widow Mrs Elizabeth Stevens. A passing reference in the Journal in September 1762 showed that this was the site of one of the public pumps from which citizens could draw water.

LAMBERT ROAD

This road presumably owes its name to the involvement of a member of the Lambert family possibly a solicitor, in its initial financing or development. County archives contain details of a Lambert family from Malvern, and an 1884 directory lists solicitor William Lambert, who had offices in Malvern and at 14 **Foregate Street**. There was a good deal of building on adjacent streets by 1884, with development backing onto this road, but the first building application in which it was named was in 1886 for six houses. These were probably the six houses called Lambert Terrace. There were applications to build another eight homes by 1894, and a listing two years later showed all 14 homes, plus a bakery on the corner of **Comer Road**, and The Dove, now a general store, on the corner of **Knight Street**. On the corner of **Bozward Street** was a Dogs' Home, with Albert Hancox as the kennelman.

The homes built included five Eva Cottages, housing a platelayer, a tailor, and two married ladies who were presumably widowed. At the two Stroud Cottages were a locksmith and a brush maker, and at a villa called Raithly lived a mill manager named William Strawson. Residents at Lambert Terrace included a china decorator, a police constable, a butcher, a railway clerk, a plumber and a smith.

LANSDOWNE CRESCENT

This street was built on land which was part of the Red House Estate. The Red House on **Rainbow Hill**, later called Marl Bank and the home of Edward Elgar at the end of his life, is said to have been the HQ of the Parliamentary forces in the Civil War, and the site at which the city was surrendered after the 1646 siege. The house was well known and the lower part of the Astwood turnpike road was sometimes referred to as Red House Hill.

The estate was a triangular land holding bounded by Rainbow Hill /Astwood Road on the east, Merriman's Hill/Green Lane on the west, and the line of Lansdowne Crescent on the south. The estate was held in the eighteenth century by William Browning Esq. He must have died before 1786, and in that year Margaret Browning, presumably his widow, split the estate between her two daughters, Ann Griffiths and Margaret Millington Browning, who received the southern half including the house, and in 1816 bequeathed it to John Watkins of Birmingham, who was first found listed as living there by 1834, though he may well have moved in much earlier.

In the early 1820s the crescent and **Lansdowne Crescent Lan**e were unnamed footpaths leading from **Lansdowne Road** to Rainbow Hill, but John Watkins must have been planning this housing development for some time, and announced the sale of lane for building in 1824. Progress was slow however, and by 1832 only two houses stood here. Before he could put his plans fully into effect, Watkins died in 1835, and though his dream went ahead it took more than 30 years to realise.

From 1824 to 1837 this was referred to on documents and maps as Prospect Crescent – presumably the name that John Watkins had intended for it - finally being referred to by its present name in 1838, suggesting someone had decided that a name reminiscent of the prestigious Bath development, Lansdown Crescent, completed in 1793 on Lansdown Hill, would better enable them to market the houses then being built here. Only Nos. 1 – 5 and 18 had been completed by that date. By around 1868 the crescent had probably been completed. Nos 1 – 16 were built on The Hill Field, and 17 and 18 were built on part of an adjoining field, mostly in Regency style.

There does not seem to have been a public auction of lots, as happened in **Britannia Square** and **St George's Square**, so presumably plots were sold by private contract. Construction seems to have been a mix of commissioned and speculative builds. Nos. 7 – 9 were built in 1861-2 by builder George Priddey, presumably as a speculative venture, but No. 16, built around the same time, was commissioned from builder Joseph Wood, who lived here at Lansdowne Villa, as the rectory for St Nicholas Church, since the rectory on **The Cross** next to the church had been sold to a bank around 1855. The new rectory was largely or totally funded by William Perrins of Lea and Perrins, who lived here, as did John Wheeley Lea at one time.

No 18 initially housed a Female Asylum or Penitentiary, which had been set up elsewhere in the city in 1825. A garden ran around the house surrounded by a high wall, and inmates were allowed to take exercise there. There were 15 inmates in 1840, though authorities bemoaned the fact that the house could have taken twice as many if the funds had been available.

This later became known as the Bishop's House, because it was the home of Bishop Gore, who became Bishop of Worcester in 1902, but disliked Hartlebury Castle and lived here instead until 1904. Other houses were occupied by solicitors, clergy, engineers, traders, shop-keepers and businessmen. Five residents held the office of mayor up to 1900.

LANSDOWNE CRESCENT LANE

In the 1820s this was an unnamed footpath, which in the 1830s became an access road to properties off **Lansdowne Crescent**, and later also to **Rogers Hill**. The west side is taken up with the rear of houses in Lansdowne Crescent, and the east side was not developed until modern times.

LANSDOWNE ROAD

This road must have long existed as a track leading from **The Tything** to the top of Rainbow Hill, where the turnpike road was an important route running north, but there was little development here until the second half of the nineteenth century. As late as 1838 this was shown on a map as an unnamed lane running through an entirely rural area. Early in the century it was referred to as *Cut Throat Lane*, a name often given to dark, lonely lanes.

The road must have taken its present name from **Lansdowne Crescent**, which had that name by 1838, though this name was not first found recorded until 1868, in a building application for four houses and a corner shop. This was the first building application found for the road, but a good deal of building must already have taken place in the early 1860s, before building control began, as was the case in **Lansdowne Street**. The road was first found listed in a street directory in 1873, and Chesnut Place, a terrace of four homes here was listed separately in that year, but further development was slow until the first six years of the 1880s, when eight applications were submitted for 33 homes.

In 1884 there were around 60 homes here, a mix of cottages, villas and some more substantial houses. At the 11 Lansdowne Villas on the south side of the road lived retired army officer Capt. William Hunter, alongside two clerks, a canvasser for GWR, a police inspector, and several widows, at least one of whom was letting out apartments. In the four villas at Chesnut Place, near the Chesnut Tree, were master mariner John Perks, coal merchant George Cullis and Edward Scott Sanderson, who styled himself a gentleman.

This development was mainly before the canal, but just beyond the canal bridge were nine cottages called Stanhope Terrace, housing an engine fitter, a smith, a clothier's assistant, a cashier and two commercial clerks. Behind this terrace was Merriman's Lodge, a substantial house split in two, to house a colliery agent and a bank clerk. There was a little more development at the other end of the road, and a couple of substantial houses on the south side, but other than that there was still much open ground around the road, which was developed at various dates from the 1920s or 30s until quite recently.

At the junction with **Flag Meadow Walk**, when both these roads were rural lanes, stood the Whey Tavern, probably dating from the eighteenth century, which was popular with city folk on summer walks. It closed about 1840 and became a lace factory. A short distance from the start of the road was a corner shop then kept by Francis Glover. At the end of Lansdowne Street is the Chesnut Tree inn, which was listed from 1873. Opposite was a corner shop, then kept by Mrs Maria Probert, which closed in the 1970s, as many corner shops did. Across the road, at the end of **Chesnut Walk** was the shop of butcher Matthew Andrews, which continued as a butcher's until the 1960s or 70s, and as a shop until at least the 1990s, but has since been converted into a house.

Builder Herbert Ashcroft, who built **Ashcroft Road** in Barbourne, and named it after himself, was living in this road in 1884 at Sabrina Villas, just east of Lansdowne Crescent, probably in a house he built himself. He became involved in other large-scale projects aside from Ashcroft Road, such as the building of 16 houses in **Waterworks Road** and **Barbourne Walk**, for which a building application was submitted in June 1888.

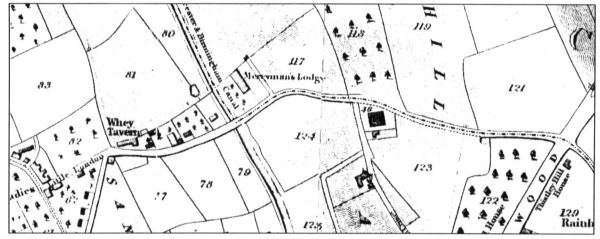

Lansdowne Road in 1838

LANSDOWNE STREET

This street must have taken its name from **Lansdowne Road**, which in turn will have taken its name from **Lansdowne Crescent**. The Journal referred to this as a new street in March 1863, though building had probably begun in the previous year or two, since by that date there were reported to be 30 or 40 houses built and tenanted. The paper added that "others are fast being built, and thanks to the city lighting committee, the street has now been well lighted with gas". The speed with which the development was going ahead may indicate an attempt to get the street up before building control was introduced in 1865, but it was not complete by that date. A building application was submitted for 12 houses in 1869, and another for five more houses in 1881, which must have been built by 1884 when a listing showed the street completed, and with a shop and three pubs in the vicinity.

In many streets new housing consisted of a mix of humble cottages and more spacious and profitable villas, but space was limited here, and this street consisted almost entirely of terraced housing for working families, packed in tightly, with modest gardens. Consequently few of the individual investors took the trouble to name the terraces of homes they had financed. The first five cottages on the east side of the street were called Chesnut Terrace, just beyond were six homes called Cheltenham Villas though they were little bigger than the neighbouring cottages, and on the other side of the street, at Nos. 14-18 was Addison Terrace, but all the remaining properties just had numbers.

Nevertheless, there was an interesting mix of residents. Aside from two prison warders, there was also the chief warder, George Barber Gibson, and three police constables at the northern end of the street. Other residents were clerks, building workers, clothing, factory and metal workers, glovers and a milk dealer. The three pubs they could readily frequent were the Chesnut Tree on the corner of Lansdowne Road, the Peep O' Day on the corner of **Cumberland Street**, and the Lansdowne, on the west side, which in 1884 also served as a grocer's shop. The other shop, on the corner opposite the Chesnut Tree, was then kept by Mrs Maria Probert. The Lansdowne survived until recently, but plans have now been submitted to turn it into housing.

LANSDOWNE TERRACE

No street directory listing was found for this street until 1884. At that time there were 14 modest homes listed here, possibly built as early as the 1860s, with residents including a cooper, a gilder, two stokers, a carpenter, a labourer, a shoe finisher, an engine driver, a carriage painter, a tailor, a painter, a gloveress and a horse hair worker, probably at Webb's factory in **Copenhagen Street**. Another five cottages were added soon afterwards, and there has been a little modern infill development.

LANSDOWNE WALK

A map of 1838 showed this as an unnamed footpath from **Lansdowne Crescent** to **Lansdowne Road**. By 1884 the northern end had been widened slightly to allow access to two terraces of five cottages on the east side, named Shrawley Terrace and Ashperton Terrace, whose residents included a machinist, a gas stoker, two joiners, two engine drivers, a laundress, a gardener and two railway guards.

The street name was not then listed, and was first found in 1896, but most of it remained as a footpath, which it partly still is. Two years later there was an application for road widening at the southern end of the street. It was submitted by Samuel Telford Dutton, after whom **Dutton Street** was likely to have been named. He was city council member for the area in the 1890s, and lived nearby at Marl Bank. **Rainbow Hill**, which was later home to composer Sir Edward Elgar. The only two building applications in his name were for creating **Rogers Hill** and widening this street.

The work must have been carried out by 1903, when there was an application for a further five houses at that end of the street, which had been built by 1905 as Hatfield Villas, housing three engine drivers, an iron moulder and a fitter. The east side of the southern end of the road was not built on for some years, and development took place at various dates until quite recently.

LARK HILL

This formed part of the manor of Perry, described under **Perry Wood Walk**. In 1814 eight acres of land here was purchased from landowner William Oldnall Russell by John Knapp of **Sidbury**. The Knapps had grown wealthy in the gloving trade. In the 1790s John Knapp senior was a partner in glovers Knapp and Lea in **Lowesmoor**.

In 1811 he and his son John were involved in the purchase of parts of the Sansome Fields estate, which in 1813 was leased wholly or partly to Knapp senior. Knapp junior was doing well enough in business at that time to mint trade tokens as change, some of which are still in existence. By 1820 both were styling themselves as gentlemen.

In 1819 Knapp junior mortgaged the property he had bought here for £3,000 with attorney William Parker, in order to develop the land, and in that same year he advertised plots of land for sale suitable for house building. Flat land for house sites had to be manually carved out of the hillside by gangs of navvies. One of the first houses to be built was Woodside, at the top of **Lark Hill Road**, which was completed in the early 1820s. It was owned by wealthy glover Joseph Burlingham, but he lived at a mansion at **St Catharine's Hill**, just down the road, so it is likely he built this house speculatively to rent out.

The finest of the villas was Heron Lodge, described under **London Road**. Knapp died in September 1823 and Parker took over administration of the project. The remainder of the properties were built speculatively as semi-detached villas, completed about 1828, first named Lark Hill Crescent, then Lark Hill Terrace.

In 1854, as a drain was being dug, a large quantity of ancient silver coins were found in this area, which were subsequently deposited in the British Museum.

In 1884 the nine villas listed were occupied by a mix of gentlemen styling themselves Esq. and executives for leading city industrial concerns. Daniel Osborne was a manager for Lea & Perrins, George Henry Williamson was from Williamson's tin plate manufactory in **Providence Street**, Henry Oram at Woodlawn was a partner at Scott & Oram, and Francis Woodward was an alderman and JP.

Neither Woodside nor Heron Lodge have been homes for many years. Woodside was occupied as offices, partly by Great Universal Stores' haulage arm, later White Arrow, until 2005, since when it has been unoccupied. Heron Lodge has also been used as offices for some years, at one time occupied by Midland Red, and is also now empty.

LARK HILL ROAD

First found in a street directory in 1930, when there were nine homes listed, though some houses here are much older, having been built as part of the **Lark Hill** development.

William Laslett - TW

LASLETT STREET

Named for Worcester lawyer and philanthropist William Laslett. Born in the city in 1801, son of a bank cashier, he became a clerk but was noticed by **Foregate Street** lawyer William Wall, and articled as a solicitor. He eventually took over the firm, and practised for some years in Foregate Street.

In 1842 Bishop of Worcester Dr Carr died in substantial debt, and there is a story that his body was seized by the sheriff's officer and held for a month until the debts were paid by Laslett, on condition that Maria, the bishop's eldest daughter, married him. The marriage was not happy, and they separated after a few years. He later moved to Grimley, then Abberton Hall near Pershore.

From 1852 to 1860 Laslett was Liberal MP for the city, and during that period he qualified as a barrister in 1856. In 1868 he went back to parliament, this time as a Conservative, and held the seat until 1874. He died ten years later.

He was a complex man, eccentric and often parsimonious in his private life, yet generous to the city of his birth. In 1868 he paid a substantial sum for the city gaol in **Friar Street** which he turned into almshouses. In 1870 he acquired the Music Hall, later the Public Hall in the **Corn Market**, and sold it to the city for a reasonable sum, and he also gave 20 acres of land for Astwood Cemetery.

The street was first found listed in 1885 when most of the land around it was still vacant, and there were just seven modest homes here, including three Rose Cottages housing a drayman, a smith and John Purchas's shop on the corner of **Gillam Street**, and two more cottages on Rose Terrace housing an iron moulder and a widow. There was also a commercial traveller and a cooper. Development was slow, with five small scale applications for 13 more homes by 1896, 11 of which were shown completed and occupied in the listing for that year.

The other two homes were completed by 1900, and two more were built soon afterwards to complete the street. Only one Rose Cottage remains, and the shop has been replaced by a takeaway on the site of the other two.

LAUGHERNE ROAD

A former farm track, this road was developed on land which was formerly part of Ivy House Farm – see **Comer Road**. The farm stood immediately north of the southern end of the road, and William Giles was farmer there in1896. A building application for a new road here was submitted in 1889. It follows the line of a farm track which led between what by then were known as **Comer Road** and **Oldbury Road**, both of which were also farm tracks not many years earlier. It no doubt took its name from the nearby Laugherne Brook, running to the west, about a mile of which is now a local nature reserve.

No building application for housing was recorded for two years after the road was applied for, and development then was relatively slow and almost entirely small-scale, with most applications being for one or two houses. Between 1891 and 1905 there were 26 building applications for a total of 45 homes, and by 1905 about 40 had been built, mostly villas, though with a sprinkling of more humble cottages.

Residents included an assistant official receiver, a nursery foreman, professional cricketer Frederick Lloyd Bowley, and William Lea, secretary of the Worcester Permanent Building Society. But there was also a potter, a painter, a butler, a builder, a draper's assistant, a letter carrier, clerks, a commercial traveller and an insurance agent. The shop on the corner of **Rowley Hill Street** still survives.

Most development continued to be on the west side of the road, with three homes there for every one on the east side in 1922. As late as 1928 there were extensive orchards to the west of the road, and on both sides at the northern end where development did not begin until the 1930s.

Lavender House, and Lavender Road in 1884

LAVENDER ROAD

Named for the Lavender family and the house that bore their name. Originally it was a track leading to Barbourne House, **Barbourne Road**, and Lavender House was then called Barbourne Villa, a late eighteenth century, stuccoed house with an ornamental wrought-iron balcony overlooking Barbourne Brook, which was demolished in the 1970s. The house was set in its own grounds, though they were not as extensive as those of Barbourne House, but the Lavenders also owned land to the west of Barbourne House. John Pearkes Lavender was born in 1792 and traded as a whitesmith or ironmonger in a half-timbered building on the corner of the **Shambles** and **Church Street**, where the business was later

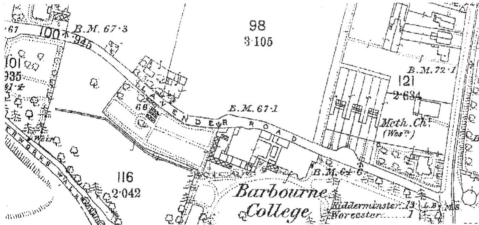

carried on by John Hall who had been his apprentice, and it remained Halls until the building was demolished in 1962. Lavender was a member of the corporation from 1821, he was sheriff in 1831-2 and mayor in the following year. He also served as governor of the

County Prison in **Castle Street** from 1820 to 1843, when he retired on a substantial pension of £149 10s. In 1823 Lavender's daughter Mary married John Gutch, a Bristol newspaper owner, and friend of essayist Charles Lamb.

In 1826 Lavender had dammed Barbourne Brook to help improve his land, but several adjoining landowners claimed their land had been adversely affected, which resulted in an inconclusive law suit, and may have led to Lavender's purchase of the Barbourne House estate in 1838, where he is believed to have lived, perhaps until his death in 1846. In mid-century the lane was christened 'Admiral's Walk' by locals, since Admiral Hastings, hero of the storming of Acre, tenant of Barbourne House and a local magistrate, was often seen pacing up and down there for exercise.

The Lavenders were partners in the Farley, Lavender, Owen and Gutch bank at **The Cross**, where NatWest Bank is now. The bank went bust in 1857, after Mr Lavender's death, but his other daughter, Jane, was horrified that some worthless notes issued by the bank had her father's signature on them, and provided her own funds to honour them. The sisters also built St Stephen's Church and school. Lavender House was leased by Barbourne College from 1894 until its closure in 1908. The land on which the road stands was part of the substantial land holding of Mrs Mary Gutch (see **Ombersley Road**) and no development was permitted on it until the 1880s, after her death.

The first street directory listing found for the road was in 1884. The residents were inevitably well-off, including a wine merchant, a solicitor, a couple of clergymen and a military officer. By 1900 there had been four applications for a total of 20 houses, and development here had doubled to around 25 homes. Another seven were added soon afterwards, but the west end of the road was not developed until later in the twentieth century.

Historic Worcester Streets

LECHMERE CRESCENT

The Lechmeres held lands in Worcestershire from the Conquest, with their home at Hanley Castle. Sir Edmund Lechmere, after whom the Crescent must have been named, was a wealthy nineteenth century banker, and MP for several Worcestershire constituencies.

He was born in 1826, and in 1852, after university, he became a partner in Berwick's bank, often referred to as the Old Bank, on the corner of **Bank Street**. In 1856 he succeeded to his father's title and estates, and two years later he married well and acquired estates in Yorkshire. During 1866-8 he was MP for Tewkesbury, during 1876-85 he represented West Worcestershire, in 1885 he was elected MP for Bewdley, and in 1891 for Evesham, which seat he held until his death three years later.

In parliament he took an especial interest in agricultural matters, and he was also keen to encourage allotments and gardening. He was one of the founders of the St John Ambulance Association, and Deputy Chairman of the Red Cross Society. The crescent was first found listed in a street directory in 1880. At this time it was surrounded by open fields and orchards, and contained only a handful of substantial detached or semi-detached villas.

Like many developments of this period, the name was actually given to a small row of villas, though the crescent had been laid out ready for development, which proved to be much slower in coming than developers probably hoped.

Residents in 1884 included Henry Webb of Webb & Exton surveyors, Inland Revenue officer James McCormick and Francis Best Loxley. There were also a small number of more modest homes. At Mount Pleasant Villa was law clerk Frederick Simms, and at Fern Dale Cottage was schoolmaster Thomas Watts.

Sir Edmund Lechmere in 1883

By 1896 there were a few more homes, but there was no dramatic growth, even by 1928. The 1930s was the decade in which the city's suburbs really began to expand, and some further building went ahead in that period, but there was still a small number of vacant plots remaining at the end of that decade, which have been built on at various dates since.

LESLIE AVENUE

The development here must have been planned and built by **Northwick Road** builder Ronald William Morris, who presumably chose the road name, perhaps for a member of his family, as must also have happened with the adjacent **Colin Road** and **Dorothy Crescent**. The road was first found in a street directory in 1937, when there were four homes here.

Hubert Leicester - TW

LEICESTER STREET

This street was named for Elgar's boyhood friend and **High Street** neighbour Hubert Aloysuis Leicester, who was mayor of the city more times than anyone else. Leicester, a chartered accountant, was mayor in 1905 and 1906, but went on to serve in the office again in 1914, 1915 and 1916, which made him the city's longest-serving mayor. No-one else in the four centuries that the city has had a mayor has equalled this record. In 1917 a presentation portrait of him was painted, to be hung in the Guildhall, but oddly it has spent many years languishing in the cellar at the museum. Hopefully it will be restored to its rightful place at the Guildhall before long.

He campaigned for the clearance of slum areas and the improvement of housing, and also gave a good deal of his time to educational and hospital work. He had a life-long interest in music, was active in many local musical societies and was choirmaster at the Roman Catholic Church in **Sansome Place** for more than 50 years.

He also published two volumes of Worcester history in 1930 and 1935. He was made a freeman of the city in 1932, and had he lived a little longer he would have been knighted, since his name appeared in the Honours List a week before his death on 15 June 1939.

This street was first found by name in a street directory in 1908, but the first few homes here were probably built in the 1860s. They were a small row of modest cottages, since demolished, which were owned by a widows' charity founded by Christopher Hebb, after whose charity **Hebb Street** was named. The street now consists of a terrace of six villas called Whistone Terrace, recalling an old name for **The Tything**. Builder Bert Ashcroft, who built **Ashcroft Road** and named it after himself, submitted a building application for them in 1901, and they were built and occupied by 1905, when they housed a porter, a coachbuilder, a glover, a prison warder, a tailor and an ostler.

Above, Lich Street 1884. Below, about 1900 - WN

Lich Street

A victim of rampant 1960s redevelopment, which replaced it with a shopping precinct, this was an ancient street, known in times past as Leach or Leech Street, which ran from **Friar Street** to **High Street**, past the Lychgate into the large Cathedral graveyard, so it was nicknamed 'the street of death', though it was actually a lively shopping street at one time. Prior to the late eighteenth century, when **College Street** was created, this was the only route by which traffic from **Sidbury** could reach the High Street. So completely was this street destroyed by the 1960s development that it is hardly possible now to even determine where it was. The best indication of the west end of the street is that it was shown on an 1884 map opposite the east end of what is now **Deansway**, which indicates that it ran from what is now the Deansway junction with College Street, across the area now occupied by a roundabout and multi-storey car park, through to Friar Street. The Lych Gate must have entered the cathedral churchyard roughly opposite the east end of the cathedral, and the site is now probably under buildings on the north side of College Street.

The buildings of the south side of the street would once have surrounded, or even encroached on the large cathedral graveyard – the only one in the city in the medieval period. The lychgate dated from the early sixteenth century, though the street was mainly fifteenth century. The buildings here had some fine

Historic Worcester Streets

timber-framed frontages, especially the house known as the Old Deanery, believed to be an early residence of the Deans of Worcester.

This was traditionally a street of tradesmen and shopkeepers, usually with a fair sprinkling of hostelries to beguile the harassed shopper. The businesses found in this street in 1790 included two cheesemongers, a cutler, two drapers, a last maker, a staymaker and a whitesmith or ironmonger.

There were also several pubs or inns. A small pub called the Three Cranes was recorded here in the seventeenth century, held by butcher John Honnyett in 1601, and mentioned again in 1690.

It was not listed in 1790 but the Black Boy and the Mitre were. Neither of these was listed a century later, but they were both still shown in 1840, along with the Duke of York, recalling the king's son after whom **Albany Terrace** and **York Place** were named.

In 1713 the Journal mentioned the Royal Arms at the bottom of the street, which seems to have been an ale house, and was said to have 'a very good Billiard-Table'. By 1840 shoemakers predominated in the street, accounting for almost half the listed businesses. There were also several clothes brokers and dealers, a woollen draper and a stonemason.

As the nineteenth century progressed however, the character of the street changed. By 1884 the New Punch Bowl opposite the cathedral lychgate, which was first listed in 1873, was the only pub left in the street – and it closed around 1912. There were still some shoemakers, but only four of them.

Above, the Cathedral Lich Gate in the 1950s. By the time it was swept away by development in the 1960s it was the only one left in England - WN

Below, Lich Street in 1954 - WN

Clothing was still here, with two tailors and a number of clothiers and clothes dealers, and there was still a stonemason, but there were others for whom this was perhaps residential accommodation rather than a shop window, such as labourer Thomas Penny, iron moulder Joseph Glover and plumber Ben Jones.

In a sign of the nineteenth century's scientific progress, there were also Public Vaccination Rooms near the High Street. After the Second World War there were a number of interesting businesses here. Older residents might remember the radio store Rediffusion, on the north corner at the High Street junction, and Beryl's Babyland at the Friar Street junction.

By the 1960s the Cathedral Lychgate no longer had a gate, and appeared to be little more than a pedestrian access to College Street, but nevertheless it **was** the only remaining cathedral lychgate in the country. That did not prevent the council's 'Lich Street Comprehensive Development Plan' receiving planning consent by March 1962, and within a few years both the street and the lychgate were demolished to make way for a controversial 1960s hotel and shopping complex, which was originally called The Lychgate, but has since been re-named Cathedral Plaza, thus ending all connection with this ancient street.

H.H. Martyn and wife Fanny - WN

The street's most famous son must have been Herbert Henry Martyn, who was born in the slums here in 1842 and was such a poorly child that a doctor once told his mother to take him home to die. But he pulled through and went on to attend the School of Design in **Pierpoint Street**. He later founded a famous Cheltenham-based architectural decorating business, and formed in 1917 what became the Gloster Aircraft Company.

LIME AVENUE

Part of a 'tree' estate, this street was first found in a street directory in 1937, when eight homes were listed here.

Lion Row

Late nineteenth century street directories listed this name, but not **Lion Walk** of which it was said to be an offshoot, which was odd, since Lion Walk seemed to be earlier, having been first found in the health board streets list of 1872, while Lion Row was first found listed in a street directory of 1885. Late twentieth century maps reversed this, and listed Lion Walk, but not Lion Row. The distinction is academic now, since the whole

Little Angel Street before it was widened into Angel Place - WN

area behind **Lowesmoor** has been redeveloped. Lion Walk continues to exist, but in name only, now effectively as an offshoot of Lion Court. An 1896 listing for this street showed 15 homes, housing six labourers, three charwomen, two carpenters, a hawker, a cab driver, a stoker and a haulier.

The meaning of the name has not been traced. No pub of this name is known in the area, so the name seems most likely to be related to the canal, perhaps a canal wharf named for a navigation company logo or trademark, but no information on this has come to light during research for this book.

LION WALK
See **Lion Row**.

Little Angel Street

Now **Angel Place**. An ancient lane running from **Broad Street** to **The Butts**, on the site of what is now **Angel Place**.

The section between **Angel Street** and The Butts was renamed in the late eighteenth or early nineteenth century, and the remainder, from Angel Street to **Broad Street**, was renamed after demolition of the east side of this street during road widening in 1913. In 1790 wine merchant William Cary, and 'taylor' and victualler Thomas Pope were listed in the street.

By 1884 occupants included the Duke of York inn, which opened about 1820 on a site roughly where the entrance to Crowngate is now, and only closed when the area was redeveloped in the late 1960s. A few doors down was Henry Adlam's Oyster Rooms (oysters were very cheap then!), and further along was William Phillips' eating house.

There was also a stationers, wine and spirit merchants, a jeweller, a hairdresser and a baker, amongst others. At the southern end of this street, on Broad Street, was the Bell Hotel, an old coaching inn, which was demolished during the road widening.

Little Boughton Street

It ran from **Nursery Walk** to **Bransford Road**, roughly where Swinton Close is now. **Boughton Street** itself began to be developed around 1811, and this street may have been developed soon afterwards, perhaps originally as housing for workers at the adjacent nursery. There was a building application for two further cottages in 1871, and it was listed in a street directory of 1880. Unlike the mix of housing in Boughton Street, the homes here seem to have been for working families.

In 1884 around 30 homes were listed here, plus a shop near Bransford Road kept by Mrs Caroline Brook, and a pub called the Gardener's Arms. Despite the pub name, and the nearby nursery, by then only a couple of the residents were gardeners.

Almost half were labourers, though some may have been working at the nursery. Other residents were building tradesmen, a blacksmith, a miller, a commission agent, gloving workers, a seamstress and a laundress. The Gardener's Arms had opened by 1850 but it closed around 1915.

The street's fate was sealed when the council's clearance plan was drawn up in 1964, and the area has been redeveloped since.

Little Charles Street

Blockhouse. This small street ran parallel with **Charles Street**, just to the south of it, and an alleyway connected the two on the west side. It was probably created as a rear access to some of the premises in Charles Street sometime between 1840 and 1865. In 1884 it had a small number of hard-working residents, including the street's shopkeeper and blacksmith Henry Andrews at Nos. 1, 2 and 8. His neighbours were a dyer, two glove cutters, a baker, a shoemaker and a hawker. The street was demolished to make way for the **City Walls Road**.

LITTLE CHESNUT STREET

Developed at the same time as **Chesnut Street**, it was first found recorded in a building application of 1872 for six houses, and by 1879 12 houses had been applied for, though when a listing of residents appeared in a street directory in 1884 there were 27 homes, plus a pub and a shop, which may suggest that building began before building control was introduced in 1865, or that some applications have been lost. The directory named it as Middle Chesnut Street, though a map of the same year used the present name.

In addition to building, factory and gloving workers, the street had a telegraphist, a china burner, a miller and a 'hotel boots' or boot and shoe cleaner. On the corner of **Chesnut Street** was Frank Osborn's ale and porter stores, which by 1900 had become the Fir Tree pub, but had reverted to an off-licence by about 1950.

On the opposite corner in 1900 was Mrs Emily Smith's shop, and Henry Burrell, at No. 13 near **Northfield Street**, also kept a shop, as well as working as a compositor.

Little Fish Street

It ran from the end of **Fish Street**, behind St Alban's Church, to **Copenhagen Street**, but fell victim to the 1960s redevelopment of the area. Residents in 1884 included a hawker, a shoemaker, a porter, a greengrocer and a bricklayer..

LITTLE HOLYWELL HILL

First found in the health board streets list of 1872, and in a street directory of 1884, which listed four residents, a carpenter, an iron worker, a labourer and a street superintendent.

Little King Street

A vanished street near the city's **Sidbury** gate, shown on a map of 1764.

Little London in 1903 by E.A. Phipson - MAG. These cottages on Talbot Row are gone, but the timber-framed cottages, left, still exist

LITTLE LONDON

It is difficult to date development here exactly, because the cottages which earned the street its name were demolished before the Second World War, but they could have been either early nineteenth or late eighteenth century, but not much earlier, since they were apparently brick built, not timber framed. Until the 1880s this street continued south to **Chesnut Walk**, until **Tennis Walk** was created around 1884.

The name was a rustic joke, from the days when this small enclave of development, which grew up near the Talbot inn and **Paradise Row**, was in striking contrast to the rural area around it. It was probably coined by farmworkers passing regularly on the way to market, or walkers returning to 'civilization' after strolling in the rural solitude of the fields around what is now **Sansome Walk**, suggesting sarcastically that this street was getting as built up as London.

The cottages were named Talbot Row and in the late nineteenth and early twentieth century most of them had been taken over by small businesses, including a fried fish shop, a sweet shop, a bicycle repairer, a greengrocer and a barber's shop. In the 1920s, on a site now occupied by the grammar school design block, was the County Garage, and above it was the King's Hall, a popular local dance school and entertainment venue where there were Friday night dances.

A family in Little Park Street in 1926 - RS

LITTLE PARK STREET

This was once a busy street, but it suffered in a 1960s redevelopment, and is now much shorter than it once was.

It was first mentioned in 1821, with building apparently going ahead around the same time as the *Blockhouse* development, though there is little detail of what was here until later in the century. The street originally ran across what is now **Dent Close** to end at *Beaver Row*, but since redevelopment of the area in the 1960s it ends at **Lock Street**.

This was a populous street in the nineteenth century, with around 40 homes here, and four courts of housing listed off it. There were also five shops and a pub called the Park Street Tavern, to distinguish it from the Park Tavern which was in **Park Street**.

This was very much a working class community, with labourers, shoemakers, building workers, a boiler maker, a basket maker, a stoker, a drayman and a range fitter living here in 1884.

It was perhaps a sign of how hard life could be for working families at that time, that around a quarter of the homes had a woman as head of household. They included Mrs Ann Ballinger who kept the pub, midwife Mrs Mary Buckingham, nurse Mrs Matilda Hobro, dressmaker Mrs Ann Sankey and

Mrs Harriett Handy, who ran a lodging house. The Park Street Tavern had closed by 1950, and much of the street was demolished around 1962.

LITTLE SOUTHFIELD STREET

This was part of the mid nineteenth century Arboretum Pleasure Grounds, with their entrance drive on **Arboretum Road**, which were sold for redevelopment in 1866. The first building application for this street was submitted in 1878, and within two years eight homes had been applied for, including the six Victoria Cottages, a housing project put forward by Joseph Fisher of **Albany Terrace**, who was responsible for a number of small scale speculative building projects. The cottages were built and occupied by 1884, when residents included a stonemason, a harness maker, an ironmonger's assistant, a tailor, a newsagent's assistant and an upholsterer's assistant. There was also a hop porter, a coffin maker and a mail cart proprietor. Living here in 1896 was Frederick Hyde, sergeant-major of the **Southfield Street**-based Worcestershire and Warwickshire Artillery Volunteers. A hop warehouse here, later occupied by Lamb's the removals firm, was once owned by wealthy local hop merchant George Gascoyne, who lived in **Barbourne Terrace**. There has been considerable recent redevelopment here.

LIVINGSTONE STREET

This street is situated in the area at the crest of Red Hill known as Oliver's Mount, since Oliver Cromwell is said to have made his camp here during the Battle of Worcester in 1651, so that he could see over the whole city and direct his troops.

It was first recorded in a building application of 1895, seven years later than **Cromwell Crescent**, though this seems to have been developed first. It is possible that the street was named for missionary and explorer David Livingstone. This might seem odd, since Stanley's famous expedition to find him was in 1871, and he died two years later, more than 20 years before this street was first recorded, but Queen Victoria's Golden Jubilee in 1887 brought many foreign potentates to Britain, and created much public interest in this country in the British Empire and those who contributed to building it. It is also possible that a family named Livingstone were involved in the financing or development of this street, but there are no records available to show this.

The first building application for this street in 1895 was for 19 cottages and a shop. By the following year a street directory listed 10 homes, and in 1897 12 more were 'under construction', which were largely built and occupied by the following year. Residents here at that time included three firemen, three railwaymen, a labourer, a pattern maker, a gardener and a warehouseman, with Harvey Banner's shop on the corner of **Foxwell Street**. On the north side of the street were six more railwaymen, another fireman, a carpenter, a bricklayer and a file cutter. There was no further building here until the modern development of the east end of the street.

Lock Street Sunday School, demolished around 1971 - RS

LOCK STREET

This small street stands just beside the canal lock variously known as Blockhouse Lock and Foundry Lock, hence the street name. This must have been built about the same time as **Little Park Street**, which was first mentioned in 1821.

In 1884 there were 22 modest homes here, plus a shop and a Sunday school. One third of the householders were labourers, while others were china, building and gloving workers, a basket maker, a charwoman, a cab driver and a shoemaker.

On the corner of **Park Street** was greengrocer Edward Wills.

The Lock Street Sunday School was at the rear of the Zion Chapel, which was run in conjunction with the Angel Street Congregational Chapel. In 1910 Robert Hussell had a small china works at No. 21. The whole area to the rear of Park Street was redeveloped in the early 1970s.

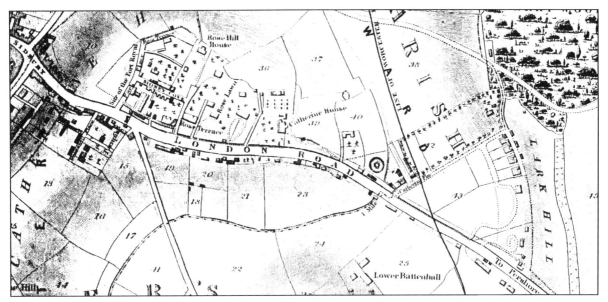

London Road in 1838, still largely surrounded by open fields

**London Road Turnpike Gate which ceased around 1870 - RS
Below, the London Road smithy and adjoining shops in 1889**

LONDON ROAD

This will have been the major approach road to the city from the south for centuries past. It seems always to have been referred to by this name in past times, though it was also called the Oxford Road in the late eighteenth century, when Worcester was a stop on the stagecoach route from Wales to that city.

This will have been the traditional approach to Worcester from the south as long ago as Anglo-Saxon times, and perhaps before, though it did not always

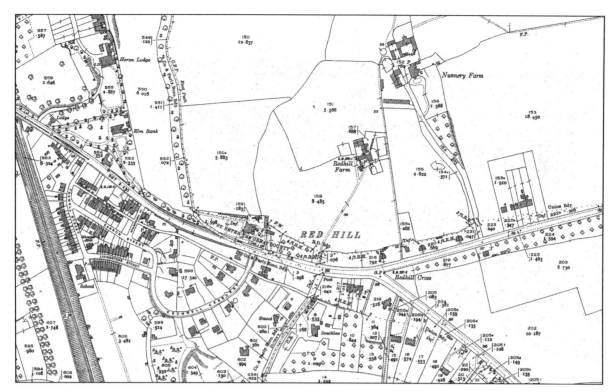

Red Hill in 1928, with ribbon development but still open fields behind

follow the same route as now. The line of the medieval road is not certain, but it probably ran in a gently curving line to the south, following roughly the line of streets running parallel with the present road. It was created in its present, straighter form as a turnpike road in the eighteenth century, cutting though part of the site of the fortifications at Fort Royal. The turnpike gate stood at the bottom of the hill, originally a joint gate with Bath Road, but it was later moved to the top, towards Mount Pleasant, a promontory with excellent views over the city, just beyond Fort Royal.

The first section of the road, leading out of Sidbury Gate, was known as Wheatsheaf Hill, from the name of an eighteenth century inn halfway up the hill, also found listed as the Old Wheatsheaf, which had closed by 1860.

The Turnpike Trust dug out the inclines here and at Red Hill, work on the latter beginning around July 1812, creating cuttings to reduce the gradients, which were previously very steep for coaches to climb, and so hazardous to descend that Gwilliam said crosses stood at the bottom of both hills until the seventeenth century, at which travellers could give thanks for their safe descent, though Hughes has regarded them as boundary markers.

When the railway came in the 1850s an embankment had to be created towards Red Hill, which has left cottages on the south side below the road level, though houses elsewhere are above the road level because of the turnpike cuttings.

A 1936 advertisement

Tradition has it that an early version of 'park and ride' existed at the Mount Pleasant, as country people left their carriages and walked into the city to avoid the toll, but the pub was not found listed until 1873, three years after the gate probably ceased to operate, though it may have existed earlier as an unnamed beer seller. The tollgate and tollhouse were demolished soon after the gate ceased to operate, and by 1918 or before the tollhouse site was occupied by the garage of one of the earliest bus companies, Marks' Blue Buses,

Heron Lodge at Lark Hill - TW

where City Motors is now. The site of the gate is also marked by Turnpike House, immediately beyond **Fort Royal Hill**.

The top section of this road took the name Red Hill from the red marl clay soil, which was especially prominent when it was dug out of the turnpike cuttings. An area to the south of the road, where **Cromwell Crescent** and **Cannon Street** are located, was referred to in past centuries as Oliver's Mount, since by tradition Oliver Cromwell stationed himself here during the Battle of Worcester in 1651, so that he could see over the battlefield and direct his troops. There was also an artillery battery nearby. In a building application of 1885, when development reached the area, it was referred to as Oliver's Mount building estate, and Red Hill Lane was shown as Oliver's Mount on a city street map of 1940.

It was in nearby Perry Wood that Cromwell met secretly with a Worcester tailor named William Guise, who alerted him to a Royalist plan for a surprise night attack on his camp. Forewarned, the Roundheads set a trap, and the Royalists suffered heavy losses. This was good for Cromwell, but unfortunate for Guise, who was discovered by the Royalists and hung from the sign of the Golden Cross inn in **Broad Street**. After the Restoration, Royalists altered the story to suggest that the Parliamentary commander had met with the devil, and sold his soul for victory in the battle.

In 1149 King Stephen laid siege to Worcester, during the war with Matilda, and built a fort on Red Hill, the remains of which could still be seen in 1820, according to local historian John Chambers, though it is questionable whether what he saw were the remains of a twelfth century fort, or of one of the Parliamentary positions from the Battle of Worcester in 1651. Public executions were carried out in this area until the early nineteenth century, and they were always referred to as being at Red Hill, though they were actually on what is now **Whittington Road**.

London Road at the Wyld's Lane junction about 1905 - RS

There will have been rural or semi-rural development on this road in past centuries, but urban development tentatively began

Historic Worcester Streets

about 1820, with fine villas at **St Catherine's Hill** and nearby Lark Hill. The finest of the Lark Hill villas is Heron Lodge, reached by a private drive just east of the railway bridge. It was said by Gwilliam to have been built by Admiral Powell, a hero of the Napoleonic wars, who commanded a captured French vessel called the Heron, and gave the name to his house. In the early years of the twentieth century, up until 1921, it was the home of William Kilbourne Kay, founder of the Kay's catalogue empire. It had been in use as offices for some time, and is currently empty. Gwilliam said that a large willow tree on a lawn beside the house was cultivated from a cutting of the tree planted at Napoleon's grave at St Helena, but it no longer seems to be there.

By 1838 spasmodic development stretched as far as the east end of Wyld's Lane, but there was virtually nothing beyond. By 1840 slightly more modest homes were being built along this road, including Catherine Place, a terrace of 10 homes near **Lark Hill Road**; Prospect Place, a terrace of seven houses near **Greenhill**, and St Mary's Terrace, a terrace of five houses, later called **Rose Terrace**. Ellen Wood lived there as a girl after moving from **Sidbury**, and other notable residents included Richard Padmore, after whom **Padmore**

John Noake

Street was named, and journalist, mayor and local historian John Noake, who didn't have a street named after him, but should have had. A number of businesses were listed here in 1840. Those probably clustered around the bottom of the hill, including cooper James Newman, schoolmistress Sarah Porritt, milliner Elizabeth Parr, earthenware dealer John Jauncey, coal dealer William Collier, coach builder and harness maker John Hadley and blacksmith Thomas Hadley.

A great deal more building took place around 1860, largely completing housing along the road, and very few building applications were recorded throughout the rest of the century. In 1884 there was fairly solid ribbon development along most of the road, though there was still much open land behind. Building continued as surrounding streets developed, and by 1890 houses were going up so fast that a new school was needed at the bottom of Red Hill. Housing was always a mix of more substantial properties taking the title 'House' or 'Villa', particularly at the lower end closer to the city, and cottages and small terraces.

In those days, though house numbering was common, almost every property also had a name. Sebright Lawn, near **Battenhall Road**, was the home in 1896 of William Temple Bourne, JP for the city and county. Elderslie, near **Camp Hill Road** was the work of architect Henry Day who designed Lindisfarne House in **Barbourne Terrace**. Each of the houses or small terraces was probably built by a different investor, and the names they chose were often redolent of their interests or the places from which they came, as was probably true of the five Pembroke Villas near **Sebright Avenue**, where cathedral organist Hugh Blair lived in 1896, and Mile End Cottage next door.

At No. 7 from the eighteenth century was The Cross Keys inn, but it and adjoining properties were replaced by a block of flats in the 1960s or 70s. Further along, on the corner of Fort Royal Hill, is a pub which was

Olympic cyclist Ernie Payne's home near Yew Tree Close - TW

probably built originally in the nineteenth century, though its name changed many times.

It was once the London Vaults, which was probably the original name, but by 1896 it had become the Ale & Porter Stores.

By the mid twentieth century it was the Fort Royal, and it had several later names including the Little Sauce Factory. The nineteenth century Sebright Arms, first found listed in 1837, recalls the family who once owned the land in this area.

At No. 1 was the former Loch Ryan Hotel, which was built about 1760 but was a private house until the twentieth century. Between 1902 and 1903 it was home to Bishop Gore, but from 1903 the

Ernie Payne at the 1908 Olympics

electric trams began running past his door, and complaining that he could not stand the noise they made, he removed to **Lansdowne Crescent**.

This road can boast some distinguished connections, aside from Ellen Wood, who achieved worldwide fame. The founder of Methodism, John Wesley, first preached in Worcester at a parish workhouse here in 1768, the location of which is unknown. And in 1884 Olympic champion Ernie Payne was born here, in a cottage which still stands at No. 221, near Yew Tree Close.

His father John was a gardener at the nearby Elm Villa, which is also still in existence. Ernie trained as a carpenter, but also became a champion cyclist, nicknamed 'the Worcester Wonder' by the national press. He won 150 races in eight years, and claimed a gold medal in the team pursuit event at the 1908 London Olympics.

The large St Martin's Church was built 1903 – 11 to replace a church in the **Cornmarket**, which was then renamed Old St Martin's to avoid confusion. Only the first 24 feet (7.3 m) of the planned southern tower were built and these now form the south entrance to the church.

LOVE'S GROVE

This name was found first on a map of 1764 as Lovesgrove, though at that time it can have existed only as a pleasant footpath across the fields behind **The Tything**, one of a number of enjoyable summer evening walks in this semi-rural area behind the affluent homes lining the main road. Historian David Whitehead suggested the name was 'a charming reference to the courting rituals of Worcester's Georgian jeuness', as well, no doubt, as a nod to the many Love's Groves, ornamented with secluded arbours and undraped classical statuary, to be found in the expensively coiffured gardens of the gentry.

Love's Grove, unnamed, on a map of 1799. By this date the Infirmary had been built, shown on the right, but this street was still just a lane surrounded by an open meadow and an arable field.

Historic Worcester Streets

At the time when this name appeared Worcester had a 'season', when the gentry would descend on the city for a few weeks of socialising at the theatre, the coffee houses, the pleasure gardens, and most importantly, at the races, so a 'gentrified' name might well be though suitable for a lane near Pitchcroft.

This semi-rural idyll didn't last long however. In 1809 the lane was very much brought down to earth when building began, immediately beside its southern end, on the new county prison in **Castle Street**, which opened in 1813. In 1820 permission was given for the pathway to be widened and improved into a road, to give access to the new housing development at **Britannia Square**, and what had begun as an eighteenth century lovers' lane became just another nineteenth century access road.

The street did not end at **Moor Street** then, but continued on to *Spring Gardens*. By the end of the 1820s development had begun around the northern end, near **The Tything**, and by 1838 it had been intensively developed as far as Moor Street, with spasmodic building throughout the length of the eastern side of the road. By 1884 the county police had a station on the west side of the street, just behind the Moor Street properties, The cramped development near Spring Gardens was in marked contrast to the properties at the southern end of the street, which were larger with generous gardens. There were almost 30 homes here then. Residents included three travelling drapers, living side-by-side at the north end, an ostler, a police sergeant, several building tradesmen, a brushmaker, a coffin maker, a seamstress, a glover, an engine driver and a groom. Thomas Saunders, schoolmaster at the prison, also lived here, as did builder James Henry Beard, and Mrs Charlotte Ann Alderton, whose occupation was monthly nurse.

On the corner of Spring Gardens was a shop kept by Mrs E.A. Bradley, and nearby was the Carpenter's Arms pub, which was first listed in 1873 and closed around 1955. On the corner of Castle Street in 1910 was the shop of baker, confectioner and beer seller Frederick Jones. By 1937 furniture maker G.T. Rackstraw was here. Sometime after the prison closed in 1922 part of the site was used for a 'labour exchange' on the west side of the Castle Street junction. The street was largely cleared and in the 1960s was shortened, when Spring Gardens was cleared. There are still two of the 1820s or 30s houses here at the north end of the street, but there is nothing else of any age.

General Lowell - CB

LOWELL STREET

This street was part of the mid nineteenth century Arboretum Pleasure Grounds, with their entrance drive on **Arboretum Road**, which were sold for redevelopment in 1866. Plots off **Sansome Walk** sold fairly quickly, but this and other streets at the rear of the estate did not begin to create interest until the housing boom of the mid 1880s, when this street and **Washington Street** began to be developed within a few years of each other.

These two streets seem likely to have been named for an heroic young American general, Charles Russell Lowell, who was killed in 1864, during the American Civil War, while defending the city of Washington. He was born in Boston, Massachusetts, and had no direct connection with Worcester, but he was a descendant of the Russell family of Worcester, who held estates at Strensham and Great Witley in the sixteenth and seventeenth centuries, and it seems likely that his English relatives had a role in developing and naming these streets.

It is clear that the English side of the family were well aware of their American cousins, since the Worcestershire archives have an exchange of letters about family history with the general's uncle, the American poet James Russell Lowell.

The first record of this street was a building application for nine houses here and in **Southfield Street** in 1886, and between 1889 and 1894 there were four applications for 29 homes here. All of them were submitted by builder William Shakespeare, who started out in business as one half of Goodwin & Shakespeare, painters and decorators of No. 7 **Lowesmoor**. Between 1885 and 1900 he submitted more than 30 building applications for well over 100 homes in the city, including some in **Barry Street**. However, in this street by 1896 there were 45 houses, so either some homes were not applied for, or some applications have gone missing. On the west side at that date were eight houses which had just been completed but not yet occupied, plus the seven West Cottages and four Floral cottages. The street consisted entirely of homes for working families. Residents at that time included building workers, glovers, labourers, seamstresses, foundrymen, an engine driver, a porter, a coach painter, a blacksmith, an insurance agent and a shoemaker. By 1910 the street was complete, with 51 homes listed.

LOWER CHESNUT STREET

A continuation of **Chesnut Street**, first found in a building application of 1879, and then as now, it began where the road widens. Up to 1882 10 houses had been applied for, but when the first full street directory listing of residents appeared in 1884 there appeared to be more than 60 homes here, so perhaps construction commenced before building control began in 1865, or perhaps building applications have been lost. The north side seems to be older, since it has terraces of cottages with quaint names such as Woodland Cottages, Rose Cottages, Exbury Cottages and Sansome Fields Terrace, all no doubt built by different developers. Residents then included labourers, iron workers, fitters, building workers, factory workers, a baker, a tailor, a prison warder and a range fitter. At the west end, on the Chesnut Street corner, was Martin Samuels' shop.

Lower Street

It was on the west side of **Hill Street**, which formerly crossed **Tallow Hill** and joined **Cromwell Street**. No building applications were found for this street, except one of 1872 for a cider house, so it must have been built prior to 1865. It was still on city street maps in the 1960s, but was then demolished along with the northern part of Hill Street, and after many years as a car park, a retail park now stands on the site.

Lower Street Walk

A footway linking *Lower Street* with **Tallow Hill**. It was first found on the health board streets list of 1872, but was not listed in a street directory until 1910, and no housing was listed. It must have been cleared at the same time as *Lower Street*.

LOWESMOOR

This street was outside the city walls, but for many centuries it could have been part of an important route into the city, since the Romans were believed to use **Rainbow Hill** and **Astwod Road** as the route to their fort at Droitwich.

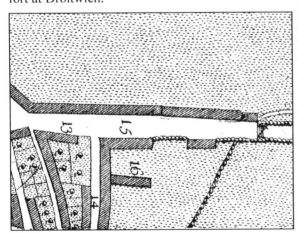

Lowesmoor in 1741, with some ribbon development up to the Turnpike Gate, but otherwise surrounded by open land

It must have been established on better drained ground, since the land stretching south from here would have been boggy moorland in the valley of the Frog Brook, which ran around Worcester to the east, and into the Severn near **Severn Street**. This accounts for the name, since *moor* had much the same meaning in Anglo-Saxon as it does now, and though *lowe* had various meanings in old languages, they most often had to do with water, suggesting the name meant wet or boggy moor. There were drainage ditches however, and a map of 1610 showed the land being ploughed and crops growing. We have no way of knowing how accurate that is, but it is possible that there were agricultural workers living in this area over the centuries.

Some urban expansion outside the city wall must have begun in the medieval period, and was shown on Speede's 1610 map as having spread from St Martin's Gate alongside the city wall and a little way along what is now this street, but all that development will have been swept away by the Royalists in the 1640s, to deny cover to attacking Parliamentary troops, and there is no sign of it on a map of the city's defences of 1651, though that is a later conjectural map. Development must have begun again not too long after the Restoration, aided by the slighting of the city walls, and a map of 1741 shows it stretching along this street as far as it did before the war.

Just before **Silver Street** was the Anabaptist's Meeting House, and just beyond it was Moore's 'Blew Coat Hospital', a charity set up about 1650 to educate 10 poor boys of St Martin's parish, who wore blue uniforms. The boys attended what became Worcester Royal Grammar School, then at St Swithin's, and lived at the

Lowesmoor in 1838, after the opening of the canal.

Below, an old cottage at 22 Lowesmoor, painted by E.A. Phipson in 1904, and later demolished - MAG

hospital with a governor. A little further on, a footpath on the right led to a large bowling green. Aside from the ribbon development on this road at the time, there was an uninterrupted vista across Blockhouse Fields to the east and Sansome Fields to the west. A street directory of 1790 lists a few 'Lowesmore' residents, including carpenter Richard Redding, glover Samuel Hardwicke, gloving firm Knapp & Lea, horse dealer Thomas Adams and R. Tasker who was described as 'governor of workhouses'. An 1851 guide to the city noted that a cattle market had formerly been held here. At the start of the nineteenth century much of this area was still open land, but with the brook diverted into the Worcester and Birmingham Canal from 1815, and the creation of Lowesmoor Wharf, the area increasingly became the focus of the industrial heart of Worcester. The port here was originally intended to be the largest canal wharf in Worcester, but there was a late change of plan, and two larger canal basins were cut at Diglis instead. Had the original plan gone ahead it would have required the use of much more of the pleasant parkland of Sansome Fields behind this street, though that land was built on anyway from the 1860s.

Despite downsizing of the development, the canal wharf drew a good deal of industry here. Coalyards, storehouses, granaries and mills soon sprang up around the wharf. Coal shipped from the Black Country accounted for a great deal of the shipping, but there were also raw materials for the new engineering plants to the south of this street, which had no other ready means of cheap transportation available until the coming of the railway in the 1850s. By 1840 there were six water carriers based here, and about 45 departures each week. There was so much traffic that there was an official Portmaster of the Port of Lowesmoor until the 1880s.

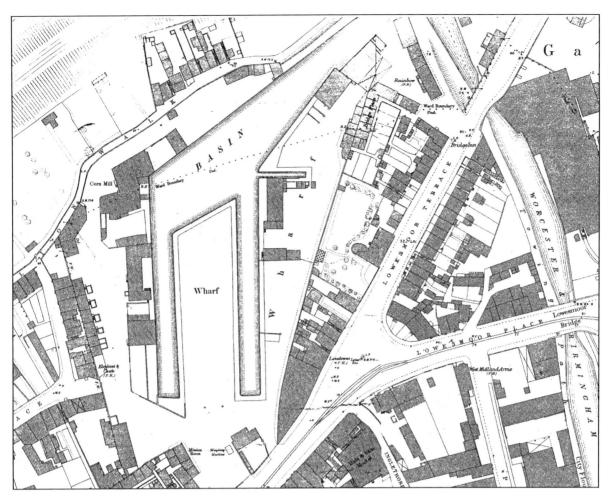

The Lowesmoor Basin in 1884, also showing Lowesmoor Terrace and Lowesmoor Place

This commerce hub must have created many jobs, and inns and commercial hotels were built to house visiting businessmen and supply the needs of workers, while mission halls cared for the spiritual needs of this busy community – the Wesleyans established a Lowesmoor Mission chapel inside the wharf gates as early as 1823. The Elim Pentecostal Church was built in the 1840s, and there was also a Countess of Huntingdon's chapel, apparently an offshoot of the ***Birdport*** chapel, opposite the wharf gates, which is still standing, though it hasn't been a chapel for many years.

By 1840 around 30 businesses had premises on the wharf, 18 of which were coal dealers. Coal was vital, not just to supply the hearths of householders, but to fuel industry. The Lowesmoor of that time was a thriving, closely-packed community, whose business residents included plumbers, coal dealers, a tailor, glovers, a straw hat maker, a timber dealer, a subscription girls' school, a cooper, a smith, a cabinet maker, a milkman, cheese factor and shoemaker Thomas Pugh and surgeon Leonard Ledbrook. All this industry and commerce came at a cost to Lowesmoor residents however. A health report of 1849 said the area was unpaved and nearly impassable in wet weather. Sewers were ineffective and it was 'abounding in filth and disease', with high levels of infectious diseases such as smallpox and typhus.

Tavern concert rooms grew into music halls in the 1850s. The two main music halls in the city were both in the Lowesmoor area, the Alhambra and the Worcester New Concert Hall, and another was in existence by 1851 in the **Cornmarket,** in what was later called the Public Hall. The Alhambra, run by the de Frece family, was in a wooden building midway between the wharf gates and **Rainbow Hill** canal bridge. It was listed as early as 1860, and by 1863 it had a resident company of performers.

The New Concert Hall, still standing just east of the wharf gates, was a much more sophisticated affair. The Navigation inn, a venue for local inquests, had long stood on the site, kept for more than 25 years by John Hill. In 1869 he took a partner and they demolished the inn, quickly building a concert hall with a curiously pointed west end, like the prow of a ship, and opening it in August of that year.

It was immediately popular, said to be filled every night 'almost to suffocation'. For a few months the two houses fought for audiences, desperate to book the best acts, but it was an uneven struggle, and the Alhambra

WORCESTER CONCERT HALL, LOWESMOOR.

Mr. JOHN HILL, Proprietor.

OPEN EVERY EVENING.

THE FASHIONABLE LOUNGE OF THE CITY.

Large & Talented Company of Artistes.

ALL THE STARS & NOVELTIES OF THE DAY.

CONCERT, BALLET,

BURLESQUE, AND PANTOMIME.

A CONSTANT CHANGE OF ARTISTES EVERY WEEK.

FULL ORCHESTRA.

OPEN EVERY EVENING AT HALF-PAST SEVEN, COMMENCING AT EIGHT.

Refreshments and Wines of the best quality

AT MODERATE PRICES.

Season Tickets for the Stalls (not transferable) issued at ONE GUINEA each, to be had on application at the Hall.

1869 advertisements for Lowesmoor's rival music halls the Worcester Concert Hall and the Alhambra

ALHAMBRA MUSIC HALL, LOWESMOOR, WORCESTER.

Messrs. DE FRECE, Proprietors.

OPEN EVERY EVENING.

THE FASHIONABLE LOUNGE OF THE CITY.

LARGE AND TALENTED COMPANY OF ARTISTES.

ALL THE STARS & NOVELTIES OF THE DAY.

CONCERT, BALLET, BURLESQUE, AND PANTOMIME.

A CONSTANT CHANGE OF ARTISTES EVERY WEEK.

FULL ORCHESTRA.

MUSICAL DIRECTOR .... MR. H. BALL.
PIANIST .... HERR JULES BENJAMIN.
CHAIRMAN .... MR. J. F. GARSIDE.
SECRETARY .... MR. G. J. SOMERS.

OPEN EVERY EVENING AT SEVEN, COMMENCING AT HALF-PAST.
Refreshments and Wines of the best quality at Moderate Prices.

Admission :—Stalls, 1s. ; Body of the Hall, 6d. ; Gallery, 3d. ; Private Box, 1s. 6d.

Season Tickets for the Stalls (not transferable) issued, available for three months, at 20s. each, to be had on application at the Hall.

closed just before Christmas 1869. For a time the building was used for a circus, but the site was subsequently redeveloped for housing.

Music Hall elsewhere went on into the early twentieth century, but not here. By 1880 the canal wharf had suffered greatly by competition from the railways. By 1884 there was just one water carrier left at the wharf, and four coal dealers. The focus of commerce had moved east, following the railway, and Lowesmoor's great days were over. The New Concert Hall closed its doors for the last time in 1880.

In 1881 the building was taken over by the Salvation Army as its Citadel, until their new building was opened in **The Trinity** in 1987.

Vesta Tilley, one of the most famous artistes of the music hall era, who was born in **Beaver Row** off **Wyld's Lane** in 1864, was said to have performed at both halls in her early days, which is just about possible, since she is supposed to have begun performing before the age of five.

In the 1890s she married William de Frece.

The street had many more pubs, totalling 11 based on directories, 1884 maps and Gwilliam's listings. The first building at the west end of the street was a pub, the Union inn, which at one time had public readings of the newspapers of the day by Mr J. Child, which was useful at a time when many working men would not have been able to read. Across the road, on the corner of **Sansome Street**, was the Old Falcon Inn. Both pubs were open by around 1820, and both fell victim to the **City Walls Road**, closing around 1970. The site of the Union is now under the wide road junction. On the north side of the street were the Boat, the Black Horse, the Alma, and beyond the Navigation was the Lansdowne. Apart from the Alma, which was first listed in 1873, all the others seem to have been early nineteenth century. Most of them closed sometime between 1950 and 1970, though the Lansdowne had gone by 1930.

On the south side of the street, beyond the Union, were the Crown & Anchor, on the corner of Silver Street, the Turk's Head and the Swan, either side the entrance to the vinegar works, more recently an industrial estate, and now a retail estate. The last of these closed by 1930, and the first two around 1950. There was also the Dove, listed by Gwilliam and said to have closed by 1851, though its location has not been determined. The street was shortened at the west end in the 1970s by the **City Walls Road**.

Numbers 13-15 are thought to be eighteenth century but are on the site of ancient buildings, whose history has been traced back for some centuries. There was a house here during the Civil War, owned by Christopher Woodward, but it was burnt down in 1645 to deny cover to attacking Parliamentary forces. In 1691 the land was leased by Edward Trovell, a relative of the Woodwards, who built the present two houses, each having a coach entrance and a courtyard at the rear. For almost two centuries the site served as a glove factory. For much of the twentieth century these houses were home to printers, including G.T. Cheshire from 1959 to 1993. Since 2005 the houses have been owned by the Worcester Municipal Charities, which spent £1m on refurbishing them, and researched their history.

LOWESMOOR PLACE

This extension of **Lowesmoor**, running from the end of that street to the canal bridge at the bottom of **Tolladine Road**, probably came into existence after the canal opened in 1815. The most likely explanation for the name is that there was a terrace of houses in the area with this name, built by or before 1815, which gave their name to the street, though the nearest to this, Bridge Place, is in **Lowesmoor Terrace**. There was no sign of any building here on a map of 1838. The name was first found on the health board streets list of 1872, and in a street directory in the following year. In 1882 a building application was submitted for a house for stonemason John Rouse, who was heavily involved in late nineteenth century housing development in the city. In 1884 there seem to have been about 15 modest homes here for manual workers, perhaps mostly on the north side of the street, but this was very much a mixed area which also had two coffee houses, the City Temperance Commercial Hotel, several businesses and surgeon Samuel Coombs at Lowesmoor Villa facing Lowesmoor, where there was a doctor's surgery until the 1980s or 90s. The West Midland Arms, on the corner of **Padmore Street**, was first listed in 1873 and still exists. The modern road scheme and redevelopment have decimated this street in modern times.

LOWESMOOR TERRACE

This extension of **Lowesmoor**, running from the end of that street to the canal bridge at the bottom of **Rainbow Hill**, probably came into existence after the canal opened in 1815. The most likely explanation for the name is that there was a terrace of houses here with this name, built by or before 1815, which gave their name to the street, though they have not been found. There was certainly building here in the early nineteenth century, shown on a map of 1829, and this name was recorded in an 1840 street directory. In 1884 there were around 35 modest homes here. Labourer was the most common occupation of residents, though there were also builders, boatmen, gardeners, clothing workers, an upholsterer and a midwife. There were also two pubs near the canal, the Bridge inn, which was first listed in 1873, but moved down the road around 1950, and the Rainbow, around the corner on the canalside, also first listed in 1873, though it had closed by 1900. The canalside and this street have largely been redeveloped in modern times.

LYTTELTON STREET

The Lyttelton family of Hagley Hall have been at Hagley since the early sixteenth century. The family member after whom this street must have been named was a leading figure in the city and county for almost 40 years. He was George William, fourth Baron Lyttelton, born in London in 1817 and educated at Eton and Oxford. He succeeded to the title in 1837, and two years later was appointed Lord Lieutenant of Worcester City and Worcestershire, and remained so until his death in 1876.

In 1846 he was Under Secretary for the Colonies, and he subsequently helped the Anglican colonisation of the Christchurch area of New Zealand, where the port city of Lyttelton is named for him. At home he is credited with founding the Worcestershire Cricket Club in 1865. He married twice and had 15 children, one of whom was headmaster of Eton, while another was a noted wicketkeeper and tennis champion.

The street was first recorded in 1884 when there were two building applications for six houses, submitted by Thomas Jevons of **Sandys Road**, who had submitted a number of applications to build new homes around that area. A map of that date showed that the land had been marked out as a potential new road, but there was no development on or around it at that time. It was first listed in a street directory in 1896, by which time

Fourth Baron Lyttelton in 1871, a caricature from Vanity Fair

there had been a further seven applications by four different developers for 26 more houses, and almost 20 had been built. In 1896 on the west side there were four homes in Levant Terrace, housing a builder, a painter and two carpenters, and two Wisteria Villas, one of which was home to a hop factor's clerk. On the opposite side there were three Parkfield Villas, whose residents included a bricklayer and a horsehair drawer, and 10 homes in Lyttelton Terrace housing several clerks and carpenters, a signalman, a leather dresser, a county court bailiff and a grocer's assistant. By 1905 32 homes had been built to complete the street.

Mall, The

Found in a 1790 directory, this name, or nickname, was given in the eighteenth century to **Foregate Street**, when it was a fashionable city promenade. The name was also given to a fine avenue of trees in nearby Sansome Fields, which ran from **Sansome Place** to what is now **Tennis Walk**, and also to a house next door to Britannia House, the former Alice Ottley School, occupied in the mid 1880s by Richard Evans Barnett, JP.

MALVERN ROAD

The historic route from **St John's** to Malvern, first mentioned in court rolls of the fourteenth century. The **Bromwich Road** is now the direct route from the city to Malvern, but this will doubtless have been the main route for many centuries. This would then have been a rural area, and urban development didn't start here until the nineteenth century.

The land on which this road stands once belonged to the manor of Wick, or Hardwick, given to the bishops of Worcester by Offa of Mercia around 790. The monks at Worcester claimed it had been granted to them by King Edgar between 961 and 975, but there is no proof that they actually did possess it until 1236, and the bishops obviously retained some rights here. The manor was a favourite with Godfrey Giffard, bishop from 1268 to 1302, who built a manor house here. He spent much time at the manor of Wick, though later bishops preferred the mansion at Hartlebury, which he also built. At the time that the parish of St John's was established in 1372, the heart of the area was part of the manor of Hardwick.

After the Dissolution the manor of Wick came into the hands of the Bromley family of Holt. According to Noake, the Hardwick manor house was burnt down during the Civil War, and so the replacement was presumably a seventeenth century building, perhaps on the same site, though there is no confirmation of this. The site of the later house has been identified as that now occupied by **Abbey Road**.

In 1746 Lower Wick was sold to the Vernons of Hanbury, who built themselves a house called Vernon Hall on this road, roughly opposite where **Hanbury Park Road** is now, which was demolished after 1884. The manor was held first by Thomas Vernon, who had succeeded to the Vernon estate at the age of 12. He took a prominent part in the establishment of John Wall's china manufactory at **Warmestry Slip** in 1751, and served as an MP. The Vernons retained Lower Wick for more than 150 years, but in the early twentieth century the estate was sold, mainly said Gwilliam, to the tenant farmers who held the remaining land. After the Vernons' mansion was demolished a house on the opposite side of the road took the name Vernon Manor, and was home in 1936 to Christopher Whitehead JP, after whom the 1930s secondary school in the road was named.

The Hardwick manor house, known as the Great House, has been identified by city council experts as standing where **Abbey Road** is now. Photographs taken in 1902 show it to have been timber framed with wattle and daub infill. Though it presumably wasn't home to the lord of the manor after 1746, it continued in use, mostly as a tannery. The Allies family seem to have held it in the late eighteenth and the first half of the nineteenth century, and by 1884 it was held by the Badgery family, but the building was empty by 1896, and it was derelict by 1904, when it was bought by the city and demolished so that the site could be redeveloped.

There is some confusion between Hardwick Manor and another manor house, which stood at Lower Wick, near what had once been the church for this area.

The chapel of St Oswald, the remains of which are behind the Manor Farm public house, is believed to have been built about 1165, but the area became deserted after the population was decimated by the Black Death in the 1340s, and the chapel was disused from 1371. It has since served as a farm building, and only a few courses of red sandstone remain from the original chapel. The manor house remained however, until

The first few courses of stonework of this farm building at Bennett's Farm remain from St Oswald's Chapel

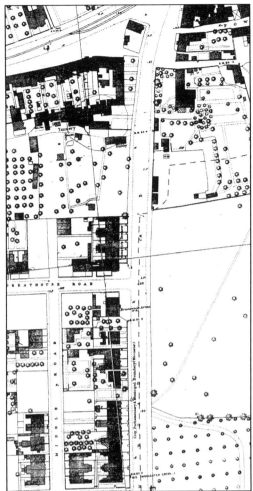

Malvern Road near St John's in 1884

probably the second half of the nineteenth century, and the fish ponds serving the manor house still exist. What exactly this manor house was is something of a mystery, but it was probably more in the nature of a farm, perhaps built by a tenant letting part of the manor estate. There seem to have been at least two successive buildings here, and the present Manor Farm, at Bennett's Dairies, is presumably the third.

In the eighteenth and nineteenth centuries there was a turnpike toll gate by the junction with **Bransford Road**. The gate ceased to operate around 1870 and in 1884 police sergeant Thomas Tolley was living in the toll house, which has since been demolished. In the early nineteenth century this was still very much a rural area once **St John's** was left behind. A map of 1838 showed an unbroken vista of meadows and orchards stretching out to either side of the road, broken only by Pitmaston House, which was built in the early nineteenth century. Much of this land was being worked by Smith's Nurseries, off Bransford Road, or the many other market gardeners around St John's. Inevitably development spread from the **St John's** end of the road, with building beginning in the 1850s or early 1860s. A building application for a public house was submitted in 1868, and the Brunswick Arms was probably completed by 1870. The Brunswick arms were the arms of the queen, who was a member of the House of Brunswick. A nearby terrace of homes called Brunswick Terrace, near the junction with Bransford Road, must have been built a few years earlier and the pub presumably took its name from them. **Bedwardine Road** and **Great House Road** went ahead either just before or soon afterwards.

By the 1880s a great deal of development had gone on in and around this road as far as **Pitmaston Road**, though there was still virtually nothing beyond. In 1884 there were around 60 homes here, varying from modest cottages for labourers and other manual workers, to substantial houses for the well-off, with the occasional row of villas for white-collar workers. On Brunswick Terrace at that time was a carrier, a commercial traveller, a law clerk, a clerk in the probate court and a china decorator. At London House on the corner of Great House Road was Thomas Monk's shop.

At the other end of the road, near Powick Mill, were the nine Mill Cottages, which were home to four labourers, three waggoners, a china grinder and a water bailiff. Nearby at Sherwood House was Maj-Gen Edward Atlay, and not far away at The Laurels was John Stallard jnr, a leading city property developer in the late nineteenth century. At the junction with St John's, on the east side of the road, was Sydney House where William Henry Waldron was a dealer in musical instruments. By 1900 development was going ahead at the Vernon Park estate, and by the end of the 1920s much of the building on this road had been completed on the east, and on the west as far as Pitmaston Road, though there was much open land behind most of the properties. The Hanbury Park development went ahead on the west side in the 1930s.

Wick Fields, near the old Powick Bridge, was the site of the first engagement in the seventeenth century Civil War, when in 1642 detachments of troopers from either side accidentally happened upon each other here, and a short but fierce fight ensued, in which more than 50 men were killed. There was also an attempt by Parliamentary forces to cross the old bridge in the 1651 Battle of Worcester, though part of the bridge was taken down to try to prevent it. Around 5,000 men from both sides died in the fighting here, and are believed to be buried in a mass grave in this area. The new bridge was built in 1837.

The best-known building on this road is Pitmaston House, a 'Strawberry Hill Gothic' mansion concealed behind its massive protective wall. The name Pitmaston is Anglo-Saxon, and is assumed to be a very common type of name from that period, showing early ownership of a farm here, ie. Pitmas of Pitma's Farm, though that personal name isn't known to Anglo-Saxon scholars. The house was built in the early nineteenth century by a nationally known horticulturalist named John Williams, who was famed for his development of varieties of potatoes and pears, including one called Pitmaston Duchess. He was very active in city and county affairs, and presented a new organ to St John's church in 1841.

Above, Malvern Road about 1900 - RS

Below, Malvern and Bromwich Roads in 1928

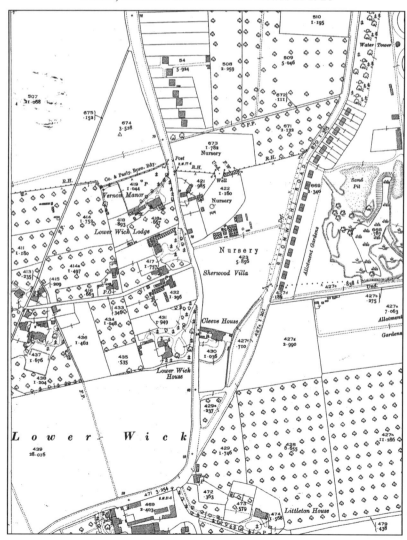

Like many old-school Tories of the time, he needlessly feared that the Reform Act of 1832, which slightly extended the franchise, would usher in an era of radical mob terror, such as had been seen during the French Revolution, and he set workmen to building a tall, forbidding, grey wall to protect his house from the mob violence which never came. It remains a striking feature of this road, and according to Gwilliam, for years afterwards passing coach drivers delighted in telling passengers the story of why it had been built.

The next long-term occupant, after Mr Williams died in 1853, was Henry Willis, founder of Cinderella shoes, based in **Sidbury** and later in **Watery Lane**. After the Second World War the gardens were used for 'rural science' lessons by the pupils of Christopher Whitehead School, and a number of John Williams' original trees were still growing here at that time. The local primary school is now to be found here.

The mock-Gothic tower beside the house was once a well-known local landmark, but it was demolished in the late 1940s.

Historic Worcester Streets

A leading nineteenth century children's author once lived at the Lower Wick end of this road. Mary Martha Sherwood, who is remembered by **Sherwood Lane**, was born in 1775, the daughter of a north Worcestershire vicar. She spent eleven years in India with her soldier husband, and when they returned in 1816 she opened a girls' boarding school here, presumably at what became known as Sherwood House, beside the Teme.

She had already written many stories, and it has been claimed that in eight years at Lower Wick she wrote eighty books! As many as 100 editions of some of her books were published all over the world throughout the nineteenth century, no doubt making her the top-selling children's author of the century. She retired to Middlesex late in life.

The first corporation power station in the country opened in 1894 at Powick Mills, by the old bridge. It had an experimental steam and hydro-electric power design said to be the first of its kind. By 1900 it supplied power to light six central streets, and the homes of 502 subscribers. However more power was needed for the electrification of the tram system, which began operating in 1903, and a larger power station was built off **Tybridge Street**. This site continued to generate electricity for more than half a century, but an upgrade of the national network was planned in 1949, and Powick Mills power station closed in 1950.

The road's secondary school opened in the 1930s and was named after long-serving city councillor Christopher Whitehead.

Christopher Whitehead-TW

MANOR ROAD

Named for the manor of Lower Wick, bought by the Vernon family in the eighteenth century (see **Malvern Road**). This road was first found in a street directory in 1937, when there were 12 homes here.

MAPLE AVENUE

Part of a 'tree' estate between **Tolladine Road** and **Tunnel Hill**, this street was first found in a street directory in 1937, when there were 44 homes here.

MARLBOROUGH STREET

Part of the Oliver's Mount estate off **London Road**. No building records have been found to give a clue to the identity of the person who developed this street or chose this name for it, or their reasons for doing so. An 1896 street directory listing for the street shows the only house here, Beaconsfield Lodge, which must have been built sometime after 1884. Rate collector William Hodges was listed there from 1896 to 1932

MARTLEY ROAD

This will have long existed as a lane leading to Martley, and was first shown in a street directory of 1880, but development was slow to reach here. An 1896 street directory listed only miller John Smith and labourer Charles Calder at Henwick Mill, just to the north of the road beside the Laugherne Brook, on a site which has since been redeveloped, and was most recently a plant hire depot. Nearby was Laugherne Farm, farmed in

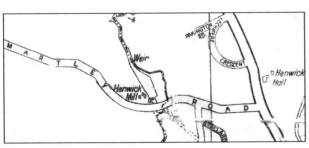

Site of Henwick Mill from a 1939 street plan - HC

1905 by Mrs James Best, who also had the house Temple Laugherne. At that date a directory also listed two Brook Cottages, housing an iron turner and a labourer, and in 1910 Laugherne Bank was home to doctor Archibald Weir. Further development had to wait until the late 1920s or 30s, and by 1940 there were around 15 properties, and a substantial crescent development to the south of them, on Farm Road and **Stallard Road**. Much more development has taken place since then to the north of the road.

MAUND STREET

There were a number of members of the Maund family around the city, most notably a local solicitor, Arthur Arrowsmith Maund. He was a city council member for the Claines ward, Under Sheriff of the city in 1896 and Sheriff in 1901, and sat on the Streets Committee. He was a partner in Maund & Coombs, which had an

A.A. Maund as High Sheriff of Worcester in 1901 - TW

office at 6 **Pierpoint Street**, and he lived at Cremyll, No. 92 **London Road**, moving to Rosslyn Villa, at No. 60 in 1896.

This street existed by 1884 or before, when it was shown unnamed on a map, though no doubt not as a made road. The gardens of homes in **Farley Street** butted onto the south side of the street, and the north side was then open land, except for a small terrace of cottages at the east end, which in 1896 were occupied by a brewer, a labourer and a gas fitter. A small amount of further development took place at the west end of the street in the 1920s, but by the 1940s most of the land to the north was still open, and was not built on until the 1970s or 80s. A shop on the corner of **Comer Gardens** has long since been converted into a house.

MAYFIELD AVENUE

No records have been found of when development of this street was begun. It was not found listed in a street directory until 1937, but it was clearly complete on a map of 1928. It will have taken its name from Mayfield Lodge or House (see **Mayfield Road**), home in the late Victorian period to David Wilson Barker, after whose brick works **Barker Street** will have been named.

MAYFIELD ROAD

Like **Belmont Street** and **Gillam Street**, this road had seen considerable development before 1884. It must have taken its name from Mayfield Lodge, a large house which once stood in its own grounds at the north end of the street. This was one of the streets which were steadily building over the fields of Merriman's Hill Farm, which ceased to be listed by 1896, though it was still here in 1884, beside what was then the west end of **Green Lane**, opposite the end of this road, with Alfred Allen as the farmer. At that time there were more than 50 homes in the road, ranging from substantial homes in their own grounds to modest cottages.

The whole development was referred as Mayfield Road on a map of that date, but was split between 'Mayfield Street' and 'Lower Mayfield Road' in a street directory of the same year. At Mayfield Lodge, or House, lived hop merchant Henry James Firkins. There was also a house called Mount Pleasant, and a Merriman's Hill Cottage. All of these, with the farm, were grouped around the end of Green Lane and must have pre-dated this road. The homes that had been newly built were modest cottages housing working families whose breadwinners were carpenters, labourers, metal workers, gardeners, railwaymen and other manual workers, with the occasional clerk or print worker. All the cottages had gardens, but they were not generous and a good sized area on the west side in the centre of the street was given over to allotment gardens.

Building records do not show who was responsible for the first phase of the development here, since they do not exist until the mid 1890s. Between 1894 and 1903 there were six mostly small-scale building applications by various investors for a total of 15 more homes. Proceeding steadily in this way, the road was still far from complete at the end of the 1920s, and infill development continued until quite recently.

A business based in McIntyre Road in 1898

McINTYRE ROAD

This road was presumably named for 1880s local MP Aeneas John McIntyre, a Scottish-born QC who as far as is known had no links to the city, other than representing its citizens in Parliament at the time when this road was being developed. Whether his name was used because he was personally involved in this development, or for some other reason, is not known. The road was part of the development spreading steadily north from **Happy Land**, onto the fields of Ivy House Farm, beside the **Comer Road/Laugherne Road** junction.

The land was divided into plots for sale, and by 1884 there were more than 30 homes here, with four more empty and probably newly built. Development had begun at the Comer Road end and progressed as far as **Buck Street** on the south, and just beyond on the north, but there were still vacant plots for around a dozen more properties between the existing houses, and beyond where development had reached there was open land on both sides of the road.

These homes were a mix of cottages and villas, all with generous gardens. They were clearly built by a number of different small investors, who put up a house or terraces of two or three homes for rent, and gave them names such as Holly Cottages, Albany Terrace, Prospect Villas, Southend House, Blenheim Cottage, Lyndhurst Villas, Sandhurst Villas and Appleby Cottage. At the oddly named Plunger Villa, opposite Buck Street in 1884, lived greyhound trainer Thomas Patrick. Not surprisingly, the name of that villa seems to have been changed within a few years!

Other residents at that time were mainly building tradesmen or shop assistants, but there were also some clerks, a tailor, a china painter, a miller, a gardener, a glover and a nurse.

The pattern of fairly rapid but small-scale development continued, with 24 applications from various small investors to build a total of 56 homes lodged up to 1899. In 1896 there were 74 homes listed, three empty so perhaps newly built. At that date Thomas Powell, caretaker of St John's Cemetery, was living at Cemetery Lodge at the end of this street.

By 1905 nearly all the building applied for had taken place, with 92 homes in existence and two more being built. Two professional cricketers then lived in the street; John Keene at one of the Fernwood Villas, and George Wilson at Laurel Villas. Thomas Attwell then had a shop on one corner of Buck Street, and on the other corner, at one of the Fernwood Villas, was John Price's grocery shop and off-licence, which had opened about 1902.

Meadow Row
Blockhouse. This name is given in a street directory of 1840, but there is no further trace of it. It was presumably a street planned for the meadow north of **Charles Street**, shown on a map of 1824, possibly **Providence Street** or **Blockhouse Street**.

MEALCHEAPEN STREET
This is that rare thing, a city centre street which has not changed its name over the centuries, at least not much, and unlike many city centre streets it was not widened in the nineteenth century. This street must have been on land held by the priory, which built St Swithin's Church in the twelfth century. Building plots were laid out on what was open land in the thirteenth century to create the street, which also then included what is now **St Swithin's Street**. The Early English name was Melchypn Strete, but it did not appear until the fourteenth century. St Swithin's Street acquired a separate name in the sixteenth century, and by 1764 this street had acquired its modern name, albeit with the variant Oatmeal-market. All kinds of flour and meal were sold at the market here. Cheap or ceap wasn't necessarily a reference to the price, it was the Old English word for a market.

This street was home to some of the leading families in the city in the fifteenth century and before, and there was considerable rebuilding at that time. Wealthy clothiers the Berkeleys were here, who founded Berkeley's Hospital in **The Foregate**, and probably the Nashs before they moved to **New Street**. By the sixteenth and seventeenth centuries these families were moving further afield, and the street thrived because of its proximity to the commercial heart of the city at the **Cornmarket**, with retail premises and several large inns.

The Red Lyon inn was mentioned in the Journal around 1714, and was for sale around 1764, when according to the Journal it was "a large well-accustomed (busy) inn". A listing of the street's occupants in 1790 gives a vivid picture of the business community here at that time. There were three hatters, two grocers, two glovers, two shoemakers, two saddlers, a barber, a brasier, a breeches maker, a florist, a hop merchant, a milliner, a patten maker, a pawnbroker and a 'toyman' or hardware store. Sheriff's officer George Wall was based here, as was the office of the Under Sheriff of the city. The post office was here, and the Reindeer inn.

The inn was by the entrance to what is now the Reindeer Court shopping arcade. The site was sequestered from the Earl of Warwick, and in 1555 was granted to the city corporation. Within five years a property on the site was let to shoemaker and brewer Thomas Tolly, who remained here until 1577. He must also have held land outside the city at Tolly's Hill, now **Tallow Hill**.

By 1653 or before it was an inn, rebuilt in the 1680s by John and Alice Houghton, and possibly called the Reindeer at that time – historian Pat Hughes suggests the name was originally the Reined Deer. By 1717 a large garden behind the inn was purchased from the Berkeley family. Later in the century more stables were built on the site, causing it to be called Stables Court. This was never a coaching inn, but probably wagons ran from here to outlying villages. Part of the stables still exist on the site, though rebuilt. The site was renovated in the 1980s before the shopping arcade opened.

A former stationery shop across the road, with a splendid eighteenth century facade to the upper floors, was also an early inn. Originally said to have been home to a family called the Johnsons, it was first licenced in 1608, and known in 1618 as The Prince's Arms, for Prince Henry, elder brother of Charles I, who would have been king but for his early death. It was rebuilt with the present facade in 1748, and was said to be one of the finest houses in the city. One of the earliest banks opened in this house on 8 January 1795. It is referred to either as Farley's Bank or Farley, Lavender, Owen and Gutch's bank since George Farley, John Pearkes Lavender (after whom **Lavender Road** was named), John Owen and John Matthew Gutch were all involved at various times in its management. It moved to the **Cross** in 1812 and went bust in 1857.

The building then became a coffee house and subsequently the Shades Tavern, where Elgar's father first stayed when he came to Worcester from London. He obviously had fond memories of his stay, since he later married the landlord's sister, Ann Greening. The city's first post office was also sited at No. 16 in 1884, and in the twentieth century it became the Shades once more. Leather seller William Shaw, after whom **Shaw Street** was named, traded at No. 7 for many years from the late eighteenth century.

According to buildings historian Pat Hughes, No. 21 was built around 1635 by cardmaker William Bradley, though the land was owned by Stourbridge Grammar School. A new front and rear range are said to date from the 1670s.

Residents in 1840 included a cheese factor, a brush maker, a schoolmaster, a baker, surgeon Richard Griffithes, clockmaker Reinea Gasper and Simmonds' eating house. The Co-op began in the city in 1881 with a bakery here, probably at 5A, at a time when many working people were worried about the high cost of bread, which they believed was caused by price-fixing. The society was formed by a joiner named James Manning, and though neither he nor any of the other founders had any business experience, and despite determined opposition from millers and other bakers, the venture was a success, and a larger Co-op store opened in **St Nicholas Street** in 1887.

MELBOURNE STREET

This street will have taken its name from the two Melbourne Cottages which stood on the south side of the **Crown Street** junction with **Droitwich Road**, probably from the 1850s or before, but were demolished in late 2011 to make way for a medical centre. They may have been named for Viscount Melbourne, who was prime minister 1835-41.

Construction here probably began in the 1860s on former orchards, with land divided into plots for sale to builders, investors and aspiring home owners, and the street was well established by the early 1880s. It looks as if building mostly spread south from Crown Street, with a small amount spreading north from **Gregory's Mill Street**, then just Mill Street. A map of 1884 shows the east side of the street largely complete except for a patch equivalent to four or five house plots towards the south end, though there was little on the west side, where a great many trees still remained. At that time a listing showed almost 30 homes here, with quite small gardens.

No information has been found on who first developed the street, but as often happened, houses were evidently built by a number of different small investors, some of whom named the homes they put up. There was a terrace of three homes called Clarence Place, a Holly Cottage, four Rose Cottages, a Kyber Cottage and an Arlington Villa where Mrs Heming had a preparatory school in 1884. Her neighbours were mostly building tradesmen, but also included a coach body maker, a basket maker, a glover, a china burnisher, a wagon builder, two labourers, an iron worker, a packer and a gardener. John Gingell at Kyber Cottage was a verger at the cathedral.

Nine of the houses – almost a third - were vacant at that time. Supply of modest new homes for rent in the 1880s boom was obviously outstripping the demand for them, and despite building applications for around 20 more homes by 1896, nothing more had been built by that date, and there was still one completed home empty. There were then 21 homes on the east side, but just eight on the west. By 1900 building had begun again, though slowly. There were around seven more homes by that date and a couple more by 1910, while by 1922 the figure had crept up just one more to 40. This was very slow progress compared to some developments begun in the late nineteenth century, and of the 35 houses for which building applications were submitted between 1888 and 1903, less than a third were ever actually built. Perhaps it was the small gardens that made the difference. Probably workers wanted the compensation of a good sized garden in return for the inconvenience of travelling further to work, and they just didn't have that here.

By 1922 Henry Holder had opened a shop at No 36 selling groceries and coal. It was still open in the 1970s, but was converted back into a house in the 1980s. A map of 1928 showed that the east side of the street had been completed, but most of the west side was still open land, though most of the trees seem to have been removed. No further progress had been made by 1940, and it wasn't until comparatively recently that that side of the street was completed.

MERRIMAN'S HILL
The name comes from the family of Merrimon or Merriman, who must have been landowners here, and gave their name to the hill which stretches from **Lansdowne Road** towards Blackpole. Almost nothing is recorded about them, other than two wills, of 1544 and 1613, and Merriman's Lodge, which is shown on a map of 1838, just east of the canal, off Lansdowne Road. The road is also shown on that map, but is only an unnamed footway following a field boundary.

No doubt this was an ancient trackway or lane, which led to or by the Merrimans' property, though it is not listed in a street directory until 1873, and this would then have mostly been a quiet rural area. This was part of the Red House Estate, on which **Lansdowne Crescent** was built, and Mr Browning was farming here in 1751. Merriman's Hill Farm was opposite the end of **Mayfield Road**.

A women's hospital opened here around 1825. A guidebook of 1837 listed the 'Female Asylum' as having two day wards, two stay wards and 14 inmates, with Dr Charles Hastings and surgeon Dr Streeten as visiting physicians. It was said to have gardens all round, in which inmates were encouraged to walk.

Even as late as 1928 there was no roadway here. A map of that date showed only fields between **Gregory's Bank**, which then followed the line of what later became the bottom of this road, and **Green Lane** which terminated at **Mayfield Road**. The two were finally linked up with this road in the 1950s.

The secondary school was opened in 1937, with separate schools for boys and girls, and was named Samuel Southall in honour of a long-serving town clerk after whom **Southall Avenue** was named. It became a mixed school in 1965, and Bishop Perowne has since taken over the building.

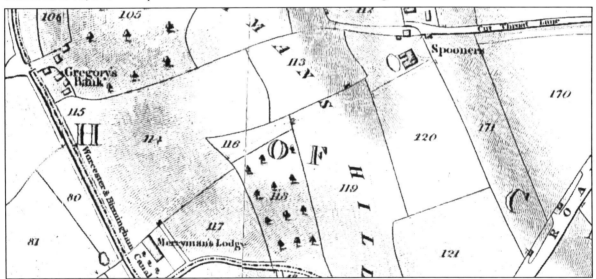

Merrimans Hill in 1838. 'Merryman's' Lodge, at bottom left, was just off Lansdowne Road, and the street, towards the top of the map, was an unnamed footway on a field boundary leading across open fields towards Green Lane, then called Cut Throat Lane

Merry Vale
Now part of **Deansway**. The name was a corruption of Mary Vale, which came from the dedication of the cathedral to St Mary. This name survived until the early 1960s when redevelopment created Deansway. This ancient street curved around the east side of All Saints Church from *All Hallows*, opposite the bottom of **Broad Street**, to roughly the Deansway entrance to Crowngate, where it joined *Birdport*. The church, with its graveyard on the east, occupied roughly half of the west side of the street. Its parish was the most populous in the city in the eighteenth century. In 1779 it had 352 houses and 1944 inhabitants squashed into the space between the river and St Andrew's parish, just along Deansway.

Situated just behind the quay, this will have been a very busy commercial street in past centuries. Occupants in 1790 included barber John Wormington, chair bottomer Ann Martin, butcher John Yarnold, grazier Richard Paine, maltsters Thomas and Joseph Meredith, whitesmith Samuel Smith, victualler Stephen Strickland and Rev Cleveland, the Rector of All Saints Church.

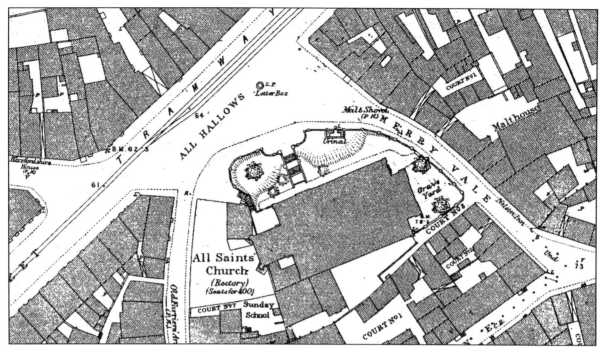

Above, Merry Vale in 1884

Below, the west side, early twentieth century - RS

An old inn here at that time, called the Pewterer's Arms, was last listed in 1820, and may have been the pub near the southern end of the street which was renamed the Lord Nelson, in honour of the great seaman (see **Copenhagen Street**). The Nelson was here until 1955. Just north of it was the Hole In The Wall, which was listed in 1820 but had closed by 1870. Near the All Saints end of the street in the nineteenth century was Strickland's lodging house, well known for accommodating a variety of unsavoury characters. There was still a hair dresser here in 1840 and some maltsters, along with a dealer in sundries, a pump maker and well sinker, a confectioner, a miller, a baker and a schoolmaster. By 1955, shortly before it was cleared, there were just three listings here. Two of them appear to have been residential, and the other was the Transport and General Workers' Union district office.

MIDDLE ROAD

The first mention found of this road was in a building application of 1868 for one house, submitted by carpenter Isaac Lippett, who built himself a home called Woodbine Cottage. Two years later there were two applications for three houses, then nothing more until 1879 – 80 when there were two applications for four houses. Nearly all of these were submitted by different small investors, and they total 15, but a map and directory of around 1884 list 19 homes, so either building began before building control was introduced in 1865, or some applications are missing. By 1884 Mr Lippett's cottage, on the corner of **Great House Road**, was next to four homes in Varna Terrace. Near **Pitmaston Road** were four homes in Eaton Terrace, and along the road were three Hamstead Villas. Residents here at that time included glovers, gardeners, a saddler, a wheelwright, a foreman, an asylum attendant, a range fitter, a seamstress and a miller.

At that date there were still around half a dozen vacant house plots on the west side and slightly more on the east. There were also quite a few trees on the vacant plots, betraying the origin of the site as former orchards.

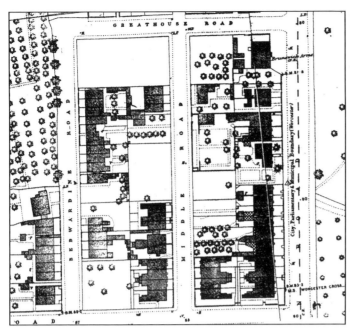

Above, Middle Road in 1884

Below, Edwardian Middle Street - RS

By the end of the 1920s the west side of the street was complete, but there had been no further development on the east by 1940, and that side was not completed until the 1960s or 70s.

MIDDLE STREET

This was part of the mid nineteenth century Arboretum Pleasure Grounds, with their entrance drive on **Arboretum Road**, which were sold for redevelopment in 1866. As with **Northfield Street**, development records began in 1870. The first application, in that year, was for two houses on a site referred to as Lot 86. Clearly a developer had divided the land up into lots for sale, though the identity of that person has not been discovered. It is unlikely to have been that first building applicant, since this was the only application he ever submitted. He was shown in the application as J. Darke, presumably John Darke, a cabinet maker and upholsterer at 8 **Foregate Street**, speculating in his one and only known property development, though he may have owned many existing properties to rent. In 1884 there was a Jeffery Darke, perhaps his son, living in the street, describing himself as a 'gentleman'.

Records suggest that development proceeded slowly at first, with no sign of further applications until 1880. Over the next four years however there were nine applications for 25 houses and a shop.

An 1884 street directory listing showed that all 27 homes had been built, but not the shop, and a map of that date showed that the west side of the street appeared complete, but there were still a few vacant house plots on the east side, which were filled by 1896. A photograph from the early twentieth century appears to show the shop, but a listing for the shopkeeper was not found.

The houses here were apparently built by a number of different investors, who named the homes and terraces they put up according to their personal taste. Three were three homes in Roscoe Place, six Mona Villas, six Avon Villas, a Fern Cottage, a Tours Villa and a Roseland Villa. This mix of different types of properties led to an interesting social mix. Residents in 1884 included a labourer and a poultry dealer next door to an ironmonger's manager; a printer's manager next door to a lithographer and a draper's assistant; a Major Steadman, an army pensioner, next door to an engine driver.

MIDLAND ROAD

It was originally created as an embankment which was part of the Shrub Hill station development, completed in 1865, though there was a temporary terminus there from about 1850. Both the station and the Midland goods yard were on this embankment. The road will have taken its name from the Midland Railway, which originally owned the terminus jointly with the Oxford, Worcester & Wolverhampton Railway, and continued to have the goods yard for many years afterwards. It was first listed in a street directory in 1880.

In 1884 the only building near this road was the Midland Railway Company's Good Offices and Bonded Stores, referred to less impressively on a map of around that time as the M.R. Goods Shed. The land to the west was open as far as **Spring Hill** and the development around the canal. In 1896 a building application was submitted

Lea & Perrins factory in Midland Road - TW

for Lea & Perrins' Worcestershire Sauce factory, which was listed by 1903. By that date there were also around 10 homes here, whose occupants included a number of railwaymen, but also a carpenter, a clerk, a fitter, a cashier and a compositor. There were also a number of businesses clustering around the goods shed, including a coal depot, an oil company and a horse keeper. By 1910 the 13 homes were here which still exist today. In more recent times part of the goods yard has been built on with business premises, but the pattern of development here is not that different from a century ago.

Mill Street

Now **Gregory's Mill Street**. This lane from Droitwich Road to the medieval mill off **Barbourne Road** must have been in use for centuries. It was listed as Mill Lane in a street directory of 1873, and as Street from 1885. By 1896 it had taken its present name. The mill stood a short distance from the canal bridge near to the end of the street.

MILL STREET

This street was first found listed in the health board streets list of 1872, and a street directory of the following year, though it will have existed for centuries as a track leading from the castle, near where **Severn Street** is

Townshend's Flour Mill in 1939

now, to Frog Mill, which was driven by the Frog Brook which is now feeding the canal. The brook originally ran just outside the city wall in this area.

In this area in the thirteenth century was a meadow called Kingsmead, which was a common duelling spot. There is a story from 1221 of Thomas, a tenant farmer from Eldersfield, near Tewkesbury, who was ordered by the Royal Justices to fight a duel as Trial by Combat at Kingsmead against his accuser in a felony case, which was watched by a large crowd of Worcester people.

He was badly mutilated, but made a miraculous recovery after praying to St. Wulfstan, and became a brother at the Commandery in **Sidbury**.

The story was reported in church circles to prove the saint's miraculous powers, and no doubt to encourage more pilgrims to Worcester, but the case was actually entered in the court records, which gives it some authenticity.

Frog Mill was probably the castle mill originally, but when the castle ceased to be used for military purposes in the medieval period (see **Severn Street**) it was probably worked by an outside miller, and was then known as the Frogging Mill. It is believed to have ceased working during the Civil War. There are some reports that it was demolished in that period, but others that it was still in existence at the end of the eighteenth century, and was then a picturesque ruin. Clearly the track still existed in the early nineteenth century, because when the canal was created a bridge was placed here. Development here might have been expected to follow quickly on the arrival of the canal, which opened in 1815, but there was still nothing shown here on a map of 1838, and it may not have been until the 1850s or 60s that this street was created. Once it was, development seems to have gone ahead fairly quickly, and building in the area was complete on a map of 1884. The Frog Mill was long gone, and by the canal corn was now being ground by the Albion Steam Flour Mills, since converted into flats, where Thomas Townshend was then the miller.

At that time there were between 50 and 60 modest homes here for working families, with modest gardens. They seem likely to have been developed by various investors and some were named accordingly. There was a row of four homes at Emily Terrace, three Albert Cottages, four cottages in Willow Terrace and seven Rose Villas. Residents included some china workers, as you might expect from the proximity to the Worcester Porcelain factory, but only a few of them. Their neighbours had a wide variety of occupations, including labourers, railwaymen, glovers, metal workers, shoemakers, building workers, tailors, a wood sorter, a cellarman, a blacksmith, a brush maker, a cabinet maker, a fireman, a brewer, a gardener, a basket maker, a laundress, a stonemason, a greyhound trainer and a sauce maker.

Towards the north end of the street on the east side was the St Alban's Home and Orphanage for Girls, now in use by Kings School as a junior school, where Miss C. Stillingfleet was then the Lady Superior. Henry Hawker kept a shop on the corner of **Willow Street**, on a site since redeveloped, and at Nos. 15 & 16, on the corner of **Posrtland Street**, was the Alma Inn, first listed in 1873, and still open in 1980, though it has closed since.

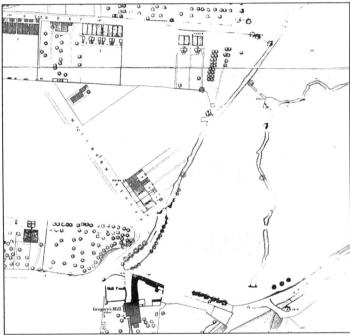

Millburn Street is on the left of this 1884 map

Millburn Street

Now **Sydney Street**. Named for the mill burn or stream, this street was first found listed in 1885, running diagonally from behind **Crown Street** towards the canal.

It consisted of the detached Snowdrop villa at the north end and six terraced Zulu Cottages at the south end, which were shown on a map of that date and named in a directory of the same year.

Boatman John Sprague lived nearest to the canal in 1885, and the other homes housed a draper's assistant at the villa and labourers at the cottages.

There was an application to build five more houses here in 1903, but no further listings of the street were found, and by 1915 it had been renamed **Sydney Street**, to form part of a poets' estate. The homes which were listed in this street have been replaced by modern developments.

Montgomery Road

The first and only listings found for this street were in 1884/5. It consisted of two homes called Stroud Cottages, off **Bromyard Road**. Residents in the mid 1880s were commercial traveller Henry Bishop and journeyman carpenter Samuel Adams. There was then a gap in the records until 1896, at which point there was no trace of this road.

MOOR STREET

Historian David Whitehead said this street was mostly built between 1822 and 1827, probably soon after **Easy Row**. It was very much a part of a small suburb that grew up in this area, of cheap housing for rent to working families. Some 59 homes plus a yard were listed here in 1884, with two courts of housing and two pubs. Cottages on the south side of the street mostly had good gardens, but few on the north side did. The yard belonged to furniture van proprietor William Winwood. At No. 16, on the south side of the street, was the

Lamp Tavern, first listed in 1873 but closed by 1908. Further along at No. 26 was the Brewer's Arms, which closed around 1960. Residents in 1884 included two prison warders, labourers, a leather stainer, building tradesmen, a marble polisher, a brewer, a machinist, a coffee roaster, a dressmaker, a locksmith and bell hanger, and many other manual jobs, plus a clerk or two, a schoolmaster and an insurance agent. At No. 59 shoemaker George Price also kept a shop. The street was 'cleared' in the 1960s, at the same time as *Spring Gardens*, and the area has since been redeveloped.

The Moors in 1884

MOORS, THE

The east side of Pitchcroft was known as The Moor Fields in times past. A Moorfield Street was also listed in 1840, which was an alternative name for this street. Upper Severn Terrace, a terrace of three houses between **Moor Street** and **Back Lane South**, was listed separately in 1840. The first intensive working class housing in the area was built at **Easy Row**. A map of 1829 showed there was development here by that date, but much more was shown on a map of 1838, though it was not listed under this name until the health board streets list of 1872, and was not found in a street directory until 1880.

A map of 1884 showed intensive development here, with about 80 homes plus a dozen courts of housing, three pubs, four or five shops, and a mission room on the corner of **Severn Terrace**. This development was primarily on the west side of the street, since the east side was occupied by access to the gardens of houses in **Britannia Square**. Clearly a number of different investors had built homes here, and in some cases named them. There were four Britannia Cottages by Back Lane South, four homes at York House Bank, near **Stephenson Terrace**, four Brickley's Buildings nearby, six Cottage Gardens, and next door to the mission hall, the Cottage of Content.

Most common occupation amongst residents was labourer, with glover and shoemaker coming some way behind. There were also clothing workers, a chimney sweep, a whitesmith, a confectioner, a hair cloth weaver, a sign writer, a seamstress, a charwoman, a laundress and a gardener.

All three pubs on this street were listed by 1873, though not all of them closed at the same time. Almost opposite Back Lane South, on the west side, was the Prince of Wales pub, near where the Swan Theatre is, which remained here until around 1970. Almost opposite was the Moors Ketch pub, which closed around 1930. At the other end of the street, on the site where new stables have been built within the last few years, was the York House inn, which closed around 1970. All these pubs will probably have gained clientele from those using Pitchcroft for leisure pursuits, as well as those people living in the area.

At the southern end of the street was a small parade of shops, with a grocer and a butcher. Near **Moor Street** was baker and provision merchant James

Mosely. Midway along the street was Mrs Mary Willoughby's shop. By 1896 the street had acquired a fried fish shop, on what is now part of the Swan Theatre site.

Most of this housing was demolished when ***Spring Gardens*** was cleared, and a terrace of houses near Back Lane South is all that remains of what was once a busy and thriving community.

MORRIN CLOSE

This street was first found in a street directory in 1937, when there were five homes listed, all on the west side, but development was obviously continuing, since all the homes here appear to have been completed in the 1930s. It seems clear that the street took the family name of someone involved with the development, but that person has not been traced in Worcestershire sources of the period. Morrin was an old Irish name, brought to this country by immigrants in the nineteenth century. The 1901 Worcestershire census lists 74-year-old Edward Morrin, who hailed from County Mayo and was formerly a general labourer, and it may have been one of his descendants who was involved in the development of this street, though they don't seem to have been living or trading in Worcestershire at the time, and no building applications have been traced.

**Councillor William
Morris in 1901 - TW**

MORRIS AVENUE

This street will have been a development of **Northwick Road** builder and city councillor Ronald William Morris, who was certainly involved in the development of **Colin Road**, and must have been involved with this street also, and gave it his family name. It was first found in a street directory in 1937, when there were eight villas listed.

NARROW WALK

Narrow though it was, and is, this path linking **Boughton Street** with **Bransford Road** had up to a dozen homes along it by 1884. It was built on former orchard land, and there were still orchards to the south of the road then. Only half the homes here were subject to building applications, so the other half were probably built before building control was introduced in December 1865. The first record found of it was a building application of 1868 for four cottages, and another two houses were applied for in the following year, though the name Regent Row, which was given for them, did not appear in the 1884 listing. There were no further building applications up to the end of the century. On the west side in 1884, a short distance from Bransford Road, were half a dozen Camden Cottages, housing a labourer, two gardeners, and two ladies probably widowed, one of whom was letting out apartments. Other residents included labourers, a charwoman, and a verger at the cathedral. Redevelopment in modern times has swept away most of these homes, and sadly this is now little more than a footpath.

NASH'S PASSAGE

This was named for wealthy Worcester clothier John Nash, who established almshouses here. He lived nearby at Nash House in **New Street**, which was built with timber left by his father.

John Nash was born in 1590, of a family which originated in Ombersley and owned mills along the River Salwarpe. He was mayor of Worcester in 1633 and MP during 1640-48. Despite living in a supposedly Royalist city, he commanded a troop of horse for Parliament during the Civil War. There is a story that while Nash was away during the war Royalist Dud Dudley from **Friar Street** moved into this house, which was much larger than his own, and when the Royalists lost the war Dudley's wife was put out of the house.

The clothing industry declined in importance during Nash's lifetime, but he had put much of his wealth into land and property, which was mainly left at his death in 1662 for the good of the poor and needy, since he never married and had no descendants. His almshouses, erected in 1664, were replacements for earlier ones erected by another charity, and were to house eight poor men and two poor women, with preference being given to those related to him. He also left money for clothing apprentices and setting young men up in business. There is a monument to him in St Helen's Church, where he was buried, with an inscription which notes that he left instructions for his will to be read annually by the Town Clerk. His almshouses were completely rebuilt in the late 1950s/early 1960s and officially reopened in 1962.

In the nineteenth century the Passage was a lane which led to the ***Blockhouse*** area, but it was cut off by the **City Walls Road**. It was listed in the health board streets list of 1872 and in a street directory of 1880. Alexandra Place, a terrace of eight houses here, was listed separately for some years from 1880. In 1884 it housed an iron worker, a tailor, a gloveress, a salesman, a nurse, a dressmaker, and a hairdresser who had a salon at Nos. 7 & 8. There are still some homes here, but this is now mainly just a walkway to **City Walls Road**.

Nedlere Street
Now **Pump Street**.

NELSON ROAD

It may have taken its name from Nelson House, one of a pair of villas which existed in this area earlier than 1884, when the building application for a new road and sewers was submitted, and no less than 10 other applications for a total of 23 homes and two shops.

Prior to that there was completely open land between **Comer Road** and the development to the west of **Henwick Road**, which were linked by a footpath called Bromyard Walk. Building obviously went ahead quickly, since the street was also listed in a street directory in that year, with 'eight houses now in course of erection'. There were five more applications for 11 homes in the following year, and four more applications for another 12 homes had been submitted by 1890. The majority of these were very small-scale applications for one or two houses, submitted by many different small investors.

By 1896 there were 46 homes listed here including Nelson House and Fern Villa, which was appreciably more than had been applied for, suggesting either that some applications have been lost, or that some investors were lax about putting in their applications.

The residents in 1896 were mainly manual workers, with the occasional white collar. There were building tradesmen, shop assistants, clerks, two shop managers, glovers, an insurance agent, a box maker, a letter carrier, a potter and a tin plate worker. Ross Billingsley at No. 3 was a sewing machine agent, and Miss Wilson at No. 11 was the district nurse for St John's and St Clement's. Mrs Helen Bleakman kept a shop on the corner of Comer Road, and Robert Barnett had a shop at No. 21, near the other end of the street. By 1910 there were 57 homes here, including six being built, and by 1922 there were 69.

NETHERTON LANE

This lane, not found named until 1896, led to Netherton Place, a terrace of 13 houses in **Infirmary Walk**, first found listed in the health board streets list of 1872, and a street directory of the following year. It still leads to a housing development, but one that was built recently, after the area was redeveloped.

NEW BANK STREET

Originally just *Bank Street*. The name was changed at the end of the nineteenth century to avoid confusion with the original Bank Street off the **High Street**. The original was named for an eighteenth century banking institution situated there, but this was probably named simply because it was on a bank. It may also have derived the name from a large house called Barbourne Bank, which stood in its own grounds off **Droitwich Road**, opposite Gheluvelt Park.

A map of 1838 showed open land here, with no sign of this street or any of the streets surrounding it, except the lane to Gregory's Mill. It was first found in a street directory in 1873, the year in which the Barbourne pub was also first listed, so development probably began around 1870 or slightly earlier.

By 1884 the street was virtually complete, with almost 50 homes listed here. No building applications were found for these houses, which is not surprising, since this area was beyond the city boundary until the 1880s. What is more interesting is that an application to create this

1922 ads for Barbourne Brewery and another business in the street

road was not submitted until 1894, which does seem a little late, even by the more lax standards of that time. It was submitted by the same developer also involved in **Sunnyside Road**.

An 1884 street directory listing suggested a number of small investors had been involved in building the homes here, and some of them had given their houses names with interesting overseas connections. At Nos.

7 – 10 were the four New York Cottages, with Brooklyn Villa at No. 6, and two Sydney Cottages at Nos. 11 and 12. There were also four Oxford Cottages, two Kettering Villas and two Rose Cottages. The only possible developer traced is William Clues or Clews, a carpenter, who was living in 1884 at Sydney Cottages, which he may have built, and submitted applications to build three houses in **Park Avenue** in 1887-8. Other 1884 residents included building tradesmen, blacksmiths, railwaymen, seamstresses, a prison warder, a telegraph clerk, a shoemaker, a coach builder and a baker.

At No. 15 then was a county police station manned by police constable Alfred Willis. Robert Allen's little Barbourne Brewery was based behind the Barbourne inn at Nos 17 and 18, and developed a successful small business for some years supplying other houses. Sadly plans have recently been put forward to turn the Barbourne into flats.

NEWMAN'S PASSAGE

A passage from **The Tything**, near the George and Dragon, to Britannia Road. There were three cottages here in 1884, housing a tinman (tin plate worker) and brazier and a 'town traveller'. The Newman family gained their wealth from gloving, and Pat Hughes said Dr John Newman had a house in Britannia Square.

New Passage

Blackfriars First found mentioned in a directory of 1873. It consisted of three cottages, occupied in 1884 by gardener Charles Parsons, labourer Richard Stanton and salesman John Watkins.

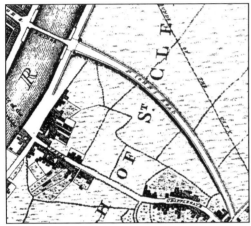

New Road, then called St John's Road, in 1799, 18 years after the new bridge opened. Below, Worcestershire cricket legend 'Tip' Foster, who captained England at both cricket and football - WCC

NEW ROAD

This road was built across riverside sheep pastures owned by the Dean and Chapter, to provide the western approach to the new bridge which opened in 1781 (see **Bridge Street**). It was listed under this name as early as 1790, but was also often referred to as *St John's Road*. Architect John Gwynn, mindful of the flood risk, raised the road on a causeway. He presented a wooden model of the road to trustees in February 1780, and soon afterwards the Journal said large quantities of earth were dug from fields below Mr Philip Moule's house in *Rosemary Lane*, now **Henwick Road**, to create the causeway.

An innovative solution by Gwynn to any further flood problems was that the road was drained by two 'grand cylinders' or flood drains, each 3'6" (roughly 1.1m) in diameter, which ran parallel with the pavements. How successful they were history doesn't record, but obviously they didn't end the flood problems here, and perhaps because of that, there was no rush to build here.

There were a couple of properties listed near the **Bull Ring** in 1790, occupied by collector of excise John Weeks and tobacco pipe maker Ann Taylor. To the east there were open fields. Almost a century later in 1884 there was little more here, though ironically **Tybridge Street**, which had been the approach road to the old bridge demolished in the 1790s, was heavily built up in places. This road was of a generous width even then, but there was room at that time for an avenue of trees at either side. Along the centre of the road ran the rails for the horse bus service to **St John's**.

At the west end of the road, with its back to the Bull Ring, was the imposing Cripplegate House, standing in its own grounds, which was home in 1884 to Rev William Ernest Bolland, headmaster of King's School. At the other end of the road, near the bridge, was a small colony of tradesmen, including sawyer Alfred Langford, salt dealer Thomas Yardley, fruit dealer John Morris and the refreshment house or cafe of Matthew Tolley. Opposite was the Bridge Mills saw mill off **Hylton Road**.

A building application was submitted in 1896 for a pavilion at the New Road Cricket Club, the proposed ground of the Worcestershire XI, and from 1899, when the club moved here from the Cinderella ground in

Historic Worcester Streets

Bromyard Road, one of the most beautiful cricket grounds in the country has yearly held the hopes and dreams of cricket lovers across the county. The early team was nicknamed Fostershire because there were as many as five of the Foster brothers from Malvern in the side, including 'Tip' Foster, the only man ever to captain England at both cricket and football. The ground was originally leased from the Dean and Chapter, but the club bought the freehold in 1976.

New Road in the early twentieth century, showing one of the toll houses, later demolished - RS

New Street, with Nash House on the left, in the 1870s - BG

202

New Street looking towards the Cornmarket around 1900 - RS

NEW STREET

The old name, Glovers Street, was used for both **Friar Street** and New Street in the thirteenth century. In the sixteenth century gloving became a mainstay of the city economy as the traditional cloth trade declined. It was in the second half of that century that this street was redeveloped and it may then have acquired its modern name, which it may have had at the time of Queen Elizabeth's visit in 1575, though it was still being referred to as 'Glovers Street or New Street' on Green's map of 1764.

Around 1714 the Journal mentioned a house here, formerly the New Inn, which was to let at that date. In 1790 the street's occupants included only two glovers, but there were two attorneys, two bricklayers, two carpenters, two 'taylors', two cheesemongers, a baker, a carpet manufacturer, a drawing master, a plasterer, a shoemaker, a surgeon, a tallow chandler and a jeweller. Christopher Hubbold, master of the Bishop Lloyd Charity School in **The Trinity**, also lived here.

The Swan with Two Nicks, then just the Swan, and the Pheasant were both here at that time. William Ford was a butcher and also kept the Seven Stars pub. At No. 48, where the goods entrance of Marks and Spencer is now, was the Greyhound, listed by 1829 as the New Greyhound, which Gwilliam said was one of the most important country carrier inns in the nineteenth century. By 1896 the Liberals had their club and local association offices here at No. 9.

Like many other city thoroughfares, this street had some fine houses, of which Nash House (see below) would have been typical, but in the eighteenth and nineteenth centuries many of them were converted into slum tenements and the gardens were built over with cramped courts. There are however some fine sixteenth century buildings remaining on the east side of the street. The original No. 1 was demolished in 1895, together with the first three houses in Friar Street, to make way for the extension of **Charles Street**.

The city's first Wesleyan chapel was built here in 1772, after John Wesley visited the city four years earlier, and found there was nowhere large enough for the crowds who wanted to hear him preach. He returned in March 1772, when the chapel opened, but in those less tolerant times he faced a hostile mob of citizens who had to be dispersed by the mayor. By 1795, four years after Wesley's death, the chapel had become too small, and the congregation moved to **Pump Street**, but a plaque records the chapel site opposite Market Passage. A pub here called the Old Chapel closed around 1980.

The Swan with Two Nicks has been serving drinks since 1764, though the building dates from about 1550, and had previously been home for almost two centuries to the Elcox family, who began as weavers but became goldsmiths. In 1784 it was known as the Little Swan, apparently not taking its present name until 1830. The name refers to 'swan upping' or marking. From the twelfth century swans were deemed to belong to the crown, but around 1550 some were split between two Livery Companies of the City of London, the Dyers and the Vintners, or wine sellers. To mark their swans the Dyers cut one nick on the bird's beak and the Vintners cut two nicks. Swan upping still continues on the River Thames, but only as an annual census of birds, and these days the bird's leg is ringed. In the nineteenth century there was still a substantial yard behind this house, which had stabling for 40 horses.

John Nash

The Pheasant is also in a sixteenth century building, and has had the same name since it became an inn in the 1770s or 80s. According to the pub's history, the first landlady was Mrs Eleanor Morris who had been at The Pheasant in **Silver Street**, where her husband had been licensee. When he died she moved to this building, obtained a licence, and since the Silver Street premises had been delicenced, she was able to use the same name here. Until the 1800s, when the 'sport' was made illegal, this was a principal inn for cockfighting.

There was a bowling green behind the inn for the city corporation (see **Bowling Green Walk**).

One of the street's most important and striking buildings is Nash House, built for John Nash, who lived in a house immediately on the south side of this building. His father, Richard, was one of the two bailiffs of the city in 1581, and when he died in 1605 he left his son the timber to build this house. John was a wealthy clothier (see **Nash's Passage**) and mayor of the city. Being childless he left this house in his will to a relative, Richard Nash of Droitwich, who made a number of alterations, adding two chimneys and coach access. It was purchased by alderman John Hughes in 1689, and has gone through various hands and various uses since. The ground floor is currently a cafe.

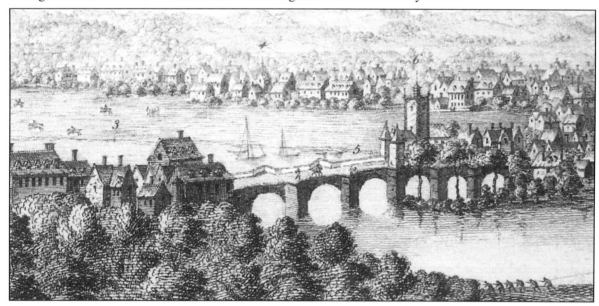

Worcester's old bridge between Tybridge Street and Newport Street in 1732

NEWPORT STREET

This is roughly on the line of a Roman road, and may have developed as a city street c. 900-1100. It was Ewport in Old English, meaning river gate; a reference to the fortifications on the old bridge. The present name was in use by 1610 or before.

Until 1781 it was the traditional river crossing approach from the city, with **Tybridge Street** forming the approach on the opposite bank.

In ancient times the river crossing would probably have been by stepping stones, which would have become accessible at times because the river was tidal. The original bridge here would have been of wood and was no doubt built before the Norman Conquest.

It is possible that there was a bridge as early as Roman times, though it was likely to have been somewhere near where the cathedral now stands. Between 1307-1319 a stone replacement was built for the bridge here, of six piers with cutwaters, similar to one still in existence at Hereford.

In the centuries that followed the city authorities probably often exaggerated the poor condition of this bridge, in attempts to wring repair funds from central government, but it did actually seem to come in for a lot of wear and tear. It was said to be damaged by boats tying up to the piers, it was certainly damaged during the Civil War when one of the piers was blown up, and in the 1680s, during a period of severe winters, the piers were damaged by icefloes! By 1768 the old bridge was said to be dangerous and decayed.

In 1771 work began on a new, wider bridge downstream, which opened in 1781, approached by **Bridge Street**, and the quays were reconstructed at the same time. The foundations of the medieval bridge were so solid that gunpowder had to be used to demolish them. The new bridge of 1781 was effectively obliterated by the widening work which took place in the 1930s, and the quays have been altered as commercial traffic on the river gave way to railway and road traffic.

In the medieval period this was an area where cloth dyers gathered, because they had easy access to the river to obtain water for dying, and to dispose of the noxious waste products of their trade. Some tanners also established themselves here for similar reasons. This was then one of the least populated areas of the city, but it gradually filled up with businesses, tenements and courts.

By the Tudor period there was a solid line of houses and businesses along the roadside, some perhaps already with adjoining tenements to the rear, but as late as 1741 there was an open vista of gardens at either side, stretching west to **Dolday**, and east to the Severn. By the end of the eighteenth century however these gardens were beginning to fill up, not least with development from Dolday, which had been almost deserted in Tudor times.

What historian David Whitehead described as one of the city's most important inns, the King's Head, stood here near the bridge in 1608, and presumably derived a good deal of its business from travellers. Though it continued for a few years after the new bridge opened, the loss of passing trade must have been fatal, and it closed in 1785, and was demolished soon afterwards. There was probably also a Saracen's Head inn here in 1577, and a Green Dragon inn here lodged prisoners during the Civil War, probably in the stables. Around 1714 the Journal mentioned an inn called the Fountain, where the landlord was Thomas Poole, and another called the Bear was also in this area, presided over by the widow Wall.

In 1790 a street directory showed three glovers working on this street, two stone masons, a baker, a basket maker, a corn chandler, a distillery, a painter, a pastry cook, a watchmaker and a boarding school run by Miss Herbert. There was also Ible's coffee house and three pubs, the Green Dragon, the Severn Galley, which the Journal had also mentioned around 1714, and the Star.

During the nineteenth century this became a populous area, tightly packed with poor housing, surrounded by no less than seven slum courts. Along this street were eating houses, pubs, shoemakers, warehouses, manufacturers, a wholesale rag merchant, fishmongers and shopkeepers. The pavements, such as they were, would have been thronged night and day with the poor and destitute of this community, and contemporaries described them in terms reminiscent of scenes from Dickens.

Much of the poor housing here was demolished around 1930. By 1965 the bus station and car parking were taking up a good deal of the street and in 1977 the remaining houses, of late eighteenth or early nineteenth century date, were mostly small shops serving travellers, though even these disappeared when the bus station transferred to the new Crowngate Centre in the 1990s.

The street had many pubs over the centuries, aside from the King's Head. Of the three listed in 1790, the Green Dragon, the Severn Galley and the Star, Gwilliam only has information on the first of these, which must have been on part of the street where flats now stand. From his note it appears that this was a substantial inn with extensive stabling, and there were ancient cellars beneath the pub with medieval stone vaulting, which must have been part of an earlier building, but presumably they were destroyed when the site was redeveloped. The pub closed around 1950.

The 1884 Ordnance Survey map shows no less than six pubs along the north side of the street. They were, from west to east, the Hope & Anchor now the Severn View Hotel on **North Parade**, the eighteenth century Green Dragon, the Boar's Head, the Prince of Wales, the Old Red Lion – these last three almost next door to each other - and the Herefordshire House. Gwilliam believed the Lion and the Herefordshire House were eighteenth century pubs, though neither of them was listed by these names in 1790. The Boar's Head seems to have opened early in the nineteenth century and closed around 1910. The Old Red Lion closed about 1955, and the Herefordshire House by 1970. All that seems to be known about the Prince of Wales is that the landlord was fined in 1868 for serving drinks after hours.

NEWTOWN ROAD

Newtown seems to have been a small settlement that clustered around the Gun Tavern. No information has been found to determine the age of either the settlement or the pub, but both were perhaps established after

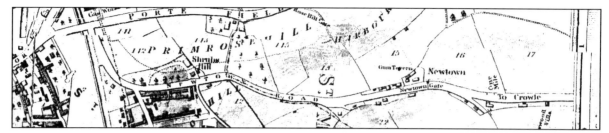

Newtown Road in 1838, and below, a close-up of the Newtown section of the map, showing the turnpike toll gate

the Turnpike Gate was put up in the eighteenth century, just beyond where the pub stands, roughly where **Ronkswood Hill** is now. Houses well above the road level at the west end of this road may be a sign that the turnpike trust reduced the gradient of the highway here. The toll gate operated until about 1870. The pub is supposed to have taken its name from a Worcestershire Rifle Volunteers' rifle range behind the pub, but the hostelry appeared on maps well before the rifle range did, so it is more likely that the name comes from a Civil War gun emplacement to the south of **Ronkswood Crescent**, more or less opposite where the pub stands.

Until the mid twentieth century this area was still largely rural. Ronkswood Hill and Ronkswood Crescent were the only discernible nineteenth century developments here. As late as 1940 the Gun Tavern was a country inn with a football ground behind, on the former rifle range. The area was known as Top Meadow, and was alive with wildflowers in the summer. There was a large pond at the base of Perry Wood, which was known for its newts, referred to locally as nazgels, but this was drained when building of the estate began in 1948. The pub must have been rebuilt during the development of the estate.

Further up the road stood Ronkswood House, which existed until after the Second World War. It was situated on the north side of the road, roughly opposite where Hillside Close now stands, and was the home of the Hills, a family of wealthy farmers and lawyers, who lived there in the eighteenth and nineteenth centuries, and had been farming 1,000 acres at Nunnery Farm from the seventeenth century or before, of which this land was part.

George Hill was a prominent city solicitor who also served as a county coroner from 1810 until his death in 1826. His son, Richard Price Hill, followed his father into the law, but not until 1847, and though he was only 22 then he was said at his death in 1898 to have been the second oldest admitted solicitor in the city.

Richard Price Hill and his wife Lucy

He had considerable property at Shelsley and Martley, Broadheath and Malvern, and also owned the Brickfields estate in Worcester. He was a church warden of Holy Trinity Church for many years, and was President of the Worcester Law Society. He and his wife Lucy, daughter of another city solicitor, had three sons and six daughters, but their marriage was perhaps not a happy one, and when she died three years after him she left instructions that she should not be buried next to him. Their eldest son John also became a city solicitor.

Work began on building Ronkswood Hospital in 1938, to provide treatment for war casualties, and 20 wards were built of 40 beds each, to care for 800 patients. Infirmary historian Miriam Harvey said the two operating theatres often had to have two operating tables in each, to cope with the demand. Even then an overflow of patients sometimes had to be sent to the Infirmary in **Castle Street**. In 1951 the hospital became a convalescent home, but also had a maternity unit from 1952. Ronkswood became part of the Infirmary in 1966, and later took over Accident and Emergency. It closed in 2002 and the hospital has since been demolished.

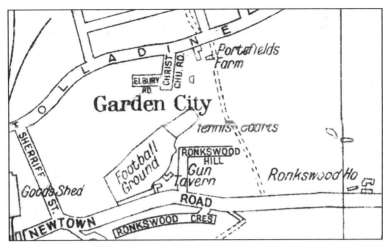

Newtown and Tolladine Roads on a 1939 street plan, showing Ronkswood House, which still existed then - HC

North Barbourne
The name used in the 1880s for the east side of Droitwich Road.

NORTHCOTE STREET
Northcote in Anglo-Saxon meant north cottages, so this could be quite an ancient name for a small settlement in this area, though there was no sign of any development nearby on a map of 1838, other than the ancient lane leading to Gregory's Mill. This could also be a family name of someone involved in the development of the street, though the name was not traced. Much development took place in what is now **New Bank Street** and on **Droitwich Road** in the 1860s and 70s, and a map of 1884 shows this as a service road to the rear of houses in both those streets. This street was not listed in a street directory until 1896. Since there was no actual development here, the only directory listing shown – until it ceased to operate - was for the entry to the Barbourne Brewery, at the rear of the Barbourne inn.

NORTHFIELD STREET
Part of the mid nineteenth century Arboretum Pleasure Grounds, with their entrance drive on **Arboretum Road**, which were sold for redevelopment in 1866. The name could be an old field name, since a map of 1838 shows a number of field divisions on Sansome Fields.

There is no record of development here until a building application of 1870 for 2 houses, then nothing more until 1871 when there was an application for five houses and a corner shop, but over the next 12 years there were 13 applications for just over 40 houses and two shops. The bulk of these, for 27 houses and a shop, were submitted by builders Henry and Thomas Dixon. Henry was based in **Lowesmoor**, but Thomas had a yard in **Southfield Street**.

Homes seem to have been built as fast as they were applied for, and a map of 1884 showed the street had been completed. Some of the homes built had been given names which were significant to the investors or builders There were three homes in Westwood Terrace near **East Street**, five Gloria Cottages, four Rosedale Cottages and a Waltham House near **Sansome Walk**. At Nos. 22-25 were the four tenements of Fleet's Almshouses.

At the west end of the street, on the corner of **Sansome Walk**, was St Mary Magdalene Church, formerly the church of the Tything parish, but now split into flats, with boys' and girls' schools behind it, which are now the rehearsal rooms of the local operatic society. Residents of the street in 1884 were a broad cross section of Victorian workers, including skilled china workers, dressmakers, building tradesmen, compositors, metal workers, clerks, glovers, an engraver, a harness maker, a member of the Ordnance Survey staff, a watchmaker, a wood carver, the manager of a boot shop, and two hotel boot cleaners living side by side at Nos. 11 and 12. At that time Edward Tillbrook was a beer retailer on the corner of **East Street**, at what became known from 1900 as the Arboretum Inn but is now being converted into flats, and Richard Weaver had a shop on the corner of **Little Chesnut Street**.

NORTH PARADE
This must have been created after the new bridge opened in 1781, since it runs off **Bridge Street**, though it was not found listed in a street directory until 1840. The Severn View Hotel on the corner of **Newport Street** is an interesting marriage of two houses of different dates. The house on the east dates from the mid to late eighteenth century, but had become an ale house by 1801, and was known as the Hope and Anchor in the nineteenth century. The house on the west was said to have been built for an undertaker between 1820 and 1840, on the edge of the city wall.

The Old Rectifying House is also of interest, though not as old. It had probably existed since the eighteenth century as the place where spirits from the distillery at the other side of the bridge were rectified or purified. It was rebuilt around 1897 and in the early 1900s was the office of a company running a number of cruise vessels on the Severn, but through most of its existence it has been a pub.

North Parade, above, the riverside, below in 1778, and steamer Holt Castle at North Parade, 1920s - RS

NORTH QUAY

An additional quay, also known in the nineteenth century as Upper Quay, existed here to supplement the often overworked **South Quay** downstream near the former St Andrews Church, where the College of Technology now stands. A city guidebook of 1837 said a fruit market was held here on Wednesdays and Saturdays.

North Street

This street of early Victorian workers' cottages, which led out of **Lock Street**, was first found listed in 1840, and was contemporaneous with the ***Blockhouse*** development. In 1884 there were 23 homes listed here, a shop, and a rear entrance to the Lame Dog Tavern. One third of the residents were labourers. Other occupations included an asylum attendant at Powick, a baker, a basket maker, an iron worker, a blacksmith, a shoemaker, a china dipper, a gloveress, an iron fitter and a carpenter. Mrs Sophia Bond had a shop on the corner of **Little Park Street**, and Mrs Jemima Hazard had a shop further along   The street existed until the 1960s, when it was demolished to be replaced by a block of flats.

NORTHWICK AVENUE

This street was created in 1898 as one of two access roads to Barbourne Works, a substantial printing works on the north side, which has since been converted into apartments.

The Works was created at a cost of £22,000 for the printing firm of W.E. Tucker, and the initials can still be seen on a cartouche above the main entrance. Mr Tucker, said to be originally from London, had a successful printing business at 15 **High Street**, but saw opportunities for expansion, and obtained a wealthy backer.

Barbourne Works, and the original press hall, from a pamphlet published by W.E. Tucker

In January 1898 a building application was submitted for the Works and two new roads, the other being **Sabrina Avenue**. The buildings were designed by Briggs of London, and constructed by Worcester building firm Bromage and Evans, who were also responsible for building the Hop Market Hotel, rebuilding the Old Rectifying House and moving Queen Elizabeth's House at **The Trinity**.   Despite these prestigious commissions, they regarded Barbourne Works as one of their largest contracts. It was centred around a massive press hall, the full height of the three-storey building, with specialist departments for production of large posters, books, legal printing, and many other requirements, and the firm tried to recruit print workers from far and wide.

Unfortunately the massive plant was not a success, and within three years the company had gone into liquidation. By 1903 the Works was a ladies clothing factory. During the Second World War parachutes were packed there for the RAF base at Perdiswell. In 1951 the Works was purchased for £45,000 by the Kays catalogue firm, for use as its main despatch warehouse, and it remained part of Kays for 50 years. Around 2005-7 the Works was converted into apartments. Despite clearly having existed by 1900, the avenue did not appear in a street directory until 1922, at which time building was complete. The listing portrayed a street of white collar workers, with few residents having to get dirty for their pay. There was a manager, a bus driver, a prison warder, a civil servant, clerks, an auditor, a tea traveller, a shop assistant, a storekeeper and a bookbinder, but there were also glovers, a stoker, an engineer, a gardener and a toolmaker.

Next door to Barbourne Works, across Sabrina Avenue, was the Yeomanry Riding School, the nineteenth century premises of the Worcestershire Yeomanry. The Earl of Dudley was its colonel, and other members of the land-owning aristocracy were also involved. Later the Yeomanry became a cavalry regiment and were called hussars. It became a parachute regiment during World War Two and was at Arnhem, but has since been swallowed up in a TA Regiment. The riding school became a biscuit packing factory, and later the premises of a paint supplier. The building was demolished around 1990, and houses now stand on the site.

NORTHWICK CLOSE

Off **Northwick Road**, this street was included on a map of 1928 when there were five homes shown, but it was first found in a street directory in 1930, when 15 homes were listed here, so development must have been going on fairly rapidly.

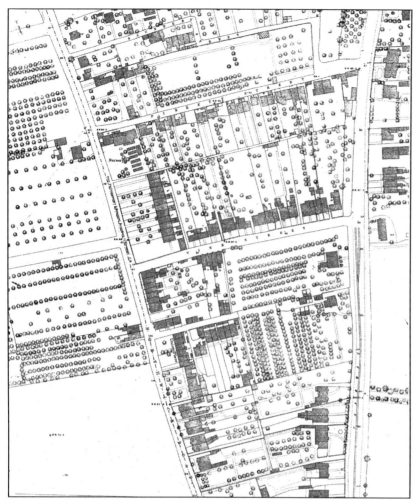

Above, Northwick and Ombersley Roads in 1884

Below, A 1936 ad for builder Ronald William Morris, who built many of
the houses in Northwick and created several streets

NORTHWICK ROAD

Northwick, or north settlement, was the main manor of the Bishop of Worcester at the time of Domesday Book, and no doubt before. There was no mention in Domesday of a manor house, but there was one in the area, which was rebuilt in the reign of Henry VII, and is believed to have been roughly at the end of Linley Close, in an area where medieval fishponds and part of the moat have been traced from old maps. A small triangular green near **Old Northwick Lane** was the centre of the old hamlet of Northwick. This manor began to lose its importance in the thirteenth century, as Hartlebury became established as the bishop's main manor.

Most of Northwick did not become part of Worcester until the 1930s, and in the mid nineteenth century this would still have been very much a rural area, with isolated country houses such as Northwick Lodge and Northwick Hall, and the occasional country cottage.

In the early 1870s it was still being referred to as Lane, but the first traces of urban development could be found. A terrace of villas named Bainsbeck Terrace, between **Vine Street** and **Pinkett Street**, was listed in 1873, and by the 1880s the east side was filling up fast, though it was still open land on the west side of the road.

Building records are almost non-existent, but an 1884 street directory listing shows the road bears all the hallmarks of modest developments by a number of different investors, who named the homes they created according to their personal taste. Aside from Bainsbeck Terrace there were Belle Vue

Cottages, Floral Villas, Clevedon Villas, Myrtle Villa, Albion Place, Union Place, Robertson's Buildings and Berrington Cottages. In all there were more than 60 homes here, whose residents had a real mix of occupations. There were clerks, gardeners, an inland revenue officer, an architect's assistant, labourers, shop assistants, building workers, an organ builder, a book canvasser, a stoker, a china painter, a stonemason, a hairdresser and a florist amongst others. Market gardener Thomas Newey had the Northwick Nursery near Pinkett Street. Development continued steadily and by 1922 there were around 90 homes here. Near **Northwick Avenue** then was the Barbourne Skirt Factory.

At Ash Cottage, on the corner of **Ombersley Road**, which must have been where the garage is now, was a shop kept in 1884 and for many years after by Mrs Elizabeth Powell. By 1922 it had been taken over by Mrs Fanny Biddle. On the corner of **Union Place** during the Second World War was Mr Jackson's general store, which was demolished in the 1960s during the development of Union Place. The Northwick Arms pub, on the corner of Vine Street, opened around 1900 and is still with us.

These homes on Northwick Road are all gone now, the villas on the right for the creation of Union Place, and the cottages on the left for road widening before the Faithful Overalls factory was built. This picture was probably taken in the 1930s - RS

NORTHWICK WALK
Off **Northwick Avenue**, this street was first found in a street directory in 1930, when 12 homes were listed here.

NORTON CLOSE
Off **Bath Road** opposite Norton Road, this street was first found in a street directory in 1936, when villas The Heritage and The Hedgerow were listed here. By the following year there were 11 homes listed.

NUNNERY LANE
Originally this would have been a path or trackway to the former Nunnery Farm, named for the White Ladies convent in **The Tything**, which held land at Nunnery Wood in the Middle Ages, possibly as tenants of the Hospital of St Wulfstan, better known as the Commandery in **Sidbury**.

Evidence has been found that parts of the wood were once ploughed farmland, but this would never have been ideal as arable land, and as ploughing was abandoned, probably after the Black Death pandemic of the 1340s, the land reverted to oak woodland. The farm was probably always a dairy farm, which may have supplied the convent with milk and other dairy products. From the seventeenth century or before, the Hills, a family of wealthy farmers who became lawyers, farmed 1,000 acres at Nunnery Farm. This land stretched as far as **Newtown Road**, where the Hills were living at Ronkswood House in the eighteenth and nineteenth centuries.

Nunnery Wood and Perry Wood were originally part of the manor of Pirie or Perry, which once held much land to the south of the city. The manor was held by the Bishops of Worcester from before the Conquest until at least 1212. It was later held by wealthy clothiers the Berkeleys, and by the Perry family, who had taken their name from the manor, and after the Dissolution it was granted to Christ Church, Oxford, which mostly still holds Nunnery Wood.

This area consisted of woods interspersed with open meadowland until the 1930s. This street was first listed in a street directory in 1937, when there were just five named houses listed. George Pitcher was the farmer at Nunnery Wood Farm then. There was a good deal more development in the 1930s, but most development in the area is modern. Nunnery Wood was partly felled in 1946, to provide timber for post-war reconstruction, and the wood now covers a smaller area than it did previously. Nunnery Wood High School opened in 1954.

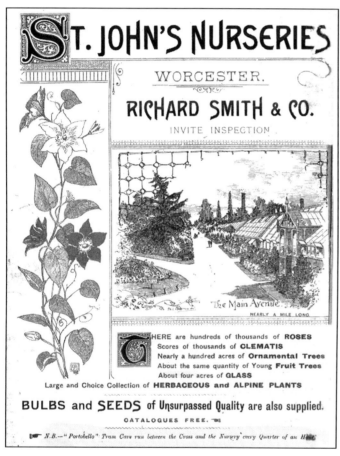

An 1896 advertisement

NURSERY ROAD

This name recalls the local nursery business which became one of the largest in the world. It was founded by Richard Smith, son of a Lower Wick nurseryman, who settled next to the park at Boughton shortly before 1820, working as a nurseryman and jobbing gardener. He supervised gardens at several large houses and quickly progressed, marrying into the Isaac family at Boughton House (see **Isaac Walk**). His son and grandson, both also named Richard Smith, each took over the nursery in turn, and at its height in the 1880s it covered 157 acres, stretching as far as Lower Wick, with a central drive 2,300 yards long, and eighteen miles of walkways between the beds, plus two and a half acres of glasshouses. The second Richard Smith popularised the Worcester Pearmain apple tree, which made a fortune for the nursery, and he married into the family of landscape artist Benjamin Williams Leader. From around the turn of the century the Victorian interest in horticulture ran out of steam and from at least 1911 nursery land began to be sold off, though this road and the adjacent **Nursery Walk** may have been built on former nursery land towards the end of the nineteenth century. Smith's nurseries shrank inexorably throughout the twentieth century, until the business ceased trading in 1993, and the last three and a half acres were sold for housing. Smith's Avenue recalls the family which once owned the market garden business.

This road was first listed in a street directory in 1896 when there were four Holly Cottages and a Poplar Cottage, all occupied by labourers, who probably worked at the nursery. These nursery cottages still stand, and a late Victorian or early Edwardian villa was added soon afterwards. But there is also a large detached villa, and two substantial terraced villas, all of which clearly seem to be from an earlier date – possibly even late eighteenth century – and oddly these were not found in the 1890s listings. In an area where most development is modern, this road serves as a reminder of this area as it must have been in the past.

NURSERY WALK

See **Nursery Road**. This road was first found in the health board streets list of 1872, and in a street directory of 1896, when there were listings for The Shrubbery, Ceylon House, Park House and Park Cottage, whose residents included a surveyor and an engineer at the power station at Powick, but everything here now is modern.

OAK AVENUE

Part of a 'tree' estate off **Brickfields Road**, this street was first found in a street directory in 1937, when 29 homes were listed here.

Oatmeal-market

Another name for **Mealcheapen Street**, listed on maps of 1610 and 1764.

OFFLEY STREET

Offley was a first name, acquired by marriage, of the Wakemans of Perdiswell Hall - see **Wakeman Street**. The best known nineteenth century member of the family was Sir Offley Penbury Wakeman, a popular figure in both Worcester and Claines, after whom several streets were named. This street was first found listed in a street directory in 1900, with just four listings. On the corner of **Crown Street** was a painter whose wife kept a shop, the site of which has since been redeveloped. The other residents were a plasterer and a thatcher. No further development took place here until around the 1970s.

OGILVY SQUARE

This street was first found in a street directory in 1940, when there were four homes here, though it must have been created in 1939 or earlier. It was no doubt named for Miss Diana Ogilvy MBE, a city magistrate and councillor for St Martin's Ward, who lived at Bishop's House, **Lansdowne Crescent**.

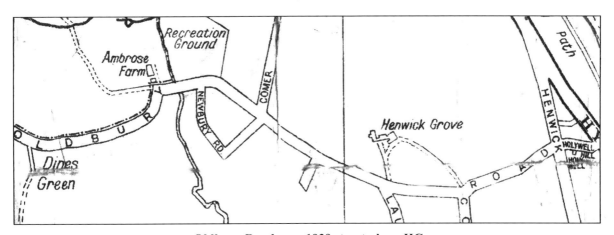

Oldbury Road on a 1939 street plan - HC

OLDBURY ROAD

This road existed for centuries as a country lane or footpath, and acquired new significance with the building of **Comer Gardens** in the 1850s, bit it was not found listed until the health board streets list of 1872, when it was still shown as Lane. It was first found in a street directory in 1880, and by then was being referred to as a road, but it was actually still nothing more than a country lane, running between fields and orchards, and ending just beyond Henwick Grove, where its route was blocked by a line of trees.

Henwick Grove was the largest house in the area, and living there in 1884, and for many years after, was Mrs Martha Binyon, while at Henwick Grove Lodge beside this road was Charles Rutter, who was listed as her gardener, though he was more likely to be her chief gardener, since she would have needed many to tend the extensive grounds around the house. Down the road at Oldbury Lodge was market gardener Joseph Day. There was the occasional villa dotted around the area, but there was nothing even approaching urban development in the area, and so it was to remain well into the next century.

By 1928 the road had progressed to just beyond Ambrose Farm, west of Laugherne Brook, but it was still effectively a farm track. A modest amount of building had spread south from Comer Gardens, and development was spreading slowly and inexorable north along **Laugherne Road** and **Comer Road** but it had not yet disturbed this rural idyll. In the 1930s however, though much of the road remained rural in character, there was much more development south of Comer Gardens. But the major development was the appearance around Henwick Grove by 1940 of six large accommodation blocks, four of which remain today. They were built for the Royal Air Force, which took over Henwick Grove as a training centre shortly before the Second World War began, in a move that changed the area forever. In 1946 the Grange and its accommodation blocks were taken over as an emergency teacher training centre, becoming a College of

Historic Worcester Streets

Education by the 1970s, later a Higher Education College and finally the University of Worcester. The road was widened and the fields and orchards around this road were finally built over from the 1950s on.

OLD NORTHWICK LANE

An ancient lane running down to a wharf or slip on the Severn. It was at this point that Prince Edward, later Edward I, was said to have crossed the river to surprise and defeat Simon de Montfort at the Battle of Evesham in 1265. There was a reference to 'Old Northwick' in 1884, and a directory then listed more than 20 modest homes here, with labourers making up around half the residents. Others included glovers, shoemakers, a drayman, a gardener, a baker, a brewer, a charwoman and a dressmaker. It seems to be referred to as 'Northwick Lane' in 1932, but the present name was not found in a street directory until 1937. Twentieth century development has left the lane with a varied mix of housing, from Victorian to modern.

OMBERSLEY ROAD

At the start of the 1880s the land here was an almost uninterrupted vista of open fields, with only the occasional building. Beyond the junction with Droitwich Road there was no building on the west until Barbourne Grange,

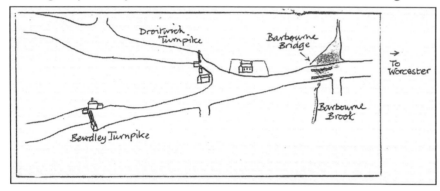

Above, the Droitwich and Ombersley Road turnpike toll gates in 1751. Below, Barbourne Grange - TW

at the junction with **Northwick Road**. This land may have been part of Barbourne in Anglo-Saxon times as far north as **Vine Street**, and it is possible that the Georgian Barbourne Grange, on a site where there has been a farming settlement for some centuries, may have been the original site of Anglo-Saxon settlement in the area. A glass bottle of about 1650 was found at one of the cottages associated with the Grange, which suggests they were built about that date.

In the late nineteenth century this road was surrounded on both sides by farmland. The land at the south end was then owned by Mrs Mary Gutch, one of the two daughters of banker John Pearkes Lavender, after whom **Lavender Road** was named.

She married one of her father's partners in the Farley, Lavender, Owen and Gutch bank at **The Cross**, and prevented any development in this area during her lifetime, except for St Stephen's Church and school. St Stephen's School was built by Thomas Wilkes, who was also the local undertaker, thanks to the generosity of Mrs Gutch and her sister.

The school opened in 1864. It was frequently a very popular school, winning praise from inspectors and parents, and it survived to celebrate its centenary, but closed soon afterwards and a housing development now stands on the site next to the church.

After the death of Mrs Gutch the land was sold and development quickly began, though it was mostly small-scale. Building applications show that many schemes were for two houses, with a fair number for just

An Edwardian photograph of a tram outside the Vine Inn in Ombersley Road, where tram services terminated - RS

one house. In total, between 1886 and 1902 there were 31 building applications for 71 homes, submitted by many different small developers or investors.

Then as now there were a number of shops. In 1884 Edward Hill kept a shop as greengrocer and dairyman a short distance along on the east side. William Pitt was a baker on the corner of **Hunger Pit Walk**, and Henry Digger was a newsagent further along. The Post Office near **Perdiswell Street** was kept by Mrs S.E. Lambert. Then as now this road had two pubs, The Vine near Vine Street, and the New Inn by **Cornmeadow Green**, both of which were said by Gwilliam to have been first listed in 1873, though he thought the latter was older.

William Kilbourne Kay who founded Kay's of Worcester, which grew into the vast mail order empire which was once the city's leading employer, lived in this road in the 1890s. He is supposed to have been at No. 115 from 1891, he was listed at Cliftonville in 1895, and at St Denis near **Victoria Street** in 1896. The stately Victorian villas spreading along this road also attracted many other local entrepreneurs, managers and professionals.

At Glenholm, near the Toll House, in 1896 lived Rev Ward, the vicar of Spetchley, between two local

George III in 1788, from a portrait in Worcester Guildhall - TW

businessmen. Not far away lived a surgeon and a bank manager, and at Ravensbury, near **St Stephen's Street**, lived the chief clerk in the probate office. At Sandoline Villa lived a mathematical master at the King's School, and at Clissold lived a manager for glove makers Dent & Allcroft.

A toll gate set up by the Worcester Turnpike Trust between 1714 and 1751, probably near where St Stephen's School later stood, made national headlines in 1788.

In August of that year George III and the royal family paid a visit to Worcester, and passed through the toll gate on their way to see the Bishop of Worcester at Hartlebury, but unfortunately courtiers neglected to pay the toll. When gate-keeper Robert Sleath saw the royal entourage returning later, he locked the gate and refused to let the king through until all the tolls had been paid for both journeys. His determined stand made his name known nationwide, and when he died in Birmingham in 1805, this epitaph appeared in the local newspaper:

On Wednesday last, old Robert Sleath

Passed through the Turnpike Gate of Death.

To him would Death no toll abate,

Who stopped the King, at Wor'ster Gate.

That gate was replaced around 1814 with a joint gate at the junction with **Droitwich Road** which ceased to operate in 1877. The area's most outstanding building is the landmark Northwick cinema, opened in 1938 under the same management as the Scala in Angel Place. Its much-admired Art Deco interior is one of only two remaining designed by gifted architect John Alexander, and RIBA still hold the original perspective drawings. By 1966 it had become a bingo hall, but it closed in 1982, and was empty until 1991. After five years as a music venue it closed once more and was empty until late 2000, when it was taken over by Grays Interiors from the **Tything**, who occupy it at the time of writing.

The former Northwick Cinems - TW

ORCHARD STREET

Cherry Orchard. This street probably began as a rear access to homes on **Bath Road**, from which the Cherry Orchard development grew. Providence Terrace, a terrace of 10 houses here, was listed in 1880. When the street first appeared – unnamed – on a map of 1884, much of the other development around it consisted of rear gardens of houses in Bath Road, though there was still a good deal of open ground.

The Worcester City Constabulary station at No. 6 Orchard Street in the early twentieth century, when PC Arthur Harry Guy was based there - RS

There were just six building applications for 15 houses between 1890 and 1901, yet in 1896, when it was first found in a street directory, there were around 30 homes here. All save two of these were on the west side, in a pattern that still continues today. There was a shop near Bath Road, kept in 1896 by William Willis.

Residents at that time were mostly manual workers, but few were labourers - most of them were skilled workers such as china gilders, china painters, a japanner (enameller), building tradesmen, shoemakers, a whitesmith (probably an ironmonger) and a clerk of works.

The Cherry Orchard Board School, now Cherry Orchard Primary School, opened in June 1883 with 38 pupils. This was not necessarily the total number of youngsters of school age in the area, because fees were then payable, and even though they were modest, some parents just couldn't afford them, and free education didn't come in until 1891.

The school gradually expanded west to **Cavendish Street**, where an attractive school hall was built in the 1940s. For many years the school was also the local branch library. The school began moving to a site off **Timberdine Avenue** in the 1970s, and all departments had moved there by 1982. The original school site is now used as a day centre.

A building application for the church here was submitted in 1902. The bell at St Mark's Church came originally from the watermen's church on a barge on the Severn, thanks to a parishioner who happened to have acquired the bell and noticed that the church didn't have one. There was a police station of the Worcester City Constabulary at No. 6 in the early twentieth century.

Orphanage Lane

This lane, leading to the orphanage off **Henwick Road**, was first found under this name in 1930, but must have been the lane formerly known in the nineteenth century as Asylum Lane. There were four homes here in 1930.

Oxford Road

An eighteenth century name for **London Road**.

Richard Padmore - TW

PADMORE STREET

Named for Richard Padmore, a leading iron founder in the city, who became Worcester's mayor and MP. He was born in Shropshire in 1789, and worked in the coalfields before coming to Worcester in 1818, to be taken on at the Worcester Iron Foundry in **Foundry Street**, run by Robert and John Hardy. In 1823 he married Emma, only daughter of John Jones, who had extensive iron-founding interests in the city, and in 1829 he became a partner in Hardy & Padmore.

He was elected a member of the city council in 1835, and within just three years he was an alderman. In 1840, with Edward Evans of the Hill Evans vinegar works, he founded the Worcester City and County Bank, which moved to the Cross in 1861 and merged with Lloyd's in 1889. He was the city's first Nonconformist mayor, elected in 1848 and again in 1852, though he refused to have the traditional procession to the cathedral or wear a mayoral robe. He was elected as the city's MP in 1860 and 1865.

Hardy & Padmore produced street furniture castings which went all over the world. Their best-known work included the dolphin lamps on Westminster embankment, London; the Blackpool Tower; and a much-admired fountain, presented to Worcester by Richard Padmore in 1858 for the market hall, now in Cripplegate Park. He died in 1881, aged 92, at Henwick Hall, and was buried at Astwood Cemetery. Hardy & Padmore closed in 1967.

Originally this street would have been a track leading to the Vulcan Iron Works (see **Cromwell Street**), from **Lowesmoor** where many of the workers may have lived. The Vulcan Iron Works, was started on a canalside site at the bottom of the street in 1857 by Thomas Clunes, as iron and brass founders. In 1861 he was joined by former railway employees McKenzie and Holland, whose company had merged into the West Midlands Railway in 1860. John McKenzie, a hard-working Scot, had been superintendent of the locomotive, carriage and wagon department of the Oxford, Worcester and Wolverhampton railway – nicknamed the 'Old Worse and Worse' – and Worcester-born Walter Holland handled accounts and administration.

The firm then began specialising in railway signal engineering. Its interlocking railway system was to revolutionise travel safety. By 1875 the company had become McKenzie and Holland, and expanded to cover the triangular site bounded by Cromwell Street, **Shrub Hill Road** and the canal, employing 480 people by 1881. Walter Holland was mayor in 1878-9, and again, by popular demand in the Queen's Golden Jubilee year, 1887. He died in the following year. The company merged in 1901 and its operations ceased in 1921. The premises off Shrub Hill Road are rented to small businesses, but there is no trace now of the original Vulcan Works. A branch of the Vinegar Works railway line from Shrub Hill ran alongside the street for 180 yards to the City Flour Mill.

The street was first listed in a street directory in 1880, and was always a street of industry and commerce. In 1884 inevitably the businesses were facing towards the canal. The Alhambra Wharf was presumably at the north end of the street and named for the **Lowesmoor** music hall. Further west on the canalside were the substantial premises of the City Steam Flour Mills of Goodwin & Sons, millers and corn merchants, and the massive Vulcan works were at the end of the street. The only resident seemed to be foreman William Farmer at Mill Cottage. The West Midland Tavern, on the corner of **Lowesmoor Place**, was first listed in 1873 and still exists.

A tram depot was built here early in the twentieth century, which was taken over by the Midland Red in 1928. Since then virtually the whole street is given over to the bus garage and parking for Midland Red employees.

Sir John, first Baron Hampton

PAKINGTON ROAD

The Pakingtons were Worcestershire land owners over a number of centuries, with a home at Powick, and there is a portrait of fourth baronet Sir John Pakington in the Guildhall. This road off **Lechmere Crescent** was no doubt named for Sir John Somerset Pakington, first Baron Hampton, born in 1799, who may have owned land here. It took him four attempts to become MP for Droitwich, which he finally achieved in 1837, but he kept the seat for 37 years, during which he twice held office as Secretary of State for War. He died in 1880.

This road was first found listed as Street in a directory in that year. An 1884 map showed two homes here, just off **Hallow Road**. Residents then were inventive **Shambles** engineer John J. Cam at South Villa, and at Eldersfield, Edward Little, gardener to J.F. Greswolde-Williams, who lived at Henwick Grange. The road saw no further development until the 1930s, and seems to have been complete by the 1940s.

Palace Row

A small street between **Palace Yard** and *Little Fish Street*, now part of **Deansway**. In 1790 organ builder and harpsichord maker James Chew was based here. By 1884 John Nicholson had taken over as organ builder, the Inland Revenue had an office here, and Josiah Stallard had a bonded store, but this was mainly then a street of glovers. Dent, Allcroft & Co. were at *Warmestry Slip*, and three other glovers had gathered here. This was the first street to become part of **Deansway**, in the late 1930s.

Palace Yard

Now part of **Deansway**, it led from the west end of **College Street**, where it joined *Lich Street*, to the north side of the Bishop's Palace, where it connected to *Palace Row*. In the nineteenth century the Bishop's Palace had larger grounds to the east than now, including a wooded area largely screening it from the road.

This street marked the furthest western extent of the ancient cathedral Sanctuary, and the site since early times of the Bishop's Palace. It has been said that there was a Bishop of Worcester living on this site before there was a king of England, which may be true since the diocese was founded in 680, though the earliest known bishop's house on the site dated from the thirteenth century.

Over the centuries the Bishop's Palace has been the home of two martyrs, four saints, several lord chancellors of England, and Egwin, the founder of Evesham Abbey. The present palace, dating from between 1200 and 1235, is said to be the oldest building in the city, aside from the cathedral, and has played host to Elizabeth I, who held her court in the Great Hall here for a week in 1575; Charles I and II during the Civil War; James II in 1687, the year before he was ousted; and George III, who

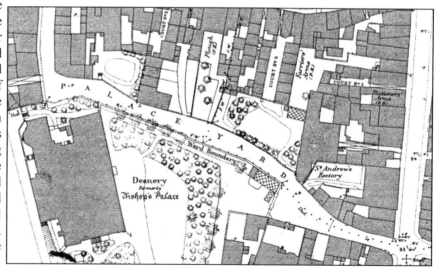

Palace Yard in 1884

stayed here with his family for almost a week in 1788, while they visited the Three Choirs Festival.

The palace ceased to be the bishop's residence in the 1840s. Church histories suggest that Bishop Pepys, a distant relative of the diarist, kindly made the palace available to the Dean because he also had a residence at Hartlebury Castle, but the decision was actually forced on him by a reforming Royal Commission who thought two palaces was one too many for any bishop. Nor was the palace given to the Dean; he had to pay £3,000 for it in 1846. It ceased to be the Deanery in 1941. Since the war it has been a diocesan office, and the bishop lives next door. This street has further fine examples of the Georgian development begun in **College Yard**. The Seven Stars inn was listed in 1775 and 1790 in 'Palace Street', which is believed to have been this street. No further mention of this pub has been found and it was not shown on the first large-scale Ordnance Survey maps a century later.

Paradise Place

A mid-Victorian terrace of houses at the south end of **Barbourne Road**, first found listed in a street directory in 1864. By 1880 the premises here were shops, and have remained so ever since. In the late nineteenth century they served the local community, with grocery, greengrocery, china, drapery and a post office, but they are now mostly occupied by specialist businesses.

Paradise Row

Listed in a street directory of 1840, though it is not a street but a row of stately Georgian town houses built in the late eighteenth century to form the High Street of fashionable Barbourne, though they were at that time in **The Tything**, since **Barbourne Road** then commenced just to the north of them. Residents in 1884 included commercial traveller George Shepherd, manager Moses Smith, Francis Shrimpton who had a grocery store at **The Cross**, Captain Locke, and two widows. The houses are now split into flats.

Paradise Row - TW

PARK AVENUE

This land was part of the estate of Mrs Mary Gutch (see **Ombersley Road**), and in 1884 it was still open land with sand pits mid-way down on the south side, but development was rapid when it began.

The first record found of this street was a building application submitted in 1886 by Kidderminster builder James Higgs, for a pair of semi-detached houses. He also applied to build two more houses here later that year and another two in 1891, but he was just one of many small investors and speculators who built homes here in the next 10 years. Up to 1896 there were 16 mostly small-scale applications to build 51 homes here, but at that date there were 44 homes built and occupied, with five others built and awaiting occupation, and six more being built, which is slightly more than the homes applied for, so perhaps an application or two has gone missing.

Many of the homes were given names by their builders or investors, which recalled places they held dear. There were Milford Villas, Glen Maye, Glen Helen, St Ann's, St Ives, Rossmoyne, Strathmore, Goodrich Villa, Algorta and Tregenna, amongst others. This was a very white-collar area. Residents in 1896 included commercial travellers and clerks, cashiers, a draper, a telegraphist, a GPO telegraph engineer, a surveyor, an insurance agent, an architect's assistant, an inland revenue officer, a draughtsman, and William Moody, finance clerk for the county. Two more homes had been built by the end of the century, and 12 more were put up between 1910 and 1922. By 1928 the north side of the avenue was complete, but the south side was complete for less than half its length, and though a little more development took place on that side of the street in the 1930s, it remained incomplete by 1940, and has only been finished since.

PARK STREET

This street was originally part of a footpath leading across the Blockhouse Fields, which is why a canal bridge was placed here. It was first mentioned in 1821, with building apparently going ahead around the same time as the *Blockhouse* development, though there is little detail of what was here until later in the century. It was then known as Great Park Street, to distinguish it from **Little Park Street**. The street was shown complete on a map of 1885, except for the land between **Derby Road** and the canal, where the Jehovah's Witnesses are now. The street takes its name from the parkland around Fort Royal House.

Residents tended to be a bit more clerical and managerial than in Little Park Street. In 1884 they included clerks, a foreman, the manager of the Sheet Dept at the GWR, a dairyman, a fruit and potato dealer, glove manufacturer Robert Bach at Nos. 13 and 14, and police detective sergeant William Underwood. The United Methodist Free Church, always known as the Zion Chapel, apparently dated from earlier than 1845, since it

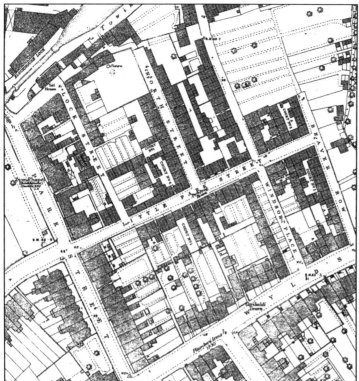

Left, Park Street and Little Park Street in 1884. Above, the Apollo Cinems in Park Street in 1918 - BG

was rebuilt in that year, perhaps because the original building proved too small as the *Blockhouse* continued to grow. The Bricklayers' Arms was built before 1908 and was still open in 1980, but has closed since.

The Zion Chapel had closed by 1911, and was converted in that year to open as the first permanent cinema in the city, the Apollo Electric Theatre, originally under the name of Evan's Picture Palace. To gain sufficient distance from the screen, the metal projection box was cantilevered out over the street. Gwilliam said the lively and not always hygienic *Blockhouse* audiences were likely to find themselves doused with a giant disinfectant spray. The Apollo closed in 1935, but the former chapel still exists and has since been converted again, this time into accommodation. There were several shops. One on the corner of Derby Road was a shoe repairers for many years, another was just south of Little Park Street, and a shop on the corner of Wyld's Lane was well known as an Italian grocery store for many years. All of these have closed, but the shop on the corner of **Lock Street** is still open as a barbers.

PARK VIEW TERRACE

This riverside terrace near Park Avenue runs to the east of marshy riverside land, and was clearly developed, probably initially in the 1880s, as a site for building superior villas in semi-rural surroundings. The only early information found about this street is a single building application of 1895 for two houses for George Gascoyne, who went on to become the largest hop and seed merchant in the city, though at that time he gave his occupation as commercial clerk. By 1905 his houses, The Elms and Riverlynne, were built and he was living in the first of them and letting the other to an analyst's assistant. Later Gascoyne moved to much grander surroundings at **Barbourne Terrace**.

The other homes here at that time were probably built prior to the 1880s, when the city boundary expanded to include this area. Not surprisingly, all the homes had names rather than

Kepax ferry about 1900 - RS

numbers. Other residents in 1905 included local businessman William Homer JP at Riverscourt, manager Herbert Knott at Kenmare, local businessman Francis Dingle at Chace Water, Herbert Spreckley of the **Barbourne Road** brewery at Cove Cottage, and local businessman Edward Hancock at Hazeldene. Mid-way along the road was the Kepax Ferry, then run by carpenter Albert Cheston, and remembered by the nearby Kepax Gardens and Ferry Villas. It was subsequently taken over by the Bailey family and became popularly known as 'Bailey's Boat'.

There was still a good deal of potential building land in the street at the end of the 1920s. Much of it at the north end was developed in the 1930s, but the southern end was only developed quite recently.

Penbury Street before it was paved - RS

PENBURY STREET

One of a number of streets named for Sir Offley Penbury Wakeman of Perdiswell Hall (see **Wakeman Street**). In the 1880s this was completely open land, worked by Barbourne Nurseries. It was first found as a street in 1899, when there was a building application for two houses. It was first found listed in a street directory of 1900 as Padbury Street, which must have been a clerical or setting error. At that time there was just one house in the course of erection, but development went ahead quickly.

In the next three years there were seven building applications for 27 houses, including five with stables. In a 1903 directory it was referred to as Penbury Road. There were then 13 occupied houses, five newly built waiting for occupants and three more being built, plus the St Stephen's Institute and Working Men's Club. By 1905 the street was finally listed with the present name, and even more homes than there had been applications for – 27 in total - with 34 by 1922. A map of 1928 showed that the street was complete but for one vacant house plot in the centre of the south side, which was not filled until around the 1960s. The east end on the south side has seen further redevelopment since then.

PERDISWELL STREET

No doubt named for Perdiswell Hall, the home of the Wakeman family (see **Wakeman Street**), since it appeared in the late nineteenth century on land which must formerly have been part of Barbourne Nurseries. The street was first found in a directory in 1884, and the south side of the street was already complete at that time, but only about a third of the north side. There were already around 35 homes here in 1884, for which there are no building records, since this area was previously outside the city boundary. Park Terrace, with 10 homes, was probably the work of a single builder or developer, but there is no indication of how or by whom the rest of the street was built.

The homes here were very much providing modest accommodation for working families, though gardens were of a good size. Residents then were mostly building tradesmen and labourers, but included a gardener, a lithographer, a brush maker, a wheelwright, a coach builder, a shoemaker, a porter, a seamstress, a laundress and a basket maker. The street was completed before 1928.

PERRY WOOD WALK

Perry Wood Walk, with the White Cottage, before Metal Box - RS

In past centuries this was a lane leading from **Wyld's Lane** to Nunnery Farm, connecting to a deeply cut pathway called the entrenchment, possibly an ancient estate boundary, which still leads through the wood. It was listed in the health board streets list in 1872, but the first listing in a street directory was not until 1932, after development began in the area.

The old name of the area was Pirywode – meaning 'wood by the pear tree' in Old English - found in annals of 1370 of the Hospital of St Wulfstan, better known to us as the Commandery in **Sidbury**, which at that time presumably held what was left of the ancient manor of Pirie or Perry, which once included much land to the south of the city.

The manor was held by the Bishops of Worcester from before the Conquest until at least 1212. It was later held by wealthy clothiers the Berkeleys, and by the Perry family, who had taken their name from the manor, and after the Dissolution was granted to Christ Church, Oxford, along with Nunnery Wood which it mostly still holds.

The Parliamentarians had a battery in Perry Wood during the Battle of Worcester in 1651, and evidence of the encampment there, usually called Cromwell's trenches, can still be seen in the area. Perry Wood Cottage, a large white cottage, possibly built in the eighteenth century, once stood at the head of this street near the present Crown Food factory, by the path through the wood. It still existed in 1924, when this was still open meadowland, with many native wildflowers growing in profusion in the boundary hedges, which are now quite rare.

In 1814 glover John Knapp bought land in this area, and five years later mortgaged it for £3,000, and offered land for sale suitable for building. Erection of large villas went ahead on **Lark Hill** in the 1820s, but development here did not begin until the start of the 1930s when Metal Box came here, and most of the homes here date from that decade.

The company had been created in 1921, with the amalgamation of four manufacturers from London and the South East, and the North of England, to create probably the largest metal container business in the UK. However the firm's involvement with Worcester began only in 1930, when it amalgamated with the Williamson tin plate manufactory in **Providence Street**. In response to foreign competition the business then began building here the fist purpose-built plant of its kind in the UK, which opened in the spring of 1931, to provide cans for the food industry, a business that Williamsons had already been in.

It will have been at this time that Perry Wood Cottage was demolished, and this street was created on the line of the former lane, as an approach road to Metal Box. The factory continued to supply the food canning industry for 70 years, and at one time employed 1,000 people, but the group which grew from it became a sprawling, diverse international corporation, in which canning had little importance, and in 1996 this business was sold to leading American food packaging company Crown Food, and its closure has been announced during the preparation of this book.

Nunnery Wood was partly felled in 1946, to provide timber for post-war reconstruction, and no doubt there was also felling here, since the wood now covers a smaller area than it did previously.

PHEASANT STREET

The street owes its name to an eighteenth century inn, though the Pheasant was actually in **Silver Street**. This might seem odd, but inns of that time frequently had substantial gardens around them, and this probably

The Hill Evans vinegar works, probably in the mid nineteenth century

began life as a lane leading to a substantial bowling green at the rear of the inn, referred to in the Journal in 1714. The licensee in the 1770s or 80s was a Mr Morris, but when he died, his wife Eleanor moved to **New Street** to set up a new pub. According to the history of the Pheasant there, she was able to use the same name because the Pheasant in Silver Street had been delicenced after her husband's death, but a new Pheasant existed in Silver Street by 1805, where the Journal reported that more than 100 cocks were being matched at the cockpit there.

In the nineteenth century the street was dominated on the west side by the massive Hill, Evans vinegar works, which expanded to cover a six acre site bounded by **Lowesmoor** and **St Martin's Gate**. It was founded in 1830 by chemists William Hill and Edward Evans, and by 1844, when the duty on vinegar was repealed, the works were probably the largest in Britain. The firm was taken over by the sons of the founders, Edward Bickerton Evans and Thomas Rowley Hill, after whom **Rowley Hill Street** was named, and was to become the largest in the world.

The stately Great Filling Hall, built in the 1850s and now occupied by a Territorial Army unit, was reputed to have as great a span as the roof of Westminster Hall. It was 120 feet by 160 feet, with a roof partly of glass, rising to a ridge height of 70 feet. From about 1873 a private railway branch line from Shrub Hill ran into it. The vats were huge, the largest being 40 feet high, holding 114821 gallons. At its height, in the early twentieth century, the works were said to be the largest in the world, producing two million gallons of malt vinegar a year in six grades, which was sold all over the globe.

Other products included vast quantities of British wine made from raisins, gooseberries, cherries, cowslips, elderberries and ginger, as well as port, sherry and quinine wine, exported to the tropics to combat malaria. The company continued to expand during the first half of the twentieth century, but was taken over in the early 1960s and closed in 1965. The last train on the branch line ran on 5 June 1964. Within a few years the site became an industrial estate, and remained so until redevelopment began in 2009.

The Filling Hall, listed Grade II in 1974, is the most striking building on the street, but the most impressive remains are said to be the vast, vaulted, storage cellars below the site, which have all the grandeur of the crypt of a great cathedral.

On the east side of the street in the nineteenth century was densely packed housing, with no less than five courts off the street. Labourer was the most common occupation of residents in 1884, followed by metal worker. There were also some shoemakers and glovers, laundresses and seamstresses. Thomas Bach manufactured gloves at the junction with Lowesmoor. There were two small shops in the street then, and three pubs shown in an 1884 street directory, the Lamp Tavern near Lowesmoor, and the Eagle and the Cock & Magpie. Very little seems to be known about any of these pubs, and the only one listed by Gwilliam is the last, which he said closed after 1930. The slum housing in this area was probably cleared in the 1930s, and most of the street has been redeveloped.

Pie Corner

This was at the north west corner of **Copenhagen Street** and *Birdport*, now under **Deansway**. It has not been found on maps but was referred to in a 1790 Worcester directory, and was traced through the Plume of Feathers pub, which stood there from the eighteenth century and was last recorded in 1896. Old London had a Pie Corner near St Paul's, which had been the site of a food market. Worcester's Pie Corner must have got its name because it was on the corner of the former *Cucking Street*, the street of the cooks.

Piercy's Alley

Listed off **Lowesmoor** in 1840.

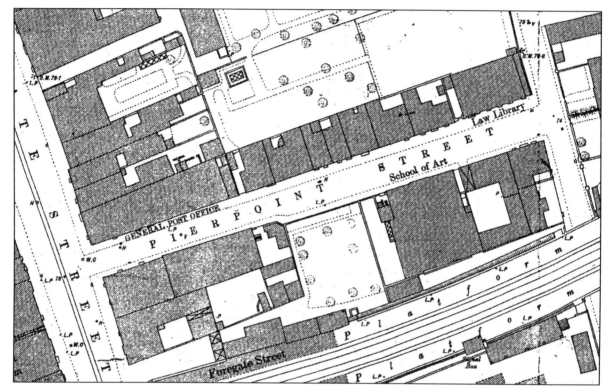

Pierpoint Street in 1884

PIERPOINT STREET

This street was named for Matthew Pierpoint, a surgeon at Worcester Infirmary in the early nineteenth century, whose house and garden occupied the site used to create the road.

Before coming to Worcester he had been elected Senior President of the Royal Medical Society in Edinburgh. He was appointed to the Worcester Infirmary in 1819, and was very active politically with Tories in the city, as well as being a surgeon in the Worcester Militia, based at **St George's Square** at one time. His hot-headed nature was shown by an action for slander he took in 1824, seeking damages of £5,000 from a young woman who claimed that his care of her sister had not been good enough. He won the case but the court clearly thought little of its merits, and he was awarded only 39 shillings (£1.95) in damages.

He took a prominent part in dealing with the cholera outbreak of 1832, which cost the lives of 79 people who were buried in a mass grave at **Tallow Hill**. He later married an heiress from Crown East, and for a time lived the life of a country gentleman. He was a familiar figure on the local social scene, but his turbulent arrogance often involved him in bitter disputes. Though he was regarded as the injured party in a violent confrontation with local solicitor Charles Bedford at Diglis Bowling Green (see **Shrubbery Avenue**), other disputes reflected little credit on him.

In 1835 the Birmingham and Gloucester Railway published a bill for a direct link between the two towns, crossing Worcestershire but by-passing Worcester, which threatened the city's time-honoured position as Birmingham's port. Pierpoint angrily opposed the scheme, and afterwards claimed he had obtained a bond from the promoters guaranteeing the route would pass through the city, but for twenty years he refused to show this supposed bond to anyone, and was subsequently accused of having deceived citizens over its existence.

In the event, the railway went ahead according to the original plan, avoiding Worcester. Pierpoint soon ran through his wife's money, and died in 'embarrassed circumstances'.

There was no sign of the street on a map of 1829, but the first section, off **Foregate Street**, is shown on a map of 1832. Around the same time a handsome new building was constructed at the

An 1869 ad for a Pierpoint Street business

west end, which housed the City and County Library. Development was swift, and a map of 1838 showed that building seemed to have been completed on the north side of the street, though there was still some vacant land on the south side.

An 1840 directory listing showed that from the start this was a street of commerce. Occupants included architect Harvey Eginton, four solicitors one of whom was James Best, commissioner of bankrupts, two insurance offices, a milliner, a dressmaker, a plumber, a coachbuilder and Mrs Gray's lodging house.

By 1884 two of the most powerful legal families in the city, the Stallards and the Hills, had moved into the street next door to each other. The Stallards, father and son both called John, were at No. 3, and both were leading figures in the city's late Victorian building boom. Next door at No. 2 was Richard Price Hill, who came from a wealthy farming family, and lived at Ronkswood House, **Newtown Road**. He owned Brickfields estate as well as much other land around the county, and by 1896 was in partnership with his son John George. At No. 1 in 1884 was the city's post office, on a site which was later a telephone exchange, where the Postal Order pub now recalls the street's past.

The City and County Library moved here from **Angel Street**, where it had opened in 1790 as the city's first public library. It was a subscription library, dependent for funds on the number of its subscribers, but the growth of its financial base had not been rapid. It had grown from 600 volumes to around 5,500 in its first forty years, but subscribers had increased by only 60 in this period to 180. In 1840 B. Bunn was the secretary and librarian.

To try to make ends meet the library let off much of the building, and Deightons, the local printing firm which then published the *Berrow's Worcester Journal*, opened a newsroom on the ground floor where the public could read newspapers of the day for a small fee. Nevertheless, by 1860 the annual subscription had risen to the not inconsiderable sum of twenty-one shillings.

In 1879, after years of public pressure, the corporation finally agreed to take over the library, and it re-opened in a building in Foregate Street in 1881, transferring to the present library building when it opened in 1896. Its building here was taken over as the Worcestershire Law Society library, whose librarian in 1896 was Miss Alice Oakey. The library was demolished in 1960 and replaced by an office building.

A building on the south side of the street, near to **Sansome Walk**, now an office building called International House, once housed the Worcester School of Design and Art, which had a national reputation in the mid nineteenth century.

Its famous pupils included leading Victorian landscape painter Benjamin Williams Leader; leading sculptor Thomas Brock, whose major body of work included the statue of Queen Victoria outside the Guildhall in Foregate Street, and the Victoria Memorial outside Buckingham Palace, for which he was said to have been knighted; and sculptor H.H. Martyn, who set up a famous national architectural decorating business, and in 1917 founded what became the Gloster Aircraft Company. The School closed around 1890.

Kay's had a photographic studio here at No. 14 from the early 1950s to the 1990s.

Though clearly there is nothing in the street older than the 1830s, a good deal of what was built at that time still remains.

Pinch, The

A notorious court which existed by or before 1764, behind a row of cottages in the area of the later fruit and veg market on **Hylton Road**, near the site of the Worcester Arena. A disastrous cholera epidemic originated here in 1832. The first victim was a travelling brazier and rag collector who lived here, and died within 16 hours of contracting the disease on 14 July.

A number of other cases here quickly followed. The epidemic continued until October, and of the 238 people who contracted the disease, 79 died and were buried in a mass grave at **Tallow Hill**. This area must have been cleared in the 1920s.

PINKETT STREET

The Pinkett family came from Fernhill Heath and may have owned land here or been involved in the development of the street. Mrs Elizabeth Hooper Pinkett was listed at Dilmore Lodge, Fernhill Heath, in 1885. Frederick Henry Pinkett was a veterinary surgeon in the city at that time, who had his surgery at 21 **Sansome Street** in 1884 and was living at 1 **Arboretum Road**.

This street had probably long existed as an unnamed lane or 'cuthrough' between **Northwick Road** and **Ombersley Road**. It was shown in this way on a map of 1859, but was not listed in a street directory until 1884 when there were 18 homes here. Residents were either labourers or small tradesmen, including two blacksmiths, a signalman, a drayman, a gardener, a laundress, a shopkeeper, a tailor and a glover. At that date the south side of the street was complete, but virtually nothing had been built on the north side where orchards still existed, and it was there that subsequent development was concentrated.

No building records exist until the 1890s, and they show that after the initial phase development was fairly slow, with only eight building applications submitted for 27 homes between 1892 and 1905. Two of these applications, for a total of six homes, were submitted by John Wilesmith Jnr, whose family had a saw mill in **Portland Street**, and offices in **Bath Road** where he put forward a number of building applications. Other applications were by various investors or speculators. All the homes for which applications were submitted had been built by 1910.

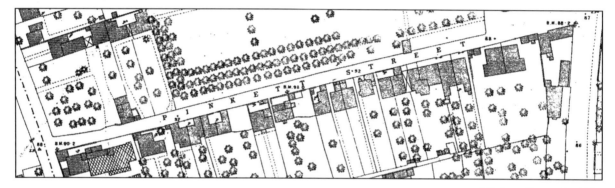

Pinkett Street in 1884

PITCHCROFT LANE

This area probably had some sporadic developments of farm cottages over the centuries, and is likely to have been known by this name long before any substantial development took place in the area, since it is a route from Pitchcroft that may have linked with **Barbourne Road** originally.

The first record of development here was a building application for two houses in 1872, which had been built by 1884, and it was first listed in a street directory in that year, when there were just those two listings, for shoemaker Frederick Vincent and labourer Charles Redding, who lived in a pair of cottages mid-way along the lane on the south side, surrounded by open fields. The Old Farm seems to be the group of buildings shown near the west end of the lane on a map of 1884, but it was empty by 1896.

In 1885-6 there were two building applications for four houses, and it wasn't until 1895 that there was a sizeable application for 20 homes, submitted by busy property developer William Henry Aston, whose family had a saw mill in *James Street*.

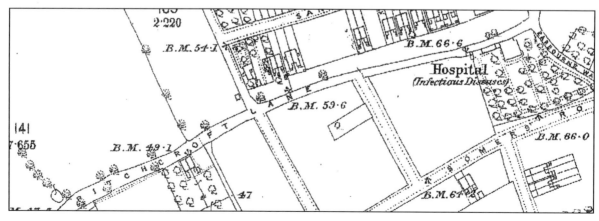

Pitchcroft Lane in 1884

There was just one additional pair of cottages by 1896, but by 1900 the homes applied for had been built, which completed the north side of the lane. In 1900 Mrs Augusta Furness was keeping a shop on the corner of **Barbourne Walk**. The existence of a number of different investors was suggested by the different names given to small groups of cottages. There were Jameson Cottages, Arno Cottages, Carola Cottages, Adelaide and Sydney Cottages. Residents in 1900 included labourers, building tradesmen, a baker, a gas meter maker, a

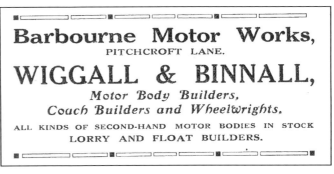

A 1922 advertisement

compositor, a letter carrier, a cellarman, a mechanic, a bootmaker, a florist and a seamstress. The south side of the lane was not developed until comparatively recently.

One of the most notable buildings in the area was Barbourne Lodge, which was on the corner of the Lane and Barbourne Walk, with its grounds backing onto **Somers Road**. Though the house was shown on an 1884 map as facing onto the Lane, it was listed in directories on Barbourne Walk. Probably a farmhouse originally, the Lodge was a bedlam, or mental institution, in the early eighteenth century, and for some years from the 1760s was home to the Burney family, relatives of novelist Fanny Burney. In the nineteenth century it was an isolation hospital, for patients with infectious diseases, and was thus so feared that in 1905, several years after it closed, it was deliberately gutted by fire, to kill any lingering germs, before being demolished.

PITMASTON ROAD

Named after Pitmaston House on **Malvern Road**, this road was first found recorded in 1866, when there were six small-scale building applications for a total of 14 homes.

Eight applications, mostly for one or two houses, with the occasional builder's application for three, four or five homes, continued into the early 1880s. There were four applications for seven homes in 1867, one application for two homes in 1868, four for 13 homes in the following year, one application for 3 homes in 1870, one for two houses in 1877, one for four in 1879, one for two in 1880, and one for nine houses in the following year. There was also a building application for a shop and bakehouse in 1889. The road was first listed in a street directory in 1880. By 1884 a total of 47 homes had been built here, and a pub called the Fox Inn, which was first listed in 1873, and is still here.

An Edwardian view of Pitmaston Road - RS

There was a real mix of occupations amongst residents. Gardeners, probably at Smith's Nurseries, were the largest group, but others were labourers, an inland revenue officer, a foreman, a basket maker, a cabinet maker, a railway inspector, a tailor, a groom, a compositor, a seamstress, a confectioner, a laundress, several glovers, an iron worker, a leather dresser, a bricklayer and an insurance agent.

The remainder of the homes applied for had been built by 1896, and the shop and bakehouse had been built next to the pub, which was then kept by John Williams.

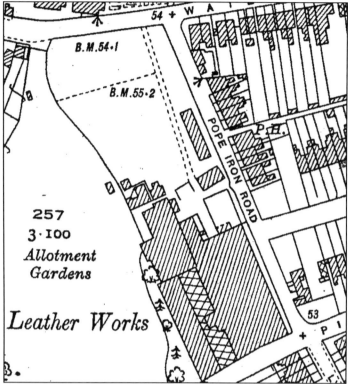

Pope Ison Road in 1928, and Ward's leather works - MS

POPE IRON ROAD

This road will have taken its name from the pub, now called the Winning Post but previously the New Pope Iron, which in turn will have taken its name from an ironworks which stood on the riverside to the north, probably founded in the eighteenth century. Iron smelting had a long history in the area, dating to Roman times, when there was a considerable iron industry along Pitchcroft, smelting iron ore brought in by river, probably from the Forest of Dean. There is no definite information about the foundation of the Pope Ironworks, but in 1751 a Bromwich and Mercy Pope owned a forge at Duck Brook, about six miles up the Severn, and they or a relative may have started the ironworks here. A plan of 1808 showed the works covering a substantial site at the bottom of what is now **Waterworks Road**, but it appeared to have ceased working by 1880, when houses were built across the riverside slipway.

The half-timbered Pope Iron inn, possibly of eighteenth or even seventeenth century date, stood on the riverside next to the ironworks. It was probably intended originally to serve river travellers, and those people waiting for low tide to ford the river to the west bank, but must have changed its name when the ironworks opened, and the thirsty workmen no doubt became regular customers.

This street was apparently created in the 1860s or early 1870s, though there was some confusion about it. The old pub on the riverside was demolished in 1895, and it has been assumed that the New Pope Iron pub was built here as a replacement around that time, and that the road must have been created at the same time. This seems to be confirmed by the fact that this street was first listed in a street directory in 1896. However the New Pope Iron pub was first listed in 1873, 22 years before the old one was knocked down. Its address was then given as **Sandys Road**, and this was referred to as Sandys Road North, which suggests that building of the street went ahead 20 or 30 years earlier than previously thought.

The 1896 listing – the first found under the present name - showed the street complete at that time, with nine homes here, plus a shop, the pub and Ward's leather works, which took up the whole of the west side of the street. Residents then included a laundress, a carpenter, a leather dresser, a bricklayer, a labourer and three stonemasons. Joshua Jones was keeping the shop on the corner of Sandys Road. The pub which gave this road its name was sadly renamed in 2007.

Ward's Barbourne Leather Works was a notable building on a substantial site at the junction with **Pitchcroft Lane**. It was founded in 1892 by businessman J.R.H. Ward, and was the only substantial tannery ever founded to the north of the city. After Ward's death about 1900 the business was taken over by Thomas William Badgery, who ran a glove leather business in the city, and had apparently been advising Ward. By 1903 the works had expanded to four times their original size, and exported high quality leather all over the world, though it was best known to local residents for the dreadful smells that came from the works, caused by some of the strange substances used to treat the hides, including bullocks' blood and dog 'muck'. Foreign competition led to the company's closure in 1978, and its premises were demolished, and that side of the street was redeveloped with other commercial premises.

PORTEFIELDS ROAD

In the nineteenth century **Tolladine Road** was referred to as Porte Fields Road, leading to the Port Fields once held by the White Ladies convent in the **Tything** – 'port' usually referred to a Roman military road. There was a Portfields dairy farm in the area, which was listed as late as 1922, when Charles Vincent Depper was the farmer. This road was first found in a street directory in 1930, when there were 71 homes listed here.

Portland Place

Blockhouse. In 1784 this was Williams' timber yard, just inside Friars' Gate, but by 1824 this small street had been created as a route between **Carden Street** and **Charles Street** and into *Little Charles Street*, and there were a number of modest homes here. In 1884 six homes were listed, whose residents were a dairyman, a bookbinder, a fitter, a porter, a leather dresser and a cabinet maker. The street was demolished to make way for the **City Walls Road.**

PORTLAND STREET

The reason for this name is not entirely clear. Port Fields, on the southern slope of Elbury Mount, were owned in the medieval period by the White Ladies convent in **The Tything**, and there may be some connection, but it seems more likely that this name refers to Diglis Port, which was created about 1815 when the Worcester & Birmingham Canal opened.

The development of **Mill Street** must have begun in the 1850s or 60s, and no doubt followed here fairly soon afterwards. The street name was first found in the health board streets list of 1872, and in a street directory of the following year. Development seems to have gone ahead fairly quickly, and building in the area was shown complete on the east side on a map of 1885, though there was still a good deal of open land on the west. A street directory of 1884 listed almost 50 homes here, most of which may have been built before building control began in late 1865, since no building records were found until 1877, and then there were only a handful of applications for 16 homes over the next 10 years. The biggest of these applications, for six homes in 1884, was submitted by Alderman Thomas Townshend of Albion Mill in Mill Street, who may well have been one of those involved in the first phase of building in the street.

The 1884 listing for 46 homes has the typical appearance of a street financed by a number of different investors or speculators who named small terraces of homes according to their taste. There were three Aucuba Cottages listed, six Fern Cottages, two Sunnyside Cottages near **Willow Street**, four Sabrina Cottages, and a Richmond House. Not surprisingly there were a number of china workers and boatmen amongst the residents, but there were a wide variety of other occupations, including building tradesmen, metal workers, labourers, laundresses, shoemakers, glovers, a basket maker, a confectioner and a couple of coal dealers.

Oddly there wasn't a corner shop then, but there was a pub, the Unicorn near Mill Street, where landlord Josiah Davis was also a cider dealer. It was first listed in 1873, but may not have been popular since Gwilliam said it had closed by 1906, though the Alma was listed here then, so it may have just changed its name. At the end of the street, beside the canal, were the Portland Street Steam Saw Mills of the Wilesmith brothers, who were also very active in property development. Later there was a shop on the corner of Mill Street, and another elsewhere.

The remaining homes for which building applications had been submitted were completed by around the end of the nineteenth century, but the street has been largely redeveloped in the late twentieth century.

PORTLAND WALK

The street was first found in the health board streets list of 1872, but that does not mean there was development here at that time. The first entry in a street directory was in 1930 when there were eight listings.

POUND WALK

Situated on the east side of Pitchcroft, skirting streets built around **Britannia Square** on what were once the Bishop's Pound Fields, this footpath was first found listed in a street directory in 1937, though it must have existed long before that.

POWELL'S ROW

This small lane was named for a builder who is said to have owned the land and built some of the houses. In 1877 historian John Noake said an elderly St John's resident remembered that around 1800 a builder in the area called Powell, purchased some houses in an ancient lane called Rotten Row, built a few more homes at the end of the row to rent out, and named the street after himself. There were a number of builders called Powell in the city around that time, but none listed in St John's, so it has not been possible to trace the builder referred to here.

This street was listed in the health board streets list of 1872, and in a street directory in 1885, when there were 18 homes listed, including three Eglantine Cottages at the east end, where the residents were an asylum attendant, a warehouseman and a piano tuner. On the **St John's** corner, presumably on the south side, was the music warehouse of W.H. Waldron. Other residents included labourers, building workers, tailors and dressmakers, a charwoman and a tram conductor. A picture postcard of the street and some of its residents was published around 1910, though the picture used may have been older. Only two of the cottages still remain, and they are much altered. These may have been Nos. 11 and 13 in 1910, in which case their occupants then would have been gloveress Mrs Jones and labourer William Birbeck.

This postcard of Powell's Row dates from about 1910 but the picture may be older - RS

Powick Lane

This lane is thought to have been named for the Powick family, who were recorded in the thirteenth and fourteenth centuries, but on maps of 1610 and 1764 it was listed as Poytes Lane, perhaps from another past landowner, though the name has not been traced. It was changing to Powick Lane by the time of the second map, since both names were listed. It ran from the junction of *Merry Vale* and *Birdport* to the **High Street**, taking much the same line that the route through the Crowngate Centre does now. By the late eighteenth century the top end of the lane had become **Bank Street**, after the establishment of the Old Bank in 1765. On the south side, with gardens on part of the site now occupied by the Countess of Huntingdon's chapel, stood almshouses founded by John Walsgrave or Walsgrove. The name appears no less than eight times in

the list of city bailiffs between the 1530s and 1560s, and a Robert Walsgrove was bailiff in 1592. It was usual for money to be left for such charitable purposes in a will, so John must have died before 1567, since the almshouses were built by that date. They were rebuilt by public subscription in 1825. Walsgrove Court almshouses were built in **Infirmary Walk** around 1900, but the almshouses still existed here, and in 1922 the six occupiers were each paying rent of 1/6d (c. 7p).

A directory of 1790 listed cooper Thomas Collins, currier (leather dresser) William Bristow, nailer William Dickens, schoolmaster Mr Esner - and two pubs, the Rising Sun kept by Mrs Williams and the Swan kept by Mrs Mansell. The first of these was near the Bank Street entrance to Crowngate, and closed around 1930. The Swan closed around 1850, according to Gwilliam, who also lists the Glovers Arms, near Merryvale, which he said had closed by 1920, and the Queen's Arms, midway along the south side of the street, which he said was first listed in 1850 and closed around 1960.

In 1884 the lane was clearly lined with shops, since half the directory entries were for shopkeepers. Other listings included tripe dresser Mrs Betsy Kirk at the junction with Bank Street, a paperhanger, a horsehair weaver, a fruiterer, a baker, a hawker, a marine stores dealer and a charwoman.

The west end of the lane was affected by the 1960s **Deansway** development, and it was entirely redeveloped in the 1990s Crowngate development.

Above, old house in Powick Lane in 1899. Below, Powick Lane in 1822.

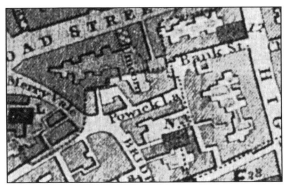

PRICE STREET

A William Price was sheriff of Worcester in 1855, and the Price family may have owned land in this area, or been involved in the development of the street, though there are no building records, partly because this area did not become part of the city until the 1880s, but mainly perhaps because, despite being listed in a street directory in 1896, this is just a back entry for houses on **Raglan Street**, and though it continues to be listed on street plans, there is not even a street sign to indicate where it is.

PRINCE RUPERT ROAD

One of several roads in this area recalling the 1651 Battle of Worcester. Prince Rupert was the German nephew of Charles I, and had a formidable reputation in European wars before he was appointed as cavalry commander for Charles I during the Civil War, at the age of just 23, eventually becoming the senior Royalist general. He was accounted an impetuous but skilled and courageous soldier against the Parliamentarians, but he was deported when Charles lost the war. He returned after the Restoration and commanded the Royal Navy, dying in England in 1682. His sister Sophia was the mother of George I.

This road was part of a development promoted by glove manufacturer Robert Bach of *Great Park Street* and six other investors, which included **Derby Road** and **Hamilton Road**.

Building began in Hamilton Road in 1871 but the first building application for 14 houses in this road was not submitted until 1885, with another for 13 homes in the following year, both submitted by Robert Bach. There was no sign of the road having been created on a map of 1885, but despite Robert Bach's death in January 1888 building went ahead quickly. But it soon became clear that plans for 27 homes here were unrealistic. By 1896 21 of the homes applied for had been built, and the street was complete. Residents then had a wide range of occupations. There were

Prince Rupert

carpenters, charwomen, labourers, a wood turner, a tinplate worker, a china fitter, a glover, a groom, a kilnman, a charwoman, a tailor, a compositor, a shunter, a cabman and a bootmaker.

PRIORY ROAD

This road was probably named because the land here was once owned by the church at Worcester. It was first found in a street directory in 1937, when there were eight homes listed.

PROSPECT PLACE

On the high ground off **Greenhill**, which no doubt gave rise to the name, this street was first found in a street directory in 1930, when eight homes were listed.

Providence Works

PROVIDENCE STREET

This street was named for a tin plate works built here in 1858 by Irishman William Blizzard Williamson, who had come from London to start a small japanning (enamelling) business in **Lowesmoor**, which he built into a large concern, producing baths, travelling trunks, lawyers' wig boxes, cash boxes, and camping washstands for soldiers in the field.

When Mr Williamson died the firm was taken over by his sons, William and George, who patented several innovations and boosted the business and the workforce. Both became mayor, William in 1883 and George ten years later. When his brother retired in 1890, George ran the company alone. He was a councillor for many years and Chairman of the Streets and Electricity Committees for seven years during which he carried out much modernisation of city streets.

The Williamson brothers, William, above & George-TW

He oversaw the widening of **High Street, Pump Street, Bank Street, St Swithin's Street** and **St Nicholas Street**; raised **Hylton Road** to try to avoid flooding; encouraged private landlords across the city to improve their properties, and oversaw the building of the first ever municipal power station, to light city streets with electricity. He eventually retired to Bournemouth and died in 1918. His son, also George, took over the firm.

In 1930 it became part of Metal Box, but the Providence Works continued to produce tin plate products until 1963. A telephone exchange now stands on the site, but the family is remembered by Williamson Road, opposite **Sherriff Street**.

Providence Works - WN

This street could largely have been built as part of the *Blockhouse* development prior to Williamson's coming here. If not, it must have been built soon afterwards, since the street's pub, the Old England on the corner of **Blockhouse Street**, clearly existed before 1871, when there was a building application for alterations to it.

Residents in 1884 included rent and tax collector S. Coney at the end of the street, plus a prison warder, a sawyer, a signalman, shoemakers, an engine driver, a railway porter, a box maker, glovers, a tailor, a charwoman, an iron worker, a fitter and a French polisher. There were two shops in the street, George Dyer's bakery and grocer's shop on the corner of **St Paul's Street**, and Mrs Mary Ann Paynter's shop on the corner of Blockhouse Street.

At the west end, on the corner of **Temperance Street**, were the St Paul's schools for boys and girls. The Old England had closed by 1965, and the area was flattened in the Blockhouse clearance.

PUMP STREET

Originally this was a narrow lane called Nedlere Strete in Old English, later Needlers Street, first mentioned in 1299, home presumably to the garment industry which once made Worcester so prosperous, but also apparently where needles and similar small items were made.

Medieval trade guild restrictions were said to have forced the needle trade out of Worcester, and it became established at Redditch, which by the nineteenth century was world-famous for its needle and fish hook manufacturing.

The street afterwards took its present name (though it was also known as 'Lane' as late as 1880) from the presence of a public pump serving this end of the city, situated at the entrance to the **Shambles**, from which people could draw water. There had previously been wells in each ward, and a city ordinance of 1551 required the appointment of 'credible persons' to ensure their maintenance, but in 1612, during a period of severe drought throughout England, the city authorities ordered that pumps be installed. The present name was shown on a map of 1764, but must have been in use long before that.

When the city waterworks moved to Barbourne at the end of the eighteenth century water was piped into the city and the pumps became obsolete. There were several other wells around the city, including one at *All Hallows* as a result of which that area was called The Well.

Pump Street in the 1930s - RS

Historic Worcester Streets

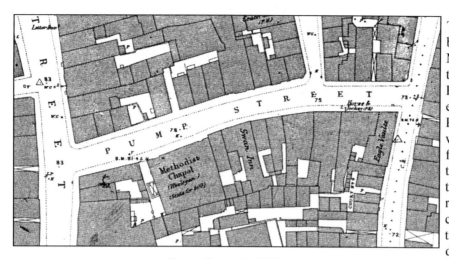

Pump Street in 1884

The bottom part of the street, between the Shambles and **New Street**, was known in the time of Elizabeth I as Ballan's Vine, and in the eighteenth century as Badam's Vine. The name was later said to be due to the fact that a large vine grew on the north side, and it was said that some rough representations of grapes could still be seen carved on the corbels of a since demolished corner house there in 1930. However the name is very similar to Ballam's Vine, a name which formerly existed in London for an area of Jewish settlement, so it is possible that the small Jewish community which existed in Worcester up to 1275 may have made its home here. The later change of name was perhaps because a house here was taken by the Badams or Badhams, who were coal dealers in **Quay Street** in 1840.

Directory listings for 1790 included baker John Day, cheesemonger John Hooper and cook Mrs Boydell, plus two pubs, the Horse and Jockey and the Crown. Five years later the Methodists, or Wesleyans as they were then known, moved here from **New Street** and have been here ever since, though of course their chapel has been rebuilt since then. By 1840 this had become the street of the shoemakers, housing five of them. Other trades included a tailor, a cabinet maker, a furniture broker, a hairdresser, a currier, a lacemaker, a tinman (tin

The side entrance to the market hall - TW

plate worker) and a bookbinder. Refreshment houses in 1884 included Walter Chaplin's Coffee Palace No. 2 near New Street.

The street was widened in the late nineteenth century, but many older buildings survived until the 1960s, though they have sadly since disappeared.

The Horse and Jockey, near the east end of the street next door to the Eagle Vaults, was owned by Spreckley Brothers brewery in **Barbourne Road** in the late nineteenth century, and is said to have closed in the 1920s. The Crown had become the Old Crown by 1840 and is said by Gwilliam to have closed by 1955. He also lists the Swan, which was midway down the south side of the street, which he said was listed in 1873 and closed around 1970.

The most notable feature of the street is the 1881 facade on the north side, which was the south entrance of a market hall which ran between the Shambles and **High Street**.

QUAY STREET

Since early times this was the main street leading to the quay of Worcester's inland port. In earlier centuries it was also known as Keyen, Cain or Key-street. The quay is now referred to as **South Quay**, to differentiate it from **North Quay** which was created in the 1780s, but through most of the city's history the quay here was the only one serving the port. The area behind the quay and along this street would have been lined with warehouses and merchants' houses, only one of which remains. The three storey early eighteenth century Merchant's House, built in Flemish bond with stone sills and keystones, was converted into flats in the 1980s. In 1790 directory listings in this area included barge builder George Ascoe, coal merchant John Daniel, merchants Thomas Hill and Edward Nott, and a pub called the Marquis of Granby, of which nothing more seems to be known. Listings in 1840 include a maltster, a cabinetmaker, a milliner, a coal dealer, a plumber, a builder and several shopkeepers. Inns listed hereabouts included in 1763 the Old Salt Scales, of which nothing further is known, and in 1840 the Old Farriers Arms, an early nineteenth century pub towards the top of the street, and the Old Severn Trow, at the junction with **South Quay**, an old watermen's inn, both of which closed around 1955.

By the twentieth century road and rail competition had largely put an end to commercial traffic on the Severn. Most of the slums behind South Quay were cleared in the 1930s, and the area was redeveloped with the **Deansway** scheme and the building of the college of technology from 1959.

Quay Street in 1822

QUEEN STREET

There seems to be nothing more than tradition and legend to support the history of this old street just inside the medieval city wall. By tradition it is said originally to have been called *Corncheapyn* or corn market, but it is unnamed on seventeenth century maps on which the **Cornmarket** is shown and named. The street was first found named on a map of 1741. It is possible that the market began here, and by the Tudor period or before it had spread out beyond the southern end of the street, into what became known as the **Cornmarket**, where there was more space. Legend has it that the street was renamed in honour of Queen Elizabeth I, who visited the city in 1575, though it may also have taken its name from the Queen Elizabeth almshouses off **The Trinity**.

This always had some businesses, but it doesn't seem to have been regarded as part of the main commercial area, and there were also residents. In 1790 broker John Chance and whitesmith Thomas Barrett were based here, and the Dolphin was the local pub, though nothing more seems to be known of it.

In 1884 this was the headquarters of the Worcestershire Rifle Volunteers, a group of part-timers, though their sergeant major, Edwin Judd, was named as a resident and was presumably a regular soldier. Other occupants included a cabinet maker, a shoemaker, a couple of labourers, a coachman, three charwomen, an iron worker and a grocer's assistant. Ironmongers J & F Hall, who had a shop on **The Shambles**, had an iron warehouse and workshop here, and hardware merchant William Bennett was based nearby. There was also a pianoforte packing warehouse, a fish stores and a solicitor. On the corner of **The Trinity** was the Old Peacock inn, which Gwilliam said first appeared in 1793, and thus could have been the Dolphin renamed. It had closed by 1912, to make way for the Worcester Co-operative Society's Hatton Buildings, and the corner premises are now an insurance office.

The east side of the street was cleared in 1966 and this is now little more than a car park entrance.

RACK ALLEY

An old alley which ran from **The Butts** opposite the former council refuse depot into **Dolday** beside the Woolpack pub. Its name came from an association with the cloth trade. In the eighteenth century there were racks on open land off **The Butts** on which cloth was left to dry, probably after dying. The alley now just leads to the back of the Crowngate car park.

RAGLAN STREET

This street must take its name from Raglan Cottage, a substantial detached villa in wooded grounds, which once stood on the west side of the junction with **Gregory's Mill Street**. No building records have been found, and an 1884 listing seems to suggest that the street was built as one development prior to 1884 when 19 homes appear to be listed on what was clearly former orchard or nursery land, which was shown on a map of that date as still retaining many trees. Residents at that time included three carpenters, two railwaymen, two tailors, a brewer, a labourer, a smith, a machinist, a coal agent, a gloveress and a seamstress, and at the east end of the street John Goodwin had a shop. However this does not tell the whole story. **Sunnyside Road** and **St George's Walk** did not exist then. A building application to extend Sunnyside Road to link with this road was submitted in 1898, creating the situation in which that road extends almost half-way up what might have been regarded as this street. There was still substantial room for further development at that time, and a good deal of modern development has taken place, but only five of the originally listed 19 homes remain here.

RAILWAY WALK

First found listed in the health board streets list of 1872, but that does not mean there was development here then, and the first street directory entry found was in 1930, when there were seven listings.

RAINBOW HILL

In Roman times this is said to have been the main route out of the city to a fort at Droitwich. The charming name must be a corruption of an Old English name, Ravenhoh or Rainow, meaning Raven Hill.

After the Romans left, their road no doubt deteriorated into a trackway, but it remained an important route, and in later centuries marked the eastern boundary of the Red House Estate to the west of the road, when it was often referred to as Red House Hill, or in the eighteenth and early nineteenth centuries as The Astwood Road. No information has been found on when the Red House was first built, but it was long a well-known landmark, probably so-called because it was originally built of red sandstone. It was situated on the west side, midway up the hill, roughly where Elgar Court is now, in an area called the Round Mount. A later house on the site was called Marl Bank, and was the home of composer Sir Edward Elgar in his final years.

Contemporary accounts have identified the Red House as the Parliamentary headquarters

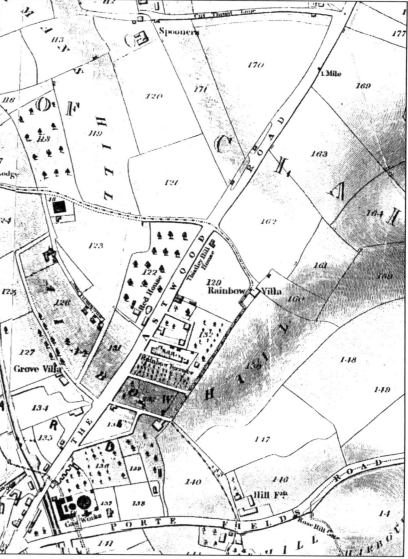

Rainbow Hill, then called The Astwood Road, in 1838

during the Civil War siege of the city in 1646, and the Round Mount was the site of the Royalist surrender. Worcester was the last city in the kingdom to hold out for Charles I, despite being besieged for four months, but running short of food and gunpowder, the stubborn defenders finally had no choice but to submit, and on 23 July the whole garrison, with flags flying proudly, marched out of **St Martin's Gate** to this spot to surrender. In the eighteenth century the Red House Estate formed part of the extensive estate of Sir Charles Trubshaw Withers of Sansome Lodge, in what is now **Sansome Walk**. An engraving of 1781 showed the area as an uninterrupted vista of open fields looking down over the city.

Sir Edward Elgar

This road as it is today is the result of the work of the eighteenth century Turnpike Trust, which dug out the roadway to reduce the gradient for carriages and carts, leaving steep marl banks of spoil on either side, which is why houses are well above the road level in places. Until the 1860s a turnpike gate stood at the bottom of the hill, where the road forks, and the hill was an area of pastures and orchards, with a small number of large houses and rural villas, such as **Rainbow Hill Terrace**, which had largely been built by 1838. As more development crept up the hill the gate was moved to the top of the hill, but probably ceased to operate about 1870. By that date **Lansdowne Crescent** had been developed to the west of the hill, and the whole of the Red House Estate would be built over during the rest of the century.

In the late nineteenth century the Red House, which was also variously known as The Mount and The Round Mount, was re-named Marl Bank, and was subsequently the home of composer Sir Edward Elgar. After his death, many in the city felt that the house should be preserved as an Elgar museum, but Sir Edward himself apparently favoured a museum at his birthplace at Broadheath, though he only spent the first year of his life there, and in the 1960s Marl Bank was demolished and the site redeveloped with flats.

In the nineteenth century, just north of the railway bridge, below Lansdowne Terrace, on the site now occupied by the Worcester Masonic Centre, stood a house called Grove Villa, which was once the home of a Dr Dixon who was believed locally to be the inspiration for the central character of an 1856 rags-to-riches novel, *John Halifax, Gentleman*, though this claim has never attracted any support outside Worcester. The doctor was a Quaker, and in 1824 played host to the popular prison and social reformer Elizabeth Fry, when she visited the city. Another local resident was Alderman William Lewis, who lived at a house called The Knoll at the top of the hill, and was the last person in the city to hold the lucrative post of Stamp Distributor at his stationer's shop in **Broad Street**.

Worcester from 'Red House Hill' in 1781

RAINBOW HILL TERRACE

According to building listings records, the 10 substantial villas here were built between 1830 and 1850, but residents have traced the sale of house plots to 1811, and completion of the first homes to 1813. Other houses were built at various dates, and a map of 1838 suggests that the street was largely complete, but one plot must still have been unoccupied, since there was a building application for a single house in 1871. The street was shown on a map of 1838 as Rainbow Terrace, with the Hill being added some time before 1884. A map of 1884 shows open land stretching away to the south as far as the railway bridge. At that time residents included Henry Grainger, of the Grainger porcelain works at **St Martin's Gate**; the Rev Philip Norton, curate of St Nicholas; commercial traveller J. Hayes; and John Orme Brettell of local mechanical engineering firm J.O. & C.E. Brettell of **Foregate Street**.

Historian and peace campaigner E.P. Thompson, famous for his work on British working class movements, was a resident here until his death in 1993, and his widow Dorothy, herself an important historian of the Chartist movement, continued to live here until her death in 2011.

City engineer William Ransom in 1931 - TW

RANSOM AVENUE

This street will have been named for council officer William Ransom, who lived for many years at a house called The Mount at 81 **Bath Road**. In 1922 he was assistant city surveyor, and by 1931 he was City Engineer. In the 1930s he would have been involved in the development of this estate on land which had been part of a dairy farm. This street was first mentioned in a street directory in 1936, and a 1937 listing showed 127 homes here.

REDCLIFFE STREET

This street name could have been taken from a Worcestershire family name or a house name in the area, but neither one has been found. It could also have been derived from a natural feature in the area, though there is nothing obvious.

There are no building records, so the date at which the street was created is impossible to determine exactly, but it was probably in the early 1890s. It was first found in a street directory of 1896 when two villas were listed, Rose Villa which was appropriately the home of florist Thomas Boon, and Florence Villa, where draper's assistant Benjamin Sealey lived. In the following year the Barbourne Bowling Green Club was founded, and was incorporated two years later, with its green and registered office here. By 1908 there was a third home here, Clifton Villa where law clerk George Ricketts lived. There was no further development until around 1920, when there was a sudden spate of building, and by 1922 there were 14 villas. The street has been completed at various dates since then.

Barbourne Bowling Club in 1911 - RS

Regent Street

This street was on the east side of **Hill Street**, close to **Cromwell Street**, and was created with industrial cottages for working families after 1829. In 1884 there were 35 homes here and four more in Regent Street Walk which gave access to **Shrub Hill Road**. Residents then included railwaymen, smiths, building tradesmen, metal workers, a tailoress, a charwoman, a glover and a 'trotter dealer'. On the north side of the street was the Ram inn, which closed in the 1960s. The street was still shown on city street maps in the mid 1960s but was demolished soon afterwards, and a retail park now covers the site.

RESERVOIR LANE

This must have existed originally as a lane leading to the Rainbow Hill reservoir, which was created after a new waterworks was built in Barbourne in 1858, in the area of the later **Waterworks Road**. The waterworks took water directly from the Severn, which was pumped up to the reservoir through a water pipe between them, which was completed by 1861. Development here must have begun soon after the reservoir was created, and must have been complete before building control regulations came into force in 1865, since the only building control record for this lane throughout the rest of the century was for alterations and additions to a house in 1872. That was the first record found for this street, and it was also shown in the health board streets list in the same year. In 1884 the only listing was for the home of Mrs Fanny Phillips Wilson, after whom **Wilson Street** must have been named, presumably a widow, at The Hermitage, with a spacious garden which filled the north side of the lane, while the gardens of houses in **Rainbow Hill Terrace** filled the south side. With landscaping to the east around the reservoir, it was a very pleasant spot. The Hermitage has since been demolished and the site of house and gardens has been redeveloped with modern homes.

RICHMOND HILL

This street was created in the 1870s, at the same time as **Richmond Road**, with which it shares much of its history. This was probably always known by the present name, but the postal addresses here were listed as part of Richmond Road until just before the First World War. The first reference to this street was found in a directory of 1912, but it was not listed separately until 1915. However the seven homes here were probably built in the late 1870s.

Building applications being submitted from 1874, mostly for a single house for small investors or aspiring home owners, mostly did not make clear which Richmond they were for, but one in 1876 did specifically refer to Richmond Hill.

By 1884 all seven homes here were listed, though as 1 – 7 Richmond Road. At No. 6 then was Henry Morgan, proprietor of a saw mill on **Wyld's Lane** where Smith Brothers were a century later, and next door to him was school board clerk, Thomas Spackman. When this street finally got its own listing in 1915 the residents were a pattern maker, two ladies who were presumably widows, a glover, a wheel examiner, a manager and a warehouseman.

RICHMOND ROAD

The Richmond name probably came from the name of a house in the area prior to the creation of the road. A map of 1838 does show a large property in the area, but no further details of it have been found. This was probably intended originally as a service lane to the rear of properties on **Wyld's Lane**, but it soon began to be developed.

This road was created in the 1870s, and listings for it until just before the First World War also took in what is now **Richmond Hill**, though there was always a certain amount of confusion in building applications, which makes it difficult to determine exactly what was being built where in the initial phase of building. One building application in 1876 referred to Richmond Hill, and many applications referred to 'Richmond Street'. The likelihood is that building was going on in both streets at the same time, and the houses on the hill may always have been referred to as on Richmond Hill, though this road was their postal address.

The first record found of the road was a building application for one house in 1874, and over the next five years there were nine more building applications submitted by various small investors or aspiring home owners, all for just a single house. Not until 1879 was there an application to build three houses. However the building records don't tally with what was actually built. By 1884, when there had been applications to build 13 homes, there were actually 19 listed, 12 here and seven on the Hill, which may suggest that some applications have been lost, or were never submitted.

An 1884 map showed that the north side of this road was occupied with the rear entries of houses on Wyld's Lane, and the south side had been fully developed.

Residents in 1884 were a mix of white collar and skilled workers, including clerks, foremen, an engine fitter, an inland revenue officer, a builder, a draper's assistant, a chine painter and a schoolmaster. The two villas on the north side were not built until 1897. At St Nimmo in 1915 was tinman (tin plate worker) William Court, and at Richmond House was a single lady, Miss Annie Pointon.

ROGERS HILL

Long before the street was built this area apparently had quite a violent history. During the 1646 siege of the city the Roundheads mounted what was said to be their principal battery here, and fired their shot a mile into the city, as far as the fortifications of the old stone bridge between **Newport Street** and **Tybridge Street**, though they can't have caused too much damage there, since the attackers had major problems trying to get through those defences into the city in 1651. This was also said to have been a favourite duelling place, perhaps because it was well away from the city.

As late as the early eighteenth century the name referred to the whole area as far as **Rainbow Hill**, and when the Red House there was offered for sale in the Journal around 1713 it was said to be "commonly known by the name of Roger's Hill". The name may have come from the Rogers family of Kidderminster, who held land all over the county, including presumably some in this area.

The building application to create the street was submitted in 1898, by Samuel Telford Dutton, after whom **Dutton Street** was likely to have been named. He was city council member for the area in the 1890s, and lived nearby at Marl Bank, Rainbow Hill, which was later home to composer Sir Edward Elgar. The only two building applications in his name were for creating this street and widening **Lansdowne Walk**.

Development went ahead quickly. In 1899 an application was submitted for 14 houses, which were shown in a street directory of 1900 as in the course of being built. There were two further applications for a total of 15 houses in 1901. The first of these applications had been submitted by David Harper, who was very active in property development around Barbourne in the 1890s, submitting applications to build almost 50 houses, though his application for 14 homes here was by far the biggest. Also involved was George Wood, who applied to build 100 houses in the city in the 1890s. Both men were clearly builders, though they were not listed as such. Both built villa residences, some substantial, and there is an interesting variety of architectural detail. All 29 houses applied for here had been built and occupied by 1903. Six of the occupants then were railwaymen. Other residents included shop assistants, a tailor's cutter, a compositor, fitters, a plumber, a fireman, two boiler makers, a shoemaker, a cabinetmaker, a blacksmith, a coach painter and a commercial clerk. Another half dozen homes were added soon afterwards to complete the street, but for a modest amount of modern infill.

RONKSWOOD CRESCENT

The name Ronkswood is Old English, and dates from the time in centuries past when the woods on this hillside will have merged with Perry and Nunnery woods. Scholars have been unable to come up with an explanation of the name, and suggest that 'Ronks' may have been the name, or more likely the nickname, of someone

who once held the land here, derived from Old English *ranc* meaning proud.

This street was first found in a street directory in 1880, but this was then outside the city, and there are no building records. A map of 1884 showed that though there were about a dozen properties here there was no roadway at that time. Residents were listed under **Newtown Road** and it is not easy to identify them, but it appears that more than half of them were labourers, probably on the surrounding farmland, but there were also two seamstresses and an engineer. Another resident at that time was Walter Holland Jnr. of railway engineering company Mackenzie & Holland of **Cromwell Street**. There was open farmland all around, and there was no other development in the area until construction of the Ronkswood estate began in 1948. A pool fed by the Perry Brook existed at the base of the hill, but it was drained when the estate was built. Just to the south there was an earthwork entrenchment of Civil War date. Everything here now is from the 1930s or later.

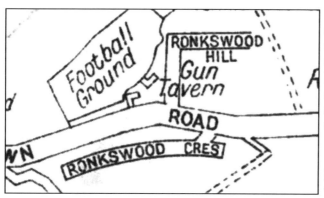

Above, an 1838 map of the area where Ronkswood Crescent would be created. Below, the same area on a street plan from a century later - HC

RONKSWOOD HILL

This street did not exist until the **Newtown Road** turnpike gate, which stood roughly at the south end, was removed around 1870, and the original development of the street must have taken place in that decade, since listing of the street was contemporary with **Ronkswood Crescent** in 1880, but identification of the residents is difficult, since they are listed under Newtown Road. All the development here now is 1930s or later. See also **Ronkswood Crescent**.

ROSE HILL

Originally regarded as part of **Cole Hill**, this street was created amongst an area of substantial, detached villas, which were broadly contemporary with those at **Lark Hill**. It must have taken its name from one of the large houses in the area, either Rose Lawn, a large house built on **London Road** around 1814, just to the east of this street, or the larger Rose Hill House, north of it, at the top of this street.

The street was first found in a street directory of 1840, but building records are almost non-existent, and residents are shown under London Road in street directories. In 1884 the Rev Robert Bourne was at Rose Hill House and Edward Gillam was at Rose Lawn. The five terraced villas of St Mary's Terrace on **London Road** were immediately to the east of this street, and residents in 1884 included Rev Richard Cattley, an hon. Canon of Worcester Cathedral, and journalist, local historian and former mayor John Noake. Given the spacious gardens of these houses, the small number of properties listed seemed to fully develop the available land. Richard Cadbury, son of one of the founders of the chocolate firm, came to Worcester to marry in 1902, and lived for a time at Rose Hill House. He also opened a coffee house in **Friar Street**.

ROSE TERRACE

It probably took its name from one of the substantial houses in the area, or more likely from **Rose Hill**. It was first found in a street directory in 1880, but it was unnamed on an Ordnance Survey map of 1885. Considering the spacious gardens, it seemed to be fully developed at that time, but had only a modest number of properties. Residents were listed under **London Road**, so are difficult to identify. There appeared to be about a dozen homes here in 1884. Only about half of the original homes remain, and there has been some redevelopment, though it is not intensive.

Rosemary Lane

The old lane that in the eighteenth century became the southern end of **Henwick Road**. At that time it was said to mark the eastern boundary of the parish of St John's.

ROWLEY HILL STREET

Developed on land which was formerly part of Ivy House Farm – see **Comer Road**. Named for a city MP and partner in the giant Hill, Evans vinegar works (see **Pheasant Street**). Thomas Rowley Hill was born in Stourport in 1816, the son of William Hill, one of the two founders of the firm in 1830, and attended University College, London.

Hill, Evans was subsequently managed by the sons of the founders, and grew into the largest plant of its kind in the world, with a private branch railway from Shrub Hill.

He was already regarded as a leading citizen in 1856 when he was first elected to the city council. He became sheriff in the following year and mayor in 1858, being appointed a magistrate in 1865. Three years later he stood for parliament unsuccessfully.

He was elected an MP in 1880, but lost his seat after five years and failed to regain it in the following year. He then quit national politics, but in 1889 he was elected to represent Martley on the new Worcestershire County Council.

He was represented on governing bodies and committees of many local organisations and charities, and gave much money to good causes, including the city's first free Public Library and Museum, which opened in **Foregate Street** in 1879.

He clearly admired the Evans womenfolk; both his wives were from the family. There was no doubt about his popularity in the city, since almost 1,000 people subscribed to commission a portrait of him for the Guildhall, painted by Frank Holl, one of the most sought-after portraitists of the day. He died in 1896 and was buried in Astwood Cemetery.

Thomas Rowley Hill - TW

The street was first mentioned in a building application three years later, and within four years there were four applications by various investors for a total of 24 houses. It was first listed in a street directory in 1900, when there appear to have been nine homes built, housing a signalman, a blacksmith and a police constable at May Villas, and a certified bailiff, a painter, two gardeners and an engine driver on the other side of the street. Applications and building moved on steadily, and by 1910 there were 36 homes here.

The street was definitely going up in the world, with a lot of clerks, and a reporter, though for which newspaper the directory doesn't say. By 1922 there were two more homes, and three more soon afterwards, mainly on the south side. Much of the north side of the street seems to have been developed by the local authority, but not until the 1930s.

Historic Worcester Streets

Rush Alley

A notorious slum alley, traditionally the market for rush sellers, said by Noake to be possibly the oldest market in the city. The alleyway was cleared in the late eighteenth century to make way for **Bridge Street**, though the market was said by Noake to have continued here into the nineteenth century.

Russell Terrace

A terrace of 20 homes off the south side of **Tybridge Street**, roughly opposite St Clement's Close. It was referred to as Street in an 1868 building application for three houses. This was the only building record found, which suggests that the remainder of the homes were built prior to the start of building control in late 1865. These were very modest homes for working families, with small yards but no gardens. In 1884 residents included three leather dressers, two carpenters, gloving workers, an upholsterer, a sawyer, a tailor, a dressmaker, a laundress, a fireman, a gardener, a drayman, a tinman (tin plate worker) and a grocer's assistant. The Terrace was still shown on a map of 1928, but was probably cleared soon afterwards.

ST ANNE'S ROAD

This seems to have been the start of a 'saints' themed estate, with St Michael's Road adjoining, but this theme was not otherwise continued in adjacent roads. This road was first found in a street directory in 1937, when six homes were listed here. The church hall on the corner is later, apparently 1950s.

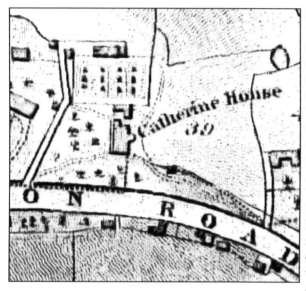

St Catharine's Hill in 1838, and an engraving showing Joseph Birlingham's house in the centre

ST CATHARINE'S HILL

Probably called Cobhill or clay hill originally, it took the present name from a chapel dedicated to St Catherine, which was formerly said to have stood near the roadside, and would have been used chiefly by travellers.

The land here was part of the estate attached to the Commandery in **Sidbury**, once owned by the Wyldes after whom **Wyld's Lane** was named. Around 1792 most of the estate was purchased by wealthy glover Joseph Birlingham, who had a glove manufactory at The Commandery.

He was an innovative businessman, and is believed to have been the first manufacturer in the city to use steam powered machinery. He built a fine neo-classical mansion here named St Catharine's Hill, which was surrounded by substantial pleasure grounds on tree-lined meadows, with a grass tennis court.

This was the home in the late nineteenth century of leading local solicitor Edward Corbett. He fell from grace in 1902 after he was caught misappropriating clients' funds. But after a long jail sentence, he reinvented himself as 'Stroller', writing local history columns for the Worcester Herald and Berrow's Journal. In the Edwardian period the house was owned by Rev Edward Gilliat. Part of the land was sold to provide a site for St Martin's Church, which opened on **London Road** in 1911, and during the First World War the house became home to Belgian refugees. The house was still in existence in 1928, but was demolished soon afterwards and the land was

redeveloped for housing in the early 1930s, though the entrance gateway off London Road still exists. A listing for the street was first found in 1936, when there were seven residents listed, including Rev Henry Bathurst, curate of St Nicholas Church, with eight listings by 1940, though all 10 homes may have been built by then.

ST CATHARINE'S VALE
This was the valley of the Pirie or Perry Brook, which runs down from Perry Wood. The valley was raised in the eighteenth century with spoil dug out of **London Road** by the Turnpike Trust to reduce the gradient. The brook is now culverted. It was developed for housing at the same time as **St Catharine's Hill**. It was included on the health board street list of 1872, and the first four homes here were probably built around that time or soon afterwards. The first street listing was found in 1936, and by 1940 the other four homes in the street must have been built, since there seemed to be eight listed then. There was a shop on the corner of **Wyld's Lane** which closed in the late 1980s.

St Clement's Square
A large area of housing at the west end of *School Walk*, and around **Bush Walk**. It was in existence in 1840, and in 1884 there were more than 40 homes listed . All of them were small and some had little or nothing in the way of gardens, though others had quite generous gardens. These were very much homes for working families, with 1884 listings showing residents in a wide range of manual occupations. Labourer was the most common occupation, providing a living for one in every six residents. There were also four seamstresses, building tradesmen, a glazier, a pump maker, a waterman, a lamplighter, an engine driver, shoemakers, a baker, a stonemason, a basket maker, a brewer, a glover, a charwoman and a platelayer. This area was still shown on a map of 1940, but was cleared around the 1960s.

St Clement's Street
Name used in the nineteenth century for **Tybridge Street**, after the new St Clement's Church opened in **Henwick Road** in 1823, though the name had fallen out of use before 1873.

ST DUNSTAN'S CLOSE
Off **St Dunstan's Crescent**, this street was first found in a street directory in 1937, when there were 21 homes listed.

St Dunstan, from a stained glass window at Canterbury

ST DUNSTAN'S CRESCENT
This street was named for a tenth century Bishop of Worcester who became a saint. An application to create the crescent was submitted in 1885 by the St Dunstan's Crescent Building Estate, as a new road off **Battenhall Road**. Sadly there is no indication in the building application of who was behind the scheme. A map of that date showed no sign of the road about to be developed, but there was immediately a string of building applications, all small-scale for one or two houses. Throughout the remainder of the 1880s there were 15 building applications for 24 houses.

Not until the 1890s were some slightly larger building applications submitted, but there was also a distinct pause in development in that decade. In 1890 there were two applications for 10 houses, one of them for eight homes from Diglis builder and active property developer William Bennett, but there was no further development until an application for one home in 1895. However between 1896 and 1903 things got back on track, with 15 applications for a total of 34 homes.

By 1896 there were 33 homes here. Residents at that time included, as you would expect, a number of managers, including George Williams Waldron, manager at Willis's shoe factory in **Sidbury**, at Malvern View. There were also clerks, shop assistants, china workers, a bookbinder's assistant, a compositor, commercial travellers and Thomas Packwood, yardsman at the Star Hotel. There appears to have been a shop on the corner of **The Hill Avenue**.

ST GEORGE'S LANE NORTH
A long established route to Merrimans Hill, originally called Flag Lane. The Flagge family were wealthy Claines landowners and Lady Alice de la Flagge was Prioress of White Ladies nunnery on **The Tything**, 1308-1328. At that time she gave a gift of land to the convent which must have included the land around the present **Flag Meadow Walk**, and may also have included land around this lane, in fact one source suggested that her gift may have included land as far as Perdiswell. As late as 1838 this was apparently known as

Historic Worcester Streets

Above, Old cottages in St George's Lane, painted by E.A. Phipson in 1905 - MAG. Below, the boys and girls of St George's School Standard 1 in 1935 - MS

Cut-throat Lane, a name found in many semi-rural areas, probably just denoting a dark, lonely lane where locals joked you might get your throat cut. It has also been suggested that the name applied to **Lansdowne Road**.

The lane changed its name after the building of a chapel of ease in **St George's Square** in 1830, and the opening of a school in the lane in 1835. The former Flag Lane was first listed as St George's Lane in 1840, and again in a guide book of 1851, but the North wasn't added until 1880.

The first curate of St George's, Rev James Tyrwhit, began the first public school in the area in a cowshed on a vacant house plot, where he engaged a master and mistress to educate 120 children between the ages of five and 13. By 1833 the house plot had been sold, and a new site was found for St George's School on what was then still called Flag Lane. By 1836 it had 90 boys and 70 girls on roll. Master in 1910 was Bertram Brotherton, who went on to become a secondary school head, mayor, and author in 1962 of a series of newspaper articles on city street names.

A map of 1838 showed about a dozen small properties scattered along the length of the lane, which then terminated at the canal, and had no connecting roads. A street directory of 1884 listed almost 60 homes here, so there had clearly been a good deal of development in the intervening period, probably in the early 1860s, since there are no building records for this development, and only a handful of small building applications throughout the rest of the century.

Residents were manual workers, including labourers, building tradesmen, foremen, glovers, gardeners, metal workers, plumbers, a baker, a seamstress, a tailor, a coach builder, a watchmaker and a blacksmith. On the corner of **Barbourne Road** was Mr Bond's shop at Westwood House, which became a branch of the Co-op between the 1890s and the 1960s or 70s. Near Gloucester Terrace builder Richard Wilkes also had a shop and off-licence. Beside the canal was the St George's Tavern, which was in existence from around 1800 and was rebuilt around 1970, and renamed The Cavalier. An 1896 directory shows another pub, called The Perseverance, at No. 4, roughly where the hairdressers is now, which had become an off-licence by 1930.

The lane was best known for many years as the home of Worcester City Football Club, which was based here from 1905. Worcester beat Liverpool here in the third round of the FA Cup in 1959, in what is still the northern club's biggest cup upset. Unfortunately the club's plan to fund a new home by selling this ground for housing went awry, and after the last game here was played in 2013, the club had to move to Kidderminster, though at the time of writing it still hopes to find a new home somewhere in the city.

ST GEORGE'S LANE SOUTH

An offshoot of St George's Lane North, which was first found in the health board streets list of 1872, and in a street directory in 1884. At that date there were six listings, including two Shrubbery Cottages housing gardener William Dobbins and shoemaker E.W. Dobbins, laundress Mrs Henry Dobbins next door at Woodbine Cottage, and Willow Terrace, housing horse keeper Robert Hill and iron fitter Samuel Hill. There was an application to build four more cottages in 1890, six more in 1901 and another three in 1903, though not all of these were built. By 1905 the ten homes had been built which are still here, and several more have been added recently.

Above, the first St George's Church 1888. Below, the former Militia depot which became a laundry and has since been replaced by flats - RS

ST GEORGE'S SQUARE

The square takes its name from the dedication of the church which stands at the far end of the square, but the land had previously gone under many other names. In the mid eighteenth century it was White Lady Field, probably once part of **The Tything** convent lands. In the early 1750s it was owned by the Cooksey family who had a long association with Whiteladies, the farm house on the convent site.

The land had a fascinating history before development began. In 1795 Holland Cooksey's widow, Elizabeth, conveyed a one-fifth share in family land holdings to her son Richard and each of three daughters, retaining one-fifth herself. Richard obviously had substantial debts, probably run up on his 'expectations' from the family fortune, since he quickly placed his share of the land in trust to protect it from his creditors. However his actual holding had not been identified, and before it could be, both Richard and his mother died in 1798. Since one of Richard's trustees had gone to the East Indies, his long-suffering creditors had to get an Act of Parliament to appoint a new trustee, before the land could be sold on 24 March 1801.

The site, by then meadow land which went under the names 'Flag Closes' and 'White Ladies', was purchased by Tything butcher George Hope for £1100, and became known as Shrubbery Meadow. George died in 1818, leaving the land to his widow, Sarah, to pass on her death to George's eldest sons, George and William, but the successful sale of plots at Britannia Square had taken place in the previous year, and the trio decided to follow suit. The cow pasture was divided into 22 lots around a central carriageway, marketed as Shrubbery Place, and an auction was held at the Star and Garter Inn on 10 January 1825, but only two lots were sold; Lot 1, now No. 30, and Lot 22, now Nos 1 and 2 though they were not built until around 1870, making them the last houses built in the square. Further auctions were held at the Talbot on 21 May 1827, and 1 October 1833, to sell remaining plots on the north and then the south side of the square.

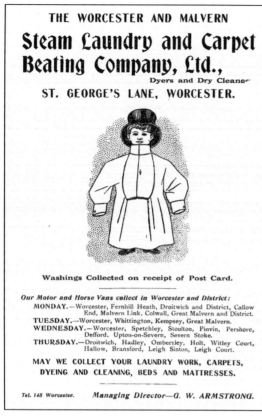

Above, a 1910 advertisement. Below, Edwardian youngsters in the square - RS

The earliest date in county archives for deeds of properties in the square, presumably drawn up on first sale of houses by the original owners or developers, is as late as 1836, but research has shown that many of the houses were speculative builds by various builders, which were then rented out.

One builder, Joseph Wood, who had built numbers 9 and 10 by 1835, and also built numbers 12 and 13, was mayor of Worcester in 1861, and **Wood Terrace** was probably named after him. The Church Building Commissioners purchased land at the east end of the square in January 1828, and the foundation stone for a chapel of ease was laid on 11 March, 1829.

The building, which opened in October 1830, cost £3,500, but was just too small. After the consecration of the chapel, the square became known as St George's Place, acquiring its present name by 1837.

Of the house plots still remaining empty at the time the church opened, one roughly in the centre of the south side of the square, still contained an open cowshed where the first St George's parish school was founded by Rev James Tyrwhitt, the first curate of St George's chapel.

On the north side of the square, close to the church, from about 1853 was a depot for the Worcester Regiment of Militia, a part-time unit which trained periodically and was ready to turn out in emergencies.

In 1878 the Militia apparently moved to Norton Barracks, and their depot became the Barbourne Steam Laundry,

which closed in the 1980s, and has been replaced by apartments.

The chapel of ease closed in August 1893 and a new church was commissioned from probably the greatest architect of the day, Sir Aston Webb, a Londoner who married the daughter of a Dr Everett of **Foregate Street**.

Historic Worcester Streets

Sir Nikolaus Pevsner, who surveyed Worcester for 'The Buildings of England' series in the mid-1960s, wrote: "Aston Webb's church is a set piece at the end (of the square) which could not be bettered".

Notable residents of the square included local historian John Noake, who was at No 11 from around 1862 to 1879. In 1851 No 12 was occupied by Worcester clockmaker and jeweller John Martin Skarratt whose apprentice, William Wilbourne Kay, subsequently founded the mail order company Kays, and took over the business he had worked for. At No. 1 in 1884 was Samuel Telford Dutton, after whom **Dutton Street** is likely to have been named. Living there in 1891 were the Spreckley family, owners of the brewery in **Barbourne Road**, three of whose sons were lost in the First World War and are remembered, with all those who fell, on the church war memorial. It is interesting that in 1905 almost half of the householders were ladies, either Miss or Mrs, probably living on money left by late parents or husbands, and quite possibly letting rooms to make ends meet, though only one was listed in that way.

ST GEORGE'S WALK

It is possible that some plots of land along the route may have been marked out as early as 1838, but the first definite record found of the street was a building application of 1874 for eight houses; the only application to be submitted by a Charles Cross, about whom nothing else is known.

Another application for five houses was submitted in 1880, but there were at least 17 homes shown on an 1884 map, so it may be that some applications have been lost, or that some homes were built before the start of building control in late 1865, or before the city boundary moved beyond Barbourne Brook in the early 1880s. There was an application to build another five cottages in 1887, but nothing else throughout the rest of the century. At that date the street already extended as far north as it does now, presumably in anticipation of the creation of **Sunnyside Road**, which was being planned at that time.

The listing for this street in an 1896 street directory showed 25 homes here, so some more applications must have gone missing, or perhaps weren't submitted. Most of the homes here at that date had apparently been built in small terraces and presumably named by proud investors. There were two Brook Villas, five homes on Cecil Terrace, eight on Gloucester Terrace and five at Shakespeare Villas, which were probably named after William Shakespeare the late Victorian Worcester builder and property developer, rather than the better known Stratford dramatist. Residents at that time included labourers, gardeners, carriage builders, a stone sawyer, a nurse, a brewer, a porter, an organ builder, a police constable, a glover, a waiter, a railway porter and a bricklayer.

A terrace of five Victorian cottages still remains here, but the rest of the street has been redeveloped. The Myriad Centre was previously a nursery, and before that a private school, but was originally part of St George's School, and by the 1920s had become the St George's Church Institute. Though it now fronts onto this street it was listed in **Henry Street** through much of its history.

St John's in 1799

ST JOHN'S

There is a good deal of confusion about this name. Today it is popularly applied to the whole suburb west of the Severn, comprising most of the St John's parish as it once was, which for most of its history was outside the city, only beginning to become part of it in 1837.

The street name however only applies to the area's 'high street', running south and east from the parish church, starting at its junction with the **Bull Ring**, and running past the end of **Bromyard Road** to the junction of **Bransford Road** and **Malvern Road**. Though as late as the eighteenth century some sources said the street ran from the Severn at the east end of what is now **Tybridge Street**.

Historic Worcester Streets

St John's Church about 1810, and St John's looking towards the church - RS

It clearly took its name from the parish church of St John the Baptist, which began its long life as one of two chapels west of the river, the other being St Oswald's on the Malvern Road, though the street is no doubt much older than the church.

It was the drove roads from mid-Wales which converged on this street, that created the prosperity of this small community. The Welsh were once not allowed to own property or businesses in the city, and were also not allowed to spend the night there, so this area supplied the lodgings and services that the drovers needed. For city folk this was a lane from the bridge through the village of St John's and on towards the bishop's manor at Wick, and Malvern.

There has been controversy over the years about the

parish name St John in Bedwardine, with the eighteenth century historian Nash suggesting that Bedwardine meant 'bread ward', where the crops were grown for the monks' bread, but the land here belonged originally to the bishop's manor of Wick, not to the monastery, and modern scholars are agreed that the name meant 'beda's enclosure', a reference to the name of what was probably the first Anglo-Saxon owner of the land.

St John's Church was established around 1165, but was then only a chapel of ease, with St Oswald's chapel on Malvern Road, beside the bishop's manor house, as the main church in the area. But in 1372, after the Black Death had decimated the population and left outlying areas deserted, it was decided to abandon St Oswald's, and St John's, surrounded by the small village which had grown up in what had become the priory manor of Hardwick by 1236, became the parish church in 1372, originally called St John of Wyke. The first known vicar of the new parish was John Troucestre.

A small amount of the original chapel remains, but most of the church is of later date. The tower was built in 1481, and once had a fine steeple, but that was shot off by the Roundheads during the Civil War, when the Royalists were using the tower as an observation post. The church was also plundered and set on fire by advancing Parliamentary forces. The Parish Office, dating from about 1600, was part of the vicarage until the church was extended in the nineteenth century.

Medieval and Tudor St John's will have consisted of timber framed houses lining the road, which have since mostly disappeared, though there are a couple of fine restored examples, one beside the Co-op store and another around the corner, which give some idea of what this area was once like. There are also some fine

St John's shops, Horton's butchers, now Narraways - IN, Miss Frances Annie Holds' hatters and milliners in 1903, was later Mutters newsagents for many years. Bottom, St John's cinema during the First World War

Georgian houses, some concealing a core of earlier construction, and though there has been development here, the street has not suffered as badly as some others in Worcester, and retains a nice mix of mostly period buildings, with some real gems.

St John's had the right to its own annual fair, which was held on the Friday before Palm Sunday, just before Worcester's fair. Under a grant of 1460, city officials were allowed to attend and would walk through St John's in a very grand procession, accompanied by the sword bearer, constables and other officers, and a band, but prior to 1837 they had no jurisdiction in the township, because it was not part of Worcester. Another important fair here was the St John's Mop or hiring fair, held at the bottom of **Bransford Road**.

Until the beginning of the nineteenth century a Piepowder Court was held at the church house, now the Bell inn, to deal with disputes between merchants, and offences committed at the fair. The name came from the French *pieds poudres*, or dusty feet, a reference to the fact that most people at the fair would be visitors who had travelled over dusty roads to get here. The court would have been presided over by the steward to the lord of the manor of Hardwick, in whose manor St John's was situated. Punishments could include fines or a spell in the pillory. The court last sat in 1814, but was revived in the early twentieth century as a historical tableaux. There was always a wide range of businesses in the area, interspersed in the past with the homes of the well-off. In 1790 the businesses here included an attorney, an auctioneer, two bakers, a blacksmith, a butcher, a barber, three carpenters, a druggist, a gardener, a nailer, a millwright, a shoemaker, a staymaker, a tanner, two tailors, a timber dealer and a wire worker. St John's Post Office was on the corner opposite the church in the 1880s.

There were also six pubs. One of the area's leading inns was the Angel which is known to have existed in 1670, but closed in the 1980s and has been best known since as a greengrocers, though it is now a carpet shop. Another local inn, the King's Head, almost opposite Bransford Road, was purchased by the Godsall brothers in 1914 and the St John's Cinema was built on the site, and was a popular local entertainment venue for more than half a century, with Harry Godsall giving an on-stage running commentary to accompany the silent movies.

Historic Worcester Streets

In 1929 it was said to have secured the first talking picture in the city, Al Jolson's *The Singing Fool*, and the queue for the evening performance stretched down to the Bull Ring. After a fire in 1939 the cinema was taken over by the Odeon chain, and it finally closed in 1959. It later became a nightclub, but has been derelict since another disastrous fire in 2007. The Bell is recorded as the church house in the seventeenth century. The other pubs listed in 1790 were the Crown on St John's Green at the end of **Bransford Road**, which closed in the 1970s or 80s, the Swan Inn, near the King's Head, which has closed since 1985, and the Cock & Cross, about which nothing further is known.

The city tram depot, is invariably referred to as having been at the **Bull Ring**, on the site now occupied by the Co-op supermarket, but that road ends at the junction with **Henwick Road**, so the site was in this street. The depot was in existence from 1881 to 1928. A large two-track tram shed was opened in February 1884. Originally the trams were pulled by horses, and services returning to the depot or serving the St John's routes needed an additional team to pull them up the steep gradient. From 1903 electric trams replaced the horses. Midland Red buses were running from here between 1914 and 1921, and by 1928 buses were ready to take over, and the tram system was shut down after just 25 years. Lancaster bomber canopies were said to have been made in the tram shed during the Second World War.

This picture was taken outside the tram depot on the last day of the horse trams on 25 June 1903 - BG

St John's Road
This was an early name used for **New Road** after the new bridge was opened in 1781 (see **Bridge Street**).

St Lawrence Lane
This medieval lane ran from the **High Street** to **Friar Street**, named for the patron saint of librarians, to whom the church of the Greyfriars was dedicated. Retail development now covers the site, but it ran off **High Street** just north of **Pump Street**. No information was found for it after the Tudor period.

ST MARTIN'S GATE
Originally the gate was known as Clap Gate, one of the three gates in the Anglo-Saxon city defences. 'Clap' meant cloth in Old English, and this was the gate which would have given the most direct access to the cloth and garment-making quarter around *Glovers Street* and *Needlers Street*. The original St Martin's Church in

Historic Worcester Streets

Cornmarket was built in the twelfth century, and the present name for the gate and this street was in use by 1610, at first without the 'St', though the old name continued in use for many years and was last seen on a map of 1829.

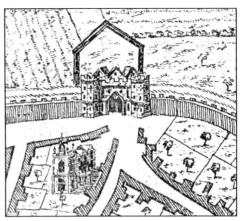

In Roman times this is said to have been the main direction out of the city to Droitwich, where there was a fort. The original Anglo-Saxon defences were probably earthworks and timber, but the walls will have been rebuilt in stone sometime during the medieval period. Nineteenth century maps show the site of the gate roughly where the roundabout on the **City Walls Road** is situated.

The line of this street was outside the city wall, but according to the mapmakers the street hardly existed before most of the wall was taken down after the Civil War. A map of 1610 showed a lane running north from the gate, parallel with the city wall, to connect with **Lowesmoor**. The present street line, running east

Above, the medieval St Martin's Gate, reconstructed from a later map. Below, the St Martin's Gate area in 1886

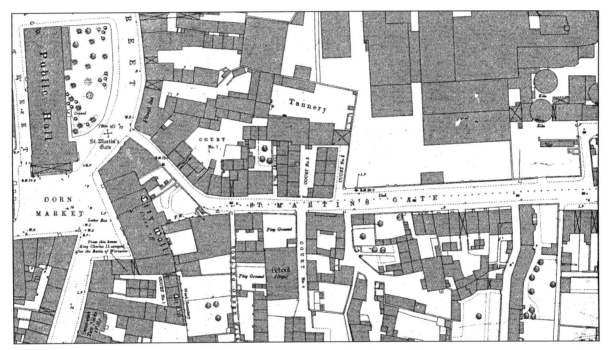

from the gate, was not found until a map of 1741, and even then it ran originally in a dog leg pattern, going south-east before turning east. The dog leg was eliminated by the **City Wall Road** in the 1970s, to create the current street line.

By the 1550s the gate was considered surplus to the city's defence requirements and was let out as accommodation. No doubt it was refortified during the Civil War, but does not seem to have been damaged and was probably let out again afterwards. On 3 September 1651, when Cromwell won the Battle of Worcester, it was the last gate to be held by the Royalists, and enabled the future Charles II to just about make a quick getaway before the Roundheads took the gate. In history also, it was probably the last city gate to go, being demolished in 1787, 85 years after the Foregate was taken down, which may suggest that this was the least used gate and there was no great pressure to remove it.

The map of 1610 showed a populous area outside the gate, but in 1790 the only directory listing here was for Mrs Ann Draycott, who may have been renting a tenement above the gate. Development probably began to gather pace with the arrival of the canal, which opened in 1815. A map of 1829 showed a good deal of development at the west end, and a map of 1838 showed it spreading east. It was certainly a populous area by 1884, when a street directory showed a mix of small tradesmen, shops and businesses, surrounded by five courts of intensive housing.

Behind a couple of these courts on the north side was a large tannery, not a type of business normally noted for the pleasant odours emanating from its premises. Near the west end was a tobacconist's shop, not far from pikelet maker Mrs Mary Wainwright, who was next door to stationer, newsagent and cabinet maker

Thomas Pheasey. Further east was a greengrocer, next door to John Hill's fried fish shop. Near **Spring Gardens** was police sergeant William Preece.

On the corner of **Pheasant Street** was the Grainger porcelain works, set up in 1809 by Thomas Grainger. It developed a reputation for high quality tableware, and under his son George, diversified into porcelain for commercial and industrial uses. The firm was acquired by Worcester Porcelain in 1889, and all the work was transferred to the **Severn Street** works in 1902. The premises were then mostly let off to small businesses, and were largely demolished in 2009, though the facade has been retained

George Grainger

A day school credited with being the first in the city 'for the children of the labouring poor' opened here in 1811, on the south side, just west of what is now the end of the street. The Lancastrian Monitorial School was based on the system created by Joseph Lancaster, and it was set up after he came to the city in April 1809 and gave a lecture at the Hop Pole in **Foregate Street**. Eight benefactors bought the land and the school was built by subscription.

The system was based on the master teaching a lesson to a selected group of pupils, who then taught all the others. It opened with one inexperienced teacher and 352 boys, but this didn't work well and the numbers had to be drastically reduced.

After this school opened, a number of others for poor youngsters followed around the city. There was a building application in 1893 for a new school here, presumably a rebuild of the monitorial school, though whether that went ahead is not known. The school lasted 105 years, closing in 1915, and the building lasted until 1975, when it was demolished to make way for the **City Walls Road**.

Around 1763 the Journal mentioned a pub originally called the Three Crowns but by then known as the Bellman, which was 'without St Martin's Gate' and was being sold in that year by the widow Mason. At No. 1 in 1855, next door to The Plough inn in **Silver Street**, was the Railway Bell, which was then listed as a beer retailer, though by 1860 it was listed as one of the city's music halls. According to Gwilliam, it closed around 1912. The courts around this street were probably cleared in the 1930s, and what remained here was decimated in the 1970s when the City Walls Road was created.

St Martin Street

This street led from **Lowesmoor** to the Hill, Evans vinegar Works, but became part of the works as it expanded, and no records have been found of residents. In 1870 the firm obtained an Act of Parliament to close off the street, and it has since served as an entrance into the site, though it was still shown in street directories, and on city maps as late as the mid-1960s. It now leads into the supermarket and retail site.

St Martin's Walk

Possibly listed as early as 1840 as St Martin's Place, it ran off **St Martin's Gate** and **Pheasant Street**, and was still there until the mid-1960s.

St Mary's Steps

Steps leading into **Edgar Street** beside the tower. Linen draper William Eyton was listed here in 1790.

St Maries Street

Old name for *Warmestry Slip*, off **Deansway**.

ST MARY'S STREET

Maps show that this street began life in the eighteenth century as an unnamed lane or track leading from **The Tything** to Sansome Fields, a popular area for summer walks. It subsequently gave access to the Arboretum, and acquired its name from St Mary's, the Tything parish church on **Sansome Walk**, which opened in 1877. It was first found in a street directory in 1880. A map of 1884 shows that there were gardens occupying the south side, and much of the north side was taken up with what was left of what had once been very extensive grounds behind the Saracen's Head in **The Tything**. The only listings were for a detached home, Airdrie Villa, occupied by vet Adam Robertson, and four semi-detached houses called St Mary's Villas, occupied by an auctioneer, a traveller, a horse dealer, and Thomas Melhuish, chief telegraph clerk for the GPO.

The south side of the street was redeveloped for council offices in the twentieth century, and the last remaining section of the Saracen's Head grounds, which had been serving as its car park, was redeveloped for a block of flats in the 1990s.

ST NICHOLAS STREET

An ancient lane leading from **Foregate** to the Trinity Gate, which may have been just a foot gate. In 1610 a map showed this street as Gaol or Gayle-lane, since it led to an old city gaol which is believed to have been in the gate tower of the Trinity Gate, which was demolished later in that century. The street name then changed to **Garden Market**, since the vegetable market was held in this street. It must have taken its present name after the church was rebuilt in the eighteenth century. It has also been suggested that it was called *Union Lane* in the nineteenth century, presumably after the House of Industry on **Tallow Hill** became the Union Workhouse.

Residents in 1790 included a cheesemonger, a gardener, a gloving firm, and two hop merchants. There were two pubs listed at that time, the Pack Horse and the Holly Bush.

The former Pack Horse inn, now The Courtyard, must be one of the oldest hostelries in the city, having held a licence since 1485, according to Bill Gwilliam, who said it was once a staging post on the Shrewsbury to London stagecoach route. It had substantial accommodation and stabling in past times, and one year, during the September Hop Fair Day, the inn stabled 119 horses in one day. In the early twentieth

Above, St Nicholas Church in the late eighteenth century. Below, St Nicholas Street in 1822.

century it had an imposing stuccoed Georgian front, but it was acquired in 1935 by Dudley brewers Hansons, who stripped off the stucco and added the mock Tudor front. The Holly Bush inn was at No. 1, near the junction with **The Cross**. It was still open in the 1980s, but in the 1990s the premises became a pizza restaurant. There was once only a narrow entry out to Lowesmoor for pedestrians, and a pub called The Dolphin is said to have stretched across most of the lane, but it is not listed by Gwilliam and no other trace has been found of it. Inquests were sometimes held at the Victorian **Yorkshire House**, opposite the end of **Queen Street**, but Gwilliam said it had closed by 1908. Next door was the late Victorian Imperial, which still exists, though not under that name.

A Militia depot is said to have stood at the east end of the street on the south side until 1838, when the building became the first city police station. It continued in that role until 1862 when a new police station was built in **Copenhagen Street**. By 1884 two companies of the Worcestershire Rifle Volunteers were based there.

The street was widened in the late nineteenth century, and the developers have been here since. All that remains of any age on the south side is the church and the Co-op building, though there is more surviving on the north side. An historic building which has dodged the developers is No. 39, now a dental surgery. It is an attractive eighteenth century house built sometime between 1736 and 1799, which supposedly stands on the site of the Trinity Gate in the city walls, where the city prison was believed to have been housed in the gate tower in 1610. The gate was demolished later in that century.

By tradition, the first church of St Nicholas may have been built by knights returning from the Crusades, since Nicholas, who was bishop

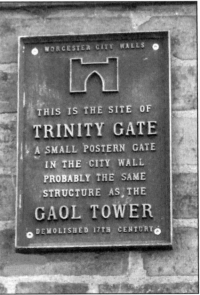

The Trinity Gate plaque - TW

of Mirca in southern Turkey, was patron saint at that time of all dangers, especially shipwreck, which was a great peril for crusaders travelling to Palestine. This tradition may well have evolved from the existence in **The Trinity** of an order of monks dedicated to freeing captives in the Middle East.

The church was built possibly in the twelfth but more probably the thirteenth century – the first known rector was appointed in 1291 - and part of the massive crypt and the lower walls may remain from that church. It may have been rebuilt in the sixteenth century, since part of the crypt may be from that date. Burials took place in earlier times simply by depositing coffins in the crypt, so it is not hard to imagine what the atmosphere in the church was like.

The rebuilding of 1730-35, which gave us the striking west front and stepped tower, was once thought to have been carried out by Guildhall architect Thomas White, but is now attributed to Humphrey Hollins, though Thomas Johnson of Warwick has also been mentioned. The tower is said to be based on a rejected design for London's St Mary-le-Strand, which was published in an architectural book in 1728. What is said to be the first recorded city Sunday School was at this church in 1785. The church underwent restoration in the early twentieth century, reopening in June 1913.

Though the parish of St Nicholas was entirely within the city, it also drew a congregation of the well-to-do from **The Tything** and Barbourne, since their parish church at Claines was remote, and was hardly fashionable for city folk. The rectory formerly stood next to the church in **The Cross**.

The Co-op has long gone from its extensive department store site on the south side, but it had been here since the nineteenth century, though the building is 1960s. The Co-op was started in the city in 1881, originally with a bakery in **Mealcheapen Street**, and the store here was established in 1887, initially to sell groceries, though it soon expanded into drapery, footwear and hardware, and the attractive Victorian building which they erected here in 1888 is proof that business must have been good.

The Co-op horrified other shopkeepers by giving dividends to customers and bonuses to employees, as well as giving staff a half-day holiday and cutting working hours, which ultimately forced other shops to follow suit and improve conditions for their staff.

The Midland Telephone Company had its offices in this street, and installed the first telephone in the city in November 1880.

St Nicholas Street in 1920; buildings on the left were later replaced by the Co-op department store

ST OSWALD'S ROAD

This was originally a pathway through St Oswald's cemetery (see **The Tything**), which extended south across land later used for offices and a car park by catalogue company Kay's. It was first listed in the health board streets list of 1872, and in a street directory of 1873, but it went only as far as the entrance to St Oswald's, and continued to **Sansome Walk** as a footpath. There was little here besides St Oswald's Hospital, though in 1884, when this was listed as St Oswald's Walk, there was a St Oswald's Cottage here which was home to a Miss Whitgrove. It must have been renamed Road after widening in 1890.

According to city historian Hubert Leicester, it was while walking here that Sir Edward Elgar met a friend and revealed for the first time that he had set the words of a patriotic poem called *Land of Hope and Glory* to music, predicting correctly that in a few months it would be heard all over the country. Leicester, as a lifelong friend of Elgar, might be thought a reliable authority, but this story is probably based on the fact that Elgar lived nearby in **Chesnut Walk** with his sister in the 1880s, whereas it is generally accepted that *Land of Hope and Glory* was not composed until 1901-2, so this claim seems doubtful.

St Oswald's in 1784

ST PAUL'S STREET

This street in the former *Blockhouse* district existed for centuries past as an old path called Withy Walk, which ran across Blockhouse Fields from **St Martin's Gate** to **Wyld's Lane**, and its route would also have taken in what became **Foundry Street**. It ran beside a drainage ditch, and was supposed to be there still in the 1850s, at least in part, though this street was shown as Denmark Place on maps of 1824 and 1838, and probably took its present name soon after the first church was opened in the 1830s.

The 1824 map showed a first short section planned from **Foundry Street** and **Charles Street**, but surrounded by open land. By 1829 a map showed some development to the south east, but development seemed to stall for a time, and it is believable that a part of the old path existed in the 1850s, though much more building went ahead in the early 1860s and the street was probably complete by 1865, since there were hardly any building applications throughout the rest of the century.

Historic Worcester Streets

Rev. Studdert Kennedy

In 1884 there were a number of shops serving the local community and four pubs. On the corner of **St Martin's Gate** was a butcher's shop, and three doors down was the Roebuck Inn. Further down, on the corner of *James Street*, was the Potters Arms Inn; on the corner of *Wellington Street* was the Vulcan Inn; and on the corner of *King William Street* was the inn of that name. All these pubs were first listed in 1873, and had probably all been built in the early 1860s. All of them closed between 1960 and 1973, but for the Roebuck which is said to have closed around 1900. There was also a sweet shop, a coal merchant and several corner shops. Residents were almost entirely manual workers and small tradesmen, with building workers, glovers, a boiler maker, a tallow chandler, a sugar boiler, an iron moulder and a rope spinner.

The first St Paul's Church opened in 1837. Like the original chapel in **St George's Square** it was a typical 'Commissioners Church', built very much on a budget, and like the original St George's, it didn't last long. A new church was built in red brick in 1885-6, which has stood the test of time, though the old church building served as a school until it was demolished in the 1940s.

The heart of its parish was the ***Blockhouse***, an area of poverty so bad that it had a soup kitchen in the 1890s. The deprivation in the area greatly concerned the parish's most famous incumbent, the Rev G.A. Studdert Kennedy. He came to St Paul's in 1914 but two years later he left to act as a military chaplain during the First World War, becoming famous as 'Woodbine Willie', for handing out bibles and Woodbine cigarettes to soldiers.

When he returned to his parish he was horrified at the conditions of poverty in which his parishioners were living. It was said he would give away his own clothes to beggars, and he began to write and preach that society must tackle the poverty in its midst. He left in 1922 to preach nationally and died just seven years later. Worcester was brought to a standstill by his funeral. The Rev Kennedy's church still exists, but there is scarcely anything else left in the street that he would recognise, following modern redevelopment.

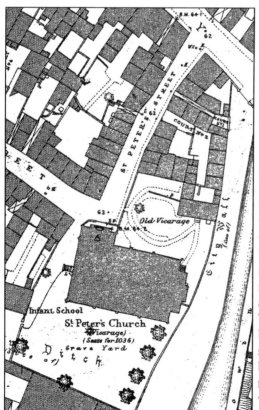

St Peter's Street in 1884

ST PETER'S STREET

The street was first found in the health board streets list of 1872, and in a street directory of the following year, but it probably existed as the lane leading to the church from some time in the tenth century, and is clearly shown on a map of the city in 1651.

It took its name from St Peter's Church, the parish church of St Peter the Great parish, which was at the southern end of the street, beside the city wall. It was called 'the Great' to distinguish it from the chapel at Worcester Castle near **Severn Street**, which had the same dedication, and so was styled St Peter the Less.

The parish may have been created as early as 969, and if so then the first parish church must have been built around that time, in a position very close to the city wall, with the vicarage beside it, which in the nineteenth century had a relatively spacious garden. The church must have been rebuilt in the medieval period and was described in the eighteenth century as small and neat but unremarkable.

The old building was demolished in 1838 and replaced by a brick-built church in early Victorian Gothic, accounted by some the ugliest church in the city. This building was ruinous by the early 1970s and it was demolished in 1976, though the remains of its foundations are said to exist still beneath what was formerly a Worcester Porcelain car park, but is now part of the Berkeley Homes development site. The part of the parish inside the walls is now part of the Worcester civil parish, but those parts outside the wall form the St Peter the Great County Parish.

Much poor housing was built for rent in this area before the Civil War. In 1746 a parish workhouse was set up in a half-timbered building here, which existed well into the twentieth century, and administered the benefit system in very different times. Supporting single mums on the parish rates was not popular in the eighteenth century, and in 1780 parish records showed the authorities moving fast when an Ann Williams claimed parish relief for herself and her new-born child. After she had been persuaded to reveal the name of the father, a warrant was issued for his apprehension by a posse of constables, and a parson was soon summoned to marry the 'happy' couple.

In 1884 the bicycle and tricycle depot of Bowcott & Co. stood where there is now a motorcycle dealer. Residents included a nurse, a verger, a chimney sweep, an umbrella maker, a laundress, a seamstress, several labourers, a painter, a shoemaker and a nail maker.

This was a narrow street of old timber framed houses within living memory, but it was well and truly 'cleared' in the mid twentieth century and sadly this old street is now nothing more than the entrance to a modern housing development.

ST STEPHEN'S STREET

This street may have long been in use as a 'cut-through' from **Ombersley Road** to **Droitwich Road**, but in the 1860s it acquired a new role as the access road to St Stephen's Church, and then St Stephen's School.

St Peter's Street and Church about 1900 - RS

Both buildings were the result of the generosity of two ladies who were members of the wealthy Lavender family, after whom **Lavender Road** was named. The family owned land around Barbourne Brook, and were also partners until around 1850 in the Farley, Lavender, Owen and Gutch bank at the Cross, where NatWest Bank is now. In 1862 Miss Jane Lavender and her sister, Mrs Mary Gutch, built St Stephens Church.

The cost was never disclosed, but the building of St Mary's, **The Tything** parish church in **Sansome Walk** in 1876-7 cost £6,000, which was a considerable sum then, and gives some idea of what St Stephen's must have cost. The school opened in 1864. It was built by Thomas Wilkes, who was actually the local undertaker, but diversified into construction, also building Claines school and many houses in the area. Conditions in the poorly-heated school were not always ideal. In 1930 there was a measles epidemic, followed by an outbreak of scarlet fever, which disrupted the work of the school for six months. The school survived to celebrate its centenary, but subsequently closed, and the site is now occupied by a block of flats.

Though the street must have existed from the early 1860s, the north side

St Stephen's Street in 1884

was entirely occupied by the church and the school, and there was no other development here immediately. The land here will have formed part of the estate of Mrs Mary Gutch, who owned much land around **Ombersley Road**, and when this street was surveyed by Ordnance Survey in 1884, there was open land on the south side. However, around that time or very shortly afterwards the land was split into plots for house building, though progress was not rapid, with just four building applications for eight houses in the period 1886-9, but that completed this small street when they were built.

In 1896 two of the eight houses were empty, presumably having just been completed, and the one on the corner of **Droitwich Road** was Samuel Ranford's grocer's shop. Residents included builder James Higgs, commercial clerk Harold Bibbs, two widows, Mrs Karn and Mrs Wolfenden, and William Newton, assistant inspector to the Chamber of Agriculture. By the 1960s the shop was Mr Taylor's supermarket.

ST STEPHEN'S TERRACE

No records have been found for the building of this small cul-de-sac, which may suggest that it was built prior to the start of building control in late 1865. It was listed as Place in a street directory of 1873, but was unnamed on an Ordnance Survey map of 1884, though its small terrace of four cottages was shown, to which two more were added soon afterwards. Residents in 1884 included glover Edward Luffman, carpenter Joseph Gould, agent Manasseh Edwards and nurse Mrs Matthews. These cottages seem likely to have been built on land which had been part of Barbourne Nurseries, and there was still orchard land to the west of the terrace, which was not built on until comparatively recently.

ST SWITHUN'S CLOSE

The first record of this small street was a building application of 1880, for a new road off **Camp Hill Road**, originally called St Swithin Crescent. It was submitted by William Good Pike of **Britannia Square**. He was an estate agent with offices at **The Avenue**, and presumably submitted this application on behalf of a client, whose identity is not known. Development was anything but rapid however. When the area was mapped five years later there was still open land here, with no sign of the street. It wasn't until 1890 that there was an application for a house and shop, but neither one was built, and there was no development here until around 1980.

ST SWITHIN'S STREET

Originally part of **Mealcheapen Street**, which was created in the thirteenth century, this street became known as Gosse or *Goose Lane* or Goosethrottle Lane in the sixteenth century, because it was the site of the city's poultry street market. It was also known as Grass Cross Lane, leading to **The Cross**. It acquired its present name in the nineteenth century. The sign at the west end of the street has no apostrophe, but the sign at the east end does and is probably the more widely used version now, so has been preferred here.

This was a busy commercial street in 1790. A directory listing of that date included Mrs Nelme, who described herself as 'pastry cook to their Majesties'. She was clearly one of those local business people who took full advantage of having gifted their products to the Royal family during their visit two years earlier. Other businesses in the street included a baker, a brush maker, a firm of glovers, a linen draper, a pawnbroker, directory printer and publisher James Grundy, three shoemakers, two tallow chandlers and upholsterer and watchmaker John Thomas.

By 1840 there were two watchmakers in the street, a straw hat maker, a hairdresser, a cabinet maker, a cheese factor, a confectioner and a solicitor, amongst others. John Perrins at No. 4 was a gun maker and a member of the Worcestershire sauce family.

Street widening was planned as early as 1884, when a dozen properties on the north side were listed as 'shortly to be pulled down'. They were housing a boot and shoe maker, a watchmaker

St Swithun's Church in the late eighteenth century

and toy dealer, a grocer, two confectioners, a brush warehouse, another watchmaker and a tea dealer. However widening was not carried out until 1890-91, when the whole of the north side was demolished. A small group of four older buildings does remain however on the south side, at the east end of the street.

The earliest known church on the site must have dated from soon after 1126, when the priory was given permission to build it. The dedication of the church to a ninth century Bishop of Winchester with no known Worcester connections, and a reputation for giving us 40 days of rain if there is a shower on his feast day of 15 July, has been regarded as odd. However, his cult was spread by a successor, Aethelwold, who was closely involved with Worcester bishops Dunstan and Wulfstan II in monastic reform, which made the dedication an obvious one for the monks who built the church.

St Swithin's Street before 1890 when it was widened - RS

It had one of the city's smallest parishes, but its parishioners were amongst the wealthiest citizens, and it eventually became the church of the governing body of the city. It was always hemmed in by shops and market stalls – at one time the herb market was here, and in 1619 the hosiery and liquor markets – leaving no room for a graveyard, meaning that parishioners had to be buried beneath the floor. John Noake noted in the mid nineteenth century that the congregation had to endure an intolerable smell during services.

The church was presumably rebuilt in the fifteenth century, since the tower dates from that period, but the remainder of the church was rebuilt during 1734 - 36. In 1764 it was said to be the only church in the city with an organ and chimes. Its eighteenth century interior especially has been much admired, but its congregation has long since moved to the suburbs, and it has been redundant as a church since 1977, though it is still used for community events and special services. Oddly the church now uses Swithun, while the street has Old English Swithin, and there is some controversy about which is older.

Berrow's Worcester Journal moved here from **Sidbury** in 1748, after it was taken over by clergyman's son Harvey Berrow,

An 1896 advertisement

though he did not add his name to the publication until 1753, after he claimed unscrupulous competitors began an opposing newspaper with the same name as his. By 1790 it was no longer listed here, and in 1820 it was in **Church Street**.

Behind the church stands a modest eighteenth century building which was home in the 1790s to the business of watchmaker John Skarratt, whose family firm later employed William Kilbourne Kay, founder of the Kay's mail order empire, which was once Worcester's leading employer. Skarratt's, which moved to **Broad Street** in 1814, was a successful business in its own right for a century, not only serving the city but supplying clocks and watches to the Great Western Railway, but its involvement with Kay's was not quite what it would appear. A plaque placed on the building in 1994 – claimed as Kay's bicentenary year - suggests that it was this business, taken over by Kay, which led directly to the founding of Kay's, but the history of Kay's, published nine years later, showed this was not actually correct. Kay started his own business after leaving Skarratts, and he only later took over the firm he had once worked for. Ironically it was Kay himself who was responsible for the confusion. He took over the Skarratt family business in 1896, and then began dating the founding of his firm from 1794, the date usually given for the establishment of Skarratt's, thus making his ten-year-old business sound much better established than it actually was.

Directories suggest that Mr Kay also got the founding date of Skarratt's family firm wrong. The year 1794 was the date at which John Skarrat set up as a watchmaker in this street, but he seems to have taken over a watchmaking business which in 1790 was run by Charles Carleton Skarratt at 63 **High Street**, where he also had a Staffordshire china and glassware showroom. That business was no longer listed in 1794, and presumably John Skarratt had taken over and moved it here. So the founding date of the Skarratt family business is not known, but it must have been founded in 1790 or before.

The Arcade Picture Palace, the city's second cinema, was built in 1912 on the site of what is now Superdrug. It took its name from the unsuccessful Central Arcade, established by 1905, which ran through to **Church Street**, and by 1912 housed Lipton's the grocers, and Foster Bros clothing store, but had several empty shops. The cinema was taken over in the 1930s by Gaumont British Picture Co., which had closed it by 1936 and opened a replacement in **Foregate Street**.

At the west end of the street was the Central Temperance Hotel and Restaurant, which was rebuilt in 1903, and is now a building society with flats above. Foster Bros moved to No. 16 and were still here in the 1950s. Here at that time were Lane's chemists at No. 2, tobacconist Frederick Wright at No. 9, two doors down from Osborne & Sharpe builders' merchants. George Mason's grocers were at No. 14, and Thorntons the jewellers were at No. 18.

ST WULSTAN'S CRESCENT

This street was named for the eleventh century Bishop of Worcester and saint, who was so respected by William the Conqueror that he was the only Anglo-Saxon bishop to retain his see after the Conquest. This is a 'modernised' spelling of his name: the correct Anglo-Saxon spelling was Wulfstan. This street was created and developed early in the 1880s, after development of the adjacent **Richmond Road** had gone ahead quickly in the previous few years. In two years from 1881 there were 16 mostly small-scale applications by various small investors to build a total of 31 houses here, though only just over 20 were actually built, with two more vacant plots being developed in modern times. By 1884 21 of the planned homes had been built, with another added by 1915. Residents in 1915 included five clerks, a potter, a glover, a ticket examiner, three skilled china workers, a fitter, a moulder, a confectioner, and picture frame maker Chas Cook at St Wulstan's House. There were also three ladies living alone, one of whom let apartments.

SABRINA AVENUE

Sabrina was the goddess of the nearby River Severn in Celtic mythology. The avenue was created in 1898 as one of two access roads to Barbourne Works (see **Northwick Avenue**).

It was not included in a street directory until 1922. There were four schoolmasters here then, perhaps at the grammar school in **The Tything**. Other residents included a number of clerks, the deputy county surveyor, a civil servant, a dairyman, a fitter, a bus conductor, railwaymen, machinists, a cabinet maker, a telegraphist, a florist's manager, a tinsmith, an engineer, a baker and commercial travellers.

SABRINA TERRACE

This street was first recorded in a building application of 1897 for two villas. By 1922 there still seemed to be only three listings, shown under **Thorneloe Road**, for the villas Southbourne, Calgarth Lawn and Woodhall. Only one resident gave an occupation – clerk. There were six listings by 1937, but the southern end of the street was not developed until later in the twentieth century.

SABRINA WALK
Off **Sabrina Avenue**, this street was first found in a street directory in 1930, when there were eight homes listed.

Salt Lane
Now **Castle Street**. The route by which salt travelled for centuries from Droitwich to a salt wharf at the bottom of this street, but the trade had ceased by the nineteenth century, and the lane was renamed after a new county prison, built in the style of a medieval castle, opened here in 1813. However the old name continued in use throughout most of the nineteenth century. As late as 1880 it was still listed in a street directory, though with the notation 'better known as Castle Street', and it finally seems to have fallen out of use in the 1890s.

**Above, Samuel, First Baron Sandys.
Below, Sandys Road in 1884**

SANDYS ROAD
Named for the Sandys family (pronounced Sands), who were Worcestershire landowners for centuries, with their home at Ombersley, which had been granted to them in 1614. Edwin Sandys, a learned but quarrelsome cleric of Elizabeth's reign, managed to rise to high office despite supporting Lady Jane Grey against her. After a brief period of imprisonment he was appointed Bishop of Worcester from 1559 to 1570, and went on to be Bishop of London and Archbishop of York.

Samuel Sandys was Chancellor of the Exchequer 1742-3, and was then created Baron Sandys of Ombersley, and became Speaker of the House of Lords. He built Ombersley Court as it is today, but for the brick front which was added in the nineteenth century. He died in London in 1770, from injuries received when his carriage overturned on Highgate Hill.

In the nineteenth century the title passed by marriage to the Hill family, one of whom was aide-de-camp to Wellington during the Peninsula War, but in 1861 the title holder changed his surname to Sandys. His son, Augustus Frederick Arthur Sandys, became Lord Sandys and held the title until his death in 1904.

It is possible that the revival of the Sandys name, or the accession of a new lord, led to the street name, which was listed in a street directory in 1873, but was first recorded in a building application of 1867, for two cottages, submitted by builder George Priddy.

There were four more small-scale applications by various builders or developers in 1871, but then nothing until an application for two houses in 1879, and the first larger application for six houses was not submitted until 1884, by builder James Henry Beard, who was also responsible for another 15 relatively small building applications over two decades. So by 1884 applications had been submitted for 17 homes, but a directory in that year suggests there were 45 homes in the street at that time, and five more being built, so more than 30 homes were presumably built before building control began in late 1865. Some confusion was caused however by the fact that nine homes in what by 1896 was called **Pope Iron Road** were listed here in 1884, described at that time as Sandys Road North.

Residents in 1884 were almost invariably manual workers. There were building tradesmen, labourers, glovers, coach workers, a laundress, a dressmaker, a confectioner, a smith, an iron fitter, a clerk, a shoemaker, a butcher, a compositor and a fireman. Fire brigade captain Thomas Sayce lived at No. 13, and Thomas Williamson had a corner shop here.

Historic Worcester Streets

In 1896, when Pope Iron Road was listed separately, 44 homes were listed here and eight more were being built. There were eight applications for 23 homes in the period 1885 to 1902. In total just over 60 fitted in here. There was a corner shop at the east end, long since converted to a home.

SANSOME FIELDS WALK
This name was originally used for what is now **Sansome Walk**, which was an old pathway beside the Sansome Fields long before it became a street. This may have been an extension of it and kept the name, though when it was first regarded as a street name is difficult to determine exactly. An 1869 building application for a single house – the only house building application found in this name during the nineteenth century - may refer to this street or to Sansome Walk. The first listing of this street name in a directory was in 1884, when there were listings for four Myrtle Cottages, occupied by a glover, a potter, a tailor and a foreman, and four Enfield Cottages, occupied by a laundress, a cabinet maker, a guard and a gardener.

SANSOME PLACE
This was originally part of Sansome Fields, and known as Sansome Stile, leading into an area which was open meadows and woodland in the eighteenth century (see **Sansome Walk**).
The Society of Friends have been established here since their chapel was opened in 1701, after they had worshipped in various places around the city and suffered a fair amount of persecution. Quaker leader George Fox first visited the city in 1655, when the Society was probably founded here, but a meeting in 1662 was broken up by militia. In the 1670s Fox was thrown into the county prison at the castle off **Severn Street** for 14 months, and in 1681 a Quaker leader in the city was imprisoned for holding an unlawful gathering in **Friar Street**.
The Roman Catholic St George's Chapel, which had opened in 1686, probably in **Foregate Street**, moved to this area by 1741, presumably to an existing building, since a new chapel was built here in 1765, near where the present church stands. It was still a dangerous time for catholics and the priests referred to it as a 'new shoppe' in their letters. It wasn't until 1791 that catholic chapels became legal. The present church was built in 1829, the year that the Catholic Relief Act was passed, but the present facade wasn't erected until 1887. The Presbytery, built in 1851, was designed by Joseph Hansom, the architect of Birmingham Town Hall and designer of the Victorian Hansom cab. Edward Elgar was appointed organist here in 1885 in succession to his father, and much of his early religious music may have been written for St George's.
There was a girls' National School here in 1861, and catholic schools behind St George's in 1884. Beside the church in that year was a small colony of solicitors, four in all, including Curtler and David, who also acted as clerks to the county magistrates. Around the corner, near what was the sorting office in modern times, was Larkworthy's agricultural implement depot, and Miss Fanny David, French corset maker. By 1896 the Temperance Hall was in this area. In 1884 there was also a gasfitter and bellhanger, a furniture warehouse, and a wheelwright, There were also manual workers tighly packed into cramped accommodation, and the Lowesmoor Iron Works near **Lion Walk**. Near the canal wharf was the Elephant and Castle pub, which Gwilliam said was first listed in 1873, and closed around 1970.
In 1896 the Worcester Cycle Works was established on a site which was later a telephone exchange, and now houses student accommodation. The works was actually a cycle factory which could manufacture all its own parts and build its own cycles, with model names such as 'Zodax' and 'Zodiac', but it apparently didn't last long, disappearing from listings around 1905.

SANSOME STREET
This was originally Portditch or *Town Ditch*, the ditched area of the ancient defences outside the city walls, leading east from the Foregate. The street had changed its name by the late eighteenth century to the present form, inspired by the nearby Sansome Fields. It was part of open agricultural land to the north and east of the city until at least the seventeenth century. There was however a medieval tile-making industry here, and ironworking somewhere nearby, since these were industries involving high temperature kilns and forges which would not have been welcome in a city of timber-framed houses, and there were probably no or low city dues payable out here.
The town ditch was probably infilled around the mid-seventeenth century, after the city walls were slighted at the end of the Civil War. A track then developed leading from Foregate to the Trinity Gate, on the line still taken by the road, and this created the impetus for development in the area, which covered both sides of the street by 1741. The old name for the street was still used on a map of 1764, but the current name, spelled 'Sansom', was listed in a directory of 1790, with the 'e' added within twenty years.

Historic Worcester Streets

Around 1620 the Inglethorpe Charity, founded by the will of wealthy city businessman Richard Inglethorpe, built almshouses for the poor on the north side of the street, on the site of what is now the Worcester Arts Workshop. Inglethorpe, who had been High Bailiff of the city in 1610, died around 1617. In accordance with his will, the almshouses were to house six poor, elderly men and one poor woman, aged at least 50, who was to act as housekeeper for the men, washing their

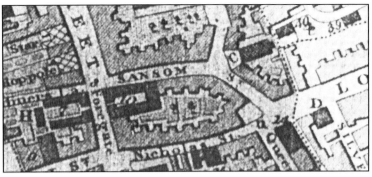

Sansome Street in 1822

clothes, making their beds and generally looking after them. His second wife, Margaret, supervised their construction in her husband's memory.

But 25 years later, during the Civil War, they were taken down by the Royalists to deny cover to attackers. Pat Hughes said they were rebuilt in **Dolday**, but that may have been another development of the charity, since they were apparently rebuilt here after the Civil War, and were certainly here in the early eighteenth century.

In 1732 they were inspected by the city surveyors, who found them 'very much out of repair'. Canny local businessman John Garway then offered to replace them with a row of dwellings in **Taylors Lane**, in return for acquiring this more valuable site. The new almshouses were built, but the land here still belonged to the charity in the nineteenth century, so Garway must only have obtained a lease. On a map of 1810 the land now occupied by Worcester Arts Workshop was still held by the Trustees of the Inglethorpe Charity, who applied in 1871 to build a warehouse on the site, and by 1884 there was a brewery there.

Richard Inglethorpe was remembered by *Inglethorpe Square* and *Inglethorpe Meadow* off **Lowesmoor**, no longer in existence, and his name is still kept alive by Inglethorpe Court off the Hopmarket.

In the eighteenth century the city workhouse occupied a substantial site on the southern corner of the street, with its entrance on **The Foregate**, on the site where the Hop Market Hotel was later built.

It was created by an Act of Parliament of 1703, to be built where the old Foregate gatehouse had stood, which had been taken down in the previous year. It had some initial difficulties however, and closed within a few years after running up a £300 debt. The corporation then let out the premises as a hop market and warehouses, and the street became the location for city hop merchants, having nine by 1820.

However Samuel Sandys of Ombersley, MP for Worcestershire for 25 years, rallied support for the workhouse, and after years of effort, managed to get it reopened in 1730. The hop market remained on the site, which was said to be the largest in the land in the eighteenth century, with proceeds from rents going to the guardians of the poor, which is why the Hop Market governors were known as Guardians. It was described as 'a capacious and beautiful structure' by 'Robinson Crusoe' author Daniel Defoe, who visited the city around 1740. The workhouse residents would have been transferred to the House of Industry on **Tallow Hill** when that opened in 1794.

In 1790 there were just two hop merchant listed here, three glovers plus a gloving firm, a 'plaisterer', and Miss Adamson, a mantua maker (a superior type of dressmaker). There were also two pubs, the Plume of Feathers, on which Gwilliam has no information, and the Golden Hart, near the Hopmarket entrance, which he said closed in the 1970s, though the building is still here. In 1840 there were eight hop merchants, a livery stable, billiard rooms, and two solicitors, including Charles Bedford of the Shrubbery Estate in what became **Shrubbery Avenue**. There was also a listing for the Old Falcon pub on the corner of **Lowesmoor**, and the 'Temperance Arms', which sounds like a temperance movement version of a pub, and wasn't here in the 1880s, though there was a temperance hall in **Sansome Place** in 1896.

For most of the nineteenth century the street would have been much narrower than it is today. Widening must have happened in the late nineteenth century, when similar work was going on in other city streets, but it had the effect of removing most of the older buildings from the street, and a spate of rebuilding removed the rest.

In 1898 Spreckleys Brewery in **Barbourne Road** submitted an application to rebuild the Golden Hart inn on the south side of the street, and in the following year an application was submitted to build the Hop Market Hotel, during which the massive foundations of the ancient Foregate were discovered.

Sadly, aside from these turn-of-the-century developments, there is little left of the street's past. Its most important feature is 'The Hop Pickers', a superb carved panel by William Forsyth of **The Tything**, situated near the west end of the street, which recalls its historic connection with hops.

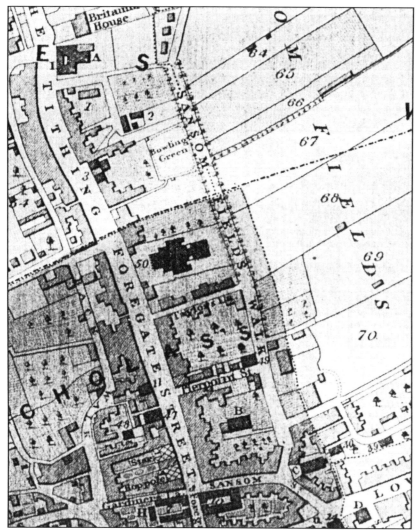

Sansome Walk, then called Sansome Fields Walk, in 1822

SANSOME WALK

Formerly Sansome Fields Walk, a perimeter path on Sansome Fields. In the eighteenth century this was a pleasant area of meadows and woodland, which stretched north as far as Barbourne, and east as far as **Rainbow Hill** and **Merriman's Hill**, and was much favoured by city folks for summer walks.

The name came from the Sansom family of dairy farmers, who must have been farming here up to the eighteenth century, and were farming at Claines from the nineteenth century. The family may have diversified into farming from blacksmithing, since John Sansom was a sixteenth century smith who lived in St Nicholas parish, the parish closest to Sansome Fields, and died about 1588. Worcester's Tudor House Museum has a pony trap sign-written 'H. Sansome, Dairyman, Claines', and there were Sansomes listed at Oak Farm, Claines in 1884, and at North Claines in 1931.

In the eighteenth century it was the estate of Sir Charles Trubshaw Withers, mayor in 1765, whose mansion, Sansome Lodge, was almost the only house in the area, and public enjoyment of this rural oasis close to the city was thanks to his generosity. His father Joseph had been mayor in 1740 and has a memorial in St Swithun's Church. Sir Charles – he was knighted during George III's visit in 1788 – died in 1804 at Strensham, where there is a memorial to him in the parish church. He was a popular figure in Worcester, and obituaries described him as 'the father of the city'. His home still exists, opposite the bottom of **Pierpoint Street**.

The nearest neighbour, on the other side of the Walk, was Ivy House, believed to date from about 1700. It acquired its name because the front was once covered in ivy, but it has since been cleared off. It is now the home of Armstrongs the tailors, who moved here in the late nineteenth century. The firm began trading in 1792, which must make it one of the oldest businesses in the city. It was founded by a Mr Turner, and had at least five other homes before moving here. The first Armstrong in the business took over in 1888, and by the end of the century the firm had branches in Stourbridge, Birmingham and Leicester, and twelve travelling salesmen covered Worcestershire and Shropshire. As a result the firm had a substantial staff, and local deliveries were carried out with a horse-drawn carriage.

A gravel path which had been widened by Sir Charles, ran along the west side of the meadows, between avenues of elms, and was a favourite walk for city folk. After the death of Sir Charles the estate was taken over by Worcestershire deputy lieutenant Thomas Blayney of Evesham, but in 1811 it was sold at auction in 10 lots. The buyers included wealthy glovers the Knapps, glover Philip Ball, and hop merchant Robert Felton. In 1813 part or all of the estate was leased for 99 years to John Knapp senior. Thomas Blayney was said to have given the Sansome Fields Walk to the city in 1815, so that may not have formed part of the land auctioned. The street was first listed in a street directory under its present name in 1840. At that time Pierpoint Street solicitor and County Coroner William Price Hughes was living at Sansom Fields House, **Foregate Street** auctioneer William Bentley was living at Sansom Lodge, and G. Woodberry Spooner was running a

Sansome Fields in the late eighteenth century, when Sansome Lodge, which still exists, was home to Sir Charles Trubshaw Withers

gentlemen's boarding school here. Soon after that date the estate was purchased by a private company and converted into pleasure grounds which opened in 1859, but they were not successful and closed four years later. The site was sold for redevelopment in 1866, though considerable development had gone ahead elsewhere in this street by 1864.

Building records paint a picture of surprisingly slow development through the rest of the century, with 15 applications for 33 homes and two shops over the next 36 years. This does not seem to fit with what was built however, since there were close to 30 homes listed here by 1884. By that date Miss Stearman had a ladies' school at Ivy House. Residents were either skilled or managerial. Alfred Mason at a villa called Bebington was a carver and gilder; George Hodgkiss at Raglan Villa was an auctioneer's manager, and Fred Stone next door at Bath Villa was a 'professional brewer' at Joseland's brewery. There were also a number of residents styling themselves as 'gentlemen'.

Rev Pilkington, the first vicar of the **Tything** parish in 1875, gave a site on the corner of this road and **Northfield Street** for the new parish church, which opened in 1877. When he and his wife first inspected the site they were horrified to find that it was the habitual haunt of prostitutes, and they rented a building nearby to set up a rescue home for 'fallen women'.

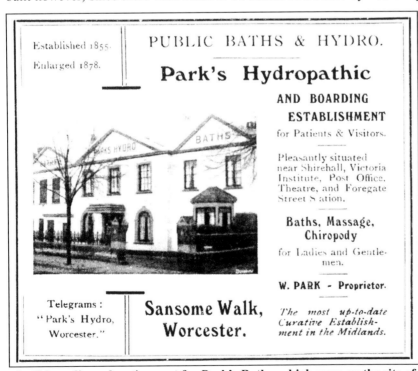

An Edwardian advertisement for Park's Baths, which were on the site of the present city council swimming baths

The new church, which was only just within the Tything parish, cost £6,000 to build, which was raised by subscription. It closed in 1977, and the Church Commissioners planned to demolish it in 1982, but after a vigorous local campaign led by architect Ian McConaghy the building was saved, and was subsequently converted into apartments. The Baptists, who had been in **Silver Street** since the early eighteenth century, moved to a new chapel built here in 1863-4, and there was an application for a chapel house and school in 1868.

The major nineteenth century development here was the School of Art, now apartments, which was part of the massive Victoria Institute complex opened in 1896, running through from **Foregate Street**. The other striking building is the public baths, which stand on the site of private premises best known as Park's Baths, which unlike the present swimming pool, stood close to the roadway. The baths here were open-air and part of a private hotel which had opened by 1854. Aside from the pool itself there were a number of 'spa' style and later Turkish baths. The premises were taken over by William Park in 1890, and his family continued to run them for many years. Meanwhile the only public bathing available was in the Severn, in primitive 'swimming barges'. A plan for the city to build new baths was reported in the Journal as early as July 1912, but it wasn't until 1971 that the city took over and demolished Park's Baths, replacing them with the present indoor pool which opened in 1972.

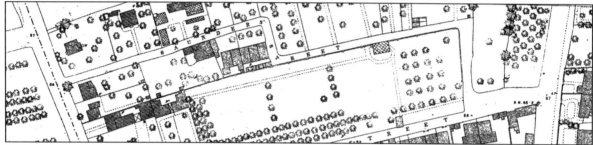
Saunders Street in 1884

SAUNDERS STREET

The county archives have records relating to a Saunders family, who held the Manor of Ombersley in the sixteenth and seventeenth centuries. It is possible that they had the land here or were involved in financing the development, though no evidence has been found. There are also no records to tell us who built the homes here, though there is an application to create the street, but it was not submitted until 1885, after the houses had been built. It was submitted by Henry Morgan, who had the Midland Saw Mill in **Wyld's Lane**. He was involved in property development, submitting 30 building applications over two decades, but all were small-scale, so it is unlikely he built all the homes here, though he may have built some.

The street was fist found in a street directory of 1884, when there seem to be 21 properties listed. It was evidently built fairly haphazardly on former orchard land, and a map of 1884 shows a good many trees still standing, over much of the open land remaining around the street, especially on the south side. Residents then were manual workers with a wide variety of occupations. They included labourers, laundresses, a carpenter, a stonemason, a bricklayer, a blacksmith, a hay trusser, a china potter, a brace maker, a glover, a railway porter, a coachman, a gardener and a brewer.

Further development was slow, and it was not until 1922 that a directory listed the 24 homes which completed the street, but for a small amount of modern development.

SCHOOL ROAD

The street looks from maps to have been built on former orchard land, probably in the 1850s or 60s, though some cottages may have been here earlier. It was first found in the health board streets list of 1872, and a street directory of the following year. The little St John's School, which gave the street its name, was situated a short distance along on the east side, on a site since redeveloped, and was handy here for the development around **Boughton Street**, which had begun early in the century, but it catered only for boys. There was space for a girls' school further along, but that didn't happen, and the larger school on **Bransford Road** took over education in the area by the early twentieth century, and by 1922 this school was being used only for boys' woodwork classes.

Much of the west side was taken up with the grounds of Boughton Villa off **Bransford** Road, also on a site since redeveloped. In 1884 there were 14 modest homes here, though some had good gardens, and there was room for more development. Though this was close to the Boughton Nursery there was little sign of nursery workers living here. Residents then included several labourers, a shoemaker, a fireman, an asylum attendant, a letter carrier, a gardener, a seamstress, a sawyer, a compositor, a baker, a porter and a cattle dealer. There was apparently no shop in the street, but there was the Berkeley Arms pub, which might be almost as old as some of the houses in Boughton Street. Because of redevelopment, the pub is all that remains of this road as it was.

School Walk

This former footway, also known as School Lane, led from the southern end of **Tybridge Street**, just west of the present St Clement's Close, past the little nineteenth century St Clement's School to *St Clement's Square*, and may have connected with **Bush Walk**, though not with **Henwick Road**. It will have been created when the school was built, and was shown in a directory of 1840. An 1884 directory listed about 16 homes here, plus a shop on the corner of **Tybridge Street** kept by Mrs Louisa Maund. The school was about midway along the walk, on the north side. At the west end of the walk, clustered around **Bush Walk**, was a substantial area of housing called *St Clement's Square*, consisting of 38 modest homes, whose residents were labourers, building workers, seamstresses, shoemakers, glovers, a charwoman, a pump maker, a waterman, a lamplighter, a brewer, a gardener, a coachman and a platelayer. The Square had been cleared by 1928 but the Walk remained, probably until the area was cleared around the 1960s.

SEBRIGHT AVENUE

The Sebright family held the manor of Besford, south of Worcester, for almost three centuries, and also enclosed land at Redhill on **London Road**. The manor, near Pershore, was acquired in 1606 for £2,750 by William Sebright, a wealthy London merchant, of a family from Blakeshall in Wolverley, and it remained with that family for two and a half centuries. By 1614 he had also acquired the Battenhall Estate.

His nephew Edward was High Sheriff of Worcestershire, and was created a baronet in 1626. He seems to have kept his options open in the Civil War. In 1642 he was Commissioner of Array for Charles I, responsible for mustering troops for the Battle of Edgehill, but four years later Charles was complaining he had changed sides, and in 1651 Edward said he had acted for Parliament whenever possible, though he was still fined the very considerable sum of £3,618 by the Roundheads.

The sixth baronet, Sir John Saunders Sebright, who succeeded to the estate in 1761, was a colonel of the 18th Regiment of Foot, later the Royal Irish Regiment, and became a Lieutenant-general, as well as representing Bath three times as an MP. His son, of the same name, represented Hertfordshire in Parliament for many years, and was a noted agriculturist whose ideas on selective breeding influenced Darwin. It may have been partly as a result of his reputation that the Royal Show, a major agricultural event, came to the area in 1863. It was sited on land owned by the Sebrights, off **Battenhall Road**, and attracted 70,000 people to the city over five days.

The last of the Sebrights of Besford inherited the Battenhall Estate in 1864, and sold it in 1885 to Frederick, Earl Beauchamp. There was then open land south of Battenhall, but events moved swiftly. The land was divided into lots for sale, and within the space of two weeks there were two separate applications to create this street, submitted by different developers. On 7 October 1885 a building application for this new road and sewers, was submitted by Worcester Land & Investment, the property development company of furniture dealer Edwin Nichols. But on 20 October a second application was submitted by Henry Morgan of the Midland Saw Mill in **Wyld's Lane**, another busy property developer, who submitted thirty mostly small-scale building applications over two decades. Whether Edwin Nichols had dropped out quickly, or whether they were competing for control of the development is not clear, but neither one applied to build any of the houses.

Over the following decade 13 mostly small building applications were submitted by various investors and developers, for a total of 33 homes. By 1896 25 homes had been built here, mostly villas, though with a few more modest cottages. Residents then were mostly a mix of manual and skilled workers. They included glovers, gardeners, a porter, an engine driver, a butler, a foreman, a wood turner, a bootmaker, a decorator, a potter, a clerk, a machine agent, a carpenter, a bricklayer, a fitter and a plumber. An application was submitted for another 10 houses in 1904, which must have been built soon afterwards. The 48 homes listed in 1922 were nearly all Victorian and Edwardian, and were nearly all at the north-east end of the street, adjoining **London Road**. The remainder of the street has been completed at various dates since.

SELBORNE ROAD

The name may be the surname of a family involved in the development of the street, but no Worcestershire record of such a family has been found. Perhaps a more likely explanation is that it was inspired by *The*

Natural History of Selborne, a pioneering ecological work by eighteenth century Hampshire naturalist Gilbert White, which was popular throughout the Victorian period, and is still in print.

No building records were found for this road, but research by a resident suggests that the earliest homes here may have been built in the 1850s, with more building in the 1870s. It was first listed in a street directory of 1896, when there were half a dozen stately villas here. Residents then included wealthy local brewer and city JP William Joseland at Milford Lodge. These were all on the west side, and a smaller plot on that side was built on in the 1950s. Development on the other side is modern.

SELBORNE ROAD WEST

This was originally known as Sharman Road West, but was renamed on 26 October 1903, and was first listed in a street directory in 1908, when there were nine homes listed here, including two large villas, Grettordene and Westbourne, the latter home to Joseph Sharman Wood, of long-established building firm Joseph Wood. There were also four villas in Crescent View, and two in Olga Villas, beside which another villa named Emlyn was built around the same time. This still left a couple of vacant plots which have had to await modern development.

SEVERN STREET

Previously this street was *Frog Lane*, named for the Frog Brook, which now runs into the canal to the east of the city centre, but prior to 1815 ran around the city wall to join the Severn near here. Until the seventeenth century this was a narrow lane running only a short distance from Edgar Street to the city wall, presumably to Frog Gate, a postern in the city wall, which was in this area.

This was one of the early working class suburbs of the city, developed originally in the early seventeenth century. Outside the wall was the Frog Mill powered by the Frog Brook. In times of drought the miller was required to divert the mill stream into the gardens of houses in this lane once a week. The mill pond dictated the line of this street. The mill was said by Hughes to have been dismantled in 1643 during the Civil War, to deny cover to attackers, but it must have been rebuilt later, since it was here in the eighteenth century, described then as a picturesque ruin.

A map of 1741 shows the lane running through a gap in the wall down to the river, which it had probably done since soon after the Civil War, when the walls were slighted. It was then bounded on the north by orchards and the castle, and on the south by Diglis fields, with the popular Diglis bowling green at the riverside, which also had assembly rooms, kept in 1712 by Allen Malpas of the Cross Keys inn in **Sidbury**.

Severn Street, then Frog Lane, in 1822, U is the castle

Frog Lane was still listed in 1790, but the name changed early in the nineteenth century, probably after 1815 when the brook was diverted into the Worcester & Birmingham Canal.

In 1790 residents included a bricklayer, a coal merchant, a sedan chairman, and two fishermen. Appropriately the pub here then was called the Fish. It was a short distance down from **Edgar Street**, on the east side, just before **King Street**, and closed around 1920. There was also said to be a pub called the Mason's Arms here in the eighteenth century, when most of the cathedral stonemasons lived in this area, but it is not shown in the 1790 listing, and no information has been found on exactly where it was. Gwilliam said it closed around 1850. Just the other side of **King Street** was the short-lived Porcelain Works pub, which Gwilliam said was first listed in 1873, but had closed by 1900. He also lists the Fountain, opposite the porcelain factory, which was shown on a map in 1884, but changed its name to the Potter's Wheel in 1979; and the Shades, a short distance west of the porcelain works, which closed before 1908.

A map of 1885 showed nine courts of housing around the street, and a street directory of around that date listed more than 50 homes here, not counting the courts. There was also Dandy Row, a terrace of meagre cottages behind the Shades. In total, there will have been hundreds of people living in this poor,

densely-packed housing. Conditions were so bad that there was a soup kitchen here in the 1890s. Called the Victoria Soup Kitchen, it was just off Edgar Street. A street directory listing of 1896 surprisingly showed only three china workers in the street, including china figure maker Frederick Evans. The most common job was labourer – almost one in three gave this as their occupation – and there were also factory workers, metal workers, fishermen, boatmen, clothing workers, a barmaid, a blacksmith, a painter and decorator and a coal dealer.

However there were also some white collar workers – a newsman and a clerk – and Mrs Mary Sebright was a certified midwife. Slum clearance in this area must have taken place in the 1950s, when **King Street** was cleared.

The castle was built by Urse D'Abitot, the first Norman lord of Worcester, before September 1069, and was probably of timber originally, though it was later rebuilt in stone. In layout it was typical of the style of motte and bailey castles built throughout England by the Normans after the Conquest, though the shape of the bailey was less usual, being a sort of odd rectangle, suggesting it was utilising an earlier defensive site.

Near the Severn was a towering motte, with an inner bailey to the east, protected on the south and east by a ditch and bank, and an outer bailey to the north, on the site of the present College Green, which caused consternation at the priory, since it was then the monks' graveyard. This was a royal castle, held by the hereditary sheriffs of the county, the Earls of Warwick. Its chapel was dedicated to St Peter, called 'the Less' to avoid confusion with St Peter the Great in **Sidbury**.

This was never one of the great Norman citadels, but it saw action on a number of occasions, though it generally seems to have had little effect in deterring attempts to take the city. It was briefly threatened in 1088, when it was held by Bishop Wulfstan against Roger of Montgomery, during the rebellion against William Rufus. During the wars of Stephen and Matilda, King Stephen burnt the city in 1150 and attacked the castle in 1151. In 1155 Hugh Mortimer fortified it against Henry II, and in 1216 William Marshall held the city and castle against King John, who took both without too much trouble. In the following year the land at College Green,

Historic Worcester Streets

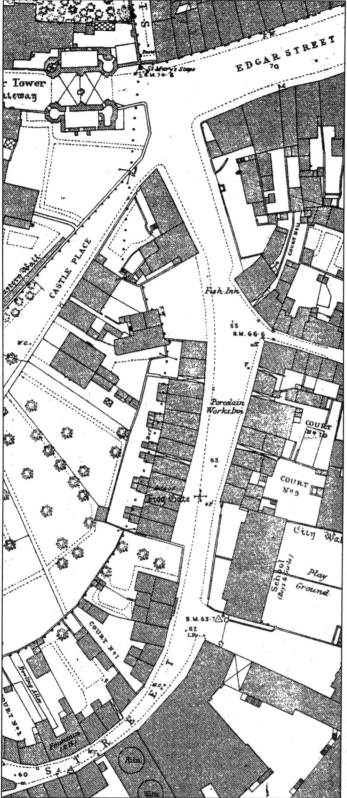

Part of Severn Street in 1884, showing the site of Frog Gate

taken from the monks when the castle was built, was returned to the monastery. This weakened the castle further, and it was easily taken by a rebel earl in 1263.

By 1397 the castle had ceased to be regarded as necessary for defensive purposes, though Constables were being appointed as late as 1540. The castle was then let to magistrates as the county prison, and executions were held at the castle gate in the sixteenth century. The site was refortified during the Civil War. In 1653 a new building was put up in the inner bailey to house prisoners, which was expanded in 1796 with the building of eighteen new cells. Its most famous prisoner was George Fox, founder of the Quakers, who was imprisoned here for 14 months in 1673-5, and is said to have written his famous Journal here. With the introduction of transportation, prisoners could easily be sent by river from here to Bristol, for transport to the colonies to serve their sentence.

Gaol fever (typhus) was rife in the gaol, and conditions were roundly condemned in 1788 by prison reformer John Howard. It was also very insecure, and in 1807 the assize judge arrived in the city to find that all the prisoners in the most important cases had escaped. The furious judge gave dire warnings of what would befall the authorities if this happened again, and in 1809 work began on a new county prison in **Castle Street,** which opened in 1813. The castle motte was taken down in 1830, and the whole site had been cleared by 1853. The King's School senior playground now occupies the castle site, and in 2010 was renamed Castle Court. Some excavation has been carried out there but nothing conclusive has been found.

Robert Chamberlain set up his porcelain works here, which later became Royal Worcester Porcelain. The firm was founded in 1751 at *Warmestry Slip* by Dr John Wall and other wealthy local investors, with starting capital of £4,500, and the intention of copying popular Chinese wares. The factory made a number of technical innovations and produced wares finer than any other factory in England at that time. The company was sold in 1783, but Robert Chamberlain, who was supervising decoration, left and set up his own factory which received an order for a service for Nelson in 1802. The two firms merged in 1840 at this site, where the factory remained until it closed in 2009, though the on-site museum is still open.

Diglis House was built on the riverside in the reign of George III, on the site of a previous house belonging to William Berkeley, which was demolished in 1643 after the Roundheads succeeded in occupying it during

Above, the Porcelain Works in 1882.

Below, Severn Street in 1905 by E.A. Phipson - MAG

an attack on the city. In the nineteenth century it was home to the family of Benjamin Williams Leader, who became a leading Victorian landscape painter, and Constable is known to have been a visitor. Later Richard Binns, the managing Director of Royal Worcester Porcelain, lived here, and after his death in 1900 it was a hostelry for some years, until it became the Diglis House Hotel in 1916. Much loved BBC cricket commentator John Arlott stayed here whenever he commentated on games at **New Road**.

SEVERN TERRACE

Historian David Whitehead said this terrace was laid out between 1817 and 1826, though development seems to have been very slow after the building boom of the early nineteenth century faded. It was shown in a street directory in 1840 when Moor Place, presumably a large house, was recorded here. In 1895 a building application was submitted for construction of 28 homes, but houses on the east side of the terrace are earlier than this date, and presumably pre-date the introduction of building records in 1865. In 1884 there were 19 homes listed, plus the Rose & Crown pub on the corner of **Easy Row**, which Gwilliam said was first listed in 1873 but closed around 1912. This was always a rather superior spot. In 1884 seven of the residents – more than a third - were living on income that was probably unearned, either 'gentlemen' or single or widowed ladies who had inherited money. The others included a foreman at a shoe factory, a foreman at a tin-plate works, a commercial agent, a coal dealer, a builder and two single ladies running ladies' schools at Nos. 3 and 9.

The Shambles around 1900 with the Butchers Arms pub on the left - RS

SHAMBLES

An ancient market street in which there is sadly little left of any age. The name is Old English, meaning a stall or market where meat was sold, but the street only acquired this name in the seventeenth century. Its medieval name was Baxter or baker Street, where bakers plied their trade. It may still have had that name in 1575 when Queen Elizabeth visited the city, but it changed as butchers became established here. Previously they seem to have plied their trade around **The Cross**.

By the end of the sixteenth century there was increasing competition between city butchers and 'foreigners', butchers from country areas. This perhaps led some city butchers to trade on Sundays, when 'foreign' butchers would not have been around,, and in 1599 the city authorities prohibited this, on pain of a fine of 6s 8d (33p). In 1601 a shambles or street market for 'foreign' butchers from villages outside the city was created at the **Pump Street** end of this street, probably where the Market Hall is now, and they were forbidden to trade elsewhere, on pain of a five shilling (25p) fine. The Worcester butchers fought back, becoming incorporated by

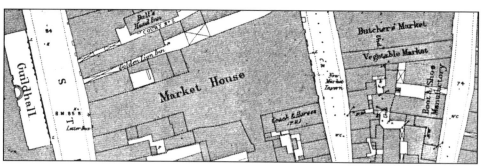

The Market Halls in 1884 - only one still exists

James I in 1604, and city butchers moved into the street throughout the seventeenth century.

In 1671 the city authorities ordered that the street market be pulled down, because it was 'a common nuisance', and the 'foreign' butchers' market moved to a yard behind the Globe Inn in the **High Street**. By 1741 the new street name was shown on a city map, and by 1790 a directory showed there were 17 butchers in the street and one baker. At that time there was also a glazier here, a glover, an ironmonger, a 'taylor', and a servants' register office. The only pub listed in the street at that time was the Coach & Horses at No. 20, which Gwilliam said closed around 1950. In 1840 there were still 17 butchers and a baker, but also a wide variety of other businesses, including a wood turner, an eating house, shoemakers, a hair dresser, provision dealers, a tripe dresser, a chain manufacturer, a trunk maker and a cheeses factor. By 1884 the street had something much more like the range of retail businesses we are used to here, including ice cream maker Henry Hull and china and glass dealer Richard Pratley whose shop was here until a few years ago, though some of them such as tripe dressers (two of them) and a rope and twine maker, would not be found here now, and there were still 14 butchers, mostly grouped around the north end of the street.

Facilities were created behind the shops for slaughtering, and as late as 1899 there was a building application for a new slaughterhouse and stables at no. 35. Street trading continued until it was forbidden after the opening of a market hall between the Shambles and **High Street** in 1804, since redeveloped into an arcade. There were still a small number of butchers trading in the street within living memory, but there are none here now. Another new market hall, backing onto **New Street**, and believed to have been built on the site of the former 'foreign' butchers' market, was opened as a vegetable market in 1849 and is still in existence. Immediately to the south of it was the New Market Tavern, which must have opened around the same time as the market, and closed in 1906.

There were a number of hostelries here, which did a roaring trade on Saturday evenings while bargain hunters waited for butchers to sell off surplus stock, which took place about 10pm, in those days of much longer shop opening hours.

Pub listings from the 1880s have been found from various

Above, an 1898 advertisement for the Cam engineering works at No. 32. Below, The Shambles in the late 1940s, with Hall's building on the right - RS

sources for eight pubs, some of which were short-lived, according to Gwilliam. From north to south there were, the Liverpool Vaults at No. 41, which was first listed in 1873 and closed around 1960; the Butchers Arms at No. 16, which opened between 1790 and 1820 and closed around 1950; the Market Hall Vaults, by Market Passage, which was first listed in 1873 but closed around 1900; the Market Fountain, almost opposite, named for a Hardy & Padmore fountain presented to the Market Hall and now in Cripplegate Park, on which Gwilliam has no information; the eighteenth century Coach and Horses; the New Market Tavern; and the Bakers Arms, location not known, which Gwilliam said opened about 1850 and closed, or perhaps changed its name, between 1870 and 1873.

By or before 1870 John Cam's engineering business, the Excelsior Works, was at No. 32, three doors north of the Market Hall. Around that date he was joined by his son, John James, who set up a notable engineering business around 1900 in **Charles Street**.

Many older people will remember the old-established hardware business J & F Hall, based in a fine sixteenth century half-timbered building on the corner of **Church Street**. The business had a long history, having been set up around 1792 by whitesmith John Pearkes Lavender, after whom **Lavender Road** was named. The business may even have gone back further than that, since Lavender may have taken over the ironmonger's business of William Hall, which was listed here in 1790. John Hall was one of Lavender's apprentices, and in 1822 he took over the business with F. Hall, trading as 'ironmongers, iron merchants and iron founders', with manufacture of water pumps a speciality, though by the mid twentieth century the store was supplying the DIY market. There was an outcry when the building was demolished in 1962. Hall's then moved to **Wyld's Lane**, but could not be traced during preparation of this book.

The street became a pedestrian precinct in February 1973.

SHARMAN ROAD

Probably named for Joseph Sharman Wood, mayor of the city in 1885, presumably the son of builder Joseph Wood, after whom **Wood Terrace** was likely to have been named. He was also a JP for the city, and lived at **Camp Hill Road** in the late nineteenth century, and **Selborne Road West** in 1908. His middle name will have derived through marriage from the Sharman family, one of the most notable members of which was Richard Sharman, a well-off brewer who bought and rebuilt a house at 50 **Broad Street** about 1640, probably as an inn, which may have been the Vintorne, recorded in 1696.

This road may originally have been intended as a service access to the rear of properties in **Barbourne Terrace**. Much of the available land here was used for a small nursery/market garden. The first record found of the road was in 1888, when a building application was submitted for four houses here, though there is no evidence of them having been built here, and they could actually have been intended for one of the streets backing onto this one. Two years later there was an application for an extension to the road, which must have been Sharman Road West, which was renamed Selbourne Road West on 26 October 1903. The first directory entry found for the street was in 1896. There were then just two listings, one for tailor William Hooper, who must have been living in a cottage here, and Joseph Peachey, who must have been the market gardener. In 1901 there was a building application for two houses, but again there is no sign of them having been built. In 1908 the only listing was for the gardener, who by then was Joseph Workman, and any development here is much later.

Walter Sharpe in 1931 - TW

SHARPE ROAD

This road will have been named for Walter Sharpe, who was Sheriff of Worcester in 1924, and a partner in Osborne & Sharpe builders' merchants at 11 **St Swithin's Street** and in **Trinity Street**. It was first found in a street directory in 1937, when there were 10 homes listed here. At that time Walter was living at Ailesworth, 94 **Bath Road**, and had apparently just retired from business and the council, though he was still an alderman, and was serving on the Education Committee.

SHAW STREET

In the eighteenth century, and perhaps earlier, it was *Gardiners Lane*, named for a Mr Gardiner, whose home may have been on the site of Berkeley's almshouses, which front onto **The Foregate**. He had died by 31 Oct 1704 when the freehold of the land on which the widow Gardiners's house stood was conveyed to the estate of Sir Robert Berkeley, for the sum of £260. This street was then only a narrow footpath between surrounding gardens. It was still listed as Gardiners Lane in 1840, but shortly afterwards city businessman William Shaw gave to the city the lease of land on the north side for widening the lane, and it was re-named for him.

He was born in 1766, and in 1787 completed his apprenticeship as a glover, and subsequently set up as a leather seller at 7 **Mealcheapen Street**, where he traded for many years. He was elected a member of the

Corporation in 1814, and remained so until 1836. He was Sheriff of Worcester in 1821, and mayor in the following year. In 1819 he had purchased Britannia House in **The Tything**, and he lived there until his death in 1843, at the age of 77.

From the early eighteenth century almost the whole south side of the street was given over to Berkeley's Almshouses, which front on to The Foregate. A building on the south-west corner, which became the Five Ways, now The Angel, was first found on a map of 1838, but the pub, which is actually in **Angel Place**, wasn't found listed until 1873.

The city post office moved here from **Mealcheapen Street** around the middle of the nineteenth century, to a single-storey building specially erected for it by wealthy builder John Hughes, who built the entire north side of the street. In the 1870s it was the only place in the city where letters could be posted and one of only two places where stamps could be bought. Letter deliveries were only free then in the central area of Worcester. The post office later moved to **Broad Street**.

At the east end of the street in 1884 was the site of the extensive premises of drapers Scott & Oram, which fronted onto Foregate Street. Above this were offices, in a pattern which still exists today. Next was estate agent and surveyor Gearge Yeates, vets Perrins & Robertson, auctioneer and valuer Nathaniel Taylor, physician and surgeon George Crowe, and William Bird, agent for the Phoenix Fire office.

SHERRIFF STREET

Named for businessman Alexander Clunes Sherriff, who had interests in ironmaking and railways. Born in 1816, he gained experience in railway management, and in 1856 became general manager of the struggling Oxford, Worcester and Wolverhampton railway, based at Shrub Hill, and thoroughly reorganised it. He was

a director of the City and County Banking Company, later Lloyds Bank, and several railway companies, as well as a Russian iron works. He was elected sheriff of Worcester in 1861, and mayor in 1862 and 1863, and in 1864, on leaving office, he presented the corporation with a valuable gold chain still worn by mayors, though they are no longer supposed to take it outside the Guildhall for insurance reasons. Later that year he was elected MP for Worcester, retaining his seat until his death in 1875. He lived for many years at Perdiswell Hall, **Droitwich Road**, but later moved to Craycombe, Fladbury. He had a reputation as a genial, hospitable man who did much to support local organisations and further the cause of Worcester business.

Alexander Clunes Sherriff - TW

The site of this road was waste land in the 1880s, but it had presumably been created by 1898, when it was listed in a street directory. The GWR goods shed was built to the west of the road, now used for a variety of small businesses, and cattle pens extended north in an area that has now been redeveloped. At the north end of the road on the east side was a brick works, which was disused by 1928. South of that, in buildings also reused for commerce in modern times, was the Progress Iron Works.

SHERWOOD LANE

This lane off **Malvern Road** took its name from Sherwood House beside the Teme, which was once the home

of leading nineteenth century children's author Mary Martha Sherwood, who opened a girls' boarding school at the house in 1816. The street was first found in a street directory in 1937, when 11 homes were listed. By this date Sherwood House had been split into five apartments.

SHRUBBERY AVENUE

The name comes from the Shrubbery estate which previously occupied the site. Shrubbery House itself was almost opposite Baskerville House, though standing some way back from the main road. The estate surrounding it was substantial, bounded on the north by St George's Lane South and St George's Church, on the south by Cumberland Street and White Ladies Close, on the west by Barbourne Road and on the east by Flag Meadow Walk.

Perhaps its best-known occupant was Regency buck Charles Bedford, a leading Worcester solicitor with a reputation for high living. His reputation,

Mary Martha Sherwood

and his practice, suffered badly after what was judged to be a very ill-matched fight with city doctor Matthew Pierpoint, who gave his name to **Pierpoint Street**. It was said that Bedford was never forgiven by local society, and he is supposed to have drunk himself to death. The last occupants were the Smith Hanson family, who were textile merchants.

The estate was still complete at the time of the first detailed Ordnance Survey map of the area in 1884, fringed by pleasant wooded areas and open grasslands, which would not have disgraced many a public park, but six years later the first application was lodged for development of the site, by city solicitor and property developer John Stallard Jnr. Construction was mostly small-scale, with 21 building applications by various developers and investors for 87 homes over the next 14 years. Around 35 of them had been completed by 1896, when the street was first found in a directory. Residents in 1896 included a number of clerks and commercial travellers, a professor of music, managers and an inspector of factories. More than 60 homes had been built by 1908. Development levelled off after that, bur continued steadily, with 67 homes listed in 1922. Residents then were largely white collar workers. Since then the number has been reduced slightly by modern development.

Baskerville Hall, midway along on the south side, took its name from Baskerville House in **Barbourne Road**, where 20 boarders from what became the Alice Ottley School in **The Tything** lived for five years from 1889. When the girls had to move out in 1894, a 'new Baskerville' was built here for 27 boarders.

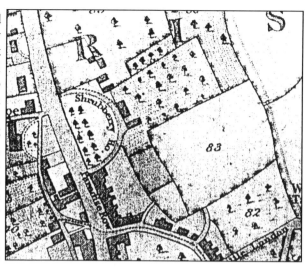

Above, Part of the Shrubbery Estate in 1884, shortly before it was redeveloped. Below, Shrubbery House

SHRUBBERY ROAD

Part of the Shrubbery estate (see **Shrubbery Avenue**), the first record of development here was a building application of 1890 for new roads and sewers, here and in **Shrubbery Avenue**. Four years later there was a building application for 18 houses here, submitted by city builder William Shakespeare, but there were only four more applications for 16 homes over the next five years, about half of which were from Mr Shakespeare again. The road was not listed in a street directory until 1908, and by then more than 50 homes had actually been built, so presumably some applications have since been lost. Unlike **Shrubbery Avenue**, career expectations were rather more modest in these attractive but smaller homes, with residents a mix of clerks and skilled workers such as a mechanic, a bookbinder, a linotype operator and a jeweller. At Heathercliff was inquiry agent Gilbert Baker.

SHRUB HILL ROAD

This road is inevitably associated with the Georgian-style station building, which was completed in 1865, though there was a temporary terminus here from 1850, but the route must have existed long before that date, perhaps originally as a trackway linking **Rainbow Hill** and **Wyld's Lane/London Road**, which could have been quite ancient, since the hill on which the station stands was fortified in ancient times and as late as the eighteenth century was known as Harp Fort, presumably from the shape of the earthworks. The road was

Crowds heading to the Worcestershire Exhibition on Shrub Hill Road in 1882

first listed as Shrubhill Row off **Tallow Hill** in 1840, and as Shrub hill in 1873, the 'Road' not being listed until 1903.

The station was originally owned by the Oxford, Worcester & Wolverhampton railway and the Midland railway. The OW&W was said to have unreliable locomotives and poor carriages, and was not highly regarded, being nicknamed the 'Old Worse and Worse'. In 1860 it amalgamated with other lines to form the West Midland Railway, which was taken over by the Great Western Railway in 1863. The company then had a carriage works at Worcester, one of only three in the UK, and the city must have seemed well placed to become a major railway engineering centre, but it wasn't to be. In November 1864 the carriage works had a disastrous fire, and the work was transferred elsewhere, causing Swindon to become the great GWR engineering centre which Worcester might have been.

The Vulcan Iron Works, founded in **Cromwell Street** in 1857, spread out along the west side of the street as far as **Lowesmoor**, expanding as railway engineering company Mackenzie and Holland, though the premises fronting the street were not built until after the First World War.

In 1865 the imposing building along the east side of the street, described by Bill Gwilliam as 'one of the finest Victorian industrial buildings in the Midlands', was completed for the Worcester Engineering Works. This was an enterprise begun by a number of leading local businessmen, including vinegar maker Thomas Rowley Hill, after whom **Rowley Hill Street** was named, and Alexander Clunes Sheriff, former chief executive of the OW&W, after whom **Sheriff Street** was named. The aim was to repair and build locomotives, and they are believed to have built around 70 over the next five years, but the orders dried up, and in 1871 the firm ceased trading.

The West Central Wagon Company then took over the building, but also went bust. In 1882 the 54,000 square feet building was pressed into service for a unique event called the Worcestershire Exhibition. It had many industrial exhibits, exclusively from Worcestershire firms, but it was much more than a commercial show, it was a celebration of Worcestershire, with Old Masters on show from many local collections, and modern work by Worcester artists such as Leader and Brock, and others who had attended the School of Design in **Pierpoint Street**.

The main entrance hall contained an organ and a stage capable of accommodating an orchestra. The exhibition ran from July to October and had 200,000 visitors, making it a great financial success, and providing funding for various educational schemes in the county. Subsequently Kay's had part of the building from 1893 to 1908, and in 1903 Heenan & Froude moved in (see **Cromwell Street**). In 1966 Kay's purchased Elgar House, near the station, which it had until the late 1990s.

A new Holy Trinity Church to serve the east of the city was built here between 1863 and 1865, beside the road just before the entrances to the industrial estate and the station, where there is now a grassed area. James Forsyth of the **Tything** was just one of the gifted artists engaged to work on the church, and it received the fine roof from the Guesten Hall at the cathedral, though it had to be altered to fit here, and half the original timbers were found to be too rotten to be used, which increased the building cost by an estimated £100. The initial plans included a tower and spire, but perhaps the additional roof cost put paid to them. However the potential congregation was moving even further out into the suburbs, and in 1965 the church closed and was subsequently demolished. Thankfully the roof was saved and went to the Avoncroft Museum of Buildings near Bromsgrove, but much of the fine carving and sculpture was apparently broken up.

SIDBURY

This street first developed as a small suburb to the Roman settlement at Worcester. It was abandoned after the Romans left, and archaeological excavations 1959-89 found no further settlement until the tenth century, but the roadway must have been in use throughout the Anglo-Saxon period. It was for many centuries the

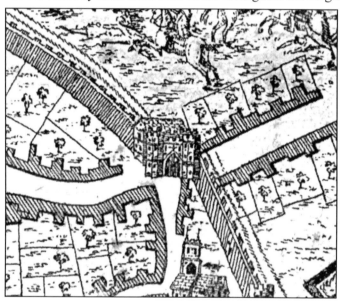

approach road to the city's main southern gate, yet it had developed partly on church land, which was not subject to city ordinances. At the city end it terminated at the southern perimeter of the cathedral graveyard, which spread out to the north of the cathedral as far as *Lich Street*. It is difficult to determine where exactly this street met **London Road** prior to the nineteenth century, but it seems certain that the junction was further south than it is now, and in the eighteenth century it may have extended as far as Green Hill. It also once extended some way up what is now **Friar Street**, probably to *Lich Street*. The first change in its boundaries came when **College Street** was created through the cathedral graveyard about two centuries ago, but the site of the junction with London Road was probably not fixed as it is now until later in the nineteenth century.

Above, the medieval Sidbury gate, a reconstruction from a later map. Below, Sidbury and the surrounding area in 1822. The turnpike toll gate at the bottom of London Road is bottom right.

To the Anglo-Saxons this was Southan Byrig or Suthbiri, mentioned in a charter of 969. This meant southern or south burg or burh, probably a southern extension of the main Anglo-Saxon defences which centred on the fort to the north of the city, possibly near what is now **Angel Street**.

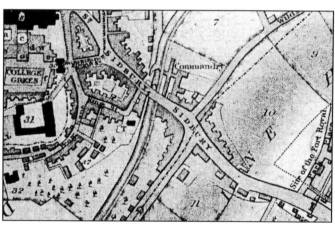

What form this southern burg or defended settlement took is not clear, but this may be a reference to the former tump on the riverside, near where **Severn Street** is now. This dated originally from the Roman period, when there was said to be a ford across the Severn here at the intersection of two minor Roman roads. It was sufficiently large for a small community to live there, as did the monks who first came to establish the church here in the seventh century. On the orders of Alfred the Great the tump was increased to 80 feet (about 24 metres) above river level, with sandstone defensive walls. It was later utilised by the Normans for the keep of their castle. When this motte was taken down in 1853, the Anglo-Saxon works were found to have covered the remains of a Roman period settlement, including a well and coins. By 1610 the name had been corrupted to Sudbury, and took its modern form by 1741, when the city was mapped by Doharty.

Historic Worcester Streets

Sidbury Gate, which was situated roughly on the present canal bridge, was one of the three main entrances to the city in Anglo-Saxon times. By the late sixteenth century it was considered surplus to the city's defence requirements, and was let out as accommodation sometime between 1577 and 1581. This judgement proved to be premature however, as it had to be refortified during the Civil War, and saw some of the heaviest fighting during the Battle of Worcester in 1651. It was largely demolished in 1768.

The Worcester and Birmingham canal in this area, which opened in 1815, took the line of the ditch outside the medieval wall. According to the Journal of June 1812, work on the canal within the city began at that time near the Commandery. The old canal bridge just about accommodated one lane of traffic each way, prevented by white railings from plunging into the canal. In the Sidbury Bridge reconstruction of 1961 a number of medieval buildings were removed and the road and canal bridge were widened. Plans for the dual carriageway leading from here to **Deansway** had received planning consent by March 1962, to be completed by September 1965.

A small group of older buildings have survived. Of these, No 107, a listed building in use for many years as a gentlemen's outfitters, probably dates from the seventeenth century, though it had a brick front added in the second half of the nineteenth century. Buildings historian Pat Hughes suggests that the door of No. 45 may have come from Greyfriars after the Dissolution.

Above, Sidbury in 1829.

Below, the old city wall in Sidbury in 1896, by E.J. Burrow

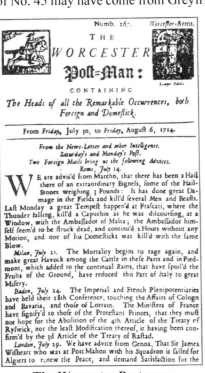

The Worcester Post-man

The parish church of St Peter the Great was off Sidbury, at the bottom of **St Peter's Street**, beside the city wall. A chalybeate spring claimed to have medicinal properties 'of exceptional virtue', was found here on the west side of the canal in 1816, but it was lost during construction of a new sewer system.

Worcester's first newspaper, which is also claimed as the world's oldest continuously published paper, was set up here in 1709 by London-trained printer Stephen Bryan, though the site is now in College Street.

The Worcester Post-man - forerunner of the Berrow's Journal – was said to have been published irregularly since 1690, but its regular appearance dated from Bryan's involvement. He took a house on the south side of the Cross Keys inn. The inn was where the Cinderella shoe factory in College Street was later built. It seems to have been demolished and rebuilt soon after Bryan arrived, and was later said by Gwilliam to have been the Horse & Groom and the Hare & Hounds.

It's possible however that Gwilliam was wrong on this one, since a map of 1885 showed the Hare & Hounds midway between **Edgar Street** and **St Peter's Street**, and there was a Cross Keys inn on **London Road** until the 1960s or 70s, so it is possible, perhaps even probable, that the inn which was here moved to London Road,

Historic Worcester Streets

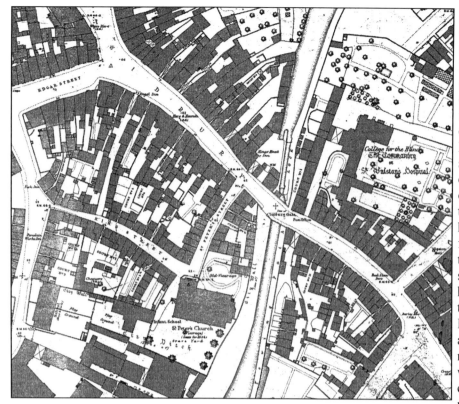

Sidbury and the surrounding area in 1884

or at least a part of it now which was then still Sidbury, when the building here was demolished during the creation of **College Street** in the late eighteenth century.

Bryan chose this location since Sidbury was on church land not subject to city ordinances. At that time it would have cost him £20 to become a freeman and trade within the city, which was a substantial sum then, and he must already have paid to become a freeman of London at the end of his apprenticeship. The newspaper remained here, with Bryan as editor, compositor, printer, and patent medicine salesman on the side, until he sold out to Harvey Berrow three months before his death in 1748. Berrow then moved the paper to *Goose Lane* in the city. Bryan's house was demolished during the creation of College Street about 50 years later.

A directory of 1790 showed this street as it was just before the creation of **College Street**, and it was certainly a busy, thriving thoroughfare. There were evidently some homes here, but it was primarily a street of commerce, and gloving was the main trade, with 13 glovers listed. There was also a legal community, with two attorneys, plus Proctor and Notary Public James Holyoake, and Jonathan Lea, Master Extraordinary in Chancery. There was also an apparitor (a servant, probably of a cathedral official), two bakers, three barbers, a blacksmith, a boarding school, bookseller Ann Gamidge, a breeches maker, a butcher, a carpenter, a chair maker, a coal merchant, a currier, a fruiterer, a haberdasher, a hallier or haulier, a heel maker, an ironmonger, a leather dyer, three maltsters, an Oxford carrier, a saddler, two shoemakers, four shopkeepers, two 'taylors' and a wheelwright. Looking after the health of this community were apothecary John Nash and midwife Mrs Dunn.

There were nine pubs listed in and around Sidbury in 1790. One of Sidbury's oldest inns, the Talbot, has been in **College Street** since that was created. It did formerly have a competitor, the Angel Inn, a few doors south of **Edgar Street**, which was first recorded in 1473 as the Angel de la Trompe. It was later the Trumpet, then the Angel, and by the twentieth century the Angel Hotel, but it closed around 1960.

Another old inn is the King's Head, which may be from the late sixteenth century, and was first recorded in 1609 as the Bell. Like many pubs, after the Restoration in 1660 its name was changed in memory of Charles I, who was beheaded in 1649, and it was recorded under the new name in 1678. Two doors along from the Bell was a house which the Journal described around 1714 as having formerly been an inn, though its name was not given. The Mitre inn was also referred to in this area around the same time as the Bell, though nothing more is known of it, and the Griffin Inn 'near Sidbury Gate' was mentioned in the Journal in November 1762. The other pubs listed in 1790 were the Red Lion, on the corner of Wyld's lane, which was still open in the 1980s, but is now a restaurant; the Chequers, which was in **King Street**; the White Hart, just north of **Edgar Street**, mentioned in the Journal of 1764, which has been rebuilt and has changed its name in recent years; and the Wheatsheaf, which was probably the pub on **London Road**. An 1840 directory also lists the Crown, probably a beer retailer, though Gwilliam has no information on it. There is also the Barley Mow, with its distinctive red brick arcading, which dates from 1898, but has closed within the last few years, and has recently become the subject of a planning application for six flats.

Next door to this street, at No. 1 **London Road**, the former Loch Ryan Hotel was built about 1760 but was a private house until the twentieth century. From 1902 it was home to Bishop Gore, but from 1903 the electric trams began running past his door, and complaining that he could not stand the noise they made, he removed to **Lansdowne Crescent**.

By 1884 the street had a post office, in part of the Commandery, presided over by Miss Amy Whiteman. At the same date the Sidbury Button Works was at Nos. 25-6, presided over by Thomas Finch, who patented and manufactured leather buttons. Cycle dealer W.J. Bladder was located at No. 69 for many years, opposite the King's Head. The shop provided all the leading brands of cycles, and as cars appeared on the roads it styled itself The Worcester Garage and went into the car repair business as well. The shop was demolished when Sidbury was widened in the 1960s.

Large gloving firm Price and Son in Sidbury was owned by Thomas Price, the father of best-selling novelist Ellen Price, who became famous as Mrs Henry Wood. She was born in 1814 and spent her early years at 55 Sidbury, named Danesbury House, which became the name of her first novel, though the house, now on the corner of **City Walls Road,** was rebuilt in 1889, two years after her death. She did not return to live in Worcester after her marriage in 1836, but many of her novels have thinly disguised Worcester settings.

Best-selling Victorian author Ellen Wood, and the rebuilt Danesbury House - TW Below, Sidbury about 1905 - RS

Sidbury's best known and finest building is the Commandery, originally a monastic hospital, believed to have been set up by Bishop (Saint) Wulfstan about 1085, probably intended in part to serve the needs of travellers who arrived after the city gates were closed, since the house was just outside the city walls. Just to the rear of the site there had been an Anglo-Saxon chapel dedicated to St Gudwal, a holy hermit in sixth century Brittany, whose cult had a following in Worcester.

Tradition has it that the building probably acquired its name due to Walter, master of the hospital until 1290, who evidently served on Edward I's crusade to the Holy Land, and thus would have had the courtesy title of Commander. In the 1530s it fell victim to Henry VIII's dissolution of religious houses. In 1539 Richard Morsyne, a Gentleman of the Royal Privy Chamber, was appointed as master to wind up the affairs of the hospital. In June 1540 he was able to buy the Commandery for about £14. Five years later he sold it to wealthy clothier Thomas Wylde for £498. The Wyldes, after whom **Wyld's Lane** was named, were one of the most prominent families in the city at that time, and held the Commandery until 1764, but their financial circumstances deteriorated from the end of the seventeenth century, and in 1695 they moved to a small estate they had inherited at

Glazeley, Shropshire. From then on the Commandery was let out to small businesses and as family living accommodation. Between 1866 and 1887 a College for the Blind operated here, the forerunner of the college at Whittington. In 1888 it was let to the prominent Worcester printing firm of Littlebury, and the family bought the building

in 1905. During their stewardship parts of the building were opened to the public. When David Littlebury retired in 1973 the building was purchased by the city, and after restoration it was opened as a museum in 1977, and is said to be the country's only Civil War centre. (For its Civil War history see **Hamilton Road**).

Smock Alley
Now **Angel Row**.

SILVER STREET

This name might suggest an area where silversmiths and other craftsmen using precious metals and stones would have worked in past centuries, but there is no evidence for this.

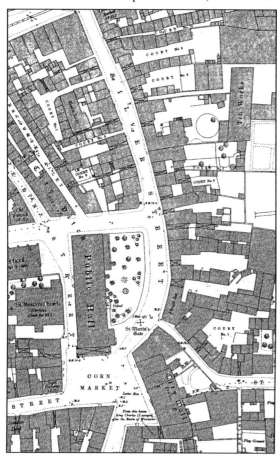
Silver Street in 1884

In the nineteenth century it ran from **Lowesmoor** to the **Corn Market**, and may have developed from the populous lane shown on a map of 1610, connecting Lowesmoor to **St Martin's Gate**. If so then it must have been in existence since the medieval period, and was probably a narrow alleyway originally. The whole area was said to have been cleared during the Civil War. By 1800 all of the street was wider but for the two ends, and they were widened in that year. Once a busy street, it was much affected by the **City Walls Road**, created in 1975, and is now just a car park entrance.

This was primarily a street of commerce, with records of businesses going back centuries. In 1644 bellfounder John Martin set up in business here, and over half a century cast around 175 bells, including over 100 for the bell towers of Worcestershire churches. He retired in 1693, and died four years later. He enjoyed ornamenting his bells and adding inscriptions, and on one at Himbleton he inscribed:
'Bee it known to all that doth wee see
John Martin of Worcester has made wee.'

The Baptists, whose records begin in 1658, had a meeting house here in the early eighteenth century, having originally met in the house of John Edwards nearby. Their chapel here was rebuilt in 1796, but in 1864 they moved to **Sansome Walk**. Their building here became a hop warehouse, and their graveyard was later built on.

The street is best-known as the site of the first Worcester Infirmary building. It originally opened in a house which is said to have been one of the first buildings to be erected in the city after the Civil War, and is the only building here to have survived modern clearance. The infirmary opened in what was then a three-storey house in the street in 1746, and was one of the first voluntary hospitals to open outside London. Bishop Maddox of Worcester was a strong supporter of the project, and encouraged subscriptions to make it a reality, but the building was just not big enough, and work began on a new site in **Castle Street** in 1768. Patients transferred to the new hospital in 1771.

Some time prior to 1788 Thomas Watkins set up a carpet manufactory here, which was visited by the royal family in that year, and afterwards Watkins styled himself 'carpet manufacturer to their Majesties'. Other businesses in the street at that time included Stephen Wilkins' vinegar manufactory, set up in 1785, two glovers, a farrier, a land surveyor and an attorney.

There were three pubs; the Crown & Anchor, which continued until about 1950; the Falstaff, probably an alehouse of which nothing further seems to be known; and the ancient White Horse, later The Plough, a large 18th century building at the end of the street opposite the **Cornmarket**, and once said to be one of 12 pubs in the area. Around 1713-14 the Journal recorded that it was 'new-built', with 'four rooms upon a floor, a very good cellar, brew-house, stables and outhouses', and subsequently reported that landlord William Frewen had moved there from the Swan in the Hopmarket. It acquired a 'black and white' exterior in the 1920s or 30s, but was demolished in the 1960s, and a Jaguar dealership was built on the site in the 1990s, which is now a furniture showroom. An 1840 directory also has the Angel, on which Gwilliam has no information.

Another inn in the area, the Pheasant, must have had substantial gardens at the rear running through to **Pheasant Street**, to which it gave its name. The licensee in the 1770s or 80s was a Mr Morris, but when he died, his wife Eleanor moved to **New Street** to set up a new pub. According to the history of the Pheasant there, she was able to use the same name because the Pheasant here had been delicenced after her husband's death, but a Pheasant existed here in 1805, where the Journal reported that more than 100 cocks were being matched at the cockpit, so maybe it

Silver Street in 1896 by E.J. Burrow, and two businesses based here, an 1896 Thomasson ad, and a later ad for Bailey & Turner

was not so much delicenced as temporarily without a licensee.

Occupants in 1840 included a stocking maker, two straw hat makers, a plumber, a leather dresser, a shoemaker, a painter, a carpenter and a furniture broker.

After the infirmary moved, the building was used for many years as Dr Simpson's Academy, a highly regarded private boys' school. In the 1850s it became the Working Men's Institute, with the intention of helping workers improve their lot in life. It had strong support from the local intelligentsia and thrived in the 1860s and 70s, though interest fell off after that, but it had provided the first adult education in the city, and helped pave the way for larger projects in the future. During the first half of the twentieth century, from at least 1904 to 1955-6, the building was occupied by ironmongers Whiteman & Co., and later by a wine warehouse.

In the late 1950s the street was as busy as ever. Occupants then included Bailey's builders' merchants, Stews City Dancing Academy, a tobacconist, commission agents, two grocers and a fruit shop, Express Sewing

An Edwardian view of The Plough in Silver Street - WN

Machines, the electrical wholesalers Newey & Eyre, Globe Taxis, a Territorial Army office, a Worcester Co-op warehouse and monumental masons H.K. Brown. Within 15 years hardly any of these businesses remained here, and the street was devastated by the creation of the **City Walls Road**.

SKINNER ROAD

An offshoot of **Skinner Street**, linking **School Road** and **Pitmaston Road**, for which there are no building records. It was shown unnamed on a map of 1885, when there were four cottages on the east side of the road, on former orchard land. When they were listed in a street directory of 1896 the residents included a gardener, a warehouseman, a labourer and a carpenter. By 1910 another four homes had been listed on the other side of the road. Much of the remaining development here seems to date from the 1930s.

SKINNER STREET

This street may have taken its name from local solicitor George Skinner, who lived in St John's, and submitted a couple of small building application in 1869 and 1876, though they were not for properties here. He may have been involved in creating the road, or in building the first houses, but unfortunately there are no early building records for this street, probably because it was created before the introduction of building control in late 1865. The street is a continuation of earlier development in the **Boughton Street** area.

An 1884 directory lists 26 modest homes here. One in every five residents was a gardener, another five were labourers, plus shoemakers, porters, glovers, seamstresses, a laundress, a charwoman, a brewer and a wheelwright. A map of around that time suggests there was room for more development on the south side of the street, and in 1894 there was an application for six houses here and in **Pitmaston Road**, three of which were subsequently built here as Llandore Cottages. Much of the present development, especially on the north side, is modern.

SLINGPOOL WALK

This name must refer to Swan Pool (see **Swan Pool Walk**), and the method of catching the fish it would have been stocked with, since 'sling' was an old term for a casting net. This must have long been in use as a footpath leading from and to the cathedral ferry, but it was not found listed as a street name until 1872, and there was no residential development here. The name was not found in street directories until the 1890s.

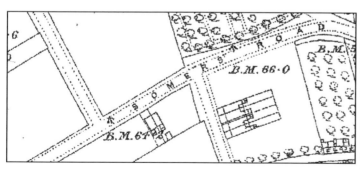

Somers Road in 1884

SOMERS ROAD

This must have been named for the family of a brilliant lawyer who spent his childhood nearby at Whiteladies in **The Tything**, and rose to be Lord Chancellor of England. John Somers was born in 1651, of a family which owned land at Severn Stoke, and bought Whiteladies in his grandfather's day. His father was a captain with the Parliamentary forces, who became a lawyer after the Civil War. John followed him into the law, being called to the bar in 1676, and quickly making a name for himself in high profile cases. By 1689 he was MP for Worcester.

He was appointed Solicitor General and knighted, and in 1697 became Lord Chancellor of England. He presided over the committee which drew up the Declaration of Rights, regarded as the basis of our modern democratic system, and he was also credited with being the chief architect of the treaty with Scotland which created the United Kingdom. He was created Baron Somers of Evesham, and tradition has it that he commissioned Britannia House in **The Tything** from Guildhall architect Thomas White, but he died of paralysis in 1716 before he could move in. The fact that this road carried the family name could mean that his descendants were involved in developing or financing it, or may previously have held the land on which it was built.

The road was first recorded in 1881, when there was a building application for five houses, by builder Thomas Insoll, who submitted 13 building applications in the 1870s and 80s, mostly for the Barbourne area.

A steady flow of further applications followed, most for only one or two homes. In total, up to 1892 there were 30 building applications for 53 homes and a shop. The first listing in a street directory was in 1884, when there were just three

John Somers

listings, for a carpenter, a clerk and a locksmith, and a map of that time showed the street marked out, but with little development in the area. However development went ahead quickly, and by 1896 there were 45 homes and a bakery on the corner of **Barbourne Road**, kept by John Morris. Further along, at Nelson Cottage, Thomas Holloway kept a shop. Many of the homes were described as villas, meaning they were regarded as superior to the more modest cottages. Residents then included clerks, salesmen, building tradesmen, coach builders, a foreman, a schoolmistress, a drayman, a cab driver and a watchmaker. Much of the street is from this sort of period.

SOMERSET PLACE

Possibly there was some involvement in the creation of this street or surrounding development by the Somerset family, who must have given the street their name. They had land at Castlemorton, and in the late nineteenth century they were involved with Worcester timber merchants the Wilesmith family, in ownership of a brickyard at Leigh. They also had links to other county land owning families, such as the Russells and the Pakingtons.

This street must have been created in the rush to get building starts before building control began in late 1865, since there are no early building records, and the later records that exist are misleading

The first record found of this street was a building application of 1868 for a single house. It was submitted by a James Tucker, and was the only building application he ever submitted, so he was probably building a new home for his family. There were no further applications until the 1890s, but a map of 1884 showed the street almost complete. A directory listing of that date showed 39 homes here.

There were a few clerks listed amongst the residents, but most were craft workers in the garment industry, coachmaking, gloving, printing and manufacturing. Ariel Constable at No. 20 was a schoolmaster at the prison in **Castle Street**.

There was some open land at the north end of the street, and in 1891 an application was submitted to build five more houses, and another six in 1894. However, by 1896 the directory noted, 'Back entrances only to houses in **Flag Meadow Walk** and **Lansdowne Street**'. How had the street gone from having 40 or 50 homes, to having none in a few years? The answer is that this had been created as a service road for houses in adjoining streets, and clearly many of the houses in those streets had been listed here through some confusion in the directory listings, which had been put right by 1896.

Historic Worcester Streets

Samuel Southall in 1901 - TW

SOUTHALL AVENUE
This street will no doubt have been named for Samuel Southall, a solicitor with an office in the **High Street**, who was a long-serving clerk to the city council, and had a secondary school at **Merriman's Hill** named after him in 1937, though Bishop Perowne school has since moved there. In that same year this street was first shown in a directory with 14 homes listed.

SOUTH PARADE
The Worcester docks were a working area, and the idea of a parade or riverside promenade must have been introduced by John Gwynn as part of his late eighteenth century scheme for the riverside, bridge and **Bridge Street**. In the event the parade was little more than an extension of **South Quay**. In 1840 corn factor J. Howell was based here, glover John Allen and solicitor Thomas Parker. In 1884 vet George Carless was at Parade House, Richard Price, proprietor of two river steamers was based here, leather dyer Richard Thompson and gloveress Miss Sarah Weston. River traffic had largely lost its importance by the twentieth century, and the area behind the quay was cleared in the 1920s and 30s, leaving this today as the sort of pleasant riverside walk that Gwynn had probably envisaged.

South Quay about 1900 - BG

SOUTH QUAY
This quay served Worcester's important inland port since early times. River transport was vital throughout most of our history, and the Severn must have been one of the busiest rivers in the country in past centuries. The Romans and the Anglo-Saxons would certainly have shipped goods to the city from Bristol, in a trade that continued for centuries. Standing at the head of the tidal race, Worcester was an important inland port for the landlocked West Midlands, with no rival until the coming of the railways in the nineteenth century. Eighteenth century views of the city often romantically depict sea-going galleons at anchor in the river, but the mainstay of the river traffic was the humble Severn trow. This was a single or twin-masted wooden vessel about 18 metres in length, able to carry up to 100 tons of cargo. Specially designed for the tidal Severn, which was extremely shallow at low tide, it had a flat bottom and demountable masts which allowed it to pass under

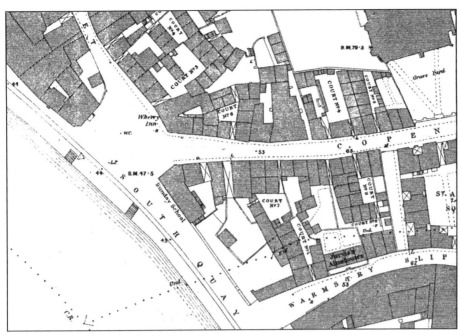

Above, South Quay in 1884

Below, South Quay about 1900 - WN

bridges. Trows were introduced to the river in the Middle Ages or before, and by the nineteenth century hundreds of them were plying between Worcester and Bristol, using bow hauliers to drag them over the shallows at low tide.

At any one time there would be a great many vessels moored along the river around the quay, waiting to load or unload. The quayside was packed with warehouses and processing plants, with properties leased by businessmen from Bristol, Gloucester, Bewdley, Bridgnorth and Birmingham. Worcester historian David Whitehead said that maltsters, clothiers, a distillery, breweries, soap works, rope manufactories and shot foundries were amongst the businesses found here, and it was no accident that the porcelain works was initially sited nearby at *Warmestry Slip*. In 1763 the Journal mentioned an inn called the Three Kings near here. In 1790 a directory listed barge builder George Ascoe here, plus coal merchant John Daniel, two merchants, and a pub called the Marquis of Granby, about which nothing more seems to be known. Businesses listed around the quay a century later, in 1884, include two corn merchants, a sack contractor, Dangerfield's iron warehouse, mineral water manufacturers Sheppard & Co, and Stallard's distillery at *Warmestry Slip*.

City records show that money was regularly spent to maintain the quays, such was their economic importance to the city. There was supposed to be a smugglers' passage leading from the quay, by which goods could reach the **High Street** overnight without ever going above ground, and something was found when old houses were demolished in *Birdport*, though it is hard to believe that this trade was very extensive.

The coming of the railways spelled the downfall of Worcester as Birmingham's port, because they made it possible for manufacturers to ship their goods direct to Gloucester's deep water docks, which could take larger and more economic vessels. To try to counter this threat, **The Butts** spur railway line was planned, to run from **Foregate Street** to **Diglis**, in the hope of persuading larger vessels to come up river. The engineers of the Worcester and Hereford Railway began work in 1860, building a sloping viaduct down to the Severn at the railway bridge, and then along the riverside and down the quay as far as **Warmestry Slip** – where it ground to a halt. The cathedral chapter decided that they would not allow the line to pass in front of the cathedral, and that was the end of the project. Even if it had gone ahead, it was unlikely to have achieved what promoters hoped, because the river was just too shallow for larger vessels. The Journal reported in July 1862, that a steamship with a full load of slates for Worcester had had to dock at Gloucester, because low tides meant it could not get up the river. Worcester never recovered its position as a leading inland port, and by the twentieth century road and rail competition had largely put an end to commercial traffic on the Severn.

SOUTH STREET

In the *Blockhouse* area. This street originally ran off *Talbot Street*, and may have been created to provide rear access to homes in **Charles Street**, which was created soon after 1820. In 1884 there were almost 40 homes in and around the street, including a terrace of six homes called Union Place, which was listed separately in street directories for much of the century. Residents then included a good many labourers, plus glovers, clothing workers, a few painters and tin plate workers, an upholsterer, a confectioner, a cab driver, a boatman and a tobacco pipe manufacturer. Poverty will have blighted the lives of many in the area, and in 1884 St Paul's Church had a Mission Room here. By 1896 there were four almshouses in the street, housing a bricklayer, a bootmaker, an insurance agent and a charwoman, endowed by Hebb's Charity, founded by Christopher Hebb, who is remembered in the name of **Hebb Street**. On the corner of **Carden Street** was the Odd Fellows Arms, named after a working men's friendly society, and possibly the meeting place of the local lodge. It closed around 1960, after which the street was cleared and redeveloped.

SOUTHFIELD STREET

This was part of the mid nineteenth century Arboretum pleasure grounds, with their entrance drive on **Arboretum Road**, which were sold for redevelopment in 1866. The first recorded building application here was in 1870 for the HQ of the First Worcester Volunteer Artillery Corps, and the street was first listed in a directory in 1873, by which time the artillery depot near **Middle Street** had been built. The unit was renamed the First Worcester Royal Garrison Artillery by 1904.

In 1870 there was also an application for 12 houses, which were named Artillery Terrace, and were listed in street directories for many years from 1880 as a separate address. Otherwise development plans progressed slowly, though building seemed to follow the plans fairly quickly. Between 1874 and 1895 there were 13 mostly small-scale building applications for 38 homes. By 1884 there were around 35 homes here, and a map of that date showed there was still a good deal of building land available, especially on the north side, east of **East Street**. By 1896 there were around 65 homes, suggesting that some building applications may since have been lost, or were never submitted in the first place.

Residents then had a wide range of mostly manual occupations, including two telegraph linemen, railwaymen including a couple of engine drivers, a police constable, boot makers, shop assistants, some clerks, a lamplighter, a wagon builder, a draftsman, an iron worker, a greyhound 'slipper', a gas fitter, a coal dealer, a compositor, a laundress, a blacksmith, a wheelwright and at least three ladies taking in lodgers. At Glyndon Villas then was Thomas Carmichael of coach builders Carmichael & Sons, who now build fire engines. There were two shops in the street then. One beside the artillery depot was kept by Mrs Ann Harwood, and the other, on Artillery Terrace, by Mrs F. Barnett. Next to the Terrace, builder Thomas Dixon had a yard.

In 1890 the Arboretum Mineral Water Works opened at No. 18. Mr H. Jones claimed to have founded the firm in the early 1870s, making it one of the oldest in the county, and it was said to be using the water from a deep spring on the site to produce its product. He also claimed to have a thriving trade in bottling Guinness and Bass ales. By 1896 the plant was being operated by Mrs Sarah Jones, perhaps his widow. It was said to have closed about 1910.

A street directory for 1896 also showed that Leonard and Harrington had moved into the street, with their attractive hop warehouse on the corner of **Middle Street**, now converted to housing. J.W. Buckland also had a hop warehouse beyond **East Street**, where the Post Office also had their telegraph stores, again now converted to apartments.

Spa Gardens

Blockhouse. This was a row of terraced cottages off open land at the bottom of *Spa Row*, and must have been created at much the same time. In 1884 occupants included a labourer, a shoemaker, a range fitter, glovers, a drayman, a lamplighter and a painter. The street was demolished in the 1960s.

Spa Row

Blockhouse. The name came from Spa Field, the field where it and surrounding streets were built. The name must have been related to a spring in the area of **Spring Gardens**. This street, off **Carden Street**, was created and apparently fully built by 1824 when it was shown on a map of the *Blockhouse*. It consisted of a dozen terraced cottages. In 1884, when there was still open land at the bottom of the street, residents included several labourers, a baker, a seamstress, several shoemakers, two draymen and a file cutter. The street was demolished in the 1960s. It was located roughly where Carden Close is now.

SPETCHLEY ROAD

Spetchley was probably an ancient tribal hundred meeting place; its name in Anglo-Saxon was Spaec leahtun meaning the clearing where speeches were made. It was referred to in a charter of 816, and was part of a manor belonging to the church at Worcester. This road had clearly been in use for many centuries as an ancient trackway, but urban development did not begin until the twentieth century, and the road was not found listed in a street directory until 1937, when there were 37 homes on the north side and just one on the south side.

The former Spring Gardens area off Britannia Road in 1884

Spring Gardens

This was a street running off **Britannia Road**, across the top of **Love's Grove**, and curving round to meet **Moor Street**, presumably named for a spring in the area, though no details of one have been found. It was first found listed in a street directory in 1840. It was a populous street, with more than 40 homes listed in 1884, plus a shop kept by carpenter John Price near Britannia Road, and the Carpenters' Arms pub at the junction with Love's Grove. Some housing was fairly intensive, including a court at the west end, but a number of houses had very good gardens. Residents at that time included builder John Bourne, after whom **Bourne Street** may have been named, who had a yard and office here, plus building workers, railwaymen, labourers, laundresses, an ostler, a furniture van proprietor and Thomas Oliver, verger, probably of nearby St Mary's church in **Sansome Walk**. The pub closed around 1950, and the street disappeared in the redevelopment of the area in the 1960s.

SPRING GARDENS

This was named for a spring which was in this area, though the exact location has been lost. This street will have been created between 1820 and 1840 when it was first listed in a street directory, though there were a few building applications throughout the rest of the century, for two houses in 1876, three in 1880, one each in 1882 and 1886, and four houses in 1898.

It was known as Cold Bath Spring in the eighteenth century, because it was the site of a spring popular with city folk in the summer, reached by a pleasant walk across Blockhouse Fields. There was a small building called Cold Bath, where people could bathe and drink the pure water, at a time when such a thing was not readily available in the city. The spring was lost when the canal was dug.

In 1884 there were around 25 homes listed here, and the site had been earmarked for the new St Paul's Church, fronting onto **St Paul's Street**. Residents were mostly skilled manual workers, though

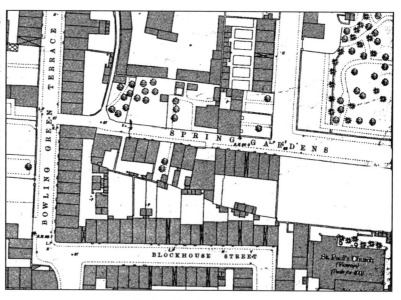

Spring Gardens in 1884

George Derham near **Bowling Green Terrace** was the manager of a coffee tavern, and William Sale, on the other side of the Terrace, was clerk to the cattle market at **The Butts**. There was also Edwin Moody, manager of the co-operative stores, and a forewoman, Mrs Elizabeth Mucklow, who worked in colour mixing for the ceramic industry. She was the only forewoman encountered in these listings, though there may have been others not listed in street directories because they were not heads of households. Other residents included a couple of shoemakers, two iron fitters, a couple of labourers, a cellarman, a warehouseman, a maltster, a couple of carpenters, a painter, a fitter, a range fitter and a tailor.

Also listed was the cooperage department of local firm George Joseland & Sons, the stores and stables of T.K. Goodwin & Sons, and horse keeper Frederick Brotheridge. Over the next decade most of these firms disappeared from the street, but in 1896 one of them had been replaced by the Piston Foundry of iron founder Charles Evans. By then there was a shop by **Bowling Green Terrace** kept by John Latham. The street was cleared in the 1960s and redeveloped.

SPRING HILL

This was named for a spring which was in this area, though the exact location has been lost. The street was first found listed in a street directory in 1840, and was surely built prior to 1865, since there are no building records. It was built between the canal and the House of Industry, alongside the **Tallow Hill** cemetery. Oddly, the street is not named on the Ordnance Survey map of 1885, but a street directory of the previous year listed around 40 homes here.

They bear all the hallmarks of having been built by a number of different investors or developers, who named what they built according to their personal taste. There were 11 homes in Carlton Place, two in Spring Hill Villas, 15 in what was effectively a court called Spring Hill Cottages, and a number of individual villas. Residents in 1884 at Spring Hill Cottages included nine labourers, plus some railwaymen, while at Carlton Place there were six railwaymen and just two labourers, plus a watchman, a seamstress and a fireman. At Spring Hill Villas were foreman William Shekell and the Misses Foster. A good deal of clearance has gone on in the area, and this street now has less than half the number of homes it had originally.

SPRING LANE

Named for a spring in the area, though the exact location has been lost. Spring Place, a terrace of 10 small cottages here, at right angle to the canal, was listed in a directory of 1840, but a canalside wharf and warehouses to the south and west of the lane, and the cottages themselves, may have been built soon after the canal opened in 1815. The lane must have been created to give access to the wharf and the cottages, but the street name was not found until the health board streets list of 1872, and was not listed in a street directory until 1884. At that time there were 26 homes listed, including those in Spring Place, and nine in New Buildings. A map of the same date showed that the newer homes all faced the canal and were larger, but none of the homes here seemed to have much in the way of gardens. There is no record of who built these homes, which clearly suggests they were erected before the start of building control in late 1865.

Residents in 1884 had a real mix of occupations. Labourer was the most common job, being given as their occupation by five residents, but there were also gloving workers, laundresses, several iron workers, a china painter, a fireman, a currier, a county court bailiff, a hairdresser, a coal dealer, a watchman, a leather dresser and an engine driver.

There was an application in 1895 to build four more houses immediately to the north of Spring Place, which were listed by 1900 as Prospect Terrace. Around a dozen Victorian cottages still remain here, including Prospect Terrace, but the wharf and associated buildings, and the remaining homes have given way to modern redevelopment.

STAINBURN AVENUE

This name is obviously linked to the adjacent Laugherne Brook, but this is a stream name from the north of England or Scotland, and what it is doing here is something of a mystery. This street was first found in a street directory in 1937, when there was just one home listed.

STALLARD ROAD

The Stallard family, originally from Brockhampton, Herefordshire, first became prominent in the city through a wine business set up by William Stallard in **Copenhagen Street** in 1808, and continued by his son Josiah and their descendants, but this road is more likely to have derived its name from father and son city lawyers, both called John, who were very active in Victorian property development, especially the son. They had an office in **Pierpoint Street** and John Stallard was mayor in 1866.

John Stallard Jnr was mayor three times in the twentieth century, the last time in the mid-1930s, about the time that this road must have been created. He died in 1961 at the grand old age of 103. This road was first found in a street directory in 1937, when two homes were listed.

STANLEY ROAD

This road is said to be named for the son of a local businessman. When James Roberts took over the Three Springs Tannery off **Wyld's Lane**, across the canal from the **Blockhouse**, in 1877, he also acquired the land between **Midland Road** and roughly where **Vincent Road** is now, and later developed it for housing. At that time, though there was some development along the canalside, and along Wyld's Lane as far as **Richmond Hill**, the land he had purchased here was completely open, save for Field House, a mansion opposite Richmond Hill. An application for creation of three roads – this road, **Cecil Road** and Vincent Road - was submitted in 1890. Tradition has it that these roads were named for his two sons, Cecil and Stanley Vincent.

Development went ahead quickly here, with 11 building applications for a total of 48 homes and a shop submitted by 1895. In 1896, when the street was first found listed in a directory, there were 40 homes here, many of them villas which attracted white collar and managerial workers, as well as manual workers at Stanley Terrace. There was also a grocer's shop on the corner of Cecil Road, and six more houses were in the process of being built.

Residents then included a locomotive inspector, an insurance agent, an organ builder, a schoolmaster, and Joseph Hughes, labour master at the Union Workhouse at **Tallow Hill**. The three schools for boys, girls and infants were opened in 1915, and are claimed to be the first council schools to be opened in Worcester. The jazz trumpeter Kenny Ball, who had a string of hits in the 1960s, attended Stanley Road school for a time, when his father worked as a bookbinder at Ebenezer Bayliss printers in **London Road** in the 1930s.

STANLEY STREET

Cherry Orchard. First found on a map of 1884, when this small street giving access to the area off **Bath Road** was already complete, though then as now, the north side was occupied by the Berwick Arms, which closed in 2011. In 1896, when it was first found in a street directory, the four homes here were already listed, though they could be appreciably older than that date.

Two of the residents then were labourers, and the other two were a painter and a carpenter. The street name could relate to a family which was involved in the development of the street, though no information on this has come to light.

STANMORE ROAD

The only link found to this name is the existence in the 1930s of three villas in the city called Stanmore, but all of them were at the other end of the city. Possibly there was a fourth one here, unlisted, which gave its name to this road, or possibly it was named by someone with a link to Middlesex. It was first found in a street directory in 1937, when three homes were listed here.

Star Lane in 1884

STAR LANE

This was named for the nearby Star Inn in **Bransford Road**, which had a back entrance on this street, and was listed as early as 1822, but is now a Chinese restaurant. This road was first found listed in the health board streets list of 1872, and in a street directory of 1880. No building records have been found, but in 1884 a directory listing showed nine homes here. Five of the eight residents then were labourers, plus a gardener and two charwomen. A map of that time showed that the homes here had been built on former orchard land, and there were still orchards to the north and east, with further room for development at the north end of the lane. Redevelopment since has left hardly any homes here.

STEPHENSON ROAD

This was a footway access to the north of Pitchcroft which may have been in existence as a footpath for some time, but was not found listed as a road until 1915. That will have been after the building of seven Edwardian villas beyond the end of **Stephenson Terrace**, which were listed here in 1922, when residents included a police constable at Lyndhurst, a solicitor's clerk, a prison warder, a storekeeper and a railway clerk.

STEPHENSON TERRACE

The street presumably owes its name to a Worcestershire family called Stephenson who may have owned the land or had a hand in financing the development, but they are something of a mystery. County records show them to have been landowners in Upton and Longdon in the eighteenth and nineteenth centuries, but no land holdings in Worcester are listed. A record of 1903 shows a William Henry Stephenson selling the goodwill in a brass foundry, but the family is not listed amongst county brass founders in directories of the period. Most likely the foundry was one of their investments, as perhaps was this street.

The building records show that all of the applications submitted for these mostly substantial villas were for just one or two homes, put forward by a variety of investors or would-be owner-occupiers. A typical example was the application of 1877 which was the first record found of the terrace. It was for two houses, and was the only building application submitted by a Mr Bolam. This must have been Thomas Bolam, manager of **Sansome Street** hop merchants Buckland & Co, who by 1884 was living at one of the two Amerston Villas, presumably having built two and sold one to recover his investment. Based on the building records, these seem to have been the first houses in the terrace.

By 1887 11 homes had been applied for. Eight villas were listed by 1884, and another two by 1896. Residents at that date included local businessman Alfred Bayliss at Field View, Vulcan Iron Works cashier Henry Little at Westcroft, local businessman William Caldicott at Dudley House, Harry Davey, manager and editor of the Journal and Worcester Daily Times at Thornville, and letter Carrier John Grimley at Leesdale. There was still a vacant plot available towards the north of the terrace, which seems not to have been built on until the 1920s.

Sudbury & *Sudbury Street*
Old names for **Sidbury**.

SUMMER STREET

This street was first found on a map of 1884, but there are no early records of its development. At that time there were two substantial cottages with excellent gardens at the north end of the street, which no doubt gave the street its name, since they were called Summer Place. There was also a terrace of five cottages to the south of Summer Place, which must be the May Cottages listed in a street directory of 1896. By then there were also another eight cottages, but no record has been found of when or by whom any of them were built. Residents at that time included gardeners, labourers, blacksmiths, a range fitter, a boiler maker and a stoker. There were two applications in 1904 to build a total of 18 more houses, submitted by developer W.H. Aston (see **Himbleton Road**), but nothing more was built until modern times.

SUNNYSIDE ROAD

The name is one which was often used in the nineteenth century as a happy name for new houses or terraces. In this case the developer apparently gave the road the name of his own house.

The application to create this road was submitted in 1894, by E.P. Evans. This was presumably Edward Probert Evans, secretary to Worcester Royal Porcelain at **Severn Street**, who

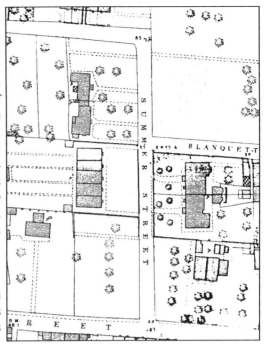

Above, Summer Street in 1885

Below, Sunnyside Road in 1928

lived at a house called Sunnyside on **Rainbow Hill**, next door to Marl Bank where Sir Edward Elgar would later live. But this application came ten years after development began here.

The road was created initially from a lengthy driveway running from the main road to the west across open land to a large detached house called Barbourne Lawn, which was shown on a map of 1884.

The road seems to run slightly further north than the driveway. The orchard or nursery land

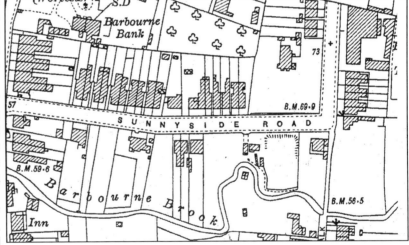

around the garden of the house was divided into building land, and a building application was submitted in that same year to build on plots 1 – 16.

In 1898 an extension was applied for, to link with **Raglan Street**, which created an awkward situation in which this road ends almost half way up that street.

In 1896 the 16 new home plots had been built on, and residents included a number of local businessmen, plus a glover, a carver, a commercial clerk and a foreman. At Barbourne Lawn then was Edward C. Corbett, who was presumably the leading city solicitor of that name who later served a long jail term for misusing his clients' funds, and then reinvented himself as 'Stroller', the local history correspondent of the Worcester Herald and subsequently the Worcester Journal.

A steady stream of small scale building applications continued, and there were 29 homes here by 1910, 37 by 1922. There seems to have been a police house on the south side of the road, possibly built in the 1930s, when the road seems to have been completed.

An application for a glove factory was submitted in 1900. Glove manufacturers A.L. Thomas were here in 1910, and I. & R. Morley by 1922. Later, probably during the Second World War, it became an engineering plant. The premises are now occupied by a training business.

Record-breaking pilot Sheila Scott, whose real name was Hopkins, spent part of her childhood here in the 1930s, living with relatives John and Kathleen Turner after her parents' marriage broke up.

Historic Worcester Streets

SURMAN STREET

This street stands on land which would once have been part of the cemetery of St Oswald's in **The Tything**, and would still have been owned by the charity at the time this street was created. It was originally a rear entry, shown on a map of 1884 as 'Back of Tything', but 12 years later it was listed in a street directory with its present name. Quite how or why this came about is far from clear.

Since this was the rear access to cottages fronting onto **The Tything**, on the corner site where Kay's built a new headquarters in 1907-8, it may well have been given the family name of the person holding those leases and letting out the properties. There was a Surman family which had been holding land in the county since the seventeenth century, but several branches of the family had developed. One local Surman was an old soldier named Thomas, who had the Lamb and Flag pub across the road in **The Tything** in the 1850s and 60s, with his wife Caroline, but they do not seem likely to have been a land or property holding family. A more likely candidate is perhaps Robert John Surman, a dentist at 48 **Foregate Street** in the late nineteenth century, who was probably a member of a well-off Fernhill Heath family.

This was never a populous street. When it was listed originally in 1896 under **St Oswald's Road** there were only three homes, one empty, the others occupied by china polisher R. Tisdale and machinist Henry Lodge. The first separate directory entry was in 1908; the only residents then were Gouldings (six) Almshouses and journeyman printer George Creese. These buildings were to the east of the street, close to **Sansome Walk**, and so were not affected by the Kay's building, but this street became just a route through Kay's car park, and the almshouses have more recently been demolished and the site redeveloped.

Swan Pool Lane

Now **Bromwich Road**. Known also as *Swan Post Lane* in the eighteenth century.

SWANPOOL WALK

This must have long existed as a lane leading to the orchards which have now been replaced with a supermarket, but formerly stretched as far as **Bromwich Road**, where this footpath also led. It will have taken its name from Bromwich Road, which in the nineteenth century was known as *Swan Pool Lane*. Land west of the river in ancient times was owned by the church at Worcester, and Swanpool was a lake, no doubt well stocked with fish and wildfowl to furnish the tables of monks and clerics. The lake was south of this lane, just west of Bromwich Road before it was straightened.

The famous Worcester Pearmain apple was found at the Swanpool market garden of William Hales in 1872. Richard Smith, who had a massive nursery at **Bransford Road**, gave £10 for the exclusive right to take grafts, and subsequently made a fortune selling the trees. Market gardeners William Daniel and Son were at Swanpool Gardens in 1884, and Benjamin Harber was market gardener at Swanpool. They were still here in 1896 when Swanpool Walk was first found listed in a street directory, but there were no residential listings. In recent years it has of course been greatly affected by the building of a supermarket.

Swan Post Lane

Eighteenth century name for **Bromwich Road**. The post referred to may have been the liberty post, marking the boundary of the city's liberties, which from the medieval period was likely to have been where **Bromwich Lane** joins Bromwich Road. By 1838, after the city boundary had changed, the name changed to *Swan Pool Lane*.

SWINTON LANE

This was originally a country path linking **Bransford Road** with **Malvern Road** near the Old Powick bridge. As late as 1838 it was shown on a map as *Cut-throat Lane*, a bit of rustic humour often applied to dark lanes. It runs along the east side of Boughton Park, former home of the Isaac family, and must have acquired its present name from John Swinton Isaac, who died in 1888. This first name was presumably his mother's maiden name. The lane was not found listed in a street directory until 1930, but presumably had this name before then. All the development here is modern.

SYDNEY STREET

This was originally *Millburn Street*, which was first listed in 1885 with six cottages and a villa. By 1915 it had the present name as part of a mini poets estate, which also includes Addison, Longfellow, Keats, Milton and Dryden – an interesting snapshot of early twentieth century poetic taste, perhaps inspired by the publication in 1900 of the popular *Oxford Book of English Verse*, in which they all appeared.

Sir Philip Sydney

Sydney, now more often spelled Sidney, was an Elizabethan courtier, soldier and poet, best known for his epic romantic poem *Arcadia*, which was reworked after his death by his sister Mary, the Countess of Pembroke, who was born at Bewdley, and had encouraged him to write it. He was killed while fighting in the Netherlands in 1586, aged just 31. *Arcadia* enjoyed wide popularity after it was published in 1590.

The street was first found listed under this name in a street directory in 1915, when there were already 26 homes here, including four empty at the end of the street, suggesting they had just been completed. Residents included glovers, labourers, a carpenter, a housekeeper, a general dealer, a brickmaker, a boilersmith, a tile maker, a horse keeper, a stone sawyer and a fruit dealer. Miss Alice Nicholls kept a corner shop at the end of the street. Around a dozen old cottages still remain here, but the original Millburn Street homes have been replaced with modern developments.

Talbot Entry

An alleyway beside the Talbot Inn, from **New Street** to **College Street**, which existed from the eighteenth century or before, but will have disappeared in the 1960s redevelopment.

Talbot Row

These were workmen's cottages on the north side of **Little London**, probably built in the early nineteenth century, many of which were used as shops by the end of the century. They were demolished before the Second World War.

The former Fownes glove factory in Talbot Street, now a hotel on City Walls Road - TW

Talbot Street

On the edge of the **Blockhouse**. The first record is a building application in 1896 for a glove manufactory for Fownes Brothers & Co. Gloving had traditionally been an outworkers' trade, but the trade was under pressure and big manufacturers survived by bringing workers into factories and streamlining production. In 1908 the only residents were Fownes and ginger beer manufacturer Joseph Parry. The Fownes factory has survived to the present day as a hotel, but the rest of the street is now under **City Walls Road**.

TALLOW HILL

This was created as a road in the late eighteenth century, but it was so altered in the late 1990s that it is difficult to relate the present street to what was once here, and all the nineteenth century housing formerly here has long gone. The street stands on land originally known as Tolly's Hill, a name listed in a directory as late as 1797, presumably on land held by the Tolly family. There was a Thomas Tolly who was one of the two bailiffs or administrators of the city in 1475, and the land may have been held by a descendant, also Thomas, who was a shoemaker and brewer in **Mealcheapen Street** in 1560, and by his son, Anthony, who was a noted joiner, living in **Friar Street**, who carved Bishop Freake's tomb in the cathedral. The name was somehow corrupted to its present form in the nineteenth century. How that happened is a mystery, but it could have had something to do with the agricultural use of the land, which inevitably would have been for sheep grazing, and mutton fat was used as a cheap form of candle tallow. This is speculation, but there was always a tendency for people to corrupt names they no longer understood into a form that made some sense to them.

In the eighteenth century this was regarded as a pleasant picnic spot by city folk, with a hillside of gorse and wild flowers, and a large pool at the base of the hill, which was drained into the canal in 1815. The road must long have been a footway leading up the hill, but it was created as a road initially to give access to a workhouse, grandly titled the House of Industry, which was built at the top of the hill in 1793-4, to ease the problems of poor relief in the city, which were reaching crisis point following the death of the cloth industry, with large numbers applying for relief. It was to take the poor of all the parishes in the city, and was erected by an act of parliament in 1792.

Above, the House of Industry on Tallow Hill in 1793

Below, the Worcester Workhouse about 1900 - WN

The land cost £2273 to purchase and the building work cost £7318. In November 1794, said the press without a hint of irony, 'the poor were first received into this comfortable asylum'. It was intended as a home and occupational centre to provide work for the unemployed, with children given apprenticeships in the making of flannels, coarse woollen cloth and especially gloves, and within a year there were 223 paupers housed there, 132 of them children. The project initially had some success, but attitudes to the poor hardened in the early nineteenth century. The Poor Law Amendment Act of 1834 compelled parishes to band together into unions to provide facilities for the poor, and the House of Industry subsequently became the Worcester Union Workhouse. The workhouses quickly became grim places, and there would have been many sad stories of the unfortunates committed there. In 1865 youngsters Emma and Henry Woolett were admitted to the Worcester workhouse after their father died and their mother deserted them. Other inmates would have been elderly, infirm, disabled, or those referred to brusquely by Victorians as 'idiots'.

The workhouse was rebuilt in 1894, and at Christmas 1911 the Journal reported there were 299 inmates. It closed in 1930, and became Hillborough Hospital, where there was a maternity unit, though it seems to have been intended chiefly as a Home for the Aged. In 1977 the Worcester Council of Churches set up St Paul's Hostel for the Homeless in St Paul's parish, and shortly afterwards it moved here, where it has been ever since.

There was a cemetery here at the west end of the street, on the site of the former pool drained by 1815, which was open for burials between 1823 and 1874, with residual interments continuing until 1895. It contributed to public health improvements by removing burials from the central area of the city. It was surrounded by a low wall, and excavations for the recent road works accidentally uncovered a number of vaults, presumably for family burials. Until recent alterations the road turned sharply after a narrow 'hump-backed' canal bridge to skirt around the edge of the cemetery area, which is now beneath the roadway, part of the retail park car parking area, and land to the south of the road. There were an estimated 4,700 burials in the cemetery, but no records have survived of where individual burials took place. In 1832 a Cholera epidemic broke out at **The Pinch**, a notorious court across the river, and spread across the city. The 79 victims were buried in the north-east corner of the cemetery, in a mass grave marked by a small wall which could still be seen in the 1920s. In October 1861 Christopher Hebb, after one of whose charities **Hebb Street** was named, was buried in this cemetery. The cemetery had been concreted over by the 1960s and there was a small, rather sad-looking children's play area at one end, roughly on the site of the cholera epidemic mass grave.

Around 40 homes with very modest gardens or yards were built on the north side of the street in the late 1820s

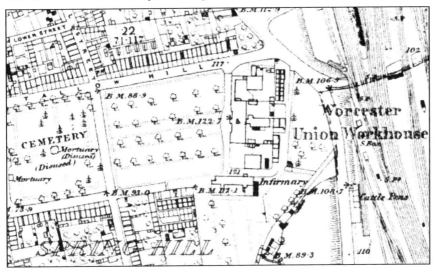

Tallow Hill in 1884

or early 1830s, and were shown on a map of 1838, but this was well before building records began, and no information has been found on who was responsible for this development. By 1884 there were 53 cottages listed in a street directory. They included five cottages in Cemetery Terrace near the canal bridge, which were then home to a labourer, a drayman, a dressmaker, a nurse and an engine driver. Other residents at that time included tinmen (tin plate workers), dressmakers, laundresses, china workers, a

fishing tackle maker, a glover, a fireman, a cutler, a carpenter, a porter, a seamstress, a timekeeper and several railwaymen. There was a day school at No. 17, and sauce manufacturers Phillips & Co. were at No. 27. There was a corner shop at the junction with **Lower Street Walk**, and another one later near **Hill Street**. On the canalside near Cemetery Terrace was the Crown Inn, which Gwilliam said was first listed in 1873 and closed around 1960. Further east, on the corner of **Hill Street**, was The Beehive pub, also said by Gwilliam to be first listed in 1873, though it may have been older than that, since there was an application to rebuild it in 1901. It remained open until the 1980s or 90s.

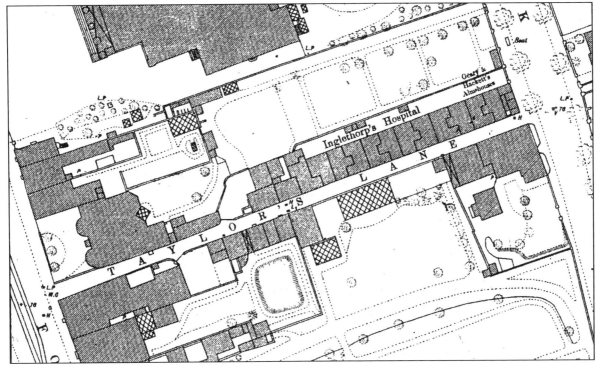

Taylor's Lane in 1884, prior to the building of the Victoria Institute

TAYLOR'S LANE

This lane was shown and named on a map of 1741, and may have been in existence from the seventeenth century or before. The name must derive from the Taylor family, who were leading citizens in the seventeenth and eighteenth centuries. James Taylor was mayor of the city in 1648. Henry Taylor was mayor in 1666, and Samuel Taylor was mayor three times in the 1730s, first in 1731, then again unexpectedly in 1732 when the incumbent died, and finally in 1737. Eighteenth century brothers Isaac and James Taylor, both gifted painters, were presumably members of this family and both achieved fame in London. Isaac's descendants settled in Essex, and one of them wrote the poem *Twinkle, Twinkle Little Star*.

Presumably this lane led to the Taylor family home in this area, probably at Ivy House in **Sansome Walk**, which was built around 1700 and is now the home of Armstrong's the tailors.

The Inglethorpe plaque in Taylor's Lane - TW

Around 1732 a row of dwellings were built on the north side of the lane, to replace almshouses built in **Sansome Street** about 1620. They were built by or for the Inglethorpe Charity, set up under the will of wealthy city businessman Richard Inglethorpe, on land which had already been used to build four dwellings for the Inglethorpe and Nash charities. In 1772 Charles Geary built two additional almshouses on a site at the east end of the lane, more recently the College of Art.

The almshouses were demolished in the 1890s, to make way for the Victoria Institute, fronting onto **Foregate Street**, which was opened in 1896, and takes up the whole of the north side of the lane. The residents then moved to newly-refurbished almshouses in **Friar Street** belonging to the Wyatt Charity. The original stone plaque set up on the almshouses in **Sansome Street** to mark Inglethorpe's benevolence went missing for more than 200 years, until it was found in use as a hearth stone at a house in Upton Snodsbury in the 1940s. It was restored and re-set in the wall of a warehouse in Sansome Street in 1951, but when that building was demolished in the 1970s it spent 30 years at the Commandery, before being set in the wall at the side of the Victoria Institute in this lane in 2002.

TEARNE STREET

County archives have some information on a family of this name, which may have been involved in the creation or financing of this street, which was first found in a street directory in 1896, under **Comer Gardens**. No building records for the street have been found, and there is no development here earlier than the 1970s or 80s.

TEMPERANCE STREET

This street took its name from the Temperance Hall, dating from the 1860s, which stood on the corner here. It was described by Gwilliam as a spacious two-storey building, with large lettering around the exterior in coloured brick reading, 'The Blessing of God Keep Us and Protect Us From All Intoxicating Drinks'. At a time when cheap gin was nicknamed 'mother's ruin' and ale was a necessity when clean water was not readily available, there were major problems with public drunkenness, and the temperance movement attempted to persuade the poor to 'take the pledge' to be teetotal.

The street must have been created around the same time as the hall, and was listed in a street directory of 1873. There was a building application to put up three houses in the previous year and another for 15 houses in 1887. By 1896 all these seem to have been built, and a few more, since 20 homes were listed in that year plus two shops. Residents were nearly all manual workers. They included building tradesmen, glovers, porters, a furniture dealer, a coal and oil dealer, a railway guard, a leather parer, a poultry dealer and a dressmaker. James Rushton kept a shop near the corner with **Providence Street**, and there was another by **Bowling Green Terrace** kept by Thomas Robinson. There was also a business near **Providence Street** called the Economic School Furniture Company, with a shop in **St Swithin's Street**.

By 1896 there was a temperance hall in **Sansome Place**, and the hall here was destroyed when the Providence Works in **Providence Street** were extended in 1900. The area was cleared in the 1960s and redeveloped.

TENNIS WALK

This name came from the 'Lawn Tennis Ground' behind Whiteladies house, roughly on the site where the grammar school has tennis courts now. The school moved to the site on **The Tything** in 1868, but it only occupied a part of the site it now has, and the Whiteladies house and tennis ground still existed separately in 1884. At that date this street was first found listed in a street directory, but the Ordnance Survey map of that time showed it as part of Little London. Clearly it must have been created as a separate street with the building of homes here, but word about the name change had not got to the map makers in time.

The 1884 directory listed 15 homes here, including nine North Cottages. There are no building records for any of these properties, or for any property in this street up to 1900, so no indication of when the first houses were built, though it was probably not long before 1884. As to the building applications, they must either have been lost since, or were never submitted in the first place. The 1884 residents included three glovers, two labourers, two shoemakers, a horse breaker's assistant, a railway wheel tapper, a sawyer, a coachman and a plumber. By 1896 the original 15 homes all seemed to be listed as North Cottages, and there were also six Gordon Villas, probably inspired by Gordon of Khartoum, built just to the north of **Lansdowne Road**. In 1900 there was finally a building application for three homes, but they seem not to have been built, since no more properties were listed up to 1922. By the early 1970s the villas had been demolished and replaced with a concrete children's playground, but the site was built on once more in the 1980s.

TERRACE WALK

In 1884 open land stretched from **Rainbow Hill Terrace** – from which this street takes its name - to the railway bridge, and this was a footway leading to a track beside the railway. It was not until 1897 that there was a building application for a new road here. It was first found listed in a street directory in the following year, with '6 houses in course of erection', for which no building application has been found. The same entry appeared for the next five years, but the houses didn't appear, and 'in course of erection' was clearly an exaggeration; 'planned but not applied for' would have been more appropriate.

There was an application to build four cottages in 1900, but clearly the plans were upgraded, and in 1905 four Malvern View Villas were listed, though one of them was still empty. The others were home to an engine driver, an insurance agent and a glover. They still exist at the top of the lane, and eight Crescent Villas run off the bottom of the lane, which were clearly built soon afterwards.

THE

See under next word.

THORNELOE ROAD

The road must have taken its name from Thorneloe House on **Barbourne Road**, best known to older residents as the Eye Hospital, the garden of which backed onto this street. The house in turn took its name from a prominent local legal family who are thought to have built it in the 1740s or 50s. They didn't stay there long, but may have continued to hold land in the area, since they crop up in a number of local names.

This was probably created originally as a lane giving rear access to homes on Barbourne Road. It was first found listed as a street in the health board list of 1872, and in a directory of the following year. In 1884 there were two directory listings, for Cedar House, on the west side at the southern end of the lane, then home to local businessmen William and Henry Caldicott; and Thorneloe Villa, home of auctioneer Richard Hobbs. There were three small applications to build a further four homes by 1896, but a directory of that date showed another five, which were already built and mostly occupied. One, Clare Lawn, was still empty, but the others were occupied by local businessmen. All the other development here is modern.

THORNELOE WALK

This pathway linking with **Thorneloe Road** must have been created at the same time, and was also first found listed in the health board streets list of 1872, but of course without any homes.

THORN AVENUE

Part of a 'tree' estate off **Brickfields Road**, this street was first found in a street directory in 1937, when 26 homes were listed.

Three springs

A pathway which led from **Tallow Hill** to the *Blockhouse* area before the Worcester and Birmingham Canal existed, and after the canal was cut between 1811 and 1815 it ran by the canal side to Foundry bridge, leading into **Foundry Street**. The Three Springs Tannery was established in the eighteenth century at the end of what is now **Vincent Road**, taking water for the tanning process from the springs, and by 1800 it was one of the three biggest employers in the city.

TILL STREET

A tithe map of 1843 shows that the land in this area was called Harp Meadow, and was farmed by Edward Till, hence the street name. Based on the records seen, it is only possible to say that the street was created and the land developed for housing within the next 40 years, but Lansdowne Lodge and Merriman's Lodge, the only two homes actually in this street, could well have been built in the 1850s or 60s, and thus the street could be said to be complete at that time. It was first found in a street directory in 1884, listed under **Lansdowne Road**, but the listing is misleading. At that time the lodges were home to a colliery agent and a bank clerk, but only Merriman's Lodge was actually listed, and the entry included the four villas occupied by a cashier, a commercial clerk and two married ladies, presumably widows, which are on Stanhope Terrace and do back onto this street, but are actually on Lansdowne Road. The first separate directory entry for this street was found in 1908, when the lodges were occupied by William Sansome and Mrs Ward, but again only Merriman's Lodge was actually listed. This is all the more inexplicable when you consider that Lansdowne Lodge is the only house here which can be accessed from this street, since the access to Merriman's Lodge is by the nearby Merriman's Walk.

TIMBERDINE AVENUE

This street name derives from the manor of Timberdon or Timberdine which consisted of lands granted at various times to the priory and convent of Worcester. The name meant woodland pasture in Old English. The manor extended down to the Severn, where there was a valuable fishery mentioned in Domesday Book, and ran some distance along the Bath Road. The manor, with the fishery and a wood called Pylgrove were granted to Sir John Bourne in 1545, with the manors of Battenhall and Barneshall. Around 1700 a timber-framed manor house was built on the corner of what is now St Peter's Drive, which after various rebuildings is now mostly late Victorian or later, and is a restaurant. By 1799 the manor was in the possession of the Lechmere family, who held it until 1912.

The Royal Show of 1863 was held on land to the south of here (see **Battenhall Road**). Timberdine farm, on which the avenue is partly built, was being farmed by Robert Atkins in 1908, and William Jones in 1932. By 1928, as car use grew, there was a Timberdine Filling Station here. The avenue was first found in a street directory in 1930, when there were 32 homes listed.

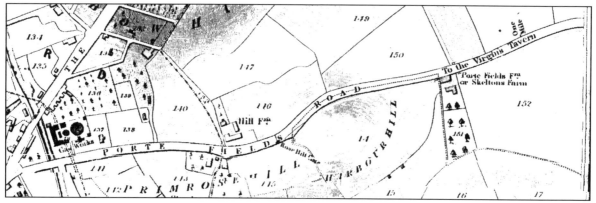

Tolladine Road in 1838

TOLLADINE ROAD

To the Anglo-Saxons Tolladine was Teolowaldingc Cote, the cottages belonging to the family of Teolowaldingc. It was referred to in a charter of 816, and was part of a manor belonging to the church at

Worcester. In the nineteenth century it was referred to as Porte Fields Road, leading to the Port Fields once held by the White Ladies convent in the **Tything** – 'port' usually referred to a Roman military road.

It was often known to locals in times past as the road to the Virgin Tavern, long a popular country inn. So commonly used was this name that it was referred to as Virgin's Tavern Road in the Worcester Railways Act 1870, though it was listed under its present name in a street directory of 1873. The tavern clearly has a long history, though the present building is twentieth century. The name probably refers to Elizabeth I, though a modern suggestion is that it had an ecclesiastical origin, since the inn was on the boundary of Claines and St Martin's parishes.

'Tollerdine', with Trotswell and Smyte, was part of the parish of Warndon, which around 1780 supported only ten farming families. The underlying clay marl formed an unyielding surface which did not easily submit to ploughing, even with a team, causing it to be nicknamed 'Horse killing land'. Consequently this was primarily pastureland. City freemen who owned cattle often had leases to graze them here.

There was a joint turnpike gate from the eighteenth century with Rainbow Hill and Lowesmoor at the bottom of the hill. Cuttings were made to reduce the gradient on the approach to Sheriff Street, hence the size of the roadside wall, and beyond Sheriff Street, where the gate was moved as development began to creep up the road.

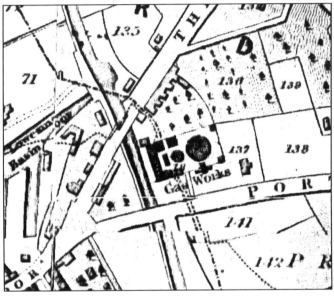

The Gas Works, between Tolladine Road and Rainbow Hill in 1838

In 1818 the city established The Worcester New Gas Light & Coke Co, funded by 750 shares of £20 each, which obtained an Act of Parliament to build a gas works in the city, only six years after the first gas works in the country opened in Westminster.

Building went ahead almost immediately, on the site where Bradfords the builders' merchants are now located, and the city was first lit by gas on 9 August 1819. A branch rail line to bring in fuel was constructed, which ran along the south side of the road, and then crossed it to turn into the works shortly before the canal bridge. Later a different route was introduced which eliminated the need to cross the road. The gas works finally closed in 1965, but the gasometers were visible for many years afterwards.

Worcester's first golf club was established here in 1898 on land at Gorse Hill then mostly owned by the Cannock Chase Company. It remained here for 28 years, until the need for more space and the complications of multiple leases caused it to move to Boughton Park, **Bransford Road** in 1927, after which the land here reverted to arable farming.

Plans for a 'garden suburb' in the early years of the twentieth century led to 22 homes, including eight bungalows, having been built on an eleven-acre site here by March 1914, but the First World War ended further development. In the 1920s a 'Garden City' was planned on the Portfields between here and **Newtown Road**, and development had begun by 1928, with a modest amount of building around **Elbury Road** and **Christ Church Road**, but Portefields Farm, a dairy farm, still existed just next door to this development, with Charles Vincent Depper as the farmer. There was still open land then stretching away on both sides of this road. It wasn't until the 1930s that there was a significant amount of development in this area.

Torcae Street
Now **Tybridge Street**.

TOWER ROAD
The name recalls the water tower which was built as part of the late eighteenth century waterworks, near where **Waterworks Road** is now, which became a well-known landmark in the area, but was demolished in 1957. No records have been found on the creation of this street. It was shown on a map of 1884, and a street directory of 1896 listed three homes here, called The Willows, Coniston and The Tower. Residents in 1922 included a J.P., an electrical engineer and two labourers. The road then had to wait until quite recently for further development.

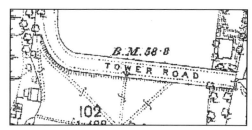

Above, Tower Road in 1884. Below, the water tower, since demolished - RS

Town Ditch

It ran around the outside of the city walls, originally as part of the defences, though in later centuries it became a handy dump for rubbish. Part of it became **Sansome Street**.

TOWNSEND STREET

This street may be named after a prominent late Victorian businessman, though there is some confusion about this, because of a change in the spelling. All the early building applications spell the name with an 'h', Townshend, the surname of Thomas, owner of the Albion Flour Mill at Diglis, who did a very small amount of property speculation in that area. The first record of this street was a building application of 1871 to create 'proposed building plots'. The identity of the person submitting this application has been lost, but it could have been Thomas Townshend, though he was not involved in any of the three house building applications found, which were submitted in 1885, 1891 and 1893 – all spelling the name 'Townshend'. However the name was always spelled without an 'h' in street directories. It seems fairly likely that the street was named after Thomas Townshend, who was also an alderman and magistrate, and it may be something as simple as a clerical error at the council or the directory publishers that led to the change of spelling which has become the accepted name.

A map of 1884 showed the road unnamed, with a terrace of four villas in the centre of the east side, which would be Fair View, dated 1881. The four West View villas are dated 1885, and are presumably the homes applied for in that year. The four villas in Sharman Terrace, may have been built under the application of 1891, and the name may suggest they were built by Joseph Wood builders (see **Sharman Road**). By 1896 a directory showed the street complete with the 15 homes which it still has. Residents then included glovers, clerks, an excise officer, a manager at a mineral water works, a grocer's assistant, a local businessman, a tailor, a plumber and an insurance agent.

TRINITY, THE

This street was first found as a lane on a map of 1610, though it probably existed for some centuries earlier. It originally ran from **Queen Street** to **The Cross**, but was cut in half by the creation of **Trinity Street** in the late nineteenth century, and the western end later became **Trinity Passage**. It was usually referred to just as Trinity, and in 1840, confusingly, as Trinity Street, though that street didn't exist for another half century.

The street seems to have taken its name from monks who may well have been involved in the establishment of a chapel and a guild here, both of which bore their name. The Order of the Holy Trinity was founded in France and approved by the Pope in 1198. The avowed aim of the order was to free captives in the Middle East, which may explain the later belief that St Nicholas Church was built originally by returning crusaders, who were perhaps giving thanks for their release. However, the Trinitarians also dedicated

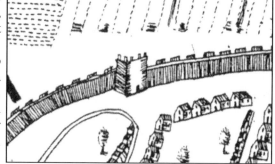

Trinity Gate 1651, from a later map

themselves to doing good deeds in the areas where they worked. They quickly set up some 50 houses throughout Europe, and definitely seem to have established themselves in Worcester at some time, though at what date is not known.

The Trinity Chapel had been established from at least 1240, and was later linked to St Nicholas Church, though the church probably hadn't been built at that time. It was situated on the north side at the west end of the present Trinity Passage, where a coffee shop now occupies the site of a former bank. It seems the chapel began as a chantry, with a priest who said prayers for dead patrons wealthy enough to have left money for

Trinity in 1838, and below, in 1884

this purpose, and there could have been a few such patrons here, since this was a well-off area. The chapel could have been established by the Trinatarians, since they were always keen to raise funds for their work abroad, but whether they were here at that time is not known.

By 1348 wealthy parishioners had founded the Trinity Guild. It was not a trade guild but a religious guild with charitable objects, one of which from its earliest days must have been the funding of the Worcester School, forerunner of the Worcester Royal Grammar School, which had existed from at least 1291, and may once have been taught by the priest of the chantry, though it later had a schoolmaster. The guild built a very substantial timber-framed hall where the school was once based, which was on the site of the building immediately on the south side at the east end of Trinity Passage. Again, it is not known if the Trinitarians were involved in the establishment of the guild, but it is highly likely that they were. The Trinitarians were removed from the city during the Dissolution, though the Order still exists in Europe, and the Guild and chantry were

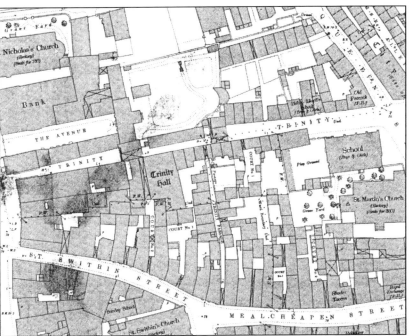

Below, old cottages in Trinity in 1902 by E. A. Phipson - MAG

abolished by Edward VI around 1546.

After the guild ceased, the hall was purchased by a group of six wealthy clothiers, and subsequently, through marriage, came into the hands of John Steynor, whose son Robert, one of the two city bailiffs in 1584 and 1586, gave it in 1612 to the clothiers guild, and it was used by them and other trade guilds for two centuries. The guild fell on hard times in the eighteenth century, and in 1790 their hall was described as 'a very old ruinous building'. In 1796 it was sold for £185 and partly demolished, most of the remainder being used as a furniture store, the school having moved to a room at St Swithin's Church.

The hall was in existence until the late nineteenth century, and was shown on the first large-scale Ordnance Survey map in 1884. It was finally demolished in the early 1890s, when Trinity Street was created, and by about 1894 the Trinity Works was built on the site, which originally housed printers Ebenezer Baylis, though it has since been turned into shops and offices. Externally the upper floors appear unchanged from when they were built.

According to the Victoria County History of

**Above, Queen Elizabeth House in 1891, being made ready to move - RS.
Below, in the Trinity in 1910 - BG**

Worcestershire, after the chantry was abolished the chapel was granted to Sir Edward Warriner and Richard Catelin. They were said to have founded almshouses on the site, but it seems more likely that they sold the chapel and used the money to build the almshouses. These almshouses were supposed to have been endowed originally by Elizabeth I for 29 poor women who each received 1s 3d (c. 7p) per month. The almshouses were later rebuilt, but no longer exist. They seem to have stood immediately to the north of the Trinity Hall, roughly on the line of the present 'Old Bridge House' over Trinity Passage.

Historian Pat Hughes believes the chapel may have been purchased by Robert Steynor, and used as a house, which after his death was converted by his widow into an inn called the Golden Cross, which was demolished in the early twentieth century, to make way for a bank, though it had probably been rebuilt in the intervening centuries.

Around 1713 the Golden Cross was kept by John Andrews, in succession to the late landlord Thomas Taylor, and must have had a reasonable amount of land attached, since an advertisement in the Journal said there was room enough for clients to turn their coach or wagon.

Historian John Noake lists this inn as one of those used in the 1734 election, but no further trace of it has been found, and in the nineteenth century the building was occupied by an outfitters, though the inn name was still used for the building. The National Provincial Bank of England, now a coffee shop, was built on the site by 1908. The original chapel foundations were said to have been found during construction of the bank.

Historic Worcester Streets

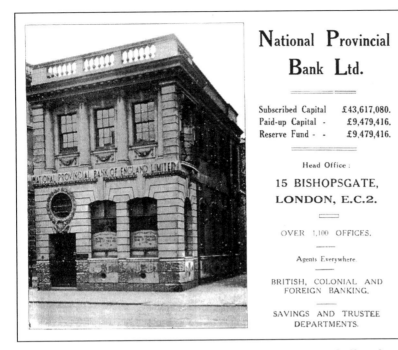

A 1920 advertisement for the bank - now a coffee shop - believed to be on the site of the former Trinity chapel

National Provincial Bank Ltd.

Subscribed Capital £43,617,080.
Paid-up Capital - £9,479,416.
Reserve Fund - - £9,479,416.

Head Office :

15 BISHOPSGATE,
LONDON, E.C.2.

OVER 1,100 OFFICES.

Agents Everywhere.

BRITISH, COLONIAL AND FOREIGN BANKING.

SAVINGS AND TRUSTEE DEPARTMENTS.

Historian Bill Gwilliam believed there might be one of the Queen Elizabeth almshouses left. He was convinced that Queen Elizabeth House, now on Trinity Street, might be the sole survivor of these almshouses, with the verandah giving access to the rooms of two residents. It has also been suggested that it was the house of the schoolmaster for the Trinity school.

Traditionally Elizabeth I is said to have addressed the citizens from the verandah during her visit in 1575, but this building seems to date from the first half of the eighteenth century, which makes it more likely that it was one of the almshouses.

By the 1890s it was in danger of demolition due to the creation of Trinity Street, but it was saved by being moved 10 metres across the road to its present position. Builders Bromage and Evans jacked up the 200 ton house and moved it on greased railway lines to its present position.

A school for poor boys and girls was founded in this street by Bishop Lloyd in the early eighteenth century, due to a murder. A Mrs Palmer of Upton Snodsbury was murdered by her own son, and since she had no other heirs her estate came into public hands and was given to the bishop, who used it to found the school, which continued until 1896. A plaque commemorating the site of the school is in an entry just off this street. On the other side, at the east end of the street in the nineteenth century, was the St Martin's Boys' School, and at the junction with **Queen Street** was the Old Peacock pub, where inquests were sometimes held in the mid nineteenth century. It was first found listed in 1790, but was gone by 1912.

Residents in 1884 included 'pig's pudding maker' Ann Taylor, bailiff Samuel Malpas and herb distiller and shoemaker E.T. Tyler, plus a porter, a seamstress, a bricklayer, a painter, a blacksmith and a dressmaker. A row of eight cottages called Trinity Gardens, stood behind the north side of the street and was listed separately in 1840.

The creation of Trinity Street in the late nineteenth century cut this street in half, and the west end later took the name **Trinity Passage**, leaving only the section of this street from Trinity Street to Queen Street, and this has seen much redevelopment since.

TRINITY PASSAGE

Originally this was at the eastern end of **The Trinity**, before it was cut in half by **Trinity Street** in the 1890s, and at that time this name was used for a back alley behind properties between **Mealcheapen Street** and The Trinity. The name was transferred to what had been the western end of The Trinity sometime in the second half of the twentieth century.

TRINITY STREET

See also **Trinity**. This street was created at the end of the nineteenth century, crossing **The Trinity**, an ancient lane which formerly ran from **The Cross** to **Queen Street**, to link **St Nicholas Street** with **St Swithin's Street**. Creation of the street probably began after St Swithin's Street was widened in 1891, and it must have been in existence by 1895, since one of the buildings here bears that date.

The ancient Trinity Hall, at the east end of what is now **Trinity Passage**, was replaced in 1894 by the Trinity Works of printers Ebeneezer Baylis, who moved to **London Road** in the 1960s. Next door, to the south of Baylis's was Osborne & Sharpe's glass and lead warehouse, built in 1895. Beyond that in 1905 was The Central Drapery Stores, and on the opposite side at that time were dressmaker Mrs Alice Parks, laundress Mrs Ella Shepherd and Miss Parsons' drapery shop. By 1940 Berrow's Worcester Jounal had moved next door to Baylis's, and remained here until it moved to **Hylton Road** in the 1960s.

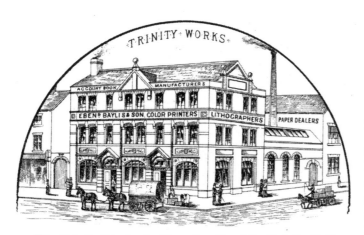

The Trinity Works, built on the site of the Trinity Hall

The oldest building here, the Church House of St Nicholas Church, dates from long before the street was created, having been built around 1750. It has been referred to as The Old Trinity House, suggesting it was on the site of the Trinity Hall (see **The Trinity**), but the two buildings were both shown separately on a map of 1884.

From 1907 the building became the diocesan office and it was at this time that additions were made and the west front reconstructed.

In the 1960s Pevsner called it 'Worcester's premier Gothic Revival house'. For almost 20 years up to 1985 it was the City Department of Health, and since about 1994 it has been a restaurant.

The west side of the Co-op building was a dominant feature of this street from the 1960s, and in recent years was occupied by the Worcestershire Local History Centre, which sadly moved to The Hive in **The Butts** in 2012.

TUNNEL HILL

This street takes its name from the railway tunnel passing under it, which was created before the opening of the first railway link to the city in 1850. Prior to that this was an area of open fields, with no development, and the tunnel was presumably dug to keep down the gradient on the line.

Gwilliam said that Tunnel Hill was previously known as Harbour Hill, a name which must come from Old English Herdeberge meaning herdsman's hill, though Harbour Hill was shown on an 1838 map as situated further south, between **Tolladine Road** and **Newtown Road**.

The present name presumably came into general use in the 1850s. The builders seem to have followed fairly quickly behind the railway navvies, and a good deal of house building probably went ahead here in the 1850s or early 1860s, but this street was not listed in a directory until 1880, when it was called Tunnel Road. By 1884 there was an established community here, with around 25 homes, and a post office towards **Rainbow Hill**, kept by Walter Nutt, who was also a baker, shopkeeper and beer retailer. This development was situated either around the west end of the street or near the west end of **Holly Mount**, and residents were mostly a mix of white collar and skilled workers.

There are no building records for this first phase of development, but the street bore all the hallmarks of having been built by a number of small investors or speculators who put up small terraces of homes, or even individual houses, and named them according to their taste. Next to the post office was Alpine Cottage, then Laurel Villa. There were three Lillian Villas, two Gladstone Villas, two Derby Villas, two homes called The Beauchamps, five homes in Apsley Terrace and four in Douro Villas. Residents in 1884 were chiefly clerks and railwaymen, but there were also two foremen, a wheelwright, a watchman, a labourer, a fireman, a compositor and a timekeeper. Thomas Brown at Fair View was a sculptor.

Within five years there were applications to build a further 17 homes, which were up by 1896, when the current street name was in use. At Sunny Bank lived Albert Hodder, headmaster of the School of Art in **Pierpoint Street**. Development continued steadily, and there were around 55 homes here by 1910, and almost 60 by 1922. There has been a good deal of further development since.

A pub called the Royal George was built here in the second half of the 1950s, to replace one of the same name which had closed in **Tybridge Street**, but it has long since closed and been converted to accommodation.

Turkey

Now **Tybridge Street**. Noake believed the name was corrupted from Tower Quay, the tower probably being the defensive gate on the old bridge between here and **Newport Street**.

TURRALL STREET

A Turrall family of Shrawley are mentioned in county archives and may have been involved in the development or financing of this street. There are no records of its early development, and four modest cottages on Barbourne Place are all that is shown on a map of 1884 and in a street directory of the same date. Residents then were a salesman, a drayman and a coach smith, plus sculptor Walter Smith, who may have been related to another sculptor with the same surname at **Tunnel Hill**. In 1889 there was an application to build two more homes, and by 1896 Nos. 1 & 2 Turrall House had been built. In 1922 Liberal registration agent Richard Fairbairn was living at No. 2. Some time after 1896 three villas were built, and they and the cottages remain, but Turrall House succumbed to modern redevelopment here.

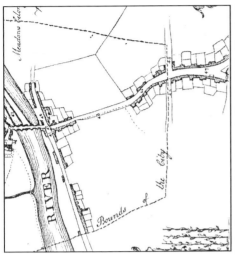

Tybridge Street in 1764, above, and 1799, below, after the bridge moved to the present site. Bottom, by 1840 development was spreading along the road, which was then called Turkey

TYBRIDGE STREET

This name is a corruption of the original Old English name. To the Anglo-Saxons it was Tubrugge Strete, the street to the bridge, since it was the western approach to a ford which had a wooden bridge before the Norman Conquest. This was an important route for livestock being brought in from Wales, and for raiders, Welsh and otherwise, trying to force their way across the old bridge, which was superseded in 1781 by a new bridge on the present crossing point (see **Bridge Street**). It was also a populous and thriving community up to the twentieth century.

It has had a number of names over the centuries, though that part leading west from the bridge had the present name in 1254. By 1741 this had changed to *Turkey*, which Noake believed was a corruption of Tower Quay, the tower being the fortification on the old bridge. The central section of the street was known as the Causeway, because it had been raised to avoid flooding, around 40 years before **New Road** was also built as a raised causeway. This work was badly needed because prior to around 1780 this road was said to be so badly worn by wheeled traffic that it was almost six feet below the level of the footpath beside it. The part leading up to the Bull Ring was Bar-gate or *Cripplegate*, though this had nothing to do with people with disabilities; in Old English it meant a gate or entry with a low or restricted opening for livestock to pass through, in this case a steep and narrow path.

By 1828 the street was divided only into Cripplegate and Turkey, which in the twentieth century, for unknown reasons, became Torcae, probably derived from Welsh, and remained so until the 1960s when the present name came into use.

The wooden bridge was superseded by a narrow but strongly-constructed stone bridge built 1307-1319. A thriving community grew up around the bridge and along this street, with a large colony of Welsh people, who congregated here because they were forbidden to own land or property within the city. This community may explain the idea that this was once part of Wales.

It might have been expected to suffer when the old bridge closed, and this street

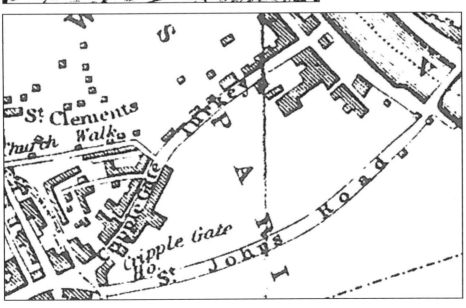

lost its traditional role as the bridge approach, but it was still thriving in the nineteenth century. Nails, tobacco pipes, shoes, ropes, tarpaulins and sails were amongst the goods manufactured here. There were also service businesses. Barber William Leadigo was here in 1790, along with haberdasher Walter Mayers, carpenter George Lee and millwright George Morris. Listed on Cripplegate were baker Simon English, bricklayer John Bennett, glover John Williams, schoolmaster John Radcliff and soap boiler Mrs Smith.

There were five pubs listed in the area in 1790. The Bear and the Royal George were at the east end of the street, and the Cock, the Rising Sun and the White Horse were listed under Cripplegate. The first of these was a seventeenth century inn, on the northern side of the junction with **Hylton Road**, which survived until around 1970, though from photographs it looks to have been rebuilt in the early twentieth century. The Royal George was almost opposite, on the riverside, but had closed by 1955, though a replacement was apparently created at **Tunnel Hill**. Of the other three, only the Cock, towards the west end of the

Above, slums in Tybridge Street in 1920 - RS Below, the junction of Tybridge Street and Hylton Road in 1930 - on the right, The Royal George, on the left, the Bear Inn - WN

street, was still serving drinks in 1884. Gwilliam said it closed around 1970. He listed the Rising Sun as closed between 1851 and 1873, but he has no information on the White Horse. He also lists, from west to east, the Lamp Tavern, which he said was first listed in 1873 and closed around 1970; a beer retailer, possibly called the Cock & Magpie, on the corner of **Church Walk**; and the Apple Tree, which was listed in 1822 and closed by 1930.

The street was surrounded by crowded courts and tenements, many of which were notoriously insanitary. Because of the risk of flooding much of this housing, even in the late nineteenth century, was clustered around either end of the street, with a much lower density of housing north of the central section of the street, and nothing on the south, where Cripplegate Park is now. Just east of the **Bull Ring**, was the substantial Cripplegate House, standing in its own grounds, but on its doorstep to the east were eight densely-packed courts of housing, and *Russell Terrace*, a row of twenty industrial cottages with not a scrap of garden between them. Some of this slum housing was clearly in very poor condition when it was photographed in 1927. It was cleared in the 1930s, and the street was subsequently straightened and widened.

The deep depression between the Tybridge Street and New Road causeways was filled in with rubbish in the early twentieth century, and the first part of Cripplegate Park was opened in 1922, with more being opened ten years later.

A modern housing development on the north side at St Clement's Close perpetuates the tradition of a local community here, but all that remains of the older housing in the street is a single property called Tybridge House, built around 1820, which was in use as offices in recent years, and is now a veterinary surgery.

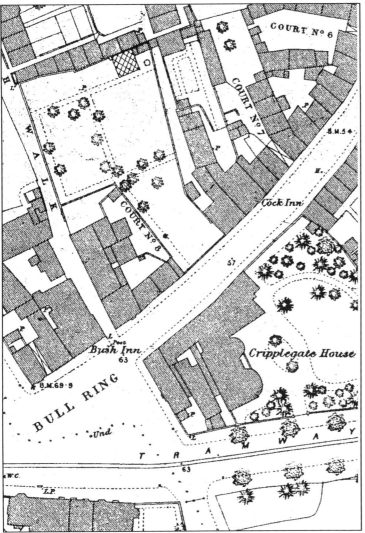

The west end of Tybridge Street in 1884

The power station which stood on a large site south of the road, fronting on **Hylton Road**, was built originally by 1903. The city had already built the first corporation power station in the country, which opened at Powick Mills on **Malvern Road** in 1894, and supplied power to light six central streets, and the homes of 502 subscribers by 1900. But more power was needed for the electrification of the tram system, which began operating in 1903. Following a decision to upgrade the national network in 1949, the Powick station closed in 1950. The power station here was rebuilt in 1942, but it was closed in 1975 and demolished in 1979. More of Cripplegate Park now stands on the site, and a retail park stands opposite where the fuel depot was once situated. The only reminder of the power station is the small riverside water inlet and pumping station on Hylton Road.

A Victorian resident of this street would scarcely recognise it now, because of the amount of change which took place in the twentieth century.

TYTHING, THE

This has been a busy and populous street for many centuries past, and was a thriving community quite separate from the city, until nineteenth century boundary changes. This entry includes Upper Tything, which was first found listed separately in 1884.

Until 1837, when city boundaries were expanded from **Castle Street** to Barbourne Brook, the Tything was outside the city, and until 1875, when the Tything parish was created, it was in Claines parish for baptisms, marriages and funerals, and part of Droitwich district for registrations. After the Tything became a civil parish in 1875, St Mary's parish church was built in **Sansome Walk** in 1876-7, but closed in 1977 and was later converted into flats. The extent of this street has changed slightly. In the nineteenth century it extended north as far as the site of **Shrubbery Avenue**, but now it ends at **Little London**.

A tithing was an ancient administrative unit which was a tenth of a hundred, but this street probably takes its name from the former tithe or tything barn on the corner of what is now Little London, which received tithes for the convent known as White Ladies, established here about 1240.

The convent was set up by Walter de Cantilupe, Bishop of Worcester from 1237, and was one of two convents established in the county in the thirteenth century by the Cistercians, a monastic reform movement. No original plan of the convent has survived, but it certainly had a chapel dedicated to St Mary Magdalene, of which there are remains, and this was the official name of the convent, though the white habits of the nuns quickly gave it the name by which it was commonly known.

The convent was not large, with probably only about six nuns at any one time, who were often older ladies who had raised their families and entered the convent after being widowed. Nor was it wealthy, but it held land at Nunnery Wood and White Ladies Aston, and Lady Alice de la Flagge, who was prioress in the early fourteenth century, brought it lands in Barbourne and perhaps beyond, including what is now **Flag Meadow Walk**. The convent was closed at the Dissolution and the site became Whiteladies farm, which in the eighteenth century was home to the Somers and Blurtons, and the Cookseys of Upton Warren. The Worcester Royal Grammar School moved to the site in 1868. The ruins of the convent chapel can still be seen here, incorporated into an eighteenth century building.

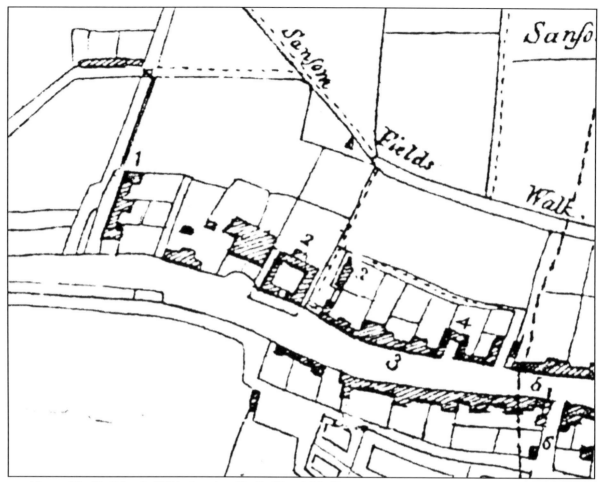

Above, The Tything in 1764, showing Castle Street (5), St Oswald's (2), and Whiteladies farm (1), but with much open land around, and starting to be more developed in 1838, below.

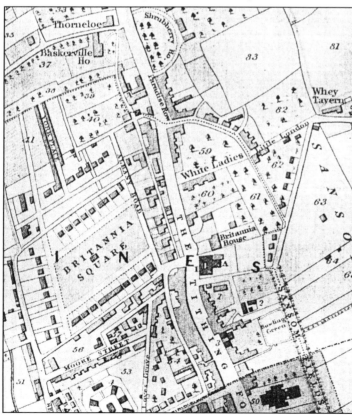

The street also had another religious community, the Hospital of St Oswald, one of the oldest charitable foundations in the country, reputedly established by Oswald himself, while he was Bishop of Worcester from 962 to 991. A sixteenth century account claimed it was originally an isolation hospital for monks suffering from leprosy, though the disease was not thought to be found in this country at that time, which could suggest strong foreign links in the age of crusading. In the medieval period the hospital's extensive cemetery, which stretched across the land to the south of **St Oswald's Road**, where Kay's the catalogue company later had offices and a car park, was the only one in the area apart from that at the cathedral, and plague victims were known to have been buried here. At the Dissolution the hospital was converted to almshouses, which still exist. At least three chapels have stood on the site, the current one was built about 1873.

In the fifteenth and sixteenth centuries thriving industries brought many people to the city and there was considerable

Above, the popular Saracen's Head bowling green in the early nineteenth century. Below, remains of Whiteladies chapel at the grammar school - TW

development here as far as St Oswald's, which resulted in slum conditions, drinking, illegal gambling and prostitution. There was little regulation because the area then lay outside the city, and only the county sheriff had authority here, which he often found difficult to enforce. The city authorities were probably not sorry to see the Tything slums cleared during the Civil War to deny cover to attacking Roundheads.

After the Restoration a few of the former residents returned and built homes – the cottages on the corner of **Little London** probably date from this period, though they acquired a fashionable brick frontage in the eighteenth century – but most of the new homes were built by the wealthy,

moving out of the densely populated city to a healthier environment.

Directory listings for 1790 show The Tything residents included attorneys, glovers and tailors, together with a butcher, a banker, a builder, a baker, a fruiterer, a gardener, a hairdresser, a tea dealer, a stay maker, a hop dealer and a livery stable keeper. It also boasted the homes of a good many of the city's most important people, including William Thomas, the Under-sheriff for Worcester. Nevertheless there continued to be a social mix of residents in the street, and in June 1812 the Journal reported that a subscription had been taken up here for the relief of the poor, which was laid out on bacon and pease (a sort of porridge made from boiled vegetables), to be sold to the poor at half the cost price.

There were five inns listed in 1790, all of which are still with us, though not all with the same names, nor are all still in this street. As the population expanded they were at the centre of providing diversions for well-off residents. At the southern end of the street was the Saracens Head which once had notable Pleasure Grounds, since built on, with a popular bowling green, and plenty of room for travelling circuses and preachers. Further along on the west was the George, subsequently the George & Dragon; then the Green Man, which has been renamed within the last couple of years; the Coach & Horses, and the Talbot, now in **Barbourne Road**.

Gwilliam also lists two more pubs still with us, the Feathers, now renamed, and the Lamb & Flag, first listed in 1822 as the Old Lamb & Fleece. The latter was held in the 1850s and 60s by old soldier Thomas Surman, the son of an Inkberrow baker, and a possible descendant of John Surman who held the Talbot inn in **Sidbury**

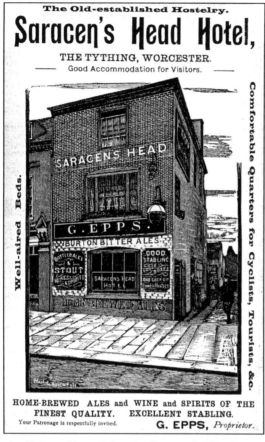

An Edwardian ad for the Saracen's Head, and Gregory's grocery store at 77 The Tything in the same period - RS

in 1730. He had served from 1813 until 1835 in the 14th Dragoons, and rose to be a Troop Sergeant Mayor. In the year after his discharge he married 20-year-old Caroline Birch of Solihull, and in 1850 they took over the pub. His sisters, Sarah and Rebecca, were at the bakery next door at the same time. By 1868 Caroline Surman was running the pub alone, and her husband died in Devon in 1872. She gave up the pub soon afterwards, and lived at No. 34 until her death in 1880.

Though the grammar school moved to its present site only in 1868, it has been in existence for many centuries. The school was associated with the Trinity Guild in **The Trinity**, and the parish of St Nicholas, and was certainly in existence by 1291 when it was known simply as Worcester School. It hit hard times after the foundation of King's School by Henry VIII (see **Edgar Street**), but in 1558 clothier Thomas Wylde (see **Wyld's Lane)** gave land at Pitchcroft to re-found the school, and a new charter was obtained from Elizabeth I in 1561. However the school remained in a room at St Swithin's Church until it moved here, and most of the buildings on the site date from then or later. Former pupils include artist Benjamin Williams Leader and leading Australian poet Adam Lindsay Gordon. The governing body, the Six Masters, set up in the Elizabethan charter, subsequently built the almshouses on the corner of **Little London**, where the White Ladies tythe barn once stood.

The former Kay's site at No. 23, bordering **St Oswald's Road**, was purchased from St Oswald's Hospital in 1907 for £620, and the business moved here from **Shrub Hill Road** in 1908, and was the headquarters of Kay's for almost

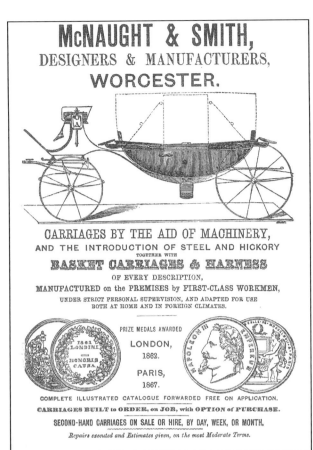

McNaught ads from 1869 and 1910

a century. The other Kay's building at Nos. 9 & 10, opened in 1938, and the entrance hall was said to be modelled on the home of Gordon of Khartoum, using entrance doors and the staircase from his Blackheath home.

The site was previously occupied in the nineteenth and early twentieth century by McNaught's carriage works, producing products with an international reputation. The company, run by James Aldren McNaught, was in existence before 1851 and made carriages for Indian princes and the Lord Mayor of London.

A disastrous fire gutted the works in the 1890s, and the company subsequently began making cars, but these did not prove as successful, and the business was wound up in 1918. It is recalled by McNaught Place, a small entry leading into what was Kay's car park. Unfortunately the Kay's building on the site suffered a similar fate, being gutted by fire in 1941, and it was not rebuilt until 1949.

A much smaller but very important business was the workshop of sculptor and carver William Forsyth, who worked next door to the Saracen's Head for 40 years. One of his best loved pieces is the tableau of hop pickers in **Sansome Street**, but his other work included fine interior and exterior work at Worcester City & County Bank, now Lloyd's, at **The Cross**, Pitchcroft entrance gates, and figures on the Perseus and Andromeda fountain at Witley Court. His brother James often worked with him here, but acquired a reputation for his work in cathedrals nationwide.\

The most notable building is Britannia House, believed to have been commissioned about 1714 by John Somers (See **Somers Road**), though he died before he could move in. He was a lawyer brought up at Whiteladies farm, who was Lord Chancellor of England under William III, The house was built by Thomas White, architect of the Guildhall. In February 1819 it was purchased at auction by city businessman William Shaw, after whom **Shaw Street** was named, and he lived here until his death in 1843, at the age of 77. In the 1860s there was a school for boys here, and in 1883 it was occupied by the Worcester High School for Girls, later renamed Alice Ottley after its first headmistress, which has more recently become part of the Worcester Royal Grammar School.

UNION STREET

This street is said to be a continuation of *St Lawrence Lane*, or Friars Lane, which in medieval and Tudor times ran from the **High Street** to **Friar Street**, but has since been built over. It was created around 1820 by widening the old lane into an access road from **Friar Street** into the *Blockhouse* area, linking with **Carden Street**.

Historic Worcester Streets

There are several possible explanations for the name. It may have come from the nearby Union Farm, off **Wyld's Lane**, or the House of Industry on **Tallow Hill**, which was run by a union of city parishes, or it may have resulted from the street uniting the city centre with the Blockhouse.

It was first listed in a street directory in 1840, when residents included a straw hat maker, a milliner, a furniture broker, an earthenware dealer, a rug weaver, a bricklayer, and the Union Inn, which opened soon after the street was created, but had closed by 1908. Also here in 1840 was the City Gaol on the corner of **Friar Street**, which was created in former friary buildings. The building was subsequently taken over as Laslett's Almshouses. No. 12 was called Moseley House in 1884 and was home to builder Joseph Compton, after whom **Compton Road** was named. The last house in the street, the link to Carden Street and the site of the Union Inn were all lost in the 1970s with the creation of the **City Walls Road**.

Upper Butts
Now **Farrier Street**. Variously known as **The Butts** and **Upper Butts**, but by1896 it had its present name.

Upper Barbourne Terrace
Short-lived extension of **Barbourne Terrace**.

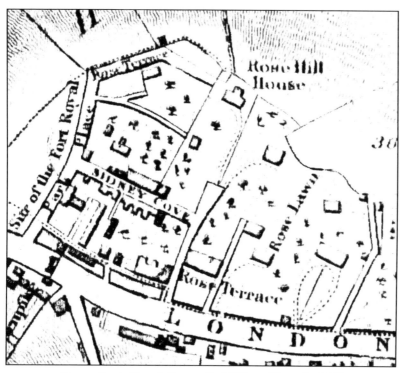
Upper Park Street, then called Sidney Cove, in 1838

UPPER PARK STREET
The present name is a variant of the nearby **Park Street**, which derived its name from the parkland around Fort Royal House.

Research by resident Christine Sylvester suggests construction of houses here began as early as 1834. The street was shown on a map of 1838 under the name Sidney Cove, the colony to which county criminals had been transported since 1787.

With no building records, it is not possible to say who developed or built the street, or why its original name was chosen.

Nor can we say why it was changed to the present version, but it had been by the time the street was first listed in a directory in 1880.

It appears that a colony of glovers lived here in the street's early days, probably working for Price's, one of the largest glovers in the city. Ellen Price, daughter of the owner and a leading Victorian novelist under her married name Mrs Henry Wood, is said to have written about them and the street under the name Honey Fair, in her novel *Mrs Halliburton's Troubles*, which first appeared in 1862, though if this is correct, the glovers must have moved in very early on, and Ellen Wood's description must have been based on her memories of the street as a young woman, since as far as we know she never returned to live in the city after her marriage in 1836.

It was perhaps a sign of the times for the gloving industry that just a single glover remained here by 1884, when there were 32 homes in the street. Residents then included six labourers, three shoemakers, two china workers, two charwomen, a fireman, a tailor, a leather dresser, a seamstress, a bricklayer, a porter, a dressmaker, an iron moulder, a packer and a coal carter.

The Park Tavern, at the west end of the street, will no doubt have done good business in its day, from families flocking to the park on Sundays. The pub was said by Gwilliam to have been listed first in 1873, and was still open in 1980, but has closed since.

A shop stood next to the pub in 1884, kept by Mrs Ann Griffiths. By 1896 there was a Park Street Mission Room listed here near **Rose Hill**, an offshoot of St Martin's Church in the **Cornmarket**, which opened for a weekly Sunday evening service.

314

In 1962 a clearance plan was drawn up, to demolish 25 of the homes in the street, and the clearance order was signed in the same year. A row of seven of the original glovers' cottages still remains, but everything else here now dates from around 1970.

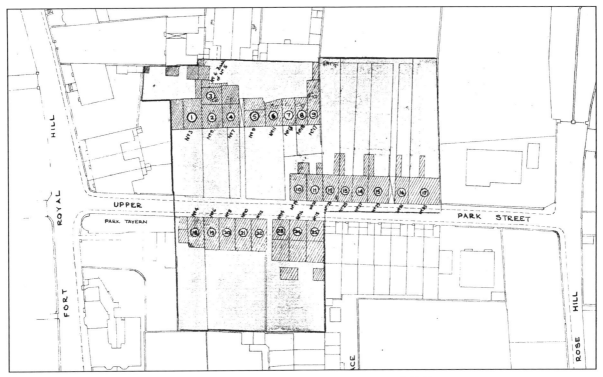

The Upper Park Street Clearance Plan of 1962

Upper Quay
It became known as **North Quay** by 1885.

UPPER TYTHING
See **Tything, The**.

VAUXHALL STREET
Named for the Vauxhall Inn on **Astwood Road**, which was in existence a few years before the road.

The pub, recently converted into a restaurant, was north of the Sansome Fields estate, a pleasant area of fields and woods much favoured by eighteenth century city folk for rural walks. This area still consisted entirely of farmland in 1838. The pub was first found listed in 1869. The pub name recalls the famous Vauxhall Gardens pleasure grounds in London, which closed in 1859, but were very fashionable in their day, and every locality at that time aspired to have its own little Vauxhall. The pub name was probably trading on the fame of Vauxhall rather than advertising what was offered here, since no evidence was found that this pub ever had pleasure gardens attached.

Development here began with a small row of five cottages called Vauxhall Terrace, which was built on the site of this street before 1884, and at that date housed a wheelwright, a signalman, a carpenter, a shoemaker and a seamstress. The road then was described as 'Newly-formed, not named', but it had been named by 1885, though no further development took place for some years. There was a building application for a shop in 1896, which had been built within two years on the corner of Astwood Road, and was being kept by Mrs Gibbons.

It was not until 1898 that there were two building applications for 17 more houses. The larger one of these, for 10 homes, was submitted by city builder George Wood, who had already been involved in similar developments at **Sandys Road** and **Shrubbery Avenue**. By 1900 all these houses had been built, and in 1901 George Wood applied to build 38 more houses. It was by far his largest application, and at that time it was the second largest application to have been submitted since building control began in 1865.

By 1903 eight of the houses were being built and eight more had been completed and were ready for occupation. By 1905 there were 48 homes here, all but one occupied. The corner shop, which had previously been a newsagents, had become a bakery. By 1908 there were 50 homes, with four more being built. There was a definite move upmarket by later investors. The name of the original terrace of modest cottages had long since disappeared from listings, and one side of the street had a series of villas, Grafton Villas, Salisbury Villas and Palmerston Villas, designed to appeal to more affluent white collar workers, though most of the residents continued to be factory workers, metal workers, fitters, railwaymen and gardeners.

An Edwardian view of Vernon Park Road, with a corner shop on the right - RS

VERNON PARK ROAD

This road was named for Vernon Park, opposite the development, beside Pitmaston House, **Malvern Road**. The Vernons of Hanbury purchased the manor of Lower Wick, which included this land, in 1746, and built themselves a house called Vernon Hall off Malvern Road, roughly opposite where **Hanbury Park Road** is now, which was demolished after 1884.

The leading nineteenth century member of the Vernon family, and the landowner who must have sold this land for development, was Harry Vernon. He was born in 1834, and as a second son he may have been intended to enter the church, since he remained at Oxford to complete an MA. But in 1859 he succeeded to the family estates on the early death of his brother. Two years later he married Lady Georgina Sophia Baillie-Hamilton, after whom **Georgina Avenue** was named, and they were inseparable for the rest of his life.

He was MP for West Worcestershire during 1861-68, but he mainly concerned himself with county affairs, being chairman of Droitwich magistrates for many years, serving in Worcestershire Rifle Volunteers for 27 years, and the Queen's Own Worcestershire Yeomanry for 33 years. He and his wife were largely responsible for founding the County Nursing Association, and were also involved with the county Red Cross. In 1885 he became a baronet. He died in 1920, and his wife died eight years later.

In 1884 this area was largely covered with the orchards of St John's Nurseries, with no sign of the streets which would be built over these rural acres within a very few years. Building must have begun on the Vernon Park Estate in the last years of the nineteenth century. By 1900 there were half a dozen villas here, including the two Vernon Villas, one of which was occupied by musician Frederick Austin; Impney, while the other was home to builder George Wood, whose career in property development in the 1890s culminated in an application for 38 houses in **Vauxhall Street** in 1901; Hadzor, home to a woollen draper's assistant; Hanbury, where Mrs Sarah Barnsley let out apartments; and Westwood, home to businessman H.C. Loach. By 1922 it was complete, with 18 homes listed here, primarily with managerial residents. S. Grosvenor at Stanage was a former police inspector; Walter Longden at Westwood was 'clerk and steward of mental hospital'; and Joseph Richardson at Tower House was an analytical chemist.

VICAR STREET

The Baptist Church on **Rainbow Hill** opened in 1881, and the building of a house for the minister may have given rise to this street and the name. It was first mentioned as 'road from Albany Road' in a building application of 1882, and first found listed in a street directory two years later. There were just four homes here in 1884, housing a butcher, a school board agent, a locksmith, and artist Albert Hodder, though oddly there was no mention of the minister, who must have been listed on Rainbow Hill. On the corner of Rainbow Hill was a shop kept by George Taylor, which by 1896 had become the Rainbow Hill Liberal Club. Two small-scale building applications were submitted in 1904 for three new houses. Only two were built, and they were listed by 1905. These were all on the north side of the street. Homes on the south side appear not to have been built until the 1920s or 30s.

VICTORIA AVENUE

In 1884 there was a driveway here on what became the southern end of the street, leading to a large house, perhaps St Catherine's Vale House though it isn't named on a contemporary map. The house was probably built in the early nineteenth century, about the same time as **St Catherine's Hill**. In 1896 it was home to Robert Clarke of Lewis, Clarke & Co., which had a brewery in **Angel Place**.

In 1897 a building application was submitted for this new road, named after the reigning monarch. The Queen's Diamond Jubilee in that year, celebrating her sixtieth year on the throne, resulted in a wave of public affection for the long widowed monarch, and her late consort, and Albert and Victoria streets sprang up all over the country. The adjoining **Albert Road** here also went ahead at the same time. Both roads were applied for by leading local property developer John Stallard Junior, after whom **Stallard Road** was probably named. The building of this road did not immediately spell the end for St Catherine's Vale House, it continued to be listed until 1903.

The first building application, for two houses, was submitted in 1898, and development continued to progress steadily over the next few years, with a mix of smaller-scale and larger building plans from a variety of investors and speculators. In the next seven years there were nine building applications for 50 more homes, six of which were for four homes or less.

Queen Victoria's official 1897 Diamond Jubilee portrait

It was first listed in a street directory in 1900, when there were 11 homes listed, but building was obviously going ahead quickly, and within three years there were 36 homes listed, plus 17 unoccupied houses which had probably just been completed, and four more being built. By 1905 there were 57 homes with a further seven unoccupied, and by 1910 it was almost fully occupied, with almost 70 homes, of which just a couple were unoccupied.

These were villas, rather than the more humble cottages found elsewhere, and all had individual names that accorded with the taste of the developers, such as Swayney House, Ritka, Blenheim, Austral Villa and Fahan. Many of the people living here were skilled workers. Residents in 1905 included glovers, engineers, china workers, metal workers, railwaymen, compositors, carpenters, fitters, clerks, foremen, a coachman, a gardener, a lamplighter, a chef, a relief station master and James Bull, manager of the Empress Tea Stores. The new St Martin's Church opened on the corner of the street in 1911.

VICTORIA PLACE

Presumably named for the reigning monarch, this was originally a rear access to properties on **London Road**, which connected with an entry off the main road, both sharing this name. There are no building records. The street was first found listed in the health board streets list of 1872, and in a street directory of 1884. The homes listed here were at right angle to the main road, sandwiched between it and **Upper Park Street**. An 1884 directory listed 17 homes here which were shown on a map of around that date, but it also listed seven homes in Park Terrace, and eight in Victoria Terrace, presumably at the southern end of the street. Residents of the homes listed in Victoria Place were mostly manual workers, including three gardeners, two seamstresses, a tailor, a shoemaker, a china printer, a charwoman, a cab driver, a porter, a coachsmith, a drayman, a coachman, a baker and a clerk. There are still around a dozen original homes here, but the rest were built recently.

VICTORIA STREET

Presumably named for the queen, this street was first found listed in a street directory of 1884, but there are no early building records. This street would have been part of the land around **Ombersley Road**, which began to be developed in the early 1880s, but was then outside the city. It was evident that the land had been split into lots for sale, since a lot No. 36 was referred to in a building application. The street was first found in a street directory of 1884, when there were 30 homes listed. Most of them were on the south, with just four on the north side, and almost all had generous gardens. Eight of these homes were empty, perhaps suggesting that they had recently been completed and were not yet occupied. Residents in 1884 were mostly manual workers, including building tradesmen, labourers, a gardener, a glover, a groom, a seamstress, a brushmaker and a clerk.

The first building application was found in 1886 for 3 houses, and between 1888 and 1895 there were five more applications to build a further 13 houses. Building went ahead quickly, and by 1900 there were 50 homes here, and another dozen have been added since, mostly in the 1930s. The shop on the corner of **Bourne Street** must have opened in the 1880s or 1890s, but has long since closed.

VIGORNIA AVENUE

The name is a Latinized version of Worcester, probably developed in the nineteenth century, though not the name by which the Romans knew the city, which was thought to be Vertis. This street was first found in a directory in 1930, when there were 40 homes listed.

VINCENT ROAD

Said to be named for the son of a local businessman. When James Roberts took over the Three Springs Tannery off **Wyld's Lane**, across the canal from the **Blockhouse**, in 1877, he also acquired the land between **Midland Road** and roughly where **Vincent Road** is now, and later developed it for housing. At that time, though there was some development along the canalside, and along Wyld's Lane as far as **Richmond Hill**, the land he had purchased here was completely open, save for Field House, a mansion opposite Richmond Hill. An application for creation of three roads – this road, **Stanley Road** and **Cecil Road** - was submitted in 1890. Tradition has it that these roads were named for his two sons, Cecil and Stanley Vincent.

An 1898 ad

There was considerable interest from developers. Property speculator Walter Aston, of the saw mill in *James Street*, submitted a building application for 47 houses here in 1892, the largest application to have been submitted since building control began in 1865. Henry Smith applied to build another 10 and Edwin Yarnold another six in the following year, and three more applications for a total of 10 homes and a shop were submitted in the next two years. By 1896, when the street was first found listed in a directory, there may have been more than 60 homes here, though an odd numbering system makes it difficult to tell.

There were few of the villas here which drew white-collar workers to Stanley Road, and residents were a mix of building and factory workers and railwaymen. There were two shops, one on the corner of Cecil Road, and another near Wyld's Lane, but no pub. Field House, between this road and Stanley Road, survived an estate being built around it and is still here today, though it is now split into flats, and its generous garden has been built on. The Rev Robert Hugh Blair, rector of St Martin's, was living there in 1884. In 1896 artist Sidney Meteyard was there, and Mrs Meteyard was running a ladies' school. The Three Springs Tannery, once a leading city employer, continued to operate at the end of the road until around 1974, and a small business park now stands on the site.

VINE STREET

The name is based on the Vine Inn on the corner of **Ombersley Road**, which was first listed in 1873, and was the northern tram terminus in the days of horse and electric trams. The Northwick Arms, on the corner of **Northwick Road** may be slightly later. The street had probably long existed as an unnamed lane or 'cutthrough' between **Northwick Road** and Ombersley Road, and was shown in this way on a map of 1859, but it was not listed in a street directory until 1884 when there were 18 homes here, a shop and the two pubs. There was a shop next door to the Northwick Arms, kept by Mrs Harriet Biggs.

The street was complete on the north side in 1884, but there was a large garden to the south, covering half the length of the street. Residents then included clerks, wheelwrights, a tailor, carpenters, a harness maker, a draper's assistant, a drayman, a porter, a glover, and retired farmer Isaac Sansome, who was probably farming the land here before it was developed, and was presumably from the family who gave their name to Sansome Fields.

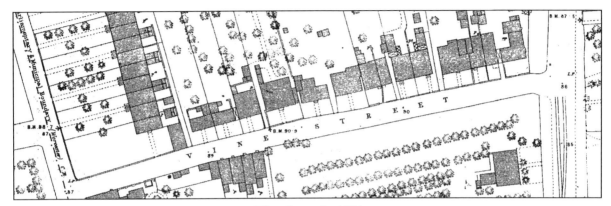

Vine Street in 1884

WAKEMAN STREET

Named for the Wakeman family, who were established at Perdiswell from at least the late eighteenth century. Perdiswell Hall was built in 1788 by George Byfield for Thomas Wakeman, who was mayor of Worcester in 1761 and owned much land in the Claines area. The family became known throughout the city as the owners of Barbourne Nurseries, which had much land north of the city under cultivation.

In the next generation Henry Wakeman confirmed the family's status as landed gentry, having a baronetcy conferred on him in 1828. He was the victim of what must have been a major local scandal at the time, when his first wife, Theodosia, ran off with a Guards officer in 1792.

The marriage was dissolved, and in 1797 he married Sarah, only daughter of Richard Ward Offley of Shropshire, and Offley afterwards became a first name for generations of their descendants, one of whom gave the name to **Offley Street**.

At his death in 1843 he was succeeded by his son Sir Offley Penbury Wakeman, who gained a reputation as a charitable man and a liberal landlord, and was said to be very well liked in Worcester. He married in 1848 and a son, also Offley, was baptised in 1850, but his wife, Mary, died in 1852, in childbirth or soon afterwards. When Sir Offley died six years later, little Offley was left an orphan at the age of eight, to be brought up by an aunt. During his minority Perdiswell Hall was let, and one of the tenants was Alexander Clunes Sherriff, after whom **Sherriff Street** was named.

The young Wakeman may have moved in later, since the hall was listed as his seat in 1870, but in 1875 the estate was purchased for £26,305 by retired manufacturer Henry Walker, who often lent the grounds, which stretched as far as Fernhill Heath, for public events. He died in 1911, and in 1919 the estate was purchased by Worcestershire County Council, though it was used as an RAF airfield during the Second World War. Fire badly damaged the hall in 1956 and what remained was demolished, but a stable block survives, now Grade II listed and used as offices, and there is also a leisure centre on the site.

The first reference to this street was in 1894, when there were two building applications for a total of 13 houses and a shop, with an application for 11 more homes in the following year. Both applications were submitted by stonemason John Rouse, a leading builder and property developer in late Victorian Worcester. The street was first listed in a directory in 1896 when there were 16 homes here, and four more being built, but by 1905 there were 27 homes here, plus a shop on the corner of ***Millburn Street***, kept by William Green, and another on the corner of Offley Street kept by Mrs Ann Langford.

Residents were mainly manual workers. In 1905 one resident in every three was a labourer, and there were building tradesmen, two lamplighters, two boilermakers, a fitter, a leather staker, an insurance agent and a gardener.

See also **Offley Street**, **Penbury Street** and **Perdiswell Street**. Probably all four streets were built on former Barbourne Nurseries land.

WALNUT AVENUE

Part of a 'tree' estate off **Brickfields Road**, this street was first found in a directory in 1937, when there 32 homes listed.

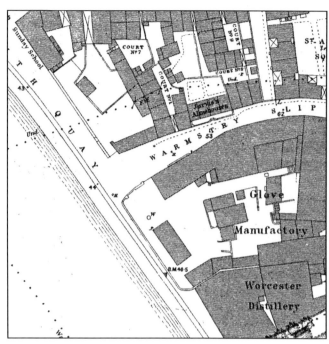

Warmestry Slip in 1884

Warmestry Slip

Also known as *St Maries Street*. Behind St Alban's Church for several centuries was Warmestry House, a substantial three-storey courtyard mansion dating from the beginning of the seventeenth century, with large gardens. Beside it was Warmestry Slip, a steep slipway leading down to the river, which in the medieval period was known as St Mary's Lane because of the dedication of the cathedral church. According to Hughes, it was known before that as Seintemarinestrete, because of the presence in the area of a long-vanished Saxon chapel dedicated to St Marina.

Members of the Warmestry family held the role of Chief Registrar of Worcester from 1544 until at least 1641, and in 1661 Thomas Warmestry became the first Dean of Worcester after the Restoration.

The house was empty by 1751, and Dr John Wall set up what later became known as Royal Worcester Porcelain there, using the Warmestry family quartered device, a crescent, as the original Worcester porcelain mark.

Warmestry House as the porcelain works in 1752

The firm amalgamated with Chamberlains of **Severn Street** in 1840, but the Warmestry factory continued working for some years, making replicas of medieval encaustic floor tiles for church restorations. Subsequently the house became Maw's tile factory, and then Dent and Allcroft's glove factory. As late as 1837 it was described as a fine example of ancient domestic architecture, and a few of the rooms were still said to be in their original state.

Stallard's had a riverside distillery and wine warehouse in the garden for some years, sending Worcester gin down the river to the port of Bristol.

In Tudor times there were also 15 or more timber-framed houses, some substantial and all with good gardens, backing onto the north side of the slip and fronting *Cooken Street*, which then ran down to the quay. The first barracks for soldiers in the city were said to have been built half-way up the slip, replaced in 1722 by Jarvis's almshouses, which were rebuilt in 1829 and continued here until the 1930s.

In the nineteenth century the Model Dwellings on *Birdport* backed onto the slip. It continued in existence until the site was redeveloped for the College of Technology, on which building began in 1959.

Warndon

Originally Waerma's hill, an Anglo-Saxon district name which, like many such names, seems to come from the name of the original owner of the land. The modern form of the name didn't appear until the sixteenth century. The manor was included in Doomsday Book in 1086 under the name Wermedun, when it was part of the bishop's manor of Northwick, and was held by the Sheriff of Worcester, Urse D'Abetot, from whom it was held by a knight named Robert, who may have been an ancestor of the Bracys who held it in later centuries. In 1594 it was sold to wealthy Worcester clothiers the Berkeleys. Around 1780 Warndon parish included 'Tollerdine, Trotswell and Smyte', and supported only 10 farming families. In 1930 Warndon has just 26 residents, plus farmers Chas Bolton, William Haughty and William Quinney. Housing development began at Warndon in the 1930s, and at Warndon Villages in the 1980s.

WASHINGTON STREET

The land here was part of the mid nineteenth century Arboretum Pleasure Grounds, with their entrance drive on **Arboretum Road**, which were sold for redevelopment in 1866, though this area close to the canal wasn't developed for another two decades.

This was probably one of the new roads off Northfield Street referred to in a building application of 1882, submitted by city solicitor Frederick Corbett. There was no immediate development, but in 1884 an application was submitted by Diglis builder William Bennett for 18 houses here and in **Southfield Street**. In that same year the street was shown and named on a map, but with no development, and a small area of the arboretum remaining on the north east. In the housing boom of the 1880s building land was in demand, and in 1885-6 there were a further seven applications for 46 homes, submitted by Bennett, stonemason John Rouse and other speculators. In 1899 a further six homes were applied for. Neighbouring **Lowell Street**, began to be developed soon after this street.

These two streets seem likely to be named for an heroic young American general, Charles Russell Lowell, who was killed in 1864, during the American Civil War, while defending the city of Washington. He was born in Boston, Massachusetts, and had no direct connection with Worcester, but he was a descendant of the Russell family of Worcester, who held estates at Strensham and Great Witley in the sixteenth and seventeenth centuries, and it seems likely that his English relatives had a role in developing and naming these streets. It is clear that the English side of the family were well aware of their American cousins, since the Worcestershire archives have an exchange of letters about family history with the general's uncle, the American poet James Russell Lowell.

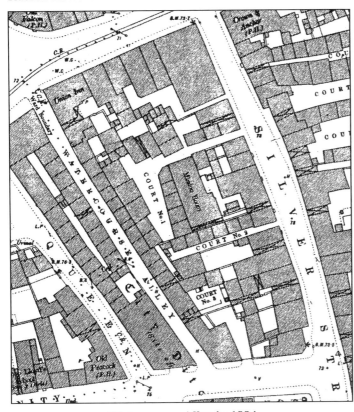

Watercourse Alley in 1884

By 1896 there were 36 homes here, and a shop on the corner of **Southfield Street** kept by Mrs Elizabeth Robinson. Residents were mostly manual workers, though many were skilled or qualified tradesmen. There were boot and shoe makers, carpenters, railwaymen, waiters, labourers, glovers, a tailor, a commercial traveller, a bookbinder, a hop porter, a fitter, an iron moulder, a cabinet maker, an upholsterer and a leather parer. Mrs Harriet Curnock at No. 3 had lodgings to let, Miss Sarah Salmon next door was a box maker at Dent's gloves, William Price at No. 16 was a 'pianoforte tuner', and Miss Cope at No. 34 was a 'lady help'.

By 1900 the street appeared to be complete with around 40 homes.

An application for a hop warehouse here was submitted in 1893 by William Charge & Co, which was then based at the Hopmarket. It was next to Kingsland Villas, and the firm was listed here in 1900, but the building was empty by 1905, and by 1910 it was listed as Winwood's furniture stores, recently converted to apartments called The Lofts. A building application for the Washington

Arms was submitted in 1901, and it was first found listed in 1908, though it has recently been converted into a house. By 1922 there was a fried fish shop at the end of the street.

Watercourse Alley

An alleyway which ran from the end of **Lowesmoor**, parallel with **Queen Street**, to *Exchange Street*. It was first found listed by name in the health board streets list of 1872, but it appears to be shown, though not named, on a map of 1741, and may have been older than that. It is assumed that the name derived from it being near the line of the old city ditch, which would once have been filled with water. In 1896 there were 15 homes listed here. Residents included five labourers, four charwomen, an auctioneer's porter, a cab driver, a carter, a fitter and two gloveresses. At the junction with **Lowesmoor** stood the Union Inn. This was a poor area, with some homes listed as condemned in 1908. The alley was still shown on street maps in the 1960s, but fell victim to the **City Walls Road** in the following decade.

Waterloo Gardens

Blockhouse. The name was listed in Bentley's Directory in 1840, but no further trace was found of it. It may have been an intended street name never used, or a terrace of homes in another street.

Waterloo Street party in 1937 - RS

Waterloo Street

Blockhouse. This street led off *King William Street*, and must have been built first, since it took its name from the canalside Waterloo Inn, at the junction of the streets, which had been there since at least 1822. The pub had been named not more than seven years after the final British victory over Napoleon in 1815. The street was first named in a street directory in 1840, but no listings were found until 1884, when residents included mostly labourers, together with a mix of working men and women and small entrepreneurs, including gloveresses, a porter, a bricklayer and shopkeeper, a cab proprietor, a firewood dealer and a salt dealer. This was never a populous street, with just 20 homes here. The pub closed around 1950, and the street was demolished in the 1960s.

WATERWORKS ROAD

This road started life as a footpath skirting around the city waterworks, which were originally sited near the bridge, but moved here around 1790. A 'cut' was created to divert water from the main Severn flow, and a quaint water tower was built, reached by an attractive stone bridge across the cut. Unfortunately the Barbourne site was also used for waste disposal, which inevitably contaminated the water supply and infectious diseases continued to spread in the city for some years. The small waterworks was also inadequate to meet the needs of a growing city, and each area was supplied with water only twice a week.

In 1858 a new waterworks was built here, but the quality of the water supply remained much the same until improvements in filtration in 1894, after which there was a drastic reduction in infectious diseases in the city. The tower of the old waterworks was demolished in 1957 and only the foundations can be seen beside the brook, though it is still remembered by the nearby **Tower Road**. The waterworks closed in 1995, was purchased by the city council in 2000, and is now an environmental centre.

The road first appeared in a directory in 1884 when there were 36 homes here. Residents then included porters, china workers, labourers, coach builders, clerks, carpenters, fitters and an insurance agent. Waterworks House or Lodge was the home of the onsite engineer, which in 1884 was George Greenway.

There was a building application for 16 houses in 1888, but development was then sporadic, with eight applications totalling 27 homes and three shops in the 1890s. By 1910 there were 56 homes here, and there seem to have been 58 by 1922, but the west end of the street has recently been redeveloped.

The old Waterworks about 1900 - RS

WATERY LANE

This must long have existed as a 'cutthrough' between **Bromyard Road** and **Bransford Road**, though the earliest record found was an 1871 application to build a storehouse for petrol, which was the only nineteenth century building application found. The name is a bit of a mystery since the nearest watercourse, Laugherne Brook, is some distance to the west. In 1884 the four listings here were for a seamstress, two labourers and a gardener.

The Cinderella shoe firm moved here from **College Street** in 1914. It had been one of the biggest boot and shoemakers in the city in the nineteenth century, but its fortunes declined in the twentieth century, as fashions changed and foreign competition increased, and the company went into liquidation in 1976. The Cinderella Works was converted to flats in 2012. Aside from the modest number of houses here, the rest of the street is industrial/commercial.

Sir Walter Scott

WAVERLEY STREET

What we seem to have behind the development of this street is a fan of Sir Walter Scott, who was one of the most popular writers of the nineteenth century. Unfortunately we don't know who that fan was, since there are no nineteenth century building records for this street, but he or she was far from being alone, since there are said to be some 650 streets in the UK which take their name from Scott's novel, Waverley, published in 1814, and more than 2,000 that take their names from one or other of his 30 novels. Waverley is the best known, not simply because it was the great historical romance writer's first novel, but because his books – which included Rob Roy, Ivanhoe and Quentin Durward – are known collectively as the Waverley novels. This came about because novel writing was still regarded by some as disreputable in his day, so he mostly wrote anonymously, and many of his novels were simply described when they first appeared as being 'by the author of Waverley'.

This was one of the earliest streets in the Cherry Orchard area, first found listed in a street directory of 1880 as 'Terrace'.

A map of 1884 shows this street, though unnamed, providing access to **Cavendish Street** gardens. There was some Victorian development visible at that time, but most development took place later, and then as now there was a large area of riverside meadow to the west.

At that time the street shrank to a footpath north of **Berwick Street** and was only later widened to give vehicle access to Diglis.

It was first listed as Street in 1896, when there were 16 mainly modest homes listed here. Amongst the residents was a traffic agent for the Severn Commission, who apparently gave his name as Julius Caesar. Labourers were the largest group amongst other residents, but there was also a drayman, a sawyer, a bricklayer, a charwoman, a valet and a foreman.

Wellington Street

Blockhouse. Named for Lord Wellington, the victor of the Battle of Waterloo in 1815, who was said by Leicester to have been given the Freedom of the City in 1816, though his name is not on the official list. The street was shown on a map of 1829, but was listed as Place in a street directory of 1840. It ran from **St Paul's Street**, almost opposite St Paul's Church, just north of *Waterloo Street.* At the bottom of the street was the Three Springs Wharf, where T. Sewell coal merchants was based, and nearby, between here and *James Street*, was the timber yard and saw mill of William Aston, a member of a family much involved in property development in the late nineteenth century. There were 16 homes here, including a terrace of four cottages called Spring Place, which in 1884 housed two labourers and two glovers, and almost all the other residents here were either labourers or glovers. The street was demolished in the 1960s, but is remembered by Wellington Close nearby.

WESTBURY STREET

It is not clear why this street name was chosen, since there is no sign of anyone with this surname being involved with the development here, or being in Worcestershire at that time. Westbury meant 'West Borough' in Old English, so it is possible that this name derives from the memory of a small settlement in this area in past times, but there is no evidence to support this theory. It seems most likely therefore that the street name derives from the name of an earlier house in this area, which has not been traced. The street was first found listed as Terrace in a street directory of 1880.

It was shown, though not named, on a map of 1884, and the 11 houses and a shop to the north of the railway were then already complete. Residents in 1884 included two labourers, two stokers, a former horse breaker, a shoemaker, a railway guard and a carman. James Rimmer kept the shop on the corner of **Southfield Street** at that time. It was finally listed as Street in a directory of 1896. Within a century the area was completely redeveloped.

WHEATFIELD AVENUE

The name is reminiscent of the fields which surrounded **Bath Road** not long before the 1930s development. This street was first found listed in a directory in 1936, when there were five homes listed, but that number had doubled by the following year.

WHINFIELD ROAD

This road seems likely to have been one of several named for a family which probably owned or held land here before development went ahead. Arthue Henry Whinfield was listed at Severn Grange, North Claines in 1904, and Elizabeth Street and Philip Street, nearby off **Cornmeadow Lane**, may also have been named for members of the family. Presumably they were landowners, since they were not listed as farmers.

This development may have been prompted by the introduction after 1903 of electric trams running on the route to the Vine on the **Ombersley Road**. The land seems likely to have been sold in plots sufficient for five villas, since there are four blocks of five villas here, which were first found listed in 1905, though they were shown under **Ombersley Road**.

At Florence Villas were a viceman, a saucemaker, a gardener, a labourer and a bricklayer; at Whinfield Villas were two ladies presumably widowed, two gardeners and a labourer; at Granville Villas was Mayor's officer Daniel Sidney, a widow, a printer, an insurance agent and a glove cutter; at Grantham Villas was a gardener, a fitter, a compositor, and two men who didn't give occupations. The development here went no further at that time, and everything else in the road is modern. The New Inn on the corner of Ombersley Road was first listed in 1873, though it may have been older than that.

WHITE LADIES CLOSE

This was clearly named for the White Ladies convent in **The Tything**. Dr John Wall, of porcelain and Malvern water fame, is said to have first set up his medical practice here in the late 1730s, but no other record of the street has been found from that time.

The street was first found in the health board streets list of 1872, and in a street directory of the following year, but building applications suggested development was slow. An application to build six homes was submitted in 1876, and another for five more in 1880, but by 1884 a total of 19 homes had been built - Shrubbery Villa was added later - which may suggest that some of them dated from before building control began in 1865, or that applications have been lost or were never submitted.

Residents in 1884 were mostly either skilled or manual workers, though Caleb Simper at No. 16 was the organist at St Mary's Church in **Sansome Walk**, and Mrs Smith next door was a cotton bonnet maker. Others included two tailors, two carpenters, a milk seller, a coachman, a laundress, a fireman, a French polisher, a railway guard, a foreman, a glover, a builder, a servant and a compositor.

WHITE LADIES WALK

Named for the White Ladies convent in **The Tything**, this street was first found listed in the health board streets list of 1872, and was shown, though not named, on a map of 1884 when the five homes in Cowper Terrace, which are the only houses in the street, were already complete. There are no building records to indicate the date of construction, and they may have been built before building records began in 1865. Residents listed in a street directory of 1896 were a laundress, a bricklayer, a nurse, a porter and a carpenter.

WHITE'S ROAD

This street may have been named for Horace Albert White, who was a county councillor in the 1930s, though no direct connection has been traced. It was first found listed in 1932, when there were 19 homes here.

WHITMORE ROAD

This street may have been named for George Edward Whitmore, who was a county councillor in the 1930s, though no direct connection has been traced. It was first found in a directory in 1930, when there were 24 homes listed.

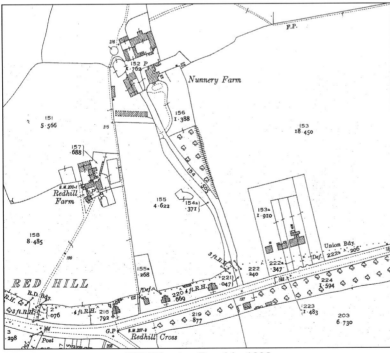

Whittington Road in 1928

WHITTINGTON ROAD

An old lane leading to the village of Whittington, which was an ancient manor belonging to the church at Worcester, known to the Anglo-Saxons as Hwitingtun, or Hwita's farm. It was referred to in a charter of 816, when Deneberht, Bishop of Worcester, granted it to Coenwulf, King of the Mercians. It was leased out several times in the tenth and eleventh centuries, including by Bishop Britheah to his brother Ailric in the 1030s, but he was dispossessed of it by William the Conqueror after 1066.

The manor was shown in Domesday Book, and some of the lands included were probably those of the manors of Battenhall and Barneshall, with which it was closely associated. It was long held by the Poer family, and was given to the priory at Worcester in 1330 by city merchant John the Mercer. It was subsequently broken up, with part of the manor being attached to the manor of Spetchley, and part to Woodhall in Norton.

Public executions were held here until a new county prison opened in **Castle Street** in 1813, though they were always referred to as being at Red Hill. The site was near the junction of two ancient roads, the London

Road, which then ran a little further south, behind the present houses, and an intersecting road which survives only as a footpath to Battenhall. This site was also convenient for gibbeting bodies beside the London Road after execution.

In 1606 a number of minor players in the Gunpowder Plot of 1605 were hung, drawn and quartered here, including Humphrey Littleton of Hagley Hall, and John Wintour, a half-brother of the Wintours of Hindlip Hall.

One of the most famous executions to take place here was that of catholic priest Fr John Wall in 1679. He was apparently treated with some respect, as a man dying for his religious beliefs, and was not gibbeted, but buried at St Oswald's in **The Tything**.

There is a memorial to him at the execution site at the rear of No. 4. According to Gwilliam, the last executions here took place in July 1809, when two men were hung for robbery with violence, though no details of the case were found in The Times. Executions were held at the new county gaol after it opened in **Castle Street** in 1813.

The land here had been waste, but at some stage it was enclosed by the Sebrights, after whom **Sebright Road** was named. This area would have been rural throughout much of its history, and something which could be properly described as urban development didn't begin to arrive here until around 1932, when the road was first found in a directory. There were then listings for eleven homes and the Worcester College for the Blind.

Wich Road

Or Wicks road. An early name, last found in 1790, probably for **Malvern Road**.

WILLOW STREET

First found listed in the health board streets list of 1872, and in a street directory of the following year, its name must come from Willow Terrace, a row of cottages on the corner of **Mill Street**, which probably took their name from their proximity to the Severn. In 1884 there were more than 20 homes listed here, for which no building records have been found, which could mean they dated from prior to December 1865. Residents in 1884 included six shoemakers, three labourers, two compositors, two glovers, a law clerk, a tailor, a tailoress, a police constable, a seamstress and a china potter.

Henry Hawker kept a shop on the corner of **Mill Street**, on a site since redeveloped, and Joseph Sylvester had a shop on Landsend Terrace. On the west side, roughly midway along the street, Hancock & Son had the Ceramic Art Colour Works, producing colours for porcelain manufacturers, and no doubt supplying much of their output to Royal Worcester in **Severn Street**. In recent years the whole street has been redeveloped.

WILSON STREET

The street must have taken its name from Mrs Fanny Phillips Wilson, presumably a widow, who lived at The Hermitage, **Reservoir Lane**, from at least 1884 until around 1897. She may have been involved in developing this street near her home, or it may have been named in her memory.

It was first shown unnamed on a map of 1884, when there was development over most of the west side, though it would be some years before any listing of residents could be found.

A building application was submitted for four homes here in 1902, and another two years later for 13 more, but a street directory listing was not found until 1910, when there were 14 homes here, mostly split into three blocks of Hallow Villas, Kimpton Villas and Reservoir Cottages. Residents then were all manual workers, including a fireman, a brass moulder, fitters, glovers, a labourer, a blacksmith and a carpenter.

WINCHESTER AVENUE

This name is something of a mystery. It looks like a street which has been named for or by an individual, perhaps a builder or developer, but no-one of this name has been traced in Worcestershire in the 1920s or 30s. Perhaps there was an intention to develop a 'theme estate' of Hampshire names, which did not materialise because adjoining streets were given other names. This street was first found listed in 1937, when there were 41 homes here.

Windsor Place

The Windsors were Worcestershire landowners for centuries, and their title of Baron Windsor is still held by the earls of Plymouth. This small entry ran off *Little Park Street* through to **Wyld's Lane**, just to the west of *Beaver Row*. In 1884 there appear to have been 18 modest terraced homes here, housing labourers, gloving workers, metal workers, charwomen, a shoemaker, a fitter, a hay trusser and a nurse. In modern times this little street shared the fate of Beaver Row.

WITHERS ROAD

As long ago as 1765 Sir Charles Trubshaw Withers was mayor of the city, and owned the Sansome Fields estate, with a mansion called Sansome Lodge, which still exists on **Sansome Walk**. Two residents of this name lived in the city at the time this road was created, who may have been his descendants, and could have had some involvement in the development of this road. One of them, Sidney Withers lived in Graham Road, St John's, and the other is **Selborne Road West**, Barbourne. First mention of the road was in 1930, but the first listing was not found until 1937, when there were eight homes here.

Wodestapestret

An Anglo-Saxon street name, apparently meaning the street of wood lathes. The street has been said by scholars to have been lost, but was identified by John Noake in *Worcestershire Relics* as an old name for **Quay Street**, though it is perhaps more likely to be a variant of the old name for *Hounds Lane*.

WOLVERTON ROAD

This may have been the new road included in a building application of 1898, and referred to then as Worthington Road. The land it stands on appears to have been a footway beside the houses and gardens in **Lower Chesnut Street** and **Little Chesnut Street** in 1884, and at that time there was open land to the south, between **Washington Street** and the canal.

The use of the Worthington name may have been a clerical error, since the brewers Worthingtons submitted an application on the same day – 25 April – for alterations at the Black Horse Inn in **Lowesmoor**. But it may also have been a clue to the name of an original backer of the development. There were several Worthingtons listed in Worcestershire around that time, but probably the wealthiest, and therefore the most likely to have been involved as an investor, was Alfred Worthington, a JP from Old Swinford, Stourbridge. The present name must be taken from two hamlets, Upper and Lower Wolverton near Pershore, one of which was presumably the home or birthplace of the person financing the development.

The scheme was a substantial one, since the 1898 application, submitted by city builder William Shakespeare Jnr, also included 31 houses, and the road was presumably intended to extend further south than it does now. The ten homes built first - four Crescent Villas and six Welbeck Villas – were shown under Lower Chesnut Street in 1903.

The road was listed under its own name in 1905, when residents included a carpenter, a clerk, a shopman, a hairdresser, a cooper, a fitter, a blacksmith, a coach finisher and two ladies who were probably widows. Unfortunately the ambitious plans did not work out, and the road remained with just those ten homes, which are still here today.

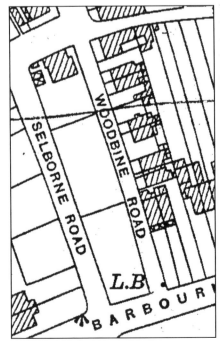

Woodbine Road in 1928

WOODBINE ROAD

Woodbine Cottage, near **Barbourne Terrace**, probably built in the late 1880s or early 1890s, was likely to have been the first home to be built here, and must have given the road its name. Woodbine was an old name for honeysuckle. The road was not shown on a map of 1884, but did appear in a street directory in 1896. At Riversdale then were a cashier and a potter, at Laburnam Cottages were a tailor and a glover, and at Glyn Villas were another glover and sculptor Charles Brown. Within four years two Rose Cottages had been added, occupied by a slaughterman and a plumber, and by 1910 another home had been added at the end of the road, occupied by coal agent Alfred Allen, which completed the east side of the street. The other side is all modern.

WOODLAND ROAD

Situated directly north of Astwood Cemetery, this road benefitted from the trees screening it, hence the name. It was first found listed in 1937, when there were seven homes here.

WOOD TERRACE

In 1962 Alderman Brotherton was satisfied that this street was named for Ellen Wood, the best-selling Victorian novelist who was born in **Sidbury**, but it is fairly clear that it was in fact named for city builder Joseph Wood, because he was behind the creation of the street.

He was mayor of the city in 1861, and his building firm took the lead in many nineteenth century city construction projects, and still exists today. In March 1867 the site on which the terrace was built was amongst five lots of land auctioned by Mr Wood at The Talbot in Barbourne, and the first building application was submitted three months later, for two cottages.

The Worcester Bowling Club at the end of the road also opened in the same year. Elgar's friend Hubert Leicester, after whom **Leicester Street** was named, was later its president.

Joseph Wood - TW

Development was slow to judge by the building applications, with just three further applications submitted during the rest of the century, each for two houses. But here as elsewhere around this area, there was a good deal more built then we have records of, leaving us to conjecture whether other applications were never submitted by developers, or have since been lost.

An 1884 street directory lists 19 homes and a shop here on the north side of the terrace, which were shown on a map in the same year. Some of the few house plots still vacant at that time appeared to have the remains of an orchard or a thickly wooded grove, giving some idea of the landscape before development began.

Residents in 1884 included four china workers, two compositors, a bricklayer, a cutler, a bookbinder, a corn dealer, a fitter, a coach painter and a coachmaker, probably from McNaught's on **The Tything**. Henry Knight at No. 3 was clerk at St Mary's Church. Edward Marchant had a shop on the corner of **Sansome Walk**, which survived in various hands until the 1970s. Further along, at Whitby Villas, was Dudfield's ale and porter stores off-licence. By 1896 several more homes had been added, totalling 23 homes and small businesses, and four more were added between 1910 and 1922.

WOOLHOPE ROAD

The reason for the name is not known, but it may derive from some connection the developer had with Woolhope in Herefordshire, or with a well-known natural history society in the county named the Woolhope Club.

There were still open fields to the east of Bath Road in 1885, but within eight years the building application for this new road was submitted by leading city property developer John Stallard Jnr, and development went ahead very quickly. A long list of large and small building applications was then submitted by developers and investors. In the five years from 1894 there were 22 applications to build 73 homes here.

By 1896 18 of these homes had already been built, and four more were going up. Residents in the street at that time were a mix of white collar and manual workers. There were two police constables and a sergeant, two glovers, three tinmen, , two boot and shoe makers, a foreman, a compositor, an organ builder, a local businessman, a railway clerk, a blacksmith, a miller, a dental assistant, a gardener, a watchman and a law clerk.

Small building applications continued to be submitted, and by 1900 there were 78 homes and three more being built, with 83 and two more under construction by 1905. When they were completed soon afterwards, it was the first time for more than a decade that there had not been house building going on somewhere in the street. In 1910 RSPCA inspector Charles Thomas was at Glendale. There is some later development at the north end of the road.

WYLD'S LANE

The name resulted from the ownership of the Commandery in **Sidbury** by the Wylde family, who had long been leading merchants in the city. The estate was purchased in 1545 for £498 by wealthy clothier Thomas Wylde, whose family was then one of the most prominent in the city. The former monastic buildings occupied a site much larger than that of the Commandery now, with gardens leading up to the hill beyond, and an avenue of trees leading to a deer park. This lane ran along the southern boundary of the property from **Sidbury**. Thomas Wylde used his wealth to adapt the former monastic buildings into a model Tudor home. He was a member of the corporation, served the senior position of bailiff in 1547 and became an alderman in the following year. There are effigies in the cathedral nave of his son Robert, who died in 1607, and his wife Margaret. His descendant, Robert, was a barrister and one of the officers who surrendered the city in 1646 at the end of the second Civil War, and the family's fortunes probably suffered during the war. His grandson,

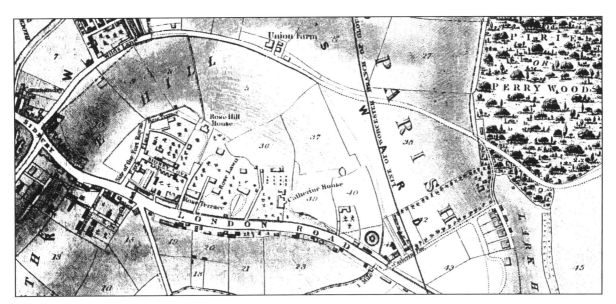

Wyld's Lane in 1838, above, and 1884 below, to near where Stanley Road and Vincent Road are now

also Robert, seems to have spent much of what was left during his tenure as city MP from 1701 to 1727. He had already moved the family in 1695 to a small estate they inherited at Glazeley, Shropshire, to let out the Commandery, and later it was mortgaged for £1,500, but the family's fortunes continued to deteriorate, and in 1764 they sold the Commandery estate, severing their last link with the city.

As late as 1838 the land around the lane was open farmland. Union Farm was a dairy farm situated just east of where Compton Road is now, and it was still listed in 1896, when Frederick Priday was the dairyman. Aside from the farm, there was nothing here except Field House, on the north side of the lane betweenthe site of **Vincent Road** and **Stanley Road**.

The lane followed roughly the course it has now, until it passed what later became **Midland Road**, then instead of curving south, to rejoin **London Road**, it veered off east to Perry Wood. To the west there was development around ***Beaver Row*** by 1864.

The lane was widened into the present road about 1863, and extended to create the upper part of the lane, rejoining London Road at the bottom of Red Hill. By that time the railway had arrived, and the lane was

The Garibaldi, scene of three murders - WN and the Cottage Homes on a 1904 map

forced to curve around sidings and a locomotive turntable immediately north of the railway bridge at **Perry Wood Walk**. The sidings will have been built to serve the Midland Saw Mill, near the bridge, which was held over two decades from the mid 1870s by Henry Morgan. Like several other timber yard owners he was also heavily involved in property speculation, and submitted 30 building applications over that period. These were invariably for two or four houses, but he did also apply to create **Sebright Road** and **Saunders Street**. The mill and timber yard were held by Smith Brothers in modern times, but the site was redeveloped for housing in the 1990s, though the business is remembered by Sawmill Close. The 1860s widening and rerouting of the lane must have given a boost to the construction of housing here, much of it in the form of cottages for working families, but by 1884 expansion still stopped at **St Wulstan's Crescent**, though there were around 90 homes up to this point, with residents including building workers, shoemakers, glovers, clothing workers, china workers, railwaymen and metal workers. Near the west end of the lane was the Commandery Nursery of James Corbett & Son. J. Coombs Snr at Hamilton House was a scripture reader, the Rev Robert Blair at Field House was the Rector of St Martin's Church in the **Cornmarket**, and James Thrupp near **Fort Royal Hill** was the assistant divisional superintendent of the GWR.

The continuing demand for housing as industries east of **Lowesmoor** continued to expand, meant that homes advanced steadily along the lane, to reach the east end by the close of the century, though there was still some vacant land not built on until later. In total, between 1867 and 1903 38 applications were submitted to build a total of 148 homes here.

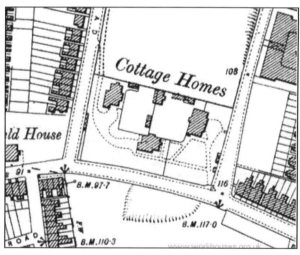

In 1893-4 the Poor Law Union built what was in effect an orphanage on a two and a half acre site off the lane, between **Stanley Road** and **Midland Road**. The Union workhouse on **Tallow Hill** was being rebuilt at this time, but alternative accommodation for children was felt desirable, and so three Cottage Homes, likened by the Berrow's Journal in October 1894 to 'three palatial villa residences', were built as separate accommodation for boys, girls and infants. Children had to share the domestic chores and the regime was strict, even brutal at times by our standards, but by the 1930s the children got a little pocket money and a sweet ration, and an annual holiday was introduced in 1945. The homes were renamed Perryfields in 1947, and were closed by 1961. The buildings were demolished in 1992, and the site was redeveloped for the Perryfields Day Centre.

The most famous past resident of this area was Matilda Alice Powles, better known as music hall star Vesta Tilley, who was born in 1864 in *Beaver Row*, just off the lane, near **Dent Close**. The modest homes there were demolished and the site redeveloped in the 1960s or 70s. The most infamous resident of the lane was probationary Worcester City police constable Herbert Burrows, who committed an horrific triple murder at the Garabaldi inn in 1925, for which he was hung in 1926. The Victorian pub, at No. 75, was rebuilt around 1950, but later burnt down and the site was redeveloped, though the house further along the lane where Burrows lodged still exists. Surprisingly this was never a big area for pubs, despite the large concentration of potential customers, and the only other hostelry listed is the Plumbers Arms, on the corner of **Cole Hill**, which is still with us.

There were a number of shops along the lane, and some remain near Fort Royal. Amongst those that have now gone are what was an Italian grocery store for many years, on the corner of **Park Street**, opposite a corner shop which is now a hairdressers, and another corner shop at **St Catharine's Vale** which closed in the 1980s.

Youngsters from York Place ready for a fancy dress party in the late 1920s. Behind them is the pedestrian gate to Spreckley's Brewery in Barbourne Road - GG

YORK PLACE

Named for Frederick, Duke of York and Albany (see **Albany Road**), this street dates from the 1830s, and was almost certainly the first built housing development in Worcester, since earlier schemes involved the sale of plots.

The original developers were Worcester businessman John Rowlands, who lived in Britannia Square, and Shropshire landowner Henry Wilding of Hall Stretton, The development was planned on land which was part of the Third Pound Field, traditionally belonging to the Bishop of Worcester. Construction began in 1831 but in November 1832 Rowlands and Wilding sold out, probably because building costs were rising beyond their ability or willingness to meet them.

The project was taken over for the bargain price of £48, by Worcester skinner, leather seller and glover William Ball, who owned other land nearby, and city investor Harvey Shelton, but they evidently had trouble attracting other investors.

By late 1833 Ball had moved to Middlesex, perhaps in retirement, and passed his share in the project to his son Philip Ball, a city glove manufacturer, his granddaughter Charlotte, and distinguished local surgeon, Christopher Hebb of Britannia Square, who is remembered by **Hebb Street**.

331

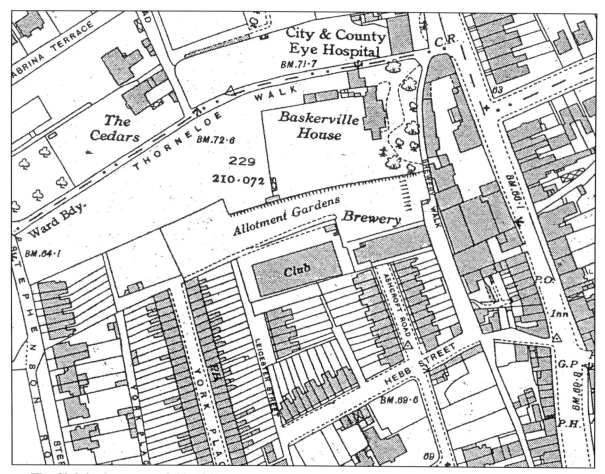

The Club in the centre of this 1940 map was secretly used during the Second World War for making aircraft parts, including turrets and canopies for Lancaster bombers

Hebb, the founder of a number of local charities, was perhaps more likely to have become involved in the project through philanthropic motives of helping provide decent homes for working people rather than for any commercial gain, but his involvement saved the project, since he was a leading figure in the local community and someone investors would undoubtedly trust. The new owners put in £500 each; and promoted The York Place New Building Society in which members paid £1-10s-0d (£1.50) a month for the construction work, and ownership of the houses in the street was decided by way of a vote amongst the members of the society. Construction of more than 60 houses was largely completed by 1835, and fully complete, and named for the first time, on a map of 1840. Each house had its own 'privy' and each pair of houses shared a well. York Place always had a fascinating social mix.

At the time of the 1881 census residents included a newspaper sub-editor at No. 1 next door to a newspaper editor, and at No. 4, 12 people squashed into one small house, including cordwainer (boot and shoe maker) John Wigley and his wife and six children and a family of four lodging there. There were also chemists, glovers, a stonemason's labourer, laundresses, a coachman, a decorator, a plumber, railwaymen, an ostrich feather dyer, a straw hat maker, school masters and mistresses, a printer's compositor from Australia on a visit, and at Nos. 45 & 46, the little Royal Oak tavern which was a feature of the street until sometime in the 1960s when small local pubs, which were once found in every street, began to disappear. There were also two local shops at various times.

As late as the 1940s there was a small-holding across the bottom of York Place and allotments surrounded a vehicle access road or track and pedestrian pathway leading into the rear of Spreckley's Brewery in **Barbourne Road**. A nearby indoor bowling alley, since demolished, was secretly pressed into service making canopies for Lancaster bombers during the Second World War. The Building Society was wound up and the houses were sold at auction around 1970.

Further Reading

Below is a listing of published sources used in the preparation of this book. Some sources are now only readily available online, and a number have been included here with current URLs, but unfortunately websites only exist as long as their hosting lasts, so some sites listed may have changed address or no longer be accessible in the future.

Atkin, M.	*The Civil War in Worcestershire* (1995)
Attwood, D.A.	*The Growth of Nineteenth Century Worcester* (Thesis, 1997) *Worcester City Planning Applications 1865-1948* (WRO)
Barker, P. et al	*The Origins of Worcester* (1970) (Trans Worcs Arch Soc Third Series Vol. 2 1968-69)
Berrows Worcester Journal	*Tercentenary 1690 – 1990* (1990)
Bridges, T. & Mundy, C.	*Worcester – A Pictorial History* (1996)
British History Online	www.british-history.ac.uk
British Listed Buildings	www.britishlistedbuildings.co.uk
Brotherton, B.	*Worcester Street Names* (*Worcester News* Feb – Nov 1962)
Bundy, C.	*The Nature of Sacrifice* (2005)
Carpenter, J.	*Victorian Worcester* (2006)
Chambers, J.	*A General History of Worcester* (1820)
Corbett, E.F.	'Stroller' in *Worcester Herald* and *Berrows Worcester Journal* (1923 – 1935)
Covins, F.	*The Arboretum Story* (Undated)
Darlington, J. and Evans, J.	*Roman Sidbury, Worcester: Excavations 1959-1989* (Trans Worcs Arch Soc Third Series Vol. 13 1992)
Doolan, B.	*St George's, Worcester 1590 – 1999* (1999)
Duignan, W. H.	*Worcestershire Place Names* (1905)
Ekwall, E.	*Dictionary of English Place-Names* (1960)
Green, B.	*Bishops and Deans of Worcester*
Green, V.	*The History and Antiquities of the City of Worcester* (1764 & 1796)
Grundy, H.H.	*A Short History of the Worcester Tramways 1881-1928* (1991)

Historic Worcester Streets

Grundy, J.,   Street and Trade Directories – Worcester and Worcestershire
Bentley, J.,   (1790 on)
Littlebury,
Kelly *et al*

Grundy, M.   *Memory Lane* (Various dates)
                   Worcester Memories (2012)

Gwilliam, B.   *Old Worcester : People and Places* (1993 & 2010)
                   A Gazetteer of Old Public Houses and Inns in Worcestershire (Unpub)
                   Coach Travel and Turnpike Roads in Worcestershire (Unpub)
                   (Ed. Pam Hinks) www.worcesterpeopleandplaces.com

Harris, J.   *The Greatest of Blessings : A history of Worcester's Water Supply* (1994) at
                        http://www.users.totalise.co.uk/~fortroyal/waterhtm.htm

Harrison, P.   *Worcester Then & Now* (2011)

Harvey, M.   *Tales from Worcester Royal Infirmary* (2012)

Haynes, C. & M.   *Old Worcester* (1987)

Hillaby, J.   *The Worcester Jewry 1158-1290*
                   (Trans Worcs Arch Soc 1990)

Hughes, P.   (Ed.) *Worcester Streets : Blackfriars* (1986)
                   Buildings and the Building Trade in Worcester 1540-1650 (1990)
                   (Unpublished PhD thesis held at Worcestershire Record Office)
                   Heron Lodge and the Development of Lark Hill (1992)
                   Worcester Walkabout – Cornmarket, New Street, Friar Street (c. 1980)
                   Report on Royal Albert Orphanage (2007) at
http://planningapps.worcester.gov.uk/images/dv_pl_files%5CL11J0117/L11J0117-SD.pdf

Hughes, P. &   *The Story of Worcester* (2011)
Leech, A.

Hughes, P. &   *Worcester Streets : Friar Street* (1984)
Molyneux, N.

Jones, A.E.E.   *Anglo-Saxon Worcester* (1958)

Jones, R.   *Pioneers of Photography in the City of Worcester and around* (2007)
                   Worcester: Past and Present (2001)
                   Worcester Through Time (2009)

Knowles, J.M.   *Lansdowne Crescent, Worcester to 1900 : a study* (1988)

Leicester, H.A.   *Forgotten Worcester* (1930)
                   Worcester Remembered (1935)

Macdonald, A.   *A Guide to the Monuments in Worcester Cathedral* (1947)

Malvern Industrial www.miac.org.uk
Archaeology Circle

Mills, B.   *Kay's of Worcester* (2003)

Historic Worcester Streets

Morriss, R.K. & Hoverd, K	*The Buildings of Worcester* (1994)
Nash, T.R.	*Collections for the History of Worcestershire* (1781 & 1799)
Noake, J.	*Notes and Queries for Worcestershire* (1856) *Worcestershire Relics* (1877) *Worcestershire Nuggets* (1880)
OUP	*Oxford English Dictionary* (1971)
(Eds.) Page, W, & Willis-Bund, W.J.	*Victoria County History of Worcestershire* (4 vols - various dates)
Palmer, R.	*The Folklore of Hereford & Worcester* (1992)
Pevsner, N.	*The Buildings of England : Worcestershire* (1968)
Poulton-Smith, A.	*Worcestershire Place Names* (2003)
Robertson, S.N.	*Worcester Golf & Country Club 1898 – 1998* (1998)
Shuard, R.	*Remembering Worcester* (1988)
Stafford, T.	*Worcester As It Was* (1977)
Standish, B.	*Once Upon a Postcard* (1987)
Stenton, A. & Mawer, F.M.	*The Place-Names of Worcestershire* (1927)
Talbut, G.	*Worcester as an Industrial and Commercial Centre 1660-1750* (1986)
Thorn, F. & C.	*Domesday Book : Worcestershire* (1982)
True North Books	*Memories of Worcester* (2000)
Turberville, T.C.	*Worcestershire in the 19th Century* (1852)
University of Portsmouth	www.visionofbritain.org.uk
Wardle, C. & T.	*The History of Barbourne* (2007)
Wardle, T.	*Heroes & Villains of Worcestershire* (2010)
Watson, W.	*An Orchard Survey of the City of Worcester* (1999) http://www.wbrc.org.uk/WORCRECD/Issue7/orchards.htm
Whitehead, D.	*John Gwynn and the Building of Worcester Bridge* (Trans Worcs Arch Soc 1982) *St Swithin's Church* (1996) *The Book of Worcester* (1976) *Urban Renewal and Suburban Growth : The Shaping of Georgian Worcester* (Worcestershire Historical Society 1989)

Historic Worcester Streets

Whitehead, D. *et al*   *St Clement's Gate : Background Papers on Local History,*
                        Archaeology and Urban Morphology (1996)

Whittaker, R. *et al*   *Studies in Worcestershire Local History* (Various dates)

Wilkes, M.   *The Impact of War on Northwick Manor*
                        http://www.wyac.co.uk/_media/northwick_at_war.pdf

Willis Bund, J.W.   *The Civil War in Worcestershire* (1905)

Winspear, S.   *Worcester's Lost Theatre* (1996)

Worcester   *Names of Streets, Roads, &c.* (1872)
Board of Health

Worcester   *An Outline Resource Assessment and Research*
City Council   *Framework for the Archaeology of Worcester* (2007)
                       Buildings of Local Significance in Worcester (2011)
                       Conservation Area Appraisals 1 – 20 (Various dates)
                       Council Yearbooks (Various dates)
                       Portraits and Paintings at The Guildhall (2009)
                       Worcester 800 – a celebration (1989)
                       Worcester City Defences – Conservation Management Plan (2007)
                       Worcester City Historic Buildings Data (2011)

Worcester   www.worcester citymuseums.org.uk
City Museums

Worcester   *Worcester at Work* (1903)
Daily Times
…............now

PICTURE CREDITS

The author owes a debt of gratitude to all those people and organisations below who have kindly loaned images for use in this publication, to enable it to provide a visual as well as a descriptive record of Worcester's historic streets and their history, and also to anyone who has made material available during the long research process, but whose name has inadvertently been omitted. All rights remain with the owners of images reproduced.

BG - Bill Gwilliam *Old Worcester : People and Places*

BS - Brian Standish *Once Upon A Postcard*

CB - Carol Bundy *The Nature of Sacrifice*

GG - the late Mrs Gladys Green of York Place

HC - HarperCollins Publishers

HL - Hubert Leicester

IN - Ian Narraway, I.J. Narraway Family Butchers

LL - Linda of Lee Design, Hebb Street

MAG - Worcester City Museums and Art Gallery

MS - Martin Smith

PG - Paul Griffith

RS - the late Ron Shuard

TW - Terry Wardle (with thanks for facilities to photograph portraits to Worcester City Council and the cooperation of Guildhall staff past and present)

WCC - Worcestershire County Cricket Club

WN - Worcester News (with special thanks to Mike Grundy)

Historic Worcester Streets

Index